FOCUSED LIVES

Simeon (1759-1836)—Strategic Mentor
Gordon (1836-1895)—Missionary Minded Pastor
Brengle (1860-1936)—Public Saint
Morgan (1863-1945)—World Class Bible Teacher
Jaffray (1873-1945)—Missionary Pioneer
McQuilkin—(1886-1952) Bible College Founder
Mears—(1890-1963) Recruiter of Leaders
Maxwell—(1895-1984) Missionary Trainer

Inspirational Life Changing Lessons From Eight Effective Christian Leaders Who Finished Well

by Dr. J. Robert Clinton

ISBN 1-932814-16-7

© 1995 Dr. J. Robert Clinton

This book is available from:

Barnabas Publishers
2175 North Holliston Avenue
Altadena, CA
91001

TABLE OF CONTENTS

Page	Contents	
1	Preface	This book is written differently than most. The preface tells you what to expect in this book and how to read this book.
15	Chapter 1.	**Interpretive Biography** This introductory chapter describes the theoretical underpinnings for the presentation of material on each Christian leader as well as an explanation for the format of a historical chapter.
27	Chapter 2.	**Charles Simeon** (1759-1836) The Strategic Mentor--Effective Change Through Mentoring
77	Chapter 3.	**A. J. Gordon** (1836-1895) A Study in Ultimate Contribution
123	Chapter 4.	**Samuel Brengle** (1860-1936) Public Saint--A Study in Consistency
175	Chapter 5.	**G. Campbell Morgan** (1863-1945) World Class Bible Teacher
225	Chapter 6.	**Robert Jaffray** (1873-1945) Missionary Pioneer Who Exemplifies Major Life Achievement After Age 57
277	Chapter 7.	**R. C. McQuilkin** (1886-1952) A Life Dominated by a Three Fold Thrust
333	Chapter 8.	**Henrietta Mears** (1890-1963) A Destiny for Challenging Emerging Leaders
391	Chapter 9.	**L. E. Maxwell** (1895-1984) The Deeper Life--the Central Hub of this Focused Life
445	Chapter 10.	**Focal Findings** Comparative Lessons From These Eight Effective Leaders
485	Glossary	
499	Appendix A.	6 Barriers To Finishing Well
501	Appendix B.	5 Things To Enhance Good Finishes
505	Appendix C.	6 Characteristics of Those Finishing Well
507	Appendix D.	An Introduction to Social Base Processing
511	Appendix E.	Biographical Genre and the Historical Model
517	Appendix F.	An Explanatory Note on Reading Venn Diagrams--Giftedness Set; Ultimate Contribution Set.
521	Bibliography--References Cited or Mentioned Not Included in Chapter Bibliographies	

Acknowledgment of Sources

I am grateful for the many sources that were available to me and for permission to reference and quote from the following works.

Bennett, John C.
   1992   **Charles Simeon and the Evangelical Anglican Missionary Movement--A Study of Voluntaryism and Church-Mission Tensions.** Doctoral thesis. Edinburgh: University of Edinburgh.
            Quotes used by permission.

Houghton, George Gerald
   1970   **The Contributions of Adoniram Judson Gordon to American Christianity.** Unpublished Th.D. dissertation, Dallas Theological Seminary.
            Quotes used by permission.

Matthews, Arthur
   1956   **Towers Pointing Upward.** Columbia, S.C.: Columbia Bible College.
            Quotes used by permission.

Tozer, A. W.
   1947   **Let My People Go: The Life of Robert A. Jaffray.** Harrisburg: Christian Publications.
            Quotes used by permission.

Tomatala, Yakob Yonas
   1990   **The Dynamic Missionary Leadership of Robert Alexander Jaffray.** Doctoral dissertation. Pasadena: School of World Mission, Fuller Theological Seminary.
            Quotes used by permission.

Baldwin, Ethel May and David V. Benson
   1966   **Henrietta Mears--and how she did it!** Ventura, Ca: Regal Books. Quotes used by permission.

Roe, Earl O., Editor
   1990   **Dream Big, The Henrietta Mears Story.** Ventura, Ca: Regal Books. Quotes used by permission.

Spaulding, Stephen Maxwell
   1991b   **Lion On the Prairies: An Interpretive Analysis of The Life and Leadership of Leslie Earl Maxwell, 1895-1984.** Unpublished pre-doctoral dissertation. Pasadena: School of World Mission. Quotes used by permission.

Other quotes were from sources in the public domain or in accordance with the fair use copyright law.

PREFACE

> Remember your former leaders. Think back on how they lived and ministered. Imitate those excellent qualities you see in their lives. For Jesus Christ is the same today, as He was in the past and as He will be in the future. What He did for them He will do for you to inspire and enable your leadership. **Hebrews 13:7,8** (Personal Interpretive Paraphrase)

This leadership mandate, to study leaders, and to follow their examples, expecting Jesus to empower, forms the Biblical and philosophical basis for this book. Comparative study of over 800 Christian leader's lives[1] has validated the importance of this mandate. What have we learned?

1. God shapes a leader over an entire lifetime.
2. God intends to develop a leader to reach the maximum potential and accomplish those things for which the leader has been gifted.
3. When using a time perspective to analyze and overview a leader's development the life can be seen in terms of several development phases, each yielding valuable informative lessons.
4. Shaping processes can be identified, labeled, and analyzed to contribute long lasting lessons and values.
5. Patterns can be identified and are highly suggestive for anticipating future processing by God.
6. As we study these lives we can expect God to use them to shape our own. These lives can be used to empower us.
7. Few leaders finish well.

The seventh observation jars one's thoughts. An initial study of a number of Old Testament leaders[2] showed that about 1 out of 3 finished well. Repeated anecdotal evidence from modern day leadership indicates that numerous leaders are failing in ministry and seems to backup the observation. That phrase, *Few Leaders finish well*, provides a chilling warning to leaders such as you and me, and indeed to all of those of us who want to finish well.

This warning should encourage us to study leaders who don't finish well to determine why this is so. We have done this. We have identified a number of obstacles or hindrances to leaders finishing well. We should also study those who finished well to determine why this is so. We have done this too. We have also identified a number of things that have enhanced leaders to finish well.[3]

But this present study goes even further. I have purposely selected a number of leaders who not only finished well but were very effective in their lives and ministries. And I do so in order to inspire other leaders to finish well. I use an approach[4] to analyzing their

---

[1] These studies have included Biblical leaders, historical leaders, and contemporary leaders with the majority being contemporary leaders.
[2] This preliminary study was written up in a paper, *Listen up Leaders!* (1989) by Dr. J. Robert Clinton. Available through Barnabas Publishers, 2175 N. Holliston Avenue, Altadena, CA, 91001.
[3] I sometimes use *we* and sometimes use *I*. That's because many of my students have helped me in research. Their case studies have provided me with a data base to do comparative analysis. While there are many complex reasons why leaders do not finish well there are at least 6 major reasons. See Appendix A. We have also identified 5 major enhancements to continuing well and finishing well. See Appendix B.
[4] This framework is called leadership emergence theory. It was developed over the past 12 years as part of my doctoral research and on-going post-doctoral research. The framework uses three major concepts (a time-line perspective, analyses of critical incidents in a life along that time-line, and comparative study of

Preface to Focused Lives							page 2

lives which identifies important lessons, values, and insights that helped focus them in their lives and ministries. I define a focused life as follows.

A focused life is
- a life dedicated to exclusively carrying out God's unique purposes through it,[5]
- by identifying the focal issues, that is, the **major role, life purpose, unique methodology, or ultimate contribution,**[6] which allows
- an **increasing prioritization** of life's activities around the focal issues, and
- results in a satisfying life of being and doing.

These that I have studied lived such *focused lives*. Their lives counted for God. And it excites me to discover major roles, life purposes, ultimate contributions, and the ways God led them to prioritize their lives and ministries around these focal issues.

So what! How can your reading of these so-called focused lives help you? Let me suggest two ways:

1. **Using the Leadership Mandate, Hebrews 13:7,8**
The Hebrews 13:7,8, leadership mandate gives one answer. As you meditate on these leader's lives you will see *excellent qualities* in their leadership such as values, principles, methods, ministry insights, and perspectives which you can apply to your own life and ministry. As the mandate states, you can trust Jesus to enable you to use these in your own situation.

2. **Proactive Use of Concepts**
Seeing the many concepts of a focused life defined, described, and illustrated in these lives will give you a working grasp of these ideas. This in turn will allow you to be more proactive in using them in your own life. That is, you can recognize symptoms of these concepts in your own life and can begin to make decisions based on this discernment which will deliberately advance you toward your focused life. You will sense God's affirmation as you deliberately take steps to focus your life around His unique purposes for you. This may mean adapting a role, clarifying a specific life purpose and using it to choose your role and sift your activities, or to clarify achievements you want to accomplish and leave behind as your legacy. Again, because of familiarity you will be sensitive to God's shaping and guidance activities that help you identify and prioritize around these focal issues.

---

patterns of development) to gain insights from a life. The framework was used to study each of the lives in this book. From these in-depth analyses I have drawn the significant values that I include for our benefit-- our empowerment from these historical mentors. For the analysis framework, see Clinton (1988) **The Making of A Leader** and (1989) **Leadership Emergence Theory**. Available from Barnabas Publishers.

[5] I am thinking primarily of full time Christian workers who have made a second commitment beyond their salvation experience dedicating their lives to accomplish God-directed purposes through them. I am not saying that non full time Christian workers can't have focused lives. I am sure they can. It is simply that this research deals with full time workers and is primarily for them. This definition may or may not hold for non full time Christian workers. I have not yet studied them in depth.

[6] These four--*major role, life purpose, unique methodology,* or *ultimate contribution*--are called the *focal issues*. Usually one or more of them dominates a focused life. A number of other factors (like giftedness, ministry insights, sense of destiny) contribute to the divine guidance which helps these leaders to prioritize life's activities around the focal issues. Both the identification of focal issues and the processes that prioritized them are given in the studies of the eight chosen for this book.

Now I do not want to intimidate anyone. I don't want to lay a guilt trip on you. I do not expect you to be or do or accomplish what these leaders did. You are you--a uniquely gifted person whom God is shaping for His purposes. But I do expect you to see some of the values that under girded these effective leaders. I want you to profit from the lessons that emerge out of their experience. I do expect you to see how God focused these leaders toward those achievements. I do expect you to get insights from your own ministry from these leaders. I do want you to be challenged to live up to the potential God has given you.

On what basis did I choose these leaders? Of the hundreds of leaders that I could have chosen, why these? There are simple reasons and more complex ones. **One**, I had in-depth case study material already done on most of these or at least a collection of materials ready for research. **Two**, all of these leaders have influenced my own development personally. **Three**, I am interested in studying the latter phases of Christian leader's lives.[7] I want to learn in order to help many more Christian leaders to finish well. These chosen did finish well.[8] **Four**, these eight leaders give a fairly good spread across a number of factors such as:

1. The ones chosen, time-wise, span from the late 1700s to the mid 1980s. Comparative lessons that repeatedly show up over different generations carry a self-authenticating force and will most likely have relevance for today.
2. The backgrounds of these eight vary ecclesiastically--Anglican, Presbyterian, Wesleyan, Baptist, Congregational, Christian and Missionary Alliance.
3. They have varied giftedness sets[9] and ultimate contributions.[10]
4. There are represented in the selection both singles and married and both male and female.[11]
5. There are church and parachurch workers as well as missionary and non-missionary types.

---

[7]This necessitates case studies of people who have already finished. It requires enough information to draw out observations. Biblical leaders with the exception of about six don't have as much information available as is needed to speak about focused lives. Contemporary leaders have yet to finish. We are narrowed to historical case studies. But this is not a limitation. There are so many rich studies of Christian leaders that fulfill the models of Hebrews 13:7,8.

[8]*Finished well* can mean different things to different people. While there are probably many characteristics that could be used to evaluate a good finish, our comparative studies of those finishing well has identified 6 characteristics. See Appendix C. Not all of these 6 characteristics appear to the same degree in all of the leaders chosen but they do help us see what finishing well means.

[9]*Giftedness set* refers to the collection of natural abilities, acquired skills and spiritual gifts. Either of these elements can dominate a life. In the case of each of these we are talking about people whose spiritual gifts dominated their lives as will be the case with many present day Christian leaders. See Clinton and Clinton (1994) **Developing Leadership Giftedness**, available through Barnabas Publishers.

[10]*Ultimate contribution* refers to categories of major life achievements. Comparative study of lives has resulted in 12 prime types (some of which focus on being and some on doing). Effective focused leaders usually have several of these prime types in their make-up. We call this the ultimate contribution set. Prime types include: **Saint** (model life), **Stylistic Practitioner** (model ministry style), **Mentor** (productive ministry with individuals), **Public Rhetorician** (productive ministry with large public groups), **Pioneer** (founds apostolic type works), **Crusader** (rights wrongs and injustices in society), **Artist** (creative breakthroughs), **Founder** (starts new organizations), **Stabilizer** (solidifies organizations), **Researcher** (develops new ideation), **Writer** (captures new ideation for use of others), **Promoter** (distributes effectively new ideation). Knowing your ultimate contribution set early can make the difference in a proactive or reactive stance toward future development. See Clinton (1989) paper, *The Ultimate Contribution--A Life that Counts*, available through Barnabas Publishers.

[11]Though I have only one female (single), Henrietta Mears, in this selection. I do not have as much case study information on females. Future works will include more female leaders.

6. And most important to me, these focused lives, all have strong value based ministry philosophies.[12]

Fifth, with such a spread I will have a better chance of appealing to readers. I know that one or two of these will strongly appeal to you.[13] And I want that to happen.

Who are these leaders? Let me share some motivational sketches that should stir you to identify with one or more of them for special study.

Charles Simeon (1759-1836) was a single, Anglican Pastor, who significantly influenced missions and the evangelical movement in the Anglican Church. He was the vicar of Holy Trinity Church, and a Fellow of King's College. His long tenure in one place (54 years at Cambridge--a major educational center in England), his strategic ministry insights, his strong mentoring ministry (e.g. Henry Martyn, etc.),[14] and his risky missions parachurch involvement make him a valuable study for leaders today. This is especially true for those who are in denominations characterized as going down hill. He can encourage one to stick it out and bring about change. He worked within the system and saw it changed significantly though it took a long time. He also had extensive ministry influence beyond it.

His perseverance against his initial negative reception and persecution in the ministry stand out as exemplary in pastoral ministry from that time to this. And this encouragement to persevere is so needed in a day when so many drop out early on after their first plunge into full time ministry.

I was introduced to this Christian leader through Gordon McDonald's lecture series at Fuller Theological Seminary in the mid 80s. Simeon is a personal hero of McDonald. McDonald actually visited Simeon's church and grave site in England. His penetrating analysis and public presentation motivated me to study this great Anglican Christian leader.

Simeon's life and the observations on what brought about focus will appeal to a number of you. Surprisingly, Simeon's life can be a great encouragement to campus workers of today as well as denominational renewal workers. His continual, deliberate, and persistent input into young leaders studying at Cambridge had a renewing effect not

---

[12]The initial impetus for this book was to do a follow-up study on ministry philosophies of leaders who finished well. I had previously done a major paper defining ministry philosophy. See Clinton (1992) *A Personal Ministry Philosophy--One Key To Effective Leadership*. Three major perspectives are involved in analyzing ministry philosophies: the *blend variable* (studies major values and how they were shaped); the *focal variable*--which looks at the factors which tend to focus the leader toward ultimate achievements and the *articulation variable* which refers to the integration of values and explicit expression of them. This book focuses more on these first two--the identification of focal values and the observations on how the leader became focused.

[13]I say this rather strongly because we have observed a major pattern summarized by the phrase, *LIKE-ATTRACTS-LIKE*. That is, leaders and potential leaders are attracted to other respected leaders who have similar giftedness, similar ministries, similar values, and like achievements (or intended ones). This dynamic happens even if the parties are not aware of it conceptually. Therefore I have chosen a broad range knowing that the *LIKE-ATTRACTS-LIKE* dynamic will be working. I even dare to hope that one or two of these might become historical mentors for you and have an on-going input in your life as you do follow-up study.

[14]Bennett (1992:17) lists as outstanding examples of mentorees that went overseas, the so-called *pious chaplains* of British India: David Brown, Claudius Buchanan, Daniel Corrie, Henry Martyn, and Thomas Thomason. Their impact on India from 1786 to 1835 was an indirect but important achievement for Simeon. Simeon actively sought chaplaincies in Asia for forty of his Cambridge students. In addition, he sent many into Anglican Pastorates all over England.

only on the Anglican Church but on England itself and even into India. Single male workers can be encouraged by this one whose deliberate choice of singleness was one factor which enhanced his focused life.

His focused life emphasizes all of the focal issues: major role, life purpose(s), unique methodology (mentoring) and ultimate contributions. The shaping forces that helped him move toward a focused life included a strong mentor influence early on.

A. J. Gordon (1836-1895) was a married,[15] missions-minded (with a name like Adoniram Judson what could you expect), Baptist pastor in the Boston area. His twenty-five years as senior pastor at the Clarendon Street Baptist Church of Boston highlight his focused life. Not only did he bring about steady church growth in the strongly non-receptive Boston area but he also extended his ministry to national influence primarily through his conference ministry with D. L. Moody at Northfield (and the networking contacts it produced).

He was entrepreneurial and encouraged and released multiple ministries flowing out of his church. These included evangelistic, social, and missionary minded ministries. He was interested in training and releasing leaders. He founded Gordon Bible Institute which was the seedbed for the Gordon-Conwell Seminary of today.

He maintained a consistent testimony for the Word of God and fundamental tenets in a time when there was a major crisis between modernists and fundamentals.[16] And yet his diplomatic bearing allowed him to have friends all across the theological continuum. And because of his winsome personality and these relationships he continued to have influence.

He did fundamental thinking which was well ahead of its time (for example his study into women in leadership, and his views on missions and missionaries). Many of his study papers still need to be read today.

I became interested in him when doing ultimate contribution research and especially when I saw that he manifested all of the prime types. He is unusual in this regard (most effective leaders have 4-6 ultimate contribution categories, not 12 like he did). But it is the inner consistency, his character and beingness, which impress me as much as his achievements. He had strong values which guided his life and ministry. Ministry essentially flows out of being. He superbly illustrates this.

---

[15]His *social base pattern* was the *release pattern* (male in full time ministry, female in full support from the home), as was common in those days. His wife was a tremendous support to him. His son wrote the definitive biography of his life. See Appendix D. Social Base Processing.

[16]One doctoral research study on his life traces the fundamentalists movement of today to his influence. While this may be true for his orthodoxic concerns his orthopraxic breadth put him far beyond the fundamental camps of today and more in line with evangelicals. See The **Contributions of Adoniram Judson Gordon To American Christianity**, by George Gerald Houghton, Th.D dissertation at Dallas Theological Seminary.

He will appeal to those:

- who espouse qualitative church growth as well as quantitative church growth,
- who want to see a turn of the century Flag Ship ministry,
- who are interested in a pastoral model with a mission minded thrust,
- who advocate a strong authoritative Biblical base in the midst of ministries which are pulling away from the Bible,
- who are interested in how to create sodality ministries and release people to accomplish their visions out of a church setting.

He was my personal historical mentor for 1990 and 1991. I appreciate his impact in my own life--especially the challenge to expand my influence-mix.

His focused life emphasizes two of the focal issues: major role, ultimate contribution. The shaping forces that helped him move toward a focused life included a variety of diverse elements.

Samuel Brengle (1860-1936) was a married,[17] Salvation Army worker who early on (mid 20s) went through a paradigm shift[18] with regard to a holy life. And it lasted all his life. This was a great encouragement to me personally. My teaching on the victorious life indicated to me that it is usually only entered into by people with 15 or more years of ministry experience and in their mid to late 30s. But here was a young person who moved into a victorious life early on.[19] I can now encourage those younger leaders who hunger for victory in their lives with this fine American prairies' product who ministered through the Salvation Army.

Eventually, his testimony of a holy life and public ministry so impacted that the Salvation Army created a brand new role for him, a unique role which took into account both his public rhetorician focus and his emphasis on a holy life. He was released to minister in this role the rest of his life.

He was married for 28 years and had a productive ministry. His wife, also a Salvation Army officer was a wonderful support in the ministry. His wife died when he was 55 and he carried on a productive ministry as a single person for the rest of his life.

His life emphasizes character as the basis of ministry. Probably as well as anyone, he illustrates that ministry flows out of being. He shows the importance of a specifically designed role to fit giftedness and experience if one is to minister in convergence.[20]

---

[17]For a short time Samuel Brengle and his wife were in the *co-ministry social base pattern*, that is, both parties in full time Christian work. But as children came they moved into the *release pattern*, with the wife maintaining the major social responsibility in the home. See Appendix D. Social Base Processing.

[18]A *paradigm shift* is a major change of perspective which significantly affects how you view some aspect of life or ministry thereafter. Paradigm shifts are often God's way of prompting a leader toward prioritizing his/her life on focal issues. See Clinton (1993) *The Paradigm Shift--God's Means of Opening Up New Vistas for Leaders*. Available through Barnabas Publishers.

[19]One does not have to totally enter into or agree with the conceptual or theological paradigm of a leader in order to admire its effects in his/her life. While not buying into Brengle's holiness paradigm, nevertheless I love his life and testimony and manifestation of the fruit of the Spirit in his life and long for those same effects in my own life.

[20]*Convergence* is the most advanced phase along the developmental time-line. It is a time of increased ministry effectiveness due to a number of factors coming together and synergizing one's ministry. Such factors as a ministry role which fits and enhances giftedness and ideal influence-mix; a mature spirituality which is the primary power base for ministry; a cogent ministry philosophy which has key values learned

I was introduced to this wonderful Christian leader by a mid-career Salvation Army Officer, Major Marg Burt, who was taking a number of my leadership classes. She gave me a copy of his biography, now well-marked, for which I shall forever be grateful. He became my historical mentor during the year 1989. I also reread the biography two years later. He is a beautiful example of one who finished well. I have deeply appreciated his impact in my own life--the motivation to finish well and especially one concept, present day faith exercised retrospectively about the long range effects of past ministry. I can still trust God today to work through my past ministry.

His focused life emphasizes all of the focal issues: major role, unique methodology, life purpose, and ultimate contribution. The shaping forces that helped move him toward a focused life included early home-life experiences, some sense of destiny interventions, some macro-contextual factors, and the aforementioned paradigm shift which accompanied a leadership committal and became the driving force of his life purpose.

G. Campbell Morgan (1863-1945) was a married[21] Congregational Pastor (Baptistic roots--a preacher's kid) who had an extended parachurch Bible Conference ministry which spanned two continents. His thirteen years as senior pastor of Westminster Chapel and his ten years of itinerant Bible conference ministry in Canada and the U.S.A., provided the environment for identifying and using his major role--the focal issue which was the driving force of his focused ministry. This world class public Bible teacher exemplifies what can happen when use of and explanation of the Bible become the central and controlling factor of a life.

His numerous ministry insights (such as his Bible Institute ministry from within a local church base, the use of a retreat center, and the spread of his influence through a written ministry flowing out of his oral ministry) still challenge us even today. His grasp of the Gospel and the person and work of Christ are thrilling.

His search for a convergent role, involving back and forth swings from church to parachurch indicates the important necessity of adapting a role which enhances giftedness, destiny calling, experience and influence-mix[22] so as to bring convergent ministry. His is a study in how God directs and develops a person toward an ideal influence-mix.

The more than 100 writings left behind are one of the ultimate contributions that still influence leaders today. He is living proof that the Bible still equips leaders in teaching,

---

throughout ministry guiding it; a sense of destiny being fulfilled. There could also be a number of minor factors which also affect this time: geographical location, integration of many past experiences, a prophecy, opportunistic situation. In Brengle's case, God's divine intervention brought about the role adaptation, not any manipulation or forcing on Brengle's part.

[21]His four sons all went into the ministry. His two daughters supported him in the ministry at various times traveling with him in his itinerant ministry. He dedicates one of this books to them in appreciation for their help in the ministry. The dominant social base pattern throughout his life was that of the *release pattern*. He ministered full time. His wife maintained the home environment. See Appendix D. Social Base Processing.

[22]All leaders influence followers. They can influence **directly**, that is, face-to-face ministry, **indirectly**, via shaping of key individuals or via materials used by others or **organizationally** via executive leadership or committees or the like. Each leader has a profile corresponding to which of these dominates or how they relate. In addition, each of the categories can be measured in terms of extensiveness (quantity), intensiveness (depth of impact) or comprehensiveness (breadth of impact). The resulting analysis of influence which relates these factors is called the *influence-mix*. Leaders are gifted to realize some potential in influence-mix. God shapes and develops a leader toward that influence-mix. Bigger is not better. Smaller is not better. Appropriate is best. Morgan is an excellent study in how God does this.

reproof, correction, and instruction in righteousness so that they can ably carry out God's intended ministry for them. He was consistent in character as well as giftedness--a legacy equally as important as his writings.

I was introduced to one of his great books, **Living Messages of the Books of the Bible** while at Columbia Bible College in the late 60s by Bible teacher Frank Sells. This book has significantly helped me in my grasp of Bible books as a whole as well as encouraged me to launch out to master each Bible book in terms of its leadership significance for our day.[23] But it was only recently, about 3 years ago after reading the one chapter treatment of Morgan in Warren Wiersbe's **Walking With The Giants** that I saw the value of having him as one of my historical mentors.

I used Wiersbe's suggested bibliography on Morgan as my starting point. Morgan has been my personal historical mentor for the years 1993 and 1994. During this time, in my day-by-day meetings with him in his biographies, his sermons, and his teaching books, Morgan has inspired me and drawn me deeper into Christ and to a renewed dedication to mastery and teaching of the Scriptures. I have appreciated his impact in my own life--especially his Christ centered ministry, which has greatly helped me to more fully understand Jesus as the Christ and to grow in my personal relationship to Him. I have also appreciated his sound hermeneutical approach to the Scriptures which has affirmed my own Bible ministry and inspired me to go on.

He will appeal to those with a teaching gift, a hunger for the Scriptures, and those who want to see the Bible as central to their ministries. In my opinion no publicly gifted minister that I am aware of has had such a simple faith in the power of the Scriptures, when carefully explained, to impact on lives as this man did. He let the Scriptures speak for themselves. He expected them to bring response. They brought response. In every ministry assignment this was repeated. Many leaders claim to have a Bible centered ministry. He did not have to claim it. He manifested it.

His focused life emphasizes three of the focal issues: major role, life purpose, and ultimate contribution. The shaping forces that helped move him toward a focused life included the modeling of parents, early home-life experiences such as personal sickness and tragic loss of his sister, a major faith challenge as a late teenager concerning the authority of the Scriptures, rejection for ordination into the Methodist ministry, some macro-contextual factors, and a major sponsoring mentor (Moody).

Robert Jaffray (1873-1945) was a married[24] Christian and Missionary Alliance Missionary to Indo-China for 34 years. On the whole this was a successful ministry experience which included heading up a Bible School, mission administration, and writing (mostly periodicals with some training materials). But it was his acceptance of a new challenge at age 58, that sets him apart, and highlights his focused ministry. At that time,[25]

---

[23] I have produced a three Volume Series in this regard: **Handbook I. Leaders, Leadership, and the Bible--an Overview**, (1993), 305 pages. **Handbook II. They Lived By Faith--Findings from Bible Leaders Lives**, (1994), 350 pages. **Handbook III. The Big Picture--Leadership and the Bible as a Whole Macro Studies**, (1993) 400 pages.

[24] Prior to marriage his wife was a single full time missionary worker hence the independent *social base pattern* (both parties in full time different work) was in effect. After marriage and a short period the social base pattern moved to the *release pattern*. See Appendix D. Social Base Processing.

[25] This *faith challenge* came at a time when most missionaries (and pastors) would be content to move toward retirement. In addition, he had two major health problems which would have derailed most of us. And yet within ten years of accepting this challenge to begin evangelization of Indonesia, he saw the church there grow to 13,093 members with 139 centers of local churches and 141 national workers. This challenge

he went through a major renewal experience[26] which led him into Indonesia, where he founded the Christian and Missionary Alliance work there (as well as several other sodality ministries not associated with the C&MA).

The tracing of this man's life and ministry is replete with lessons for leaders today. I was introduced to Robert Alexander Jaffray through the efforts of Yakob (Yopi) Tomatala, a doctoral student of mine during the years 1988-1990. It did not take me long to get interested as I began to read Tomatala's dissertation chapters. I began to see why he was studying this great leader and why he wanted to capture the heritage so as to inspire the present church in Indonesia. The title of Tomatala's dissertation is, **The Dynamic Missionary Leadership of Robert Alexander Jaffray**. And that's what it is-- dynamic.

The study of his life will appeal to older Christian workers, who may be facing the last ten to fifteen years of their active ministry life, and they want to dare hope to do the most effective work of their entire lifetimes. What an exciting challenge, for older Christian workers to think, "My most important work is yet ahead!" It is in the mature stage of our lives, that our spiritual authority is at its height. Though our physical stamina may be down, our strategic perspective may allow us to do more than in earlier days when physical stamina carried the thrust of our tactical ministry. It will also appeal to those who want to see evangelistic outreach but as facilitators of rather than direct evangelism only.

His focused life emphasizes especially two of the focal issues: life purpose, and ultimate contribution. He is one of two exceptions to major role and long tenure in focused ministry. But close scrutiny will show that his 31 years as missionary trainer and administrator provided a networking base, experience and spiritual authority which converged in his geographical shift and new role. The old role emphasized training while espousing evangelism. The new role emphasized evangelism and espousing training as evangelism happened. It was this last role that particularly manifested a focused ministry. The shaping forces that helped move him toward a focused life, particularly the last years of extremely effective evangelistic ministry, flowed from his inspiring destiny revelation experience with God.

R. C. McQuilkin (1886-1952) can inspire lay workers who are thinking of switching to full time Christian work. This missions minded Presbyterian Sunday School teacher did just that. While as a dedicated church layman he was challenged by Charles Trumble, then the head of the Sunday School Times, a parachurch organization to accept Christ as his life, the source of victorious living. This challenge, accepted, eventually led to work in that organization and then on to Bible conference ministry with the deeper life message as its thrust. He was a married worker whose wife supported him fully via ministry in the home.

An aborted attempt, over several years time, to go to the mission field was part of the process to narrow McQuilkin to a focused ministry. His call to found Columbia Bible College provided the format for his focused ministry which brought about the convergence of all his interests--proclaiming the victorious life, providing a center for facilitating materials for the victorious life, and stimulating missions interest as well as challenging many to go.

---

came not only late in life (age 58) but during a major depression in the U.S.A. the major source of finances. See Tomatala (1990:338).

[26]See Appendix B where *renewal experience* is defined. Tozer's biography on Jaffray vividly describes this *destiny revelation* (1947:90, 91).

I became interested in McQuilkin when I was a student at Columbia Bible College and used to see his picture hanging in the administration building. I also was impressed with his son, Robertson McQuilkin, for whom I was a teaching assistant. Since I was deeply attracted to the victorious message I read Trumbull's book and later McQuilkin's biography where I saw the connection between the two. It was in the early 80s when I did a comparative study of three men who spanned almost the same time period, who had a deep impact on world missions, and yet none of the three had been a missionary. That study compared McQuilkin, Dawson Trotman, and A. W. Tozer.[27] It is from that comparative study that I draw the lessons, insights, and values of his effective focused ministry.

McQuilkin will appeal to Bible teachers, because of his long and popular and solid Bible teaching ministry.[28] His systematic, hermeneutical approach is a challenge to all Bible teachers who want to be contextual in their use of Scripture. His acceptance of many faith challenges in initiating Columbia Bible College and seeing it grow are also inspirational to apostolic types who need to be encouraged in ventures of faith. His missions minded thrust is still the heartbeat of Columbia Bible College and Seminary, the legacy of his work. He will especially appeal to those who are missions minded, probably can't go themselves, and want to mobilize others to the great unfinished task of world evangelism.

His focused life emphasizes three of the focal issues: life purpose, major role, and ultimate contribution. The shaping forces that helped move him toward a focused life flowed out of an experiential paradigm shift concerning victorious living and the dramatic guidance factor which blocked his move to the mission field.[29] That perspective was at the heart of all of his efforts and eventually led to a major role and ultimate contributions.

Henrietta Mears (1890-1963) is my only woman leader considered in this study. Three biographies attest to the power and influence of her life. She was a single woman[30] lay leader who at age 38 and after about 15 years of teaching in public schools went into ministry as a staff member of the First Presbyterian Church of Hollywood. Her thirty-five years of full time pastoral/educational work was filled with accomplishments including the challenging of 100s maybe even 1000s into full time Christian work from collegiate ranks, the founding Gospel Light Publications, 1933, the founding of Forest Home Christian Conference Center, 1938, and GLINT (Gospel Literature International), 1961.

---

[27]All three were extremely missions minded and influenced the world missions movement through their ministries. McQuilkin (along with some others) founded Columbia Bible College which has sent many people on to the mission field. Trotman founded the Navigators an organization now which has work in more than 60 countries. A. W. Tozer was part of the Christian and Missionary Alliance, a movement become denomination which has more churches and membership abroad than in the U.S.A. due to its heavy mission emphasis. He was also under consideration as one of the persons to be studied for this book but when I narrowed to eight I omitted him as well as Kenneth Strachan, a parachurch worker in Latin America.
[28]His parables book was a great help to me as I worked through my own hermeneutical principles for studying parables. This out of print book is sometimes available in Seminary and Bible College libraries. See *Studying Our Lord's Parables*, Columbia: Columbia Bible College, 1933.
[29]There had been a number of obstacles, especially health ones over a period of years, that slowed the McQuilkins from going overseas. The final blow, however, was dramatic. The boat they were to sail on overseas, with all their missionary barrels on it, sank in the harbor just days before they were to embark. This was the final guidance that opened them to consider God's plan for them in the U.S.A.
[30]She had one of the best social base situations I have seen in a single person. Her every need was taken care of so as to release her totally to pursue a word gifted ministry. See Appendix D. Social Base Processing.

Preface to Focused Lives   page 11

Early on in her Bible teaching ministry to students as she reflected on her own desire to be a missionary she realized, as she watched student after student go into full time Christian service, that her ultimate purpose would be to train many, many leaders, to nurture them in spiritual growth and to mobilize them to penetrate the world with the Gospel. This ultimate purpose became the major focal issue for her life. (Roe 1990:91).

I first became interested in Henrietta Mears when a student of mine, Karen Klebe, did a case study on her. Here was a powerful woman leader with a Bible centered ministry which impacted many and shaped some of the most influential Christians of our time.[31] Later, I was given a copy of the latest biography by Cathy Schaller. As I began to study it and note its many, many value laden statements concerning ministry philosophy, I knew I must include the study of her life in this book. From time-to-time Bob Munger and I chatted about her ministry, which he had experienced first hand, being part of the revival/renewal work among college age students in the early days of Forest Home. His personal insights about Dr. Mears and her ministry only heightened my desire to study her life in-depth.

Henrietta Mears will appeal to many: mobilizers, word gifted people, entrepreneurs and apostolic types, and those seeking how to discover and use ministry insights[32] in a ministry. Of particular interest is the study of how she motivated people.

Although her focused life emphasizes three of the focal issues, life purpose, major role, and ultimate contribution, it is life purpose that dominated. Her shaping processes toward a focused life involved value laden ministry experiences, step-by-step guidance, and call to a role which culminated the guidance and provided a platform for use of those values in a geographical location which allowed for convergent ministry.

L. E. Maxwell (1895-1984) was a rural Kansas boy whose radical conversion as an adult forever changed his life goals. After a short two year military stint near the end of World War I, he attended a small Bible institute in Kansas City for three years after his conversion and prior to any full time Christian ministry. The institute barely outlasted his student days. But mentors in that school helped to form his greater life message and ministry philosophy.[33] It was this message, a deeper life message, which was at the core of his life purpose, the major ministry focus issue.

---

[31]In **Dream Big--the Henrietta Mears Story**, Earl Roe's editorial commemorative edition observing the 100 anniversary of the birth of Dr. Mears, the first four pages of the book are testimonials to the ministry of Dr. Mears. Those attesting to her impactful ministry (many of them meaning personal impact) include: Dr. Billy Graham, the Honorable Mark O. Hatfield, Dr. Lyle E. Schaller, Dale, Roy and the Rogers family, Dr. Charles E. Fuller (previously given), Dr. Richard C. Halverson, Colleen and Louis H. Evans, Jr., Dr. Bill Bright, Dr. Jim Rayburn, Ruth Bell Graham, Dr. Steward P. MacLennan, Dr. David Allan Hubbard, Dr. Robert Boyd Munger, Vonette Bright, Dr. Warren Filkin, Dr. Larry Ward, and Ethel Barret.
[32]*Ministry insights* is a technical term from leadership emergence theory referring to breakthroughs in how to accomplish ministry. These are tailor made to the giftedness and destiny of the individual discovering them. Often they involve a *paradigm shift* about how to do ministry. Trotman's discovery of discipleship as a multiplication process is just such a breakthrough. Mears was phenomenal in seeing and carrying off new ministry insights including how to organize and release collegiates into responsible positions of ministry, motivational activities and events, etc.
[33]This institute, Midland Bible Institute, was founded by W. C. Stevens of the Nyack Bible Institute. According to Spaulding (1991:39) it actually graduated only one male student--Maxwell. However, E. V. Thompson, founder of Worldteam, my own mission, also studied under *Daddy Stevens* so well known for his treatment of Romans and the deeper life, victorious message. So this small Bible institute, which lasted only a few years, had long lasting influence through these two great products, Thompson and Maxwell. Stevens and Dorothy Ruth Miller, another experienced ex-Nyack faculty member provided the mentoring

Eventually, in the early 20s, he went to Canada and in a step-by-step leading over several years founded a Bible institute. He was powerfully gifted as a Bible teacher right from the start. This institute grew to become Prairie Bible Institute. When the tremendous missionary window opened after World War II, Prairie Bible Institute was in place and ready to train. In the years immediately following the Second World War, the school experienced the greatest student body influx of its history. The post-war period meant a whole new movement in world missions. Prairie was a leader in this thrust. Maxwell's travels abroad heightened his vision for missions. Whereas by 1948, 373 career missionaries had been sent out from the entire alumni, by 1959, only twelve years later, the number totaled 1200. (Spaulding 1991:69)[34]

I had known of Maxwell because of his book **Crowded to Christ** which Frank Sells had mentioned when I was at Columbia Bible College. My good colleague and friend, Jeff Imbach, was from Prairie. His folks were on staff there. A number of missionaries I respected in my mission had trained there. So I knew a bit about Prairie and its reputation for rugged discipline, missions emphasis and deeper life teaching. But it wasn't till Steve Spaulding, the grandson of L. E. Maxwell studied with me and wrote a doctoral dissertation on Maxwell that I became interested in Maxwell. This brilliant and candid analysis by an *insider* piqued my interest and shed tremendous insight into why Maxwell had a focused life.[35]

Maxwell will especially appeal to four kinds of people: those with strong word gifts, pioneers who may have to start a needed work from scratch, those who are missions minded and want to mobilize people toward the Great Commission, and those who propound the victorious life message. His ministry insights, though perhaps not directly transferable to today, will prompt your search for functional equivalents for today.

His focused life emphasizes all of the focal issues: life purpose, major role, unique methodology, and ultimate contribution. The shaping forces that helped move him toward a focused life flowed out of his mentoring experiences leading both to victorious living and a Bible Institute methodology for training and mobilizing. His early character shaping brought about need for the reality of victorious living.

Well, there you have it. Eight leaders whose lives have important lessons for us. Your study of any one, two, or as many as you want to do, will lead you into insights for your own life. You will be moved, yes, but even more you will have ideas that will challenge you, that you can use. And perhaps even some life-changing values.

If I were to condense the book as a whole into a subject and major ideas, here is how I would word it.

---

which shaped Maxwell. There Maxwell also learned a comprehensive inductive Bible study methodology (much like G. Campbell Morgan's methodology) which stood the test of time in his own Bible teaching ministry. Dorothy Ruth Miller went on later to teach with Maxwell at Prairie Bible Institute.

[34]Spaulding goes on to say that six of these were from the Maxwell household. In my own mission, when I went to the field in 1971, there were numerous alumni of Prairie in the West Indies.

[35]See Stephen Maxwell Spaulding's **Lion On The Prairies: An Interpretive Analysis of the Life and Leadership of Leslie Earl Maxwell, 1895-1984.** Unpublished manuscript to be submitted for a Doctoral Dissertation at the School of World Mission, Fuller Theological Seminary.

Focused Lives, As Seen In These Eight Christian Leaders,
include some common elements such as
- long term ministries in a major role crafted to fit the leader, or an expanding, changing role in a long term geographic locale, and/or use of a unique methodology to accomplish purposes which may include,
- a lifelong involvement of serving Christ to fulfill some specific destiny purpose, and/or
- a concentration on achieving certain important goals which left behind legacies for the on-going work of Christ, and
- an importance on the Word of God for personal growth and ministry, and
- the shaping work of God to move these leaders toward their focus, all of

which **reflect insightful lessons and values helpful to present leaders.**

. Read again the underlined portion. That's what I want to accomplish in your life. My intent is for you, the reader, to meaningfully interact with one or more of these historical mentors so as to be empowered by the lessons, values, and/or insights. I want you to know the inherent power promised in Hebrews 13:7,8 and the enabling work of Christ in your leadership. And of course I want you to see symptoms of a focused life in your own experience so that you can deliberately make decisions enhancing your focus.

Let me suggest how you should read the book. The book is organized in a straightforward manner. Chapter 1 explains the basic format used to structure each interpretive biographical chapter. Chapter 10 concludes with comparative lessons drawn from Chapters 2-9. Chapters 2-9 each give interpretive biographical information on the 8 leaders that I have introduced in the preface. After chapter 10, I include a glossary of important terms that are used throughout the interpretive dialog. I usually *italicize* them for easy reference. The footnotes carry a good bit of the interpretive framework. If you are not technically inclined, skip them. But if you are interested in the interpretive framework of leadership concepts I use to exegete these lives and you want to be connected to further leadership materials then glance at these handy-to-get-at footnotes.

If you read chapter 1 you will know **what kind** of interpretive information I am going to include in each of the biographical chapters. In that chapter I will explain the **importance of the kinds of information** I will give. Once you have that under your belt you should feel free to read at your leisure any **one** or **more** of the biographical chapters. Each will stand alone and contain valuable cognitive information as well as motivational information. Because of the LIKE-ATTRACTS-LIKE dynamic my guess is that you will be attracted to 2 or 3 leaders. Read them expectantly. I expect God to challenge you with concepts He wants to put in your ministry. But be prepared to invest time. Know that an hour or hour and a half is involved in the reading of a single biographical chapter, that is, if you are carefully reading for lessons for your own life.

Finally, after reading as many biographical chapters as you want, go to chapter 10 and see my final comments which give comparative highlights. Some of those highlights may cause you to go back and read other biographical chapters. Or, if you are old fashioned, just read the whole book in sequence. I'd like it if you read the whole book. Don't forget the leadership mandate as you read.

> Remember your former leaders. Think back on how they lived and ministered. **Imitate those excellent qualities you see in their lives.** For Jesus Christ is the same today, as He was in the past and as He will be in the future. What He did for them **He will do for you to inspire and enable your leadership.** Hebrews 13:7,8 (Personal Interpretive Paraphrase)

Acknowledgments

I am thankful to: Gordon McDonald who connected me to Charles Simeon; Major Marg Burt who gave me Samuel Brengle's biography with a word of exhortation to read and use it; Frank Sells who first introduced me to G. Campbell Morgan's works and Warren Wiersbe whose chapter encouraged me to study Morgan's life; Dr. Yopi Tomatala whose love for and research into the life of Robert Jaffray, the founder of his denomination in Indonesia, linked me to Jaffray; Steve Spaulding, whose doctoral level research dissertation on his grandfather, L. E. Maxwell, challenged me with the all consuming passion of this great teacher; Karen Klebe Goldfain who first did a case study on Henrietta Mears, a heroine of hers, and Cathy Schaller, who gave me the latest biography on Henrietta Mears, **Dream Big--The Henrietta Mears Story**. I believe it providential that I was linked to each of the eight leaders who are the object of this study. These eight historical mentors[36] have inspired me.

I am also grateful to Dean Dudley Woodberry and my faculty of the School of World Mission of Fuller Seminary (and of course the board) for my sabbatical which enabled in-depth research into these eight leaders lives as well as time to write.

My thanks also go to John Bennett for permission to copy and use his Doctoral Dissertation on Charles Simeon. I have referenced his outstanding dissertation on Simeon many times in Chapter 2.

Disclaimer--Writing Style, Use of Past Present and Future Tenses

Sometimes when I write I subconsciously put myself back into the time frame of the person I am writing about. I then write using present tense language or future tense language from that time-frame's perspective. This is sort of a *past present tense*. Since I already know what will happen in the future I sometimes foreshadow by using a *future tense seen in the present*. I did this unconsciously. I have so lived with each of these biographical persons that it is as if I were there. I found out about this when I shipped Simeon's chapter to Betsy Glanville, whom I knew had selected Simeon as a historical mentor for the year 1994. She caught this and pointed it out to me. Now I had two options. I could correct each occurrence and put past tense language in its place--this I have done from Chapter 7 on (after Betsy gave me the feedback). But upon going back and reading Charles Simeon and other earlier chapters I find I like the quaint feel of these quasi-tenses even if they are not exactly seen regularly in English. The like-notions of flashbacks and foreshadowings somewhat give precedence. So I decided not to go back and change these rather stylistic descriptions in the earlier chapters. Could I ask your indulgence? Read through these and feel with me as I frequently put myself back there and describe from a present tense framework.

Referencing

I use the missiological approach to reference bibliographical entries. I give author, year, and page number(s) of sources I quote or draw information from. Refer to bibliography entry using the author and year. Example: (Clinton 1989:217) indicates **Leadership Emergence Theory**, page 217. I note permission to quote these sources, where required, in the bibliographies of each chapter.

---

[36]See **Connecting--Finding the Mentors You Need To Succeed In Life**, by Paul Stanley and J. Robert Clinton. Chapter 10 deals with *historical mentors*. Of course, one of my purposes in this book is to show you how rich are the insights that can be gained from historical mentors. I hope to connect you in to the notion of historical mentors. They are always available. Real live mentors aren't always there.

Chapter 1.
Introduction to Interpretive Biography

Remember your former leaders. Think back on how they lived and ministered. Imitate those excellent qualities you see in their lives. For Jesus Christ is the same today, as He was in the past and as He will be in the future. What He did for them He will do for you to inspire and enable your leadership.
                    Hebrews 13:7,8 (Personal Interpretive Paraphrase)

Introduction

In this chapter I am going to explain my approach to analysis of Christian leaders using available biographies and materials. I am going to answer the question, from my perspective, **How shall we remember these former leaders?** Some readers do not need this. They don't require or need an explanation of my approach to presentation of material. If that is the case with you, then by all means move on to chapter 2 and Charles Simeon or to the chapter of your choice. Each chapter stands alone. Its information is useful and understandable as is. But if you are interested in an explanation of the structure of a chapter, the concepts I use, and the underpinnings of my overall approach, then read on.

In my opinion, all biographical work presents biased material. It involves selection of material. It involves presentation of material. It is a second hand, selective look at some small pieces of reality. Not all the reality is even available to a biographical writer. No matter how objective an author claims to be, that author brings a personal analytical framework to the task of presenting material, a personal worldview that affects what is seen and communicated. I recognize that. I am not negative about this. For me it is simply the way things are. Those very biases that authors have will enable them perhaps to see things I would not or you would not.

In doing historical analysis of Christian leaders who have passed away this is compounded further. For the most part, I am working with materials of others who have written about these leaders.[1] With all this in mind, how can we be sure of what we are presenting or you of what you are reading? The final answer is you can not for certain. The question then, in the final sense, is not, "Is this exactly true, what I am reading?" At least for the non-academic, non-professional scholar. More precise and appropriate, I believe, are the questions, "If this were valid and true, is it useful? Does it violate Biblical norms? Does it violate conscience? Is it in harmony with truth as I understand it?" And that is the basic mind-set I use as I read the biographies and analyze the incidents recorded.[2]

---

[1] I am also studying first hand writings of these leaders, themselves, so that I get their viewpoints on many things--particularly some of their Biblical views and some of their stated values underlying their approach to ministry.

[2] I realize that there has been a major paradigm shift with regards to biography. From the Christian side of things, Elizabeth Eliot's work No Graven Image and her biographical work on Kenneth Strachan as well as Amy Carmichael illustrate the new standard which prefers to look at people *warts and all*. Prior to this paradigm shift, Christian authors usually painted only the rosier side of some character with a few minor exceptions. Presentations often overwhelmed readers. They knew they could never be like those heroes or heroines as presented. The Christian audience today accepts as more valid, material which shows the down side as well as the up side. Frequently, my students are troubled by this rosy picture of Christian heroes or heroines. I apply my criterion ruthlessly. If it were true, could we use it? For I recognize that all biography is biased.

Chapter 1. Introduction to Interpretive Biography

So up front I am admitting to an approach called interpretive biography.[3] Most biography is interpretive anyway, by default. That is, the selection criteria of the author is one form of interpretation. Choosing what to include is one of the strongest forms of interpretation, even if you do not comment on the selections. Most biography follows a linear approach to presentation of selected materials with anecdotes or vignettes containing actual happenings in the life. The linear approach then traces the life in terms of time periods. Chapters follow apparently natural phases of time. Finally there is usually several chapters that then go on to highlight the author's view of the value of the life. All in all, this is interpretive biography but without an adequate framework to guide it.[4] The value of the work, then, depends on the intuitive quality of the researchers. Some do well. Others not as well. I realize my presentation will be biased by my understanding of leadership, use of available materials, writing style, and view of historical biography. But I at least have a framework guiding my attempt toward consistent interpretation and evaluation.

The usual critical vignette approach to biography picks certain vignettes from among many possible which represent in some fashion the different phases of the life. The vignettes will be ordered chronologically. Very little interpretation is given. Perhaps there will be explanation to fill in the holes between the selected vignettes. Now this leaves any interpretation, evaluation, and application to the reader alone. Some readers prefer this.

But I have found that most readers can not actually interpret, evaluate or apply very well anyway. So for most, the reading of a biography is entertaining and perhaps moves the heart, but little else happens. I prefer to interpret for the reader and suggest values, lessons, insights and potential applications. I want to not only move the heart but to also give perspectives, explicit concrete ideas, which may allow a change of understanding as well. After all, I have accumulated a level of expertise of evaluating lives. Who better to do it? This is generally true of all biographers. They have lived with the source materials and have immersed themselves with the character they are studying. Who better can draw out observations and conclusions? Having acknowledged, then, my bias toward interpretive biography, let me explain my framework of analysis.

Overview of Leadership Emergence Theory

I define a leader, from a Biblical perspective, as a person with God-given capacity and with God-given responsibility who is influencing a specific group of God's people toward God's purposes for the group. I then look at how God develops such a leader that He has invested in. How does God take a leader from potential to accomplishment of His purposes through that leader?

The assumption of this theory is that as a Christian with this leadership capacity responds to the shaping activity of God through life's circumstances and decisions, the leader gains in responsibility, influencing those entrusted to his/her leadership toward God's purposes. Given human frailty and failure, the processing and responding take

---

[3]Norman K. Denzin's 1989 work, **Interpretive Biography**, Newbury Park: Sage Publications lays out the rigorous academic framework for this form of biography. My own study and research into leader's lives uses a qualitative analytical research approach called grounded theory. My research results and my own framework for analysis is in harmony with Denzin's careful description though I happened on to Denzin long after my basic research was done.

[4]See Appendix E which gives 5 types of biographical genre: vignettes, linear vignettes, critical vignettes, chronological/interpretive, themes of a life. My approach is chronological/interpretive.

Chapter 1. Introduction to Interpretive Biography

varied amounts of time. As faithfulness is demonstrated, the leader is given greater responsibility, though this is not necessarily measurable quantitatively. An effective leader, responding appropriately to God's developmental interventions will approach ever new levels of effectiveness, reaching a degree of ministerial convergence in which one's skills, gifts, roles and sphere of influence are merged for the greatest effect.

The development of a Christian leader has at its core a spiritual formation of character and intimacy with God which cannot be calibrated from an external perspective but which is equally as or more important than the development of externally measurable leadership skills and influence.

In our comparative study of many leaders we have identified three major overall categories to help us understand the development. These three include a time-line perspective, analyses of critical incidents in a life along that time-line, and patterns over time. We then analyze these critical incidents and patterns for lessons, values, and insights that help us understand the shaping effect of these upon the life and ministry. We are particularly interested in the shaping activity of God in the life and ministry. For purposes of categories, we delineate three kinds of such shaping activities: 1. Spiritual Formation, those which affect leadership character; 2. Ministerial formation, those which affect leadership skills; 3. Strategic formation, the shaping of an overall ministry perspective, a ministry philosophy, which interweaves lessons learned into an increasingly clear ministry framework that gives direction and focus and ultimate purpose in a leader's life.

Comparative studies among many lives have produced a generic time-line, the identification of various kinds of critical incidents and some common patterns. As we compare a specific unique analysis of a given person with these generic findings, we frequently get other suggestive insights for further probing. Further research along these suggestions often opens up new findings. And so it goes, the theory affects our findings and the findings develop further the theory.[5] I collect many of the theoretical notions, sometimes introduced in the text or footnotes in the glossary.

So then in my presentation of these eight Christian leaders I assume a strong providential working of God in their lives. I analyze their lives and construct a time-line for each. I analyze critical incidents along that time-line for lessons, values, and insights that help explain the leader's life and ministry. I identify patterns. I use evaluation categories and methods that have arisen out of comparative studies of many leaders. Now I can not put all of this information in one chapter. It would require a book length treatment to do that for each of the leaders chosen in this book. Instead I select from that analysis some important items which can help us understand their focal issues and God's directive destiny toward those focal issues. I go on to give my opinion, my own evaluation of their ultimate contributions. All of this with a view toward identifying, as carefully as I can, ideas which may be transferable to my readers.

If I must select from a mass of information only a few things, what are they? What interpretive biographical information will I include? How will I display it? That is the

---

[5]As with any new theory, leadership emergence theory contains many definitions and descriptions unfamiliar to a new reader of it. The theory is fairly far along in its development though there is always the tweaking of definitions. I am introducing the theory, as illustrated in these lives, in this book. The footnotes, for the most part carry on a running dialogue which gives the concepts I introduce and where you can find them for further study. I also give numerous interpretive comments in the footnotes. I italicize the labels for definitions and concepts in these footnotes for easy referencing. I also collect them all in a glossary which follows chapter 10.

objective of the next section. I will show you the basic organization of my display of information for a biographical chapter.

Basic Structure of A Biographical Chapter

I use the following 11 headings to help me organize my presentation. I will list them first, then give a brief explanation for each. The basic sections include:

1. Title,
2. Two Attention Getters, called Opening Illustration 1 and 2,
3. The Time-Line (though I mention the time-line here in the order of items as I use it to organize the biographical narrative of item 4 which follows, it will usually be included at the end of the chapter as a reference aid).
4. Highly Condensed Biographical Narrative,
5. Critical Incidents Identified, and/or Explained,
6. Values,
7. Ministry Insights, Lessons, and General Values,
8. Contributions,
9. Overall Lessons from the Life,
10. Implications for a Focused Life,
11. Where To Go and What To Do For Further Study.

The Title

For each of the Christian leaders concerned I give a title. Some are cumbersome and lengthy. These are complicated people I am describing. Notice in doing this I have already interpreted what I think is something central to that person. Each title was agonizingly chosen (some changed several times). The carefully chosen titles are suggestive of something about the leader that I think needs to be emphasized. For example,

> Chapter 2. Charles Simeon (1759-1836)
> A Man in the Right Place, Strategically
> A Study in Sphere of Influence and
> Effective Change Through Mentoring

Usually the significance of the title will be explained along the way or at least in categories 7, 8, 9, or 10. In this case, you would need to know what I mean by a mentor. You would have to know what I mean by strategic as over against tactical. And you would need to know some things about change dynamics. All of these will be discussed in the chapter. The point I am making now is that *these titles are suggestive*. They anticipate what is to come. They foreshadow in a motivational way. Scrutinize them carefully. Then read the chapter looking forward to an explanation of these hopefully intriguing titles.

Again note, my selection of a title is certainly a facet of **interpretive** biography.

Attention Getters

Gregory's second law of teaching, the Law of the Learner, states,

A LEARNER IS ONE WHO ATTENDS WITH INTEREST TO THE LESSON.

Chapter 1. Introduction to Interpretive Biography

Or stated as a rule,

> GAIN AND KEEP THE ATTENTION AND INTEREST OF THE PUPILS UPON THE LESSON. DO NOT TRY TO TEACH WITHOUT ATTENTION.

I label attempts to do this, Attention Getters, called Opening Illustrations 1 and 2. I never teach without using them. And the way I will do it in each chapter is to give one or two real life incidents right at the beginning of the chapter. You have probably noticed that the technique is in vogue in popular Christian literature. Hardly any chapter begins without some kind of illustrative example. I follow suit. I want you to see critical incidents. I want you to feel as well as to understand. And so I begin with an attention getting incident or two. These range in size from a few paragraphs to a couple of pages. But these are not just random. They each have an important teaching point. Each vignette I so choose will be representative of an incident which shaped a *focal value* or was a *focal factor*. What is a focal value and what is a focal factor?

definition   A **focal value** is a dominant controlling perspective which interweaves itself throughout a person's ministry.

definition   A **focal factor** is an incident which helps give strategic guidance in terms of role, life purpose, unique methodology, or ultimate contribution of the leader.

Once identified, a focal value can be illustrated in many diverse aspects of the person's ministry. In fact, the more it is seen across the person's ministry, the more certain that it is a focal value. A focal point describes the time or actual prompting incident(s) that crystallized the value. Analysis of a focal point includes describing the incident that prompted the discovery, evaluating the providential shaping activity, describing explicitly the value, and showing the result of this value in the ensuing ministry. Such values, when abstracted into a clear statement that can grasped by others, often prove to be transferable almost immediately in someone else's ministry. That is, readers can learn vicariously in a second hand manner without the actual experience which prompted the first learner. The focal factor points the leader to one or more of the focal issues. Sometimes the focal factor is embryonic in form and will be reinforced in other critical incidents.

Perhaps more fundamentally, we should ask the question, what is a value? I have studied some experts in order to get at the notion of a value.[6]

definition   A **leadership value** is an underlying assumption which affects how a leader behaves in or perceives leadership situations or issues.

Some examples of such values include:

Example 1   Small group structures are necessary in the church for believer's to learn about their spiritual gifts.

Example 2   Spiritual authority must dominate a leader's power bases--i.e. those means used to influence followers toward God's purposes.

---

[6] I was especially helped by Paul W. Taylor's (1961) work clarifying the language used in describing values. Others values oriented authors I profited from include Sidney B. Simon (et al 1978). Hunter Lewis (1990) and Christopher Hodgkinson (1991) bring up to date my reading on value theory. But when all is said and done I simplified the technical descriptions and definitions to the one included here. I am not too far off base in capturing the essence of a value in doing so.

Example 3   Ministry must be personal.

Values can affect all three of the kinds of God's shaping formational activity--leadership character, leadership skills, and leadership strategic thinking.

The Time-Line

The integrating concept of a leadership emergence study is the time-line around which the study is oriented.[7] Usually this time-line is given along a horizontal axis. The time-line is broken into increments referred to as development phases, identified with Roman numerals. Where possible these increments are dated or in some way marked in terms of time. These phases are usually labeled with descriptive phrases which point out the central thrust of the development that happened in the phase. A given leadership emergence study on a leader will produce a time-line that is unique to that leader. There will be a foundation period in which God works sovereignly. There will be a transition time into full time Christian work. From there on, time periods will vary with each leader. They will fit God's development for that leader. Development phases should be labeled to capture that uniqueness.

The **time-line** is the linear display along a horizontal axis which is broken up into development phases. A **unique time-line** refers to a time-line describing a given leader's lifetime which will have unique development phases bearing labels expressing that uniqueness.

A time-line representing the life of a leader can usually be broken down into units which are related to a significant segment of development. These significant portions of time are called development phases. Development phases are usually indicated by Roman numerals and a label describing the thrust of development going on during the phase. Further sub-divisions of development phases are called sub-phases, which are indicated by capital letters. Development phases and sub-phases have similar characteristics which will be described and discussed later. A **development phase** is a marked off length on a time-line representing a significant portion of time in a leader's life history in which notable development takes place. A **sub-phase** is a marked off length on a time-line within a development phase which points out intermediate times of development during the development phase.

A development phase represents a unit of time in a person's life. Sometimes it can be identified by noting major changes in sphere of influence, roles, or geographical locations. **Sphere of influence** refers to the totality of people being influenced and for whom a leader will give an account to God which includes those people under direct personal influence (face-to-face present ministry), those under indirect influence (non-time-bound influence), and those under organizational influence (influence flowing through organizational structures.) **Influence-mix** refers to the descriptive profile of a person's sphere of influence at any given time in their ministry. It is my assumption that God's intent is to develop a person to reach his/her maximum potential. Shaping activity if responded to will do this.

---

[7]Here I give a brief introduction to the notion of a time-line. Two articles give extended treatment and in fact spell out the details I used in studying these eight Christian leaders. See *The Time-Line, What It Is and How To Construct It* (1993) and *Getting Perspective, By Using Your Unique Time-Line*, both available through Barnabas Publishers.

Chapter 1. Introduction to Interpretive Biography

I developed detailed time-lines for each of the Christian leaders studied in this book. These time-lines helped me put into perspective the shaping activities and movement toward focal issues.

Highly Condensed Biographical Narrative

I use the time-line divisions, that is the labels for phases and sub-phases to break up my narrative description of their lives. This description, called a capsule, is a highly condensed overview of the major events, activities, and people that shaped the lives in these phases. You need this, sometimes, to put in context when and how the incidents that shaped them occurred. I try, where ever I can, to include the critical incidents that form the vignettes for focal values, and/or the focusing direction that leads to a focused life.

Critical Incidents Identified, and/or Explained

Critical incidents are important shaping activities in which either a focal value is imparted or some pivotal career guidance occurs. Because of the highly condensed nature of the biographical narrative I need to give further information describing critical incidents or to explain the critical incident. This section allows me that freedom. In this section, I attempt to trace and give interpretive comments on the focal points and focusing activity that channeled the leader toward a focused life. I usually label a critical incident with a name that points to its central thrust, give the age of the leader at the time of the incident, and give an explanation as to which formation is being affected.

Values

In this section, I attempt to identify and state some important values that shaped leadership character, leadership skills, and leadership strategic ministry. In short I attempt to give my interpretations of values that under girded the focused life.

Ministry Insights, Lessons, and General Values

I have already described what a value is--an underlying assumption which affects how a leader behaves in or perceives leadership situations or issues. I include these in this section along with lessons and ministry insights. Lessons are statements reflecting observations of how these values may fit into other leader's lives. Ministry insights refers to special breakthroughs that allow a leader to deliver his/her ministry to others in a more effective way. These insights flow from an understanding of giftedness as well as an understanding of new leadership skills and how they can be used. Often, they are paradigm shifts, major perspective changes. All leaders learn ministry insights over their lifetimes. It is these breakthroughs that move leaders to new levels of potential.

This is a highly interpretive section in which I try to give meaning to what I see. I draw upon my past experience in studying leaders, my knowledge of what leadership is, and needs for insights to today's leaders to help me select what I present in this section.

Occasionally under this section I will give a list of quotations or sayings attributed to the leader. Especially do I do this if I think they are worthy of copying down and displaying on a bulletin board in your office to inspire you.

Contributions

I give three kinds of contributions in this section. One, I comment on what this chapter, that is, this study of the life of the Christian leader contributes to our understanding of leadership concepts in general and developmental theory in particular. Two, I give specific contributions, probably unique, of the life. Three, I talk about the ultimate contribution set of the Christian leader.

An ultimate contribution is a lasting legacy of a Christian worker for which he/she is remembered and which furthers the cause of Christianity by one or more of the following: 1. setting standards for life and ministry; 2. impacting lives by enfolding them in God's Kingdom or developing them once in the Kingdom; 3. serving as a stimulus for change which betters the world; 4. leaving behind an organization, institution, or movement that can serve as a channel for God to work through; 5. the discovery of ideas, communication of them, or promotion of them so that they further God's work.[8] Twelve general types of such legacies have been identified, labeled and defined. This kind of information is helpful, not only in affirming the life work of these Christian leaders, but in its suggestive power to bring focus to a present life or ministry that is already contributing. Such futuristic thinking can help a leader to mold an ideal role and to focus more deliberately on that which God wants to accomplish, long term, through the leader. The twelve types are not exhaustive. They apply mainly to full time Christian workers, pastors and missionaries. Additional research is needed on lay workers and Christians in secular work. Further types are likely and will be added as research unearths them. Table 1-1 below identifies the twelve prime types of ultimate contributions.

Table 1-1. Legacy Types--Ultimate Contributions

Prime Type	Major Thrust of the Type	Historical Example
1. Saint	A Model life, not a perfect one, but a life others want to emulate.	Samuel Brengle R. C. McQuilkin
2. Stylistic Practitioner	A model ministry style; a flagship church or ministry organization which effectively delivers the ministry output of a leader.	A. J. Gordon G. Campbell Morgan
3. Mentor	A productive ministry with individuals.	Henrietta Mears Charles Simeon
4. Public Rhetorician	A productive ministry with large public groups.	G. Campbell Morgan Samuel Brengle
5. Pioneer	Founds apostolic type works.	Henrietta Mears Robert Jaffray
6. Crusader	Rights wrongs and injustices in society	A. J. Gordon
7. Artist	Creative breakthroughs.	Henrietta Mears A. J. Gordon
8. Founder	Starts new organizations.	R. C. McQuilkin L. E. Maxwell

---

[8]See position paper, Clinton 1989, *The Ultimate Contribution*, which gives the results of a comparative study of 40 outstanding missionaries in terms of legacies left behind. Details patterns, descriptions, and definitions with examples are given there.

Chapter 1. Introduction to Interpretive Biography   page 23

Table 1-1. Legacy Types--Ultimate Contributions continued

Prime Type	Major Thrust of the Type	Historical Example
9. Stabilizer	Solidifies organizations.	G. Campbell Morgan R. C. McQuilkin
10. Researcher	Develops new ideation.	G. Campbell Morgan A. J. Gordon
11. Writer	Captures new ideation for use of others.	G. Campbell Morgan Henrietta Mears
12. Promoter	Distributes effectively new ideation.	L. E. Maxwell Samuel Brengle

Effective focused leaders usually have several of these prime types in their make-up. We call this the ultimate contribution set. I will display the ultimate contribution set with a pictorial diagram which emphasizes the importance of the various elements and the relationship to each other. I do this for a purpose. I want to familiarize you with the notion of ultimate contribution set with hopes that you will tentatively identify your own and hence make deliberate proactive decisions toward accomplishing it in the future.

Overall Lessons from the Life

Here I attempt to focus what I have been saying in terms of observations that allow for transfer into ministry today.

Implications for a Focused Life

What have we learned from this life that helps us understand a focused life? That is the question I attempt to answer in this section. When we study a focused life we are in fact looking for a number of *focal factors* leading to one or more of the four *focal issues*:[9]

1. giftedness development,
2. destiny processing,
3. identification of key ministry insights,
4. identification of major values that uniquely fit one's ministry,
5. integration of personality factors so as to identify a focused or ideal role that moves toward convergence,
6. social base processing,
7. ultimate contribution set,
8. ministry philosophy concepts,
9. future perfect time paradigm,
10. boundary processing which helped focus,
11. paradigm shifts which helped focus,
12. windows of opportunity.

---

[9] I mentioned earlier in footnotes in the preface, that I was looking for factors that make up the focal variable of a ministry philosophy. The focal variable describes those factors which help the leader prioritize life's activities around focal issues (major role, life purpose, unique methodology and/or ultimate contribution). These given here are an initial list of such factors.

Now I realize that not all of these concepts are familiar to you now. But I hope they will be after I have introduced them in terms of real life examples. It is in this section that I will discuss these items as they apply to the lives of the eight Christian leaders.

Where To Go and What To Do For Further Study

Finally, I hope to interest you in further study of one or more of these eight Christian leaders. In this section, I will suggest materials you can use to adopt one of these as your historical mentor. I will usually give comments explaining what I think is the value of an entry. Where only one biographical source exists I will sometimes point out the value of the individual chapters. Appendix E was included in this book just in case you want to do follow-up work. It contains specific details on how to get a historical mentor and learn from that life.

Charles Simeon
(1759-1836)

A strategic change agent via mentoring

Chapter 2. Charles Simeon (1759-1836)
A Man in the Right Place, Strategically
A Study in Sphere of Influence and Effective Change Through Mentoring

> Remember your former leaders. Think back on how they lived and ministered. Imitate those **excellent qualities** you see in their lives. For Jesus Christ is the same today, as He was in the past and as He will be in the future. What He did for them He will do for you to inspire and enable your leadership.
> **Hebrews 13:7,8** (Personal Interpretive Paraphrase)

Let's remember Charles Simeon,[1] a pastor who brought evangelical renewal to the Anglican Church. We can learn much about change dynamics from studying his life. Can one leader affect an entire denomination? Here is Barclay's assessment.

> Now, what was his influence?[2] It has been described like this. When he started preaching in 1782 there was really only a handful of evangelical ministers left[3] in the Church of England. I don't know an exact figure, but it was probably a few dozen. When he finished, 54 years later on, one third of the pulpits in the Church of England were said to be occupied by evangelicals and the vast majority of those were men who had been influenced directly by Simeon in Cambridge.[4] Many of them had been converted through him, or else they had come under his influence in some way. His influence on the evangelical cause in the Church of England was absolutely staggering.
> (Barclay 1986:9)

How did he do it? It began first of all with God's foundational work in his own life. It continued with an important and timely mentoring experience in his own life. Mentoring as

---

[1] Most Americans are not aware of Charles Simeon nor of much about the Anglican Church. Bennett gives some idea of his importance. "In the one and a half centuries since his death in 1836, Charles Simeon has been the central subject of a host of funeral sermons, one memoir, two full biographies, more than ten 'remembrances' or limited biographies, and at least five thematic assessments." Bennett lists 17 contemporary accounts on Simeon and 27 secondary sources on him (such as the two main biographers I use in this study). None of the other seven leaders in this book has received as much attention and study as has Charles Simeon.

[2] Barclay's question is a most important one for Simeon. Barclay gives a result of that influence in a quick summary statement referring basically to extensiveness and intensiveness (of British society). But we want to examine it in more depth. How did he do it? This chapter should answer that question and more. *Sphere of influence* refers to the totality of people being influenced by a leader. A closely related term is *Influence-mix* (Clinton 1989:378). This involves a profile describing how and who leaders influence. All leaders influence followers. They can influence *directly*, that is, face-to-face ministry, *indirectly*, via shaping of key individuals or via materials used by others or *organizationally* via executive leadership or committees or the like. Each leader has a profile corresponding to which of these dominates or how they relate. Simeon will have great indirect influence, through many key individuals, on the course of Christianity as reflected in the Anglican Church. Bennett (1992:16) quotes Macaulay's 1844 letter to his sister indicating something of Simeon's influence. "As to Simeon, if you knew what his authority and influence were, and how they extended from Cambridge to the most remote corners of England, you would allow that his real sway in the Church was far greater than that of any prelate." Simeon did not choose positional authority as his basis for influence. *Power-mix* (Clinton 1989: 378) has to do with the major means a leader uses to influence followers. We will examine how he influenced. And we shall be surprised to discover the importance of personal authority, competent authority, and networking power as demonstrated in Simeon's life. A concerted deliberate program to select, recruit, and influence key individuals over a period of time can pay great dividends.

[3] *Left* is a significant word. Evangelicals in the Church of England were frequently persecuted and exited to dissenting churches--out of the established church altogether.

[4] At the end of this chapter I will comment on Simeon's impact more specifically.

Chapter 2. Charles Simeon (1759-1836)

means of growth, so important to him, became a pattern he would use to exert influence and bring about change in a whole denomination.

Opening Illustration 1
Renewal Begins With One
Charles Simeon's Personal Conversion--Touched By God

Age 19 (2 Corinthians 5:17)

Just three days after his arrival at Cambridge, Provost Cooke let Simeon know that he would be required to participate in the communion which would be coming up during the term. Feeling quite unprepared for communion--even though he was not sure what it meant--he then bought several books to study in preparation for taking communion. These books brought conviction about sin in his life, but no relief. The conviction of unworthiness grew. Simeon saw himself as a sinner.[5] How could he partake of communion being what he was? Finally, after several months and urgent seeking through prayer, fasting and study, Simeon found relief just in the nick of time. Light broke upon him as he meditated on a remark in Bishop Wilson's writing on the Lord's supper.

> "But in Passion Week, as I was reading Bishop Wilson on the Lord's Supper, I met with an expression to this effect--'That the Jews knew what they did, when they transferred their sin to the head of their offering.' The thought came into my mind, What, may I transfer all my guilt to another? Has God provided an Offering for me, that I may lay my sins on His head? Then, God willing, I will not bear them on my own soul one moment longer. Accordingly I sought to lay my sins upon the sacred head of Jesus; and on the Wednesday began to have a hope of mercy; on the Thursday that hope increased; on the Friday and Saturday it became more strong; and on the Sunday morning, Easter-day, April 4, I awoke early with those words upon my heart and lips, 'Jesus Christ is risen to-day!' From that hour peace flowed in rich abundance into my soul; and at the Lord's Table in our Chapel I had the sweetest access to God through my blessed Saviour." (Moule 1892:13,14 quoting from a private memoir of Simeon's in 1813)

His recognition of sin in his life, his conviction of it, and his acceptance of Christ's provision for it were all done individually, alone, apart from human intervention, except for the writings of several. With this conversion, this genuine personal religious experience, he was on his way into the very small evangelical Anglican community.[6] He would find himself out of sorts with the mainstream of Anglican ministers and communicants. But his personal relationship with God through Christ became the anchor for his vision of renewal in the Church of England.

---

[5]This whole experience is amazing. Simeon came from a very nominal church family. Sin was not an issue. His time at Eton had not brought him in any serious contact with sin and salvation. Communion would have no significant meaning for him. None of his biographer's even speak of confirmation. He was at Eton when this should have happened. I don't think it did.

[6]Bennett stated that evangelical Anglicans for the most part shared a common theological foundation which included a belief in human depravity, justification by faith alone, and holy living as evidence of that faith (Bennett 1992:8,9). In this incident Simeon entered in experientially to the doctrine of justification by faith alone. A personal conversion experience validated an evangelical's view of these doctrines.

Chapter 2. Charles Simeon (1759-1836)

Opening Illustration 2.
Mentored In Order to Mentor
Henry Venn, Godly Perspective

Age 23-37 (Philippians 4:9)

For more than three years Simeon grew in his Christian experience on his own. He learned early of the necessity of a devotional life. He disciplined himself to work on his perceived weaknesses. Toward the end of the three years he attended regularly St. Edward's Church nearby. The Vicar there, Christopher Atkinson, linked Simeon to John Venn, a young evangelical, who in turn introduced him to his father Henry Venn. Venn was to prove to be the upward mentor who would solidify Simeon's foundations and advise him through the roughest part of his early ministry days. When Simeon first met Henry Venn, he was 58 and a godly example of a servant leader. Catch the mentor heart of this man as Moule describes him.[7]

> Henry Venn ... was the descendant of a long line of clergymen, and himself as true-hearted a minister as the English Church has ever owned....After a laborious and singularly fruitful pastorate at Huddersfield, finding his strength decline, he had accepted Yelling in 1771, and there lived a life of apostolic simplicity, preaching week by week to a congregation of shepherds and ploughmen, writing on spiritual subjects to a large circle of correspondents, and now latterly welcoming visits from the Cambridge friends of his son John. If Henry Venn's conversation may be judged by his letters, it was no wonder that these men were glad to walk or ride over from Cambridge to the primitive village Rectory. They found there an elder friend who combined the deepest religious experience and the purest and firmest faith with a natural character as strong and genial as possible, and with a great wealth of admirable good sense.
>
> ...
>
> [After several visits with others Simeon invites himself to visit Venn alone] "I propose with the blessing of God, riding over on Tuesday morning next, before 8 o'clock, or at furthest a quarter after. To converse with your father has long been my desire."[8] He came, "and stayed till past eight at night." No record remains of that long summer's day; but it was a bright epoch for the young curate of St. Edward's, the first day of a friendship of fourteen years which left a profound impression. Many a morning did he ride to Yelling, over the then almost hedgeless

---

[7]*Mentoring* is a relational experience in which one person called the *mentor*, empowers another person, called the *mentoree* via a transfer of resources. Nine types of mentor functions have been identified. One of these is the modeling function of a contemporary Christian leader respected by the mentoree. The *contemporary model* serves as a sort of Christian hero/heroine who inspires the young leader. The mentoree tends to emulate and imbibe values from the *contemporary model* and tends to live up to the genuine expectations that person sets out. (See Clinton and Clinton, 1991, **The Mentor Handbook**). Venn not only served the mentoring function of a *contemporary model*--and that was desperately needed as most of Simeon's contemporaries were nominal Christians, at best--but he served other mentor roles as well: *spiritual guide, counselor, teacher,* and *sponsor*. He did *distance mentoring*. Note his correspondence ministry which would be dominantly spiritual guide, counseling and teaching. Mentoring is an important shaping process that God uses in the life of a developing leader. There is a large drop out from ministry in the first several years in full time Christian work. For the ones that make it through this trying time (first 5-8 years), 4 out of 5 experience mentoring help.

[8]How do mentors get connected up with mentorees? Three basic means include: 1. TOP DOWN RECRUITING (Mentors recruiting mentorees), 2. BOTTOM-UP RECRUITING (Mentorees recruiting mentors), 3. LINKERS (Someone with mentor eyes recognizes potential mentorees and mentors and links them in a sponsoring fashion). Atkinson provides an initial linking function. But for the most part, here we have an example of bottom-up recruiting. Simeon takes the initiative. He is attracted to the godly model, Venn. We also see the linking function when Venn takes the time to connect (sponsor) Simeon to John Berridge. When I discuss this more fully we shall see that Venn connected Simeon also to John Newton and John Thornton, in addition to Berridge. This family of mentors shaped his life significantly during the first 15 years.

country, and in Henry Venn's holy wisdom, kind humour, and entire freedom from eccentricity, he found guidance and correctives at many critical moments in his early years of difficult ministry. His attachment to this venerable friend grew till it was a sacred passion."

...
    To John Venn, after his father's death, he wrote... Scarcely ever did I visit him but he prayed with me. Scarcely ever did I dine with him, but his ardour in returning thanks, sometimes in an appropriate hymn, and sometimes in a thanksgiving prayer, has inflamed the souls of all present so as to give us a foretaste of Heaven itself; and in all the years that I knew him, I never remember him to have spoken unkindly of any one, but once; and I was particularly struck with the humiliation he expressed for it, in his prayer the next day."
    ...to another of Venn's grandsons...he writes, "I wish you had known your honoured grandfather; the only end for which he lived was to make all men see the glory of God in the face of Jesus." (Moule 1892:25-28)

Here is how the initial relationship developed or looked from both Venn's viewpoints.

    John Venn's Diary tells of the process [of meeting and helping Simeon]:
    "1782, June 1. Drank tea at Atkinson's with Simeon, an undergraduate Fellow of King's, a religious man.
    "June 2 (Sunday). Drank tea with Simeon (who preached his first sermon to-day at St. Edward's) and Atkinson."
    ...
    "On Trinity Sunday was ordained Mr. Simeon, Fellow of King's College. Before that day he never was in company with an earnest Christian. Soon after he was visited by Mr. H. Jowett, and my son, and two or three more. In less than seventeen Sundays, by preaching for Mr. Atkinson in a church at Cambridge, he filled it with hearers--a thing unknown there for near a century. He has been over to see me six times within the last three months: he is calculated for great usefulness, and is full of faith and love. My soul is always the better for his visits. Oh, to flame as he does with zeal, and yet be beautified with meekness! The day he was a substitute for Mr. Atkinson, he began to visit the parishioners from house to house. Full of philanthropy was his address; 'I am come to inquire after your welfare. Are you happy?' His evident regard for their good disarmed them of their bitterness; and it is amazing what success he has met with." (Moule 1892:26-29)

The Time-Line

See the time-line at the end of this chapter for a one page overview of Simeon's life with critical incidents and other important summary information. Note that there are just two phases--one of 23 years and the other of 54 years. This is rare indeed. Simeon rooted in one place, Cambridge, and stayed there for the duration. It was a strategic location. From there he exerted influence on the up and coming leadership in the country and the Anglican Church.[9]

Simeon's life is straightforward. He was educated at boarding school, Eton, in preparation for Cambridge. Then to Cambridge. Following graduation he was ordained for the ministry and accepted a pastorate at Trinity Church in Cambridge. Simeon followed a modified pre-service pattern into ministry.[10] His first few years at Trinity Church, along with his mentoring relationship with Venn, provided the real training for the ministry.

---

[9] Of course, Oxford, the other major university center could have been strategic also. But it was to Cambridge (Eton-->King's College-->Cambridge-->fellow at Cambridge) that Simeon went.
[10] Most leaders emerge via one of three major training patterns. Each pattern has some advantages and some disadvantages. Three of the eight, Gordon, Jaffray and Maxwell, fit the pure *pre-service pattern* (Clinton 1989:354). They receive formal training for ministry prior to ministry. Three fit the second pattern the *in-service pattern* (Clinton 1989:356), that is, they learn on-the-job and finally after proving their abilities take on full time responsibilities. The third pattern is a *modified in-service pattern* (Clinton

Chapter 2. Charles Simeon (1759-1836)

The 54 years of the second time period do not break down into neat, clean increments. There is overlap in the major emphases and purposes being carried out by Simeon in each of the smaller time divisions. But each small division does highlight some important emphasis. Simeon's focused life was dominated by a two fold purpose (both having to do with renewal) and an ultimate contribution. His major roles, pastor of a University church and teacher in the university were means to his purposes. His mentoring approach was the methodology that produced the most results toward those purposes.

Highly Condensed Biographical Narrative

The following running capsule, organized around the two major time increments of Simeon's life indicates important activities, people, and events that shaped Simeon's life. For some of the earlier small time periods there is little information. We pass over them and move on to those time periods where more information is available.

I. LONELY WELL-TO-DO FOUNDATIONS-- UPPER CLASS WORLDVIEW
(1759-1782); Age=Birth to 23

A. Lonely Home Life
(1759-1768); Age=Birth to 9

Charles Simeon was born at Reading, September 24, 1759. His father, Richard Simeon was a rich and successful attorney. His mother was Elizabeth Hutton. In the family history, both lines, mother and father, there were clergy. He was the fourth and youngest son. His mother died when he was a very young child. His father died when he was 25.

His oldest brother died when young Simeon was 23. His other brothers were successful--one as a minister in parliament and the other as a wealthy merchant. The family was "respectfully religious." But the interests of God and the Kingdom were not their primary priority.

Little can be said of the shaping influences of the family on Simeon. His family, well-to-do in terms of wealth, was of the respected upper classes.

B. Shunted to Eton--The Boarding School Experience
(1768-1778); Age=9-19

At 9, Simeon was enrolled in Eton.[11] He was there till he was 19. These were years of discipline including the usual hazing of lowerclassmen by upperclassmen. Simeon

---

1989:357) in which the leader first gets ministry experience, then interrupts it for formal training, and then resumes it with periodic interruptions for training. Brengle fits a modified form of this last pattern. Simeon would have to be categorized with Maxwell, Jaffray and Gordon as pre-service. Though there were no seminaries as such, people who were pre-service went to Cambridge or Oxford and then into ministry. They would be trained in languages but very little else theologically or of a ministry nature. It was a very weak pre-service training approach. Most learned as curates (assistants) under some other minister if at all.
[11]Moule gives the age of Simeon as 9 when he went to Eton (Moule 1892:4). Hopkins gives the age as 7 (Hopkins 1970:11). Perhaps all English lads think their boarding school experience is rough. But in later years Simeon looked back at this and classified it as a horrible experience. Moule (1892:5) quotes probably his real feelings about this time in his life. "Simeon said in his later age, that he would be tempted to take the life of a son rather than let him see the vice he had seen at Eton."

Chapter 2. Charles Simeon (1759-1836)   page 32

was not a particularly adept scholar. He was above average in Latin, but was not as good in Greek. He was active in the usual outdoor sports including cricket, but again was not above average. He developed a good reputation as a horseman. He was not particularly religious. We can surmise that he learned basic analytical skills and was exposed to the various classical works of literature then in existence. But most important was the privilege associated with a graduate of Eton. They had special privilege at Cambridge. It was easy to get in and they were exempt from certain examinations.

C. Elitist Education-- King's College, Cambridge Foundations for Strategic Change (1778-1782); Age=19-23

At King's College, life turned around for Charles Simeon. Here he met God. He grew even though isolated from other Christian fellowship. He decided for the ministry. He was linked into his next steps. Let me summarize it. Four things happened at King's College which significantly altered the focus of Simeon's life.

1. Conversion and early Growth
2. First Steps in Ministry
3. Links to Atkinson and Venn
4. Becomes a fellow

I'll cover the first two of these in this time period. These latter two occur as part of the boundary transition into the next time period. I will discuss them there.

Conversion and Early Growth--the Giving Seedbed

It was here that critical incident 1 occurred. As Simeon's conversion was alone--so were the first years of his Christian experience. For almost three years Simeon had no fellowship with other Christians. The University was such that a semi-isolated atmosphere pervaded. He literally did not know any others who had Christian views such as his. Moule (1896:21) referring to Simeon's diary does indicate that he did develop a discipline about his inner life, one of the first symptoms of an emerging leader.

> "Though by nature and habit of an extravagant disposition, I practised the most rigid economy; and in this I was very much assisted by allotting my small income so as to provide for even the minutest expense, and at the same time consecrating a stated part of my income to the Lord, together with all that I could save out of the part reserved for my own use.[12] This made economy truly delightful, and enabled me to finish my three years of scholarship without owing a shilling, whilst others, my contemporaries, incurred debts of several hundred pounds." (Moule 1892:21).

Hopkins relates further inner life growth (Hopkins 1977:22,23). He describes how the extravagant worldly pleasures which had first place in Simeon's life brought him under conviction. His extravagant attire, his love for dancing, and his attraction to the horse races

---

[12]In the inner life growth stage, the time preceding transition into leadership, an emerging leader is dealt with in terms of character. God begins to work in what He will work out. One of the first areas frequently dealt with is money and giving. Who owns the resources? Surrender on these issues is very important, especially when God is going to entrust control of large resources in the future. A leader who learns these lessons early can be used of God. See Clinton and Raab (1985), **Barnabas**. Lack of these early lessons often comes back to haunt a leader in later years. The financial obstacle may well waylay them from finishing well. See Appendix A. Six Barriers. See also Clinton (1988) **The Making of A Leader**. Simeon becomes one who can be entrusted with finances. He becomes a great giver and one who channels resources into the Kingdom. Note his personal giving and his use of patronage.

Chapter 2. Charles Simeon (1759-1836)

all were very important to him. On one occasion when going to a dance Simeon and a friend, after a long hot dusty ride, stopped off at another friend's house. They were refreshed from the long hot ride with some alcoholic beverage. Simeon apparently without knowing it drank too much. When they remounted and continued their long journey to the dance he was drunk. He fell once. Along the way his horse turned in to an inn. The innkeeper saw that he was drunk and took him in for the night and put him to sleep. The landlady of the inn in casual conversation mentioned that recently she had heard of a gentleman from Reading (Simeon's own hometown) who had been killed by a fall from his horse while drunk? Simeon was immediately struck by the words and with intuitive insight knew this was a warning from God. He changed his ways. Those things which had in the past gripped his life and had first place began to drop by the wayside.

First Baby Steps in Ministry

Immediately after his conversion he testified to the change and sought ministry.[13]

> What were the immediate results of the spiritual revolution? ... On the one hand he began at once to try to do good in a quiet way around him. He confided his discovery to his college friends. And as he found that his bedmaker, or chamber-woman, was seldom able to go to church, he offered to "instruct" her, and any others who would join her, on Sunday evenings; a time when worship was then unknown in the Cambridge churches. Several of the women came and the young scholar read "a good book" with them, and some of the prayers of the church.
>
> The Long Vacation arrived, and he went home, full of the same longing to impart; an instinct inseparable from a discovered joy in God. His father never gathered the household for prayers, nor did the eldest son, Richard, who lived at home. Charles had no hope that either father or brother would institute family worship at his request, so he proposed it to the servants themselves, and began. To his joy his brother cordially approved, and regularly joined the company morning and night. His father was of course aware, but never expressed either approval or displeasure. (Moule 1896:19,20)

Charles is growing. He has not quite finished his undergraduate degree. But he decides for the ministry. But that forms part of the story of the next period.

II. THE LONG SIEGE--RENEWAL OVER THE YEARS, 54 YEARS OF MINISTRY IN A CONVERGENT LOCALE (1782-1836)

At this point, Simeon is about to graduate and will be awarded a fellowship.[14] He has opted for the ministry but how this will all work out is not known. He has just

---

[13] These early attempts at ministry are called *ministry tasks* (Clinton 1989:137) in leadership emergence theory. A *ministry task* is an assignment from God (though not always recognized as such) which primarily tests a person's faithfulness and obedience but often also allows use of ministry gifts in the context of a task which has closure, accountability, and evaluation. Usually these tasks come while under the influence of local church ministry and are assigned by people in the leadership structure. Self-initiated tasks are highly indicative of leadership. These initial attempts to give out some of what he was taking in and feeling were self-initiated.

[14] Being a fellow at King's College gave him an "in" with the University scene. It provided a place for room and board. But it also required singleness as a requisite for holding a fellowship. Sometime during these next several years as Simeon recognizes the strategic import of his location and influence and as he considers the responsibilities of ministry **he opts for a single life.** Hopkins (1970:68,69) sheds some insights on Simeon's decision for prioritizing **university ministry** over marriage. In Hopkins references we see clearly Simeon's perception of married life as he saw it around him (it wasn't very

Chapter 2. Charles Simeon (1759-1836)

established his contact with Atkinson, the Minister of St. Edward's Church. And this has led him to Henry Venn. What happened next?

A. Rejection in The Ministry--Off on a Bad Foot
12 Years of Conflict
(1782-1794); Age=23-35

Charles Simeon's start in the ministry was disastrous. Any lesser person would not have persevered but have fallen by the wayside.[15] His ministry began in conflict in 1782. Eight years later, 1790, it abated somewhat. Finally in 1794, general reconciliation was complete. Simeon is ready for the expanding influence to come.

During this period of 12 years a number of important shaping activities, that is, critical incidents, brought focus into his life and ministry. I'll discuss seven of these issues following along chronologically as they happened. You will see that several cluster around 1782 and following. Several occur in 1792 a pivotal year of harbinger like pointers.

These critical incidents laid the foundations for a wide sphere of influence that was to come. Simeon's initial assignment in ministry, his nurturing by mentors during the formative period of his parish leadership, his creative ministry insight, his development of Bible centered disciplines, his life long involvement in missions in India, his initial meeting with Charles Grant, and his breakthrough in pulpit ministry all are forming him for the future. Encompassing it all, God sovereignly overshadows and clarifies for Simeon the path leading to his focused life.

1782--Against All Odds (Psalm 37:3,4)

After his conversion, for three years, he grew primarily without the advantage of encouragement of fellow evangelical Christians. He did attend the local churches. We do not know about the details of his call to ministry. But sometime during the three years at King's College he decided on dedicating his life to the ministry. He saw the great needs around him in reaching these privileged upper class sons who for the most part were not evangelical. Yet he knew they would eventually rise to places of power in England. In his memoirs we have at least a hint of God's preparation in his heart about this time in his life. And we see, in seed form, the beginning of a strategic purpose.

---

positive; he didn't want to perpetuate his own family background and what he saw around him was basically negative). He desired to be freely focused on ministry without the distractions of a wife and family. But we are not given the details of his making the decision or the exact time when he made it. This decision is a critical incident and I do include it on the list of items. Bennett credits some of this decision to Berridge's influence (1992:123). I do not have access to the correspondence he refers to. Had we this detailed information, I would have included an explanation of it here in these first several years as that is where I think the decision was made. I do know it was made, though I don't have the details--and particularly his interaction with God on the issues. So I do include this choice of celibate lifestyle for ministry sake as a critical incident. Certainly this decision for a celibate life focused on ministry is a major key to what Simeon accomplished. There are positives and negatives involved in this, as reflected in Simeon's life. This choice let him devote himself to students--almost an open door policy. But the processing and shaping of a family on a life--relational lessons, smoothing off the abrasive edges, being stretched to demonstrate Christian reality in a most intimate context, and a gut-level accountability--is missed by Simeon.

[15]Today there is a rather large dropout of pre-service trained Christian workers in the first 5 years. How would today's Christian workers have fared in this setting. Not very well I think. But Simeon knew the system very well. He knew he could weather the storm as long as the Bishop above him was behind him.

Chapter 2. Charles Simeon (1759-1836)

> "I had often," he says..., "when passing Trinity Church, which stands in the heart of Cambridge, said within myself, 'How should I rejoice if God were to give me that church, that I might preach the Gospel there and be a herald for Him in the University.' But as to the actual possession of it, I had no more prospect of attaining it than of being exalted to the see of Canterbury." (Moule 1892:35)

We know from the above that Simeon desired to be used of God. We do not know the details of his call,[16] but we do know he was ordained deacon by the Bishop of Ely on May 26, 1782 and that he took his ordination seriously. The next step was a curacy.[17]

St. Edwards; Atkinson's Help

He had been attending St. Edwards where he had enjoyed Christopher Atkinson's ministry and felt it closest to his own evangelical beliefs. Atkinson was pivotal in Simeon's life at this critical juncture--in two ways. He introduced Simeon to Henry Venn, who lived about 13 miles away. This wise, older, evangelical Anglican pastor, provided opportunity for a hungry young emerging leader to gain insight. Simeon thus leapfrogged ahead in learning about life and ministry--learning what otherwise may have taken years to learn. Atkinson also invited young Simeon to take charge of his church for the summer months as he intended to be absent on holiday for an extended time of three months.

Simeon jumped at the chance to minister in Atkinson's church. St. Edward's was to be his Jericho--a faith building early victory. Here, in three months of preaching and door-to-door visitation in the small parish, he first tasted of success in the ministry.[18] Simeon's ministry flourished. He won the hearts of many with his concerned pastoral visits in the homes. His preaching attracted the largest crowds in that church in over a hundred years. The news spread rapidly. Henry Venn was excited by the news of this young evangelical's first ministry. He contacted John Newton and John Berridge, other evangelical Anglicans, and expressed his joy and affirmation of young Simeon (Hopkins 1977:34,35).

This was an honorary curacy. That is, he was not assigned to this officially by the Bishop in charge of this region. While it did show some of Simeon's potential it would not "count" on an official resume for future purposes. Theoretically, if Simeon was to go into the Anglican ministry he would have to serve a longer term as a curate and gain experience and time under a supervising minister.

---

[16] We know from what he taught to his own mentorees that a call must be clear, personal, inward, and certain (Bennett 1992:129,130). Surely these would have been true for him. A certain call is one of the anchors that will take a leader through hard times, such as Simeon faced in the first 12 years.

[17] A curate is a clergyman who assists a Vicar or Rector. It is an assistant pastoral role. A curate would usually serve a number of years before becoming a Vicar (usually an endowed office with a stipend) or the Rector (holds the rights to tithes in a parish). In the Anglican Church, this assignment potentially allowed for a form of in-service training, an internship. With a conscientious minister a curate could receive excellent training. However, few did. And some potentially prominent leaders were buried in this role and never appointed as full ministers of a parish, a sometimes political plum, dished out by Bishops to those of prestigious or influential families.

[18] Two shaping activities are especially seen in this three months of ministry. This was a *ministry task* (Clinton 1989:137)--a successful one. And Simeon received *ministry affirmation* (Clinton 1989:267). *Ministry affirmation* is a shaping process in which God gives approval to a leader in terms of some ministry in general or some ministry experience in particular which results in a renewed sense of purpose for the leader. Here Simeon sees results. He knows God's hand is upon his life. This good ministry experience is needed--especially in light of what is to come.

Chapter 2. Charles Simeon (1759-1836)

At the end of the summer, after Atkinson's return, Simeon did not have any definite future prospects. He was fully resigned to go home and take care of his father, something the family had suggested.[19] Just at this time, Henry Therond, Minister of Holy Trinity Church died. For some reason Simeon felt he should try for this prestigious position. Whatever possessed Charles Simeon that he should think he could be appointed to this pastorate? Hopkins (1977:36) points out that this was probably the most unusual, unexpected and highly irregular of all appointments in the strange history of patronage by Bishops in the Church of England. Four almost insurmountable barriers hindered his appointment: 1. Simeon had not served a curacy--there were plenty of more experienced, capable Curates out there that may have deserved this role. He was basically inexperienced and not ready for such an important role; 2. Simeon was only a deacon, not ordained as a priest, hence he could not administer Holy Communion. 3. He was not quite 23 the minimum age for ordination. 4. He was an evangelical. Most Bishops were decidedly against any who took evangelical stands. To them this hinted of "Methodism." It was against all the odds. But here was a door of opportunity. Simeon went for it.[20]

He wrote his father and asked him to intervene with the Bishop of Ely. Richard Simeon knew the Bishop of Ely personally. He did just that and wrote a letter asking that his son be given the assignment. The situation was complex. The parishioners wanted the present curate, John Hammond, to be appointed and petitioned the Bishop to do so. They met with Simeon and told him they didn't want him. Simeon explained that he was not in it for the "living,"[21] but was interested in the position because he wanted to minister and care for the people. They were still adamantly opposed. Simeon agreed to reconsider and think it over and reflect on their views. He said he was basically a man of peace. If after thinking about it he deemed it improper to continue he would write the Bishop and withdraw his name.

He actually went so far as to write a letter to that effect but he missed the post on the day he wrote it. He was somehow constrained not to mail it for several days. In the meantime these vociferous parishioners wrote the Bishop and said that Simeon had already retired. They pressed their candidate again. Simeon then heard from the Bishop who did not appreciate the manipulative actions of the parishioners. He stated clearly that he would not appoint Hammond even if Simeon withdrew. Simeon figured something like this. They are not going to get their choice whatever happens. It might as well be me. So he accepted the position. And now comes his Ai--except it wasn't a simple defeat but an extended problematic entrance into leadership.

---

[19]In fact, he was in the process of packing his books and vacating his new rooms in the Fellows' Building (Moule 1892:30) when Henry Therond, the Minister of Trinity Church passed away. In retrospect, we can see the divine timing. In just two weeks Simeon would have gone home to take his older brother's place to take care of his dad. He would not have tried for Holy Trinity Church. Simeon's older brother died around this time. The other two brothers felt that Simeon should come home and take his place. The father died just two years later when Simeon was 25.

[20]Hopkins (1970:36,37), the most recent biographer of Simeon, is amazed that Simeon would even try for this. He asserts that it was Simeon's brash boldness that propelled him to do so. Hopkins also estimated that the chances that the Bishop would make this appointment were probably 1 in a 1000.

[21]*Living* is a term referring to the stipend (benefice) that comes with the job of minister. At that time many Anglican Pastors were in positions for just that reason. Frequently they did poor jobs in caring for their flock. Simeon was actually willing to cede this stipend over to Hammond and let him continue as curate under Simeon as the minister. Simeon's concern was for their spiritual welfare.

Chapter 2. Charles Simeon (1759-1836)

> The parishioners were then dead set against Simeon. They immediately appointed Hammond to the post of lecturer as was their right.[22] Moule describes the anti-Simeon scene.

> > I need not explain how very unpopular the appointment was; it was very plainly shown to be so. The parishioners chose Hammond Lecturer at once. By the usage of the office he thus had a right to the pulpit every Sunday afternoon, leaving only the morning to Simeon. That right he exercised for five years, and was then followed for seven years by another clergy man, equally independent. Not till 1794 was the Minister chosen to be Lecturer also. And on Sunday mornings the church for a long while was made as inaccessible as possible to him and his hearers. The pew doors were almost all locked, and the should-be occupants were absent, leaving only the aisles for any congregation that might assemble. On the first Sunday indeed aisles and pews alike were nearly empty when the service began, a bitter trial for the lately popular young clergyman; but after a while people trooped in; and "multitudes," as the weeks went on, were unable to find room. Simeon set forms in the aisles, and even put up open seats in nooks and corners at his own expense; but these the church-wardens pulled down and threw into the churchyard.
> > To visit his people at their homes was impossible of course for the present; scarcely a door would open to Charles Simeon. "In this state of things I saw no remedy but faith and patience. The passage of Scripture which subdued and controlled my mind was this, 'The servant of the Lord must not strive.'" (Moule 1892:37,38)

And thus, not wanted, Reverend Simeon began his 54 years of ministry at Holy Trinity of Cambridge. He was ordained a priest on September 28, 1783. In addition to his role as parish priest he was a Fellow at King's College in Cambridge. Though unpopular, with his local parishioners, Bishop Yorke supports his important role. He has located in a strategic center of influence from which he will increasingly radiate evangelical vitality.

1782ff--Mentoring Circle--Wise Counsel of Henry Venn, The Tolerant Mentor

It is at this point that the mentoring seen in Incident 2, *Mentored In Order to Mentor*, takes powerful affect. Henry Venn's wise counsel from time-to-time probably saved Simeon for the ministry in general and certainly so for the Anglican Church. His long years of service gave him perspective and wisdom. He was tolerant. He knew that the shaping activity of God would mellow his zealous and brash young friend. One illustration shows his tolerance and long range perspective. Apparently Simeon was not only brash but slightly arrogant and ill-mannered--something Henry Venn's family noticed quite readily. They did not want their father inviting him over.

> Henry Venn's daughter used to tell a story which shows us Simeon at that time,
> ...He had just ridden away after a visit at the Rectory, and first one Miss Venn and then another exclaimed about his manner. "Come into the garden, children," their father said, and led them out into that favourite school-room. "Now pick me one of those peaches." But it was early summer, and "the time of peaches was not yet"; how could their father ask for the green fruit? "Well, my dears, it is green now, and we must wait; but a little more sun, and a few more showers, and the peach will be ripe and sweet. So it is with Mr. Simeon." (Moule 1892:45)

Wise mentors see long term potential in an emerging leader even among youthful immature traits which turn others off to their potential leadership. Venn saw this. He saw Simeon more in terms of what he would become and what he would accomplish than what

---

[22]*Lectureships* were Sunday afternoon messages, a recognized function of the church, controlled by the parishioners and funded by them separately. Usually the minister appointed by the Bishop was also the lecturer. Here we have a split situation. It forebodes a divided congregation. This will continue as a thorn in Simeon's side until 1794.

Chapter 2. Charles Simeon (1759-1836)   page 38

he was. That kind of mentoring attitude does much to encourage the actual becoming and achieving. Venn encouraged Simeon in his preaching and in his study of the Bible. And he modeled a godly life--one filled with wisdom and kindness. His influence on Simeon continued for the first 15 years of Simeon's parish ministry. His importance in shaping Simeon life and vision of renewal probably can not be overstated.

That Venn was constantly and deeply concerned for Simeon is seen in his warning about Simeon's Sunday evening services. This incident is typical of his concern. Simeon's innovation to produce effective ministry in his parish bordered on the edge of acceptable practices among Anglicans.

1782--Necessity--The Mother of Invention and Alternative Ministry Forms--Mentoring Results

Venn had a right to be concerned. For Simeon was about to begin a practice that could have brought ecclesiastical judgment and ended his Anglican ministry.

At this point a pattern emerges that becomes typical of Simeon. When opposition, tradition, or even ecclesiastical rules or procedures thwart Simeon from accomplishing something needed or something he feels is right, he reacts. **He will find an alternative way to get it done.** Frequently, the approach will be on the **fringes of that which is accepted** by the Anglican Church.[23] It is this kind of pressure which will bring forth numerous ministry insights, that is, innovative breakthroughs for delivering ministry. Simeon introduces a number of these over the years.[24]

Simeon does what he can to get people in his church though the majority of parishioners are boycotting his Sunday morning services and locking their personal pews. He begins to attract people from further around, even outside his own parish. They have very few seats; the aisles are crowded. Simeon tries several things to get around these problems--all are thwarted by these people, especially the church wardens, those responsible for locking the church.

Simeon begins a Sunday evening service--basically for the poor who work at the University and can't attend morning services. The church wardens lock the church on Sunday night. He rents a room in the parish and goes on with his meetings. Soon he has outgrown the room. There is not a room big enough to rent in the town. So he goes to a neighboring parish and rents a room.[25] It was at this point that Venn called in his younger friend and advised him on the situation. Venn was concerned. He wanted Simeon to be an

---

[23] At this point in time, the English religious scene has the established church, the Anglican Church which is funded by the government and in league with the government. The government funds and protects the Anglican Church and the church in turn helps preserves the social order. But there is also the dissenters (Methodists, Baptist, Quakers, etc.), that is, those churches which have resulted from leaders breaking away from the Anglican Church or from other movements. These folks also push for social change. Governmental restrictions are hard on them. They are discriminated against in many ways. They can't get into the universities, etc. Religious liberty is at stake, as far as they are concerned. Because of these powerful tensions existing, Anglican Priests such as Simeon had to be careful and follow the guidelines of the Anglican Church.

[24] In fact, Bennett (1992) calls Simeon an intrapreneur (an entrepreneur who works within the system).

[25] This is infringing on someone else's territory. In this case the parish had an absentee minister who did not object to Simeon's efforts. But he could have. These services were essentially unlicensed and hence illegal, and could bring punishment on Simeon. Public religious meetings held in an unlicensed location were called coventicles. A charge of coventicle was serious.

Chapter 2. Charles Simeon (1759-1836)

evangelical voice in the Anglican Church and did not want him to be forced out. Simeon respectively listened and pleaded his case. Venn after discussing all the options cautioned Simeon but blessed him and allowed him to make his stand. Simeon continued these Sunday night meetings though they changed in form and function as these years went by. They became the base for his *lay societies* that is, the lay leadership of his parish.

Venn, Berridge, and Newton continued to encourage young Simeon and to affirm him. Bennett points out that for a decade and a half Simeon was mentored by these godly men (1992:128). What were some of the things he imbibed from these first generation evangelicals? Bennett quotes from Simeon's autobiography.

> Henry Venn, rector of Yelling and in semi-retirement, exerted more influence on Simeon than any other person during his life.[26] Perhaps Simeon's friendships with Thomas Thomason and Henry Martyn were emotionally closer, but Venn was father, tutor, and model to Simeon until Venn's death in 1797. Henry Venn also introduced Simeon to three others who shaped his life and work: John Berridge, John Newton, and John Thornton. In his autobiography Simeon credits much of his character development to these elder evangelicals. From Berridge, vicar of Everton, Simeon learned evangelical zeal, sympathy for parishioners, a benevolent spirit, and the value of celibacy. John Newton, then rector of St. Mary Woolnoth, instilled in Simeon a prudent and moderate evangelicalism. From the patron of Clapham and its patriarch, John Thornton, Simeon was confronted on three fronts: "Humility...Humility... [and] Humility."
>
> The influence of Henry Venn et al. was not directed toward Simeon's theological development. Existing correspondence between Simeon and his mentors rarely addresses the theological distinctives of evangelicalism. As previously suggested, Simeon's theological convictions were already in place by the time he made the connection with the Venn family. Rather, Simeon's mentors contributed to his pragmatic side, including the formation of his principles of churchmanship[27] and pastoral methodology. Perhaps most important to Simeon's future life and work, Venn and his colleagues were crucial to the positive development of his personal character.(Bennett 1992:122,123)

Simeon had a solid base of mentoring experience on which to build. This was foundational to a focal issue, his unique methodology of influence, which was to arise over the years.

1782--Early Bible Centered Ministry Habits

Read Simeon's preface to his 17 volume *magnum opus*, **Horae Homileticae**, the comprehensive edition done in the last years of his life. You can not help but be impressed with Simeon's view of, respect for, and means of using the Bible in his ministry. In the preface he states how he must let the Bible speak for itself. He indicates that it is the preacher's job to discover the things of God in his own long hours of personal Bible study. And from that study he must learn to expound in clear and simple language that which he has found. Where did he learn this? It was in these first years of parish ministry that he began his life long discipline of rising early and studying the Scriptures. It did not come natural to him.

---

[26] In leadership emergence theory the final years of an effective leader are often referred to as Afterglow years. In this time, a respected godly leader often has great influence not via positional power but by spiritual authority via networks of relationships. Such is the case with Venn. Simeon was just one of numerous ministers he influenced during this final 20 years or so of his life.

[27] The term churchman or churchmen refers to Anglican Church clergy. Churchmanship is the operation of a churchman within the polity, procedures, traditions, and etc. of the Anglican Church. Simeon was a Churchman. He believed deeply in the liturgy of the Anglican Church. He thought its prayer book an outstanding work. He followed its policies--though he would stretch them sometimes to push his evangelical views. He respected the authority of its governance. His problem will always be how to promote his evangelical beliefs while staying within the framework of churchmanship.

Chapter 2. Charles Simeon (1759-1836)

Hopkins (1977:69) describes the extreme disciplinary measures Simeon imposed upon himself to learn to arise early. He wanted to devote the early hours, arising before dawn, to Bible study and prayer. Most of his contemporaries, the other Fellows, slept on. He decided to fine himself a small amount of money each time he overslept. He was good intentioned about this. He would collect the fines and give them to his maid from time-to-time. But this wasn't punishment enough so he decided to up the fee and throw away a golden coin worth much more into a nearby small river. Only once did he so "waste" his money. His habit enabled him to study in depth the Scriptures over the years.

In 1785 he bought **Brown's Self-Interpreting Bible**, then a six-inch thick version which had cross-references for verses. Hopkins (1977:67) states that this study Bible became his constant companion his whole ministry. Simeon's neatly written remarks are on almost every page of this Bible. Hopkins goes on to say that Simeon was so pleased with this discovery and found it so useful that he immediately ordered forty copies from the publishers to give away to poor clergymen who could not afford such an important treasure.[28] Behind each of his sermons there was serious Bible study.[29] And behind that study was a value. *The Bible is the authoritative Word of God. It is important to study it and proclaim its truth to one's followers.*[30]

1787--Kindling a Missionary Flame,
Brown, Grant, and the 1787 Plan--Destiny Moment for Simeon

Simeon had persevered 5 years in the pastoral ministry. He was opposed. He was criticized. He was ridiculed because of his evangelical stand. Thankfully, during this period, he had no major responsibilities in the University. Thus, he was free to focus on personal disciplines, to make his first efforts at learning about homiletics, and to preach round about the region. He spread both evangelical thinking and his personal reputation and testimony as an evangelical. He was being affirmed by Berridge on these "extracurricular activities" and being cautioned by Henry Venn about them. And by all of his mentors he was encouraged to guard his own inner life and to make sure he was growing personally as a Christian minister.

At this time, a letter arrived from David Brown posted from Calcutta on September of 1787.[31] It challenged toward missions. Brown was an India Company chaplain and

---

[28]Hopkins (1970:67) points out that this study Bible had an excellent introductory section by the editor and a copious marginal reference to parallel Scriptures. This discovery is an illustration of the providential shaping activity called *literary processing* (Clinton 1989:184) in which God brings across a leader's path written materials at a timely moment so as to meet special needs, give important information, or otherwise alter life or ministry. Frequently, mentors provide this function of giving important materials to mentorees. In this case, we do not know how Simeon happened upon this important study Bible.

[29]Hopkins (1970:67) cites Bishop Daniel Wilson of Calcutta, a long time friend of Simeon, as stating that "behind each sermon lay at least 12 hours of study."

[30]I want to point out here (and I will continue to do so in each biographical chapter), as I will do again in the final chapter of the book, of the central role the Bible played in the eight leaders studied in this book. Each studied the Bible regularly and deliberately all their lives. They studied it devotionally for their own lives. They studied it to exhort others. They studied it to know of God and His purposes and to teach them to others. This will not be true for all focused leaders. But all of the eight leaders chosen in this book were *word gifted* leaders. See Clinton and Clinton (1994) **Developing Leadership Giftedness**, where we develop the concept of word gifted, power gifted, and love gifted clusters of spiritual gifts. All eight leaders in this book had spiritual gifts as the *focal element* of their giftedness set and word gifts as the dominant spiritual gifts.

[31]David Brown is identified as one of the first of Simeon's so called *Pious Chaplains of India*. He entered Magdalene College at Cambridge in 1782, the same year Simeon was made a Fellow of King's College. Simeon's relationship to Brown differs somewhat from the others. He was more of a lateral mentor with

Chapter 2. Charles Simeon (1759-1836)

former student who had been influenced by Simeon. He had arrived in India in 1786. There he had quickly been introduced to "evangelicals" who helped influence his assignment to the prestigious post of chaplain at the garrison at Ft. William. The evangelicals included William Chambers, George Udny, and Charles Grant (Bennett 1992:218). Primarily it was Charles Grant who served as the all important mentor sponsor for Brown. These men burned with a mission passion for India. They were prominent leaders in the India Company--though a minority. Bennett describes something of their vision. He also alludes to their wisdom concerning change dynamics. I will comment on this after the quote.

> ...Sharing an evangelical spirit, and motivated [through Grant] by the failure of Coke's initial efforts,[32] the four men drew up a "Plan for a Mission to Bengal and Behar." The essence of the "Plan" was a proposal for India Company Patronage of missionaries in the same way as the East Indies Company supported its chaplains. The scheme called for the posting of an English clergyman in each of the eight divisions of Bengal and Behar "to establish schools, employ catechists, and establish churches."
> With the "Plan" drafted, it remained to secure the approval of the Company's Court of Directors. Being already an adept politician, Grant knew that Company approval would be gained through Parliamentary influence. Thus, on September 17, 1787, Grant and company sent the "Plan" to William Wilberforce, then Member for the county of Yorkshire and the leading evangelical in Parliament. In recognition of the ecclesiastical infrastructure of the "Plan," a copy of the proposal was forwarded to the Archbishop of Canterbury. Further religious input was sought through copies to Thomas Raikes and the Countess of Huntingdon.
> Then, being pragmatic men, Grant and Brown also considered the consequences of success. If Wilberforce was victorious and the Court agreed to patronize missionaries, what kind of missionaries were the Directors likely to approve? The answer would naturally parallel Company policy on chaplains. The East Indies Company would employ Churchmen. How would evangelical Anglican clergy come to India? By the encouragement of their elders, mentors, and friends. The "Plan" needed a clerical agent in England, one who could influence senior ministers to recommend India to their juniors, and one who might challenge those training for holy orders to consider serving the Established Church as a missionary. A name came to the mind of David Brown in the midst of this discussion: Charles Simeon, vicar of Holy Trinity Church, and his own mentor in Cambridge. In September of 1787, Brown wrote to Simeon on behalf of the authors of the "Plan," inviting him to serve as their clerical agent in England (Bennett 1992:219-221).

These men were wise change agents. They had a future vision they wanted in place and they prepared a bridging strategy to get it in place.[33] One of the elements of this

---

some downward mentoring functions into Brown's life. Both gave input into each other's lives. The others of the Pious set were all mentorees receiving primarily downward mentoring from Simeon. See Clinton and Clinton (1992), **The Mentor Handbook** for the categories of upward, lateral and downward mentoring. Suffice it to say that Brown had *the right* to challenge Simeon as he did in this letter.
[32]Bennett gives the background leading to the letter. "The Wesleyans really were the first off the mark in the race to establish an evangelical missionary movement from Britain. Fully eight years ahead of Carey and the Baptists, at least one Methodist was actively seeking to send missionaries to India. In 1784 and again in 1786, Thomas Coke was in correspondence with an India Company official in Calcutta, Charles Grant, in order to arrange for transit licenses for Methodist missionaries. Coke attracted Grant's attention, if not also his encouragement. ...[Coke was not successful in getting Wesley's backing for his missionary vision and as a result the missionary agenda was delayed for three decades.] However, Coke's temporary failure stimulated Charles Grant to act on his own." (Bennett 1992:217,218)
[33]*Change agents* must know the system they are dealing with inside and out. Grant did. They must know the change participants and the roles of the major change agents. Wise change agents think through the steps necessary for moving the system from *where it is* to *where it ought to be*. This is called a *bridging strategy*. Part of the bridging strategy involves the ramifications of success and failure. These men thought

strategy included the recruitment of missionaries. It was at this point that Brown, providentially in place, could link to Simeon. The challenge was made.[34] Simeon accepted it. He is launched in his interest in missions. This will grow significantly over his lifetime until it becomes one of his dual life time purposes. Bennett notes the acceptance of the challenge.

> Across the top of Brown's letter is Simeon's own annotation, written in 1830.
> "It merely shows how early God enabled me to act for India; to provide for which has now for forty-two years been a principal and incessant object of my care and labour."
> ... His own autobiography and other contemporary sources agree that Charles Simeon rose to the challenge of his new 'diocese.' (Bennett 1992:207, 221)

Many of Simeon's accomplishments owe their birth to this foreign mission challenge. For over twenty years he will grapple with the problems of founding the Church Missionary Society. He will sponsor the British and Foreign Bible Society even though it is outside Anglican favor. He will sponsor Chaplains in the East India Company. He will rejuvenate a Jewish mission. This mission passion also brings Simeon to the attention of Charles Grant--in my opinion, along with Wilberforce and Thornton, some of the most influential lay Christians of all time.

Why should Simeon even rise to the challenge? Probably there are numerous reasons. There are usually no simple answers to such a complex question. We do not have all the information to answer the question thoroughly. But from what we do have, we see the critical importance of timing. The timing was perfect. Simeon was shut out of his own church--at least from productively accomplishing all that he wanted to. The majority of his parish were against him. He had lots of youthful energy and plans for ministry which were being thwarted. He was already starting to do itinerant preaching outside his parish--a thing somewhat necessitated due to the blocking situation in his own church. He had not yet started his deliberate in-depth mentoring ministry at the University.[35] He was ready, in the timing of God, for some challenge--why not an interest in missionary effort. And from this strategic location in Cambridge he will greatly help influence the English people toward a responsible missionary viewpoint.

1792--Charles Grant, An Influential Evangelical Partner

Charles Grant modeled what powerful influence a Christian businessman can have on the Christian movement within a country.[36] In 1792 he crossed paths with Simeon.[37]

---

ahead. In fact, Grant already had some alternative schemes in mind in case the "Plan" failed. Wise change agents always have more than one egg and more than one basket. When the "Plan" does fail, Grant begins to work on two different alternative schemes. See Clinton (1992), **Bridging Strategies--Leadership Perspectives for Introducing Change.**

[34]This is a *ministry challenge* (Clinton 1989:226), one of the expansion cluster of process items. *Ministry challenges* are one of the means God uses to expand a leader to a wider sphere of influence and development toward realization of potential leadership influence.

[35]In addition to the timing, Bennett (1992:208-217) lists six major macro-contextual pressures that would have influenced Simeon toward a missionary spirit: 1. Utilitarianism, 2. Social Responsibility, 3. Theocentric Influence, 4. Wider Views of the World, 5. Eschatology and 6. Churchmanship.

[36]While this book is dedicated toward full time Christian leaders who are effective and have finished well, any book which treats lay persons--especially successful businessmen--who led focused lives and counted greatly for the kingdom--would certainly have to include this great man. Where are the many biographies about him? Bennett (1992:218) at least points us to one by H. Morris. He certainly was an important synergistic force on Simeon's influence.

[37]Of course, he had been introduced to Simeon from afar in the correspondence over the "Plan." But it was in 1792 that they met face-to-face. Grant was a *divine contact* for Simeon. *Divine Contacts* (Clinton

Chapter 2. Charles Simeon (1759-1836)

His partnership with Simeon provided a synergistic, dual, secular/clerical base of power from which to influence the Church of England for missions. Who was he? How did they meet? What was their partnership? What were the results of this partnership? Bennett gives us insight into the person, the heartbeat and the influence of this man. It is worth taking space and time to introduce this solid Christian entrepreneur. It will help us appreciate a catalyzing force for increasing Simeon's sphere of influence.

> Until 1780 Grant served as secretary to the Board of Trade in Calcutta, a body that had been created to coordinate the East India Company's commercial operations in India. Tiring of an administrative role and looking for a more lucrative activity, Grant became Commercial Resident at Malda. While directing the Company's trading concerns in his territory, Grant was able to enter into a number of advantageous personal contracts. This was common practice for Company officials. By such private trade Grant amassed a significant fortune and rose in influence among the Company's officials in India.[38]
>
> In addition to increasing his wealth and status, Charles Grant became a committed evangelical during his residency in India. His spiritual renewal originated out of the deaths of his brother, his uncle, and both of his daughters in 1775, 1776. Grant's new faith had direct effect on the use of his fortune and his rank. Grant bought the Kiernander's Old Mission Church in 1787 and thus provided an evangelical pulpit for Calcutta.[39] Grant also used his position to encourage Thomas Coke's plan to send Methodist missionaries to Bengal in 1784, 1786 (Bennett 1992:296,297).

He was involved in the "1787 Plan" with Brown. He tried one of his alternate schemes, personally recruiting and placing a missionary in India. This plan too failed.[40] After returning to England, he was influential in numerous evangelical enterprises including missionary efforts. India House and Parliament were the major settings for Grant's efforts on behalf of the Christianization of India. He was elected to the company's Court of Directors in May 1794. His influence after that date was immense (Bennett 1992:298-300). Notice Bennett's insight into Grant's change dynamics procedures.[41] It is this

---

1989:260) are special kinds of mentors. They intervene in the life of a mentoree at a timely moment to provide linkage to resources or affirm some plan of action or reinforce some touch on the life by God. The timeliness of the intervention, as well as the actual function done, validates the person as divinely sent, that is, a divine contact or means of contact with God's divine intention. Grant will connect Simeon to vast resources and a power base from which to insert evangelical missionaries and/or ministers into India. He will also introduce Simeon to an important *ministry insight*, how to use wealth and position to affect patronage and placement of evangelicals.

[38] He acquired a major power base (large reservoir of wealth), modeled a successful business career (which added to his influence in the secular world), and was introduced to the great spiritual needs of people all over India. Once he became an evangelical he saw the sovereign hand of God in this provision and determined to use his power for God. Would that there would be hundreds of talented *busters* who with deliberateness would enter business with kingdom motives and with such a vision as Grant had. Creative financing for mission effort is desperately needed now, in these days of repeated appeals to the same overworked financial base for missions.

[39] This was the start of a *ministry insight* in how to use wealth for evangelical influence. Simeon will pick up on this later.

[40] The missionary endeavor of recruiting, training, financially backing and getting to the field and into effective ministry is an involved process that is difficult to understand in its entirety. Grant did not have the relational skills nor the perspective of the whole process to pull it off. In fact, it is not till later when Simeon recruits missionaries, that the difficulty of selection processes becomes clearer after several failures.

[41] This is an example of what we term in change dynamics theory, as *coffee cup diplomacy* (I suppose we would have to use an equivalent phrase--*tea cup diplomacy* for our British friends). See Clinton 1992, **Bridging Strategies--Leadership Perspectives for Introducing Change**. Effective change agents are aware of the personal involvement and relationships with influential people in order to get things done. Both Simeon and Grant were especially aware of this important feature of *networking power*. Grant did thorough research as well--another characteristic of successful change agents. After returning to Britain

Chapter 2. Charles Simeon (1759-1836)

meeting that really launched the partnership of Grant and Simeon. I'll talk more about the partnership in the next time period when Simeon began to assert influence in missions.

> Not unlike Simeon, Charles Grant exerted much of his influence on the "mission business" through various private discussions and meetings. One such engagement--and a crucial one as far as this study is concerned--was a dinner with Simeon in Cambridge in October of 1792. Claudius Buchanan of Queens' College, a student of Simeon's, was also present. (He later became the Rev. Claudius Buchanan, D.D. Vice-Provost of the College of Ft. William in Bengal.) The meeting afforded an opportunity for Simeon to meet the senior author of the "1787 Plan" for the first time. Prospects for missionary activity in India were discussed, with Buchanan expressing his hope "to be qualified for [such] work." Moreover, it is certain that Grant and Simeon discussed ways and means for filling East India Company chaplaincies with Simeon's students. Although Simeon and Grant shared Wilberforce's hope for the patronage of missionaries by the Indian Government, the two men had been considering alternatives for more than a year. In 1791 Simeon had inquired of Grant regarding a chaplaincy for Samuel Marsden. Grant declined the suggestion on the grounds that Marsden was too young, but he took the opportunity to reply to specifically ask Simeon to help him to identify prospective chaplains. Buchanan, for example, became one of the chaplains that Simeon helped to send to India in 1796 (Bennett 1992:299,300).

Grant and Simeon hit it off well. Both Grant and Simeon were get-it-done type of people. They were not afraid to attempt change of the system. They found alternative ways to do things. They shared much in common such as an appreciation for evangelical dissenters, an implicit trust in each other's judgment, and most of all a desire to see India evangelized. This God-given informal partnership with its synergistic interplay has dynamics which can be just as effective today.[42]

1792--Pulpit Breakthrough--Discovery of Jean Claude's Essay; A Ministry Insight for Public Ministry; A Methodology Easily Passed On By Mentoring

Many wealthy upper class British men and women are introduced early on to oratory. It is part of their upbringing in the home. Social events provide the opportunity for oratory to be observed and practiced. In their boarding schools they are further introduced to it. Simeon was no stranger to public speaking when he took over the pulpit of Holy Trinity Church. There is overlap between public speaking and preaching. But there is also a vast difference between public speaking and pastoral responsibility for a public ministry which changes lives over the long haul. Simeon was untrained as a pulpiteer. Neither his Eton background nor his Cambridge background prepared him for a pulpit ministry. Formally, he was untaught in this as were all the other ordinands and young men entering the ministry. He struggled with this. He did not lack zeal or passion.

---

in 1793 he researched and wrote *Observations on the state of society among the Asiatic subjects of Great Britain* which he published in 1797 (Bennett 1992:299). This research gave backing for his argument for Company financial support for missionary activity in India. Once he became a member of the Court of Directors--the executive leadership of the East India Company--he was able to bring about much change. This was especially so when he was chairman or vice-chairman, positions which rotated among Court members.

[42]Mission minded full time Christian workers need the political savvy, resources, connections, and power bases that dedicated lay Christians can provide. The lay Christians need the strategic theological insights and practical savvy involved in placing and developing Christian work and workers.

Chapter 2. Charles Simeon (1759-1836)

He did not lack heart. But he needed to learn effective communication from the pulpit which would convict, edify, impart truth, and honor the Savior.[43]

Pulpit practice in these days included the following. Some sermons were read verbatim. Frequently, these were lifeless.[44] Many sermons were written out and then memorized. They were repeated verbatim from the pulpit.[45] What a burden! Simeon sought to change ineffective pulpit communication and to impart a different burden--one for responsible public ministry which proclaims the Word of the Lord.

The breakthrough for Simeon came in a surprising way. He discovered a classic book on preaching--one more than a hundred years old--yet still presenting useful information.[46] It was not an Anglican book. In 1792, ten years into his struggling pulpit ministry he happened on to a little booklet by Jean Claude, a Huguenot notable (1619-1687); *Essay on the Composition of a Sermon*. This discovery refreshed Simeon in at least three ways. One, Claude affirmed many of Simeon's own principles learned by experience. Two, Claude systematically arranged his preaching principles so that they made an integrated whole which could be easily taught to others. Three, Simeon was inspired to write up materials which used Claude's work as a base. He not only improved upon Claude's work but added to it illustrative sermons and/or sermon outlines which flowed from the principles. This gave him a solid base of transferable concepts and a major training manual (originally published as **Skeletons** in 1796) he could use in his mentoring efforts which were just about to begin as a deliberate and major thrust of his ministry. Later he will continue to improve upon this manual until it becomes a major contribution that he leaves behind.

1794--Summary of Focal Issues and Shaping Toward Them

In 1790 the tensions in his church eased a bit. The wardens in a conciliatory gesture allowed Simeon to use the church for his Sunday evening meetings. In 1794 the church as a whole went a step further. They returned to Simeon the lecture. His ministry is at this time flourishing in his own parish. And Simeon is much further along toward his focused life. A home base exists upon which to build a very influential ministry. Let's summarize the focal issues and the means for prioritizing, the focal factors, to this point.

At this point Simeon has been sovereignly led to a major role within the Anglican Church, a ministerial position in Holy Trinity Church, and a strategic location from which he will be able to influence greatly over the next period of time. He has seen the power of a personal conversion experience in his own life. He knows that the Church of England

---

[43] Simeon was not a poor pulpiteer. Even early on he demonstrated an innate ability to move people. He was probably one of the better public rhetoricians in the region. But he struggled with it until this breakthrough. Need is one of the major factors in discovery of *ministry insights*.
[44] Hopkins records incidents of some Vicars simply plagiarizing sermons of earlier greats and reading them in the pulpit (Hopkins 1977:56).
[45] "Memorized sermons" were referred to as *the mandated text* method. Simeon sought to eliminate this method as he felt it limited spontaneity and enthusiastic presentation of material. He did not, however, recommend pure extemporaneous speaking. He was for thorough preparation. After doing thorough preparation and using outline notes to guide one for several years he felt one could then, still after preparation, speak more freely.
[46] When we talk about *ultimate contributions*, particularly writing ones, we speak of contemporary and classic contributions. Contemporary meet the need of the hour. Classic deal with issues that fundamentally hold even long years after. This is a classic contribution. Both contemporary and classic contributions are important. But classic ones will be useful long after the authors have passed on. See position paper by Clinton (1989) *The Ultimate Contribution*.

Chapter 2. Charles Simeon (1759-1836)

needs pastors who have experienced this kind of personal relationship with God. His ultimate purpose is becoming clear. The mentoring influence of the first generation of evangelicals, Venn, Thornton, Newton, and Berridge, has done two things. It has helped him see the need for an evangelical renewal within the Church of England. Further, it has modeled the importance of and power of the mentoring concept. He has personally been empowered by mentoring. He will be able to empower others. He has been introduced to a second ultimate purpose--the cause of missions, especially in India. It is in seed form now. But this purpose will further grow and dominate his next two major periods of time.

Eight critical incidents have influenced him progressively over this period. They helped shape some very important values. They have led him to his major role. They have highlighted for him, in seed form, two ultimate purposes for his life--a renewal focus in the Church of England and a desire to mobilize the church toward missions. They have given him the unique methodology he will use. Critical incidents generally do two major things-- they describe the means for shaping of crucial values; they describe the ways that God identifies the focal issues in the life. These eight performed those two major functions.

In Simeon's case, four of the eight, were dominantly **value incidents**: Incident 1. *New Creature*--the value, *renewal begins with a vital relationship with God*; Incident 2. *Henry Venn, Evangelical Renewal Vision*--The value, *a growing band of like minded ministers who think strategically can indeed affect renewal*; Incident 3. *Singleness, Concentrated Focus on University Ministry*--The value, *Sacrifice can be made if the goal is worth it*; Incident 4. *Jean Claude Essays, Effective Pulpit*--The value, *renewal pastors can be trained to effectively communicate from the pulpit and lead many others to renewal*.

Four of the eight were focal factors, i.e. **strategic guidance** incidents. They helped narrow Simeon toward the focal issues: Incident 2, *St. Edwards*, gave affirmation in the pastoral role; Incident 3, *Against the Odds*--shows how God sovereignly intervened to provide the location, Holy Trinity and King's College, Cambridge, and major role that will insure the possibility of Simeon's development of his leadership potential. Incident 6, *The 1787 Plan*--inspires Simeon to the wider task of an effective renewed church reaching out to the world. It will be the springboard for his future mission activity. Incident 7, *Charles Grant,* provides a linkage to a yet future but powerful ministry.

B. The Strategic Years--Seeding the 3rd Generation of Evangelicals, Leadership Selection and Development Through Mentoring, Gaining a Missionary Interest--India, the Focus
(1794-1816); Age=35-57

Simeon has accumulated 12 hard years in the ministry. But he now has a base from which to exert increasing influence on the Anglican Church. He further clarifies a life purpose which will dominate all that he does. That purpose is to bring evangelical renewal to the Anglican Church. He is in the process of developing his other life purpose with initial attempts to initiate change projects involving missions and the Anglican Church. Ultimately he will be frustrated in this but will find alternative means of flaming this passion.

He is part of the second generation of evangelicals. He will develop a methodology for sowing and planting the third generation of evangelicals. These *Simeonites* will drastically influence the Anglican Church, the ongoing evangelical movement, and missions in the 19th century. The foundations for this on-going 19th century influence are laid down in this development phase in Simeon's life--the years from 1794-1816. These years are bounded on the front end by the firm establishment of his parish base in 1794 and on the closing end by Charles Grant's final retirement in 1816. Still this is not a clear cut

Chapter 2. Charles Simeon (1759-1836)

time period. There is overlap of items from the previous time period, 1782-1794, and there will be overlap into the next time period, 1817-1836.

Though there is overlap I will focus my description in terms of two emphases:

1. (1794-1805) Simeon's influence via Cambridge and evangelical networks which are steps toward his **renewal purpose** for the Anglican Church, and
2. (1805-1816) Simeon's efforts toward furthering the **worldwide mission aims** of the church.

1. The Cambridge Years
Early Renewal Efforts--Cambridge Sermons, Sermon classes, Mentoring,
Ministry Innovations,
Networking Power of Evangelicals--the clerical societies,
Isaac Milner--Evangelical Gatekeeper,
Early Mission Efforts--Developing CMS,
Obstacles to Recruiting--Inflexibility and Personality Conflicts
(1794-1805); Age=35-46

Renewal does not come easy in any situation. I want to identify several means Simeon used to bring renewal. These can be grouped under four headings: public ministry--in the parish and University; value based training via mentoring; ministry innovations--renewal in small things; networking with evangelicals--outside and inside the University.

Public Rhetorician--The Power of Oratory to Promote Renewal

Simeon used his pulpit ministry in his own church, in other parishes, and upon occasion in University sermons to propagate many of his renewal ideas. He became an accomplished speaker. Many of his sermons were printed and circulated. In 1787 he was asked by the Vice-Chancellor to address the Cambridge University with the first of his sermon series. This was a great honor. This continued throughout his 54 year tenure. He gave some 10 of these 4-lecture series during his lifetime. He frequently used these series to get renewal thinking out in the public as well as reinforce his stand with the established church. Some of these University sermons stirred up public debate.

In addition, Simeon used his own pulpit to great advantage over the years. Large numbers of Cambridge undergrads attended his church. His pulpit ministry brought some to Christ, edified many toward growth in their Christian lives, modeled the importance of a pastoral calling and challenged many of them into life changing decisions for ministry. His public ministry in his own church was often a means for recruiting and inviting promising young leaders into his mentoring fishing pool, the Sunday night meetings.

Mentoring--The Sermon Classes, 1792 Onward

Simeon developed his unique methodology for bringing renewal into the Anglican Church, mentoring, during this period of time. He simply personally influenced up-and-coming potential clergy by mentoring them during their Cambridge years. Over and over, year in and year out, he persevered in inspiring young men to accept the claims of Christ on their lives and to serve Him. This is the most important renewal means that Simeon

Chapter 2. Charles Simeon (1759-1836)

employed. He touched individual lives.[47] He built renewal values into their lives. Then he sent them out to the highways and byways to bring renewal to the rank and file of the Anglican Church. Later he will develop powerful resources to actually place them in important pulpit positions.

One of his most important means for mentoring involved his Sunday night Sermon classes. This was not a formal class scheduled by the University but an informal one attended by mentorees. This class was held in Simeon's personal quarters. Entrance to the class was by invitation only. The class began in 1790 as a gathering for undergraduates. After Simeon's discovery of Claude's essay, in 1792, he began to instruct on homiletical principles. Out of these early classes he developed his materials to publish **Skeletons** in 1796 and updated versions in later years (Bennett 1992:164).

Simeon had profited greatly from the mentoring he received from the first generation of Anglican evangelicals--Venn, Berridge, Thornton and Newton. Particularly was this true of character formation as well as early insights into ministry methodology. These early experiences helped shape his own mentoring methodology and content with those emerging leaders in Cambridge. Bennett points out that Simeon focused his mentoring on several important values to be implanted in mentorees. He lists 9 important topics on which Simeon concentrated: 1. A Call to Ministry; 2. Fidelity to God; 3. Dependence on the Holy Spirit; 4. Exercise of Proper Authority; 5. Submission to Proper Authority; 6. A Spirit of Moderation; 7. Compassion in the Parish; 8. Diligent Effort; 9. Perseverance in Adversity (Bennett 1992:129-145).

From the number of students attending his church, sermon classes, and later, his conversation parties, Simeon always selected an inner core for special treatment. Bennett describes this special in-depth sharing of Simeon's life with his close mentorees.

> ...Simeon established special bonds of friendship and concern with a relatively small circle of his students during his years in Cambridge. Thomas Thomason, one of those students, recorded that "Mr. Simeon watches over us as a shepherd over his sheep. He takes delight in instructing us, and has us continually at his rooms"...Abner Brown, a student of Simeon's in the late 1820s, noted that Simeon was extremely close to a small number of students, often relying on them for advice and assistance in such weighty matters as evaluating the fitness of a fellow student for appointment to a curacy.
> Some of these students from the "inner circle" became, themselves, curates to Simeon. These included Thomason and Henry Martyn, later India Company chaplains; Thomas Sowerby; Matthew Preston; James Scholefield, later Regius Professor of Greek at Cambridge; and William Carus, Simeon's biographer. It was Simeon's custom to spend a portion of Sunday, over supper, with his curates and close student friends. There they would discuss the day's activities and receive Simeon's advice for the coming week. It was also a meaningful time for Simeon, for these men were his 'family.'...Over the years, Simeon's "inner circle" grew in number, stature, and influence (Bennett 1992:165,166)

---

[47]Bennett (1992:121) states it well. "Charles Simeon did not aspire to or achieve higher office in the Established Church. Only infrequently, and with reluctance, did Simeon accept official roles at King's College or in the University....Based on the facts, it appears that the vicar of Holy Trinity Church was no institutional leader. Nevertheless, Charles Simeon was one of the most influential clergymen in the history of the Church of England. This achievement was realized through Simeon's commitment to and perfection of the model for leadership employed by first-generation evangelicals: Charles Simeon made disciples. Above all other accomplishments, Charles Simeon was a mentor." Bennett devotes a whole chapter, 47 pages to Charles Simeon the mentor. He also devotes another 43 pages in a later chapter to describe Simeon's most important mentoree's and their impact upon India in particular and missions in general.

Chapter 2. Charles Simeon (1759-1836)

Leadership Selection Methodology--Funneling the Response

Simeon's relationships with students can be thought of as a series of concentric circles which form a systematic approach to leadership selection.

In the **outermost circle** there was the entire student body at Cambridge which could be potentially influenced by Simeon in his duties at Cambridge or as pastor. This included especially those students who attended his church regularly. In the early days those who attended were ridiculed by others. But this changed. As the years went on this number greatly increased--several hundred each Sunday.

Then the **next smallest circle** contains those involved in the *Conversation Parties* (which I shall describe shortly). Those who were most interested in following up had opportunity for further contact with Simeon. This would be 60 to 80 on a weekly basis. Up to this point the student chooses to be involved. But from here on Simeon chooses who will be involved.

Then in the **next yet smaller circle** there were those who were really considered mentorees. These would be *invited* to the weekly sermon class. About 15-20 made up this select and privileged group.

Next closest to the center was the "inner circle" of 6 to 8 who met weekly for supper and evaluative conversation. They spent several hours and chatted reflectively on what they had learned during the week and what to expect in the coming week.

Finally, in the **very center small circle** there was a select very few who became co-workers with Simeon as curates. These men at first were in effect serving internships. They learned ministry by watching, by personally interacting much with Simeon, by accepting increased responsibility, and finally by being released into ministry. They were able to learn of his parish ministry and his ministry outside. They saw how he handled parish problems. They saw how he related to other ministers--both evangelicals and non-evangelicals in the Anglican Church. They noted also his warm relationships with evangelicals outside the Anglican Church. They saw his willingness to be involved in voluntary organizations for promoting the Gospel both home and abroad. In short, they were introduced to the full sway of his churchmanship. They imbibed Simeon's values which made up his ministry philosophy.

It was from the co-workers, the inner circle, the preaching classes, and the conversation parties that the vast majority of Simeon's recommendations for the mission field and the pastorate came. Occasionally he would recommend someone who had not been involved in this selection process.

Impact Training--The Informal Theorem

There is a major *impact dynamic* involved here. A person engaged in extensive mentoring will have *levels of intimacy*. The closer the intimacy, the more time is spent together. The level of instruction moves from more formal to less formal as the circles decrease--with much more interaction in the smaller circles. The rule is--*the more informal is the instruction medium, the deeper the impact of values in the life.*[48]

---

[48]This same kind of dynamic is seen in Christ's ministry training: the crowds, the greater fringe of disciples, the 500 disciples who followed hard, the 120 who formed the core of the first church, the 12, the three, and the one. In addition there were levels of intimacy in his social relationships: the band of those supporting him in ministry; Mary, Martha, Lazarus; Mary.

Chapter 2. Charles Simeon (1759-1836)

There is always the danger of favoritism when the *differing levels of intimacy* dynamic is employed. But it is worth the risk of being accused of showing favoritism. It is really not favoritism. It is simply responding to those who are more responsive and who will profit more from training. It is an important selection process. There is great power in recognizing that impact training increases with an increase in informality. In two statements the values seen in *levels of intimacy* can be summarized. 1. *The more informal the training medium the more potential for in-depth impact in the life of the trainee.* 2. *Invest more in those who respond to training--give them more training and take them deeper into it.*

Simeon's intent in mentoring was consistent with his purpose of helping the Anglican Church recover its spiritual vitality. According to Bennett (1992:148) Simeon had pinpointed two problems that he would attack. The weak Anglican Church was plagued with ministerial non-residence and incompetent clergy. His mentoring activity dealt primarily with the second of these problems. His patronage schemes, which develop more fully later, help deal with the first problem.

I will return to Simeon's mentoring when I talk about his results of mentoring for missions--especially his influence in India through the Pious Chaplains.

Ministry Innovations--1794-1813

I mentioned a Simeon pattern earlier. When **thwarted** in some way **he would find alternative means** for accomplishing something. Simeon was more pragmatic than theoretical. He found ways to solve practical problems. His solutions often were innovative. Being at a center of learning and influence he was aware that many new methodologies were being introduced in various parishes. He did not necessarily embrace them all. But he was open to these innovations. He recognized the need for creativity in parish work. He was prepared to change traditional ways if it helped progress the evangelical cause.

His major innovation was that of mentoring men for the ministry. But he was involved in many others, some of which he did not create but simply promoted.

Innovations Simeon promoted or introduced for parish ministry included: better worship singing, Sunday evening lectures, lay oriented training societies, laity assisting in parish visitation, methodologies for dispensing help for the poor in the parish, organization of stewards for managing church finances and charity and relief, summer retreats for clergy.

Innovations Simeon used in connection with his renewal efforts include: various kinds of small groups for use in mentoring, training in homiletics--the sermon classes, production of training materials for preaching, the formation of clerical societies of evangelicals, personal fund raising for various organizations, beating the bushes--carrying his ideas for promoting organizations out to leaders far and wide.

Recruiting Innovation--The Conversation Party

I want to describe one of these innovations, the "conversation party." Though it comes later in time, it was an insight that served as a fishing pool for potential mentorees. It was a natural extension of the mentoring going on during this period of time.

In 1812, after 30 years in residence, Simeon moved to larger quarters at King's College. He began what he called "conversation" tea parties. These were held on Fridays

Chapter 2. Charles Simeon (1759-1836)

at 6:00 p.m. Any students at Cambridge could come to these. Simeon served tea. After a time of informal chatting Simeon would bring the meeting to order. He invited questions from the group. There was no lecture or prayer. That avoided the accusation of an unlicensed church meeting. Eventually the Sermon classes of 15-20 students were scheduled for 8:00 following the "Conversation party." Bennett (1992:165) states that it was primarily through these two events and his Sunday pulpit that Simeon helped train Anglican ministers and missionaries for a generation and a half.

Let me give some observations on this informal means of training. The methodology, using open questions, requires experience and wisdom. Simeon is dealing with university students some of them with innate intelligence greater than his. This is not an easy method to use. One must become adept in answering all kinds of questions. This is risky. One can look like a fool. However, with the development of careful diplomatic skills to field questions and with a reservoir of answers to repeated questions, question and answer sessions can be used to great advantage. Much can be taught via this method. And potential mentorees can be challenged to want more. The scheduling of the sermon class directly after the *Conversation Party* meant that in the 60-80 attending there would be a solid empathetic core of 20 or so who were on Simeon's wavelength. These *Simeonites* also could use this Friday night event as a means for recruiting new potential mentorees.

Each of these ministry innovations were in their own way *Simeon statements of renewal*.

Networking Power of Evangelicals--the Clerical Societies

Part of Simeon's scheme for renewal involved recruiting and getting evangelicals into the University scene. They were generally discriminated against. They could not obtain high paying jobs. Many simply did not have finances needed for further education. Simeon found ways to solve these problems. Bennett describes Simeon's efforts in these regards.

> Simeon's work as a mentor did not begin when his students arrived at Cambridge and found their way to his church or College rooms. Neither did Simeon's efforts on behalf of his disciples end when they left the University. Through an active role in the formation and operation of a number of evangelical clerical societies, Simeon was enabled to recruit the students he would later mentor. Then, through his famous activity in patronage trusts and in recruiting chaplains for the East India Company, Simeon assisted his students to find appropriate "spheres" of ministry and Christian service. These aspects of Simeon's labours as a mentor were brilliantly coordinated with his direct discipleship of students during their residency in Cambridge.
> Owing to the limited means and influence of most evangelical Churchmen in the eighteenth century, it was not easy for their sons to secure a place at Cambridge or Oxford in Simeon's early days. It was equally difficult, if not more so, for evangelicals to secure a respectable living after taking a degree. Access to the Universities and to good parishes upon graduation was essential to resolve the evangelical's dilemma: the choice between poverty and multiple charges. Simeon worked tirelessly to rectify this situation.
> In order to give evangelical students greater access to the Universities, Simeon gave active support to the development of clerical societies.[49] (Bennett 1992:151)

---

[49] Venn, his mentor, had paved the way in this by forming a fellowship for Yorkshire's evangelical ministers in 1767. Later in 1771 after he moved to Yelling, the fellowship organized under George Burnett to become the Elland Clerical Society. They were able to get their first student into Cambridge in 1782 with the help of an evangelical sympathizer on faculty--Professor Farish (Bennett 1992:152).

Chapter 2. Charles Simeon (1759-1836)

These societies were composed of evangelicals who met regularly to encourage one another. They also attempted to assist young men in preparation for ministry. This involved selection of promising students and providing them with scholarship aid. They also used their connections to get them accepted.

Venn suggested to Simeon in 1786 that they should form a society nearby. Simeon took up the cause. The West Norfolk Society was the first of Simeon's efforts. He was later instrumental in starting others.[50] These would be important in encouraging evangelical efforts in their locales. They would also provide fellowships in which Simeon's mentorees could find the same nurturing mentoring environment that had been provided him in his first years in ministry.

One other networking innovation that Simeon introduced was summer retreats for pastors and their wives. This he continued from 1796-1817. His efforts at renewal were not just limited to mentoring future leaders. He also saw the need to provide retreats for present day clergy. This was indeed an innovation at this time.

1788--Isaac Milner--Evangelical Gatekeeper

In change dynamics theory, a gatekeeper is one who controls access to something whether information, flow of activities, or other resources.[51] Both Oxford and Cambridge were controlled dominantly by non-evangelical Anglican Churchmen. This meant few evangelicals could gain entrance for study and eventual placement in the established church. Isaac Milner became President of Queen's College, Cambridge in 1788. Bennett describes this important turning point which helped open the gates to evangelicals.[52]

> The turning point for the evangelical clerical societies was the appointment of Isaac Milner, a friend of Simeon's, to the Presidency of Queen's College, Cambridge, in 1788. This event, combined with Farish's influence at Magdalene and Simeon's at King's, opened wide the doors for evangelicals at the University. Much larger numbers of students subsequently came to Cambridge, sponsored by the societies, to prepare for parish work under the tutorial care of the evangelical dons. Nevertheless, even with the formation of the Bristol Clerical Society in 1795, demand consistently exceeded supply. In a letter of 1814 to Thomas Thomason, Simeon observed that the societies were able to meet only a tenth of the need for "pious curates." (Bennett 1992:153)

A growing number of evangelicals made possible the organization of these societies. And the societies in turn spurred on the growth and placement of more young evangelical pastors. This networking power worked hand-in-glove with Simeon's personal mentoring efforts at Cambridge. Though there were other evangelicals already in Cambridge, Milner, with his power position, was the key that ignited the critical mass and allowed this cycle to happen.

---

[50]Another influential one was the London Clerical Education Society which was formalized in 1816.
[51]We have identified 9 or so change participants by function. The gatekeeper is one important one. We have also pinpointed 4 major change agent roles: catalyst, solution giver, process helper, resource linker. Simeon was dominantly a catalyst and resource linker. See Clinton (1992) **Bridging Strategies.**
[52]Though this event actually occurs in the previous phase, the momentum of it began to take effect in the time period being presently described.

Chapter 2. Charles Simeon (1759-1836)	page 53

2. The CMS Disenchantment, The India Years
The Missions Life Purpose Develops
The Pious Chaplains and Others
Other Missions Interest
(1805-1816)

While Simeon's mentoring also increased during this period, from 1805 on he increased his involvement in missions in several ways including his most important accomplishment for missions--his placement of chaplains. You will remember that Simeon's response to the "1787 Plan" launched him into a missions focus. When that "Plan" failed, Simeon set about to create a mission society that would be acceptable to the Church of England.[53] This again illustrates the Simeon pattern of **frustrated plans/ innovative alternatives** at the fringe of acceptability. His hope was that the Anglican Church would support this venture. Thus began a long period of efforts, more than eleven years, by Simeon in cooperation with others to bring into existence such a mission organization.

A number of important issues are involved with the starting of an organization. There is of course the need for leadership both in bringing into existence the organization and then those who will operate it. There is the convincing of a constituency to back it. There is the need for funds. There is the diplomatic efforts in getting it accepted by the established church. Then there is, in this case, the recruitment and deployment of the missionaries. This involves further liaison with the receiving countries powers to be. In all these kinds of issues Simeon was involved. In 1799 the organization was up and running. Bennett notes Simeon's involvement.

> It had been eleven years since Simeon had been invited by David Brown to foment a missionary movement among evangelical Churchmen. At last there was something to show for Simeon's efforts.
> ...Charles Simeon was in every sense a true founder of the Church Mission Society. He had been constantly at work in the background as he drummed up support for the new venture. Simeon had also been a participant in almost every major event leading up to the formation of the Society. Many of his contributions to these meetings resulted in important course corrections in the development of the CMS. Simeon had been instrumental in securing the support of evangelical Anglican clergy for the Society. He had recognized when headway would only be gained through the lay activism of Clapham. He had comprehended the growing disenchantment of many of his fellow ministers with the London Missionary Society and therefore he steered things toward a voluntary society for Churchmen. And Simeon had urged his fellow founders to embrace the "catechist plan" in order to avert further delay over the availability of ordained missionary candidates (Bennett 1992:238,239).

Bennett next traces the disenchantment of Simeon with the society, its on-going leadership, and its earliest decisions. In short, after going through the energy draining process of helping this organization come into existence over an eleven year period of time, Simeon gradually withdrew his pursuit of the mission cause through it. While there are numerous complicated reasons for this (rejections of his innovative ideas by the leadership, problems in recruiting missionaries, problems in gaining acceptance with the established

---

[53]This whole arena is the focus of Bennett's doctoral dissertation: **Charles Simeon and the Evangelical Anglican Missionary Movement--A Study of Voluntaryism and Church-Mission Tensions.** Voluntaryism refers to the private support of societies formed to advance specific causes. That a minister within the established church could openly support an organization outside the church was a fact, though it did create tensions as Bennett so expertly analyzes.

Chapter 2. Charles Simeon (1759-1836)

church, foot dragging in general, personality clashes)[54] the point is that Simeon lost heart for the venture.[55] During the next six years after its formation Simeon attempted to recruit missionaries for the organization. Numerous barriers to recruitment arose not the least of which was the financial support level of a missionary. Simeon recognized that the level would have to be raised in order to get top candidates. He could not convince the leadership of the CMS. Further, he recommended a top flight candidate, Samuel Lee, of comparable linguistic skills with Henry Martyn and William Carey. The CMS foot dragging and ultimately rejection of him, was typical of the kind of opposition Simeon felt from the CMS. True to his pattern of **frustrated plans/ innovative alternatives** at the fringe of acceptability Simeon turned to another approach to realize his mission purpose.[56]

Mentor Sponsoring, The India Missionary Focus--11 Fruitful Years

It is at this point that critical incidents 6, *Brown Links Simeon to India*, and 7, *Partnership for India--Charles Grant*, come into play. Simeon links hands with Charles Grant to recruit and place chaplains with the East India Company. He began to recruit and recommend from his contacts and mentorees those he felt were qualified for missionary work in India. His standards were high. He learned through several unsuccessful attempts to recruit that he would need high standards. From 1805 to 1812 he recommended about eight men in addition to the special five, called the Pious Chaplains. From 1813 to 1816 the number tripled to twenty-four. All in all, Simeon encouraged over forty of his students to consider an East India Company chaplaincy through the patronage of Grant. Twenty-one of his students responded successfully to this call.[57]

I should say a word about Simeon's most influential placement of leaders in India. In the literature they are called the *pious chaplains of India*.

---

[54]Bennett (1992:289) in reviewing Simeon's relationship to the CMS and his views of it 1824, many of which were valid during our time period now being discussed, lists numerous reasons including: 1. the progress of the Society for Missions to Africa and the East; 2. his own inability to recruit missionaries for the Society; 3. the rejection of the "catechist plan;" 4. the tendency of the Society's leaders to turn away from the universities as a source of personnel; 5. the General Committee's inability to recognize that salary comparisons with English clergy were relevant issues; 6. interpersonal conflict with key personalities associated with the Society; 7. the lack of interest of fellow clergy in the missionary cause; 8. all the delays such indifference had produced; 9. his geographical distance from the centre of the action in London; 10. the opposition of the hierarchy of the Church toward the CMS; 11. the Society's open challenges to the proper authority of the bishops; 12. his success in recruiting chaplains for India and his failure to enlist missionaries for the country; 13. the contrast between the access that chaplains had to India and the limits placed on missionaries; 14. the nonchalance of the Society with respect to his recommendations of personnel; 15. Society's promotional operations at home; 16. the ring of truth in the attacks of some of Society's harshest critics.

[55]This is a recurrent pattern seen in change dynamics situations--*the last straw syndrome*. When a change takes a long time to implement and there are many battles won and lost along the way, advocates who brought in the changes often lose energy to pursue them further. Sometimes further opposition of any kind becomes the last straw, the one that breaks the camel's (change agent's) back.

[56]Bennett (1992:207-290) traces Simeon's efforts and the disenchantment process. The 83 pages devoted to this show its importance. We are dealing with a fundamental drive in Simeon to accomplish a life purpose which is being thwarted. Toward the end of his life, Simeon will again intervene to help the CMS when he gets the head of the CMS, Henry Venn--grandson of his own mentor, and Bishop Daniel Wilson of India together to iron out problems concerning India. Eventually they worked out a concordat which established a good working relationship between the society and the established Church in India (Bennett 1992:29, 389).

[57]Bennett (1992) list all forty by name. He also describes their eventual ministry postings.

Chapter 2. Charles Simeon (1759-1836)

The most prominent connection between Charles Simeon and British India was his relationship with five India Company chaplains in particular. David Brown, Claudius Buchanan, Henry Martyn, Daniel Corrie, and Thomas Thomason became known as the 'pious chaplains of India.' The appellation reflected their standing in India as the foremost evangelicals of their day. In one sense they were simply among the first of Simeon's twenty-one East India Company chaplains. This, however, is an incomplete assessment. The strength of the bond between Simeon and these five men suggest that something more than mere patronage was at work. Simeon's association with them reveals the true intensity of his work as a mentor and a patron (Bennett 1992:325).

Table 2-1 Summarizes The Pious Chaplains and their assignments and accomplishments in India. Information has been adapted from Bennett (1992:326-360, Appendix I).

Table 2-1. The Pious Chaplains

Name	To India	Assignments/ Summary of Achievements
David Brown (1763-1812)	1785	Bengal chaplain (1785-1812) Ft. Wlliam, Calcutta, 1786-94 Sr. Chaplain, Calcutta, 1794-1812 Provost, Ft. Wm. College, 1800-1807 **Achievement**: Linked Simeon to missions in India. Strong mission activity including founding of Calcutta Bible Society.
Claudius Buchanan (1766-1815)	1796	Bengal chaplain (1796-1808) Barrackpore, 1797-99 Jr. Chaplain, Calcutta, 1799-1800 Vice-Provost, Ft. Wm. College, 1800-07 **Achievement**: Modeled Simeon's churchmanship in India; Mission strategist; worked for establishing ecclesiastical structure in India.
Henry Martyn (1781-1812)	1805	Bengal chaplain (1805-12) Dinapore, 1806-08 Cawnpore, 1809-10 Furlough, 1810-12 **Achievement**: Most famous of Pious Five; even more well known than Simeon; ultimate contribution= Saint; brilliant linguist who translated Persian and Hindustani New Testaments; modeled apologetic ministry to Islamic scholars; Mentored indigenous converts--most famous, Abdul Masih

Chapter 2. Charles Simeon (1759-1836)   page 56

Table 2-1. The Pious Chaplains continued

Name	To India	Assignments/ Summary of Achievements

Daniel Corrie (1777-1837)	1805	Bengal chaplain (1805-35)
		    Chunar, 1807-09
		    Cawnpore, 1810-13
		    Agra, 1813-14
		    Furlough in England, 1815-17
		    Benares, 1817-1819
		    Sr. Chaplain, Calcutta, 1819-23
		    Archdeacon of Calcutta, 1823-35
		Bishop of Madras (1835-37)
		Achievement: Most successful of Simeon's mentorees in ecclesiastical structure; Outstanding churchmanship; worked ecumenically with others outside Anglican Church; placed evangelical chaplains in good posts;

Thomas Thomason (1774-1829)	1808	Bengal chaplain (1808-29)
		    Old Church, Calcutta, 1808-26
		    Chaplain to the Governor-General, 1814-15
		    Furlough, 1827-28
		    Old Church, Calcutta, 1829
		Achievement: linked to Simeon; helped CMS; outstanding pastor to expatriates at Old Church, Calcutta

The most effective years in getting the chaplains placed were the windows of opportunity when Grant was either chairman or vice-chairman of the Court--which occurred three times during this interval. Bennett gives the sad words, which he sub-titles **The End of an Era for Simeon**, describing the conclusion of this fruitful period.

> The conclusion of Grant's final term as chairman of the East India Company Court of Directors marked a major change in the pace of Simeon's efforts to recruit chaplains for India. Without the control of official patronage that Grant's station provided, Simeon lost the ability to secure posts in India for his students. He might encourage men to consider an overseas chaplaincy, but he could no longer place them in such positions with ease (1992:368).

It was a good ride while it lasted.

1816--Summary of Focal Issues and Shaping Toward Them

What of the focal issues[58] have been cleared up by this time? The major role is set. It is a dual role--a respectable parish ministry in the established church and a college Fellow allowing influence at Cambridge. One of his life purposes is clear--he must bring evangelical renewal to the established church, the Church of England. The other is becoming clear. He wants to motivate England toward missions. Especially is he interested in India. He has discovered a unique methodology by which he can work on both purposes--mentoring of emerging leaders in the context of small groups. At least several of

---

[58]Remember that the focal issues refer to one or more of the following around which one prioritizes activities in order to fulfill a satisfying life: major role, life purpose, unique methodology, or ultimate contribution. Simeon actually has something of each of these issues in place. He is focused.

Chapter 2. Charles Simeon (1759-1836) page 57

his ultimate contribution areas are identified: *public rhetorician*--he is an effective public communicator; *mentor*--he will influence by close individual relationships; *promoter*--he will constantly motivate and bring change concerning renewal and missions.

In summary, by 1816, Simeon is in a well established dual role--pastor of an influential in a town church in Cambridge and a fellow at the University. He has opted for a single life style which allows him to fully engage in the double role. He occupies a strategic location giving him access to potential leaders. During this period of time he deliberately focuses on his mentoring of emerging leaders. His frustrations with the Church Mission Society lead him to look elsewhere to fulfill his missionary passion. He is able to recruit and place key leaders in India with chaplain posts.

Five critical incidents were touched on during the discussion of this time period. Four of the five were focal factors pressing Simeon toward accomplishment of one of his major life purposes--that of promoting the mission cause in Britain and more particularly his interest in India. Two of the four focal factors were previous incidents already discussed but which now come into full swing. They are Incident 6, *Brown Links Simeon to India*, and Incident 7, *Partnership for India, Charles Grant*. The other two focal factors include Incident 9, *Disenchantment*, which was negative preparation for his whole hearted involvement in the Grant partnership, and Incident 10, *Mentor Sponsoring to India*, his major means of fulfilling his personal destiny for India.

The other, a ministry insight, reinforced important values dealing with recruitment and training. That was Incident 11, *Conversation Parties*, a major means of recruiting mentors and extending his renewal ideas among college student leaders.

C. The Strategic Years--Preparing the Future in England
   Eschatology and the Jewish Mission
   Placing 3rd Generation Evangelicals in England Parishes
   (1817-1836); Age=58-77

Because of Simeon's now well established dual role, his long tenure, his networks of evangelical influence, and his acceptance as an evangelical churchman he has his most fruitful ministry during this period. But rather than touch on all his leadership influence endeavors I want to concentrate on just four items for this time period: His involvement in *The Jewish Mission* in London, his provision for long term evangelical influence via patronage, his production of **Horae Homileticae**, and his triumphant finish.

The Jewish Mission--1815 Onward

In his study of the Bible over the years, Simeon had come to see things about the Jewish nation in Scripture. His early versions of his sermon manuals contained a number of sermon outlines on the role of the Jewish nation. He believed that the Gentile Church had become the people of God because of the failure of the Jews to fulfill their spiritual mandate. So for the moment the Gentiles were in, the Jews were out. But Simeon believed that it was God's destiny for the Jewish people to be recalled as a nation in order to spur the Gentiles to faith. Because of these beliefs Simeon, in his latter years, came to see that the evangelization of the Jewish people was strategic for the overall progress of the Gospel. For this reason, a Biblical conviction, he became interested in a Jewish mission agency in greater London area, the London Society for the Propagation of Christianity

Chapter 2. Charles Simeon (1759-1836)

Amongst the Jews [LSPCJ]. What a title! To simplify things, I'll refer to it as *The Jewish Mission*.[59]

The Jewish Mission had been formed in 1809 in order to promote evangelical Churchmen and Dissenters in the evangelization of Jewish people. Simeon joined in this effort in 1810, primarily because of his growing theological convictions. He was on the fringes. But in 1815, because the Mission was about to collapse for lack of financial backing Simeon took an active hand. He felt he could bring some organizational stability. He helped it re-organize along the lines of the Church Missionary Society. By 1819 the organization was led by and backed by Churchman. The fundamental change that allowed this to happen was the stipulation, pushed by Simeon, that all members of The Jewish Mission be members of the Church of England.

Once over the hurdle of acceptance by Churchman, Simeon supported fully The Jewish Mission. Between 1811 and 1836 he spoke at least on 46 public occasions to gain acceptance of the Mission and/or to raise funds for it.[60]

Simeon also helped *The Jewish Mission* strategize a plan for expanding onto the Europe continent. Bennett comments on this.

> Simeon was also credited with helping the Jews Society develop its ministry strategy for Continental Europe. He urged the Society's workers to seek individual converts among the Jews, baptize them, join them in witness to their families, and assist them with vocational training. Such education was deemed to be necessary in view of the loss of status and employment that generally accompanied a profession of Christian faith in a Jewish community. This last component of the scheme reveals the careful thought that Simeon gave to the cultural implications of Jewish evangelism.
> The intensity and thoroughness of Simeon's efforts on behalf of the LSPCJ were measures of his commitment to the Jewish cause. The evangelization of the Jewish people had become an authentic priority for the Old Apostle of Cambridge. In turn, Simeon had identified another genuine alternative course for this contributions to the British missionary movement (Bennett 1992:375,376).

Simeon's missionary agenda included arousing the Church of England to its missionary obligations, the participation in mission efforts by voluntary organizations to stir up others for missions, and the special interest in getting trained Churchmen into India to help advance the state of Christianity in India.

---

[59]Bennett (1992:370) carefully points out that this is a different starting point for Simeon. Simeon's other ministry purposes flowed naturally out of his mentoring efforts with students. This one had a theological base which spurred it on.

[60]Bennett (1992:375) points out correspondence that indicates Simeon's fund raising endeavors. Over a period of 5 years on an annual basis he wrote a personal letter to one donor giving an up-to-date evaluation of *The Jewish Mission* along with its developmental plans and needs. This was also a thank you note for her contributions. Evidently she was a large donor.

Chapter 2. Charles Simeon (1759-1836)

Simeon's Involvement in Patronage--Thornton Trusteeships/ the Simeon Trust, Thinking Toward the Future of The Evangelical Movement

Earlier I had mentioned that in his attempts to bring renewal in the Anglican Church, Simeon attacked two major problems. The weak Anglican Church was plagued with ministerial non-residence and incompetent clergy. His mentoring activity dealt primarily with the incompetent clergy. There were several reasons for the non-residency problem. Frequently, ministers would have multi parish ministries due to the low pay involved in these small rural parishes. Sometimes a minister would accept a benefice but delegate the day-to-day responsibility to a curate or even lay minister. In any case, there existed many parishes not well cared for. Finances were a major reason. In addition, the more lucrative benefices were usually withheld from evangelicals as the Bishops or patrons controlling these assignments were wither non-evangelicals or anti-evangelicals or both.

Simeon was interested in the plight of the evangelical Churchman. Many of his earlier mentorees had gone on to small non-strategic parishes and were buried there for a lifetime. Simeon set about to do something about all three of these related issues: non-residency, low finances, and non-strategic appointments for evangelicals.

God brought across Simeon's path a ministry insight, which took advantage of an English cultural pattern in the established church. I have identified this insight as Critical Incident 12, *The Thornton Trusteeship*. The cultural custom was rooted in feudal days. A godfearing feudal lord would put up a church for his village and assign someone to minister there. The villagers were glad the landlord, usually a Squire, would take the responsibility to build their church, appoint a parson to take care of their spiritual needs and provide the financial support for the minister. Usually this responsibility was passed down to the son. Gradually it became a valued privilege to make these appointments. Frequently, there were benefices attached, that is, an endowed income attached to the privilege. In time the right of appointment came to be regarded like a piece of property. It was inherited by a son from his father. They could also be given away or sold to someone who wanted the privilege. The whole system is referred to as patronage, that is, the right to appoint a minister to a position, usually endowed.[61]

Simeon had seen Charles Grant use wealth to purchase the right of appointment of Kiernander's Old Mission Church for 1000 pounds. This allowed Grant to have an evangelical pulpit for Calcutta. Simeon helped supply chaplains for this church. But he himself got involved in this practice and saw its potential use in a round about way. John Thornton was an influential evangelical businessman and one of Simeon's early mentors. He was one of the first in England to purchase advowsons for evangelical purposes. At Thornton's death in 1792 a trust was set up to administer the advowsons he had purchased over the years. His son Henry was the prime trustee. John Venn was also a trustee. Charles Simeon was an alternate trustee. In 1813 at John Venn's untimely death he became an active trustee. In 1814 Henry Venn passed on. So Simeon found himself in effective control of 12 "livings." (Bennett 1992:154,155)

From this time on, Simeon set about to purchase these "livings." He was particularly interested in placing evangelical clergy in every growing population center or other center of influence. He came to the conviction that the securing of a fruitful ministry in a strategic location would justify any outlay of money. He paid 3000 pounds for one important church in a growing population center. When ever an important pulpit would

---

[61]Advowson is the technical name given to the right of appointment. "Living" is another name referring to the income derived from an advowson or benefice.

Chapter 2. Charles Simeon (1759-1836)

come available for sale he would take a risk, make a bid and then find a way to raise funds. He inherited a legacy from his brother. He used the better part of those funds for this purpose. Hopkins (1977:218) mentioned that in response to appeals Simeon raised contributions of 10,000 pounds, 9,000 pounds, 8,000 pounds, 4,000 pounds and the like.

In 1833 Simeon formally created a Patronage Trust and wrote up the guidelines for administering it. He had managed over the years since 1814 to merge Thornton's holdings and his own. In 1835 The Municipal Corporation Act forced burroughs to divest themselves of church patronages. This made many come on the market. Simeon and his backers picked up a number of important livings at this time (including one which cost 6330 pounds). (Hopkins 1977:219). By the time of his death, Simeon with his Patronage Trust controlled over 40 livings (Bennett 1992:156). Eventually this trust grew to control over 140 "livings." Now while this may be a drop in the bucket in terms of total number of parishes and pulpits involved, remember Simeon also chose strategic ones that were influential. Strong evangelical presence in them would also affect many other parishes around them.

Thus, Simeon taking advantage of an English custom, which seems strange to American church thinkers, was able to place evangelical ministers in important posts and to see that they were provided for with adequate financial support.

His mentoring activity did much to solve the problem of getting competent evangelical pastors trained for ministry. His creative risk taking in purchasing advowsons placed them in strategic posts. Simeon went a long way toward bringing evangelical renewal in the Anglican Church.

Simeon's Magnum Opus--Horae Homileticae,

In 1792 Simeon discovered Claude's work on preaching. It revolutionized his thinking about training young ministers to preach effectively. He published his own version of that work and added 100 sermons outlines/ illustrations, **Skeletons**, in 1792. He continued to study the Bible, prepare sermons and sermon outlines all his life. In 1801 he republished it, calling it **Helps to Composition**. Now he included 500 sermon outlines. In 1819 he published another expanded edition of 17 volumes, called **Horae Homileticae**. Thirteen years later he published his final edition, now expanded to 21 volumes and containing 2536 sermon outlines covering the whole Bible from Genesis to Revelation. This originally sold well bringing in 5000 pounds total. Simeon donated these royalties to three societies. Simeon presented a copy of this work to the King. He also personally presented each of the archbishops a copy. He sent copies to all of the chief libraries in Europe and America and to each of the Cambridge college libraries.

This work did not stay in print after Simeon's death. But it was widely distributed during the last years of his life. And it typifies his interest in the Scriptures and effective pulpit ministry. So in producing this magnificent work Simeon modeled something of the importance of pulpit ministry.

Simeon's Triumphant finish.

Simeon ministered for 54 years in his dual role. For the first 30 years he faced a great deal of opposition, various kinds of discouragement, and very little acceptance in the wider church. During that time he faithfully turned out evangelical pastors and seeded them all over England. He worked with other evangelicals, influential men in the business and political world as well as within the Anglican Church. Together they saw evangelicalism

Chapter 2. Charles Simeon (1759-1836)

spread until it was no longer an unacceptable position. In the last twenty-five years of his ministry he received cooperation, fellowship and profound respect far and wide. So that by the time of his death he was as Barclay and Macaulay indicated, one of the most influential men in the whole of the Church of England.

In this analysis, I have concentrated on Simeon's change dynamics, his sphere of influence and his unique methodology of mentoring prospective ministers. I have not said much of Simeon the man. Earlier I quoted Venn as being farsighted and looking beyond the young brash, arrogant vicar, Charles Simeon, and seeing the ripened peach. At the end of his life the peach indeed had been through much rain and sun and ripened magnificently. He was a godly person. He still had some of his eccentric ways but he was recognized for his godliness. He was gentle and expressed a heart of love toward others.

In 1829 he celebrated his fiftieth year as a Christian. It was a special time; 2 days set aside to be with a special few and to meditate together on the goodness of the Lord. Three years later he again had a celebration--this time of his fifty years in ministry. Again a time in which this old saint was honored by his parishioners. But the crowning celebration was in June of 1836 when he toured as many churches as possible which had his mentorees of days gone by in their pulpits. It was an eight week tour and covered hundreds of miles by coach. It was a demanding, tiring tour but one filled with satisfaction as he looked back to see achievement of his aim to bring evangelical renewal to the Anglican Church.

He was clear thinking till the very end. Hopkins (1977:212,213) describes his funeral as the most remarkable that Cambridge has ever seen. The town closed down. School at Cambridge was canceled. The chapel was filled, more than eight hundred present inside and another 800 in the college hall. The bells tolled. The old Apostle was honored. He finished well.

Critical Incidents Identified, and/or Explained

Critical incidents are shaping activities which can affect **values** relating to all three types of formations--spiritual (leadership character), ministerial (leadership skills) and strategic (total direction in life and ministry). They also give **strategic guidance** toward the focal issues and hence accomplishing of life's objectives.

There is a sense in which many, many incidents in a leader's life affect **values**. But from that large identifiable number a few should be highlighted and recognized as very significant. Usually a lesser number affect **strategic guidance**.

Here is a list of these that I have so identified from the materials that were available to me. Table 2-2 indicates these. I number them for convenience of referencing later when I comment on them.

Chapter 2. Charles Simeon (1759-1836)

Table 2-2 Listing Of Some Critical Incidents In Simeon's Life

Incident(s) Name	Age	Formational Type Dealing With Basic Value/Thrust
1. New Creature Passion Week Conversion Experience (see page 28)	19	Spiritual--Simeon experiences conversion. This is foundational for his ministry. It also gives in embryonic form strategic guidance toward a life purpose--to bring renewal to the Anglican Church.
2. St. Edwards; Atkinson's Help (see page 35)	22	Ministerial, Strategic--Simeon learns the value of a caring personal ministry. He gets his first experience of pulpit work. This introduction to ministry also affirms strategic guidance toward a role--that of the pastorate in the Anglican Church.
3. Against the Odds Appointment to Holy Trinity (see page 34-37)	22	Strategic--This focal factor is the prime factor. The pastoral role in the Anglican Church in this strategic center of influence is a necessary pre-requisite for the renewal ministry involving mentoring and for the missionary recruiting that is to come.
4. Henry Venn--Early Contemporary Mentor (see page 29-30, 37,38)	23	Spiritual, Ministerial, Strategic--This critical incident involves both focal values and focal factors. Simeon character is shaped by this wise mentor. His ministry perspective is broadened. He is connected into the first generation of evangelicals. And he moves toward bringing about evangelical renewal within the Anglican Church.
5. Singleness--a Sacrifice to Focus on Ministry (see page 33 fn 14)	23-28	Strategic--This focal factor narrows Simeon's personal responsibility and allows him to give himself without reservation to the students he will mentor toward pastoral roles or missions.
6. 1787 Plan/ Charles Brown Links Simeon to India (see page 40-42)	28	Strategic--This focal factor kindles a missionary heart in Simeon. He will from this time on be vitally interested in moving the Anglican Church toward a responsible interest in missions and will personally take an interest in the mission cause in India.
7. Partnership for India Charles Grant/ Powerful Business Sponsor (see page 42-44)	33	Strategic--This focal factor connects Simeon to power resources and windows of opportunity that will help him fulfill his desires for missions.
8. Jean Claude Essays Training of Preachers (see page 44-45)	33	Ministerial, Strategic--Simeon is affirmed in many of his pulpit communication principles he has learned through trial and error. A major value is imparted. Preaching can be taught. He is inspired to teach others via a unique methodology of Bible centered preaching.

Chapter 2. Charles Simeon (1759-1836)   page 63

Table 2-2 Listing Of Some Critical Incidents In Simeon's Life continued

Incident(s) Name	Age	Formational Type Dealing With Basic Value/Thrust
9. Disenchantment/ The Chaplaincy Alternative (see page 53-54)	41-46	Strategic--This focal factor involved recognizing a closed door. It paved the way for him to openly embrace an alternative means of fulfilling his mission vision--the chaplaincy post in India.
10. Mentor Sponsoring To India (see page 54-56)	46-57	Strategic--This focal factor enabled Simeon to fulfill a major portion of his destiny purpose of promotion of mission causes through his placement of 21 influential mentorees in the East India Company chaplain posts.
11. Conversation Parties (see page 50-51)	53	Ministerial, Strategic--This focal factor describes a special ministry insight--a means for recruitment and training of mentorees.
12. Thornton Trusteeships/ Systematic Patronage/ Simeon's Trust (see page 59-61)	54	Strategic--This focal factor describes one of Simeon's most important means for insuring that well trained evangelical pastors would be placed in important and strategic ministries. He was named as alternative trustee for Thornton's Trust in 1792. In 1814 he was the only surviving trustee. This catapulted him into patronage and his means for insuring renewal in the coming generation.

Values And Critical Values

Usually I will use this space to identify the shaping of a leader in terms of spiritual formation (leadership character), ministerial formation (leadership skills) and strategic formation (strategic direction). I identify a fairly large number of values associated with these kinds of formation. But with Simeon I have done something different. He was such a superb change agent that I want to capitalize on that. I have identified some selected values from Charles Simeon which I think have relevance for today, especially for those who desire to introduce renewal or change in large somewhat decadent systems.[62] In parenthesis I identify the related topic or incident(s) from Simeon's life most closely allied to the change value. All of these were critical in my opinion.

1. **Personal Conversion Experience**
   Renewal must begin with genuine individual conversions which reflect a personal relationship with God. If you have personally experienced something and it has radically altered you, you can recommend it to others with conviction and force.

2. **Mentoring Methodology**
   A leader ought to approach changing the system as a whole by personally changing as many individuals as possible over a continued long period of time.

---

[62]I realize I am highly subjective here and am probably reading back into Simeon's life change dynamics ideas seen elsewhere. Yet I think each of these ideas can be demonstrated as being vital to Simeon even if he might not have expressed them explicitly as I have here.

Chapter 2. Charles Simeon (1759-1836)

3. **Early Mentoring By Venn et al; formation of Clerical Societies**
   Groups of others of like-mind from within the system must be organized in order to encourage, to give perspective, to moderate, and to combine power resources to bring about renewal.

4. **Singleness--Celibate Life Style**
   Sacrifices are necessary and can be made if the end result is embraced with passion.

5. **30 years of Opposition by non-Evangelicals**
   Attacks on personal character, ministry reputation, and ideation must be expected and can be weathered if your loyalty to the system is manifested and your role within the system is stable.

6. **Clerical Societies; Clapham Saints; Partnership with Grant**
   Coalitions and partnerships with people of resources both within and without the system must be sought in order to bring to bear influence from numerous directions on the system.

7. **Sunday evening lectures; Voluntary societies; Chaplancy Efforts**
   When you are introducing innovative ideas and methodology and find yourself blocked by obstacles the system raises you must find alternative methods for demonstrating the validity of the ideas while attempting to give appearances of staying within the systems accepted methods. Remember at the fringes the system's rules and regulations are not as clear and can be stretched outward to bring in change.

8. **Patronage**
   You must find acceptable practices already available in the system and exploit them to introduce your own changes.

9. **54 Years of Ministry Eventually Brought Recognizable Results**
   A good change agent must expect opposition and persevere within the system over a long period of time always keeping the end result in mind. Remember change takes longer than you expect even when you expect it to take longer than you expect.

10. **Simeon's Example over his lifetime; his triumphant finish**
    A Spirit-led change agent should expect to be triumphant if he/she is faithful over a lifetime. The victory may or may not occur in your lifetime nevertheless that is the attitude that should permeate throughout your lifetime.

Overall Ministry Insights

Simeon's life highlights some important leadership insights. I will discuss two major areas: sphere of influence, and two major leadership lessons.

Ministry Insights into Sphere of Influence from Simeon's Life

I want to comment on some important insights about a leader's influence that are illustrated in Simeon's life. Before doing that I need to introduce some concepts that will allow us to specify more clearly the lessons in Simeon's life.

Chapter 2. Charles Simeon (1759-1836)　　　　　　　　　　　　　　　　page 65

Each leader we have studied has God-given giftedness and a capacity to lead.[63] *Sphere of Influence* (Clinton 1989:227) refers to the totality of people a leader influences. All leaders influence followers. They can influence *directly*, that is, face-to-face ministry, *indirectly*, via shaping of key individuals or via materials used by others or *organizationally* via executive leadership or committees or the like. Three measures help assess these kinds of influence: 1. extensiveness--which refers to quantity; 2. comprehensiveness--which refers to the scope (breadth) of things being influenced; 3. intensiveness, which speaks of the depth to which influence extends to each item within the comprehensive influence. Extensiveness is the easiest to measure and hence is most often used or implied when talking about a leader's sphere of influence.

Influence-mix (Clinton 1989:378) refers to the attempt to measure sphere of influence including the three kinds and three measures. It has to do with how and who leaders influence. Each leader has a profile corresponding to which of these dominates or how they relate. Simeon's profile provides a most provocative approach to influence. He counters the prevailing tendency to rise in hierarchical position in order to influence. He does not use positional power to influence. His profile showed a relatively large direct influence--via his public rhetorician ministry, an impressively large indirect influence via individual mentoring and networking power with key evangelicals, and a somewhat unusual organizational sphere of influence. Let me explain each of these briefly.

Simeon's pulpit ministry in Holy Trinity Church allowed a **direct influence**, that is, repeated face-to-face, with 600-800 on a weekly basis. His occasional University sermon lecture series reached another several hundred. These were often also put in print and circulated. He did itinerant preaching. All of these were an important part of his influence but while fairly extensive (quantity) they were limited as most public rhetoricians to a relatively small comprehensiveness and even smaller intensiveness.

But Simeon's **indirect sphere of influence** merits our careful attention. His mentoring affected hundreds, maybe even more than a 1000 individual leaders in their earliest years--when they are most pliable to key ideas. The comprehension was broad-- dealing with a full range of character issues and with a broad based ministry philosophy for an effective evangelical ministry which embraced a solid churchmanship. And the intensity was deep. Many of these emerging leaders imbibed deeply of Simeon values which they reflected all their lives.

Simeon's **organizational influence** also contradicts standard approaches. Rather than serving as an organizational leader or on executive committees as so many do with good effects he preferred to work through informal leadership blocs. Power coalitions such as the Clapham saints or associations such as his clerical societies or individual partnership with those in organizational influential positions such as Grant gave Simeon access to power albeit by informal and quasi-organizations. Frequently, he could bring to bear on the Anglican Church influence from without.[64] Evangelical interests in parliament grew over the years and became a major factor in opening up India to

---

[63] Ephesians 2:10 speaks of the uniqueness. Romans 12:3ff speaks of the capacity of giftedness. Leadership emergence theory has affirmed the concept of leader's being shaped by God to accomplish His purposes through them at the level of their capacity. The shaping activity of God moves toward both of these goals. Bigger influence capacity is not the goal. Nor is small influence capacity. Appropriate influence capacity is. Some leaders fail to respond to God and operate below their capacity. Others, perhaps with ambition, seek to influence beyond their capacity. Ministry essentially flows out of being. Giftedness and influence capacity are part of this beingness as are personality and one's destiny.
[64] He seemed intuitively to know Mintzberg's power structure theory particularly the outside forces for influence. See his **Power In And Around Organizations**.

missionary effort both from the established church and from dissenter groups. Simeon exemplifies the importance of networking power as an alternative to formal organizational power.

Power-mix (Clinton 1989: 378) has to do with the major means a leader uses to influence followers. Simeon exemplified a dual power base--personal power and competency. His authority to influence was dominantly spiritual authority which uses modeling, persuasion, and competency to influence. *Spiritual authority* (Clinton 1989:192-197) is the right to influence conferred upon a leader by followers because of their perception of the spirituality of that leader. It flows from one or the other of a combination of a leader 1. who models godliness, 2. who knows God (and His purposes and ways) via deep experiences, and 3. who demonstrates gifted power. Simeon influenced, not by position, but because his followers were attracted to his life and dedication to serving God. Over the years his growing reservoir of wisdom was increasingly heeded.

Simeon Exemplifies Two Major Leadership Lessons

Simeon magnificently illustrates two of seven major leadership lessons seen in leadership emergence theory.[65]

EFFECTIVE LEADERS VIEW LEADERSHIP SELECTION AND DEVELOPMENT AS A PRIORITY FUNCTION IN THEIR MINISTRY.

EFFECTIVE LEADERS SEE RELATIONAL EMPOWERMENT AS BOTH A MEANS AND A GOAL OF MINISTRY.

I have already commented on the concentric circles Simeon set up as a means of recruiting via a natural selection process. He responded to those more responsive leaders he could influence. His mentoring methodology was the priority function of his ministry. That he empowered these mentorees relationally can be seen especially in the Pious Chaplains. But what is seen there could be multiplied extensively had we a list of all the pastors he influenced.

Contributions

This chapter contributes to the general field of leadership development in the following ways:

1. It portrays how God can use a person to stay within a large organization of which he/she is a minority in terms of ideas, doctrinal stand, or methodologies and bring change in that organization.
2. It pictures alternative means of exerting influence to bring about leadership results.
3. It depicts a leader who had all four focal issues come into play in his lifetime. **Life purpose** was the driving force. An established **major role** was the means. A **unique mentoring methodology** provided the spark that continued to ignite this leader. **Ultimate contributions** were both means and ends.

---

[65]The other five include, Effective Leaders: 1. maintain a learning posture throughout life; 2. value spiritual authority as a primary power base; 3. have a dynamic ministry philosophy; 4. evince a growing awareness of their sense of destiny; 5. view present ministry in terms of a life time perspective.

Chapter 2. Charles Simeon (1759-1836)

What were Simeon's contributions? We are interested in both specific/unique contributions and his ultimate contribution set. His ultimate contribution set is one of the simplest of all the leaders in this book. This is partly so because of the extremely narrow focused life. His profile in diagram form is given below.[66]

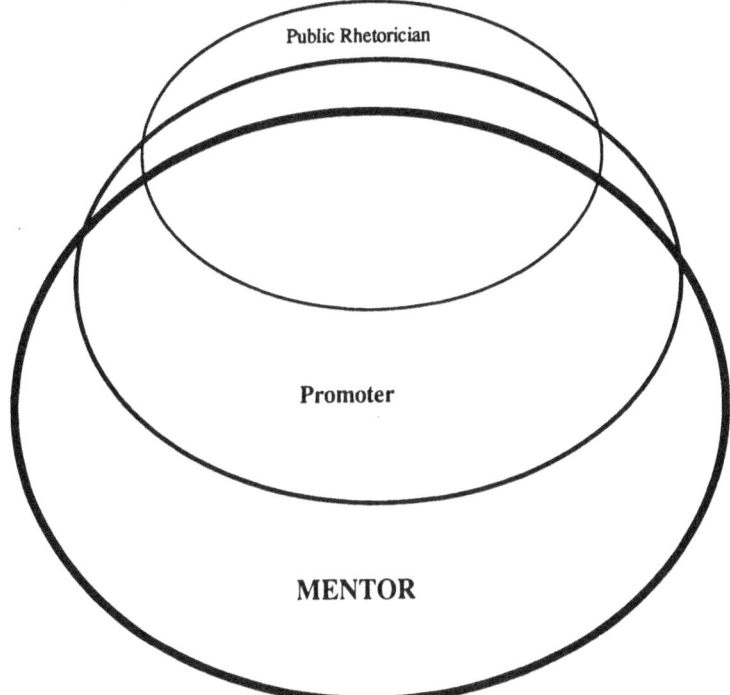

From an ultimate contribution perspective, the most important results of Simeon's life were the pastors and missionaries he mentored who influenced the course of the evangelical movement in Britain in the 19th century. He also left a much more renewed Anglican Church in terms of evangelical tenets and fervor than was the case when he began his renewal work. His public rhetorician contribution involved both the promotion of his renewal and missionary causes, the building up of Saints in his parish and his perfecting of homiletical skills which he passed on in his mentoring.

His specific and unique contributions to the cause of Christ and the on-going of the Christian movement include at least the following:

1. He pioneered modern homiletics.
2. He led many nominal emerging leaders into an evangelical experience which permeated their ministry within the Church of England.
3. He helped found the Church Missionary Society--though he did not help develop it.

---

[66]The diagram which describes his ultimate contributions in pictorial form is called a Venn Diagram. See Appendix F for an explanation of how to read Venn diagrams.

Chapter 2. Charles Simeon (1759-1836)

4. He promoted various missionary causes via voluntary organizations.
5. He modeled a leader who finished his course with satisfaction.
6. He laid the foundations for evangelical impact in the 19th century.
7. He affected the course of Christianity in India and Australia.
8. He brought about major change in the Anglican Church, a large organization.
9. He provided a means (patronage) for on-going influence of evangelicals in the Anglican Church by providing job opportunities and financing for them.

Overall Lessons from the Life

In addition, to the ten change values I have previously identified, I want to emphasize three important lessons concerning change dynamics.

Probably the most encouraging lesson from Simeon's life involves change dynamics. Change can be implemented in a large organization by individual effort. But that individual effort must be linked with others to effectively introduce change. Our present studies in change dynamics have led us to recognize that the introduction of planned change into a system requires an interlocking quartet of change roles.

Charles Simeon was primarily a **catalyst** change agent--that is, one who opts for changes in the system and stirs up the scene to call attention to the changes. He was secondarily a **resource linker**, one who can link resources into the change scene to help promote those changes. He was able to network with **process helpers**, those who are wise to the total change process and can guide it, moderate it, and bring closure to aspects of it along the way. Finally, he networked with **solution givers**, those who have ideas for solving the problems and planning for the end results.

A second lesson is in the form of a warning. Change takes a toll on a change agent. He/she must be prepared to endure criticism and persevere through, spurred on by the end results as a driving vision.

A third important lesson encourages and warns. Change can be introduced. But it will take longer than you expect it to take even when you expect it to take longer.

Implications for a Focused Life

What have we learned from this life that helps us understand a focused life? From a comparative study we have categorized 12 screening issues which help us think about focus in a life.[67] I will first use the 12 screens that help us to probe how focal factors happen. I weigh them relatively speaking in terms of their effect of Simeon's focused life. Then I will summarize lessons about his focused life.

---

[67] These include: 1. giftedness development; 2. destiny processing; 3. Key Ministry insights; 4. Major values uniquely fit to the leader; 5. Personality factors; 6. Social Base processing; 7. Ultimate contribution set; 8. ministry philosophy concepts; 9. Future Perfect Time paradigm; 10. Boundary Processing; 11. Paradigm Shifts; 12. Windows of Opportunity. Of these, 11 affected his focused life, two only tangentially (giftedness development and destiny processing). Boundary processing basically did not affect at all (his entrance into ministry was a rapid boundary which was opportunity driven).

Chapter 2. Charles Simeon (1759-1836)   page 69

1. Giftedness Development

The following diagram[68] represents Simeon's giftedness set. His dual role basically enhanced this giftedness set from the beginning. The set itself was not that significant in contributing to focus as it would have been if Simeon had been in a role thwarting this set. Also giftedness was not known in the late 18th and 19th centuries as it is today.

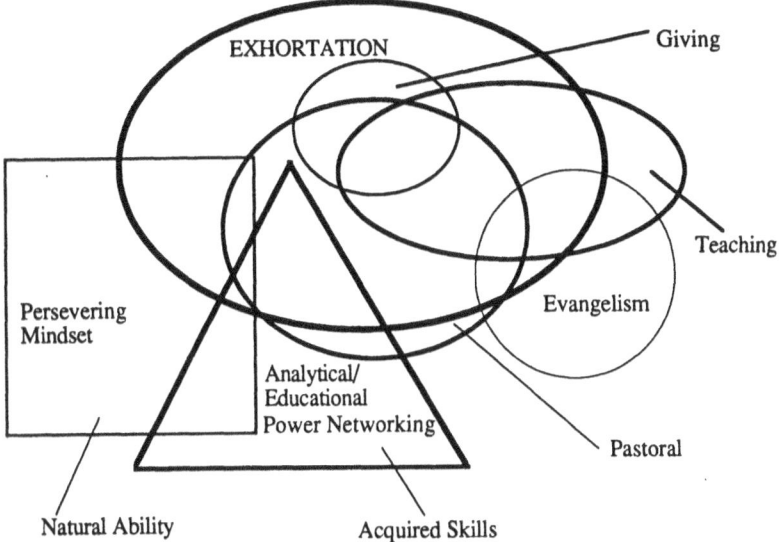

2. Destiny Processing

Simeon coming from a very non-charismatic bias would probably not even recognize a sense of destiny perspective. Yet his two life purposes were in fact destiny goals. The pattern is there even if not known by Simeon. There was destiny preparation flowing from his conversion and first three years of isolation growth. There was destiny revelation as the first generation evangelical Anglicans mentored him concerning renewal. And there was tremendous destiny fulfillment as seen on Simeon's final tour of pulpits with *Simeonites* and his triumphant finish with its honor and recognition.

3. Identification of Key Ministry Insights

Mentoring was the key ministry insight that emerges from Simeon's life. An additional twist on it was the extent in which he used group processes in mentoring. His mentoring became a major focal issue--a unique methodology--which he perfected and used powerfully to move toward his life purposes.

4. Identification Of Major Values That Uniquely Fit One's Ministry

See my previous discussion on change values important to Simeon.

---

[68]The diagram which describes his giftedness set (natural abilities, acquired skills and spiritual gifts) in pictorial form is called a Venn Diagram. See Appendix F for an explanation of how to read Venn diagrams.

Chapter 2. Charles Simeon (1759-1836)

5. <u>Integration Of Personality Factors So As To Identify A Focused Or Ideal Role That Moves Toward Convergence</u>

Simeon's own family environment, his sibling position, his physical appearance and his personality probably all contributed to make him a person who could be happy without the social base of marriage and family. This shaping of his focus overlaps with social base.

6. <u>Social Base Processing</u>

Simeon, early on, opted for a single life style. This brought tremendous focus in terms of control of time, schedule, priorities, etc. He was able to give himself whole heartedly to his mentoring efforts. Other social base issues were primarily taken care of him by his living situation on campus.

7. <u>Ultimate Contribution Set</u>

I have previously commented on his ultimate contribution set. Simeon was extremely focused. Mentoring dominated his attempts to promote his causes. His public oratory ministry secondarily formed a part of the set.

8. <u>Ministry Philosophy Concepts</u>

Simeon was a churchman. He was convinced of the importance of the established church to order in society. His ministry philosophy developed around key values which promoted the established church and evangelical interests. The latter would take precedence but only within well ordered parameters. His change values formed an important part of his ministry philosophy. Simeon was a well disciplined person who followed his framework of convictions both as to the church, missions, and evangelical interests. He was able in the latter years to articulate well many of his values and to deliberately pass them on to mentorees. This was an important factor in bringing focus to his life.

9. <u>Future Perfect Time Paradigm</u>

Simeon visualized a Church of England replete with evangelicals and vital to the cause of Christ and missions. While he would not have explicitly known the concept of future perfect thinking, his clear-cut vision revolving around his two fold life purposes essentially functioned life a future perfect paradigm.[69]

10. <u>Boundary Processing Which Helped Focus</u>

This focusing issue played little or no part in bringing focus to Simeon.

11. <u>Paradigm Shifts Which Helped Focus</u>

Simeon's conversion was a radical experience which contained in seed form his vision for renewal in the Anglican Church. His early mentoring by Venn et al fed this paradigmatic change in Simeon until his role in bringing about renewal fully materialized.

---

[69]See Clinton (1992) **Bridging Strategies** for the notion of a future perfect paradigm, that is, an apparent future situation not yet in reality but in place to the eye of faith. The faith reality controls decisions which solve the basic problems in reaching the vision.

12. Windows of Opportunity

When patronages became available Simeon took advantage of them.

SUMMARY ON FOCUSED LIFE INSIGHTS FROM SIMEON'S LIFE

Let me summarize what we have learned about a focused life from Charles Simeon.

A <u>focused life</u> is
- a life dedicated to exclusively carrying out God's unique purposes through it,[70]
- by identifying the focal issues, that is, the **major role, life purpose, unique methodology,** or **ultimate contribution**,[71] which allows
- an **increasing prioritization** of life's activities around the focal issues, and
- results in a satisfying life of being and doing.

All four of the focal issues played an important part in Simeon's life. The **major role**, a dual role provided an accepted status and a locale from which to operate. That role was used to carry out a twofold **life purpose**, bringing about evangelical renewal in the established church and awakening a mission interest--especially for India. His mentoring was a powerful unique **methodology**. Three of the **ultimate contribution** set fit him.

Specifically we see a natural order that worked well for Simeon. He found his combination dual role first. He then consolidated that dual role so that it was stable and secure. He then began to expand out from that two-fold role toward effective attempts to reach his two-fold life purpose. His unique method flowed naturally from his own life and grew with importance as his role stabilized.

Simeon was able to pull off a dual role right from the beginning--a role which fit his giftedness. Most effective leaders struggle to adapt a role to fit giftedness.

Simeon shows how life purposes move over time from a vague affective desire to a clarified cognitive aim that has strong volitional intent behind it.

Focus requires perseverance. When facing opposition, ridicule, persecution, and frustrations, one can persevere if that perseverance is tied to a strong enough life purpose.

A single life can be satisfying if the life is focused around divine purposes.

Remember the last concept of a focused life, **it results in a satisfying life of being and doing**. Simeon along with Brengle, more than any other of the eight lives studied, exemplifies this concept of **a satisfied life**. When in the last year of his life, he looked back on his accomplishments, he was satisfied.

---

[70] I am thinking primarily of full time Christian workers who have made a second commitment beyond their salvation experience dedicating their lives to accomplish God-directed purposes through them. I am not saying that non full time Christian workers can't have focused lives. I am sure they can. Grant, Thornton, and Wilberforce certainly did. It is simply that this research deals with full time workers and is primarily for them. This definition may or may not hold for non full time Christian workers. I have not yet studied them in depth.

[71] These four--*major role, life purpose, unique methodology,* or *ultimate contribution*--are called the *focal issues*. Usually one or more of them dominates a focused life. A number of other factors (like giftedness, ministry insights, sense of destiny) contribute to the divine guidance which helps these leaders to prioritize life's activities around the focal issues. Both the identification of focal issues and the processes that prioritized them are given in the studies of the eight chosen for this book.

Chapter 2. Charles Simeon (1759-1836)

Closure--Lets Really Remember Charles Simeon

Well, I have attempted to apply the Hebrews 13:7,8 leadership mandate.

Remember your former leaders. Think back on how they lived and ministered. Imitate those **excellent qualities** you see in their lives. For Jesus Christ is the same today, as He was in the past and as He will be in the future. What He did for them He will do for you to inspire and enable your leadership.
Hebrews 13:7,8 (Personal Interpretive Paraphrase)

We have remembered Simeon! We have seen some excellent qualities. Let's close with **really remembering** his two-fold life purpose, that so satisfied him. How did he do in terms of his two life purposes? Bennett, in the conclusion of his dissertation analyzing Simeon's missionary influence, gives fitting tribute to Charles Simeon's life time of his mission effort--one of the driving life purposes. Note my boldfaced emphasis.

> The first decades of the evangelical missionary movement were marked by significant challenges. Chief among these wee the need for missionary personnel and the necessity of a solution to the church mission tensions faced by the movement. Both of these difficulties were created in one way or another by the opposition of the Established Church to the initiatives taken by the progenitors of the CMS and the other evangelical voluntary societies. As documented in this study, Charles Simeon's world-view--his evangelicalism, his concern for order in society, and his commitment to mentor others--allowed him to embrace the voluntary missionary movement while also addressing the challenges to its progress.
> Simeon's contemporary legacy to the British missionary movement was two-fold. First, Simeon made disciples and thereby helped to people the evangelical Anglican missionary movement. His most fruitful efforts in this regard came in the form of a partnership with Charles Grant in sending evangelicals to Asia as India Company chaplains. Second, Simeon exemplified limited voluntaryism. He recognized when voluntary principles threatened to produce social disorder or excessive ecclesiastical irregularity. His voluntary efforts always stopped short of such a point. Moreover, Simeon urged evangelical Anglicans to assume a conciliatory posture toward the hierarchy of the Church. He believed that such an attitude would enable evangelical Churchmen to negotiate frameworks within which limited voluntary activity would be possible.
> **No evangelical Anglican in the early nineteenths century exercised a greater strategic influence on the course of the British missionary movement than did Charles Simeon of Cambridge. That act that he did so while maintaining his reputation as a committed Churchman is the measure of his uniqueness** (Bennett 1992:393,394).

And finally here is the last thing I want you to remember. How did Simeon do in terms of his life purpose of bringing renewal to the Anglican Church? We have remembered Charles Simeon a pastor who brought about evangelical renewal in his denomination, sadly lacking it at the beginning of his entrance into ministry. Can we hope for renewal in the midst of a nominal denomination? Consider again the quote with which I began. Then note my encouraging closing remarks.

> Now, what was his influence? It has been described like this. When he started preaching in 1782 there was really only a handful of evangelical ministers left in the Church of England. I don't know an exact figure, but it was probably a few dozen. When he finished, 54 years later on, one third of the pulpits in the Church of England were said to be occupied by evangelicals and the vast majority of those were men who had been influenced directly by Simeon in Cambridge. Many of them had been converted through him, or else they had come under his influence in some way. His influence on the evangelical cause in the Church of England was absolutely staggering. (Barclay 1986:9)

Chapter 2. Charles Simeon (1759-1836)

Barclay estimates that 1/3 of the pulpits of the Church of England were said to be occupied by evangelicals. What does that mean? Let me guess. In 1799 Bennett (1992:148,149) points out that there were about 11,194 parishes. About 33 per cent of these had resident ministers. The rest were served by an itinerant curate, lay reader or occasional minister. Thirty years later, at the closing years of Simeon's ministry there were 10,478 parishes. He estimates that only 40 per cent were served by a curate who was employed by a non-resident minister. That implies that perhaps 50-60 per cent were served by resident ministers. Perhaps on the high end of guessing this means that somewhere around five thousand ministers were in the Church of England. On the low end maybe two or three thousand. But even on the low end, if nearly 2/3 of them were evangelical--then fifteen hundred to two thousand of these were evangelicals if Barclay's statement holds. From twenty-four to over fifteen hundred. That is quite an accomplishment.

What brought it about? Basically: An ultimate purpose--renewal in the church; faithfulness toward that purpose over the years even in the midst of opposition; a methodology of mentoring emerging leaders of great potential; a willingness to take or find creative opportunities to bring it about such as his sponsoring of evangelicals into mission situations and pastors into prepared situations. May God grant that some today in main line denominations would become increasingly effective for the cause of Christ or some in campus ministries, who feel their best ministries are behind them, might imitate this effective change agent and mobilize many by a mentoring ministry.

Where To Go and What To Do For Further Study

You'll have trouble getting most of these listed works. For follow-up work, do three things. One, buy the **Bridging Strategies** Manual on change dynamics and familiarize yourself with its change concepts. Two, get Moule's biography and read it with a change focus. You will really appreciate Simeon if you do that. Three, buy **Evangelical Preaching**. Read Editor's Note on Simeon and John R. W. Stott's biographical chapter--do so with my biographical chapter in mind. Go through the sermons however you want to. Remember they were long winded in those days.

Barclay, O. R.
    1986   **Charles Simeon and The Evangelical Tradition--the Evangelical Library Annual Lecture of 1986**. London: Focus Christian Ministries Trust.

Bennett, John C.
    1992   **Charles Simeon and the Evangelical Anglican Missionary Movement--A Study of Voluntaryism and Church-Mission Tensions**. Doctoral thesis. Edinburgh: University of Edinburgh.

Hopkins, Hugh Evan
    1977   **Charles Simeon of Cambridge**. London: Hodder and Stoughton.

Houston, James M.
    1986   **Charles Simeon: Evangelical Preaching**. Portland, Ore: Multnomah Press.

Moule, H. C. G.
    1892   **Charles Simeon**. London: Methuen & Co.

Simeon, Charles
    1833   **Horae Homileticae**. Self-published by Simeon.

Chapter 2. Charles Simeon (1759-1836) page 74

I. FOUNDATIONS LONELY WELL-TO-DO UPPER CLASS WORLDVIEW				II. THE LONG SIEGE--RENEWAL EFFORTS OVER THE YEARS 54 YEARS IN A CONVERGENT LOCALE		
September 24, 1759	1768	1778	1782	1794	1816,17	1836
Age	9	19	23	33<-------------------- 54 years -------------------->		
A. Lonely Home Life (1759-1768) B. Shunted to a Top Boarding School (1768-1778) C. Elitist Education-- King's College, Cambridge Foundations for Strategic Change (1778-1782)				A. Rejection in The Ministry--12 Years of Rugged Conflict (1782-1794)	B. The Strategic Years-- Seeding the 3rd Generation of Evangelicals, Leadership Selection and Development Effective Use of Mentoring (1794-1816) 1. The Cambridge Years Mentoring Develops (1794-1805) 2. The India Years--Mentor Sponsoring (1805-1816)	C. The Strategic Years-- Looking to the Future: Getting 3rd Generation Evangelicals into Parishes; Eschatology And the Jewish Mission; (1817-1836)

ULTIMATE CONTRIBUTION SET:
MENTOR, PROMOTER
PUBLIC RHETORICIAN

MAJOR ROLES--TWIN ROLES
1ST MAJOR PURPOSE
2ND MAJOR PURPOSE
UNIQUE METHODOLOGY

Henry Venn   Charles Brown
John Berridge   Thomas Thomason
John Newton   Claudius Buchanan
John Thornton   Henry Martyn
          Charles Grant Daniel Corrie

C1 New Creature (1779)   C9 Disenchantment, CMS
  C2 St. Edwards, Atkinson   C10 Mentor Sponsoring--India (1796-1816)
    C3 Against the Odds (1782)   C11 Conversation Parties (1812)
      C4 Mentoring/ H. Venn (1782-1797)   C12 Thornton Trusteeship/
        C5 Singleness (1783,4,5?)   Insights for Patronage (1813-->
          C6 "1787 Plan" David Brown
            C7 Partnership/ Charles Grant (1792)
              C8 Jean Claude Essays (1792)

A. J. Gordon
(1836-1895)

A value based leader with balance

Chapter 3. A. J. Gordon (1836-1895) A Study in Ultimate Contribution, Values, And Sphere of Influence

Remember your former leaders. Think back on how they lived and ministered. Imitate those **excellent qualities** you see in their lives. For Jesus Christ is the same today, as He was in the past and as He will be in the future. What He did for them He will do for you to inspire and enable your leadership.
Hebrews 13:7,8 (Personal Interpretive Paraphrase)

Let's remember A. J. Gordon, a person of integrity, strong values, one who left many lasting achievements behind and whose influence was long lasting.

The following vignette illustrates how a paradigm shift can radically affect a value and elevate it to a central place in a life. It shows also how a leader can know something theoretically, but not see its power until he/she knows it experientially. This is an unusual occurrence since it is a revelatory experience by a non-charismatic leader. He almost apologizes for its happening. But he can't, because it was so life-changing.

Opening Illustration 1.
A Foundational Ministry Value
A Sense of Destiny Experience Forever Changing The Church Service
A Paradigm Shift--The Presence of Christ[1]
Age 36?[2] (Acts 18:9,10)

> Not that I attach any importance to dreams or ever have done so. Of the hundreds which have come in the night season I cannot remember one which has proved to have had any prophetic significance either for good or ill. As a rule moreover, dreams are incongruous rather than serious, a jumble of impossible conditions in which persons and things utterly remote and unconnected are brought together in a single scene. But the

---

[1] This incident is taken from Gordon's own spiritual autobiography published after his death. Gordon was not a charismatic. This was a revelatory experience that present day charismatics could identify with. This dream was so real for him as to change forever his awareness of Christ in his public ministry. This is an example of a critical incident having two major shaping experiences, one called *destiny revelation* (Clinton 1989:220) and the other called a *paradigm shift* (Clinton 1989:190; see also Clinton 1993 position paper--*The Paradigm Shift--God's Breakthrough Means of Opening New Vistas for Leaders*). In this case the breakthrough is a revelation from God concerning the public ministry service. From this point on Gordon will never again view public ministry the same. This night-time encounter taught experientially something Gordon knew cognitively. His learning it affect wise and experientially constitutes the paradigm shift, that is, a change in perspective which allows him to view something much different than he did previously. He will retain a value from this processing. *Jesus is always present in our public services and what we do must please Him.* This is also confirmation of a macro-lesson identified in every one of the six leadership eras in the Bible. *The essential ingredient of leadership is the powerful presence of God in the leader's life and ministry.* This experience validates that major lesson which occurs across all Biblical eras of leadership. See *Presence Macro-Lesson* in Clinton (1993), **Handbook I. Leaders, Leadership, and the Bible--An Overview.**

[2] This date is uncertain. Houghton (1970:94) guesses it to be after the Moody meetings, 1977, and before the Conference ministry at Northfield (1982ff). I place it sometime during the first years of his ministry at Clarendon Street since the revelation itself has to do with approval of Jesus of the church and its public ministry. At that time Gordon was grappling with the numerous changes all of which were opposed by different powerful groups in the church. The revelation to me deals with approval of Gordon's changes. The issue is, who should it please. The answer, the living Christ--not Gordon, not the opponents of change.

Chapter 3. A. J. Gordon--(1836-1895)

one which I now describe was unlike any other within my remembrance, in that it was so orderly in its movement, so consistent in its parts, and so fitly framed together as a whole. I recognize it only as a dream; and yet I confess that the impression of it was so vivid that in spite of myself memory brings it back to me again and again, as though it were an actual occurrence in my personal history.

And yet why should it be told or deliberately committed to print? "I will come to visions and revelations of the Lord," says the apostle. His was undeniably a real, divinely given, and supernatural vision. But from the ecstasy of it, wherein he was caught up into paradise and heard unspeakable words, he immediately lets himself down to the common level of discipleship. "Yet of myself I will not glory but in my infirmities." God help us to keep to this good confession evermore; and if perchance any unusual lesson is taught even "in visions of the night when deep sleep falleth on men" let us not set ourselves up as the Lord's favorites to whom he has granted especial court privileges in the kingdom of heaven. No, the dream is not repeated as though it were a credential of peculiar saintship, or as though by it God had favored me with a supernatural revelation; but because it contains a simple and obvious lesson, out of which the entire book which we are now writing has been evolved.

It was Saturday night, when wearied from the work of preparing Sunday's sermon, that I fell asleep and the dream came. I was in the pulpit before a full congregation, just ready to begin my sermon, when a stranger entered and passed slowly up the left aisle of the church looking first to the one side and then to the other as though silently asking with his eyes that some one would give him a seat. He had proceeded nearly half-way up the aisle when a gentleman stepped out and offered him a place in his pew, which was quietly accepted. Excepting the face and features of the stranger everything in the scene is distinctly remembered--the number of the pew, the Christian man who offered its hospitality, the exact seat which was occupied. Only the countenance of the visitor could never be recalled. That his face wore a peculiarly serious look, as of one who had known some great sorrow, is clearly impressed on my mind. His bearing too was exceeding humble, his dress poor and plain, and from the beginning to the end of the service he gave the most respectful attention to the preacher.

Immediately as I began my sermon my attention became riveted on this hearer. If I would avert my eyes from him for a moment they would instinctively return to him, so that he held my attention rather than I held his till the discourse was ended. To myself I said constantly, "Who can that stranger be?" and then I mentally resolved to find out by going to him and making his acquaintance as soon as the service should be over. But after the benediction had been given the departing congregation filed into the aisles and before I could reach him the visitor had left the house. The gentleman with whom he had sat remained behind however; and approaching him with great eagerness I asked: "Can you tell me who that stranger was who sat in your pew this morning?" In the most matter-of-course way he replied: "Why, do you not know that man? It was Jesus of Nazareth." With a sense of the keenest disappointment I said: "My dear sir, why did you let him go without introducing me to him? I was so desirous to speak with him." And with the same nonchalant air the gentleman replied: "Oh, do not be troubled. He has been here to-day, and no doubt he will come again."

And now came an indescribable rush of emotion. As when a strong current is suddenly checked, the stream rolls back upon itself and is choked in its own foam, so the intense curiosity which had been going out toward the mysterious hearer now returned upon the preacher; and the Lord himself "whose I am and whom I serve" had been listening to me to-day. What was I saying? Was I preaching on some popular theme in order to catch the ear of the public? Well, thank God it was of himself I was speaking. However imperfectly done, it was Christ and him crucified whom I was holding up this morning. But in what spirit did I preach? Was it "Christ crucified preached in a crucified style?" Or did the preacher magnify himself while exalting Christ? So anxious and painful did these questionings become that I was about to ask the brother with whom he had sat if the Lord has said anything to him concerning the sermon, but a sense of propriety and self-respect at once checked the suggestion. Then immediately other questions began with equal vehemence to crowd into the mind. "What did he think of our sanctuary, its gothic arches, its stained windows, its costly and powerful organ? How was he impressed with the music and the order of the worship?" It did not seem at that moment as though I could ever again care or have the smallest curiosity as to what men might say of preaching, worship, or church, if I could only know that he had not been displeased, that he would not withhold his feet from coming again because he had been grieved at what he might have seen or heard.

We speak of "a momentous occasion." This, though in sleep, was recognized as such by the dreamer--a lifetime, almost an eternity of interest crowded into a single solemn moment. One present for an hour who could tell me all I have so longed to know; who could point out to me the imperfections of my service; who could reveal to me my real self, to whom, perhaps, I am most a stranger; who could correct the errors in our worship to which long usage and accepted tradition may have rendered us insensible. While I had been preaching for a half-hour he had been here and listening who could have told me all this and infinitely more--and my eyes had been holden that I knew him not; and now he had gone. "Yet a little while I am with you and then I go unto him that sent me."

One thought, however, lingered in my mind with something of comfort and more of awe. "He has been here to-day, and no doubt he will come again"; and mentally repeating these words as one regretfully meditating on a vanished vision, "I awoke, and it was a dream." No, it was not a dream. It was a vision of the deepest reality, a miniature of an actual ministry, verifying the statement often repeated that sometimes we are most awake toward God when we are asleep toward the world (Gordon and Pierson 1896:3-8).

Opening Illustration 2.
A Foundational Missionary Value
Age 48 (Matthew 28:19,20; 2 Corinthians 8:14)

One might hope that Gordon's name might have destiny implications.[3] It did. Though **Adoniram Judson** Gordon did not go as a missionary overseas he was missionary minded. And that value was communicated to his church. The following vignette vibrates with this mission passion and manifests both a value and an ultimate contribution. It also is filled with other important values.

In the fall of '84 the Livingstone Inland Mission, founded by Mr. and Mrs. Grattan Guinness of London, was handed over to the American Baptist Missionary Union. This mission was organized immediately after Stanley emerged from the gloom of interior Africa in '77. By this time its stations were planted all up and down the Lower Congo. Twenty-five men and women were in the field, acclimatized and instructed in the vernacular. Translations of a large part of the Scriptures had been made into many Congolese dialects. Schools were in running operation. A steamer for itinerating purposes plied from station to station. All the preliminary expenses, all the discouragements of frequent sicknesses and early deaths, which accompany missionary pioneering, had been borne by the founders. The mission with all its equipment was bequeathed without conditions to the American Baptists, who had been contemplating opening work in Africa as to "those who believe in maintaining every word and ordinance of God."

---

[3]One major lesson we have identified with effective leaders states: EFFECTIVE LEADERS HAVE A GROWING AWARENESS OF THEIR SENSE OF DESTINY. A *sense of destiny* is an awareness that God's Hand is on the life for special purposes and will lead to and enable those purposes. We have identified a three fold pattern: destiny preparation, destiny revelation, and destiny fulfillment. Destiny preparation involves incidents that foreshadow and point to a destiny. Destiny revelation clarifies the path, the things to be accomplished, the methodology, etc. Destiny fulfillment sees them come to pass. Here in illustration 1 we have a revelation experience. In illustration 2, Gordon's name is part of destiny preparation shaping and the Congo Missions incident is part of destiny fulfillment (Clinton 1989:350). In fact, his son, E. Gordon, stresses his missionary passion and its outworking as the distinctive and most important contribution of Gordon's life, as we shall see (E. Gordon 1896:229).

Chapter 3. A. J. Gordon--(1836-1895)

The gift was accepted at the Detroit meeting of the denomination in '84. A reaction of timid conservatism, however, followed soon after. The value of the gift did not seem to be fully appreciated. The difficulties ahead loomed large against the black sky of boundless African heathenism. A cry for "concentration of interests" went abroad, and pressure was brought to bear from many quarters looking to the return of the missionaries and the abandonment of the field.

It was at this juncture that Dr. Gordon set himself to stem the tide. Earnestly did he appeal to his own church and to local conferences to resist the entrenchment. With his pen he addressed the denomination at large. A pointed tract, "The Ship Jesus," emphasizing the American debt to Africa was written, and became widely influential. Finally he took the field with Dr. Sims, who had worked many years in this mission, and went from city to city over all the country east of the Mississippi, pleading for the evangelization of the Congo Valley. With statesman-like prevision he showed the strategic opportunities of the mission. With burning words he denounced the proposed desertion of those who were holding the outposts. He aptly recalled the history of the great and flourishing Telugu Mission and the demands for its abandonment which had been made in its days of weakness. He denied the "lack of interest" which many were urging as a reason for withdrawal. "When the doctor would feel the pulse of a patient," said he, "he lays his finger on the wrist, where the walls of flesh are the thinnest. Who will say that we may not detect the missionary pulse and learn something of the moving of the Spirit by noting the expressions of Christ's poor saints who have sent up their little gifts--in some instances the widow's all--because the burden for Africa is on their hearts? I have rarely read anything more touching than some letter of this sort which have been received; and there have been hundreds of these small donations. How can the Union, having opened its treasury and invited contributions to the Congo Mission, and in response having received gifts from hundreds of donors, many of them, as I know, the fruit of the most conscientious self-sacrifice, fail now to fulfill the trust which the acceptance of such gifts involve?"

"No! let us, pastors and editors, laymen and workmen for Christ, shut our ears to this talk about 'giving up,' and raise the cry, 'Give.' Let us emphasize the cry by entering upon a course of self-denial which we have not known before, in economizing in our living and cutting off our luxuries, that we may have more to give. The American Baptists need the Congo almost as much as the Congo needs them. They need the tremendous appeal of its misery, its darkness, and its ruin to rouse them to their old-time heroism and self-denial. Ethiopia is at last stretching out her hands to God; she is also stretching out her hands to us. How can we answer at the bar of God if, with all our yet unused resources, we turn away from the call, and withdraw our hands from Ethiopia?"

The response to these appeals was such as to place the Congo Mission beyond even the suggestion of abandonment. Gordon was able to write from Asbury Park, where the question came up for final settlement at the annual meetings of the denomination, the following triumphant words:

"Praise the Lord! The Congo Mission has gone up with a shout--gone up, that is to say, with the strong and unanimous voice of all the people to possess the land. I wish you could have seen and heard the enthusiasm of the meeting yesterday. The Lord hath done great things for us, wherof we are glad."

"Dr. Gordon's best monument," wrote after his death one who knows more of this crisis than any other, "is the Congo Mission. He saved it!" (E. Gordon 1896:158-160)

This incident contains a number of important values--dealing with missions, lifestyle, and integrity. We will come back to these in the section detailing critical values.

The Time-Line

See the time-line at the end of this chapter for a one page overview of Gordon's life with critical incidents and other important summary information. Note that there are three major time phases of length 21, 12, and 26 years. Gordon's time-line follows the pre-

Chapter 3. A. J. Gordon--(1836-1895)

service training pattern of entrance into ministry.[4] That is, he basically was trained prior to actual ministry as a full-time Christian leader. His first pastorate, in essence, was his informal training and transition into leadership. His second pastorate was a major one lasting almost 26 years. The last 18 years of this pastorate were increasingly focused ministry years. Gordon illustrates the importance of tenure in a geographical locale. A long tenure at Clarendon Street Baptist Church was needed to build credibility, resources in the church, and to overcome the chilling non-receptivity of the people in the Boston area.

Highly Condensed Biographical Narrative

The following running capsule, organized around the three major time increments of Gordon's life indicates important activities, people, and events that shaped Gordon's life. Gordon's ministry is straightforward. He grew up in a Christian home, made an adult decision for Christ, and was called into the ministry. He did thorough educational preparation for that ministry. A six year pastorate confirmed his leadership. It gave him his actual foundational training in leadership. Following that, he began his life's work at Clarendon Street Baptist church where he matured into a focused leader with an effective ministry, a Flagship Church, and numerous ultimate contributions. His ministry was so broad based and effective that he left manifestations of all 12 prime type ultimate contributions in spite of the fact of an early death due to an illness.[5]

I. New England Heritage/ Destiny Foundations
(1836-1857); Age=Birth-21

**A. Family Influences/
New England Heritage/
Destiny Foundations**
(1836-1853); Age=Birth to 17

Adoniram Gordon was born of Puritan pioneer stock the 19th of April, 1836 to John Calvin Gordon and Sallie Robinson Gordon in New Hampton, New Hampshire. His very heritage foreshadows a sense of destiny for him.[6] He came from a long line of

---

[4]We have identified three major training patterns through which most leaders emerge. Four of the eight, Gordon, Maxwell, Jaffray and Simeon (somewhat) fit the *pre-service pattern* (Clinton 1989:354), that is, they receive formal training prior to ministry. Three fit the second pattern, the *in-service pattern* (Clinton 1989:356), that is, they learn on-the-job and finally after proving their abilities take on full time responsibilities. The third pattern is a *modified in-service pattern* (Clinton 1989:357) in which the leader gets ministry experience, then interrupts it for formal training, and then resumes it. Usually this pattern will include further interruptions for training down road. Brengle fits this pattern somewhat.

[5]I am speaking humanly with this statement. He died under sixty years. All seven of the other leaders in this book lived beyond that. McQuilkin died at age 66. The six others lived 77, 76, 81, 72, 73, 89 years. His was the shortest life of the eight. But one of the most productive.

[6]A *sense of destiny* is an unusual awareness of God's hand on a life. A long line of staunch Christians, especially praying ones, often pray for the future generations and influence their life choices God ward. Gordon's great-grandfather first chose the Baptist position. He was a rugged individual who stood on his convictions all his life. Gordon's grand-mother was a woman of prayer who majored in two books, **Pilgrim's Progress** and the **Bible**. She was a prayer warrior who obviously showered A.J. Gordon with prayer and affected his life (efficacious on-going prayers, Revelation 8:3). Gordon's father, John Calvin Gordon lived up to his namesake. A. J. Gordon's mother had a "genius for goodness." (E. Gordon 1906:15,16) Her unselfish modeling of the Christian life was always before young Gordon as he grew up. The name given Gordon, *Adoniram Judson*, belonging to that great American missionary hero whose stories were making it back to America and thrilling God's people, showed the missionary fervor which was

Chapter 3. A. J. Gordon--(1836-1895)

Christians who were known for character. Gordon worked for his father in the family run woolen mill as he was growing up.

Gordon attended the Baptist church with his parents. His dad was a senior deacon in that church. At age 15 young Gordon went through a night of conviction and accepted Christ as his personal savior the next morning. His father was with him part of the time. He sealed this inward act with the outward form of baptism by immersion in the old millstream that fed the family run mill.

His conversion was radical. He began now to study and read, a thing previously studiously avoided. He nursed an inward growing conviction that he should enter the ministry. When he was sixteen he testified to this conviction in his church.[7]

> One who was present has described the scene to the writer. A warm evening in late spring; the sounds of the wakeful world of the lower creation coming in the open doors and windows; a shy; awkward boy, yet with a light on his face, announcing, with much difficulty and stumbling, his purpose to devote his life and best powers to his Savior's work...(E. Gordon 1896:19-29).

The local school in the village while adequate technically was not appropriate politically or Christian wise. Gordon decided to go for preparation for college at the denominational school some 34 miles away.

> The decision made, the first step to be taken was preparation for college. ...The boy was sent, therefore, by his staunchly Calvinist father to a trustworthy denominational school at New London, N.H. (E. Gordon 1896:20-21).

B. Preparatory Training At:
New London--Basic Analytical Skills
(1853-1857); Age=17-21

Little is known about this period of time except that Gordon was behind when the entered the New London school. He did part time work while in school to help pay his way. He was grounded in Greek in preparation for seminary studies later and the ministry to come. Houghton (1970:6) notes that he graduated with honors--having caught up his lack of preparation to enter. We know little or nothing of the shaping activities of this time, that is of his personal growth in the things of God. Neither biographer comments on these matters.

II. Thorough Preparation and First Steps in Ministry; Years of Formal and Informal Training
(1857-1869); Age=21-33

A. Formal Training
1. At: Brown University--Classical Education
(1857-1860); Age=21-24

Gordon was grounded in the classics, exposed widely to literature, and developed early a love for devotional literature (E. Gordon 1896:27). While we know little of the

---

moving in America at the time. This name is a *destiny preparation* shaping activity that foreshadows a future interest of young Gordon. He will someday be one of the great advocates of missionary activity.
[7]This is called in leadership emergence theory a *leadership committal* (Clinton 1989:146-149).

Chapter 3. A. J. Gordon--(1836-1895)

actual shaping processes at this time we know something of the character being shaped. His roommate (previously at New London and also at Brown) comments, looking back years later on A. J. Gordon as a person.

> I wish to bear testimony to the majestic character and exalted worth and influence of my classmate and lifelong friend, Dr. Gordon. For six years in academy and college--a portion of that time as room-mates--we lived in relations of tenderest intimacy. The same serenity of disposition, the same fine equipoise that has marked his riper years was characteristic of his youth. I cannot recall, during all this period of uninterrupted intercourse, a single instance of petulance or irritation. I cannot remember a single utterance from his lips that he might have wished unspoken. His religious life was steadfast, cheerful, and uniform, free from short-lived raptures on the one hand, and seasons of luke warmness on the other. The unfaltering purpose of declaring the gospel of the grace of God, with which his own life had been enriched, dominated him completely, and from this he never, amid the ambitions and temptations of college life, for one instant swerved. He was a moral and spiritual leader in college, apparently without the slightest thought of being such, and without any special effort on his part, just as he has since been in the broader sphere of life. He realized more perfectly than any man I now recall the high ideal of a deep, genuine, uncompromising piety, without the least trace of austerity or sanctimoniousness or asceticism. There was in him a delightful vein of humor, always, however, so graciously tempered that it never descended, as is frequently the case, to the level of coarseness or levity, and was never suffered to become an occasion of wounding the feelings of the most sensitive. He was withal so natural, so consistent, so magnanimous, so charitable, that he won the love and admiration of all; yes, even of those who were utterly ignorant of or indifferent to the heavenly grace that dwelt so richly in him (E. Gordon 1896:30).

Even recognizing that later remembrances are not always accurate (we tend to remember what we want) and that folks tended not to evaluate *warts and all* in those days, still this is a fine testimony.

It was at Brown when he met and began a courtship with Maria T. Hale who was to become his bride and helpmeet later on.[8]

A. Formal Training (continued)
2. At: Newton Theological Institute
(1860-1863); Age=24-27

At this time there were the tremendous currents sweeping across the U.S.A. concerning slavery and secession. Gordon read the anti-slavery books and materials coming out and being published widely. He was certainly swayed by them. Coming from a strong abolitionist background, Gordon's desire was to join a New Hampshire regiment. But his family which had invested in his education and was behind his preparation for the ministry decided he should stay in school. He followed this advice (E. Gordon 1896:35).

During this seminary training four things are worthy of note--at least from a developmental perspective.

---

[8]Years later on a return visit to Brown, Gordon thought back to his very first days of courtship with Maria Hale. E. Gordon (1896:31,32) records a letter written in 1882 but remembering back to 1860. There one can sense the depth of love and appreciation Gordon had for his wife who had added so much to his life and ministry. It is clear she was a shaping force for the good in his life.

Chapter 3. A. J. Gordon--(1836-1895)   page 84

1. Mentor Teacher/ Word Centered Model--Dr. H. B. Hackett[9]

Dr. Hackett, his New Testament Professor in Exegesis, made a deep impression on Gordon. He was a godly, Word centered professor who modeled an on-going learning posture and a love for the New Testament, particularly in the Greek. He inspired his students to study it, to believe that meaning could be found with diligent study, and to seek careful use of the text.

> It was said of Hackett that "He never went into his class, during the whole forty years of his career as a teacher, without a new investigation and revision of the lesson for the hour," ... From him Gordon learned that "every phrase of the New Testament has a meaning definite and single--a meaning that can be accurately ascertained and clearly expressed according to fixed and settled laws of human speech." From him he got "that reverent regard for divine revelation which, on the one hand, brooks no mystical importation of human fancies into the sacred text, and, on the other, does not permit the smallest Greek article or conjunction to be treated as an idle or ambiguous thing in that Word, which holy men of old wrote as they were moved by the Holy Ghost." (E. Gordon 1896:37).[10]

Contemporary models are very important during the early stages of the development of an emerging leader.[11]

2. Inner-life Growth through Literary Processing

Morgan pursues God via the inspirational writings of historical mentors.[12] His inner life develops.[13] He sees the importance of relationship with God as an important base for his ministry.

---

[9]*Mentoring* is a relational experience in which one person called the *mentor*, empowers another person, called the *mentoree* via a transfer of resources. Nine types of mentor functions have been identified. One of these is the modeling function of a contemporary Christian leader respected by the mentoree. The mentoree tends to emulate and imbibe values from the contemporary model and tends to live up to the genuine expectations that model sets out. Hackett was just such a timely example for Gordon.

[10]E. Gordon's description of Hackett is a quote from a memorial address by Dr. A. H. Strong on Horatio Balch Hackett, D.D.

[11]See Clinton and Clinton (1991), **The Mentor Handbook**, which describes the importance of contemporary models early on to demonstrate the authenticity of a Christian role. A contemporary model serves as a sort of Christian hero/heroine who inspires the young leader. Hackett was that for Gordon. He authenticated the authority of the Scriptures. He modeled serious study of it. He modeled a learning posture. He seriously prepared for his teaching. In all these things he set patterns which impacted young Gordon. Other types of mentors (coaches, teachers, sponsors, spirituality, etc.) will be needed during Gordon's lifetime. But this godly, scholarly, New Testament professor was the model who was there at the right moment to influence a very serious student toward excellence.

[12]*Historical mentors* refer to leaders who have gone before and exert influence on present leaders via biography or other writings. *Literary processing* (Clinton 1989:184,185) refers to the vicarious learning that comes through interacting with godly authors. God greatly uses, at least in a culture which stress literacy as opposed to an oral culture, writings to influence the growth of leaders. Early on, Gordon found the importance of devotional literature. He read those early Christian writers who stressed relationship with God as a primary pre-requisite of ministry. Note particularly his interest in music in the devotional life. Growth through literary processing is an important symptom of a learning posture. One of the seven important lessons discovered early on in our comparative study of effective leaders states, "Effective leaders maintain a learning posture throughout their lifetimes."

[13]*Inner life growth* is one of the symptoms of a leader beginning to emerge. Inner life refers both to character and to an inner sensitivity or awareness of God in things. It is a preliminary step leading toward or accompanying first attempts at ministry. Some of the character traits referred to by Gordon's roommate are evidently a result of some of this shaping activity.

Chapter 3. A. J. Gordon--(1836-1895)

We find him more deeply immersed than ever in hymnology, devotional literature, and the Fathers. Krummacher, "The Hymns of the Ages," and à Kempis fed his spiritual life. Patristic literature he searched to find, not buttresses for ecclesiastical pretension, but fellowship in a common love and service.

"I have been reading," he says, "with a delight which is to me of the very highest kind, the writings of the old Fathers. Their quaintness is only equaled by their sweetness. I have perhaps a peculiar taste in this respect, and were I to buy all my favorite books, I am sure my library would be of quite an antique cast. St. Augustine's 'Confessions' afford delineations of almost seraphic raptures. They give one an idea of what Christianity is able to impart to him who is willing to bear its sternest self-denials...I feel, with him, what we most of all need is the power to commune with God. I know of no greater attainment than the ability to hold unbroken communion with the Savior, closing up those avenues through which sinful thoughts and vain desires steal in, and, as à Kempis says, making of the soul a tabernacle with but one window, and that for Christ."

Of those other Fathers, the Fathers of Reformed Christianity, he made fast friends. Rutherford's "Letters" were discovered in an old issue of 1826, uncut and thick with dust. Its jewels of meditation and ecstasy were gathered with eager hands. This volume held him throughout life with the charm of an abiding fascination. Reference is made again and again, in his Newton letters, to "sweet Rutherford." (E. Gordon 1896:35,36)

3. Practical Training[14]

He preached in surrounding churches on Sundays.[15] These were learning experiences. He was getting on-the-job training in public ministry--including feedback. He also was making contacts in the Boston area. But probably most importantly, this practical training leads eventually to his next step--a full time ministry assignment. E. Gordon points this out.

> The seminarist was now beginning to preach in small country and suburban churches--entering upon a sort of pastoral clinic introductory to his coming career. He had preached occasionally in the church of his own village. ...
> The Sundays were spent in this way among the various churches of eastern Massachusetts. Now and again he felt disheartened. "There seems to be so little real appreciation of what has cost so much toil of brain, and so little apparent good from the words spoke." At other times he was greatly encouraged. (E. Gordon 1896:39,40).

---

[14]One of the problems of Seminary training is often the lack of balanced input. From training model theory we identify four elements that need to be balanced for training to be most effective. They are input (cognitive focus--seminaries high on this), experience (using the input in life--seminaries weak on this), dynamic reflection (an evaluation process which tests ideas of input with use in life and which generates new ideas from experience--seminaries weak on this since they are usually slanted toward pre-service--i.e. anticipation rather than immediate use) and formation (that is the deliberate focus on building of leadership character, skills, and strategic thinking--seminaries weak on this). Gordon provided experience on his own in week end supply work. We know that at New London character was stressed. We see in the literary processing that spiritual formation was taking place. We do not know about dynamic reflection. See Clinton (1984) **Leadership Training Models** for Holland's Two Track Analogy which gives this balanced model for training.

[15]These are most likely self-initiated *ministry tasks*. Probably they were prompted by a desire to learn to communicate, to give out some of what he was taking in, and by need for money. A *ministry task* (Clinton 1989:137) is an assignment from God which primarily tests a person's faithfulness and obedience but often also allows use of ministry gifts in the context of a task which has closure, accountability, and evaluation. Usually these tasks come in the context of local church ministry and are assigned by people in the leadership structure. Self-initiated tasks are highly indicative of leadership.

He was growing. Discernment of communication impact points to a leader who wants an effective pulpit ministry. Gordon was sensitive to his communication efforts.

4. Guidance Value--Its Step-By-Step

He continued to correspond with Marie Hale. In one of his letters he states a guidance value which stood him in good stead all his ministry. This reinforces the notion already mentioned of inner life growth as well.

> I have concluded to avoid brooding over any anxieties. I have learned to believe it wrong. It is gathering and pressing together into an intolerable burden the troubles which God has mercifully scattered over years of time. I confess I cannot see so far and so distinctly the path of my future life as I was confident I could in boyhood, before I thought of the possibility of such a thing as adversity or disappointment. Still when I have taken one step I have always had light enough to see where to take the next. So I try quietly to adopt the words of Christ, 'Take no thought for the morrow.' 'Do the duty that lies nearest to thee' has become quite a motto for me. We need to be patient above all things. I am anxious, too, that you as well as myself may learn that generous and self-denying labors for others bring the sweetest and richest rewards. The smallest action may thus be made noble, and the very drudgery of life become divine. I sometimes hope that it is one of the lessons which experience is gradually teaching me, that if I am to be anything that is truly good and noble, it must be by conquering those narrow and sordid ambitions by which the world is so much controlled. Still I am aware I have enough of them." (E. Gordon 1896:38).

The value-*Guidance is a step-by-step matter. Be obedient in the things at hand. If I follow the light I have, the next will come when I need it.* And it did.[16]

B. Informal Training/ Real Leadership Transition
At: Jamaica Plain Baptist church
(1863-1869); Age=27-33

One of the churches he preached in during his weekends while at Newton was Jamaica Plain Baptist Church on the outskirts of Boston. Just as he was finishing at Newton he received a call from this church. He was ordained in that church on June 25, 1863.[17] Soon after he was married to Marie Hale with whom he had continued his courtship while in seminary--though mainly from a distance.

The basics of pastoring were learned in this church. He conducted marriages and funerals. The daily discipline of study, visitation, and pulpit work filled his time. This was a small church. He developed strong informal familiar relationships with his congregation. During the Friday night prayer meetings he exhorted to consecrated living, giving a series of sermons on the development of the higher life. He learned to improve his tone of voice in the pulpit. He learned how to choose preaching topics. He took strong stands on the slavery issue and the war. Three children were born to A. J. Gordon and his wife Marie while at Jamaica Plain Baptist Church (E. Gordon 1896:43-45).

---

[16]The quaint King James Version of Genesis 24:27 captures the idea. Abraham's servant who has been led to find a wife for Isaac says, "I, being in the way, the Lord led me." Other translations say led straight. The basic idea is we follow the Lord in terms of what we know and we trust Him to show us as we go. He will direct us to our destination.

[17]Various dates in June are given for this ordination but Houghton (1970:7) seems to have studied the various dates and arrived at 25 June as the most legitimate. See his footnote 1 page 7 for details.

Chapter 3. A. J. Gordon--(1836-1895)

The guidance value comes into play again at this point. It comes in the form of a faith challenge which stretches a comfortable Gordon in a warm loving atmosphere of a small church.[18]

> Seated alone in his study one evening in the fall of '67, writing on his Sunday sermon, ...he was suddenly startled by.. the door-bell. ...it was the first summons to a new field of labor....an important pastorless Boston church, ...came to tender him a call "hearty and unanimous." Should he accept? Impossible! No man was ever more loved by his people. No home was ever dearer to father and husband than the one where he was sitting. No field of usefulness could offer more opportunities for a measured, yet none the less vital, religious activity. His declination was given out of hand, and was soon followed by a more formal and decisive refusal. But the end was not yet. A year passed, and still the city church was without a head, and still the delegations continued to call at the suburban manse. [Away on a visit he writes back to his wife] "Why will they not let me alone," he writes, "and not press their suit? I wish I were out of it. If you will go to them and get me off in my absence, and agree that they shall never trouble me again, I will give you half of my kingdom. I am well-nigh insane over the matter. Tell all my flock how I love them, and how I loathe the pastures of Boston and the bulls of State Street, which are worse than those of Bashan. Thank God, their call cannot divide me from you, though it may thrust me forth from my Paradise. What a comfort it must have been to Adam that, though expelled from Eden, Eve went with him!" At the expiration of the first year he yielded, and wrote out a letter of acceptance. ...The letter was torn to pieces with many expressions of self-recrimination for his disloyalty to the church of his first love. Finally, however, the pressure became too strong, and, after two years of waiting, he agreed to become pastor of the Clarendon Street Church. In the month of December, 1869, amid the universal mourning of the flock, he left Jamaica Plain to take up the work the completion of which was to constitute the capital achievement of his life (E. Gordon 1896:45,46).

Gordon accepted the challenge. That it was a challenge can be seen by the reforms that must come--at least as Gordon saw it. In 1890, he describes the progress of the church after 20 years of his pastorate. One can simply reverse the assessment to see where it was in 1870.

> We believe we have learned much, through divine teaching, as to the true method of conducting the affairs of God's church; we have proved by experience the practicability of what we have learned; and have largely united the church in the practice thereof. *Innovations* have from the beginning been strongly urged. 'Innovations'? No! that word implies newness; and God is our witness that in theology, in worship, and in church

---

[18]A *faith challenge* (Clinton 1989:223) is an assignment from God in which the leader will be stretched to trust God to see the assignment fulfilled. This Boston Church was in a non-receptive region assailed by Unitarianism and strong anti-Protestantism from Catholics. The church itself was the most important of the denomination in Boston. E. Gordon (1896:70) summarizes it: It was indeed a church of a well-defined and easily recognized type--a church which has its counterpart in every city of Protestant Christendom. It summarized, as all of its class, the admirable traits of Protestantism--comfort, order, intelligence, affluence, reserve, a not too aggressive religiousness. The challenge--how to make this into an effective church which is winning people to Christ, building them up in the faith, and reaching out to the world. This incident also involves an *influence-mix* challenge. *Influence-mix* (Clinton 1989:378) has to do with how and who leaders influence. All leaders influence followers. They can influence *directly*, that is, face-to-face ministry, *indirectly*, via shaping of key individuals or via materials used by others or *organizationally* via executive leadership or committees or the like. Each leader has a profile corresponding to which of these dominates or how they relate. Gordon's potential influence-mix will include a large direct face-to-face in terms of pulpit ministry, a large direct face-to-face ministry in conferences and speaking at various churches and universities, a large indirect influence via his writing for journals, and a large organizational influence via executive leadership on numerous boards. Clarendon Street is the geographic locale that will allow his expansion to potential.

Chapter 3. A. J. Gordon--(1836-1895)

administration it is not the new to which we have been inclined, but the old. *Renovation*, rather, is what we have sought. With a deep feeling that many of the usages which have been fastened upon our churches by long tradition constitute a serious barrier to spiritual success, it has been my steady aim to remove these. In general, we may say, it is our strong conviction that true success in the church of Christ is to be attained by spiritual, not by secular, methods; by a worship which promotes self-denial in God's people, and not by that which ministers to self-gratification; by a cultivation of the heart through diligent use of the Word and of prayer, and not by a cultivation of art through music and architecture and ritual. And with the most deliberate emphasis we can say that every step in our return to simpler and more scriptural methods of church service has proved an onward step toward spiritual efficiency and success." (E. Gordon 1896:71,72)

We can assume that the following changes were needed:[19]

1. get rid of secular means for achieving success,
2. move to a true worship,
3. primarily have a strong Word and prayer ministry central in the church,
4. do away with secondary attractions such as art, music, architecture and ritual,
5. move back to simpler and more scriptural methods of church service.

Gordon's challenge loomed large. We know from the foregoing assessment that he got there. But how? That is the story of the next development phase which will see Gordon move toward an effective and finally a focused ministry which achieved much.

III. Unique Ministry At Clarendon Street/ Increasing Fruitfulness/ A Flagship Ministry Emerges (1869-1895); Age=33-59

The ministry at Clarendon Street can be broken into three time increments:

1. (1869-1877) Stony Ground/ Reforms Begun / Worship, First Reform
2. (1877-1882) The Turning Point--Moody's 1877 Ministry; Creating a Flagship Ministry/ An Increasingly Effective Ministry
3. (1882-1895) Powerful Focused Ministry

Each of these periods contain challenges to change and breakthroughs with ministry insights.[20] Lets work through them and trace Gordon's development.

A. Stony Ground/ Reforms Begun / Worship, First Reform (1869-1877); Age=33-41

First Several Years--Attempting Change Slowly

The new minister had made one condition upon his acceptance of the call.

It was forgotten that the only condition which the new minister had made in accepting this charge was the disuse of what he called the ice-chest, i.e., the quartet gallery, and the substitution of hearty singing by the whole congregation for the delegated worship there carried on. (E. Gordon 1896:74).

---

[19]Houghton (1970:83) lists five areas of change: worship, music, amusements, finances, and administration--essentially what I have surmised above.

[20]*Ministry insights* (Clinton 1989:198) are breakthrough concepts which help a leader deliver ministry to followers. I will point out a number of these as we move through the time increments.

Chapter 3. A. J. Gordon--(1836-1895) page 89

Opposition to music changes flourished. Gordon wanted a lively congregational participation in worship singing. The choir, especially the quartet, mostly professional and paid, performed on Sunday mornings. One thing really rankled Gordon. To him it was an unbiblical practice. Some of the professional singers were not professing Christians but simply took part as a job for which they were paid. Gordon's approach to change included:

1. editing a modern collection of hymns and tunes,
2. instructing the people via a series of sermons on worship including "singing, responsive reading, giving, and the ministry of silence,"
3. patiently waiting over the years for the changes to take hold.

Gradually most changes came in little by little over a period of about 13 years. Besides straightforward Biblical teaching on the issues underlying each of the needed changes, Gordon clearly modeled in his own life obedience to the convictions he was exposing.

Priorities Right--Pursues Spiritual Formation in Midst of Tough Sledding

Normally when a pastor moves into a situation like this which demands change, he/she becomes engrossed in activities toward those ends. There is usually a loss in spiritual formation with the increase in ministerial formation that happens.[21] Gordon is unusual. He specifically maintains a balance. His spiritual life is important to him. It is the basis out of which will come spiritual authority. In the midst of instituting change Gordon sought to grow. E. Gordon comments on A.J. Gordon's growth in spirituality and in ministerial perspective during the early years of the Boston ministry.

> Soon after coming to Boston, Gordon published a remarkable study in the identities of Christ and the believer. "In Christ" was the fruit of much deep meditation, the distillation of many late hours in the Jamaica Plain manse. It is, perhaps, the most nearly perfect in form and content of any of his works, quintessential in its compression, rich, finished, and imbued with mysticism, the mysticism of the New Testament....
> The Pauline phrases, "created in Christ," "crucified with Christ," "risen with Christ," "baptized into Christ," "sanctified in Christ," "the dead in Christ," are taken as melodic themes upon which to work out the variations of a sober, fruitful exposition (E. Gordon 1896:82,83).

Gordon's view of sanctification would be what is called today progressive sanctification. "If we are in Christ we have the earnest of our sanctification." But "though this grace is conferred on each Christian as soon as he believes, it is nevertheless a gift held on deposit, 'hid with Christ in God,' to be drawn on through daily communion and gradual apprehension." (E. Gordon 1896:83) Gordon moved into union life, that is, living a life identified with Christ, that of the message of this writing. Later he will be one of the advocates of the American Keswick movement which stresses this deeper life.

---

[21] The three formations, spiritual (leadership character), ministerial (leadership skills), and strategic (leadership vision) usually alternate in terms of priority. Their order varies over a lifetime. In leadership transition it is spiritual formation, ministerial formation and strategic formation. In early leadership it is usually ministerial formation, spiritual formation, and strategic formation. In latter effective ministry it is usually spiritual formation, strategic formation and ministerial formation. In focused ministry leading toward afterglow it is usually strategic formation, spiritual formation, ministerial formation. One of the reasons for the large drop out in ministry during first efforts at leadership are because spiritual formation is neglected for ministerial. Gordon is very unusual here. He is developing a base from which will come spiritual authority.

Further growth comes through,

1. Practice of spiritual disciplines--a consistent devotional life,
2. Participation in an accountability/ growth group for pastors,[22]
3. Further literary processing,[23] including some excellent historical mentors,
4. Getting perspective, a study into movements of the times, evaluating for effectiveness.

Early Passive Mentoring--Historical Mentor, David Brainerd

Gordon was a young man of 33 years age. He was moving into a locale and church containing ample opportunity. Of particular importance at such a time is perspective, something a young man with only six years ministry experience does not yet have. Historical mentors are one source of breadth and perspective. Gordon comments on the impact on his life by Brainerd's, one of his important historical mentors that he revisited many times over his lifetime.

> Does it savor of saint-worship or superstition to be thus exploring old graveyards, wading through snow-drifts, and deciphering ancient headstones on a cold day in midwinter? Perhaps so, on the face of it; but let us justify our conduct. What if the writer confesses that he has never received such spiritual impulse from any other human being as from him whose body has lain now for nearly a century and a half under that Northampton slab? For many years an old and worn volume of his life and journals has lain upon my study table, and no season has passed without a renewed pondering of its precious contents. 'If you would make men think well of you, make them think well of themselves,' is the maxim of Lord Chesterfield, which he regarded as embodying the highest worldly wisdom. On the contrary, the preacher and witness for Christ who makes us think meanly of ourselves is the one who does us most good, and ultimately wins our hearts. This is exactly the effect which the reading of Brainerd's memoirs has on one. Humiliation succeeds humiliation as we read on. 'How little have I prayed! how low has been my standard of consecration!' is the irresistible exclamation; and when we shut the book we are not praising Brainerd, but condemning ourselves, and resolving that, by the grace of God, we will follow Christ more closely in the future. ... If ardent piety and enlarged benevolence, if supreme love to God and the inextinguishable desire of promoting His glory in the salvation of souls, if persevering resolution in the midst of the most pressing discouragements, if cheerful self-denial and unremitting labor, if humility and zeal for godliness united with conspicuous talents render a man worthy of remembrance, the name of Brainerd will not soon be forgotten.
>
> But our interest in Brainerd's grave lies especially in this: that, standing there, we stand at one of the fountain sources of modern missions. We doubt if any single life has given such powerful and such permanent impulse to the great movement for the

---

[22]This is a case of lateral mentoring in a group context. E. Gordon lists (1896:84) a number of prominent full time Christian workers in the Boston area at the time including: W. R. Nicholson, rector of St. Paul's, George C. Needham, Dr. H.M. Parsons. These men studied various books such as Gurnall's "Christian Armor," Charnock's "Wisdom of our Fathers," and other Puritan literature. They met semi-monthly in Gordon's house to spur each other on in the deeper themes of scriptural teaching.

[23]Throughout his ministry Gordon will feed himself upon the writing of the great saints of old--literary processing. E. Gordon (1896:84, 85) includes the following as saints that Gordon read and profited from: Van Oosterzee's "Person and Work of the Redeemer," Vinet's "Outlines of Theology," Alford's works, the "Horae Apocalypticae" of Elliot, Edersheim's "Sketches of Jewish Life," the journals of Eugénie de Guérin, Uhlhorn's "Conflict of Christianity with Paganism"; the poems of Henry Vaughn, of Herbert, of Quarles, and of Donne; the works of Rothe, of R. Stier, of Birks, of Flavel, of Archer Butler, of Wescott, of Guinness, of Harnack; the lives of Joseph Alleine, of Robert Moffatt, of John Woolman, of Henry Martyn, and of David Brainerd. The career of the last named exerted a powerful and lasting influence upon him.

Chapter 3. A. J. Gordon--(1836-1895)

world's evangelization which we are now witnessing as that of this young man, who died at less than thirty years of age." (Gordon 1893:269, 270)[24]

Getting Perspective--Current Movements and Their Implications

Gordon studied two prominent movements during this foundational time of growth in his life--Brethrenism and Tractarianism. Both were movements aimed at bringing reform to Christian life in England. He noted two important things in comparing these movements. One, he saw how Brethrenism contributed to Biblical interpretation and Biblical literature. Two, he noted the apostolic character of the Brethren leaders. Tractarianism, while meeting some contemporary felt needs, did not make a lasting influence. It lacked these two qualities of Brethrenism. From these movements he gained perspective--especially the importance of creating an on-going lasting influence through leaving classical contributions behind.

In summary, the first period of time at Clarendon Street Church, Gordon began to instigate changes. The external climate was stony. Internally he faced opposition. He concentrated on personal growth and building a faithful track record as he patiently waited for the changes to take hold. Little by little he gained ground and respect for his views. But it was to take a power breakthrough to turn the corner. Two spiritual forces in the persons of Uncle John Vassar, and D. L. Moody were to provide the sparks that would turn the Clarendon Street Church around.

B. The Turning Point--Moody's 1877 Ministry; Creating a Flagship Ministry/ An Increasingly Effective Ministry (1877-1882); Age=41-46

Active Mentoring, Evangelism Coach--Uncle John Vassar Lays Foundation

Gordon credits Uncle John Vassar, a personal evangelist for five years at Clarendon Street Church with the foundational emphasis which led to the turning point. Note his description of this faithful worker.

> Among all the influences which touched and vivified the early ministry at Clarendon Street, none was stronger than that of Uncle John Vassar, a devoted laborer for souls. "Far beyond any man whom I ever knew," wrote Gordon, "was it true of him that his citizenship was in heaven, and so filled was he with the glory and the power of the heavenly life that to many he seemed like a foreigner speaking an unknown tongue. I have never been so humbled and quickened by contact with any living man as with him. Hundreds of Christians, while sorrowing that they shall see his face no more for the present, will bless God as long as they live for the inspiration which they have received from his devoted life."
>
> For five successive years, off and on, "Uncle John" labored with the Clarendon Street Church in his peculiar work of "spiritual census-taking," going through the streets of proud, cultivated, self-righteous Boston, ringing every door-bell, and confronting every household with the great question of the new birth....He would literally travail in prayer for the unconverted. "The nights which he spent at my home," writes Gordon, "were nights of prayer and pleading for my congregation and my ministry. Again and again would I hear him rising in the midnight hours to plead with God for the unsaved, till I had frequently to admonish him that he must not lose his sleep." And so he wrought and prayed and instructed the young minister, meekly teachable before such a master of spiritual things, in those hard-learned and rarely acquired secrets which open the way to the heart of hearts of sinful humanity (E. Gordon 1896:94,95).

---

[24]This is written in retrospect but shows the impact of this historical mentor throughout Gordon's lifetime. It also reveals something of Gordon's passion for the modern mission movement.

Chapter 3. A. J. Gordon--(1836-1895)   page 92

It was this groundwork, by this mentor coach to Gordon, which ushered in the major break through which came in 1877.[25]

1877 Year of Breakthrough--
Moody as Mentor, Contemporary Model of Gifted Power

In 1877, D. L. Moody brought his evangelistic fervor to Boston for a prolonged campaign--it was extended to six months. His tabernacle was within 100 yards of the Clarendon Street Church which was used for overflow and "inquiry" meetings. E. Gordon describes the happenings.

> The Tabernacle was thronged night after night by audiences of from five to seven thousand. People of all ranks and conditions attended. Excursion trains brought in thousands from all parts of New England. Seventy thousand families in Boston were personally visited. Great noon prayer-meetings were held daily in Tremont Temple by business men. Meetings were organized for young men, for boys, for women, for the intemperate--in short, for all classes in the community that were ready to help or be helped.
> At the center of all these operations stood the Clarendon Street Church, like a cemetery temporarily occupied by troops in battle. What a shattering and overturning of weather-stained, moss-grown traditions followed! What experiences of grace, what widening vistas of God's power, what instruction in personal religion, resulted from these six months of revival! A new window was built into the religious life of the church. The true purpose of a church's existence began to be emphasized. Drunkards and outcasts were daily reclaimed, and brought into fellowship. Christian evidences of the best sort, evidences which had to do with the present potency of a saving Christ, were multiplied to affluence, strengthening the faith of believers. The duty and opportunity of all in the work of the inquiry-room were asserted. A great education in methods of practical religious work resulted (E. Gordon 1896:95,95).

The results at Clarendon brought radical change.

> Before the meetings were ended nearly thirty reclaimed drunkards had been received into the Clarendon Street Church. The general opinion was that these men would not stand even to the end of the year. Yet Gordon was able to say some time after..."Of those who have continued their residence with us, all have remained steadfast, as consistent, as devoted, and as useful members as we have, a demonstration that God can instantly change a man the vilest and worst drunkard to one in the way to the highest saintship (Gordon 1896:100, 101).

Gordon identified this revival as the cause of the turning point in his ministry at Clarendon Street. From here on he moves clearly toward bringing about the changes. He will now begin to build a Flagship ministry.[26] We'll look at one example in depth because

---

[25]Gordon learned about evangelism from Uncle John Vassar. But it was his heartbeat, his value for souls, his intercession for them, his efforts to reach them that touched Gordon. From this time onward his church would be concerned with souls. It is in the first few years of a new assignment that a leader especially needs a mentor coach who can instruct and show him how to operate effectively. Vassar was that for Gordon. (See Clinton and Clinton 1991 for the importance of various mentor types at different times in the development of a leader).

[26]By a flagship ministry is meant a full orbed church ministry model which is having regional and national impact and becomes a pattern or ideal for other aspiring leaders to aim at. Clarendon Street will have social ministries applying the Gospel to all kinds of social issues like alcoholics and prohibition, relief for unemployed, freedom of speech, emancipation of women, protection of Chinese immigrants. It will have evangelistic ministries. It will publish Christian literature. In short, it will have an impact on the entire

Chapter 3. A. J. Gordon--(1836-1895)

of its personal effect upon Gordon's growth. Then we'll simply summarize some of the influential ministries coming from this church.

Boston Industrial Home--Ministry to Down and Outers, A Major Result
The Faith Challenge for Gordon--1877ff

One result from the Moody campaign was a ministry to down and outers, one always fraught with problems. The Industrial Temporary Home was begun. This was a rehab home used to test out the validity of those having made professions of faith. The resultant financial load and constant turnover of workers and trustees became finally the sole burden of Gordon. It was in connection with this burdensome problem[27] that Gordon learned one of his great lessons. Notice the means of solution.

> For a term of years he carried almost alone the heavy weight of a work the only assured fruit of which was the annually recurring deficit. Burdened with this great care, he left the city one summer to take a brief vacation in the hill-country. A sense of deep disheartenment pressed heavily upon him. An undertaking promising, useful, necessary, was trembling on the edge of disruption. There was no human help in sight. he was driven, therefore, into the arms of God. Every morning during the whole summer he withdrew to a quiet place in the woods, a spot still, sun-dappled, and there laid before the Lord the discouragements and the needs of the work. Summer passed, and in early September he was back again in the city. (E. Gordon 1896:106,107).

Now note how God moves in answer to Gordon's prayerful response to the faith challenge. E. Gordon continues with the story.

> Seated in his study a few days after his arrival, he was handed a note in unfamiliar writing, requesting an immediate interview. Replying to the summons and hunting up the address, he soon found himself in the chamber of an old man, in a quarter of the city long deserted by residents and given over now to the roar of traffic. The man was an entire stranger, a relic of a rapidly passing generation, inordinately fond of his properties, as was afterward learned. There he sat, dry, wizened, in skullcap, surrounded by a clutter of dust-covered documents and papers, a bottle of brandy at his left hand. His intentions were soon made known. He had learned during the summer of the Industrial Home, and become convinced of the reasonableness and expediency of its method. He wished, therefore, to make provision for it in his will, and to get suggestions from Gordon looking toward the enlargement of the work and the placing of it upon a secure basis.
>
> This day's interview was the first in a series of events which resulted in the complete solution of this problem of many weary years. The bequest when paid amounted to over twenty thousand dollars. A strong cabinet was formed for the more efficient care of the institution, composed of men able, generous, reliable--men who have stood by to the present day. As a result of further earnest prayer, a superintendent of exceptional ability and consecration, a converted horse-jockey, was brought unexpectedly to Dr. Gordon's notice, one who for many years has not only conducted the Home with superior executive skill, but has also helped to found homes of a like character in many of our Northern and Western cities. In a short time the institution was on a paying basis....

New England region. It will become multi-staffed with specialization ministries. It will release lay people into ministries. It will train and send missionaries including women. Its Senior Pastor will have ministries outside the church which highlight his strong evangelistic concerns about the deeper life, the second coming, and the importance of the authority of the Word. One strong aspect of a Flagship Ministry is a strong staff who can operate in specialty ministries. John A. McElwain, served as Gordon's assistant for 18 of his 25 years at Clarendon Street church. He was strong in visitation ministry including personal evangelism (E. Gordon 1896:81,82).

[27] This is another instance of a *faith challenge*. Gordon's taking of a mini-sabbatical is a *ministry insight* which needs to be emulated today.

Chapter 3. A. J. Gordon--(1836-1895)   page 94

> "It was the greatest lesson in faith I have ever had," said Gordon once, in recounting the experience. "From that day to this I have prayed with the greatest assurance of God's intervention in practical matters." (E. Gordon 1896:107,108)

Gordon Honored--1878

Brown university conferred an honorary doctorate upon Gordon--certainly an indication of his growing influence on the east coast. He was only 42 years of age, but like Morgan, he was recognized early for the rising influence he would have on American Christianity.

Other Ministries Emerge As Needed

In addition to the Industrial home other ministries which applied the Gospel to social settings included monthly publication of an evangelical paper, **The Watchword** which produced news from a Christian standpoint. In the early 1880s there was a campaign to close saloons and a continual fight for prohibition. Gordon was a crusader, pioneer and a founder--that is, he stood on his convictions to correct things in society contrary to the outworking of the Gospel. He saw things that needed to be done and found ways to do them, even if it meant having to formulate a new organization. This will be characteristic of Gordon throughout the focused ministry years to come.

C. Powerful Focused Ministry
(1882-1895); Age=46-59

Gordon Enters Power Gate--Life Power Spilling Over to Gifted Power

About 1880,[28] Gordon entered a power gate.[29] His comments show it to be an appropriation by faith, that is a receiving of the Holy Spirit in his life for sealing, filling, and anointing.[30]

---

[28] The exact time of this critical incident is not known. Since Gordon describes his first seven years of ministry at Clarendon Street as spiritually lethargic (1869-1877), and since Moody's ministry was a turning point (1877), and since he taught on the Spirit life and manifested it in the Northfield Conferences from 1882 on it seems likely to me that somewhere around 1880 he must have experienced that which is described here. His experience follows basically the Keswick approach which was emerging in seed form around this time--and was later publicly preached in Moody's conferences.

[29] This experience is a *power gate* which functions to open the participant to a new level of awareness of God's power in the life. Two kinds of power gates are typically described: *life power* and *gifted power*. This has symptoms of both--I lean toward life power. The participant wants power from God to live a righteous life. There are several patterns for power gates including three major ones: a Wesleyan, a Keswick, and a Pentecostal. This power gate seems to be close to the Keswick pattern. In the next chapter we shall see Brengle go through a power gate, the entire sanctification paradigm. The Keswick power gate is a surrender/faith appropriation one. Later after the turn of the century there will be another type of power gate the Pentecostal Experience, the Baptism of the Holy Ghost. All essentially do the same function--open the way to new experience with God. None guarantee an on-going successful ministry. They are simply gates that open the way for a new relationship with God. We will see the Keswick type power gate also with McQuilkin and Maxwell. Jaffray, somewhat like Brengle, manifests a modified form of the entire sanctification paradigm. The gifted power gate experience is similar except that its participant is seeking for power in ministry. Finney's, Moody's and Torrey's experiences are of this type.

[30] Gordon does not call it a baptism of the Holy Spirit for he believed that referred to a once and for all experience in which the Church was baptized by the Holy Spirit. Here he is talking about an individual deliberate appropriation of the Holy Spirit (a la Luke 11:13)--a kind of 2nd work of grace after salvation. Houghton differs (1970:40) here doctrinally from Gordon, though in sympathy with him, holding that the

Chapter 3. A. J. Gordon--(1836-1895)

Gordon's own crisis was striking in its simplicity. James Francis, Gordon's later successor at Clarendon Street, and a preacher of electrifying power, told some of us that once he and several other young men asked Pastor Gordon how the Spirit came to him. Gordon answered, "I simply knelt and said, 'O God, Thou hast said by the lips of Jesus that Thou art more ready to give the Holy Spirit to them that ask Thee than we are to give good gifts to our children. Father, I take Thee at Thy word. I ask Thee in Jesus' name for the Holy Spirit." Then I got up and went about my work." The young men asked him, "Was that all?" "What more was necessary?" said Gordon. "But I can say this, that from that hour, as I have gone about my parish, and to and from hospitals and meetings, it has often seemed that my feet hardly touched the sidewalk." (Gordon 1951:11)

It seems he did not have an experience with the Holy Spirit for power in ministry as D. L. Moody did. This experience related above is the only power gate experience we have.[31]

Low Key Healing Ministry--mid 70s Onward

Yet Gordon did exercise *power ministry*[32] but with caution. He believed in the ministry of the Holy Spirit in healing. He seemed to be active in it from the late 70s onward. Notice his careful wise approach.[33]

> Curiously enough, while prayer for the sick is almost the commonest form of petition among Christians, a belief in the efficacy of such prayer and in the direct answer to the call for healing is freely counted as fanaticism. "Therefore we need," said Gordon, "less praying for the sick rather than more; only the less should be real and deep and intelligent and believing." The divine help is not to be invoked lightly or as a substitute for God's natural provision in medicine and hygiene. Nor is it a grace for those without depth of spiritual life or for those with whom exercise in prayer is not habitual and prevailing. Yet if the superior faith of prophets and apostles is brought forward to discourage this practice it should still be remembered that to the injunction in James to "pray one for another, that ye may be healed," is added a significant note on the powerfully effective prayers of Elias, "*a man subject to like passions as we are.*"
>
> To the objection that prayers for the sick are often apparently, unanswered, he replied with a disarming *tu quoque*. "Holding such views as we Christians do," he would say, "in regard to the efficacy of prayer for the conversion of souls, and resting on the plain declaration of God our Savior that he will have all men saved, how can we explain the fact that the mass of men go down to death unreconciled to God? We must remember both Melita and Miletum. In one place Paul healed the father of Publius by his prayers; in the other he left Trophimus sick."

---

believer has the Holy Spirit upon becoming a believer. See Gordon's book, **The Ministry of the Spirit**, for a complete explanation of his views.

[31]Frequently people who enter a life power gate will also thereafter evidence power for ministry as well. The reverse does not always seem to be as true. People who go through a gifted power experience may or may not have a walk evidenced by an increasing manifestation of the fruit of the Spirit.

[32]*Power ministry* , in general, refers to use of any of the power cluster gifts. Spiritual gifts for corporate purposes of evaluation of a full orbed ministry can be categorized into three clusters: Word, Power, and Love. The power cluster includes word of wisdom, work of knowledge, faith, gifts of healings, workings of powers, prophecy, discernings of spirits, kinds of tongues, and interpretation of tongues. These power gifts authenticate the reality of the unseen God. Gordon only used deliberately one of these gifts--gifts of healings and then basically as a Christian Role (James 5). He, implicitly used Word of Knowledge and Word of Wisdom from time-to-time, though he would not have called them that.

[33]One must remember he was operating in an era when Christian Science was making inroads. He had written a major polemic pamphlet about it. To advocate healing by faith was risky business in these days. He was criticized by many evangelicals for his stand on faith healing.

Chapter 3. A. J. Gordon--(1836-1895)

> He realized, nevertheless, the great perplexities in the whole matter. "I have little to say in regard to the principles of divine healing," he says in a letter, "but am looking constantly for light. It is a subject full of difficulties, and I shrink more and more from undertaking any philosophy of it. I do my best with every case which comes before me."
> When the sick sought him out he prayed with them in quietness and reserve. Many remarkable answers were vouchsafed (E. Gordon 1896:143).

E. Gordon then goes on to give 4 striking testimonies to divine healing including cancer, paralysis of a thigh, badly curved spine and its ramifying effects, and consumption. Let me illustrate so that you can sense Gordon's involvement in this ministry. I relate the cancer episode[34] since it also apparently contains an interesting case of word of knowledge and a shaping incident involving a word check and obedience check for the participant, the Reverend Joseph C. Young of Boston.[35] This vignette takes place in 1887 but is typical of cases earlier on and later on as well.

> "In 1887 there appeared a growth on my lip. When first noticed it was very small, but gradually increased until it seriously interfered with my preaching. A physician of good standing, after two examinations, told me that it was cancer and that I had better put my house in order, as he believed I had only a short time to live. Though believing in healing by faith, I had no appropriating faith to claim the promise *for myself*, yet I constantly sought divine guidance. For a week I had no light. At the end of this time the promise in James v.14 came into my mind like a new revelation. I had read and quoted it to others hundreds of times, but now it came direct to me with an indescribable force. I believed it immediately. Then came a perplexity--who were the elders of the church? Who could offer the prayer of faith for me? I knew many in Brooklyn, my home, and in New York, who professed faith in this promise, but I had no inclination to call them. I made the matter a subject of special prayer for some days, and the name of Dr. Gordon, with whom I was only slightly acquainted, was so vividly thrust into my mind that I accepted it as an answer to my prayer. The appointment was made to meet him in Boston with Mr. McElwain and Dr. Peck. I told them why I had come, and asked if they could take the promise in James and pray in faith for my healing. They replied that they could, and Dr. Gordon prayed, anointing me according to the instructions. I was in the study only a short time, and went away almost immediately after the prayer. I had no more pain or trouble from the cancer, and within a few weeks all signs of it had disappeared. It has never returned. The promise was believed, the prayer was offered, I was healed...I give this testimony with some reluctance. It is not a subject to be too much advertised. The Spirit heals according to the will of God, not according to our will. There has been too much fleshly formulating of theories on this as on all other teachings of the Bible, and for that reason less of the power of God manifested." (E. Gordon 1896:144,145)

Gordon's belief in the ministry of healing and the ministry of the Spirit was not just theoretical. He did not claim total understanding of the Bible about healing. Yet he was willing to risk failure and pray for healing. This was not a public ministry with fanfare, self-glory, and excesses but a quiet application of the Scriptures to specific cases. Not all were healed. But many were.

---

[34]Houghton (1970:45) relates an even more striking case of breast cancer being healed about 1876.
[35]*Word of knowledge* (Clinton and Clinton 1994) is a spiritual gift of the power cluster in which a believer with that gift receives information from God in a situation. An *obedience check* (Clinton 1989:129-132) is a shaping process in which God conditions attitudes of submission and obedience in a leader. God uses the *word check* to teach a leader sensitivity to His speaking and trustworthiness in what is said (Clinton 1989:133-136).

Chapter 3. A. J. Gordon--(1836-1895)   page 97

Conference Ministry--Moody as Mentor Sponsor--1882

In 1882 D. L. Moody first organized a conference at Northfield, Connecticut which was to have major influence on American Christianity. Evangelists, Bible teachers, Missionaries and other Christian leaders of high standing provided input to lay Christians as well as Christian workers who would gather from all over. Dr. Gordon was a prominent part of this conference. He was a speaker of renown.[36] He also was part of the beginnings of the Student Volunteer Movement which began at Northfield in 1886. From time-to-time when Moody was absent the administrative oversight would be picked up by Gordon.

Outside Public Rhetorician Ministries--1880s Onward

Gordon's own pulpit work, his writings, his various organizational associations and his conference ministry with Moody made him a well known figure who was often invited to speak outside his own pulpit. This outside ministry increased greatly over the last ten years of his ministry. His outside speaking included:

1. The Boston Monday Noon Lectures[37] hosted at the Tremont Temple,
2. Temperance Meetings,
3. Bible Conferences, from 1876 Gordon was regular part of, was a backer and an important contributor in Bible Conference ministries (examples: Niagara Bible Conference and Believer's Meetings in Clifton Springs, N.Y.),
4. Prophetic Conferences; these were instrumental in moving the return of Christ back into prominence (there were two major international ones and other regional ones),
5. Moody's Northfield Conferences; These were summer conferences. Gordon spoke repeatedly in these[38] and actually administered a number of these in Moody's absence when he was away on campaigns. These conferences had sessions for full time Christian workers, for young collegiates, and some for lay Christians.
6. Meetings of Seminary Students and University Students (Yale, Amherst, Rutgers, Mount Holyoke, Williams, Brown, Princeton among others).
7. Evangelistic Meetings; like Moody's Chicago meetings at the World Fair.

He spoke in major cities all over the United States and Canada. I want to give some excerpts from a letter written to his wife on February 4, 1884 from Princeton, N.J. where he addressed students. This gives a feel for the spiritual tone of Gordon and his gifted power.

> My Dear Wife: I will give you a little account of the work, thanking God for what he has graciously given. The first day was the toughest experience I have ever had. The students have been free, hitherto, to come to the prayer-day services or not--they have largely chosen not to come--till this year their attendance was made compulsory. My first

---

[36]Dr. A. T. Pierson said this of his address on the Holy Spirit. "Among all the renowned speakers at the Northfield Conference, he was *facile princeps*; and the address he gave there last summer on the Holy Spirit has been pronounced by competent judges the most complete ever given, even from that platform of great teachers." (E. Gordon 1896:175) This Conference ministry networked Gordon into many such similar types of events which greatly expanded his sphere of influence. I'll say more on this when I evaluate his contributions.

[37]He chaired this lectureships for 12 years and spoke often. The lecturers spoke on various topics relating to Church and state and other Christian issues (Houghton 1970:116).

[38]He used part of his own vacation time each summer to do this ministry.

Chapter 3. A. J. Gordon--(1836-1895)

address was to this compelled crowd, many of them disgusted that their holiday had been turned into a holy day. They sat before me facing at all angles, ogling and squirming and showing plainly enough that they did not propose to be solemnized. I was never so taken off my pins in my life. I sweated and floundered about and made an utter fizzle. All the grave and dignified faculty sat ranged on either side. I came home and dried my clothes and went back to the evening service with fear and trembling. That was not compulsory, and I got on much better. Still, I was so discouraged that I determined to start for home on Friday morning. But I feel that the Lord overruled my rash purpose. A large delegation of students, who appreciated exactly the trial under which I had labored, came to see me, and insisted that I should stay. I consented, and began to visit the young men at their rooms. Sunday morning I preached again before students and faculty. There was a great change; no compulsion, but all were out and very attentive. In the afternoon again deeply solemn meeting. The good old president arose and made a most solemn appeal, saying, 'Young men, you have heard the gospel to-day so plainly declared that you are without excuse if you do not accept Christ.'

"In the evening the students who were Christians planned for meetings in their rooms, inviting those in their respective halls to come in. I started at seven o'clock to visit these meetings. I found them all crowded. In the first one I struck, ten rose at my invitation to indicate their purpose to follow Christ. I went from building to building among the meetings, finding in almost every one those who were ready to stand up. I visited six of these, and I judge there must have been twenty who confessed Christ in different rooms. My reception among the students was most cordial and affectionate.[39] I think the Lord has given me their hearts, and my first discouragement has been turned into great joy. I have addressed the theological students and have met many of them in private for prayer and conference. A good work has certainly begun. I shall stay to-day at least to see it furthered. It has been a peculiar and valuable experience.

"Much love to you and to all. The Lord bless you. Pray, all of you, that I may not labor in vain or run in vain.

Yours Affectionately, Gordon
(E. Gordon 1896:150151)

1885-The Common's Incident--A Stand Upon Strong Convictions

In 1885, Gordon made a stand on freedom of speech for which he was arrested. This strong stand was typical of many that he took for various other issues such as prohibition and women's rights, For many years, in Boston itself, there had been evangelistic open air services by numerous church and parachurch groups. They simply had to apply for speaking permits which were given. Then came a period of time in which the groups having political power in Boston began to discriminate against evangelical groups and no permits were allowed. This happened for several years. Finally in the

---

[39]This is an illustration of a *ministry insight* (Clinton 1989:198) a breakthrough technique, methodology, or structure that allows a leader to deliver powerful ministry. That this is so is seen in the design of the Brown university meetings which occurred in 1891. "The School paper announced that according to the usual custom, the second week in November will be observed as the week of prayer for young men. Dr. A. J. Gordon, of Boston, will be at Brown the entire week, and will hold meetings for the students every evening during the week at 7 p.m. A method successfully tried at Princeton will be used in addition to the seven o'clock meetings. This plan is to hold meetings in each of the dormitories, of half an hour each, between nine and eleven o'clock in the evening. Each division will have a meeting of its own. The different meeting will be so timed that Dr. Gordon may be at each of them. This will be a grand opportunity to increase the religious interest in the college. Those who have heard Dr. Gordon and have felt the power of his presence need no urging to attend all the meetings. Those who have not heard him are sure of a treat, for he is one of the most powerful preachers in the Baptist denomination. (Houghton 1970:158,159 is quoting from the **Brunonian**, November 7, 1891). This delivery breakthrough suited Gordon's evangelistic gift which operated both publicly and individually. Like Brengle he was very comfortable in small groups and with individuals as well as before large groups.

Chapter 3. A. J. Gordon--(1836-1895)

spring of 1885, Gordon spoke on the Boston Commons. He was willing to be arrested in order that he could appeal the case to the supreme court on the basis of denying freedom of speech and religious liberty. Gordon was whole heartedly backed by his congregation in taking this stand. E. Gordon describes it simply though from a biased viewpoint.

> For the simplest, devoutest, and most peaceful preaching of the word of the "Son of man" on Boston Common Dr. Gordon was summoned to court and fined by the same city government... (E. Gordon 1896:117).

Two major things resulted from a series of incidents of which this was a part. One, the city government, while not rescinding the law, became more lenient in issuing permits where before they had discriminated against Protestants in particular. Two, the New England Evangelistic Association, was formed as a group that would advocate for evangelistic freedom of speech.[40] One can not wonder at the grass roots evangelism that flowed out of this church, when a pastor models so passionately for evangelism. One also must admire a leader who will stand on convictions.

Missions Involvement and Influence

Critical incident 2, given as opening illustration 2, concerning Gordon's monumental work to save the Congo Mission occurs about here. This incident was typical of a missionary passion that burned within Gordon throughout all his ministry. His interest in missions included fund raising, giving, training and sending missionaries,[41] speaking at missions conferences (regional, national, and international), writing a book on the Holy Spirit and missions, serving on executive boards of mission organizations (such as the Baptist Missionary Union), helping to engender mission movements,[42] writing for missions periodicals.

He was not only a strong advocate for missions, but was a mission strategist. He had decided values about what mission is, how it operates, and what it is to achieve. Many of his articles for the **Missionary Review of the World** were critiques of mission thought, analysis of missionary movements, and proposals of values that should underlie missions today.

He served on many boards or committees that were involved in missions including: Executive Committee of the American Baptist Missionary Union (ABMU) for 24 years, chairman from 1888-1895. He was on the Home Board of the Massachusetts Baptist Convention. E. Gordon sees this missionary passion and its outworking in Gordon's life as the distinct contribution of his life (E. Gordon 1896:229). In fact, E. Gordon, gives 4 chapters in his book to discussion of missions. I will identify a major value in Gordon's life from his missions involvement.

Typical Founder Contribution--1888, Jewish Mission

As typical of his pioneer bent and his interest in Jewish evangelism let me mention his part in the founding of a Mission to the Jews.

---

[40]Gordon was part of the instigation of this pioneer group. This is typical of his helping to form new organizations, institutions, or movements to promote unique causes.
[41]This involved eventually the founding of a Missionary Training Institute which I will describe later.
[42]Gordon was at Northfield in July of 1886 with the Student Volunteer Movement was begun. He also spoke at a number of their conventions over the next several years.

Chapter 3. A. J. Gordon--(1836-1895)

A work was also begun involving Jewish evangelism. Thiessen says that "a mission in Boston was founded by Dr. E. S. Niles in 1888, in cooperation with Dr. A. J. Gordon." (E. Gordon 1896:106)

By 1890 it had grown and money had been raised for construction.

> Gordon announced in **The Watchword** that:
> Rooms were dedicated on September 30th in the Jewish quarter of Boston at No. 18 Portland St., for the work of preaching Christ to the Jews. This, so far as we aware, is the first station ever opened in our city for this work. It is begun, not because someone has given a fund for this purpose, but because the Word of God, and the present remarkable awakening among God's ancient people, both seem to call for it.
> ...
> By April, 1891, Gordon reports:
> We express our cordial thanks to those who have contributed for carrying on this work. The first Hebrew convert in connection with the mission was recently baptized in the Clarendon Street Church. To the baptismal question "Does thou believe on the Lord Jesus Christ?" he responded in Hebrew, "I believe that Jesus is the Messiah, the Son of God." It was an effecting scene and made a deep impression on the audience (Houghton 1970:106,107 quoting from **The Watchword**).

Typical Founder Contribution--1889, The Missionary Training Institute

Gordon was interested in the Bible Institute movement and saw it as a means of mobilizing Christians to reach out and complete some of the unfinished tasks that churches were not doing. He was an occasional visiting lecturer at the Moody Bible Institute. In 1889 he began his own training institute in Boston. Its name signifies something of its purpose--The Boston Missionary Training School. Its major purpose was to train lay workers who would go on the mission field (home or abroad).

The school provided Biblical and practical instruction which was primarily functional, spiritual, and oriented to shaping character and getting people on the field who might not otherwise have made it. There was denominational opposition. It was labeled as a short cut method to the ministry, a training which lacked depth, and too premillenarium in its teaching, etc.

Gordon was interested in getting people trained and on to the mission field. Seminaries were not turning out missionaries. Many lay workers with a call of God on their lives would never go to seminary. But they might be able to do the missionary institute training and proceed on the field. The need was great. People who knew their Bibles and had experience in life with a trade frequently made the best missionaries in rugged pioneer places. And there were women as well as men who felt the call of God on their lives. The school, right from the first, trained women as well as men. He was its President until he died in 1895. How did it do?

> In the month of June in 1895, there was given the following report of the activities of the school's alumni.
> And as we look over the lists of those who have been in the School in the past years, we can discern about one hundred who may well be reckoned as such living epistles. Of these, twenty-five have gone to foreign shores, and...the large majority are faithfully heralding the good news in the far-off places of the earth--in Africa, India, China, Korea, Japan, and the West Indies. Fifteen are in the ministry in this country mostly efficient pastors. A few of these took some advanced study in other institutions, but most of them went direct from us into the work. Twenty others are in home-mission, city-mission and rescue work of various grades, from chapel-car management in the far West and teaching in southern schools to parish visitation and slum work in our

Chapter 3. A. J. Gordon--(1836-1895)   page 101

large cities. A noble army of about twenty-five are in evangelistic work, mostly in the destitute regions of northern New England. In apparent results, this is perhaps the most marked work that our students have engaged in. Hardened and neglected communities have been penetrated, and converts are reckoned by the hundreds...Fifteen others are still studying in institutions of higher intellectual grade; but gratefully remembering the scriptural basis and spiritual uplift which they received when with us; as one of them writes, that he feels "that it was a good thing to have come to us first to get something to live by while studying elsewhere." (Houghton 1970:209,210 quoting the Gordon Missionary Training School).[43]

Summary of Flagship Ministry

Let me summarize. I have stated that Gordon built a flagship ministry, that is, a church whose resources were large and whose ministry was full orbed and which influenced other churches to emulate it. In addition to church growth, some of the manifestations of a flagship church are captured by Houghton who summarizes 25 years of ministry by Gordon. He is quoting from the *Clarendon Light*, the church newsletter of 1894.

> At the end of his ministry, Gordon left Clarendon Street Church a spiritually aggressive and evangelistic work. Whereas membership of the church when Gordon came in 1869 was 358 members; he left it twenty-five years later with 1,083 members. In 1869 there were 4 baptisms; in 1894 there were 41 baptisms. In 1869 the church supported 1 foreign missionary; in 1894 it supported 12 missionaries. In 1869 the church supported 1 evangelist; in 1894 it supported 12 evangelists. In 1869 the church's extension work included a colored mission, a young peoples' society with 60 in attendance, and a ladies' benevolent circle; in 1894 its extension work included the Ebenezer Baptist Church (the former colored mission) with 200 members and property worth $25,000, a young peoples' society (Christian Endeavor) with 130 members active in the following ministries: Meetings in the Home for the Aged, services at the Massachusetts Home for Intemperate Women, services at car stables, services at wharves, services at lodging houses, services at Meonah Mission, services on Boston Common, Jewish work, Messervey's Mission at Ashland Place, "Farther Lights" Mission Band, Boys' Mission Band, Kings' Daughters, Junior young peoples' group, and Boys' Brigade. Other church activities in 1894 included the Chinese Sunday School, a Chinese Y.M.C.A., the ladies' benevolent circle, a Woman's Foreign Missionary Society, a Woman's Home Missionary Society, support of the Boston Missionary Training School with 140 students, the Pitts St. Mission, Washington Street Rescue Mission, and the Redeemed Men's meetings (Houghton 1970: 103,104).

Certainly there was lots of activity. But was it quality activity? What about the spiritual tone? Listen to Gordon's own appraisal in 1890.

> With regard to the active ministry of the church's young people, Gordon stated in 1890: As I go to the church at nine o'clock on Lord's day morning to get ready for the services of the day, I generally find a company of from twenty to thirty young men and women on their knees in the vestry, seeking strength from the Lord for the morning's work. These soon separate into companies, and go forth to carry the gospel to such as are rarely, if ever, found inside a church. One band goes to the car-stables, where the conductors and drivers are congregated, getting ready for the day's work on the horse-railroad, work which offers no opportunity for Sabbath rest or for hearing the Word in the house of God. By the singing of the young men and women their attention is arrested; they hear the gospel from these earnest Christians; often their hearts are opened to receive the Word, and not a few of them have been won to Christ. Other bands go to the

---

[43] Shortly after Gordon's death the name was changed to honor him, its first president. Dr. A. T. Pierson became its next president.

Chapter 3. A. J. Gordon--(1836-1895)

> wharves, where are found the sailors on board their ships, and a nameless crowd of loungers hanging about the dock. Here again the gospel is preached by these young Christians, and though the congregation seems unpromising, surprising results are sometimes witnessed. One of the young men reports that on a recent Sunday he saw no less than seven of these wharf-listeners so brought under the power of the Spirit that before the services ended they were on their knees in tears, crying to God for mercy. The leader of the service informs me that during the past year he took the names of seventy who gave credible evidence of conversion, in connection with this work at the docks (Houghton 1970:104,105).

This is a mighty tribute to Uncle John Vassar's ministry of almost twenty years ago. Note also the impact of Gordon's mission passion as given in his statement assessing only one facet of mission effort.

> With regard to missions, Gordon is also able to say in 1890 "that there are three New England states in each of which the combined contributions of all the Baptist churches for Foreign Missions last year were less than that of this single church." (Houghton 1970:105)

Other ministries out of this Flagship Ministry included a Chinese Sunday School begun in 1884, which grew to over 200 by 1894 and was supporting 3 Chinese pastors in China. There was also a Jewish Mission Board founded for evangelism among Jews in 1888.

In addition to sodality ministries flowing from the church there was the widespread ministry of A. J. Gordon himself. He was a public rhetorician of widely recognized reputation.[44] I will reserve my comments on this to the section when I talk about his ultimate contribution as a public rhetorician. He also served on numerous boards. For example he was a trustee of Brown University from 1874 till his death. He was a trustee of Newton Theological Institution from 1868 until his death. He was not only on these boards, but an active participant on them.

Houghton gives an appropriate closing assessment honoring this great man of God, a person of integrity and values, who achieved much. I close this biographical segment with this tribute.

> One cannot help but be impressed when Gordon's ministry in the city of Boston is reviewed. Entering a downtown church which contained elements of worldliness and formalism, the young preacher sought the benediction of God and ended his ministry there twenty-five years later with an active pastoral and evangelistic ministry which reached throughout the laity. Thus, upon his death, it could be written:
> For twenty-five years he stood in the heart of Boston as the pastor of one of its most influential and successful churches, a church which under his ministry has become conspicuous for its spiritual power, its philanthropic work, and its missionary zeal. No church in Boston has been its superior as a center of healthy spiritual life, and no church in our denomination in the world has equaled it in the extent of its devotion to ministerial education and Christian missions (Houghton 1970:126).

---

[44]*Public Rhetorician* is a term used to describe someone whose dominant ultimate contribution, that is, a major legacy, or achievement for which the person is remembered, focuses on a public ministry usually to large groups. Of the eight, five stand out as public rhetoricians: Simeon, Gordon, Brengle, Morgan, and Maxwell. Perhaps McQuilkin should be added too. Brengle and Morgan more so than others since they spent much of their focused ministry exclusively given over to public rhetorician ministries. I will say more about Gordon's public rhetorician role when I speak of communication values.

Chapter 3. A. J. Gordon--(1836-1895)

Critical Incidents Identified, and/or Explained

Critical incidents are shaping activities which can affect values relating to all three types of formations--spiritual (leadership character), ministerial (leadership skills) and strategic (total direction in life and ministry, leadership vision). There is a sense in which many, many incidents in a leader's life affect values. But from that large identifiable number a few should be highlighted and recognized as very significant. Here is a list of these that I have so identified from the materials that were available to me. Table 3-1 indicates these. I number them for convenience of referencing later when I comment on them.

Table 3-1 Listing Of Some Critical Incidents In Gordon's Life

Incident(s) Name	Age	Formational Type Dealing With Basic Value/Thrust
1. Early Destiny Heritage and Call (see pages 81,82)	0-16	Strategic--Godly heritage. Parents give prophetic destiny name. Gordon has growing conviction of ministry. He makes a public leadership committal. He is affirmed in his own church and preaches in it as a lad of 16. He deliberately sets forth a plan of education preparing for ministry. This is in a time when few attended university. Apparently none of his heritage did. This is a major focal factor.
2. Call To Jamaica Plain-- Step-By-Step Guidance (see page 86)	27	Strategic--Gordon learned an important personal value of career guidance. It is as he ministers that God will clarify the next step. Guidance is step-by-step. Minister at what God gives you now; He will open the next thing up. This is a focal value and a focal factor.
3. Pressed To Clarendon-- Providentially Challenged (see page 87)	33	Strategic, Spiritual--Gordon experiences the next step in guidance--to move to a nearby city church in Boston, the elite of the denomination, but nominal in its worship and ministry. He responds to this focal factor finally after two years of pressure from the church (but sovereignly in terms of influence-mix and faith challenges). This places him in a locale and prestigious church which if he can turn into a live evangelical church will allow him to reach his potential and accomplish God-directed achievements.
4. Opposition to Changes (see pages 88,89)	33ff	Ministerial, Strategic--Even when people say they will change it does not mean they want to. Gordon's changes were opposed. He learned a major change value: Change always takes longer than you think even when you think it will take longer than you think. He moved from a tactical approach to change to a strategic one. Some of the changes (removal of pew rental as means of income to church) took over 20 years. But Gordon backed off pushing for immediate changes; he modeled, patiently taught, and waited for the changes to come, which they did. This teaches a number of focal values.

Chapter 3. A. J. Gordon--(1836-1895)

Table 3-1 Listing Of Some Critical Incidents In Gordon's Life continued

Incident(s) Name	Age	Formational Type Dealing With Basic Value/Thrust
5. Ministry Flows Out of Being--Spiritual Formation A Priority (see pages 89-91))	33,34	Spiritual--Gordon, in the midst of tough sledding sees the importance (perhaps is driven to) grow in his spiritual life. This focal value leads him to spend time with historical mentors and uses literary processing as well as lateral mentors to shape his inner life. This on-going process enables with spiritual resources to meet tough challenges of leadership in a resistant church.
6. The Dream/ When Christ Came To Church (see pages 77-79)	36	Spiritual, Ministerial--The mystical focal value taught that the most important thing about the church is not innovations, not changes that will make it more effective, but that Christ is there. What a leader does must first of all please Him and be in accord with what He wants
7. Uncle John Vassar-- Revival's Foundations (see pages 91,92)	36-41	Ministerial, Strategic--Gordon has a mentor coach in evangelism who lays the foundations for the revival that is to come. He learns the importance of having a church centered on soul-winning. He sees the ministry of intercession, learns visitation methods and how to talk to people to open their hearts to the Gospel. These focal values will hereafter spur an evangelistic thrust as part of his church.
8. Revival Power--God Breaks through in Boston--Moody's Campaign (see page 92)	41	Ministerial, Strategic--Gordon sees God unleash His power in non-receptive Boston. He sees that God will bless a ministry that is centered on reaching people. Gordon credits this revival with bringing about a spiritual transformation in his congregation which allowed the changes that he had longed for. This turning point signals the building of a Flagship Ministry. Powerful focal values.
9. A Burdensome Problem/ The Industrial Home Faith Challenge (see pages 93,94)	44ff	Spiritual, Ministerial--A sodality ministry out of the church to reach alcoholics and down and outers, The Industrial Home, falls back on Gordon's care, time-after-time. He retreats into isolation and prays to God to solve the problem. God's answer is unexpected, the recluse who wills property and money to stabilize the work. An important faith value emerges in Gordon. Practical aspects of ministry must be brought to the Lord for His work in them. Involves a powerful focal value.
10. Appropriation of the Holy Spirit (for life power and gifted power) (see pages 94,95)	44?	Spiritual, Strategic--Gordon has a simple, second work beyond salvation experience, in which he appropriates the Holy Spirit (His sealing, filling, and anointing for ministry). Significant focal value.

Chapter 3. A. J. Gordon--(1836-1895)   page 105

Table 3-1 Listing Of Some Critical Incidents In Gordon's Life continued

Incident(s) Name	Age	Formational Type Dealing With Basic Value/Thrust
11. Linked to Broader Audience; Moody Sponsors (see page 97)	46	Ministerial, Strategic--In this focal factor, Moody sponsors Gordon in a conference ministry to expand his sphere of influence well beyond just Clarendon Street Church. Gordon sees the power in such a ministry (a focal value--ministry insight).
12. The Belgian Congo-- A Missions Passion (see pages 79,80)	48	Strategic--Missions ventures are vital to local churches. Our investment, financial wise, shows our commitment to missions. Designated giving must be honored or not accepted--corporate integrity is involved. Represents a focal value and focal factor.
13. Arrested in Boston Commons Incident (see pages 98,99)	49	Strategic--Public stands for Christ must be made. Refusal of granting speaking permits for open air evangelism was unjust. Gordon takes a stand. This deeply imbeds a focal value.
14. Prophetic Value (no page given)	50	Ministerial, Strategic--Gordon participated in international prophetic conferences and took a stand for pre-millennialism. This was also part of his motivation for missions. His interest in prophecy and its impact on present living and missions dates well before this age but I list it here because he took such strong public stands on it here. A focal value.

In analyzing the critical incidents from a perspective of focal issues it seems that Gordon first experienced God's focusing activity toward a role--that of the pastorate and particularly introducing people to the Gospel. He next felt God's burden for certain issues which led to at least two major life purposes--missions, home and foreign, as a major responsibility of the local church and clarifying prophecy in order to alert the church to be ready for the return of Christ and as a stimulus to missions. Finally, ultimate contributions, some implicit and some explicit, begin to emerge as Gordon saw end results that flowed out of his role and purposes.

Incidents 1, 2, 3 and 11 dominantly deal with God's shaping activity concerning the role. Incident 1 drew Gordon to the pastoral role--though a simple concept of it. It was to a broader role than just a simple role of a pastor in a small local church. Incidents 2 and 3 expanded his view of the role. Incident 11 showed the breadth of ministry that a pastor of a prestigious church could have outside the church. It involved a large sphere of influence, ministries within and outside the local church. It involved organizing new missions and other activities. It involved stabilizing organizations. It involved promoting missions. It was not a simple pastorate but a complex one.

A number of incidents shaped Christian character and made Gordon a leader with a sound spiritual base and from whom would come spiritual authority. Incident 5, typical of these shaping activities, showed Gordon's sensitivity to spirituality and some resources for getting help to develop along the lines of that sensitivity. He quickly saw the empowerment that could come through historical mentoring and through literary processing. He instinctively knew that ministry flows out of being and he was drawn to

God for shaping of that inner being. He further deepens his relationship with God in the faith challenge over the *Industrial Home*, incident 9. This fundamental insight, to get alone with God and in prayer learn to trust him for crucial ministry burdens was fundamental to his ministry of seeing a Flagship Church emerge. Always after that shaping incident he could respond to faith challenges and believe God for them. His *appropriation of the Holy Spirit* for power in his life, incident 10, was for him a simple act of faith in obedience to what he was seeing in the Scriptures about the Holy Spirit. Not only did he walk in victory in his personal life but he began to minister with gifted power.

Two mentors helped Gordon learn ministry skills. They imparting values. One connected him to a greater sphere of influence. *Uncle John Vassar*, incident 7, imparted skills, values, and a burden for the lost. He deeply encouraged Gordon in his spiritual gift of evangelism. He showed that winning of souls involved spiritual warfare at the intercessory level. He demonstrated the hard work involved as he faithfully plodded and confronted people with the Gospel in his visitation evangelism. His early coaching shaped foundational values. He expected God to work, even in a non-receptive field. His faith paid dividends. When Moody came, the gates opened up. Moody demonstrated gifted power for Gordon. A Holy Spirit empowered ministry brought breakthroughs. The Gospel changed lives. The *Revival Power*, Incident 8, was key to bringing about the vision of a changed Clarendon Street Church. A demonstration of God's power often does more to bring about a paradigm shift toward faith than 1000s of words.

More so than usual, the larger majority of these incidents concentrate on imparting focal values, key ideas that will hold up life purposes rather than directing toward the focal issues of major role, unique methodology, or ultimate contributions. Incident 4, *Opposition To Changes*, will give Gordon perspective not only for changing a large church, but for bringing renewal changes to the larger body of Christ. He learns patience about bringing change. This conditions him to deal with difficulties, criticism, cynicism and opposition. These values learned early on in Clarendon Street will serve him well when he moves toward renewal of the larger Church toward the Hope of Christ's return or the training of missionaries in a Bible Institute. Incident 12, *The Belgian Congo--A Missions Passion*, simply reflects values about missions that had long been a part of Gordon. "We need the Belgian Congo Mission as much as they need us." This statement shows how much Gordon saw that missions minded churches were churches that God blessed. They catch the passion on His heart. Incident 14, *Prophetic Value*, shows an inner passion that had already existed to be alert to Christ's return. This value of being ready and of promoting holy living as we wait was also part of the motivating factor for Gordon's mission passion.

Three of the incidents point to paradigm shifts. Incident 8, *Revival Power*, changed Gordon's expectations for God's working through him and in his situation. His *Appropriation of the Holy Spirit*, incident 10, so simply done and with such a receptive faith, brought with it an experiential paradigm shift following the volitional one. But it is Incident 6, *When Christ Came To Church--The Dream*, that was the foundational paradigm shift, that paved the way for Gordon's broad based effective ministry. This encounter with Christ and its result, a desire to please Him in all things and to acknowledge His powerful and influential presence, was the prime focal incident that affected the development of Gordon's life.

Values And Critical Values

With Gordon I want to list what I think are ten critical values which changed his life and/or ministry fundamentally. Table 3-2 contains these values.

Chapter 3. A. J. Gordon--(1836-1895)

Table 3-2: Critical Values For A. J. Gordon

Value	Name	Explanation
1	Ultimate Motivation	A Christian leader must first of all please Jesus Christ in his/her ministry and recognize that Jesus is present in all ministry.
2	Forward Looking	A Christian leader must expectantly await the Lord's return with a conviction that affects personal conduct and evaluation of ministry.
3	Effective Outreach	A primary reason for local church existence is reconciling lost people to God through Jesus Christ. Therefore, evangelism in all its various forms must be a vital priority and people must be released into evangelistic ministries. Evangelism is caught from models.
4	Missions	The Evangelistic Mandate to reach the world applies to local churches--they must be a vital part in that program in whatever way possible. God blesses churches which participate in world mission.
5.	Training	Where needs are great, as pioneer missionary fields, training should be designed as practical as possible and to impart character, give basic Bible habits and foundational understanding, stress the task, and release people to these tasks in as short a time as possible. Lay people so trained can impact the world for Christ. Women, who are gifted by God, as well as men, so gifted, should be released and sponsored into leadership roles for accomplishing the great task of the evangelistic mandate at home and abroad.[45]
6.	Spiritual Formation	A Christian leader must guard his/her personal relationship with God. Inner life growth should be a constant expectancy. Many resources are available including historical models, contemporary models and accountability relationships with fellow leaders.
7.	Social Gospel	The Gospel affects all of life. A leader must from time-to-time take risks to apply the Gospel to societies' problems, even if standing on that conviction brings legal ramifications.
8.	Faith Challenge	A leader who wants to be used of God to maximum potential must be sensitive to God's voice in problems and opportunities and learn to trust God, taking the risks necessary to make that trust vital and real, and see God work. Such trust will bring expansion and development to that leader.
9	Jewish Concern	A church must be concerned for the salvation of the Jews and for God's working out his purposes for the Jews in history. Such a church will be blessed of God.
10.	Success and Problems	Success always brings with it problems. Part of the success involves responsibly dealing with the problems. Leaders must be conditioned to see this as normal. That's part of being a leader.

---

[45]Gordon's Biblical beliefs on women in leadership were way ahead of his times and even challenge us.

Chapter 3. A. J. Gordon--(1836-1895)

Ministry Insights, Lessons, and General Values

The most important lesson from Gordon's life came from his *dream* incident. The sensed presence of Christ in ministry and the ultimate motivation of pleasing Christ dominated his standards of evaluating ministry. Gifted people have many motivations for accomplishing what they do. None are so important as this one. None are so revolutionary. It is a simple lesson on the one hand but if it really penetrates beyond the cognitive and moves through the affect to the experiential it will change ministry.

A second major lesson to be drawn from Gordon's life flows from his guidance value. *Guidance is a step-by-step matter. Be obedient in the things at hand. If done, if I am living up to the light I have, I can expect the next step to open up in God's timing.* Gordon was not an ambitious person. He simply followed God and obeyed in each ministry situation. Yet God used him greatly. He leaves behind more ultimate contributions than any other single leader studied in this book. We should see then that the goal is not accomplishment, that is a by-product. The goal is perceptive obedience. That should not, however, keep us from making wise decisions that lead to roles and achievements for which we are gifted and prepared. It should, however, caution us to make sure our ambition is Holy Ambition.

Gordon, probably as well if not better, than any other leader studied in this book emphasizes the *conviction* characteristic of finishing well. We do well to emulate him in this. His believed the Bible was the authoritative efficacious Word of God. He took public stands on important issues. He had strong convictions about women in ministry, the return of Christ, and the importance of missions. These convictions helped make him the great leader he was. He lived this major lesson.

TRUTH IS LIVED OUT IN THEIR LIVES SO THAT CONVICTIONS AND PROMISES OF GOD ARE SEEN TO BE REAL.

Quotable Quotes

The best prayer-book is a map of the world (E. Gordon 1896:233).

I prefer a little man with a great gospel to a great man with a little gospel (E. Gordon 1896:264).

To electrify a hearer is one thing; to bring a hearer prostrate at the feet of Jesus, quite another (E. Gordon 1896:284).

In all these things we are more than conquerors. How? Plainly thus. The man who is victorious through victory is a conqueror; but he who is victorious through defeat is more than conqueror (E. Gordon 1896:293).

The uplifted gaze without the outstretched hands tends to make one visionary; the outstretched hands without the upward look tend to make one weary (E. Gordon 1896:264).

When men get careless and easy-going in their opinions they drift into what is called liberalism as inevitably as water runs downhill. You never find men backsliding into orthodoxy (E. Gordon 1896:264).

The promises of God are certain, but they do not mature in ninety days. (Gordon 1893d:322)

Chapter 3. A. J. Gordon--(1836-1895)

Contributions

This chapter contributes to the general field of leadership development in the following ways:

1. It portrays an above average leader who accomplished great things for God in a relatively short life, not because he was ambitious, but because he held so many values close to God's heart.
2. It shows how God, in a step-by-step manner, can gradually adapt a pastoral role to that of a convergent role.
3. It shows a leader who had three major life purposes: apply the Gospel effectively in a church situation so as to impact for God, teach and influence the present Christian generation to look forward with joyous anticipation to the Lord's return, mobilize churches and church leadership to the cause of world missions.
4. It depicts a leader who has contributions in all 12 prime types.
5. It exposes a prime motivational value in ministry: the pleasing of an always present Lord in our ministry.

What were Gordon's contributions? We are interested in both specific/ unique contributions and his ultimate contributions. His ultimate contribution set is given in pictorial form in the following diagram.[46] It is a complicated diagram. For Gordon is the most versatile and balanced productive leader in terms of the prime contribution types. He represents all of the prime types. I follow that then by giving some of his specific contributions to the cause of Christ. Gordon is unique in that he contributed in so many of the prime types of ultimate contributions.

---

[46]The diagram which describes his ultimate contributions in pictorial form is called a Venn Diagram. See Appendix F for an explanation of how to read Venn diagrams.

Chapter 3. A. J. Gordon--(1836-1895)

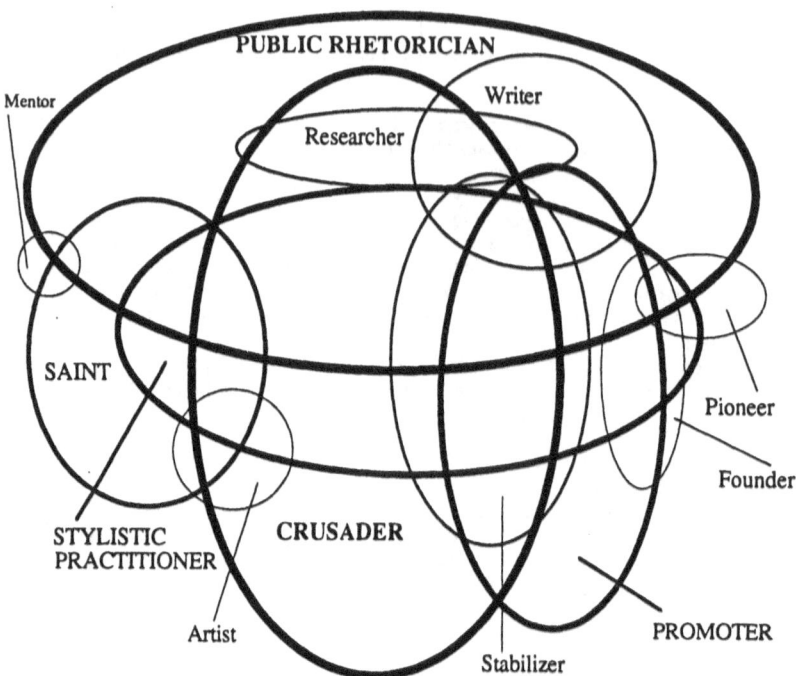

Gordon was a **Public Rhetorician**. This is the largest category and dominates his ultimate contributions. Gordon was a great orator. This ability was developed over the years. He was a large man with a commanding presence in the pulpit and a penetrating eye contact with his audiences. His voice (which was not always so) was soft and melodic yet carried. He was able to engage an audience and hold its attention during his entire address. He usually spoke without notes (though like Morgan was always prepared first). He was Bible centered in his messages. Like Morgan who was to come after him he preferred not to defend the Bible but to use it and believe in its power to accomplish what it claimed. Gordon's philosophy of preaching contained at least 5 important planks (adapted from Houghton 1970:121-125):

1. **Communicate to the Individual**--If you can't communicate with one you can't communicate with a large group.
2. **Purpose of Sermon--To Reach the Heart of the Listener**
   Sermons should not detract from their purpose by calling attention to the speaker.
3. **Illustrate Well.** His four rules for illustration. Use directly without an introduction. Don't use elaborate extended illustration. Illustrations should be easy to understand. Be open to Spirit prompted illustrations, unplanned ones, which emerge as you communicate.[47]

---

[47]Houghton (1970:123) quotes from Gordon's writing in the **Northfield Echoes** of 1894 a wonderful word of knowledge, impromptu, Spirit-led example of this fourth rule. It was the second Sunday in last February. I was preaching, and it occurred to me to illustrate what I was saying by an anecdote which I had

Chapter 3. A. J. Gordon--(1836-1895)   page 111

4. **Let The Bible Speak for Itself.** Don't defend it; use it.
5. **Focus on Spiritual Matters--Biblical Themes.**

Gordon was a strong **Crusader** and **Promoter**. I am going to combine these two categories since there is a high degree of overlap. Gordon's crusading zeal for convictions he held concerning the Gospel and social issues of his time have already been mentioned. But this same burning spirit spilled over in his efforts at missions. He promoted the cause of missions with a crusader zeal. His son captures this crusader/ promoter zeal when he describes why he wrote the biography of his father. This high tribute pulsates with mission fervor.

> ...Were it not for the fact that he [Gordon] was one of the very foremost figures of his day in America in the agitation for a world-wide propaganda of Christianity, his career would not, perhaps, be of such distinction as to require particular record. He would be remembered as a useful pastor, a gifted preacher, a friend of the poor, a man of exalted saintliness. His labors, however, in behalf of missions were, during the last decade of his life, incessant; they constituted his absorbing interest, his inspiring enthusiasm. In journeyings often, in labors of missionary tours, in labors of conventions, in labors of committees, as coeditor of the leading American missionary review, as author of missionary literature, as pastor of a church unsurpassed in missionary efforts, as the executive head of the denominational missionary organization, as founder of a training school for missionaries, he toiled to the full measure of his strength. Even after his death--suggestive, indeed, of faithfulness to the end! --there was found in his ulster pocket an appeal in behalf of the little blind girls of Canton who live in the slavery of enforced immorality! (E. Gordon 1896:228,229).

He was a **Stylistic Practitioner**. He modeled a pastoral role and developed a type of church that set an ideal for pastors of his denomination and indeed beyond it. Churches can have a variety of ministries. They can train and release numerous lay people into ministry. They can start institutions and organizations for getting needed jobs done. Gordon's 25 years at Clarendon Street Church brought changes which took it to a Flagship Church--a model for city churches which want to be a shining beacon for what God can do to a committed corporate group of people.

Gordon was a **Saint**. His warm relationship with God, his familiarity with powerful saints of old, his focus on worship, and his continual practices of spiritual disciplines throughout his life to maintain his relationship with God signal him as a **Saint**. His was a life that demonstrated the fruit of the Spirit. He merged life power and gifted power so that the ministry of the Spirit flowed through him. Being and doing were equally important in his life.

---

read long ago and had quite forgotten, until I went into the church that morning." I said, "Now sinner, you have been saying in your heart, 'O preacher, you have been urging me to believe in order to be saved, but I cannot believe; you have told me to accept Christ, I cannot accept Him; my faith is so lame, my hands are so weak that I cannot take hold.'" I said, "If that is so, just tell Jesus that you cannot take hold of Him and He will take hold of you," and this story had come into my mind. Professor Blaikie of Edinburgh called upon a student to recite. The student held his book before him in his left hand. The professor said, "Take your book in your right hand." He blushed and stammered, and went on reading, and then the professor thundered at him, "Young man, don't you know manners? Take your book in your right hand." Then the young man lifted up the stump of his right arm and said, "I have no right hand, Professor." The class was greatly moved and the professor came and put his arms around that young man and begged his pardon. "So," I said, "if you cannot take hold of Jesus Christ, He will take hold of you and lift you up." I finished, and a young man rose up, and lifted up the stump of his arm and said, "I am that very young man." I brought him into the pulpit, and with the mutilated right arm he enforced all I had been saying. How did that illustration happen to flash into my mind that morning? The impression of the truth and force of what I had been saying about being taken hold of when we cannot take hold, was tremendous."

Chapter 3. A. J. Gordon--(1836-1895)

Gordon was a **Stabilizer**. This ultimate contribution has to do with helping organizations become more effective in managing their affairs, effectively carrying out their missions, and surviving. Gordon served on boards. He salvaged missions. He recruited leadership to keep some organizations going. He build his own church into a Flagship church, a many faceted and complex operation which effectively carried out ministry. He was able to raise finances for many of his *stabilizing* activities.

He was a **Writer**. Houghton describes him as a prolific writer and attributes sixteen books to Gordon (three of these co-authored). His books include the following grouped in terms of Houghton's classes (Houghton 1970:15):

I. Music and Worship (4):
  1. Congregational Worship,
  2. The Service of Song for Baptist Churches (with S. L. Caldwell),
  3. The Vestry Hymn and Tune Book,
  4. The Coronation Hymnal (with A. T. Pierson).

II. The Person and Work of Christ (3):
  1. In Christ,
  2. The Twofold Life,
  3. The First Thing in the World.

III. Prophecy (2)
  1. Risen With Christ,
  2. Ecce Venit

IV. The Person and Work of the Holy Spirit (3):
  1. The Ministry of Healing,
  2. The Ministry of the Spirit
  3. The Holy Spirit in Missions

V. Sermons (3):
  1. Grace and Glory
  2. Yet Speaking
  3. Great Pulpit Masters

6. Spiritual Autobiography (1):
  1. How Christ Came to Church (with A. T. Pierson).

In addition to his books he edited a monthly journal, **The Watchword** for 17 years (1878-1895). This journal promoted evangelical writing dealing with fundamentals of the faith written from an experimental standpoint rather than a technical academic standpoint. It also promoted the second coming, that is the personal re-appearing of the Lord from heaven and stressed orthopraxic concerns--focusing on love. Over the years Gordon contributed at least 80 articles, editorials, book reviews and/or reports. Gordon also served as a contributor to or on the editorial boards of **The Christian Herald, Signs of Our Times, The Missionary Review of the World.** He also wrote for **The Baptist Missionary Magazine, The Baptist Quarterly, The Watchman, The Sunday School Times, Red Oak Herald, The Christian Herald and Signs of Our Times, The Episcopal Recorder, The Expository Times, The Homiletic Review, The Presbyterian Review.** He published 100s of articles, some news articles, and some book reviews. He also published at least nine pamphlets on a variety of subjects. His articles include many on missions, many on prophetic themes,

Chapter 3. A. J. Gordon--(1836-1895)   page 113

some sermons, the Holy Spirit, some biographical, many on various aspects of the Christian life, some on training, some on preaching, fundamental Bible doctrines and others.

He was a **Researcher**. Research was not his primary interest but he researched missionary subjects, many of the crusader topics he advocated, and some of the historical subjects he wrote on. His research is most evident in his journal articles and in his books on the Holy Spirit. He was well read.

He merged the **Founder** and **Pioneer** contributions. Founders begin organizations. They see a need for them and start them. They may or may not continue with them. **Pioneers** usually start new works--sometimes uniquely new, frequently church planters are of this type. Gordon did both of these. Where an organization was needed he found a way to do it or cooperate with others to bring it in to existence. His Jewish Mission was this sort. A number of evangelistic ministries connected with his Flagship Ministry were pioneer types. Organizations did not necessarily arise from them. But new works were engendered, leaders released and ministry accomplished.

Gordon was an **Artist**. His creative talent expressed itself in two ways--church music and poetry. In addition to the hymnals already mentioned under a writing contribution, Gordon wrote both music and lyrics for hymns. Houghton (1970:85) lists 12 hymns (words only), 4 hymns (music), and 1 with both hymn and music. These were published hymns. Probably many others were written. Two are still extant today for which he wrote the music--*My Jesus, I Love Thee* and *In Tenderness He sought Me*.[48] Gordon also wrote poems and since he was on editorial boards was able to get them included from time-to-time.[49] This aspect of his being highly influenced his desire to get his congregation meaningfully involved in worship singing rather than delegate it to paid quartets and choir soloist.

Gordon was less explicit about this contribution, that of a **Mentor**. Public rhetoricians frequently do not have much in the way of individual relationships, particularly relational empowerment with individuals. And that is the general case with Gordon. Gordon, however, operated as a mentor counselor in a number of ways. One was in his relationships with individuals who sought him out for advice. His godly wisdom carried much weight because of respect for his spirituality and experience with God. He also carried on an extensive correspondence work. His letters were frequently laced with two things, encouragement and godly advice--both part of the empowerment repertoire of mentor counselors. Particularly was this seen in his distance mentoring with missionaries. Missions was a passion with him. He was interested in it in all its facets. His letters were frequently very timely.

> He was, furthermore, constantly writing letters of encouragement to lonely and isolated missionaries...
> When alone in the mountains of Assam, I received from him, **In Christ** and **The Twofold Life** with the autograph and the love of the author on the fly-leaf of each. Words can never tell what these two books were to us in that mountain fastness.

---

[48]Both *My Jesus, I Love Thee* and *In Tenderness He Sought Me* are included in **Great Hymns of the Faith** a fairly widely used hymnal in the 1980s.
[49]For example, see his poem, *Where Art Thou?*, in the October 1979 issue of **The Watchword**.

Chapter 3. A. J. Gordon--(1836-1895)

Gordon's specific contributions are many and include:

1. He helped stop the American Churches' slide into modernism. Houghton credits him with being one of the founders of fundamentalism.
2. He left behind the top church in his denomination, the American Baptist, at the time of his death: a giving church; an evangelistic church; a church that promoted missions; a large church with many resources.
3. He left behind materials, books and articles, which deal with important topics on missions, prophecy, and the ministry of the Holy Spirit.
4. He modeled a focused life which is role based but which developed three life purposes out of the role, and achieved many legacies.
5. He models the validity of the pre-service track of training for entry into ministry showing all its advantages and showing how its disadvantages can be overcome.
6. He founded a number of organizations for carrying on specific ministries, one of which exists today as a powerful training institution.
7. He greatly encouraged four major movements by his participation in them: the Bible Conference movement, the Prophecy movement, the Bible Institute movement, and the World Missions movement.
8. His involvement with leaders from outside his own denomination promoted Christian unity.
9. He finished well.[50]

Overall Lessons from the Life

Three thoughts suggested by Gordon's life should provoke our interest. One concerns long tenure in a locale. Another involves encouragement for change agents. A third, exhorts us to be ready.

His life shows forth the benefits of a long tenure in one place. Where a leader is continually growing, expanding his/her role, and seeing God's hand of blessing on a ministry over the years, there is an accumulation of testimony, a cumulative force for power, accruing to that leader, which will allow tremendous accomplishment beyond expectation in those latter years. We are cautioned, therefore, unless God is clearly leading to a series of short ministries (as in Brengle's case) that we should not make premature departures from ministries because they are hard or not to our liking. Both Simeon and Gordon, though not as tough as Simeon's situation, highlight the importance of going on through a difficult start and persevering until the effects of tenure can be felt. So we should be prepared to hang in there--rather than give up--in order to see God's blessings poured out in years down road.

If we would be change agents, we must be prepared to stay with a situation long enough to see them in. Gordon had about five major changes he wanted to see happen when he first went to Clarendon Street church. They took time. They were opposed. We must be prepared to withstand the psychological effect of resistance to change since that is the normal reaction. We must patiently model, teach, and little-by-little move toward our changes. Many will have to wait till opponents move off the scene. Some of Gordon's 5 changes came within 10 years. The longest took about 23 years. He models for us an

---

[50]His son, E. Gordon (1896) certainly a critic who should know him well, inside and out, writes so highly of his Christian character. Two whole chapters are given over to his personal life. I recommend Chapter XV, A Character Sketch especially for insights into a godly character in the home, in daily life, as well as in ministry. But the whole book is filled with illustrations of his giving, his sacrifices for others, and in general the fruit of a life empowered by the Holy Spirit.

Chapter 3. A. J. Gordon--(1836-1895)

effective change agent in action. If the changes are important enough, then they are important enough to devote enough time to see them come into place.[51]

Gordon died unexpectedly. His life was cut short after 59 years. He contracted an infection in his lungs which led to ramifications and a quick death. He was ready to go in one sense. God seemingly gave him a Word of Knowledge-like premonition.

> On the 27th of December, 1894, Gordon completed the twenty-fifth year of his pastorate in the Clarendon Street Church. The anniversary was observed by his people with appropriate exercises, a reception, and a tea, followed by addresses from his colleagues in the ministry of the city. The eulogy which ordinarily characterizes such occasions was rebutted by him in a brief speech, half humorous, half serious. He distributed the praise heaped on himself to his people and to his "splendid cabinet of deacons," contending that the growth of a tree is due, not to its own excellence, but to the excellence of the soil at its roots, and that his only merit consisted in his staying so long where God had placed him and where conditions were so favorable. He reminded his hearers, on the other hand, of the danger which lay hid in all eulogy of one whose record was not closed, and of the possibility which shadowed himself as well as the great apostle of becoming a castaway on the dark seas of unfaithfulness.
>
> In the evening, while sitting with his wife at home, he took down the "Life of Andrew Bonar," which he had been reading, and, after commenting on the events of the day, opened to these words, saying, "Here is something which just expresses my feelings":
>
> "Last night's jubilee passed over very pleasantly in one way, but was to me at the same time very solemn and humbling. I see in the retrospect so much that was altogether imperfect and so much that was left undone. But it was a great gathering and most hearty on the part of all the friends who came. May the Lord save me from the danger that lurks under praise and laudation of friends. I had no idea that I had so many friends in so many parts, and that the Lord had been pleased to use me in so many ways...The anniversary was carried through in a way that interested the people, but as for myself, when I returned home and sat in the evening alone I felt deep and bitter regret at the thought of my past. I think I felt what is meant by being ashamed before God, as Ezra expresses it. And all this was aggravated by the thought of all the immense kindness of the Lord to me and to mine. I have been thinking to-night that perhaps my next undertaking may be this, appearing at the judgment-seat of Christ when I give an account of my trading with my talents..."
>
> It was a singular suggestion, a strange premonition, as if he had caught a glimpse of the dark cloud on the distant horizon (E. Gordon 1896:367,368).

Gordon's work at Clarendon Street Church was finished after 25 years. It was a good work. It was a completed work in many ways. But his death was unexpected. He finished well because he was living well. We must live today, well, exhibiting the fruit of the Spirit (not hoping that in our old age we will somehow change and be better), knowing that what we are doing today is important, and ready to go. We may not have time to carry out our plans--to adapt a role for a focused life, to carry out some life purpose, or to bring off the achievements we dreamed of. But we always have time to love the Lord, to walk in the Spirit, and to have a daily testimony pleasing to Him.

Implications for a Focused Life

What have we learned from this life that helps us understand a focused life? That is the question I attempt to answer in this section. Of the 12 factors I will comment on 7 which I think were relevant to Gordon's movement toward a focused life.

---

[51]See Clinton (1992) **Bridging Strategies--Leadership Perspectives for Introducing Change** for discussion of change dynamics principles and particularly for time perspectives for bringing in change.

Chapter 3. A. J. Gordon--(1836-1895)

1. Giftedness Development

Gordon's giftedness set is shown below.[52] It is important to note that he, like Brengle, operated evangelistically in large group or small group settings. He continued to use the gift of evangelism all his life. He was particularly good in motivating others into evangelism and helping them develop and be released into effective evangelism. This may be due to the excellent coaching and motivation to development of his own evangelistic gift by Uncle John Vassar. His exhortation gift was identified first and developed via use. His evangelism gift came into play with the forceful example of Uncle John and D. L. Moody. His leadership giftedness took hold in his late 30s and early 40s and became more prominent and effective as he moved through 50.

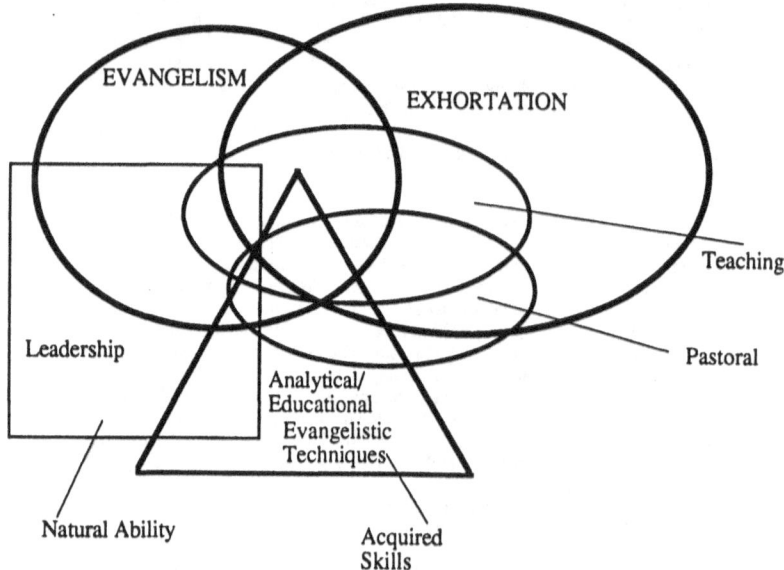

4. Identification Of Major Values That Uniquely Fit One's Ministry

I have listed previously 10 important values that I think greatly contributed to focus in Gordon's life and ministry.

6. Social Base Processing

Marie Hale Gordon was obviously a major support for Gordon. They basically operated in the release pattern. She primarily was responsible for the home base and freed up Gordon to pursue ministry outside the home. She did accompany him on some of his important trips to conference ministry. She also spoke at women's meetings.

---

[52]The diagram which describes his giftedness set (natural abilities, acquired skills and spiritual gifts) in pictorial form is called a Venn Diagram. See Appendix F for an explanation of how to read Venn diagrams.

Chapter 3. A. J. Gordon--(1836-1895)

7. Ultimate Contribution Set

I have previously described Gordon as a very capable and multi-talented person in terms of achievements that will stand as legacies to him. He contributed in all 12 prime types. Some of these contributions were significant and affected his focus in ministry--others were by-products of an effective role with a three-fold life purpose.

11. Paradigm Shifts Which Helped Focus

All three major paradigms helped bring Gordon into his focused ministry: 1. the Moody demonstration of gifted power, 2. the appropriation of the Holy Spirit for power, and 3. the recognition of the living Christ as the evaluator of ministry. It was the third one by far that was more focal.

Where To Go and What To Do For Further Study

The following are important works about Gordon or by Gordon. Glance through my comments about them then read my suggestions for follow-up. These biography entries about Gordon are basically unavailable except when checked out from some Bible College or Seminary Libraries. The dissertation done at Dallas Theological Seminary is available on inter-library loan from them. The articles from the periodicals are usually available in most Bible College or Seminary Libraries. I mention just a few to pique your interest. He did many more articles.

Gordon, A. J.

1892   *Decentralization in Missions* in **Missionary Review of the World.** July 1892, pages 492-496.

Comments: This article, while not negating the work of mission organizations, points out that the primary responsibility for missions can not be centralized in these agencies alone. That responsibility must continue but also be decentralized to churches and the vast labor force in them. Churches and individuals in them must be mobilized--the task is too great for a few mission organizations. He also suggests what happens when churches become involved in missions. He cites three cases of churches really involved: 1 sending out and supporting 350 missionaries over 30 years; one commissioning and maintaining 141 at present; and one sending out 100 in a single year.

1892   *Forerunners of Carey I*, in **Missionary Review of the World.** November 1892, pages 839-843.

Comments: Delves into the men who foreshadowed all the main principles of the coming age of mission as seen in Carey and others. Such greats as John Eliot and Brainerd are covered in this article.

1892   *Forerunners of Carey II*, in **Missionary Review of the World.** December 1892, pages 905-910

Comments: In this article he notes that 1292, 1492, 1792 and 1892 mark epochs in the history of missions. Raymond Lull and others are highlighted.

1893a   *Forerunners of Carey III*, in **Missionary Review of the World.** February 1893, pages 101-104.

Chapter 3. A. J. Gordon--(1836-1895)

Comments: Von Welz is honored in this article.

1893b *The Overflow of Missions* in **Missionary Review of the World.** March 1893, pages 167-172.

Comments: It is interesting that at the turn of the last century there was a great push for mobilizing missionary effort as there is in our time. Commonalties exist: 1. there was a growing tendency for single churches and individual Christians to take up direct missionary work. 2. a wide use of lay workers on foreign fields. He cites the work of A.B. Simpson as an example of a movement raised up for mission work.

1893c *At a Missionary's Grave* in **Missionary Review of the World.** April 1893, pages 269-275.

Comments: Honors David Brainerd, his historical mentor.

1893d *Missionary Memorabilia* in **Missionary Review of the World.** May 1893, pages 321-326.

Comments: Wonderful illustrations and quotes from sacrificial missionaries.

1893e *Education and Missions* in **Missionary Review of the World.** August 1893, pages 584-589.

Comments: He starts this article off with a striking quote. "The only organized opposition which Christianity has yet had to meet has been from the efforts of the Hindu graduates of our universities." Thus he begins his criticism of education as a means of missions. He closes with 5 objections to education as a major mission means to evangelizing people.

1893f *D. L. Moody and His Work* in **Missionary Review of the World.** October 1893, pages 754-758.

Comments: A great perceptive analysis of Moody's giftedness as one way of explaining why he accomplished so much.

1893g *Education and Mission II* in **Missionary Review of the World.** December 1893, pages 881-888.

Comments: He begins this article with this attention getter. The Roman Catholic theory has been: "Bring men into the Church, in order to bring them to Christ." The Protestant theory has been: "Bring men to Christ, in order to bring them into the Church." He closes by discussing the 4 major reasons why some say use education as a means. Finally he gives a three-fold statement which is his advice on the matter.

1894 *Three Weeks with Joseph Rabinowitz* in **Missionary Review of the World,** January 1894, pages 11-17.

Comments: Joseph Rabinowitz was one of the greatest Russian converts to Christianity. He was a hero of Gordon. This article honors him and shows Gordon's interest in mission to Jews.

Chapter 3. A. J. Gordon--(1836-1895)

Gordon also has articles on missions in:

1878-95 **The Watchword.** [He was editor from 1878-95. These were unavailable to me.]

The Baptist Missionary Magazine. [These were unavailable to me.]

Sermons, Addresses, and other articles available at the Archives, Winn Library, Gordon College.

1871-95 *Annual Reports* of the American Baptist Missionary Union also carry information on or by Gordon.

Gordon, A. J. and A. T. Pierson
1896 **How Christ Came to Church--A Spiritual Autobiography** Philadelphia: American Baptist Publication Society.

Comment: A. T. Pierson edited this and published it after Gordon's death.

Gordon, Ernest B.
1896 **Adoniram Judson Gordon: A Biography.** New York: Fleming H. Revell.

Comment: This major biography on A. J. Gordon was done by his son Ernest.

Houghton, George Gerald
1970 **The Contributions of Adoniram Judson Gordon to American Christianity.** Unpublished Th.D. dissertation, Dallas Theological Seminary.

Robert, Dana L.
1987 *The Legacy of Adoniram Judson Gordon* in **International Bulletin of Missionary Research**, October, pages 176-181.

Comment: A quick overview of Gordon and his contribution to Christianity.

Russell, C. Allyn
1985 *Adoniram Judson Gordon: Nineteenth-Century Fundamentalist* in **American Baptist Quarterly.** March 1985, pages 61-89.

Comment: A thorough short review of Gordon from a fair minded critic who is much less conservative than Gordon.

Suggestion: If you want to follow up on Gordon as a historical mentor here is what you can do. Read carefully the chapter I have written. Select out issues to follow up on (quotes to chase down, topics, etc.). Then get E. Gordon's biography from a Bible College or Seminary library and ransack it. Don't read it. Just pick and choose those things you want to follow up on. There are a number of chapters that are worth reading in their entirety. Then get some copies of a number of his articles. Use an article for a devotional time with Gordon. You can expect him to challenge you with an applicational thought from an excellent article. Read it as if he were there talking with you about the issue. Then imagine if you asked him, "What would you say I need from this article?" what he would say. Jot it down. Be blessed!

Chapter 3. A. J. Gordon--(1836-1895)

I. NEW ENGLAND HERITAGE/ DESTINY FOUNDATIONS	II. THOROUGH PREPARATION AND FIRST STEPS IN MINISTRY	III. UNIQUE MINISTRY AT CLARENDON STREET/ INCREASING FRUITFULNESS
1836 1853	1857 1860 1863	1869 1877 1882 1895
Age 17	21 24 27	33
A. Heritage/ Family Influences/ Destiny Foundations (1836-1853)	A. Formal Training At: 1. Brown University-- Classical Education (1857-1860) 2. Newton Theological Institute--Pre-Service Formal Theological Training (1860-1863)	A. Stony Ground/ Reform Begun/ Worship, First Reform (1869-1977)	B. The Turning Point--1877 Moody's Ministry Toward The Flagship (1877-1882)	C. Flagship (1882-1895)
B. Preparatory Training At New London (1853-1857)	B. Informal Training At Jamaica Plain Baptist Church (1863-1869)			

Learning By Doing 5 Major Changes Sought------------>Some Changes   All
The Persistent Call   In------------> Changes
3 Paradigm Shifts:
1. The Dream 2. Evangelistic 3. Life
                   Power   Power

Name--Adoniram Judson
Maria Hale
H. B. Hackett--Mentor Teacher

C1 The Name, The Call
C2 Call To Jamaica Plain
   C3 Pressed To Clarendon
   C4 Opposition To Changes
   C5 Ministry Flows Out of Being
       Spiritual Formation a Priority
       C6 The Dream
       C7 Uncle John Vassar
       C8 Revival Power--Moody
       C9 Burdensome Problem
          C10 Holy Spirit
              Life Power
          C11 Moody Link
          C12 Belgian Congo
          C13 Arrested--
              Boston Commons
          C14 Prophetic Value

Samuel Logan Brengle
(1860-1936)

A consistent life--public and private life in Holy Harmony

Chapter 4. Samuel Logan Brengle (1860-1936)
Public Saint

Remember your former leaders. Think back on how they lived and ministered. Imitate those excellent qualities you see in their lives. For Jesus Christ is the same today, as He was in the past and as He will be in the future. What He did for them He will do for you to inspire and enable your leadership.
Hebrews 13:7,8 (Personal Interpretive Paraphrase)

Let's remember Samuel Logan Brengle, a Christian leader whose inner consistency was on public display, whose life displayed holiness unto the Lord. Let me begin with two focal incidents that display shaping forces at work to fundamentally produce a public rhetorician who lived what he believed.[1]

Opening Illustration 1.
Leadership Committal--The Call,
A Hinge to Destiny, Ambition Harnessed by God

Age 22 (Philippians 3:7)

Let me first give enough background so you can appreciate the incident. Brengle was an ambitious college student at Depauw University. It was a day when oratory flourished. It was an era of great speakers--secular and Christian. Names like Prentiss, Beecher, Phillips, Conkling, Blaine, Hill, Ingersoll were eloquently holding forth in fiery speeches all across the country (Hall 1933:35).[2] He wanted to be a great orator--a great public leader who influenced many. He decided on law as the means for becoming a great orator.

Brengle disciplined himself to study and practice oratory. Early on he began to win speaking awards. He won contests in various state competitions. His ambition was to be a leader in the country. He saw that many political leaders first started as lawyers. He set his goal on that. What better means to use oratory. He joined a prominent fraternity, Delta Kappa Epsilon which had many young men of promise, future prominent leaders in the country. He was a well known and prominent figure on campus.[3] He was known as a talented and ambitious student who knew what he wanted and would most likely get it.

During his college years he was active for Christ, teaching a Sunday School class and leading every one of its members to Christ. And during the several years of college from time-to-time, Brengle would feel inner promptings toward the ministry--remembering the haunting thought of his father having been called to preach, but having drawn back; of his parents having dedicated him to the ministry when he was only a baby; of the fact that

---

[1] *Public Rhetorician* is a term used to describe someone whose dominant ultimate contribution, that is, a major legacy, or achievement for which the person is remembered, focuses on a public ministry usually to large groups. Two public rhetoricians in this book are Brengle and Morgan. I will refer to Morgan often.
[2] These names do not impress us today but these were giants in their day: Prentiss was a great preacher (Wiersbe includes one of his great sermons in his work); Beecher was also a well known American preacher; Phillips was an abolitionist orator; Conkling was a U.S. senator, Blaine an American Statesman, Hill a senator, Ingersoll--a lawyer, lecturer, great orator and exponent of agnosticism.
[3] Hall comments that oratory being what it was then, his activity brought him into the limelight much as college football or basketball stars would be looked to today. Brengle represented his university in various state competitions and was pitted against some of the ablest young men in the midwest (Hall 1933:36).

Chapter 4. Samuel Logan Brengle (1860-1936)

whenever now he heard a preacher expounding the Word it rang in his ears with almost irresistible appeal (Hall 1932: 38). Hall vividly describes the destiny moment when personal ambition went by-the-by and God's unmistakable call blocked Brengle's path and demanded a decision. And He used a less-than-perfect motivation to bring about this moment of focus in Brengle's life, to focus his oratorical ambition in another direction.[4]

> It happened in Providence, Rhode Island, where Delta Kappa Epsilon was having its annual convention. An important matter--one involving the very life of the DePauw chapter--had to be brought before the convention and Brengle, as the chosen delegate from his university, had come half way across the country to attend. In order to solicit the support of other chapters, he had spent considerable time on the way, stopping off to visit many of the leading colleges between Greencastle and Providence.
>
> He was met at his destination by the delegates from a chapter particularly opposed to his, who informed him flatly, "We will fight you to the death." Going to his room in the Narragansett Hotel, Brengle felt the weight of his mission. Never before, he told himself, had he undertaken a task so responsible. His own destiny, the destiny of his fraternity chapter, the very honor of his university, depended, he felt, upon his being able to carry the convention.
>
> Heavily burdened and scarcely able to collect his thoughts for the attempt he had to make to save his chapter, he went out into the street, walked awhile, and then came back to his room where, exasperated by this inexplicable depression, he threw himself upon his knees and besought God to help him win. He seemed, however, to gain nothing by the exercise; his soul was lonely, and within all was dark as night. He rose, went out on the street again, returned, knelt again, prayed again. Still the loneliness, the depression, the darkness. Yet a third time he went out on the street, returned, prayed. While praying this time, the thought of preaching was suddenly presented to his mind. Considering the idea irrelevant he sought impatiently to shake it off--but without success. A tremendous inner battle occupied the following minutes, but when at length he exclaimed aloud, "O Lord, if Thou wilt help me to win this case, I will preach!", the whole room seemed instantly to flame with light.
>
> The next day, his soul bathed in a peculiarly comforting feeling, he went to the convention hall, delivered his speech from the floor, offered his motion, and to his intense surprise the very men who had sworn they would fight him "to the death" rose to support the motion that meant reinstatement and recognition for his chapter. His victory was sweeping and entire. Furthermore, after the session many crowded about him to say that if the convention had not already been organized that speech would have ensured his being elected its president.
>
> ...the die was cast. God had kept His part of the contract made in the Providence hotel. Brengle, too, would keep his.
>
> With his life's work now clear before him, almost feverishly Brengle devoted his time to preparation for the ministry. The careful studying and teaching of his Sunday school lessons during the past four years had helped him. With others of the students, he established a noonday prayer meeting; some of the professors came in to take part; and a

---

[4] The shaping activity interpreting this processing includes *leadership committal* (Clinton 1989:146) an abandonment to God for service in any way He desires. The more clearly the divine involvement in such a shaping process, the more certain it is that the leader will persevere when the pressure times come. This shaping activity was also a destiny process item, called *destiny preparation* (Clinton 1989:103,104), the sense of God's involvement in directing the life. This is one indication foreshadowing what is to come. Cumulative recognition of a number of these process items will build a *sense of destiny* (Clinton 1989:349), an awareness that God's hand is on the leader in a special way. That Brengle was already aware of this was the flashback to his parents dedication of him as a child and his father's regret at not going into ministry, and the inner attraction to public preaching. As well as any of the eight in this book, Brengle illustrates one of the 7 major leadership lessons we have identified, "Effective leaders evince a growing awareness of their sense of destiny." For further study of the shaping activities described in all the footnotes such as this one, see Clinton (1989), **Leadership Emergence Theory**.

Chapter 4. Samuel Logan Brengle (1860-1936)   page 125

tangible satisfying result was that a revival--later to be appraised as one of the greatest ever to shake the university--was born and flourished for months. (Hall 1933:39-41)[5]

Opening Illustration 2.
Character Shaping--A Fundamental Priority to All Ministry
Shiny Black Boots

Age 27   (1 Peter 5:5,6; James 4:10)

Clarence Hall describes a most humiliating ministry task[6] that was pivotal in the life of Brengle. I quote at length so you can feel with Brengle. Brengle is a college graduate, a polished and trained orator, a preacher with circuit experience, an itinerant evangelist and a theological seminary alumnus. He is 27 years old. He has dedicated his life to helping the down and out. He has chosen to go with The Salvation Army--a rugged non-educated group of people, serving in inner-city work. He could have chosen a wealthy city church pastorate. He makes a trip to The Salvation Army headquarters in England to be accepted by them as a worker. That is the background leading to this incident.

> On June 1, 1887, at The Army's International Headquarters in London two men sat in an office, facing each other. Twinkling hazel eyes of Samuel Logan Brengle, twenty-seven, looked deep into piercing grey eyes of William Booth, fifty-eight.
> "General, I have come."
> A moment of silence. No handclasp, no warm words of welcome. An observer would have remarked that the General surveyed his candidate rather coldly, seeing the latter had dropped a promising ministry and had come 3,000 miles to give himself to The Salvation Army. Finally the General spoke:
> "Brengle, you belong to the dangerous classes. You have been your own boss for so long that I don't think you will want to submit to Salvation Army discipline. We are an Army, and we demand obedience."
> "Well, General, I have received the Holy Spirit as my Sanctifier and Guide. I feel He has led me to offer myself to you. Give me a chance."
> After this manner did they thrust and parry--the cultured young preacher of the schools and the gruff and fiery apostle of the world's down-trodden. Two days later, Brengle, in a letter to his bride, described the remainder of the interview:
>> He quoted Scripture to me, paternally advised me not to take any vows upon myself hastily, assuring me that The Army presented only a field for hard work and self-denial, and that the greatest of all must become the servants of all. I managed to get in a few words "edgeways," told him I had never sought a place but once, and that was before I entered the ministry at all, that I knew my only way up to Heaven was by going down to the lowest of the low, and that I wanted to go. That seemed to inspire him with some confidence that I was not wholly dangerous, and grasping my hand, he said, 'God bless

---

[5]This clearly illustrates the *positive testing pattern* (Clinton 1989:352), one of 23 repetitive patterns we have identified in our research on leaders. Frequently, God tests character, as in this case, and then depending on the response either brings remedial training (the negative testing pattern) or expansion if a positive response. Brengle is challenged by God, responds, and God brings expansion, thus confirming the divine affirmation in the processing. In this case, the expansion was the outbreak of revival. Frequently with young leader's the expansion is immediate and easy to connect to the test in order to build the young leader's faith.

[6]A *ministry task* (Clinton 1989:154) is an assignment from God which primarily tests a person's faithfulness and obedience but often also allows use of ministry gifts in the context of a task which has closure, accountability, and evaluation. Early ministry tasks (like this incident with Brengle) are more to test and train the recipient than to help those being ministered to. As a leader matures the ministry tasks become short term assignments which primarily help those being ministered to (like Titus to Crete). This incident was also an instance of an *obedience check* (Clinton 1989:142, 129), a shaping process testing one's response to God's desires.

you!" He then advised me to see the Chief [Bramwell Booth] soon, invited me to the "all night of prayer" at the Congress Hall, and kindly dismissed me. I love him. He's a dear old man.

...

When finally he was able to see the Chief of the Staff, he was at first received with scarcely more enthusiasm than that which had been displayed by the General. Again he was told he belonged to "the dangerous classes" (evidently a stock phrase for describing candidates of his type), with the added prediction: "You will probably stay with us for a year or two, and then you will get out. In that case, you will have just lost all that time. Really, we think you might as well stay out."

Finally, however, when the Chief saw that his enthusiastic candidate was not even remotely interested in the suggestion that he should "stay out," he agreed to give him a trial, sending him to Leamington, one of the field training depots where cadets were given part of their instruction.

At Leamington he expected to enter at once upon a continuous round of soul-saving work. He was hardly prepared for the blow to his illusions which came when he was assigned to his first duty: he was told to black the boots of the other cadets! See him:

Down in the dark little cellar he found himself with eighteen pairs of muddy shoes, a can of blacking, and a sharp temptation. It was not the lowliness of the duty but the apparent waste of his time and talent that had wounded him Remembering his Lord's story of the man who buried his talent, he prayed, the while his brush moved inexpertly across the toe of a clumsy boot: "Lord God, am I burying my talent? Is this the best they can do for me in The Salvation Army? Am I a fool? Have I followed my own fancy 3,000 miles to come here to black boots?"

As if in direct answer, in imagination he saw a picture: Jesus was the central figure, and he was washing the disciples' feet! His Lord--Who had come from the bosom of the Everlasting Father and the glories of heaven and the adoration of its hosts--bending over the feet of uncouth, unlearned fishermen, washing them, humbling Himself, taking the form of a servant!

In the light of this revelation, Brengle's heart was bowed low. "Dear Lord, Thou didst wash their feet; I will black their boots!" And with an enthusiasm heretofore unknown to the boot-blacking profession, he tackled his job, a song on his lips, peace in his heart.

Years later he would say:

I had fellowship with Jesus every morning for a week while down in that cellar blacking boots. It was the best training I could have had. I was humble, but now I was practicing my humility. I saw what The Salvation Army stood for--service. My new prayer was, "Dear Lord, let me serve the servants of Jesus. That is sufficient for me." And, do you know, that experience put a key in my hand to unlock the hearts of lowly people all round the world! (Hall 1933:71-75)

I will come back to both of these critical incidents later, pointing out where they occur in the developmental time-line. I'll refer to them also when I talk on the section tracing out important values. But notice the second incident. This awareness, a sensitivity to God in daily incidents, is typical of Brengle. It will become a repetitive pattern with him to see inner life lessons in daily events and to seek consistency with his values.

The Time-Line

See the time-line at the end of this chapter for a one page overview of Brengle's life along with critical incidents. Note that there are three major time phases of length 23, 14, and 39 years with numerous smaller periods within the phases. The distinctively unique item of this time-line is the third phase, a convergent phase. It is distinct for three reasons. One, Brengle entered into convergent ministry with an ideal role at age 37. Most do not do this until late 40s or mid 50s. Two, the role lasted such a long time. Many leaders may have a combined time of effective ministry plus convergent ministry that lasts 20 or so

Chapter 4. Samuel Logan Brengle (1860-1936)

years. But it is very rare to have convergent ministry for more than 30 years. Third, there was no transition to this role. Normally there is a period of time during which a person attempts to adapt toward an ideal role. In this case, the role came, divinely, and ready made for Brengle's convergent ministry. All of his experiences fit to make him effective in the role. And it came, through no seeking of his own, but because of his faithfulness and effectiveness.

Highly Condensed Biographical Narrative

The following running capsule, organized around the time increments of Brengle's time-line, indicates important activities, people, and events that shaped Brengle's life. Brengle's ministry experience is fairly straightforward. His early Christian experience was local church, Wesleyan. He was ordained into the Methodist Episcopal Church, a church of Wesleyan persuasion. His major focal point, the prime focal incident of his life was essentially Wesleyan in perspective. But his major ministry was with The Salvation Army, though it was basically Wesleyan in viewpoint.[7] He moved up the hierarchical structure until he was recognized as uniquely gifted and experienced for a special ministry. He was released into this special convergent role and carried it out for the rest of his life. High level leadership in The Salvation Army took the lead to move Brengle to a convergent role. His case is one of the few in which the convergent role is recognized, designed by and totally supported by the leadership of the group, rather than the individual.

I. RUGGED PRAIRIE FOUNDATIONS
A Drive To Learn Focused Toward An Oratorical Ambition
(1860-1883); Age=Birth to 23

A. Frontier Obscurity/ Rugged Start
(1860-1868); Age=Birth to 8

Samuel Logan Brengle was born on 1 June, 1860 in the rural village of Fredericksburg, Indiana to William Nelson and Rebecca Anne Brengle. Both father and mother were of pioneer stock. They came from a long line of frontier people. There was Presbyterian and Methodist roots in the family lines. Both parents were strong Christians. His parents dedicated him to the Lord before he was born.[8] His dad had received a call to be a preacher but had not followed it.[9] He became a teacher. His wife, Rebecca, had been one of his students before they were married. When Samuel was two years old his dad left for the Civil War. He served bravely as an officer and was wounded in the siege of Vicksburg. He died shortly after. Samuel's mom took over the school and for a period of time was a single parent to Sammy. She was a spiritual person and inculcated spiritual ideals in young Brengle. She remarried. The step-father was a restless man whose best venture was always just ahead. He was not successful at anything.

---

[7]Actually this is a parachurch ministry which began as a sodality, pure parachurch organization, and institutionalized to become a modality, in this case a denominational structure. Though it still had some parachurch activities. So then Brengle was essentially working in a denomination which had strong parachurch activities. And his convergent ministry was essentially parachurch in nature. See Clinton's position paper (1981), *Structural Time--A Change Dynamics Variable*, which traces the institutionalization processes of churches and parachurches.
[8]This is the first of several *destiny preparation* (Clinton 1989:103,104) process items. The second is the Abraham wagon episode given next.
[9]That he regretted it is indicated by Samuel Brengle's anxious thoughts about it when he was considering his own call. In the family line there were several preachers.

Stars In the Sky

When Sammy was eight, his step-father decided to try farming. The family moved to Harrisonville more than 80 miles away from Fredericksburg. It was on the wagon trip to Harrisonville that Samuel Brengle was personally first impressed with a sense of destiny, though he would not have called it that at the time. Hall tells the story.[10]

    A man and woman occupy the only seat, just back of the straining flanks of the horses. The man is full-bearded and square of jaw; beneath the brim of his shapeless hat are eyes that connote restlessness, eyes that have a way of focusing themselves upon far horizons. Though the woman's visage is of softer texture, her appearance is that of a woman whom frontier hardship can mark but not deface, fag but not coarsen.

    Immediately behind them, alternately standing to ejaculate over some unfamiliar object along the way and sitting back again upon pieces of household bric-à-bac, are two boys, bare of foot and freckled of face. One of them, addressed as "Sam" by the other, is about eight years of age.

    They are "movers,"--though historians will later refer to them by the more genteel word "pioneers,"--one of many families following the receding line of the frontier, seeking richer farm land, blacker soil, with its promise of a greater yield of corn to the acre.

    Packed in the wagon, tied on and around it, are all their worldly possessions. Inside are beds, a few chairs, a bureau, a rough table or two roped together. Outside, swinging and jangling with every jolt and lurch of the wagon, are pots, pans, kettles, axes, plowing implements. The wagon creaks under its load, and, when the going is hard, Sam follows his half-brother and stepfather over the side to walk ahead, leading the horses.

    Soon the lengthening shadows from the great oaks and beeches indicate that it is time to camp for the night. The horses are turned into a clearing and unhitched. A few things necessary for supper and sleeping are unpacked. The woman busies herself with the pots and pans, and the boys gather wood.

    After supper, Sam's mother opens the Bible, and all are silent while she reads a portion by the light of the campfire. The reading is from the Book of Genesis; it has to do with Abram's going into another land, an unknown place. The lesson is aptly chosen; it is good to dwell upon such passages; it helps to make the "movers" going easier. One verse especially strikes into the boy Sam's imagination; it is:

    Look now toward heaven, and tell the stars, if thou be able to number them: and He said unto him, So shall thy seed be.

    For the benefit of the boys, the reading is explained in simple, primer language: the man Abram, listening to the calling of God, is to become, he is told, the father of children, "spiritual" children, so numerous that they would be like the stars for number! But the boy Sam does not understand. Like the stars? How could that be?

    And that night, lying on a straw pallet thrown from the wagon and placed for the boys beneath the trees, he stays awake for hours, looking up through the leaves to the twinkling stars high above. The words of the Bible reading turn and twist in his mind. The man Abram...doing God's will...becomes the father of many people...like the stars....

    What does it mean? (Hall 1933:11-13)

---

[10]The very fact that we even have the incident, that is, that Samuel Brengle remembered it in old age and referred back to it, affirms it as a *sense of destiny* shaping activity (an awareness of God's intervening hand in a life for His purposes), in this case *destiny preparation*--and one day it was fulfilled in an applicational sense in Brengle's ministry. General Evangeline Booth mentions its fulfillment in passing in her foreword to the book. "Countless multitudes of men and women were drawn to him in their distress and appealed to him in their pain." (Hall 1933:vi) Hall closes the book with a reference to the tremendous accomplishments in Brengle ministry and a flashback to this Abrahamic promise incident (1933:253,254).

Chapter 4. Samuel Logan Brengle (1860-1936)   page 129

This experience, on the road, the *Abraham/ Stars in the Sky* incident, was one of the lasting memories from this harsh time of poverty.

B. Farm Years/ Early Motivation to Learn
(1868-1872); Age=8-12

Brengle's early formal education was basic. Farmers needed family for planting and harvesting so that it was only in the winter months, 4 months at most, that children could be educated. A long walk through the snow, to and from the log cabin made the education even that more valuable. Somehow during these few short months each year between the years of 8 and 12 there was born a desire to learn.

During the winter months families were basically isolated to their log cabins. Reading was a major diversion. Brengle's basic education included not only learning to read but acquiring an attitude to learn through reading. Books that were read and reread during the long cold winter months included **Pilgrim's Progress, Plutarch's Lives,** Stephen's **History of Methodism,** Dickens' **Pickwick Papers,** the works of Josephus, Scott's **Ivanhoe,** and a **History of our Wars** (Hall 1933:24).[11] Hall points out that farm life tends to build in an isolation and wilderness silence. This is a natural force for cultivation of the imagination. He credits this early time of mental growth as partially the answer to why Brengle could later paint such word pictures and communicate to the uneducated. What motivated Brengle to learn? Hall does not give an answer to that but does show that the desire was there.

> His constant reading and re-reading developed gradually within him a love for the vehicles of expression. Lyrical phrases, euphonious words, musical sentences--these pleased his inner ear as his mind-pictures pleased his inner eye. So avid was his desire to know that, when he had read and read again all the other books on the shelf, he would take down Webster's Unabridged Dictionary and find fun in toying with words and their meanings. He would try them out on stumps and cornstalks and furrows, and then take them to bed with him to brood over their meanings.
> An inner eye that could make pictures in his head, and an inner ear that could hear and enjoy and pursue words and their meanings--these were Sam Brengle's possessions as a boy, possessions which then helped to relieve the monotony of prairie life, later made of him an orator, a painter of word pictures, and later still helped to make of him a preacher of power, with the ability to present vividly and realistically the tragic terrors of hell and the transcendent delights of heaven (Hall 1933:24,25).

It is this desire to learn that will take Brengle on for further education.[12]

---

[11]This is an interesting collection having quite a breadth about life and life's meaning. **Pilgrim's Progress, the History of Methodism,** and **Josephus' Works** gave solid religious background. A framework for interpreting the Christian life and the critical incidents in it would be imbibed from Bunyan and Methodist History. The need for solid academic work would come from Josephus. **Plutarch's Lives,** dealing with biography, would have created an innate sense of destiny, that lives can count for something. Scott, Dickens and the **History of Wars** would have given insights into life, the good and the bad--the problems and accomplishments of it. They were a poor family. These were the books they had. It is amazing that they would even have these and the unabridged **Webster's Dictionary.** Repeated reading would be natural. This basic education would give perspective.

[12]This motivation to learn is something that I would pursue if I had access to resources that could help me unlock this motivational drive--like a diary or Brengle himself or his children. Perhaps it can be accounted for in part by the fact that both mom and dad were teachers and highly valued education. Perhaps Brengle's going on for high school and college were partially fulfilling their dreams. In any case, it singles out Brengle as highly unusual in his day. Very few went on to University--usually only the rich and elite. He is the archetype of a leader who "maintains a learning posture all his life" one of the symptoms of an effective leader.

Brengle learned from life as well as books. Basic skills of all kinds must be acquired for one to farm the land. Brengle knew these by the time he was 12. But at age 12 he was to learn something that was basic to his essential being.

C. Conversion/ Expanded Drive To Learn/ First Ministry Experience (1872-1874); Age=12-14

Two harbingers stand out in his early conversion experience and the sensitivity incident given below. They will be a part of who Brengle is all his life. I'll come back and mention them after I relate the incident.

Spontaneous Anger--The Sensitivity Incident

He had experienced church going. He knew about preaching. He knew that many went forward to the mourners' bench and prayed through till God met them. They claimed that conversion changed their lives. He saw this as well in the day-to-day testimony of those who were converted. As he grew older he was aware of a tendency to flare up and lose his temper, especially with his step-father. This displeased his mom. In short, there was growing awareness of his need for "conversion." At a series of Christmas nightly revival-type meetings he went forward on five consecutive nights to the mourners' bench. He hoped for some kind of unusual experience that would revolutionize him. On the fifth night, his mother went forward and knelt beside him and told him that now that he had gone forward he must "trust" God and take his stand for God. But still he had felt nothing. Hall records the moment when Brengle sensed God's acceptance.

> Weeks passed, with nothing to tell him he was a Christian except that he had gone to the mourners' bench. Then one night, while on his way to prayer meeting, there came the "witness." He and his mother, walking together across the broad and desolate prairie, were talking about a proposed move to Texas that had been given up some months ago. Sam, musing on this recent decision, said, "I'm glad we didn't move to Texas, Mother. If we had, I might have fallen in with a rough, drunken lot of fellows, and lost my soul. But we have stayed up here, and I have become a Christian." Scarcely had the words left his lips when there came into his heart an inexplicable feeling. Not an inrush of glory, not a sweeping sensation of having entered some seventh heaven; but a sweet, deep, pervasive sense of peace, quietness, rest, blessedness. Instinctively he knew now that God had accepted him. Though he had heard no voice, it was as though something had just been said to him, loud and clear, something that had settled once and for all any doubt as to whether he had a right to call himself a Christian. (Hall 1933:28)

Shortly afterwards Brengle was to have another experience, one which would condition him for his *Personal Pentecost* that would come eight years later. I call it the *Sensitivity Incident*.

> For days, weeks, months, Sam walked in the enjoyment of an exquisite sense of God's favor, anxious to show to the whole world, and more especially to his boy companions, how Christ-like his life was henceforth to be. In the flush of his new life, he felt that it was virtually impossible for him to want to be other than like his Master.
> Then one day he discovered in himself the presence of something that did not want to act like Jesus. That disturbing revelation came to him one afternoon when he, with three other boys, was going home from school While playing along the way, one of the boys took offense at something done by Sam, and, drawing angrily away, called him ...a name. In a flash Sam forgot he was a Christian, or ignored the fact, and struck the offender a swift blow. ... Instantly, with the striking of that blow, the inward witness had been withdrawn. Conviction of sin now flooded his heart; and with the vanishing of the sense of God's favor, a sense of Divine displeasure overwhelmed him.

Chapter 4. Samuel Logan Brengle (1860-1936)

In time, after much sorrowing and praying, he got back his consciousness of peace and forgiveness. But he had become possessed of a new and disquieting knowledge: there still remained in him something that under provocation would make him act unlike his Lord. There was no one then to tell that the carnal nature can be destroyed, that constant victory is a possible experience.

Hence, eight years must pass before he would be rid of the continual struggle to keep his experience, and to act at all times like Jesus. (Hall 1933:25-30)[13]

Brengle had an unusually sensitive nature to the things of God. He also learned first hand of the power of sin to break that sensitive relationship with God. These two truths were first experienced and felt, then later understood conceptually. Brengle also knew that one's experience with God should be personal and real. He perceived, perhaps almost instinctively, that the mourners' bench represents a methodology of bringing about committal and that personal experience with God.[14] He was strongly conditioned to the responsibility of the participant to seek God. These kinds of perspectives would later enhance his evangelist gift and efforts.

Following his conversion, Brengle entered into a growth spurt that was conditioned by church activity. He took up systematic reading of the Bible. He became a dedicated participant of the Sunday School, seriously studying the lessons. At fifteen he substituted for the teacher of the men's Bible class who was absent. He next became assistant superintendent of the Sunday School (Hall 1933:30). His serious study of the Bible was a continued fulfillment of the basic motivation to learn that was in him. His activity in the church setting indicated his serious intent for discipleship in the only form of it he knew about.

D. Basic Education/ Olney/ Claremont
(1874-1877); Age=14-17

Hall chronicles the educational drive further, particularly emphasizing the early interest in rhetoric and grammar. This educational drive is intensifying and will be the major guidance means that God will use to move Brengle toward focus.

> The hunger to know, the power and leadership which he saw come to those who did know--these made him determined to acquire all that was possible to him of the learning of the schools. Having gathered all that the little country school could offer him, he enrolled in 1874 as a student of the Olney high school.
>
> Especially was he interested in grammar--the right use of words, their meanings, their marshaling into phrases and sentences that set the mind singing and dancing as do the melodies of an orchestra. He wanted to know how to handle words, how correctly to use them so that, when put on paper or printed in books, they would create pictures a boy could carry behind his eyes, or, spoken from the lips of an orator, could echo and re-echo

---

[13] I added these last two paragraphs which give a decidedly Wesleyan view of sanctification though my own view of sanctification differs considerably. But this was the paradigm that Brengle worked out of. It enhanced his sensitivity to God and helped make him the Christian evangelical mystic that he was. See the later section explaining critical incidents and the comments on sensitivity and the evangelical mystic. I repeat, one doesn't have to be whole heartedly in agreement with a given paradigm in order to see its strengths and results and appreciate them.

[14] This is an early *ministry insight* (Clinton 1989:198) which he imbibed from his church experience. He will later modify it (called by Hall the Penitent Form, a public altar call with personal help from counselors or evangelists) and use it with great effectiveness in his public ministry--especially his years as a campaigner in convergent ministry. Again I point out. He first learned it affectively and experientially (with perhaps a little cognitive explanation from **Methodist History**). This is a pattern of learning with Brengle.

Chapter 4. Samuel Logan Brengle (1860-1936)　　　page 132

in a boy's head in rhythm which would transform even plowing and harrowing into agreeable tasks (Hall 1933:30,31).

Having learned all he could from the local log cabin school he attended the Olney high school for a year. It was about 7 miles away from his farm. At the end of the year he was told he should study with Professor Hinman eight miles beyond Olney, in Claremont. Brengle boarded for two years with Hinman who became his mentor coach, mentor teacher and longtime friend. They focused on grammar and rhetoric. Toward the end of this two year period of time, Brengle's mom died. He was essentially alone now. He buried himself in his studies. He knew that he wanted further education. University was next-- something rare for a farm boy.[15]

E. Harnessed Ambition at Depauw University
(1877-1883); Age=17-23

In the fall of 1877 he entered into DePauw University in Greencastle, Indiana. He prepped for two years to make up entrance requirements. He became a regular member of College Avenue Church. For five years he led the college age class and built it into the largest and most vibrant in the church. Over this period of time he led every member, without exception, to a profession of faith in Christ as Savior and Lord and membership in the church (Hall 1933:34). His evangelism gift emerged early. We shall see him active in this gift throughout his whole ministry.[16]

To his strong natural inclination for communication and oratory Brengle added skills through discipline. Hall brings out the discipline and sets the stage for the focal incident with which I opened the chapter.

> In young Brengle, oratory found a faithful zealot. With an assiduity born of intense love, he would respond diligently to her demands for long hours of study and practice. A speech with a prize at stake often would require months of memorizing, cultivation of voice, rehearsal of gestures. For years he made it his practice to sit at a piano or organ, often for hours at a stretch, striking the tones of the scale and following them with his voice, thereby developing gradually a resonant, organ-like tone with depth, flexibility, and volume.
> When preparing a speech he was careful in his choice of words; they must be tuned to the particular effect he wanted his speech to register. Especially did he like sonorous words of the type that would give his voice tones full play.
> Brengle had not gone far with his studies in the arts of speech before rewards, one by one, began to fall into his lap. By the time he had advanced to the freshman degree in the university proper he could look back with pride upon a long list of achievements on the platform. Through his public speaking he attracted attention to himself, became popular and widely-known among the undergraduates (Hall 1933:35).

---

[15] When he told his step-father of his plan for further education he was ridiculed with the words that college was a waste of time. Eventually he was able to get some money (owed to him by his step-father from money left by his dad) from the sale of the farm. This was enough to get him started.

[16] This is what is called a vested gift, that is, a spiritual gift which is part of the permanent set of spiritual gifts which are exercised. The permanent set of spiritual gifts is called the *gift-mix*. There are other spiritual gifts which come and go (called non-vested gifts). See Clinton and Clinton, 1994, **Developing Leadership Giftedness**. Frequently the evangelism gift is exercised early on as part of one's initial ministry experience but fades away as a leader moves into the late 30s and ministers in a more permanent situation. Not so with Brengle. This gift, both public and private, was exercised with gifted power throughout his entire ministry.

Chapter 4. Samuel Logan Brengle (1860-1936)

During the nearly three years more leading up to *The Call*, Brengle socialized in his fraternity, networked with friends who were to become important leaders, and diligently advanced in his studies. He led some of these influential leaders to Christ.

Then came *The Call* which makes up Focal Incident 1 with which I began the chapter. That call harnessed Brengle's educational and oratorical interests into another avenue for their expression. Law and politics went by-the-by. Ministry, the pulpit and public campaigns, would be the means for harnessing this natural ability and drive. And to these were wedded spiritual gifts that would bring forth much fruit.

II. DESTINED FOR THE SALVATION ARMY
Faithfulness and Consistency Through The Ranks
(1883-1897); Age=23-37

A. Circuit Preacher--
Northwest Indiana Conference--Methodist Episcopal Church
(1883); Age=23

Hidden Guidance

Brengle was ordained into the Methodist Episcopal church in 1884 and was assigned a rural circuit by the Northwest Indiana Conference for a year of quasi-internship as his first ministry assignment. This first assignment was in itself part of the sovereign guidance that was to teach Brengle the Joseph lesson--*the way up is first down*.[17] Upon graduation and application to the Methodist Episcopal Church, Brengle had been led to believe by the presiding elder of the Greencastle District that he could be placed in a desirable little city church with a brand-new parsonage. He was initially assigned this promising appointment by the District leader. With its cultured and refined people, this certainly was a wonderful starting point for an educated preacher/ orator of such promise. But the appointment was overridden by the Bishop. The rural circuit involved horseback travel between two villages, Brookston and Chalmers, with a community made up of mostly simple illiterate farmers.[18] How did Brengle respond to this?

> While the thought of the city church with its new parsonage and cultured congregation had appealed strongly to him, Brengle was not many months on his circuit before he realized that both happiness and spiritual stature had come to him through that appointment. Years later he said in retrospect:
>> Losing that city church was the best thing that could have happened to me. If I had gone to that appointment to work among those cultured and refined people, I should have swelled with pride, tried to show off my spread-eagle oratory, and doubtless would have accomplished little. But out among the comparatively illiterate and uncultivated farmers of my circuit, I learned the foundations of true preaching: humility and simplicity. (Hall 1933:42,43)

---

[17]See Clinton (1985), **Joseph: Destined To Rule--A Study in Integrity and Divine Affirmation** for the classic *integrity check* with Potiphar's wife and the downward pattern which leads to the throne. The *way up is down*, will be repeated several times for Brengle. It is a major means of harnessing ambitious leaders.

[18]Hall mentions these two towns. In *Looking Backward and Forward* a reflection on his 70+ years of life, Brengle mentions that there were 4 preaching places on his circuit and that there were blazing revivals in three of them(Brengle 1934:115,116). This is an illustration of the *Joshua Affirmation Syndrome*. An early success is often needed so as to affirm leadership and foster faith for other ministry which follows.

Chapter 4. Samuel Logan Brengle (1860-1936)

I call this incident *Hidden Guidance*. God was sovereignly directing through the Bishop. Brengle was destined for The Salvation Army--a rough and tumble inner-city ministry. Brengle may never have made it had he gone the velvet lined pulpit roadway.[19]

Back To School

After a year in this assignment Brengle was recognized as someone with great promise--in fact many thought he was on his way to being one of the youngest Bishops ever. Bishop Joyce, formerly his pastor in Greencastle during his college years recognized future promise and as a mentor counselor recommended to Brengle that he should go on for further studies in a theological seminary. With his sponsorship, Brengle applied to and was accepted in Boston Theological Seminary, one of the three great Methodist seminaries in America. (Hall 1933:43).[20]

B. Formal Training--Faith Challenge As Evangelist
Boston Theological Seminary/ Personal Pentecost/ Evangelistic Ministry in New England
(1884-1887); Age=24-27

At age 24, Brengle entered seminary. Five things standout from this almost two year stint of training:

1. **Hard work.** Brengle is older than most of his fellow students.[21] And he has some experience. He studies with an intensity they don't have.
2. **Meaningful Ministry.** He was learning experientially as well as cognitively.[22]

---

[19]*Sovereign guidance* (Clinton 1989:359) is the general process item label given to those divine moments of guidance when God opens and closes doors behind the scenes. Sometimes it is years after that the Hand of God can be traced. This is also an illustration of *the foundational ministry pattern* based on the Luke 16:10 little/big principle which describes a cycle of faithfulness in little things leading to expanded ministry. Brengle was faithful in this first assignment. It led to expansion. I believe the recommendation for seminary was that expansion and was a direct result of Brengle's positive response to this assignment.
[20]God supplied finances for this venture through a loan from friends who recognized his faithfulness and potential, one a banker friend who was a member of the Greencastle church who had observed his 5 years of Sunday School ministry. This is an example of *networking power* (Clinton 1989:240) the connections of contacts and friends through which God accomplishes His purposes by linking leaders to resources and opportunities.
[21]We have identified three major training patterns through which most leaders emerge. The third is a *modified in-service pattern* (Clinton 1989:357) in which the leader gets ministry experience, then interrupts it for formal training, and then resumes it. Usually this pattern will include further interruptions for training down road. Brengle fits this pattern somewhat. Four others of the eight, Gordon, Jaffray, Maxwell, and Simeon (somewhat) fit the *pre-service pattern* (Clinton 1989:354), that is, they receive formal training prior to ministry. The remaining three fit the *in-service pattern* (Clinton 1989:356), that is, they learn on-the-job and finally after proving their abilities take on full time responsibilities.
[22]From training model theory we identify four elements that need to be balanced for training to be most effective. They are input (cognitive focus), experience (using the input in life), dynamic reflection (an evaluation process which tests ideas of input with use in life and which generates new ideas from experience) and formation (that is the deliberate focus on building of leadership character, skills, and strategic thinking). The seminary mainly focused on the cognitive. Brengle supplied the experience via a part-time pastorate and occasional preaching. His own previous experience and on-going ministry while in seminary helped him dynamically reflect. His *Personal Pentecost* experience, his second year, fundamentally shaped his leadership character, skills, and strategic direction. See Clinton (1984) **Leadership Training Models** for Holland's Two Track Analogy which gives this balanced model for training.

Chapter 4. Samuel Logan Brengle (1860-1936)   page 135

3. **Personal Pentecost.** It was here that Brengle experienced his entire sanctification experience, which led him on to be a great Apostle of Holiness.
4. **Holiness Spill Over.** He spread his holiness experience. Brengle was the catalyst of a Holiness Revival that spread all over the campus.
5. **Ambition Test.** There was a necessary preliminary step leading to his selection of The Salvation Army Ministry as his lifelong pursuit.

It is the third which will prove to be the prime focal incident of his life. The fourth will characterize his ministry from now on. The fifth will continue to teach him the Joseph lesson--*the way up is first down*. It is the springboard to ministry in The Salvation Army and a forerunner of his convergent role which he will begin 10 years later.

Personal Pentecost

Let me comment at length on the *Personal Pentecost* incident since it is the prime focal incident of Brengle's life and will affect his spiritual, ministerial, and strategic formation radically for the rest of his life. He was primed for this event.[23] Timing is everything in this great power gate experience.[24]

Hall describes his state of mind and preparation for this experience. The time is very early in the morning on January 9, 1885. The place is his dorm room. Brengle is there with elbows on his study table. He has a prayerful like attitude.

> ...For several days conviction that he should be sanctified has lashed his soul into restlessness, rendering sleep almost impossible; for weeks he has searched the Scripture, ransacked his heart, cried to God almost day and night. Today, he tells himself, he must obtain--or be lost forever.
>
> No longer does he doubt the existence of such a blessing. Through exhaustive study under the personal guidance of Dr. Daniel Steele, he has become mentally persuaded that sanctification is a doctrine gloriously possible of incarnation in human life...[He has

---

[23] He was primed in at least three ways. 1. Hall had mentioned that eight years earlier his *Loss of Presence* experience showed him his need for victory in his life. This was a continual need he saw as he continued to grow. 2. There were tremendous currents exhorting to deeper Christian living in these days. They followed hard on the awakenings and revivals of the mid 1800s. There was the Keswick deeper life movement. There was the Wesleyan emphasis stirred strong by Finney's revivals. Pentecostalism had not yet arisen but its seeds were there in the Nazarene, the Holiness, and the Alliance movements. The sum is that there were macro-movements sweeping both sides of the Atlantic which were calling for a higher consecrated life of holiness and victory. 3. And finally, Brengle had been mentored by a godly Wesleyan scholar on faculty at the Boston Theological Seminary, Dr. Daniel Steele, Professor of Didactic Theology and noted Greek New Testament authority. This incident is one of the few major occasions when Brengle learned something cognitively first and then experientially affirmed it.

[24] This kind of experience is typical of a number of like *paradigm shifts* (See Clinton position paper, 1993, *The Paradigm Shift--God's Means of Opening New Vistas for Leaders*). This experience is a power gate which functions to open the participant to a new level of awareness of God's power in the life. Two kinds of power gates are typically described: life power and gifted power. This is a life power type. The participant wants power from God to live a righteous life. The entire sanctification paradigm is one of several power gates including the Keswick power gate which is a surrender/ faith appropriation one, and later the Pentecostal Experience, the Baptism of the Holy Ghost. All essentially do the same function-- open the way to new experience with God. None guarantee an on-going successful ministry. They are simply gates that open the way for a new relationship with God. We will see the Keswick type power gate with McQuilkin and Maxwell and somewhat with Gordon. Jaffray, somewhat like Brengle manifests a modified form of the entire sanctification paradigm. The gifted power gate experience is similar except that its participant is seeking for power in ministry. Finney's, Moody's and Torrey's experiences are of this type.

Chapter 4. Samuel Logan Brengle (1860-1936)

> read of the experiences of Wesley, Fletcher, D. L. Moody, William McDonald and Catherine Booth. Booth's booklets seem to penetrate deeply.]
> In his search after holiness, he has been aided, too, by his membership in the Octagon Club, a religious coterie not unlike the "Holy Club" founded by Charles Wesley at Oxford in 1729...The Octagon Club is composed of a select group of the more intellectual students, who meet each morning for prayer and the discussion of religion in its deeper manifestations. Among the members are some who avowedly have been seeking sanctification, Brengle one of them.
> Under a variety of terms--Holiness, Sanctification, Perfect Love, Second Work of Grace, Baptism of the Holy Spirit, Blessing of a Clean Heart, etc.--he has seen this experience written about, expounded, testified to (Hall 1933:46,47).

What has brought him to this point of need, beside the study and the fellowship of like minds, has been his own inward battle with self and his selfish ambitions.

> The more closely he has looked at himself the more diametrically opposed to the spirit of the Cross has he seen the "I" in him to be. Seeing the "I," therefore, and feeling its insidious, overmastering power, he has hated it and, bit by bit, has cast it from him.
> Even in his seeking the Blessing, the "I" endeavored to cross his wires so that, hearing the voice of his own ambition, he might mistake it for the voice of God. For example, after listening to Moody, whose simplicity and power stirred him deeply, the thought had come: "If I can only be a great preacher like Moody! He ascribes his power to the Baptism of the Holy Spirit. Perhaps if I seek this Baptism, I shall have this power!" But even as he held the thought the light of the Spirit had fallen upon it, revealing its grossness, and he threw it from him as an unholy thing, saying later: "I was seeking the Holy Spirit that I might use Him, rather than He might use me."
> Yet now, wrestling alone in his room at the break of day, he finds that the battle is still with the "I." The "great preacher" ambition dies hard...
> [Finally after debating back and forth about this ambition and the glory it would bring the Lord, Brengle makes a preliminary surrender.] ... "Lord, if Thou wilt only sanctify me, I will take the meanest little appointment there is!" (Hall 1933:48,49)

After further struggle attempting to disguise ambition as bringing glory to God, there comes the final surrender.

> "Lord, I wanted to be an eloquent preacher, but if by stammering and stuttering I can bring greater glory to Thee than by eloquence, then let me stammer and stutter!"
> *Let me stammer and stutter!* Surely here is the final step in self-surrender for this man whose every waking moment and every sleeping dream since boyhood has been toward the refinement of the arts of speech. So hungrily does he yearn for complete cleansing and holiness that the very vehicle of his destiny is thrown upon the altar. (Hall 1933:49)

He is ready. But nothing has happened. He anxiously awaits thinking that he doesn't have the right technique for finding it and thinking that he is ineffective in his efforts.

> And suddenly there comes up from his heart a voice speaking words that are old, but that bear a gloriously new meaning:
>
> *If we confess our sins, He is faithful and just to forgive us our sins, and to cleanse us from all unrighteousness.*
>
> "...to cleanse us from all unrighteousness!" The words break across his heart like a sky rocket, illuminating the fact that since God is "faithful and just" his promised blessing must now be received by simple faith in those attributes of God's character. Instantly the

Chapter 4. Samuel Logan Brengle (1860-1936)

Grace and faithfulness of God dawn upon him, and as he drops his head in his arms and murmurs confidently, "Lord, I believe that!" a great sense of peace flows over his soul.

Is this the Blessing? He need not put the question twice. Like a great, wordless, all-enveloping "Yes!" he gets the answer from every chamber of his body and soul. It is as though all nature, visible and invisible, had nodded its head in testifying assent, and in the next instant has begun the movement of a cool, refreshing breeze within him and started springs of sparkling waters bubbling up all through his being. Whereas all previous blessings have been transitory, coming and going, this experience has the 'feel' of permanency (Hall 1933:49,50).

Two students saw him separately, immediately after this. Both knew something had happened. They could see it and sense it in his bearing and excitement. The following Sunday he preached in his student pastorate from Hebrews 6: "Therefore leaving the principles of the doctrine of Christ, let us go on to perfection." (Hall 1933:51). He gave his testimony--his *Personal Pentecost*. Immediately there was a positive response that was affirming. This put him on record. He could only go forward. Was it real? Fifty years later he testified.

I have never doubted this experience since. I have sometimes wondered whether I might not have lost it, but I have never doubted the experience any more than I could doubt that I had seen my mother, or looked at the sun, or had my breakfast. It is a living experience.

In time, God withdrew something of the tremendous emotional feelings. He taught me I had to live by my faith and not by my emotions. I walked in a blaze of glory for weeks, but the glory gradually subsided, and He made me see that I must walk and run, instead of mounting up with wings. He showed me that I must learn to trust Him, to have confidence in His unfailing love and devotion, regardless of how I felt (Hall 1933:53).

Results of this experience spread. It was seen in Brengle's daily life, his testimony to others, and most of all in his preaching. "Before sanctification, preaching meant honors for Brengle; now it was to mean glory for Christ." (Hall 1933:54)

William Booth, the founder of The Salvation Army came to Boston. Brengle had been aware of him and his work. From time-to-time he had inward feelings about that work. Brengle attended and was deeply impressed with his spiritual power as he spoke. Booth invited all to an all night prayer meeting. Brengle attended. The next day, Booth spoke at the Boston Theological Seminary. Brengle felt a drawing to this man of God.[25] But there was one last test he must pass. It would prove that his *Personal Pentecost* was real and had really dealt with his ambition.[26]

Attractive Offer

He was feeling a need to get on with ministry. His experience had left him with a desire to minister to others and encourage them. The classroom seemed dry and sterile.

---

[25]The timing of Booth's visit, just after Brengle's sanctification experience, and the impression he made with his penetrating eyes, powerful sermons and the flaming red shirt with *blood and fire* on it mark out this visit as one timely in Brengle's thinking. Booth is evidently a *divine contact*, one who brings guidance or affirms something. Brengle had known of this movement for eight years and been strangely drawn to it. He is on the verge of making a decision. This visit along with his meeting Elizabeth Swift shortly afterward tab this as a divine contact experience. Brengle was evidently impressed with this founding Apostolic leader. There is a like-attracts-like dynamic going on here.

[26]Though the experiences are totally different one can not but help but compare this dealing with ambition in Brengle's life with pride in Morgan's life. Both were powerfully gifted and wanted to make a name for themselves. Both positively responded. God greatly blessed both.

Chapter 4. Samuel Logan Brengle (1860-1936)

But Brengle faced an integrity check[27] which will be a final key to his learning of the Joseph lesson--*the way up is first down.*

> In the midst of his urge to be up and doing there came a brilliant and tempting offer. Out in South Bend, Indiana, a man named Clement Studebaker, builder of wagons and of a fortune that had soared into many millions, had recently built also a beautiful church, claimed by South Benders to be the finest Methodist edifice in Northern Indiana. In casting about for a suitable pastor, Studebaker had appealed to Dr. Gobin, vice-president of DePauw University, for a recommendation. Dr. Gobin had written by return mail: "Brengle is the man you want." A few days later Brengle was surprised by receiving three letters, one from Dr. Gobin, another from the district superintendent of the Methodist Church, and a third from Studebaker himself, each asking him to accept the pastorate of the "Studebaker Church."
>
> What an offer! Here was honor, here a way out of the debt into which he had had to plunge to come to Boston and the seminary, here a large and wealthy congregation, here an immediate and instant leap over the poor appointments and small memberships and perplexities that have to be hurdled by the average preacher before reaching so desirable a goal. But he made no hasty decision. Better hold his answer in abeyance for a few days, he reasoned within himself, until he could return to earth, think clearly, pray intelligently (Hall 1933:57,58).

At this juncture he took off 10 days and attended a holiness conference. At the conclusion of it he preached on a Sunday morning at the oldest Methodist church in Baltimore. There were good results which convinced him of his giftedness as an evangelist. He felt a definite call to do evangelistic work. He battled back and forth between doing evangelistic work or accepting the affluent position in South Bend. The South Bend ministry would clear up his financial situation. The evangelistic ministry in the New England area was fraught with difficulties. There was no sponsoring organization or denomination. Could he get ministry opportunities? How could he get finances? In the midst of this deliberation he was prompted from within by the Holy Spirit.

> His mind was led to Jesus' words in the sixth chapter of Matthew: "Take no thought, saying, What shall we eat? or, What shall we drink? or, Wherewithal shall we be clothed? ...your heavenly Father knoweth that ye have need of all these things. But seek ye first the Kingdom of God." The Spirit then took him over into Exodus, where he was reminded how God had led out from under the iron hand of Pharaoh a million Israelites with their wives, children, herds, and fed them for forty years in the wilderness. Thus pliant to the Spirit's guiding, Brengle thought he heard God Himself whisper to his heart: "Can you not trust Me? If I could care for those Israelites in a desert land, cannot I supply all your needs in rich New England?" (Hall 1933:58,59)

He successfully passes the integrity check.[28] He chose the evangelistic ministry. For almost two years he carried on a powerful evangelistic ministry including camp meetings,

---

[27] An *integrity check* (Clinton 1989:125) is a process whereby God tests heart intent to evaluate consistency between inner convictions and outward actions. This is a foundational part of character shaping. Kinds of checks include temptation (conviction test), restitution (honesty testing), value check (ultimate value clarification), loyalty (allegiance testing), guidance (alternative testing--better offer after Holy Spirit led commitment to some course of action), persecution (steadfastness check). It is used to see follow-through on a promise or vow, to insure burden for a ministry or vision, to allow confirmation of inner-character strength, to build faith, to establish inner values very important to later leadership which will follow. In this case it was a guidance type (alternative better offer after a commitment to giving up ambition and doing whatever God wanted).

[28] Again this is similar to Morgan's decision to go to Westminster Chapel rather than Wannamaker's church. Here two other shaping activities are also in focus, an *obedience check* (Clinton 1989:129) to the

Chapter 4. Samuel Logan Brengle (1860-1936)

revival services, and preaching in conferences. God blessed this ministry greatly. He also supplied the finances needed even to paying off the school loan, a matter that had made the Studebaker offer so tempting. Hundreds were converted and sanctified under his preaching. During these meetings he would sometimes receive hints of his next ministry assignment. He was still drawn to The Salvation Army. When he would pass a Salvation Army open-air meeting or conduct a campaign in an Army Hall, or associate in other ways with the uniform, he would have an inner sense, "These are my people!" But it would take a divine contact to link him in with The Salvation Army.

C. Salvation Army Recruit/ Boot Camp
God Tests for Servant Leadership
(1887); Age=27

Divine Contacts--Connection to The Salvation Army

How would God bring about the focusing activity that would lead to The Salvation Army, the ordained place for Brengle to carry out his life work? God graciously did so by answering Brengle's prayer for a life partner. Here was his prayer.

> The prayer, oft-repeated, was first made shortly after his sanctification. On his knees he had discussed the question with his Intimate Friend: "Lord, if Thou dost want me never to be married, let me know Thy will. But if it be Thy will that I marry, I have one request to make: *help me to find a woman who will love Thee supremely*, for then I am sure she will always love me. Because of her love for Thee, she will put me into the proper place in her affection and devotion. Choose for me, Lord." (Hall 1933:62)

Notice his sensitivity to holy standards regarding marriage. His mother had long ago conditioned him toward God's choice of woman for him, one he would make unspeakably happy (Hall 1933:62). His standards flowed out of the ideals seen in his mother and his understanding of Bible requirements.

> I came to feel that part of my mission in life, one of the objects of my being, was to make some one little woman happy; while to injure a woman, to mar her life and blast her happiness, seemed to me--and still seems--the supremest cursedness and treason against the most sacred rights and claims of humanity. From mother I unconsciously got a high ideal of gentle sweetness and purity, and all womanly virtues which adorn a home and make it a haven of rest and a center of inspiration and courage and noble ambition.
>
> One of the safeguards of my adolescent years, during those lonely periods after mother died, was the thought of a wife to whom some day I wanted to give myself as pure and unsoiled as I hoped to find her. When tempted to run after forbidden pleasures, that thought was one of the great restraints in my life--one of the supreme protective influences. I wanted so to live that I could open my heart and tell my wife my whole life without shame (Hall 1933:63).

The standard clarified for him while he was in seminary. Later he wrote these words in a brochure entitled, *Why I Wanted My Wife To Be My Wife*.[29]

> It was while continuing my professional studies in an Eastern University that the conviction possessed me that my wife must not only have sweet womanly virtues, be adorned with refinement and the culture of the schools, but that she must be genuinely religious, must love God and His law supremely, for without this I realized we should fail in the highest fellowship. But with this love and loyalty we could not fail.

Matthew 6 passage and a *faith check* (Clinton 1989:143). These shaping activities instill values about God and ministry that will affect Brengle throughout life.

[29] This brochure is given in full in Brengle's (1929) work, **Ancient Prophets**, pages 13-21.

Chapter 4. Samuel Logan Brengle (1860-1936)

> But where could I find such a woman? Solomon was a very wise man and had a very wide marital experience, and he said, "A prudent wife is from the Lord." If she is from the Lord, why not ask Him for her? Why not pray to Him to find her? And this I did (Hall 1933:63).

God not only answered that prayer but used the answer to link Brengle to The Salvation Army. One of Sam's friends, D. A. Hayes,[30] discovered this potentially prudent one and rushed to say, "Sam, I've found just the girl for you." Sam went to one of The Salvation Army meetings, saw her, and as they say today the rest is history. He immediately fell in love with her and was convinced she was God's answer for she met every one of his standards.

However, God hadn't yet told Elizabeth Swift of this arrangement. A godly courtship began. It was a warm Christian friendship on Elizabeth's side but a growing love on Sam's side. Finally, when she was about ready to go to England to do research on a Salvation Army book she was writing, Brengle proposed marriage to her. He was greatly surprised at her negative answer. But he was undaunted and continued to believe she was God's answer. She left for England. Upon return he re-proposed. She spent some time in prayer and God gave her the answer and affirmed it with a verse: He shall choose our inheritance for us." (Hall 1933:67)

Days of planning followed including ministry in the future. Brengle and Elizabeth were convinced of God's leading them to minister together in The Salvation Army. As there was no training facility in the U.S. Brengle would have to go to England. This he did very shortly after they were married. This required a separation. It was at this point that the second Critical Focal Incident, *Shiny Black Boots*, given earlier, occurred. The prayer uttered in his response to that incident was answered all through his life, but supremely so in his convergent ministry. "Dear Lord, let me serve the servants of Jesus. That is sufficient for me."

As a cadet he experienced The Salvation Army on the streets at grass roots level. Marching, testifying, preaching, selling the *War Crys*, and participating in many street meetings daily. He fulfilled the essence of the little/big Luke 16:10 principle in all these activities. *He that is faithful in the least will be faithful in much*. This was to be true of each of the short ministry assignments which would follow.

Inklings of his destiny were being revealed, even in the midst of these ministry activities. He had an inward conviction from God. After less than two months in The Salvation Army he wrote back to Elizabeth.

> I don't know yet, of course, what kind of a little place God has for us in The Army, but I feel that my work will be particularly to promote holiness. I should like to be a Special to go about and hold half-nights of prayer just to lead people into the experience of holiness (Hall 1933:76).[31]

---

[30]Later during convergent ministry, Hayes who has become Professor D. A. Hayes and on faculty at Garrett Biblical Institute, at Evanston, Ill, one of the three most important Methodist training institutions in the U.S.A., will sponsor Brengle on that campus and Northwestern University for a number of visits. This connection for *networking power* was developed early. It later allowed Brengle to have more of an influence upon Methodism than had he stayed in it (Hall 1933:158).

[31]This is a *destiny revelation* activity in its earliest stages. A *special* was one who did specialized tasks beyond the standard corps pastoral and evangelistic role. But little was Brengle to guess that it would be at national level that he would be freed to do the special ministry of evangelizing and promoting holiness. He did not manipulate toward it. But it was a case of, "I being in the way, the Lord led me!"

Chapter 4. Samuel Logan Brengle (1860-1936)

Shortly afterwards, an outward assignment brings confirmation of this inner conviction--a form of double confirmation.[32] It came as he was being given a new assignment as a cadet in the Leamington depot.

> I find that my work is to be principally with solders and officers. Staff-Captain tells me this morning that I am to do considerable work in his district and that he wants me to do nothing but conduct holiness meetings. Glory to God! How I do thank the dear Lord that He is opening the way for me to do this work. Just the work I would choose.[33] O Lord, give me wisdom, love, and the fullness of the spirit! I sometimes wonder if God means me for a kind of holiness evangelist to The Army....!
> Pray much for me, that I may be used to quicken the spiritual life of *the whole Army*. I want to be so definite and so burning that God will be manifested wherever I go. ... I have been led from the beginning to pray that I might be a blessing, not simply to some little corps, but to the whole Army (Hall 1933:76).

There is still ambition here. But it is now a harnessed ambition, a holy ambition.

> I say *led*, God has led me thus to pray, and I believe He will answer, but I do not anticipate that in answering He will necessarily give me some prominent place where everybody can see me. *On the contrary, I see that He can easily answer that prayer and yet keep me in obscurity, and if He so chooses I shall rejoice.* (Hall 1933:77)

God blessed this ministry activity. In these special meetings in scattered locations, many were converted and many were sanctified. His overall training was assessed. He was told that he needed additional skills, specialized training. These included learning to be shorter in his messages and to speak with spiritual punch. He was to observe the Booths and their brief Blood-and-Fire sermons and talks. He was also found lacking in the area of administration and business skills. These were needed for executive leadership. He worked on these.

He was ready for assignment. God had given him a burden--a life purpose which flowed out of his personal experience and his giftedness. This life purpose will be a beacon focusing him throughout the next 10 years of ministry activities and will finally shine brightly in his convergent ministry assignment.

> He filled my heart with a burning desire for America. O such desire! I see it now. My desire to return has heretofore been in large measure selfish--not so much for His perishing sheep as for you, my darling. This morning he has put prayer in my mouth and in my heart for America. My whole heart longs for the dear people there, to help them, to stir them up, to pray with them and for them, and above all to insist upon holiness of heart and life among them. That's my work. Wherever I am placed, in whatever part of the field, that is the one thing God asks me to do (Hall 1933:78).

Just before leaving England and his assignment in America he spent a half hour with the General. The General blessed him with heart warming encouraging words of vision.

---

[32]*Double Confirmation* (Clinton 1989:262) is a form of certainty guidance in which God assures a person via more than one channel of His intent. Usually it is an inner conviction affirmed by some outside source unaware of the inner guidance.

[33]This is an instance of mini-convergence which I shall explain when I introduce his third development phase.

Chapter 4. Samuel Logan Brengle (1860-1936)　　　　　　page 142

D. Experience as Corps Officer: Taunton, South Manchester, Danbury (1887-1892); Age=27-32

During the first nine months of his Corps assignment he established a basic approach to Corps work. His first essential was to build up the quality of leadership, then use that leadership to reach out to others. His conviction was that battles would be won only with quality soldiers. But this training was done in the midst of Salvation Army activities aimed at evangelism and promoting holiness.

He and Elizabeth co-ministered in the Taunton Corps until her health restricted her involvement. He faced the usual difficulties of grass roots ministry: conflict of all kind, financial problems, envy, jealousy, and lack of commitment on the part of some of his soldiers. But he learned.

South Manchester, his second assignment was a short one. It impressed upon him the most important need--that of getting the soldiers sanctified.[34] This became his focus for this short assignment. He saw that activity alone, and there was plenty of that, would not "root and ground" the soldiers for the long haul. Almost the entire group of soldiers of this Corps were sanctified under Brengle's ministry. Many in later years pointed back to this time as the foundational time in their lives.

Danbury, his third ministry assignment, proved tough. Brengle was separated from his wife who had gone home to have their first child. There was debt. There were no soldiers. The quarters were poor. There were stacks of unsold and unpaid-for *War Crys*. There had been a scandal just before Brengle arrived which seriously damaged the reputation of the Army and made it difficult to promote public meetings. Brengle started with what he had and ministered faithfully.[35]

He was then assigned the Boston Number 1 Corps in November of 1888. This tested his pride. He was well known in Boston. The location of Boston Number 1 was in a poor section near a saloon. What would his wide circle of friends think? A word from the Lord eased his heart and he gave himself to Boston Number 1. The location of the saloon meant that many of the meetings were disrupted with rowdy drunkards. Yet there were blessed times as well.

One ministry insight[36] was the monthly all-day holiness meetings he initiated here. These proved to be a means for Brengle to fulfill his life purpose--*to insist upon holiness of*

---

[34]By sanctified, Brengle meant leading them through a holiness experience like he himself had gone through. It is sometimes called the *Blessing of the Clean Heart*. It is a religious experience in which the penitent seeks God's inner cleansing work and has an experience, usually a strong affective one, in which there is the sensing of God's presence, a release of guilt, a feeling of inner cleanliness and the enabling presence of the Holy Spirit. In Brengle's ministry format penitents would go forward at the end of the service to an altar and would kneel, confess, otherwise pray and wait expectantly for the experience. In old time Methodist circles this was frequently referred to as *praying through*. As I have mentioned before I evaluate it as a powergate through which a person comes to experience God's power at a higher level than before and opens up possibilities for living an exemplary Christian life.

[35]Hall does not give much detail on this assignment. He does point out the meager resources, leadership wise with which Brengle had to work--a Negro lieutenant and a hunchback girl--and an incident singing a song, *We're the Army That Shall Conquer*. It is an almost Gideon-like allusion. In the concluding chapter he refers back to this pair again.

[36]*Ministry Insights* (Clinton 1989:198) are breakthrough concepts which help a leader deliver ministry to followers. This breakthrough would be the equivalent today of a combination of day of prayer with a workshop on a holiness paradigm shift.

Chapter 4. Samuel Logan Brengle (1860-1936)   page 143

heart and life--with many in the Boston area. These meetings were attended by Salvationists--officers and soldiers, and Christian friends, and poor people. Many looking back saw this as the turning point in their deeper walk with Christ (Hall 1933:88).

The Boston Brick

It was during his Boston Number 1 assignment that Brengle received a setback that was almost permanent. One of the drunkards who had been evicted from a meeting waited outside till the meeting was over and then hurled a brick at Brengle as he came through the door. The brick hit Brengle head on. He very nearly died as a result of this attack. He was isolated from ministry for a period nearly two years recovering. During his convalescing Brengle wrote a series of articles which were later collected into his booklet, **Helps to Holiness**.[37] His message on holiness was getting a wider hearing through this indirect sphere of influence. Elizabeth symbolically noted this advancement in ministry.

> After returning from the health resort, Brengle one day found his wife painting a text on the brick. She had kept it, saying that she intended making a collection of all the bricks with which her husband would be knocked down....The text she had chosen was that word from Joseph to his brethren who had sold him into Egypt: "As for you, ye meant it for evil; but God meant it for good to keep much people alive." (Hall 1933:90,91)

God turns a terrible life threatening incident into a time of advancement, ministry influence-wise. Such is the enabling grace of God. Brengle himself saw this as an important result of his isolation time. He would often respond when people mentioned how much **Helps to Holiness** had meant to them. "Well, if there had been no little brick, there would have been no little book." Isolation processing is often used as a turning point in a boundary.[38] During his recovery time he toured the division, at the request of the new division commander, holding holiness meetings. The new commander's invitation came as a result of his reading Brengle's writings. His corps days end, with this almost two year boundary time, when he is appointed as a District Officer for Maine and New Hampshire.

E. Higher Level Leadership
Experience at District and above/ Executive Administration/ the Crisis (1892-1897); Age=32-37

Following the *Boston Brick* incident and its accompanying isolation, Brengle was appointed as a District Officer for Maine and New Hampshire. He was 32 years old, had five years of experience with the Army. He knew the problems that Corps officers face. He knew the ministry challenges. He had seen God work to deepen the lives of soldiers and officers and to expand ministries in a number of corps. His next challenge--to shepherd those who did the work he had been doing the past five years. He thought back

---

[37] This book had a wide circulation including translation into more than a dozen languages. Thousands of this book were sold, maybe over a hundred thousand. It was also called Hints To Holiness.
[38] This event has two major and one minor shaping activities going on. *Life Crisis* (Clinton 1989:278) was the first. It focused Brengle on the fundamental essentials of what life is all about. When time is short one thinks of the most essential issues. A second process involved *isolation* shaping (Clinton 1989:274, 275). This is a setting aside from ministry for an extended period of time. One result of this is a time of reflection, a gathering together of things learned, and frequently writing these lessons for others. See Paul's prison epistles which are marvelous products of isolation processing. Of the three types of isolation, the undeserved ones in which leaders are set aside are the toughest to take. Brengle responded to this processing with the result that God produced in him and through him that which He intended. This little book, **Helps to Holiness**, will serve as an important link to the man who will sponsor him to his convergent role. And of course, the minor shaping was the *influence-mix challenge* (Clinton 1989:229) an almost natural by-product of the first two, and which resulted in the booklet.

Chapter 4. Samuel Logan Brengle (1860-1936)

to his destiny prayer, *Lord, let me serve the servants of Jesus.* This was the guiding motive. Servant leadership was the core value of his district leadership. This meant sacrifices of all kinds. He led by serving and served by leading. He modeled and drew his followers upwards rather than authoritatively driving them.

He continued to uphold his basic value--develop the spiritual quality of the leaders and the work will progress.

> In his personal dealings with his officers the order always was: first the man, then his work. One officer recalls this:
>
> His first question, upon visiting our corps, and when we were alone together, was "How are you in your own soul, Captain? In the midst of your responsibilities, are you keeping close to God and allowing the Heavenly Father to pour His love afresh in your heart so that you are fit to deal with your soldiers and the poor lost souls of dying men?" And following such questions we would pray, his arm about my shoulders, his voice talking to God in that intimate, conversational way of his. Let me tell you, I would arise from such a season of helpful prayer with a feeling that I'd rather die and be lost than have him find me lax, either in my own experience or in my corps work! (Hall 1933:94)

This approach was key in inspiring leaders. The district prospered under his 2 and 1/2 years of leadership.

Brengle was next promoted to Staff-Captain and given the Western Massachusetts and Rhode Island Districts to supervise. His leadership there was again inspirational and productive but cut short.

American Split--Tolerant Firmness

The Salvation Army in America went through a crisis--a split in which Ballington Booth, son of the General and Commander-in-Chief of the Army in America resigned and split off some groups of followers with him. Hall does not belabor the causes but shows how Brengle stepped in and helped pick up some of the pieces. He was sent to Chicago and had temporary duties which lasted for 3 and 1/2 months as General Secretary for the North-Western Province comprising Chicago, S. Michigan, Wisconsin, and Indiana (Hall 1933:97). He was a busy man in the midst of the crisis.

> ...he threw himself and his every energy into the breach. Due to necessary frequent absences of his Provincial Commander, much of the responsibility of the Province devolved upon him. During the day he interviewed officers, talked with newspaper men, kept the Province's books, straightened corps accounts, untangled legal difficulties, conducted officers' councils, wrote articles for publication, organized a stirring camp-meeting on the shores of Lake Michigan, and traveled through his command. His evenings and Sunday were taken up with public meetings, church services, more officers' councils, all-nights of prayer, holiness campaigns--at all points leading enthusiastic attacks on sin and carnality. (Hall 1933:97,98)

In many situations he met up with former Salvationists who had split off. Always he was tolerant, stressed the business of soul winning, and avoided conflict with them. During these days of stress and turmoil he wrote a series of articles for *The War Cry* on the subject of "Soul-Winning." These were collected and formed into a book entitled, **The**

Chapter 4. Samuel Logan Brengle (1860-1936)

Soul-Winners Secret. This booklet was timely and turned the minds of salvationists from the split to the essential purpose of the agency (Hall 1933:99).[39]

Brengle served well in the months of the crisis. He was promoted to Major and a month later appointed as General Secretary of the Central Chief Division, under Lieutenant Colonel George French. He had learned much as a District Officer and as a temporary General Secretary in Chicago. He now had an appreciation for the larger view of the organizational structure, its problems, its administration, its leadership.[40] Hall catches the tenor of this paradigm shift, an appreciation for the bigger picture of leadership.

> Reading in his Bible the text, "Thou shalt feed my people Israel, and thou shalt be ruler over my people Israel," he drew his pencil under the words "feed" and "ruler over," as though telling himself that now he understood more clearly the dual relationship of a leader to those under him. His changed attitude is seen too, in his prayers; according to a diary entry of November 3, 1896, "high spirituality and high efficiency in business" had become twin subjects of his petitions:
>
> I have been thinking and praying today over high spirituality and high efficiency in business. I want to succeed in combining the two. Paul and Wesley and Moses and Daniel and Joseph did it. My heart is full of love for Jesus today. Bless God! He is mine and I am His. Paul says, "I was not a whit behind the very chiefest apostle." I want to be like that. Not selfishly, but for God's glory and the good of man. (Hall 1933:100)

He was a leader who spent much time with his officers. He solved problems. He encouraged those ready to quit. On the wall of Brengle's office there hung a text. It symbolized his dealings with his leaders. "Behold an Israelite indeed, in whom there is no guile." (Hall 1933:101) His leaders affirmed how true this was for Brengle.

At the end of eleven months he accepted what he thought was to be a temporary assignment to help out a situation on the Pacific Coast. This was to prove to be the front end of a boundary leading him to his destined convergent role.

III. NATIONAL SPIRITUAL SPECIAL/ HOLINESS CAMPAIGNER
Divinely Given Convergent Role
(1897-1936); Age=37-76

I have suggested previously that this entire third phase is a time of convergence for Brengle. I have pointed out how unusual it is for a leader to enter into convergence so early and to minister so long in this effective time of ministry. Usually a leader moves into convergence during a transition time of several years beginning at earliest during the late 40s in which there is adaptation toward a convergent role. Usually the ideal convergent role does not exist. And because of this, frequently, the organization or constituency will oppose the leader trying to formulate the role since it differs from traditional expectations. Brengle is totally unique in all of these matters. He entered into convergence early. There was no transition time and adapting of a present role toward the idea. There was an intervention, clearly by God to develop the role and free Brengle to operate in it. Let me

---

[39] This book like, *Hints To Holiness*, came out of the midst of ministry pressure and experience. It was applied life experience. Almost all of Brengle's writings were just such sharing of life experience.
[40] He is moving through what is called in leadership emergence theory, *the strategic barrier*, in which he sees the importance of indirect ministry as well as direct ministry. Indirect ministry means the shepherding of those in direct ministry and involves problem solving, administration, setting strategic direction, keeping vision alive for the whole movement, etc. It is not always as satisfying as leading souls to Christ, or building them up through Bible teaching--tactical ministries. But without strategic leadership the direct ministry efforts may well indeed falter.

Chapter 4. Samuel Logan Brengle (1860-1936)

discuss briefly what I meant by convergence then I shall show how the intervention came via a divine contact.

Convergence (Clinton 1989:380-381) refers to a period of effectiveness in a leader's life characterized by a number of factors coming together (merging, converging) so as to bring about that effectiveness. The major factors include:

1. **Giftedness**--The leader has a mature grasp of giftedness including natural abilities, acquired skills and spiritual gifts and sees this set working synergistically with the focal element enhanced and gift-mix matured as a gift-cluster.[41]
2. **Role**[42]--The role of the leader has been adapted to maximize giftedness and fit influence-mix and power-mix.[43] This was the most important major factor that was lacking in convergence for Brengle. He had experienced numerous transient assignments which focused on a kind of role, an evangelistic holiness concentration in public ministry. These mini-convergences[44] of role and giftedness primed him for the one that is to come at this time in his life through the divine contact, Commissioner McIntyre, Territorial Commander, Central (U.S.A.) Territory.

---

[41] In the giftedness set composed of natural abilities, acquired skills and spiritual gifts, one usually dominates. That one is called the *focal element*. In this case it was spiritual gifts (evangelism, exhortation, word of wisdom, pastoral). Further, the gift-mix is mature, that is what a *gift-cluster* is, working together. See Clinton and Clinton 1994, **Developing Leadership Giftedness**. For Brengle, evangelism and exhortation were co-dominate and supported by pastoral and word of wisdom. One of the unusual features of Brengle's gift-cluster was that both evangelism and exhortation were active publicly and privately. The pastoral and word of wisdom strongly supported the private use of evangelism and exhortation. At this point in his life Brengle was operating with gifted power--that is, sensing the supernatural empowerment of these gifts in ministry.

[42] Brengle's last assignments at high level executive leadership did not enhance the use of these gifts, especially in light of his major purpose *to instill holiness in heart and mind*. But they did give experience that would allow him to meet holiness needs of upper level leadership. Had he continued in these roles he would have frustrated his life purpose. Those roles would have hindered it simply because the essential tasks in them were time consuming and emotionally draining.

[43] *Influence-mix* (Clinton 1989:378) has to do with how and who leaders influence. All leaders influence followers. They can influence *directly*, that is, face-to-face ministry, *indirectly*, via shaping of key individuals or via materials used by others or *organizationally* via executive leadership or committees or the like. Each leader has a profile corresponding to which of these dominates or how they relate. Brengle had an extensive direct influence both private and public and an extensive indirect via his writings (flowing from direct). Organizational influence was not part of Brengle's profile except as he influenced spirituality of the whole organization. *Power-mix* (Clinton 1989: 378) has to do with the major means a leader uses to influence followers. Brengle's was dominantly spiritual authority which uses modeling, persuasion, and competency to influence. *Spiritual authority* (Clinton 1989:192-197) is the right to influence conferred upon a leader by followers because of their perception of the spirituality of that leader. It flows from one or the other of a combination of a leader 1. who models godliness, 2. who knows God (and His purposes and ways) via deep experiences, and 3. who demonstrates gifted power. All three were dominant in Brengle's life. His deep experiences of personal holiness with God were an anchor in his spiritual authority.

[44] *Mini-convergence* (Clinton 1989:380) is the leadership emergence theory term pointing to early symptoms of convergence. Ten common mini-convergent pairs have been identified as helpfully pointing to convergence. Each of these pairs involves a sense of unusual success or completeness: 1. some aspect of giftedness matched with ministry task; 2. some aspect of giftedness matched with some role function; 3. some aspect of giftedness matched with influence-mix; 4. giftedness matched with power-mix; 5. role matched with geographic location; 6. role matched with some past experience; 7. role matched with personality so as to balance out positive and negative personality traits; 8. destiny matched with special opportunity; 9. destiny matched with experience; 10. destiny matched with geographical location.

Chapter 4. Samuel Logan Brengle (1860-1936)

3. **Influence-Mix**--the leader has reached appropriate capacity for influencing followers. Influence-mix has right combination and depth (i.e. appropriate extensiveness, intensiveness, and comprehensiveness). This factor needs enhancement. McIntyre sees that Brengle's influence needs to be nationally affecting the whole Salvation Army and wants to sponsor him toward that. The role he suggests will do that.
4. **Upward Dependence**--the leader has a deep relationship with God and from which flows power in ministry. *Upward Dependence* refers to a leader who essentially ministers out of being rather than doing. This usually means a norm of union life. In Brengle's case this was manifested via consistent holiness in life (personal and public) and ministry.
5. **Ministry Philosophy**--The leader has a clear focus in what he/she is to accomplish and how to do so. Articulated values undergird the ministry. Brengle has developed this over a long period of time including means for actually seeing people enter into holiness (with emphasis on cognitive, affect, and especially volitional). His use of the penitent-form[45] and personal counseling were outstandingly effective.

The above major factors 1, 4, and 5 were relatively complete at this point. It is factors 2 and 3 that McIntyre, the divine contact, will resource.[46]

Divine contacts frequently come along at a time in which God is going to move a leader into something new--a boundary time in his/her life development. The person may or may not be aware of all that this boundary time means. But along comes the divine contact and opens up perspective on the new and gives authority to that timely intervention so that God is sensed as being in it. The experience may even border on a destiny experience. Such is the case with the following. McIntyre, as a divine contact, was the key to Brengle's convergence. A divine contact is a mentor whom God brings in contact with a person at a crucial moment in his/her development in order to authoritatively facilitate along the lines of one of the following empowerments:

1. to *affirm* either the person or some idea as legitimate and meeting with God's approval,
2. to *encourage* leadership *potential*,
3. to give *guidance* for some *crucial decision*,
4. to give *perspective* that will *clarify* some situation,
5. to *link* the person with some resource such as a person, finances, or information,
6. to link the person with some *opportunity*--for ministry, or for training, for personal development.

---

[45] A form of public altar call utilizing personal counseling as a persuasive focus.
[46] Leadership emergence theory has also identified six minor factors that sometimes occur in order to complete or complement convergent ministry. The five major factors, given above, are essential and have some manifestations for any convergent leader. Some of the six minor factors may be essential to some in convergence but not for all. These six minor factors include: 1. past experience hitherto unexplained now fits into place and contributes; 2. The unique personality of the leader fits the situation: negative personality factors are minimized in the role and positive personality factors are enhanced by the role; 3. The leader is located in a geographical center which helps radiate the influence; 4. There is a special window of opportunity that opens for a time period--it must be taken advantage of or lost; 5. There may be a prophecy in the past which now is fulfilled and/or now clarifies the guidance leading to the convergent role; 6. Previous destiny experiences come to fulfillment in convergence. Numbers 1 and 6 were especially true for Brengle.

McIntyre especially fulfilled divine contact functions 1, 5, and 6. He will deal directly with convergent factors 2, Role, and 3, Influence-mix.

McIntyre--Divine Contact Leading to Natural Spiritual Special Role

At this point, Brengle is a Major who has operated for 11 months as General Secretary of the Central Chief Division. He has answered an appeal from the West Coast for a time of ministry, holding a holiness camp meeting. He sees it as a Macedonian Call, a momentary welcome relief[47] from executive administrative detail. Catch the excitement of this divine intervention as related by Hall.

> "Major, when I asked that you might come to California, I had a double purpose in mind. I wanted you for the Trestle Glen camp-meetings; but I wanted you for myself as well. I've read your writings, sensed your spirit and I believe you can help me. I've grown a little dry in my own soul. I didn't expect to approach you here in the office; I intended rather to wait and lead the way to the penitent-form [altar call] at the camp. But I can't wait." After this frank confession of heart hunger, the two men went to their knees.[48]
>
> In such a manner was the way paved for what turned out to be, according to the San Jose **Mercury,** "altogether the most successful meeting of its kind ever held on this Coast." The camp-meeting, opening in a blaze of revival fervor, ran for two weeks, during which more than four hundred came to the penitent-form seeking deeper spiritual experiences.
>
> When the camp had closed, Brengle spent an additional four weeks conducting short campaigns in other parts of the Pacific Coast Chief Division (Hall 1933:102,103).

Now note the divine contact intervention and its affirmation of Brengle's long time growing awareness of a sense of destiny.

> It was while on this tour that Brengle became privy to a bit of information that again set ringing within him the bells of a long-lived hope:
>
> He [McIntyre] surprised me this morning by saying that since the Trestle Glen camp-meeting he and Marshall and Dunham had bound themselves in a prayer covenant, to pray that God would put me altogether in spiritual work. He is writing Colonel Higgins to suggest strongly that I be used for this work exclusively.[49]
>
> Having learned of this prayer covenant, he allowed his thoughts, for the first time in several months to dwell on the ambition that had lived with him for years--lived down deep in the cleansed recesses of his heart where in some men dwell selfish aspiration and passion for position. Was his Lord after all going to lead him into evangelistic work? During his stays in Chicago and New York, it had seemed that the Lord was closing that road to him and opening another that tended to leadership of an administration, as well as spiritual, character.
>
> . . .

---

[47]Crossing the strategic barrier, that is, moving from a basically direct ministry to an indirect ministry is difficult for two major reasons. 1. **A Training Problem:** Usually leaders are trained for direct ministry but not indirect. 2. **A Psychological Affirmation Problem:** They also receive tremendous satisfaction from using their giftedness in direct ministry. There is an affirmation that is seldom felt in indirect ministry. So then, one of the coping ministries of those in indirect ministry is forays--back into direct ministry. Brengle was on such a foray when the intervention hit.

[48]This is a typical example of opportunistic private ministry. Brengle did this kind of ministry repeatedly both for commitment to holiness and in evangelism for commitment to Christ for salvation.

[49]This is also a beautiful illustration of mentor sponsoring (Clinton and Clinton 1991) and of *networking power* (Clinton 1989:240).

Chapter 4. Samuel Logan Brengle (1860-1936)

Now, however, significant questions presented themselves: What of these hungry hearts calling him across the country to feed them? What of God so abundantly blessing his labors in this direction? And what of men binding themselves in covenant to pray him into evangelistic Work? Were these the finger of God, beckoning him at last to the type of service which, had he chosen for himself, he would have entered upon ten years ago?

A few days later, while engaged in his closing meetings on the Coast, he received a message from New York that brought joy to his heart and a shout to his throat: he was instructed to return to that city at once to farewell from his office as General Secretary for the Central Chief Division--this in order that he might begin immediately upon his new work as the "National Spiritual Special!" (Hall 1933:103,104)

The ideal role has been designed. It will provide room for reaching his ideal influence-mix. He has been assigned a national roving role to hold holiness and evangelistic meetings all over. He is free from administrative detail. The organization is sponsoring the role. This means help in scheduling and sponsoring meetings. The organization will open the doors. It will be ultimately responsible for the financing too. Notice how this also carries deep spiritual meaning. It is the fulfillment of a sense of destiny that has been growing for a long time.

At last--an appointment consonant with his specialized training, his most fervid and secret longings. Back in his Cadet days, three months after joining the Army, he had written: "I sometimes wonder if God means me for a kind of holiness evangelist to The Army..." and through the years that wondering had been ever-recurrent, till now, the appointment in hand, he wondered no more.

National Spiritual Special... In those words he saw, not just another appointment, but destiny. Reviewing the path along which he had come, Brengle could see clearly the successive steps of God's leading and training. He had given him humble birth, that he might be one with the poor. He had subjected him early to toil, that he might always understand and be able to speak the language of the toiler. He had equipped him with the learning of the schools, that he might be able to enter into the mind and problems of the scholar. He had lifted him high toward ecclesiastic position, that he might be familiar with the ministry of those among whom he was largely to labor. He had brought him low in humility, introduced him to persecution and the hardships of small Army corps experience, that he might be wise regarding the trials of his comrades. He had given him executive position, made him a "ruler over" the flock, that he might have fellowship with staff officers in their multiplied cares. Every step indeed, along his whole diversified path had contributed to his development, deepened his understanding, widened his knowledge, expanded his sympathies. He had been "all things" and in all places among all men, that he "might by all means save some."

True, the path of his development had been widening, overhung with shadows sometimes, the next step often difficult of discernment. But God had been in it all, and because His man had not faltered nor turned back, He could now lead out into the open road (Hall 1933:104-105).[50]

Note the place of McIntyre in this process. He was one who benefited from Brengle's ministry and saw potential that should be unleashed. He wrote a letter to headquarters with the suggestion of a national full time position that would free Brengle up

---

[50]This illustrates an important guidance principle, *God's guidance is clear guidance*. It is not always seen as such in the midst of it but retrospectively, one who has honestly sought God's will can affirm this statement. And because it is true one can trust a sovereign God in the midst of the confusion when it does not seem so clear.

Chapter 4. Samuel Logan Brengle (1860-1936)

from the normal higher echelon duties in The Salvation Army. And he covenanted in prayer with other faithful comrades to see God bring it about.[51]

This role was first explored and developed geographically in the U.S.A. It then expanded overseas primarily to Europe but also to the Southwest Pacific. Finally, it culminated in a time of powerful ministry in the U.S.A.

A. First Campaigns--
Breaking New Ground/ Pioneer Role in U.S.A.
(1897-1904); Age=37-44

Lack of Chronological Treatment

It is impossible to cover the next several time periods since they involve itinerant ministries and travel to so many different locales. Rather than attempt any treatment of chronological coverage I will rather comment on some of the important issues he faced during these periods or the important shaping activities.[52]

General Character of the Ministry

This period of time was characterized by travels all over the United States. For only short periods of time did Brengle enjoy the comforts of home. But his life experiences, numerous moves during his growing up time, numerous short ministry assignments over the ten years with the Army, had prepared him for just such sacrifices and inconveniences. He did not receive all the organizational support he needed during these early years. Particularly was this true of publicity and advance planning for his meetings. Several times he would be met at scheduled activities with small turnouts. One remark that Hall includes shows his sense of humor. Asked on one occasion what was the smallest number he would speak to, Brengle replied, "Well, I usually draw the line at two. But--have you fewer than that?" (Hall 1933:111).

A Public Rhetorician's Nemesis--Problem of In-Depth Follow-Through

He was troubled at first by the brief periods of his stays while on the road. He would spend three days or less, occasionally one week. In such a short time what can be done? This is a problem that all Public Rhetoricians have to deal with sooner or later.[53] As

---

[51] This is a superb example of two forms of mentoring--*divine contact* and *sponsor*. There is a sense in which all forms of mentoring are divine contacts. However, the essential thing that makes a divine contact unique is the sensed presence of a God-given timely intervention. The mentoree is primed by circumstances and experience so that when the mentor appears the situation is touched with the Divine and sensed as such. The key to this type of mentoring is sensitivity to God's timing in bringing intervention in lives. Brengle had responded faithfully in every ministry assignment. This had given him experience all up and down the leadership levels. He was now, after two stints of upper level leadership prepared to offer his ministry of holiness to the whole Army. All of us as leaders need to develop the sensitivity to divine contact mentoring both as recipients of God's grace and as those through whom it will come to others.

[52] I have not yet seen an adequate biographical treatment or model for covering chronologically the itinerant ministries of public rhetoricians. There are so many activities, important events, speaking engagements, results, etc. that an adequate treatment seems impossible. Morgan's biographers, J. Morgan, Harries, and Murray (doesn't claim to) do not adequately do this. Morgan and Brengle are the two leaders in this book with extended itinerant time periods.

[53] Billy Graham dealt with this nagging problem by getting help from Dawson Trottman who seconded an experienced disciple maker, Charlie Riggs, to head up counselor training of church participants weeks prior to a campaign. They also rigged up information systems for follow-up in conjunction with these trained counselors and churches so that after the campaign, there was follow-through on decisions. Ken Strachan

Chapter 4. Samuel Logan Brengle (1860-1936)

he ministered repeatedly like this he began to develop a means of coping with that troublesome, nagging feeling. In fact, it was a ministerial and strategic value which emerged. He describes his discovery of it.

> At first the thought that he could do little more than a superficial work in so short a time had tempted him to feel that what he did would not last. In this, however, he had quickly detected what he termed a "failure to believe in the vitality of the Word." In one of his first letters to Mrs. Brengle after beginning his service [as National Spiritual Special]...he had written:
> One difficulty that I see is that my time is so short. I must reprove, rebuke, exhort, instruct, inspire--all in a day or two--and then run away and trust the Lord to do the rest through such material as the officers may be. I wound people, cut out abscesses, amputate arms and legs, and take out eyes, but cannot stay with my patients to see how they will heal. However, that is the way Jesus went about, and Wesley, and the General. God can help people without me, and He will. Pray that He will help me to so preach the truth that people cannot escape its power, and that it may so sink into their hearts and lay hold of their understanding, judgment, will and conscience, that it shall have *cumulative force and influence* in their lives (Hall 1933:112,113).

It is the words *cumulative force and influence* that signal the basic paradigm shift in which he distinctly accepted the faith challenge to trust God to follow-up. The expansion following acceptance of this faith challenge is reflected on by Hall.[54]

> Later experience proved conclusively that his work did have *cumulative force and influence*. Doubling back on his trails of former days he was ever to meet the accumulated forces and influences of his original work. From wherever people had sat under his preaching there would spring up reincarnations of himself and his spirit--Brengle reproductions; in miniature, perhaps, but reproductions nevertheless. So his soul has marched on where his feet have never come. Men preach his sermons and tell his stories in cities he never has visited; and thus his words go on winning victories for his Lord, even in unknown corners and far-away places (Hall 1933:113).

It is this cumulative effect that made his third period of time, 1911-1927--his repeat campaigns in the U.S.A--his most powerful.

Preparation--Ministry Flows Out of Being

During this itinerant ministry there were heavy speaking responsibilities. Important values concerning them come out in his answers to two questions.

> On one occasion, when a field officer, harried by a multitude of duties that left him but little time for sermon-making, asked Brengle this question, "If you had but ten minutes to prepare for a meeting, how would you spend it?" He received a reply in two words: "In prayer!"
> When a young theologian one day asked him, "What preparation do you make for preaching?" Brengle gave answer...

---

designed Evangelism in Depth as a means of by-passing this problem. This saturation evangelism program was local church centered and sponsored for that very reason--on-going follow-through prior and after campaigns. Morgan, a public rhetorician though not an evangelist but a Bible teacher could count on two things. Most people coming to him were committed church members so there was a chance for follow-up and he had many materials and books available for their study after his public conferences.

[54] This is a mature *faith challenge* and follows the standard *positive testing* pattern of test, response, and expansion. But being a mature leader the expansion does not necessarily come immediately as would be needed to encourage a younger less mature leader.

Chapter 4. Samuel Logan Brengle (1860-1936)

> My lifetime has been a preparation for preaching. But, more particularly, I prepare my sermons for others by preparing my own heart. In this, prayer and Bible study are the chief factors. When I read books other than the Bible, they are read not that parts of them might be included in my address, but to enrich my own thought and to quicken and inspire my faith. Thus I spend a great deal of time preparing myself for preaching. Many make the mistake of giving more time to the preparation of their addresses than to the preparation of their own hearts, affections, emotions, and faith; the result often is beautiful, brilliant words that have the same effect as holding up glittering icicles before a freezing man. To warm others--and is not that your purpose in preaching?--a man must keep the fire burning hot in his own soul? (Hall 1933:114)

One must remember, in addition to the above essential advice, the cumulative effect of preparing for public ministry over the years.

A Bible Centered Person--Personally and Publicly

An important consideration of what made his convergent ministry so powerful can be seen in the following:

> The large place that the Bible occupied in Brengle's preaching was patent to all who heard him. Scripture quotations were so interwoven through all he said that to lift them out would be to make his address almost unintelligible. One hearer sharply etched Brengle when he said of him: "This man is a walking, talking edition of the Bible." Herein, doubtless, lay the tone of authority that pervaded his utterances, causing men when hearing him to think they were listening to a veritable oracle of God. (Hall 1933:114,115).

I quote this because it highlights a commonalty of all eight of the Christian leaders dealt with in this book. They were students of the Scriptures for their own lives first and for others secondarily. The Bible was first of all real to them personally. When this is so then it will permeate all the rest of the ministry--as with Brengle, "a walking, talking edition of the Bible."

Repetitive Ministry And the Plateau Problem

How did he handle the plateauing problem[55] that often waylays the public rhetorician? I think in three main ways:

1. recognition of it as a problem,[56]
2. a deliberate attempt to learn and be fresh,
3. much personal interaction with people.

Two quotes help us see his recognition of the problem. A sensitive spiritual awareness of the problem is a major first warning about it. Brengle had that sensitivity and made it a matter of prayer to seek out renewal and freshness as he continued the repetitive activities involved in evangelism and holiness ministries.

---

[55]In the preface I alluded to six major barriers or problems to finishing well. See Appendix A. Public Rhetoricians, worship leaders, and other public music talents are especially susceptible to one of them, the plateau barrier, because of the repetitive nature of their ministries which focuses on such limited areas.
[56]When reading the biography of Henry Drummond, he underlined in red those important words which were discerning about public evangelists and their inability to finish well. "A criticism of professional evangelism: A few years of enthusiasm and blessing, then carelessness, no study, no spiritual fruit, too often a sad collapse." (Hall 1933:118).

Chapter 4. Samuel Logan Brengle (1860-1936)

> The evangelist must confine himself to a certain line of subjects and he must in every new field of labor--which means every week or so--begin all over again. He aims at immediate results. He cannot wait to see the unfolding of character following the preaching of the truth, and gradually loses far vision and becomes spiritually near-sighted. (O Lord, help me. Broaden me out and deepen me in my soul's experience and give me a statesman-like view of truth and of Thy plans for the future of The Army and the Church.)
> The evangelist, may, by much prayer and meditation and faithfulness, cultivate in himself a sense of responsibility, but the tendency of his work is to destroy or atrophy that sense. He moves about largely care-free. If people do not like him, he does not feel the responsibility of adjusting himself to them, for he soon passes on and hears of them no more. His opportunities for study are limited. He works at high pressure, is surrounded by people, has many public and private engagements, lives in a hotel, or is entertained in some private home, and is away from his library and books of reference. How can he study and make quiet, careful preparation? (O Lord, help me. Keep me fresh and full of compassion and humility and teachableness!) (Hall 1933:118)

During this period of time three books were published: (1897) **Heart Talks on Holiness**, (1902) **The Way of Holiness**, (1903) **The Soul-Winner's Secret**.

B. Growing Influence--Campaigns
Abroad/ Europe and S.W. Pacific
(1904-1911); Age=44-51

During this period of time his ministry was largely abroad in Europe. I mention two highlights, one a contemporary contribution that is a legacy to Brengle's public ministry and the other a discovery of an unusual application of faith to public ministry. These in no way adequately treat this period of time but like road maps they point the way to the kinds of things that were involved.

Special Contribution To the Cause of Christ--Atonement Sermon[57]

Some think one of the finest achievements of his entire life was one sermon he preached in the midst of doctrinal controversy in Norway in 1907. The problem was a persuasive New Theology that was sweeping sincere Christians away from orthodoxy. Their tenets denied publicly the divinity of Christ and the inspiration and authority of the Scriptures. There had been public debates by leading pastors with the leader of the movement. That leader from a prominent family was so eloquent and demonstrated such extensive learning that the pastors were thwarted in their public debates. Brengle was invited to champion the cause of orthodoxy.

Brengle, as was usually the case, rather than attacking the negative heretical doctrines instead presented the positive truths and with such an appeal that there was no place for rejoinder. His sermon, The Atonement, almost totally extemporaneously given, was hailed by the crowd as the most important thing that they had ever heard on the divinity of Christ. This one sermon is a most illustrative example of an ultimate contribution which met a specific need for its moment (contemporary contribution) but will not be remembered beyond its day (as classic contribution would).[58]

---

[57]This sermon was reconstructed somewhat and published in Brengle (1934:9-42), **Guest of the Soul**.
[58]Had this sermon been recorded in written form (Brengle did it from some hastily scribbled notes on the back of an envelope) it may well have been a classic ultimate contribution like Pastor Bob Munger's Sunday night sermon, *My Heart, Christ's Home*, which has been reprinted in the millions.

Chapter 4. Samuel Logan Brengle (1860-1936)

Ministry Insight--Retrospective Faith Concept

An important insight into one of his ministerial values, I call it the *Retrospective Faith or the Backward Faith Look* is seen in his comments about meetings in Denmark during a particularly tough time of ministry involving a split due to tongues elitism.[59]

> Working his way toward Bergen, seat of the other radical departure, Brengle achieved victory in virtually every town where he campaigned. His spirits were high; neither did they droop when there came a slump in results at Fredrikshald, where for several days running he saw few at the penitent-form. Instead of complaining, he put the resultless meetings in God's hands, with the remark: "He can work backward as well as forward. He can still bless those meetings and bring much fruit to many souls out of them. I do believe, and I rejoice in hope." (Hall 1933:176)

During this period one writing achievement was involved--(1909) **When The Holy Ghost is Come.**

C. Follow-Up Campaigns--
Powerful U.S.A. Ministry
(1911-1927); Age=51-67

This was Brengle's most effective ministry time ever. The *cumulative effect* was there buttressing his every ministry activity. Everywhere he went he was following up on the foundations that had been laid over his lifetime. I mention two items: Brengle's recognition and his deep processing. This deep processing occurred throughout his whole ministry but several critical ones occurred during this final campaigning era.

Honored[60]

The way *up is down*! This Joseph lesson was learned several times in the early days. He knew the *down side* well. When he was 54 he saw some of the *up side* of that equation. He was always surprised at such honors. He was one who knew God as *the lifter of his head*.

> In a nice letter from Dr. Gobin, vice-president of DePauw, I am told the university is proud of me as a Salvationist. Why, when I joined The Army I thought they would almost want to blot my name off the Alumni Register!
> But his surprise reached even greater heights when, on June 10, 1914, DePauw called him to her chapel to receive the degree of Doctor of Divinity. Again, upon hearing that at a reunion of the class of 1883, which numbered many who had attained eminence in almost every field, it had been the consensus that "Sam Brengle is the greatest success of our class," he only smiled his incredulity. But when he was apprised of the fact that on one Founders and Benefactors Day at DePauw a renowned speaker had stated to ringing

---

[59]In the early days of Pentecostalism, the so called First Wave, tongues as the initial sign of the Baptism of the Holy Ghost, quickly created an elitist attitude which seemed to imply that those who did not have this evidence were missing something in their Christianity. This elitism attitude caused splits in churches. Second and Third wave phenomenon do not seem to cause splits as readily as did the First Wave. Splits were happening as Pentecostalism, just getting off the ground, was spreading in Scandinavia. Brengle was asked to speak to these issues. His sanctified diplomacy and his more traditional approach to life power via the Wesleyan model of entire sanctification was more acceptable than the new tongues/Baptism of Holy Ghost model. Brengle's ministry was deeply appreciated.

[60]An honor which occurred later in his afterglow ministry was one he prized highly. He was inducted into the Order of the Founder--sort of a Hall of Fame of Salvationists' heroes and heroines who have ministered over their lifetimes faithfully and who are finishing well. This was September 23, 1935, at age 75, a year before his death (Hall 1933:244).

Chapter 4. Samuel Logan Brengle (1860-1936)

applause that "the two alumni of DePauw who are most outstanding in what they have accomplished for the world's good are Count Chinda '81,[61] and Commissioner Brengle, '83--he refused to believe that anyone "could make such a mistake." (Hall 1933:159)

Part of the recognition and honoring of Brengle was due to his highly respectable educational background at DePauw and Boston Theological Seminary. During this time of highly effective convergent ministry Brengle was frequently asked to speak at Bible Institutes, Seminaries, Colleges and Universities. His talks were always apropos and fit the level of educated listeners he spoke too. But they always had a spiritual punch too. Some of the institutions of higher learning at which he had impact include: Garrett Biblical Institute (now called Garrett-Evangelical Theological Seminary), Northwestern University, Asbury College, John Fletcher College, DePauw University, Denver University, Grant University, the State Normal School of Emporia, Kansas, Presbyterian Seminary, and of course the 4 training colleges of The Salvation Army in the U.S.

Deep Processing--Maturity and Spiritual Authority

Isolation via numerous sicknesses or physical problems were numerous in the life of Brengle. Note Brengle's philosophy on these.

> Manifold trials call for manifold grace; manifold grace works for us manifold experience; manifold experience gives us manifold testimony, enabling us to meet manifold needs...
> God does not make pets of His people, and especially of those whom He woos and wins into close fellowship with Himself, and fits and crowns for great and high service. His greatest servants have often been the greatest sufferers (Hall 1933:210).

Hall's commentary explains these manifold trials; these sanctifying influences:

> Sicknesses, ailments, abrasions, accidents--in severity and number far above those which visit the average man in his lifetime--came to him. His had not been a single thorn in the flesh, buffeting him with repeated attacks; rather had he felt the pricks of an infinite variety of thistles. He could think, for example, of these:
> The injury to his head wrought by the Boston tough's brick...The scores of illnesses brought on by exposure, by his exhaustive labors and wearying travels, and by preaching in crowded and ill-ventilated little halls when scarcely able to keep to his feet. His undergoing three major operations and many minor ones. Teeth troubles that took him into dental parlors in many lands, enabling him to remark: "I could get up a most comprehensive and authoritative dental directory of the world!" The agonizing and dangerous malady (rheumatic fever) which took him close to death's door when in Denmark in 1908. Stubborn ailments of one kind and another which he kept under only by the most careful attention to diet, exercise and self-doctoring. And, on top of all these, a shocking automobile accident which, coming upon him at the age of sixty-four, swept him nearer the River than he had ever been before (Hall 1933:211,212).

But it is Hall's appraisal of the shaping influences of these trials that is most interesting.

> More interesting, however, than the fact that such trials came to him, is the question: How did they leave him?

---

[61]Brengle had been a mentor for Chinda, who became a high ranking Japanese Diplomat (Ambassador to German, 1908; Ambassador to U.S., 1911-1916; Ambassador to Great Britain, 1916-1920; Privy councilor and grand steward to Prince Regent; Japanese representative at Versailles Peace Conference, 1919). Brengle had networked him into the undergraduate leadership of the College, had shown him the basics of the educational system, and had been his friend (chess partner) (Hall 1933:37).

Chapter 4. Samuel Logan Brengle (1860-1936)

> It is not too much to say that, in looking at his manifold sufferings and trials, we are looking at the things which largely made him Brengle (Hall 1933:212).

Brengle's own evaluation of these life reverses was given to a newspaper interviewer. Note the words moral fiber and then Hall's commentary.

> I am a constant student in God's school, the University of Hard Knocks. I have forgotten much that I learned in two universities, much of the Latin, the Greek, and the Hebrew. But I will never forget the lessons I have learned in God's school It is there that moral fiber is developed. When I get to heaven I'm not going to ask Daniel how many featherbeds he slept upon in Babylon, but I am anxious to ask him about the night he spent in the lions' den. And the first thing I am going to ask Paul is about the shipwreck, and the times he spent in prison. It takes these things to make a man.
>
> Again and again when sickness interposed itself, cutting athwart his plans, checkmating his moves, he would still his soul into quietness by anticipating God's greater glory, through the trial (Hall 1933:212,213).

I have mentioned previously that spiritual authority comes through three sources. One involves knowing God by having gone through deep experiences with God (2 Corinthians 1:3,4). One reason for Brengle's spiritual authority was this shaping activity he calls *manifold trials*.

> Most valuable of all the assets his physical sufferings added to him, however, was the new understanding of, and new entrée to, the hearts of those who otherwise could not have been reached by him. With the passing of each of the "manifold trials," he invariable found that it left in his hand "another key to the hearts of my fellows." And so varied and numerous were his experiences that his keys were many (Hall 1933:215).

An extreme example of these *manifold trials*, that is, maturity processing,[62] occurred in 1915. Brengle was recovering from a very painful operation. In the midst of his hospitalization Mrs. Brengle had a complete health breakdown. With the following diary entry, Hall probes the depth of Brengle's feelings and response to the news that his wife lay dying.

> A thousand times in distant lands and lonely hours, I have been stabbed by the thought that possibly my darling might die before I could cross oceans and continents and reach her side. Now, lying only a hundred miles away, she was dying--and I was at the point of death and couldn't go to her. It seemed as though my heart would break, and it seemed as though God didn't care if my heart did break. But I did not go by appearances. I had preached all round the world that God *does care*, that all things do work together for good to them that love the Lord, and I didn't cast away my confidence and charge God foolishly. I was very weak, but I took my Bible and songbook and I read the promises and nestled down upon them, and I read the hymns of comfort and guidance and heaven and I nestled down into the will of God. I said, "O Lord, Thou knowest how I love my darling and how desolate I shall be if Thou dost take her, but I don't know what is best for her or for the dear children or for myself. Thy will be done." And peace entered my heart (Hall 1933:217,218).

Shortly afterwards, Brengle was allowed to go to her. She died on April 3, 1915. Thereafter, he had no permanent home and ministered as a single the rest of his life.[63]

---

[62] In leadership emergence theory, *crises, life crises, isolation, conflict*, and *ministry conflict* are processes which are recognized as deepening the life of the leader and leading to both spiritual authority and the concept of ministry flowing out of being. These kind of shaping activities are called life maturing activities or maturity processing.

[63] This one of the most tender moments in the book. Hall covers it well. I commend it to you. Particularly touching is the reference to the wedding ring and the prophetic motto inscribed on it, *Holiness*

Chapter 4. Samuel Logan Brengle (1860-1936)

During this period of time, two written works were published: (1923) **Love Slaves**, and (1925) **Resurrection Life and Power**.

D. Afterglow Years--
Continued Itinerant Ministry/ Less Rigorous/ Official Retirement
(1927-1931); Age=67-70+

During this time Brengle continued his correspondence ministry, personal consultation and counseling with officers and some itinerant ministry. His health was generally good. One writing effort was finalized, **Ancient Prophets (and Modern Problems)**.

E. Continued Afterglow--
Meditation/ Correspondence/ Counseling
(1931-1936); Age=70-76

Two writing projects were edited in this period. In 1934, **Guest of the Soul** was published. His part of **God as Strategist** was done though it was not published till 1942 after Brengle's death.

Toward the end of his life his eyesight failed. He met this trial as he had always done, with a positive undaunted spirit. His inner life was so rich, his knowledge of the Bible so sweeping and his memory replete with the Saints who had gone before him that though he was lonely, he was not.

> My eyes are bad, and I am getting weaker, but, hallelujah! On I go to see the King in all His beauty and the Land that is afar off--and yet not far off! Glory to God in the highest!"
> ...I have sweet fellowship at times in my own room. The saints of all the ages congregate there. Moses, is present, and gives his testimony, and declares that the eternal God is his refuge and underneath are the everlasting arms.
> Joshua arises, and declares, "as for me and my house, we will serve the Lord." Samuel and David, my dear friends Isaiah, Jeremiah, and Daniel, Paul and John and James, and deeply humbled and beloved Peter, each testify to the abounding grace of God. Luther and Wesley and the Founder and Finney, and Spurgeon and Moody, and unnumbered multitudes all testify.
> Blind old Fanny Crosby cries out: "Blessed assurance, Jesus is mine!" So you see, I am not alone. Indeed, I can gather these saints together for a jubilant prayer and praise meeting almost any hour of the night. Hallelujah forever, and glory to God!" (Hall 1933: 246-248)

Brengle finished well.[64] He is my own personal inspirational ideal of a godly leader who finished well. I cite two quotations from his twilight years which have personally inspired me for years.

> O Lord, as I grow old, help me to understand Thy mind for me and Thy will. I realize that each state of life--youth, manhood, old age--has its own problems. Help me to understand the mysteries of old age. I have not passed this way before. Help me to be wise, to make no mistakes, to be serene, patient, hopeful and unafraid.

Unto the Lord, so symbolic of their life testimonies, individually and together. See Hall 1933:216-223, Chapter XXV, entitled *Vanished Hand*.

[64]*Finished Well* can mean different things to different people. Six characteristics of finishing well are given in Appendix C. Of these six Brengle scores high marks on all six: personal vibrant relationship with God, learning posture, Christ likeness in character, Word centered faith, ultimate contributions, fulfilled sense of destiny.

O Lord, as old age overtakes me, save me from two evils: on the one hand, the querulous, critical, fault-finding habits into which so many old people fall; and, on the other, the soft, gullible spirit. Keep my eyes wide open to the weakness, foolishness, guilefulness and sin of men; yet keep my heart tender and sympathetic and hopeful. Help me to be firm and steadfast in my loyalty to truth, and always clear as to what truth is. Don't let me be deceived. Don't let me go astray the very least in my old age. Don't permit me to fall into even a little folly that, like a fly in a pot of ointment, will spoil the influence of a life devoted to Thee. Help me, O Lord (Hall 1933:236,237).

Brengle's final words just before he passed into unconsciousness were a text: "The angel of the Lord encampeth round about them that fear him..." (Hall 1933:249) That angel was surely there, for this *Apostle of Holiness*, *a Public Saint*, certainly feared the Lord.

Critical Incidents Identified, and/or Explained

Remember, critical incidents are important shaping activities in which either focal values are imparted or some pivotal career guidance occurs or sometimes both happen. Hence they are often important pointers to the focusing activity of God. They are shaping activities which can affect values relating to all three types of formations--spiritual (leadership character), ministerial (leadership skills) and strategic (total direction in life and ministry). There is a sense in which many, many incidents in a leader's life affect values. But from that large identifiable number a few should be highlighted and recognized as very significant. Here is a list of these that I have so identified from the materials that were available to me.[65] Table 4-1 indicates these. I number them for convenience of referencing later when I comment on them.

Table 4-1 Listing Of Some Critical Incidents In Brengle's Life

Incident(s) Name	Age	Formational Type Dealing With Basic Value/Thrust
1. Stars in the Sky--Early Destiny Items (see page 128)	Birth, 8	Strategic--Parents pre-birth committal, early exposure to Bible, The Abraham Passage--Stars in in the Sky. This is a focal factor.
2. Spontaneous Anger, The Sensitivity Incident (see pages 130)	12	Spiritual--Brengle's loss of temper broke his joyful relationship with God. Brengle senses that sin does this. This leads to a focal value.
3. The Call, Harnessing Ambition (see pages 123-125)	22	Strategic--Brengle's public communication drive is channeled toward ministry, a first step toward a convergent public communication role. This destiny experience, a leadership committal, would be an anchor. This is a major focal factor--value involved.

---

[65]As with other leaders studied I continue to make the disclaimer. These critical incidents are not exhaustive. Had I more data (like access to Brengle's diary, letters, etc.) or even different slants than Hall gives I might easily identify other critical incidents. But these identified are certainly important and help us understand God's ways in shaping a focused life.

Chapter 4. Samuel Logan Brengle (1860-1936)

Table 4-1 Listing Of Some Critical Incidents In Brengle's Life continued

Incident(s) Name	Age	Formational Type Dealing With Basic Value/Thrust
4. Hidden Guidance (see page 133)	23	Spiritual, Ministerial, Strategic--Ambition is curbed by a lowly appointment to a rural circuit when a city pastorate had been promised. This is preparatory to a later call to the lowly with The Salvation Army. It teaches communication skills with simple people. A positive attitude in accepting the assignment makes it a springboard to expansion and Boston Theological Seminary. Sovereign focal factor.
5. Back To School-- God supplies. (see page 134)	24	Strategic--Bishop Joyce is conscious of leadership selection and training. He recognizes in Brengle potential that can be greatly used of God. He sponsors Brengle back to a top, respected seminary. This is in harmony with Brengle's educational drive and with God's plans for him to meet needs later, all up and down the leadership levels.[66] Two mentor sponsors help with the finances. Major focal factor.
6. Personal Pentecost (see pages 134-137)	25	Strategic and Ministerial--Once having experienced this major sanctifying experience Brengle went on to minister it to others. His personal pattern enabled him to preach it to others with spiritual authority. A major focal value.
7. Attractive Offer, The Faith Challenge, (see pages 137,138)	25	Strategic--Brengle's inner call to regional itinerant evangelistic work without financial guarantee or organizational sponsorship is contrasted sharply with the Studebaker offer which takes care of his financial difficulties and catapults him into high position, ahead of the normal experiential track. Brengle chooses the lowly faith route in response to a Word, Matthew 6. The way up is down, integrity check and faith challenge, insures Brengle of the next guidance step--meeting Booth and Elizabeth Swift and inner confirmation of The Salvation Army as his people he will identify with. A major focal value. Opens door for major focal factor to come.

---

[66]Leadership emergence theory identifies five basic levels of leadership in terms of sphere of influence, role, and status as full time Christian worker or not. Type A and B are either lay leaders or bi-vocational leaders at local church level. Type C is a full time Christian worker. Type D is a full time Christian worker like a senior pastor at a large influential church having regional or national influence or a national role like Brengle's in his first campaign. Type E is a full time Christian worker influencing across nations. Type A and B (both non-full time) differ from C (full time). Types A, B, and C differ from D in that D is involved in in-direct ministry as a prime means of influence while A, B, and C are basically face-to-face direct small influence. Brengle in his convergent role ministered to leaders of all types, A, B, C, D, and E. His pastoral internship, Corps and local evangelistic experiences gave him experience and empathy with types A, B, and C. His educational background, administrative and executive leadership and itinerant ministries in the U.S.A. and abroad gave him insight into higher level leadership needs, Types D, E.

Chapter 4. Samuel Logan Brengle (1860-1936)   page 160

Table 4-1 Listing Of Some Critical Incidents In Brengle's Life continued

Incident(s) Name	Age	Formational Type Dealing With Basic Value/Thrust
8. Divine Contacts (See pages 139)	25,26	Strategic--William Booth and Elizabeth Swift are used to attract and connect Brengle to The Salvation Army, the group that will facilitate his life purpose-- to insist upon holiness of heart and life. Major focal factor.
9. Shiny Black Boots (see pages 125-126)	27	Spiritual, Strategic--Brengle catches the tone of The Salvation Army. It is servant leadership from an obedient heart. He responds with a prayer request which is fulfilled all through his ministry and especially in his convergent ministry role. "Dear Lord, let me serve the servants of Jesus. That is sufficient for me." Significant focal value imbedded in an important focal factor.
10. The Boston Brick-- Stimulus to Broader Influence (see pages 143)	30	Spiritual, Ministerial, Strategic--Isolation and life crisis brought on reflection, evaluation and deeper committal to life purpose. It gave time to organize thinking and to write what he had been teaching orally on holiness--a natural move to expand his influence-mix to beyond just direct face-to-face. An important focal factor pointing to important indirect sphere of influence.
11. American Split-- Tolerant Firmness (see pages 144)	36	Ministerial, Strategic--Crisis in upper level leadership has ripple effects throughout the whole Army. Brengle learns the best way to solve a major problem like this is to unify around an important task--strong evangelistic effort. Brengle handled ex-salvationists with a tolerant attitude but held firmly to his own basic convictions. He never denigrated the ex-salvationists. He gains upper level leadership experience and a strategic view of leadership. This will stand him well in his ministry to higher level leaders. Important focal values.
12. National Spiritual Special (see pages 147-149)	37	Ministerial, Strategic--McIntyre, as divine contact, sponsors Brengle into a role fulfilling his destiny. He will operate in this role for the rest of his life. This is the key focal factor. Notice that it is a major role and life purpose that are the primary focal issues in Brengle's life. But it is the role which was key to carrying out the life purpose. There were ultimate contributions but they were by-products of these primary focal issues.

Critical Incident 1, *Stars in the Sky*, presages an unusual sensitivity to spiritual things, a curiosity about the supernatural and an introduction to a sense of destiny. This is further confirmed in Critical Incident 2, *Spontaneous Anger, the Sensitivity Incident*. and Critical Incident 9, *Shiny Black Boots*. Many, many incidents could be cited showing his unusual sensitivity to God. Brengle was an evangelical mystic in the best sense of the

Chapter 4. Samuel Logan Brengle (1860-1936)

word. Wiersbe (1993:227) points out four characteristics of an evangelical mystic.[67] The evangelical Christian mystic has 1. a consciousness of the spiritual world beyond the physical, 2. a success standard which focuses on pleasing God rather than those in the world, 3. a bent toward developing an intimate relationship with God and its concomitant, an unusual sense of His presence everywhere; and 4. a mindset toward constantly relating this unusual experience with God to the practical things of life. Christian mystics of this ilk, with this unusual sense of God, tend to think that all Christians have this same awareness. Not all do. But these kind of people were attracted to Brengle.[68]

It is this special awareness, this sensitivity of conscience, that made Brengle so effective as an evangelist and holiness worker. He knew what blocked this sensitivity and could put his finger on it, both in terms of sin generally and specific sin(s), when dealing with individuals. This sensitivity to God will be the bedrock of his destiny as an *Apostle of Holiness, a Public Saint.* It is this sensitivity to God that also constantly forces consistency between his inner and outer life--because he did not want to lose this inner awareness of God.

Critical incidents 3, 4, 5, 7, 8, and 12 all are powerful career guidance, pivotal points. Note the variety of means God uses to focus this leader: personal individual sensitivity and responsiveness to God and His dealings, the Bishop's overriding providential blocking of a door, an alert mentor sponsor (Bishop Joyce) who sees potential and advises toward and connects Brengle to a top notch school,[69] the ministry challenge (call to evangelism) flowing out of ministry (preaching in the Baltimore church), and the use of divine contacts.

Brengle is archetypical for illustrating a leader with a growing sense of destiny.[70] Table 4-2 points out the buildup of the destiny pattern.

---

[67] He is describing A. W. Tozer (Wiersbe 1993:224-230) when he digresses on this description of a mystic. To Wiersbe, mystics are not just people who hear voices and have visions but are people who have an unusual sensitivity to God, the things of God and awareness of God in things where an average Christian would not have that same sense of God. Throughout the book Hall implicitly highlights this sensitivity with such phrases as *suddenly the preacher's face became lighted with an unutterable glory* (1933:27), *visit him with some spectacular acceptance, there came into his heart an inexplicable feeling* and *instinctively he knew that God had accepted him* (1933:28), *exquisite sense of God's favor* and *the inward witness had been withdrawn* (1933:29), *suddenly there comes up from his heart a voice speaking words that are old, but that bear gloriously new meaning* (1933:50), *a great sense of peace flows over his soul* (1933:50).

[68] In addition to those that had major needs due to sin, there were many at the penitent-form in meeting after meeting, who were sensitive to God and wanted that holiness that Brengle had. It is the dynamic seen repeatedly that like-attracts-like.

[69] Brengle will be at this school at just the right window of time: there is a Professor who is on fire with holiness concepts, there is a group of like-minded spiritually sensitive students who band together to form the Octagon Club, and General Booth, the founder--just happens to come during this window. In retrospect, these are all cumulative evidence of the providential hand of God on Brengle's life, steering from behind the scenes toward that destiny for him.

[70] In leadership emergence theory we have identified 7 major descriptions referring to effective leaders. One is, effective leaders evince a growing awareness of their sense of destiny. Brengle did. He illustrates fully the total destiny pattern (Clinton 1989:349,350) of destiny preparation, destiny revelation, and destiny fulfillment.

Chapter 4. Samuel Logan Brengle (1860-1936)

Table 4-2. Sense of Destiny in Brengle's Life

Incident	Label	Destiny Pattern, Destiny Indicated
1	*Stars in the Sky*	Destiny Preparation: Parents dedication and trail incident with Genesis 12. God is going to use him like Abraham to reach many.
3	*Harnessing Ambition*	Destiny Revelation: Further clarification: God puts a spiritual touch on what had been a strong natural bent for years. The constant drawing toward public preaching attracts Brengle. God reveals, in *the Call*, that this oratorical ability is to be channeled for God.
6	*Personal Pentecost*	Destiny Revelation: Brengle will always preach out of his experience. God who is going to use him as an Apostle of Holiness gives the holiness experience which will contain the content of one of his two major thrusts--particularly the one that will serve the whole Army so well. This will help focus the life purpose.
7	*Attractive Offer*	Destiny Revelation: Here Brengle sees the first half of his life purpose, evangelism. He receives his call as a persuasive evangelist.
9	*Shiny Black Boots*	Destiny Revelation: Brengle sees that the second part of his life purpose will be serving his fellow soldiers in the Army.
12	*National Spiritual Special*	Destiny Revelation/ Destiny Fulfillment: Here Brengle gets the role that will allow him to minister the twin prongs of his life purpose: evangelism and holiness. He will be a help to the whole Army.

As he continued to minister over the years as a National Spiritual Special, Brengle increasingly saw actual destiny fulfillment as many, many people were affected by his evangelism and holiness ministries both in the U.S.A. and abroad.

Critical incidents 10 and 11 represent stimulus to important values. In incident 10, *the Boston Brick*, Brengle began his writing of materials that would influence others. The dominant value inculcated was that writing should flow out of experience and be helpful to the common struggling Christians. This method of expanding his sphere of influence beyond the direct will continue all his life. Critical Incident 11, *American Split*, stimulated the paradigm shift through the strategic barrier (moving from direct to indirect ministry). This culminated Brengle's preparation to minister all up and down the leadership levels.

Chapter 4. Samuel Logan Brengle (1860-1936)

Finally, note the prime focal incident. Critical Incident 6, *Personal Pentecost*, is the prime focal incident of Brengle's life. The experience of it, its values, and even the means of entering into it all proliferate his ministry activity thereafter.

Values And Critical Values

Below I have identified what I think are important values in Brengle's life. Some seem to be crucial and appear throughout all his ministry. He seems to emphasize them in his talks to others. These I call critical values. I mark them with an asterisk (*). I have identified what I think is the focal value, the dominant critical value with a double asterisk (**). I have grouped these values in terms of spiritual formation, ministerial formation, and strategic formation.[71]

<u>Spiritual Values</u> (those dealing more directly with leadership character):

*1. Sensitivity to God in everyday life ought to be the natural outcome of one's following hard on God. This sensitivity can be broken by sin.
2. Obedience to anything God reveals must be the response if spiritual sensitivity is to be retained.
*3. Using one's giftedness to help others ought to be the essential attitude of a leader (The Servant Leadership Model should dominate one's ministry.)
4. Ambition must be given over to God and if He pleases channeled for His glory. Particularly will this be tested in terms of financially attractive offers.
5. The Bible must be studied and used for personal enrichment on a daily basis if one expects to use it powerfully with others.
*6. A leader ought to be that which he/she expects and demands of followers.
7. Consistency between inner values and daily life must be the expected norm of those walking in holiness.
8. A leader should expect to see God in everything and hence be shaped by God in them toward God's purposes.

<u>Ministerial Values</u> (those dealing more directly with leadership skills or insights):

*1. Commitment in response to preaching ought to be cultivated and should be the expected norm.
*2. Services ought to be focused toward the commitment time with no detracting elements.
*3. A Christian leader who wishes to communicate with power must discipline himself/herself to learn basic communication skills and be submitted to the notion that effective communication takes work. Some standards ought to be:
   a. Use simple language
   b. The flow of communication should use persuasive logic.
   c. Read your Bible so as to put life in it and gain attention.
   d. Use spontaneous dramatic vignettes from time-to-time.
   e. Have forceful pictorial illustrations which fit the points being taught.

---

[71] Brengle catches the spirit of what a value is when he talks about the difference between theology and meaningful core doctrine. "There is a sense in which every thoughtful, studious, prayerful Christian ...works out, under the leading of the Holy Ghost, his own theology, and discovers what he believes to be the true doctrines of the Bible. He may accept the teachings or doctrines of his parents and religious leaders, and hold them intellectually, but his theology [for us read values] is really limited to those articles of faith which vitalize his life, guide and inspire his conduct, mold his spirit, comfort and guard his heart, purify his nature, and kindle his hope for the future." (Hall 1933:143)

f. Maintain powerful eye contact with the audience.
g. Don't be afraid to use your knowledge of human personality.
h. Identify sympathetically with the audience.
4. The Bible ought to be read publicly with clarity, proper enunciation, emphasis and attention getting power.[72]
*5. In public ministry a communicator must be able to size up an audience, on the spot, and extemporaneously vary communication to fit the level of the audience.[73]
**6. A leader should have victory over sin and can do so if willing to accept God's cleansing of it and empowerment over sin. Such a desire should lead one to an experience in which that empowerment for holiness is known and experienced.
*7. Altar calls or other form of definite commitment should be the central focus of a public meeting and should be used to allow definite advances in people's Christian experiences.
8. A leader should expect effective ministry in even short assignments.
*9. A leader should give the best he/she has no matter what the size of the group being ministered to. The size of a group receiving ministry should not affect the quality of the ministry.
10. A leader must discover the best way to bring about holiness like the use of an altar call or extended times (like a full day) for just that focused purpose.
*11. Writing ought to capture learning from life experience and be directed primarily to the common Christian.
12. Even in short assignments a leader ought to concentrate first on upgrading quality of available leadership. This focus should be done in the midst of on-the-job training.
13. A leader ought to by faith expect blessings even from past apparent fruitless ministry. God can work backwards as well as forward.

---

[72]Both public rhetoricians in this book, Morgan and Brengle, held strongly to this value though their application was distinctly different. Hall (1933:115,116) catches the flavor of Brengle's public reading of the Scripture. "In his public handling of Scriptures, he was graphic, pictorial. While reading Bible stories, his mind would quickly translate the printed narrative into dramatic movement on the screen of his imagination. On many occasions he would break through indifference and frigidity right at the start of a meeting by his ingenuous method of clothing a text with such action. Beginning to read his selected passage in an indeliberate manner, he would break off suddenly to take part in the picture. Thus: 'Peter, an apostle of Jesus Christ...' What's that, Peter, how can you make such a claim? Did you not deny Him in His bitterest hour? Did you not turn coward, and curse and swear?' etc. Forthwith there would be a conversation between Peter and Brengle with the rugged fisherman telling in a broken voice of the loving look and the infinite compassion of his Master which gave him reinstatement as an apostle. Or again: 'Paul... unto the church of the Thessalonians which is in God ...' Wait, Paul, Haven't you got your sentence mixed? Don't you mean 'The Church of God which is in Thessalonica?' etc. And in this utter naive exegesis the crowd saw the church and caught at once the significant difference between the readings." Morgan was especially noted for his ability to read the Bible publicly in a rich sonorous voice that brought emphasis and life to the passage he read. He preferred to read the Bible passage himself and not let someone else do it. Both held to the basic formula given Timothy, 1 Timothy 4:13, προσεξε ανα attention to the public reading), παρακλησει (exhortation, application), and διδασκα explaining, clarifying) though the order was varied.

[73]Morgan the other public rhetorician held firmly to this also. Both men prepared well but when in the pulpit spoke extemporaneously from that preparation (Brengle more so). Morgan said on this, "To be able to confront an audience, and immediately to detect the general level of its ability to follow, and to be able therefore to adapt oneself in the use of language and illustration, so as to convey essential truth to that audience, is the supreme quality of great teaching." (Morgan 1910:94)

Chapter 4. Samuel Logan Brengle (1860-1936)   page 165

<u>Strategic Values</u> (those dealing with overall leadership guidance and achievement):

*1. Submission to God through authority is necessary in an authoritarian organization. Faithfulness in assignments ought to be the essential attitude of a leader. Such an attitude will lead to more challenging assignments and eventually to a role for effective ministry.
*2. A leader should recognize that God's guidance is clear guidance even when assignments which teach humility seem to be below one's status and apparent potential. When positively responded to these assignments will be stepping stones for God's next appointments.
3. A leader ought to expect that God will use contacts and friendships made all throughout ministry to open doors and link to further resources and opportunities down road. Serve and relate to folks to help them. Later God may use them to enhance your ministry. That is, a by-product of servant leadership will be expansion later on via important contacts that were served.
4. A leader ought to regard those who differ from himself/herself in doctrine or ministry emphases with as charitable an attitude as possible without compromising one's own core beliefs and values.
5. Honor, reward, status ought to be the by-products of servant leadership not the goals of life.
*6. A leader should be aware of the potential dangers in a given type of ministry (like plateauing in itinerant ministries) and should take deliberate steps to offset these dangers.

Ministry Insights, Lessons, and General Values

We can not overlook the importance of a mother in shaping, early on, in the life of her child, spiritual influences that will dominate later in life. Brengle's mom inculcated a genuine appreciation for spiritual things. She submitted to God as best she knew how in the myriad of trials that came her way in the rugged pioneer life and especially in terms of a restless life partner who did not succeed in life. Brengle imbibed her attitude toward life--especially her learning to make the best of it.

Probably one of the more important lessons to learn from Brengle's life is his convictions about ministry. He used his experiences with God as deliberate foci for his ministry. He believed his experiences with God were real and valid. They were life changing for him. He believed then that God could use those same life changing interventions with others. So he ministered toward actual response. Today, I do not see many Wesleyan leaders who believe in a sanctifying experience like Brengle's. There is little distinction between their churches and others. Brengle believed in this life changing paradigm. He saw results in his own life and in the lives of others.

Another important lesson from Brengle's life concerns his learning style. He primarily learned from experience first, usually via the affect. He was later able to formulate the cognitive underlying his learning. This is a valid pattern. Morgan dominantly learned via cognition first. We should be encouraged that leaders will have unique learning styles. Are we learning? That is, the valid question. If we are, then the learning style is appropriate whether it be volitional first, affect first, experiential first, or cognitive first.

We should be encouraged that Christian Protestant mystics are legitimate. Brengle is a model of a Christian mystic. He illustrates all four of Wiersbe's positive characteristics of a Christian mystic. The essence of his mysticism was his sensitivity to God. This is a value that even less mystically inclined leaders can emulate.

Chapter 4. Samuel Logan Brengle (1860-1936) page 166

Brengle is a public rhetorician who finished well. His end game responses to God are worth studying in depth. Each of the six major characteristics of finishing well can be explored in depth with Brengle and with good profit.

Contributions

This chapter contributes to the general field of leadership development in the following ways:

1. It portrays a very gifted leader who entered into a convergent role very early in ministry and maintained a very effective ministry over a long time period.
2. It portrays a public rhetorician who had an itinerant ministry that involved sacrifice of home life, sacrifice of a comfortable life style, and dangers inherent in such a ministry and yet who finished well. In fact, he is an archetype of a leader who finished well.
3. It identifies some important communication concepts and highlights that hard work is needed beyond just native talent for effective public communication.
4. It points out the importance and power of a definite paradigm, in this case the holiness paradigm, in focusing one's ministry.
5. It shows the importance of a life purpose as a focusing issue and how it develops over time. In this case there was a two-prong life purpose-- evangelism and holiness.
6. It shows the necessity of a unique role as a focusing issue in order to enhance a life purpose.
7. It highlights the foundational ministry pattern, faithfulness in each ministry assignment as a stepping stone to next ministry, until leadership potential is reached.
8. It shows that one can have a focused ministry without long tenure in one locale.

Brengle's ultimate contributions were by-products of the primary focal issues in his life--life purpose and major role. Never-the-less, his contributions to the cause of Christ and the on-going of the Christian movement were impressive and are profiled in the diagram given below.[74]

---

[74]The diagram which describes his ultimate contributions in pictorial form is called a Venn Diagram. See Appendix F for an explanation of how to read Venn diagrams.

Chapter 4. Samuel Logan Brengle (1860-1936)

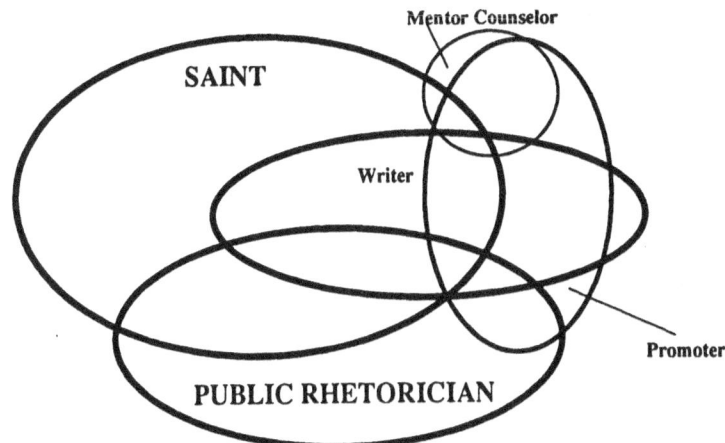

He was a **saint**. His dominant contribution was his model of a holy life. Sensitivity to God, obedience to God, and a life devoted wholly to pleasing God were an inspirational stimulus to all who knew him and to all of us who profit through study of his life. He demonstrates the reality of living a life above the controlling authority of sin. He shows that God is real and can change a life.

But he was a **public rhetorician** who led many people to Christ through his public ministry. He led many people to experience the holiness powergate and opened for them the possibility of living a holy life. His pulpit work was both effective in itself and in the model he left for those who want to communicate effectively in the power of the Spirit. He merges oratorical natural abilities and acquired skills with powerful evangelism and exhortation spiritual gifts. His most powerful pulpit material as been revised and published in the form of written material. So though we do not capture the affect and volitional power of his public ministry we do have much of its cognitive content. His sermon, the Atonement, was a major contribution in a moment of time and will have eternal results which we shall yet see someday.

He was a **writer**. His written achievements captured life experiences-- personally with God and from public ministry. His was not theoretical treatment of subjects but an experiential understanding of them. These writings were part of his activity to promote holiness and sensitivity to God. They were dominantly for the common person, the seeker or Christian needing help in his audiences. But it is amazing to see, from testimonies, just how much these practical writings also helped leaders.

He was a **mentor** who related to people personally and gave good counsel. His personal ministry was probably as powerful as his public ministry. His spiritual gifts of evangelism, exhortation, and word of wisdom were powerful in private ministry. He dealt well with individuals in formal and informal times of counseling. His servant leadership is probably seen best in his giving of himself to others in individual ministry. As Hall says he was instant out of season as well as in season.

He was a **promoter**. The dominant idea he promoted was holiness--*to insist upon holiness of heart and life.* He advocated a holiness paradigm through which people could

Chapter 4. Samuel Logan Brengle (1860-1936)

enter into that experience. He was strongly focused in this. This was the focal element and probably the more dominant of his two pronged life purpose--evangelism and holiness.

Brengle's specific contributions to the cause of Christ and the on-going of the Christian movement include at least the following:

1. He led many people to know Christ as their personal Savior.
2. He led many people to experience the Holy Spirit's power for living.
3. He pioneered a new ministry role within The Salvation Army, which role was passed on after his retirement.
4. He left behind materials in written form to promote holiness.
5. He modeled the foundational ministry pattern--faithfulness in ministry assignments.
6. He showed that even in short term assignments (his longest assignment before National Spiritual Special was 3 years or less) a leader can have effective ministry if he/she concentrates on developing available leadership.
7. He modeled a focused life with two focal issues dominant--major role and life purpose.
8. He is an ideal type of a leader who finished well.

Overall Lessons from the Life

In light with his being an archetype of a leader who finishes well, Brengle highlights all the characteristics of a good finish. One of the most inspiring is characteristic 4, Truth is lived out in their lives so that **convictions** and promises of God are seen to be real. From the moment he entered into holiness, and believed in a victorious life he lived out that conviction. And his life was on display demonstrating that his conviction was real.

Implications for a Focused Life

What have we learned from this life that helps us understand a focused life? That is the question I attempt to answer in this section. Of the 12 factors I use to evaluate a focused life, I believe six were significant in Brengle's life.

1. Giftedness Development

Brengle's giftedness set is given below in diagram form.[75] Spiritual gifts were the focal element. His major natural ability (voice, motivational ability, core communication drive) and his acquired skills (many in the area of public communication) strongly supported his spiritual gifts. Evangelism and Exhortation were twin dominant spiritual gifts in his gift-cluster. Development of these were dominantly via on-the-job experience. His convergent role was ideally suited to this giftedness set.

---

[75] The diagram which describes his giftedness set (natural abilities, acquired skills and spiritual gifts) in pictorial form is called a Venn Diagram. See Appendix F for an explanation of how to read Venn diagrams

Chapter 4. Samuel Logan Brengle (1860-1936)   page 169

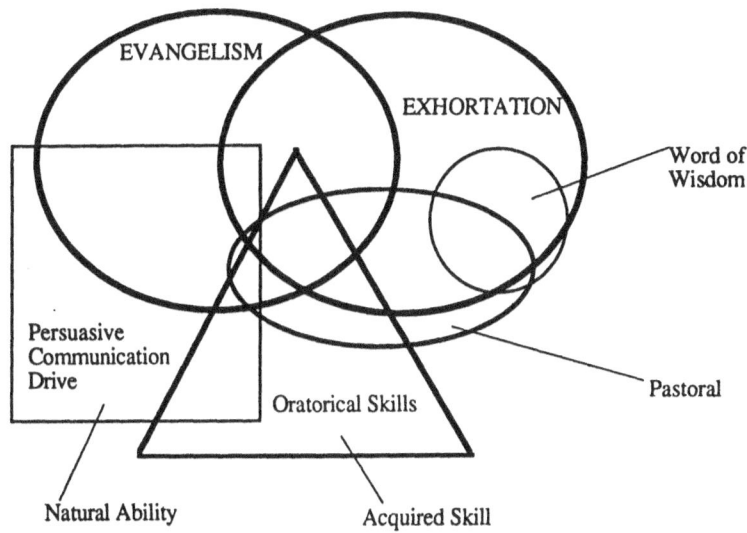

2. Destiny Processing

I have already talked at length on Brengle's sense of destiny and its development. This was a very significant factor in focusing to convergence.

3. Identification of Key Ministry Insights

The penitent-form and its use in facilitating commitment both toward evangelistic and holiness goals were a major focusing factor. Brengle utilized this powerfully as a means of achieving life purpose.

4. Identification Of Major Values That Uniquely Fit One's Ministry

I have previously identified the following, **A leader should have victory over sin and can do so if willing to accept God's cleansing of heart and empowerment over sin. Such a desire should lead one to an experience in which that empowerment for holiness is known and experienced,** as the prime focal value which was very significant in focusing Brengle's own life and his ministry.

6. Social Base Processing

Apart from Elizabeth Swift's willing compliance to fulfill the release pattern (see Appendix D) as her major ministry, Brengle could never have operated in an itinerant ministry for 18 years of their married life like he did. She was totally supportive of him. She was also his most important confidant and served as a downward mentor, particularly in communication skills. Her feedback was a great stimulus to growth and ministry.

11.   Paradigm Shifts Which Helped Focus

There were two significant paradigm shifts that helped focus Brengle. The first was the experiential entrance into the Holiness paradigm at Boston Theological Seminary which forever changed his life and ministry. The second, not as significant, but important in terms of later ministry was his movement through the strategic barrier as a leader--that is, seeing the importance of strategic leadership involving problem solving, movement through crisis, doing the things necessary to enable leaders under him to succeed. This new perspective on the bigger picture of leadership enabled him all during his convergent ministry to meet the needs of upper level leaders as well as lower level leaders.

SUMMARY ON FOCUSED LIFE INSIGHTS FROM BRENGLE'S LIFE

Let me summarize what I think can be learned about a focused life from Samuel Logan Brengle. Remember,

A <u>focused life</u> is
- a life dedicated to exclusively carrying out God's unique purposes through it,
- by identifying the focal issues, that is, the **major role, life purpose, unique methodology,** or **ultimate contribution,** which allows
- an **increasing prioritization** of life's activities around the focal issues, and
- results in a satisfying life of being and doing.

Two focal issues dominated and were equally important. **Life purpose** increasingly grew in importance and was clarified and done to some extent in ministry assignments. But it was when the **major role**, National Spiritual Special, was assigned by the organization, that the life purpose could be carried out not only freely but with the organization's backing.

We have learned from Brengle's life that a leader does not necessarily have to adapt a role in order to obtain an ideal role. Strong mini-convergence experiences can sensitize upper level leadership to the possibilities of an ideal role.

As we shall see also from Morgan's life in chapter 5, we have seen that a life does not necessarily need tenure in one location or position in order to be focused. In fact, focus for this uniquely gifted leader, with his destiny involved, demanded an itinerant ministry in locales all over.

We have seen the importance of a controlling paradigm to produce effects in lives. Brengle's paradigm of holiness and his ministry insight of use of the penitent-form honed his ministry to produce powerful results toward fulfilling life purpose.

We have seen the importance of divine contacts to move a person to focus.

We have now remembered Brengle a la our mandate of Hebrews 13:7,8. What have you remembered that may profit your life and ministry?

Where To Go and What To Do For Further Study

The following are important works that will help you greatly if you want to be mentored by Brengle. I suggest scanning my chapter again and then simply reading through Hall's work. His chapters are small. You could do one a day in your devotional time in addition to other things. See Appendix E, Devotional and Applicational Methods. Then browse among Brengle's actual works. Remember they are all books that flow out of his experiences in ministry. They are not meant to woo academics. They are meant to move people toward holiness, something academics hardly ever do. All of these are

Chapter 4. Samuel Logan Brengle (1860-1936)

available at the time of this writing from The Salvation Army Supplies and Purchasing Department of Atlanta, Georgia.

Brengle, Samuel Logan

1897 **Heart Talks on Holiness.** (reprinted 1988). Atlanta: Salvation Army.

Comments: Contains 27 meditations related to Brengle's holiness paradigm, a second work of grace freeing from sin.

1902 **The Way of Holiness.** (reprinted 1988). Atlanta: Salvation Army.

Comments: This booklet focuses systematically on holiness.

1903 **The Soul-Winner's Secret.** (reprinted 1990). Atlanta: Salvation Army.

Comments: A collection of evangelistic articles written for *The War Cry*.

1909 **When the Holy Ghost is Come.** (reprinted 1988). Atlanta: Salvation Army.

Comments: This is Brengle's theology of the Holy Spirit

1923 **Love Slaves.** Atlanta: Salvation Army.

Comments: A set of unconnected meditations. *The Dangers of Middle Age*, which points out barriers leaders face in the middle game, is especially helpful.

1925 **Resurrection Life and Power.** (reprinted 1981). Atlanta: Salvation Army.

Comments: Various articles by Brengle.

1929 **Ancient Prophets (and Modern Problems).** Atlanta: Salvation Army.

Comments: These are rich meditations of one almost 70 years of age. Particularly helpful to me were the meditations: the Ancient Prophets, Retired (helpful thoughts as one moves into Afterglow ministry), A Word to Those Who Are Growing Old, Our Mothers, The Future of The Salvation Army.

1934 **Guest of the Soul.** (reprinted 1982). Atlanta: Salvation Army.

Comments: Written after age 70 these meditations carry winsome perspectives. The first meditation *Atonement* summarizes his important ultimate achievement sermon given in Norway in 1907. *Looking Backward and Forward* was a blessing to me--especially the challenge he received from his father-in-law.

Hall, Clarence

1933 **Samuel Logan Brengle, Portrait of a Prophet.** Atlanta: Salvation Army.

Comments: This is Hall's biography of Brengle. He had access to Brengle the last three years of his life (also personal papers, letters and Brengle's diary). He intersperses actual Brengle quotes liberally throughout the entire book. These quotes make the work live.

Chapter 4. Samuel Logan Brengle (1860-1936)

SAMUEL BRENGLE (1860-1936) Critical Incidents

I. RUGGED PRAIRIE FOUNDATIONS
(A Drive To Learn Leading To An Oratorical Ambition)

1860	1868	1872	1874	1877
Age	8	12	14	17

A. Frontier Obscurity Rugged Start (1860-1868)
B. Farm Years (1868-1872)
C. Conversion/ Drive To Learn (1872-1874)
D. Basic Education/ Olney/ Claremont (1874-1877)
E. Harnessed Ambition at Depauw University (1877-1883)

II. DESTINED FOR THE SALVATION ARMY
(Faithfulness and Consistency Through The Ranks)

1883			1897
23	24	27	32	37

A. Circuit Preacher--Northwest Indiana Conference--Methodist Episcopal (1883)
B. Formal Training--Boston Theological Seminary (Entire Sanctification) (1884-1887)
C. Salvation Army Recruit/ Boot camp (1887)
D. Experience as Corps Officer (1887-1892)
E. Experience as District and above/ Executive Administration/ the Crisis (1892-1897)

III. NATIONAL SPIRITUAL SPECIAL/ HOLINESS CAMPAIGNER
(Divinely Given Convergent Role)

			1936
44	51	60s	76

A. First Campaigns--Breaking New Ground/ Pioneer Role in U.S.A. (1897-1904)
B. Growing Influence--Campaigns Abroad/ Europe and S.W. Pacific (1904-1911)
C. Follow-Up Campaigns--Powerful U.S.A. Ministry (1911-1927)
D. Afterglow Years--Continued Itinerant Ministry (1927s-1931)
E. Continued Afterglow/ Meditation/ Correspondence/ Counseling (1931-1936)

C1 Early Destiny Items:
  1. Parent's Covenant
  2. Abraham's Promise Stars in the Sky
C2 Spontaneous Anger, The Sensitivity Incident
C3 Harnessed Ambition
C4 Hidden Guidance
C5 Back to School
C6 Personal Pentecost
C7 Attractive Offer
C8 Divine Contacts:
  1. William Booth,
  2. Elizabeth Swift
C9 Shiny Black Boots
C10 The Boston Brick
C11 American Split
C12 National Spiritual Special

G. Campbell Morgan
(1863-1945)

"Did not our hearts burn within us as we heard him teach?"

Chapter 5. G. Campbell Morgan (1863-1945) World Class Bible Teacher

Remember your former leaders. Think back on how they lived and ministered. Imitate those **excellent qualities** you see in their lives. For Jesus Christ is the same today, as He was in the past and as He will be in the future. What He did for them He will do for you to inspire and enable your leadership.
           Hebrews 13:7,8 (Personal Interpretive Paraphrase)

Let's remember G. Campbell Morgan, a world class public Bible teacher.

I struggled over the title for this one. I considered various alternatives: a rhetorical question, *What is a Biblical Ministry?* or *the Foremost Bible Teacher in the first Half of the Twentieth Century* or *A Search For Convergence* or *Equipped By God--A 2 Timothy 3:16,17 Man*. Jill Morgan's sub-title of her biography, *Man of the Word*, persuaded me toward the above title. Morgan is probably the most intellectually astute and most publicly gifted of all of the eight leaders in this book.[1] That is why Focal Incident 1 below was so timely and important in his life.

Opening Illustration 1.
Leadership Character Value--Giftedness and Pride

Age 15 (Proverbs 27:6,17)

> Let it not be imagined that such gifts, even in potentiality, were unrecognized by the teen-aged boy himself. He knew himself to be gifted in the use of words, and to be the possessor of a voice which was, in itself, a powerful agent in gaining and holding the attention of a group. Practice was already reaping rewards. The consciousness of power over others was like wine to him, and might have resulted in disaster, but for the instrumentality of a friend. A colporteur, David Smith by name, was considerably older than the boy he had accompanied from Cheltenham to Birdlip, a nearby hamlet, where the two were to conduct a cottage prayer meeting
> In telling the story many years later, Dr. Morgan says: "David Smith conducted the meeting and I preached. The walk home was by moonlight, and six miles long. It seemed longer, for David Smith made full use of it to point out to me the uselessness of speaking before people merely that they might be given an opportunity to discover my ability.[2] I rebelled at first, but finally I was convinced..." It was a stiff blow to the boy's self-confidence and pride. He returned home chastened and very thoughtful. But the kind intention and Christian spirit of his friend could not be misconstrued. Through the intervening weeks he spent much time in reflection and prayer. Some time later he returned with the same companion to the cottage for another service. He took as his

---

[1] One could argue for A. J. Gordon or even Charles Simeon as equally intellectually adept.
[2] Three process items, i.e. shaping activities of God, from leadership emergence theory are in focus here two having to do with influence means and the third to an inner character value associated with public ministry. *Authority insights* (Clinton 1989:172), the discovery of how to influence people is in focus. Morgan is learning about power. More specifically Morgan is in stage 1 in the *spiritual authority discovery process* (Clinton 1989:196), that of learning about personal authority--its use and abuse. This is also an example of *mentoring* (Clinton 1989:186). Smith is acting as a mentor and correcting a character flaw relating to giftedness and pride. Morgan's response was positive. While he definitely learned something about giftedness and pride, he will continually be processed in this as his popularity increases. This will be an on-going shaping that God will repeatedly deal with. This frequently is the case with leaders who are powerfully gifted for public ministry.

Chapter 5. G. Campbell Morgan--(1863-1945)

theme the words of Jesus: 'Come unto Me, all ye that labour and are heavy laden, and I will give you rest.' This time self was forgotten; the message of the text captured him so completely that he broke down, and was not able to finish. As a result, two or three of his listeners professed their faith in Christ. It was an experience he never forgot, and for which he never ceased to be grateful to David Smith. (J. Morgan 1972:37,38)

Opening Illustration 2.
His Foundational Ministerial Value
A Faith Challenge Leading to an Authoritative Word of God

Age 19-21 (2 Timothy 3:14-17, Hebrews 4:12, 1 Peter 4:10,11)

Until he was sixteen years of age, Dr. Morgan declared it had never entered his mind to doubt the authority of the Bible. At home and in school it was held in reverence as the only revelation of truth. "I did not think," he said, "there could be any honest and respectable man who could doubt that the Bible was the Word of God. Then I went out into a world of which I had no knowledge up to that time...The whole intellectual world was under the mastery of the physical scientists, and of a materialistic and rationalistic philosophy. To quote names is enough--Darwin, Huxley, Tyndall, Spencer, Bain. I was as honest then as now, and gradually faith, while not undermined, was eclipsed. When the sun is eclipsed the light is not killed, it is hidden. There came a moment when I was sure of nothing.

For three years this young man, seriously contemplating a future of teaching and ultimately of preaching, felt the troubled waters of the stream of religious controversy carrying him beyond his depth. He read the new books which debated such questions as, 'Is God Knowable?' and found that the authors' concerted decision was, 'He is not knowable.' He became confused and perplexed. No longer was he sure of that which his father proclaimed in public, and had taught him in the home.

At last the crisis came when he admitted to himself his total lack of assurance that the Bible was the authoritative Word of God to man.[3] He immediately canceled all preaching engagements. Then, taking all his books, both those attacking and those defending the Bible, he put them all in a corner cupboard. ... He went out of the house, and down the street to a bookshop. He bought a new Bible, and returning to his room with it, he said to himself: 'I am no longer sure that this is what my father claims it to be--the Word of God. But of this I am sure. If it *be* the Word of God, and if I come to it with an unprejudiced and open mind, it will bring assurance to my soul of itself.' "That Bible *found* me," he said, "I began to read and study it then, in 1883. I have been a student ever since, and I still am (in 1938)."

At the end of two years Campbell Morgan emerged from that eclipse of faith absolutely sure that the Bible was, in very deed and truth, none other than the Word of the living God. ...

With this crisis behind him and this new certainty thrilling his soul, there came a compelling conviction. This Book, being what it was, merited all that a man could give to its study, not merely for the sake of the personal joy of delving deeply in the heart and mind and will of God, but also in order that those truths discovered by such searching of the Scriptures should be made known to a world of men groping for light, and perishing in the darkness with no clear knowledge of that Will. (J. Morgan 1972:38-40)

I will come back to both of these focal incidents later in the section that traces out important values. But notice the second incident. Frequently, the first half of this second vignette is true of many pre-service students who go to seminary. Critical studies and

---

[3] Two process items, i.e. shaping activities of God, from leadership emergence theory are in focus here. This is a personal *crisis* (Clinton 1989:210) in which his foundational belief in God and His revelation is at stake, and there is a *faith challenge* (Clinton 1989:222). Critical incidents are usually described by several processes. Out of this shaping will come a complete trust in God's revelation of Himself through the Bible. This will lead eventually to a full time committal to teach this Word.

Chapter 5. G. Campbell Morgan--(1863-1945)

technical exegesis bring about a lack of confidence in the Scriptures, a time of confusion, and a dryness of soul. All too often they never experience the second half of the faith challenge and come out convinced by God alone that the Bible is the authoritative Word of God and is worthy of study and exposition and giving one's life to exposing to a needy world. This incident is worthy of repetition in its fullness in the lives of those preparing in Seminary.

The Time-Line

See the time-line at the end of this chapter for a one page overview of Morgan's life and detailed expansions of two major phases dealing with the time of his effective focused ministry. Note that there are five developmental phases of length 25, 13, 19, 14, and 9 years. Phases III and IV represent focused ministry, one in a church environment, the other in a parachurch role. I have included his most important published writings on the time-line.

Highly Condensed Biographical Narrative

The following running capsule, organized around the time increments of his time-line, touches on some of the highlights of Morgan's life. Morgan's ministry experience is complex wavering between church and parachurch bases from time-to-time. And while operating from each of those bases he was constantly on the go with various kinds of ministry excursions outside the pale of the base.

His ministry included a wide preaching ministry, Bible teaching in churches, conferences, retreat centers, Bible Institutes and Seminaries as well as pastoral ministry in local churches. He traveled many times between the U.S.A. (and Canada) and England.[4] And on these sometimes extended trips he would minister in many states or locations. He ministered for two different times, about 3 years, and then about 14 years from home bases in the U.S.A. He had aborted attempts at faculty positions in Bible Colleges and Seminaries both in England and the U.S.A.

All in all, his was a complicated ministry. His was a restless search for a convergent role. Dr. John Henry Jowett (who replaced Morgan at Westminster) captured it well. "I can never decide whether Morgan's greater opportunity lies in a settled pastorate, or in a wider ministry in many lands (Murray 1938:43)." And neither could Morgan, in my opinion. Later I will discuss what I think was an *ideal role* [5] for Morgan. For that reason, the tremendous complexity of his life, the time-line (see end of chapter) which integrates the flow of his ministry is very important. I follow that time-line in organizing the running capsule of Morgan's life.

---

[4] Wagner mentions that he crossed the Atlantic fifty-four times (Wagner 1957:23).
[5] *Convergence* is a time of highly effective ministry which builds upon past experience and brings together a number of factors in a synergistic way. One of those factors is an *ideal role*, that is, a role which matches giftedness, personality, influence-mix, destiny, and experience so as to enhance a person's ministry (Clinton 1989:419).

Chapter 5. G. Campbell Morgan--(1863-1945)

I. Born to One Book
(1863-1888); Age=Birth-25

A. Family Influences
(1863-1873); Age=Birth to 10

Early Destiny Items--Parents, Preaching To Lizzie's Dolls

G. Campbell Morgan was born on 9 December in 1863 in a small village, Tetbury, England. Before his birth, his parents George and Elizabeth Fawn Brittan Morgan, knelt and made a vow to God dedicating the *yet to be born Campbell Morgan* to God for His service.[6] His sister Lizzy was four years old at the time of his birth.

His father, Reverend George Morgan was a Baptist preacher who resigned his Baptist pastorate after being influenced by teachings of the Plymouth Brethren, especially by George Muller's life of faith. Robert Chapman, the consistent godly preacher, whose writings, model life, and ministry deeply influenced many, many lives of church leaders as well as his own parishioners, also influenced George Morgan. George Morgan was a strong minded person who lived by his convictions. He was a man of one book, the Bible. He had unshakable convictions that it was the Word of God.

His mother was described as saintly, gentle, radiant and full of peace. She was small, dainty and fastidious in her personal habits and evinced strong religious fervor and integrity (J. Morgan 1972:24). Her modeling had impact on Morgan. She influenced Morgan and Lizzy toward the importance of reading.

As a child Morgan was physically frail. So he was home schooled, at least for the earliest part of his education. His only playmate was his sister. She died of an illness when he was eight. This was a time of deep grief for him. Shortly following this Morgan had pneumonia and nearly died. Morgan, probably by temperament, and certainly by circumstances lived his earliest years in a childhood isolated from interplay with other children. His conversations were with adults. It is easy to see why he was so reflective in his thinking.

Early on, young Campbell Morgan showed interest in preachers and preaching. His attendance at the local Methodist church brought him in contact with contemporary models of preaching: George T. Perks, Gervase Smith, and Richard Roberts (Harris 1930:21). At age seven he and his sister set up a church service in the nursery and Morgan preached to Lizzy and her dolls (1930:23).[7] Jill Morgan describes the macro-contextual pressure of oratory and great preaching and some of the contemporary models who impacted Morgan during this important time in England's history.

> Campbell Morgan became the connoisseur of a good sermon at a very tender age. It was an era of great preaching. Eloquence and oratory in the pulpit were the rules rather

---

[6]This illustrates one of the destiny process items, called *destiny preparation*. It is one indication foreshadowing what is to come. Cumulative recognition of a number of these process items will build a *sense of destiny*, an awareness that God's hand is on the leader in a special way (Clinton 1989:103).

[7]Murray adds detail to this destiny preparation activity (1938:134). Morgan reminiscing on a visit to his home in Cardiff (where he lived at age 7 and 8) said, "In that room I preached. I had one living person in my audience and quite a number that were not alive. I preached regularly there week after week and time after time to my sister and her dolls. It was then that there was born with me the passion to become a preacher."

Chapter 5. G. Campbell Morgan--(1863-1945) page 179

than the exception. During the holidays the boy was taken, by his father, to hear many of those whose names, forgotten now, were then famous in religious circles....

An event of the greatest importance occurred in 1873, an event which moved England in her national as well as in her religious life, for it was in the summer of that year that Mr. D. L. Moody and his equally gifted companion, Mr. Ira D. Sankey, came on their first preaching mission. "I saw neither of them during that visit," Dr. Morgan says, "but like thousands of others, came as a boy under the influence of the ministry of song."...

Mr. Moody's preaching had tremendous effect upon England, and a great religious revival swept the country. The whole tone of preaching, too, was modified under his influence. ...

Whatever may be the influences of his environment, a small boy soaks them up like a sponge. This child had lived his few years in an atmosphere of preaching. Plain living and an absence of almost all counter-attractions, few friends of his own age, together with a sensitive nature which had already felt the basic shock of loss, combined to make him thoughtful and introspective beyond his years. It is impossible not to believe that he possessed a natural gift for using words to express thought. (J. Morgan 1972:29-31).

Contemporary models are very important during the foundational stage of an emerging leader.[8] Morgan had several, many who were pulpit orators.

B. Basic Analytical Skills
(1873-1883); Age=10-20

Morgan never received formal theological training at a Bible College or seminary.[9] But he was a well educated person. His basic education was thorough. Typical of the British system, the days were scheduled heavy, there was strict discipline, and a rigid expectation with regards to studies. The Principal of the school was Mr. Joseph Leonard Butler. Both J. Morgan and Harries pay tribute to the impact of this man in Morgan's life. He was a contemporary model of a different sort than the pulpit orators. He was a teacher, whose strong expectations impacted Morgan's life. In later life, Dr. Morgan paid high compliments to this man for the solid educational background he attained there. Jill Morgan describes, in her opinion, the lasting *values* of Butler's model as a teacher as reflected in Morgan's own teaching ministry.

> Dr. Morgan became, in turn, one of the greatest teachers of his generation. He understood the psychology of teaching--that knowledge of one's subject is limited by the ability to impart it. He understood the patience that is every teacher's first requirement; the long waiting for results which, perhaps, he himself never sees. He knew the price paid in preparation and application, the daily discipline of the mind, the toil that precedes the achievement, the drudgery behind every success. He knew the reward of honest and enduring effort--the word spoken, perhaps years afterwards, that made him know that the labour was not in vain; the thanks in letters from all kinds and conditions of people in

---

[8]See Clinton and Clinton (1991) **The Mentor Handbook**, which describes the importance of contemporary models early on to demonstrate the validity of Christianity or to challenge to a Christian role. The contemporary model serves as a sort of Christian hero/heroine. Other kinds of mentors are needed at different times of development over a lifetime.

[9]Of the eight chosen for this book Gordon, Jaffray, and Maxwell had formal training for ministry. They attended Bible Institutes, Bible Colleges, or Seminaries prior to their full time ministry. Brengle also attended seminary, but after an assignment in full time ministry. All the rest were trained via non-formal and informal training models on-the-job. I personally think this lack of formal education resulted in an inferiority complex which was behind Morgan's several attempts for ministry on faculties--which would give him the affirmation he needed that his training indeed had been adequate (as Dale told him in Birmingham in his third pastorate).

Chapter 5. G. Campbell Morgan--(1863-1945)

> all kinds and conditions of places; the joy of knowing that, because of his teaching, others were teaching better, and good seed was bringing forth fruit--some a hundredfold.
> Who can trace results back to their ultimate sources? We say, 'here was a great teacher,' and sometimes forget that somewhere, and at some time the gift was discovered, and that someone else had a part in its awakening and development. (J. Morgan 1972:28,29)

J. Morgan goes on to speak of this grounding and its long term impact on Morgan.

> In later years Campbell Morgan was often cited as an example of a man who had never received a conventional education; who, never having been to College, sat upon two College faculties, and became the President of another. Yet it would be far from the truth to call the boy who graduated from Gratton House uneducated. Indeed, Mr. Butler saw to it that none of his students left him without the most thorough grounding he was capable of giving them in the basic principles of education.
> This foundation, in Campbell Morgan, was yoked to a quick mind, and an insatiable desire for additional knowledge, which he acquired by reading, not only in youth but all through his life. (J. Morgan 1972:35)

Morgan demonstrated the essential ingredient of a truly educated person--a learning posture.[10] He had good basic skills and he built upon them all his life. He learned from life, from people, from his ministry experiences and especially from books and of course from the one Book, the Bible. He was well read. You will see scattered throughout his writings numerous references to books and materials which he had digested.

On August 27th, 1876 just before his 13th birthday, he preached his first formal sermon, *Salvation*, at the Monmouth Methodist Chapel, to a small group of men and women, with boys and girls of his own age (J. Morgan 1972:31). This was one of several special meetings arranged for by the members of the church. There was a short lull and then a continued preaching activity until age 19 and the faith crisis. At 21, in 1884, he began again to preach and never quit until (more than 23,000 sermons and/or Bible Teaching presentations later) just before his death in 1945.

Morgan involved himself in numerous self-initiated ministry tasks,[11] one of the early symptoms of leadership. He attended services in village chapels near Cheltenham and took part in them. He attended and participated in small group meetings--cottage-meetings. At fifteen he was spending his Sundays and part of his holidays preaching in country chapels to rustic congregations. These early ministry experiences added to his desire to devote his life to the work of the ministry (Harries 1930:28).

Focal incident 1 given at the beginning of the chapter occurred about here in Morgan's development. He learned that giftedness comes from God and should be used for the service of God and His ends and not to build up the holder of such gifts. This lesson on pride was needed, especially for Morgan, for he was so gifted. Pride, unchecked early

---

[10] In our research we have identified 7 major lessons concerning effective leaders. One states, "Effective leaders maintain a learning posture all their lives." Morgan did.

[11] A *ministry task* is an assignment from God which primarily tests a person's faithfulness and obedience but often also allows use of ministry gifts in the context of a task which has closure, accountability, and evaluation (Clinton 1989:137). Usually these tasks come in the context of local church ministry and are assigned by people in the leadership structure. Self-initiated tasks are highly indicative of leadership. Most of Morgan's were self-initiated.

Chapter 5. G. Campbell Morgan--(1863-1945)

on, may easily become a barrier later on--a barrier preventing in the long run, a good finish.[12]

Recognizing the necessity for providing finances both for himself and to help his folks, Morgan took an appointment first as a teacher at the Wesleyan Day School at Islington, Birmingham and later as a Assistant Master in the Jewish Collegiate School in the same city (lasted for three years). These posts allowed for him to develop teaching skills and to gain knowledge, particularly in the Jewish school, which built up Morgan's understanding of historical background of both the Old and New Testaments, so important in study of the Bible. Yet during these years he continued to gain ministry experience on his vacations, with mission-work in country places, and preaching on Sundays in mission-halls. Albert Swift, became a friend and companion on many of these ministry activities. Their lives would be intertwined as the years wound on.

C. Leadership Transition
(1883-1888); Age=20-25

This was the crucial period, the pivotal time, in Morgan's life. A number of events occurred which give background for understanding the shaping of values in his life as well as providential leading toward the focused life.

Critical incident 2 which I quoted to begin the chapter occurs about here. This faith challenge, to accept the Bible as God's word occurred as part of the boundary[13] processing that would lead Morgan on to new heights. This incident is the prime focal incident of his life.[14] The importance of the Bible, its authority and of God's convincing use of it was the foundational value of G. Campbell Morgan's life and ministry. He never wavered on Biblical authority hereafter. He believed it had power, if presented clearly, to change lives. It was central to his ministry.[15] He never defended the Bible. He just used it. He believed in it. It brought results just as he expected. He knew it could do it because God had done it first in his own life.

In 1883, at age 20, Morgan saw Moody during his second visit to Birmingham (Bingley Hall). He was a volunteer worker in these three weeks of meetings. (Murray 1938:35; J. Morgan 1972:44). This made a deep impression on his life. Both Moody and Sankey were contemporary models who impacted young Morgan. He was to connect with them later. But these early favorable impressions set the stage for what was to come later. He saw in action a different kind of preaching--a preaching that moved people to committal. This preaching to the will was to be realized in Morgan as a major value concerning public

---

[12]Appendix A lists all 6 barriers of which *pride leading to a downfall* is one. It is through character testing such as this incident illustrates that God shapes early on and foundationally a correct attitude toward achievement resulting from giftedness. Unchecked or unheeded at this early stage, inordinate pride can become a menace to godly use of spiritual authority.

[13]Boundaries are the transition times from one sub-phase or phase to the next. These have been studied in detail. This was the turning point in this boundary. See Clinton (1992), *Boundary Processing--Looking At Critical Transition Times in Leader's Lives*.

[14]Wagner (1957:7) quotes Alan Redpath, in the Foreword, who is in agreement with me on this point. "Unquestionably, Dr. G. Campbell Morgan was the outstanding expositor of the first half of the twentieth century. This Volume reveals how he came into this pre-eminent position through the remarkable preparation of the early years of his life, and perhaps most of all because of the conflict of mind which he faced, at one time, concerning the authority of the Word of God itself."

[15]See his sermon, *Christ and the Bible*, in the Baker Book House edition (1972) of **The Best of G. Campbell Morgan**, edited by Ralph Turnbull. This sermon clearly states his convictions about the Bible.

ministry and its purpose. Morgan did not omit the affect or intellect, in fact his ministry was always highly thought provoking and a challenge to the intellect. But that was always subservient to the will. He preached and taught to move people to committal.[16]

In 1885, Morgan began keeping a daily diary in which he included his ministry activities. It is through entries in this diary that one pieces together his early explorations into ministry activities that continued to give him affirmation about entering full time into ministry. We will refer to this diary later when we talk of his ultimate contribution as a public rhetorician.

Forced Out--Mr. Levy and Certainty Confirmation

There was a growing conviction that he should be in full time ministry. His leadership committal experience, what is called in leadership emergence theory a double confirmation,[17] was a destiny experience that God was clearly in. It laid the foundations for his ministry of faith to come. Both of his major biographers refer to it. Here is Harries view on it.

> For two years the conviction was growing upon me that I would have to be set free from all other occupation, [he says], so as to devote myself wholly to the work of preaching the Gospel. I could not bring myself to the point of decision, for there was always the possibility of mistaking the voice of my own desires for the voice of God. Could I have been sure of God's will in the matter, I would not have hesitated, for then I would not have feared for the future. After two years I decided that I dared not take the step, because of others that might suffer. My father and mother were dependent upon me. Before I slept on that unforgettable night, I said in my prayer to God, "*If I am to go out as Thy messenger, Thou wilt have to force me.* (italics mine)." By that, I meant that, if for any reason apart from my own choice, my appointment at the school should be ended, I would give myself entirely to the work of an evangelist, but until then, I would continue my work as schoolmaster.
>
> Next morning, after school-hours, the Principal called me to him, and said: "I am awfully sorry, Mr. Morgan, but I am compelled to dispense with your services. Our school will have to be closed. The development of King Edward's Grammar Schools has made it impossible for us to continue, and it would be well if you sought another appointment. You may take your time about it, for the school will not be closed just yet." In that moment I knew God had taken me at my word--"If I am to go out as Thy messenger, Thou wilt have to force me."
>
> "Thank you, Mr. Levy," I answered. "And now will you hear my story?" I then related my experiences that led to the crisis of the night, and of decision taken before I slept. "And now," I said, "I can do no other but take this as the will of God. I bow before it, and submit."

---

[16]In his book, **Crises of the Christ**, Morgan talks about humankind as essentially spirit and having three centers of influence: the will, the emotions, and the intellect. He saw the will as primary though he saw that the will could be reached via the intellect and the emotions. His grasp of these essentials is not far off from modern learning theory which details cognitive, affect, conative and experiential taxonomies as basic categories through which people learn.

[17]*Double confirmation* is a special guidance process in which God makes clear, certainty guidance, His direction for a leader. Usually double confirmation involves an inner conviction to a leader which is then confirmed by some outward circumstance or person unaware of the inner dealings. This guidance process was given to make certain his leadership committal. *Leadership committal* is a critical process item in which a leader commits himself/herself to serving God as the primary role in life. The more clearly the divine involvement in such a shaping process, the more certain it is that the leader will persevere when the pressure times come. This shaping activity was also a destiny process item, called *destiny revelation*. God clearly reveals the next step toward full time Christian ministry.

Chapter 5. G. Campbell Morgan--(1863-1945)

> Taking my trembling hand in his, my Principal said, with a voice full of passion: "The God of Abraham is not dead. Go, and be blessed!" (Harries 1930:30)

Morgan realized that God had closed the door to academic teaching. So he made himself available to various ministry opportunities feeling confident that God would direct. He gave himself to evangelism and conducted many local missions.

Gipsy Smith--Divine Contact; Certainty Guidance

He first thought to go with the Salvation Army, which he had admired for some time. They asked Morgan to do follow-up work for a Gipsy Smith evangelistic campaign in Hull, in an inner city district among poor people. This he did. The original suggestion had been for Morgan to do a two week follow-up but it became a thirteen month project. Morgan learned many valuable lessons in this time--particularly the power of the Gospel to free from all kinds of debilitating sinful practices. Morgan was about four months into this ministry when he actually met Gipsy Smith for the first time--an acquaintance which built into a friendship that lasted sixty years (J. Morgan 1972:56,57).

He confided in Gipsy Smith concerning his desire to work with the Salvation Army. Gipsy Smith, a *divine contact*,[18] gave prophetic advice. He felt that Campbell Morgan, like himself, would do his best work alone (J. Morgan 1972:57). Morgan took the advice after asking for special guidance from God. This is another example of certainty guidance--this time via two distinct guidance processing activities, the divine contact and the double confirmation. These kinds of focal incidents are anchors to which a leader will return time and again later to give assurance that God is in the ministry.

> A few days after the conversation with the Gipsy he records, at the end of a day's entry in his diary: "I made it a special matter of prayer to-night as to my future, requesting an answer by post." The next morning there arrived in the post a letter from his mother. The contents of that letter are not revealed. All we know is that "Mother's letter is the answer to last night's prayer." Campbell Morgan revoked his first resolve to unite with the Salvation Army, because he believed that in doing so he was following the pathway of the divine Will. (J. Morgan 1972:56,57).

Methodist Rejection--Morgan Fails Preaching Exam

For about two years, Morgan worked as a lay evangelist for the Macclesfield District of the Wesleyan denomination. This was a busy time. He was involved in much evangelistic and preaching activity. He was pursuing ordination. Then occurred one of those focal incidents of guidance upon which a lifetime of ministry hinge. Jill Morgan describes this incident fully. It is worth recording in its entirety since upon it hinged a new direction for Morgan and his lifework and it foreshadows one of the factors, influence-mix, in ministry that was important to convergence in Morgan's public ministry.

> The requirement for the Wesleyan Methodist ministry in those days was that candidates should first submit to an examination, which, if passed successfully, would authorize them to become lay preachers. The other qualifications needed, in order to become eligible for the ministry itself, involved the preaching of a *trial sermon* before qualified examiners. Though young in years, Campbell Morgan had had an unusual amount of experience as a preacher, and the months as an evangelists in Hull had demonstrated his ability to capture and hold the attention of a congregation. This latter part of the examination held no terrors for him. The former, on the other hand, brought

---

[18]A *divine contact* is a special kind of mentor, whose timely intervention, usually is perceived as having a divine word concerning some aspect of guidance or ministry. See Clinton and Clinton (1991).

Chapter 5. G. Campbell Morgan--(1863-1945)

home a consciousness of a lack of education along theological lines, but if this could be remedied by reading and study, he was willing to try. December, 1887, was the date set for the preliminary test, and beginning in October he set himself an intensive course of reading, and stuck to it with thoroughness and determination, sometimes spending six hours at a time in study. On December 12 he sat for the *Local Preacher's* examination and passed it successfully. The next objective--to preach the *trial sermon*. Should the candidate pass this goal, it was then recommended that he take a course at a theological college. How the latter was to be managed Campbell Morgan did not know, for since relinquishing his teaching appointment he had no steady income. However, exceptions were made in some cases, and it might be possible, for a time, to undertake active ministerial work provided the examination could be passed successfully.

Campbell Morgan was one of a hundred and fifty young men who sought entrance to the Wesleyan ministry that year, and he was instructed to report at the Lichfield Road Church, in Birmingham, on May 2nd, 1888. It was a large building, with a seating capacity of a thousand. In the vestry, sharpening a pencil, was one of the three ministers who had been deputized to report on his sermon. It looked as though he meant business, and the young man's heart sank as he realized that this was not going to savour any of the inspiration of an evangelistic meeting. Things looked even less promising as the examiner turned to him and said: "Now I am ready for *you*! But it was when the candidate stepped into the pulpit that the biggest blow fell. The seventy-five people before him, lost in the vast auditorium, regarded him with a critical eye which seemed to say: "Make good, or we shall make short work of you!" ...

Suffice it to say that, two weeks later, in the list of the hundred and five who were rejected for the Wesleyan Methodist ministry that year, was the name of G. Campbell Morgan. (J. Morgan 1972:57-60)

Did Morgan see God in this? Did he learn from it? Harries helps us see that Morgan did indeed see this as part of God's training for him.

When that door of hope was closed against me [he says]--a door through which, for two years, I had been seeking an entrance and beyond which I thought lay the largest opportunity man could have--God said to me, in the weeks of loneliness and darkness that followed: "I want you to cease making plans for yourself, and let Me plan your life." So far as I know, from that day to this, I have made no plans for myself, nor attempted to arrange my future. I have always attempted to leave myself free, so that when the wind, that bloweth where it listeth, should catch the outspread sails, I might be carried in a Divinely controlled direction. It was a tremendous crisis in my life--the moment when the one string upon which I tried to play the music of my ministry lay stretched under the bow of my life; the will of God first and last. And I thank God, to-day, for the closing of that door of hope, because, when he turned my feet in another direction, I found the breadth of His commandments, and the glory of His service.[19] (Harries 1930:36)

Out of this low time in late 1887 and early 1888, God met Morgan in another way. The girl with whom he had an understanding apparently pulled back from the relationship because of the failure of the examination and thus the closed door to the Methodist church. God brought Nancy Morgan into his life. They became engaged in June and married in August. She was willing to start with him at the bottom of the ministry ladder. He offered her nothing but the shared experiences of a wandering evangelist. She became a supportive asset to Morgan's ministry from that day onward for 58 years.

---

[19]Wagner, as I do, sees this as a critical turning point in Morgan's life. "The Wesleyan Methodist's rejection of Campbell Morgan's application for entrance to their ministry had a far-reaching result in the development of the Morgan method.... Providence, however, may be better understood by the realization that acceptance by the Methodists would have resulted in a formal theological training. Such a turn of events could conceivably have altered the development of the special technique that characterizes the Morgan method." (Wagner 1957:21)

Chapter 5. G. Campbell Morgan--(1863-1945)   page 185

II. The Foundational Bible Years--Focused Intake
(1888-1901); Age=25-38

A. Stone Pastorate
(1889-1891); Age=25-28

Morgan's way had been blocked to a parachurch organization. It had been blocked to a denomination and formal theological training. It seems natural then, that along with Gipsy Smith's prophetic advice, and his father's own independent ministry background that Morgan would choose a situation which allowed much freedom and independence in ministry, yet granted a respectable ecclesiastical covering and some financial stability. And that was the case. After a year of largely itinerant ministry and establishing his relationship to his new wife, G. Campbell Morgan was called to the pastorate of the Congregational Church at Stone, a small town in North Staffordshire. He began his ministry there August 18, 1889. (Harries 1930:39). None of the biographical materials share the actual details of how Morgan was directed to this congregational church.

Conflict--Choosing to Submit to Restrictions

In this ministry assignment,[20] which lasted for two busy years, Morgan progressed substantially in a number of areas. He was ordained in this church on September 22, 1890--certainly a public confirmation of his earlier leadership committal to serve God. He learned about conflict[21] in a church setting. Early on, he displayed his penchant for ministering beyond the bounds of his own local church. He ministered to many of the surrounding small churches and brought about the renewal of one faltering congregation, the Eccleshall Church, a foreshadowing similar efforts that would occur in later situations.[22] At a critical juncture, December of 1891, in the conflict over his extraneous activities he received a note from the deacon board which commanded him to discontinue any outside activity without the consent of the deacons. Morgan received wise advice from Mr. John Crake, a mentor counselor (J. Morgan 1972:69,70), which he followed.[23]

---

[20]This is an example of shaping activity, a process item, called *ministry assignment* (Clinton 1989:200). A ministry assignment describes a ministry experience which is more permanent than a ministry task yet has the same basic pattern of entry, ministry, closure, and transition out of the ministry situation and through which God gives new insights to the leader so as to expand influence capacity and responsibility toward future leadership. One can trace developmental progress across a ministry assignment by noting before and after evaluation of items.

[21]*Conflict* (Clinton 1989:276) is one of the surprising processes that young ministers in their first assignment learn about. Conflict shapes a leader as few other processes do. The difficulty is to see God in it and learning lessons in it that will make the leader a better person in the years to come.

[22]The conflict in the church revolved around a long standing difference between two major factions in the church. Morgan had to walk a tightrope. The conflict was further heightened by Morgan's ministries outside his own local church--something which came naturally to a leader who was relatively interdenominational in breadth and who had ministered in his leadership transitional time in many varied situations. Morgan was a leader. He saw needs. He found ways to self-initiate ministry to meet those needs.

[23]There is a relatively large drop out of young pastors in the first or second ministry assignment. Of those who make it past 5 years, all can point to a mentor who helped them adjust to the many differences and disappointments of their expectations and reality in the ministry. J. Morgan comments on this. "It may be added here that Dr. Morgan made a practice all through his life of talking over his problems with those he could trust, and in whose advice he placed confidence (J. Morgan 1972:70,71)." This mentoring intervention throughout life affirms the need we assert for a balanced constellation model of mentors throughout life. See Stanley's thesis explained in chapter 12, The Constellation Model, in Clinton and Clinton (1991).

He discovered several ministry insights, particularly structures and activities to reach young people (J. Morgan 1972:71,2).[24] Finally after months of patiently following Crake's advice, which included cutting back on outside activities and not manipulating the situation or a call to get out of it, Morgan received a call to a church at Rugeley, about fifteen miles away, his second ministry assignment.

B. Rugeley Pastorate
(1891-1893); Age=28-30

Self-Study To Master The Scriptures--Discovers Own Methodology

The title of this development phase is **The Foundational Bible Years-- Focused Intake.** It is at Rugeley that he began the deliberate and scheduled life long pursuit of mastery of the Word of God. It was here that he began to discover his own unique approach to the study of the Bible.

> Dr. Morgan, at the age of seventy-six, made a most significant observation as he stood in the church at Rugeley and glanced over the empty building. "This is the place," he remarked, "where I had those two quiet years, when I did the spade work of all my Bible studies." He repeated this as he sat out in the car remembering the old days, and one felt that this place marked the real beginning of, 'This one thing I do--' the study and teaching of the Bible to which he was to devote the rest of his life. (J. Morgan 1972:73)[25]

Again as at Stone, this was a busy time. Morgan was young and had lots of energy. He involved himself in social issues to which he felt the church should address. He even spoke in political campaigns. He continued to maintain mentoring contacts including developing a friendship with Gregory Mantle, a Methodist minister, in fact, one of those who had voted to reject Morgan.

Ego Check--Sermons To Ashes

He involved himself in many preaching missions outside the church, with the approval of the church. But it was this activity and a growing popularity that led to a significant encounter with God, reminiscent of Focal Incident 1 with David Smith. This shows that public recognition and acclaim can foster pride. This sort of processing will often be repeated from time-to-time with leaders who are so gifted. Harries describes the incident and shows the on-going notion of it.

> These were great and strenuous days. But they were days, Dr. Morgan tells us, when he felt the hand of God to be definitely fashioning and moulding him for his future life of service....
> All this was not the matter of a moment [says Dr. Morgan] but of years. It began in the days when, as yet, I was but an evangelist; it continued after I had been ordained to the Congregational ministry, and was rapidly becoming one of the popular young preachers of the denomination. God was speaking to me, that I knew, and the crisis in which His voice rang out clearly, almost peremptorily, making known to me His will, came at Rugeley, one Sunday night, after service. I had preached, and we had held an after-meeting, in which men and women had decided for Christ.

---

[24] He organized a debating group, in which all kinds of topics including religious and secular were debated (J. Morgan 1972:71).

[25] The winter was long and snowy and conducive to study in the library. Morgan spent these important days of study in absorbing Greek and doing his original studies in the Scriptures. He studied Dickens and Kingsley as well (J. Morgan 1972:73,74). But most important was the establishment of a habit of study, giving the best hours of the day to study.

Chapter 5. G. Campbell Morgan--(1863-1945)   page 187

> At the end of the day I went home to my own study, and sat there alone. As clearly as though it had sounded in the room, a voice put this question, "What are you going to be, a preacher or My messenger?" For a moment I knew not what it meant, except to realize that the Spirit of God had created a crisis. I stood at the parting of the ways. Presently I began to ponder that night's sermon--to review my ministry. To my dismay I discovered that the desire to become, and be known as a great preacher, was beginning to get the upper hand.
> "What are you going to be, a preacher, or My messenger?" For hours I sat, vainly endeavouring to answer the question, but not until the night had died down, and the light of morning glinted through my study-window, did I arrive at a decision. It was a night of conflict between a man and his God. It was my brook Jabbok--the place where God met me, face to face. Just as the light of morning scattered the darkness of the night passed, so did the light Divine stream into my soul, and joyously I cried out, "Thy messenger, my Master--Thine!"
> But the victory was won, only when the ashes of a bundle of sermons lay in the study fireplace. The work of many years was destroyed on that golden morning, when I stepped out to follow God at all costs, determining to do so without those sermons. During the night hours I came to see that they had been moulded and made so as to include a large element of self. For that reason they were destroyed. As they burned, I said to my Master: "If Thou wilt give me Thy words to speak, I will utter them, from this day forward, adding nothing to them, taking naught away. Thine whole counsel I will declare, so help me God. " So did the Lord prevail. (Harries 1930:45,46).

This important lesson gave Morgan a new conception of his work as a Christian minister.

The over activity led eventually to a physical breakdown and an enforced rest.[26] It was during this compulsory rest, that Gregory Mantle, one of Morgan's mentors, in this case a mentor sponsor, linked Morgan to the Westminster Road Congregational Church in Birmingham. I believe this whole sequence, the challenge to inner-life growth, the isolation period, and the leading to Westminister Road Congregational Church to be an excellent illustration of the positive testing pattern.[27] Morgan had responded well to the test. The call to Birmingham was the expansion. God is taking Morgan into a new situation which will expand his potential and allow development of a wider sphere of influence.

C. Westminster Road Pastorate, Birmingham
(1893-1897); Age=30-34

Morgan began his ministry at the Westminster Road Congregational church on June 11, 1893. It is just before his 30th birthday. He has had two major ministry assignments, both in small rural type pastorates, behind him. He has learned from both. Now he will move into a large metropolitan area where he will move from a local church sphere of influence to a regional influence. Immediately he makes friends with Dr. R. W. Dale, long time pastor in the Birmingham region. Dr. Dale becomes a mentor counselor and friend who encourages Morgan concerning his training, "You must never say that you are untrained," he said with some sternness. "God, who has many ways of training men, has trained you, and I pray that you may have great joy in His service." (Harries 1932:50) Dale went on to encourage his personal study of various books and materials.

---

[26]This is a form of *isolation processing* (Clinton 1989:274), a setting aside of a leader, by God in order to draw the leader to God and to focus the leader to reflect on life and ministry. Isolation processing frequently accompanies boundary times and forms a stimulus to move on to God's next assignment.

[27]The positive testing pattern is one of 23 repetitive patterns we have identified in our research on leaders. Frequently, God tests character, as in this case, and then depending on the response either brings remedial training, if negative response, or expansion if positive response. This test, an *integrity check* (Clinton 1989:125, 352) focuses on an inner-life value, previously taught at a lesser level.

Chapter 5. G. Campbell Morgan--(1863-1945)

His health was not yet up to par so after about a year at Westminster at the recommendation of a physician he and his family took off three months and rested at the island of Stark and later at the Isle of Man. It was here that Campbell and Nancy lost a child, Gwennie, their first born. This sad event shaped him empathetically. He always loved children and had a special place in his heart for them in all his ministries. He was warmly welcomed back after the rest.

He came into a church situation that was troubled. Doctrinal differences and other problems had scattered the church members. He built back the church with a good pastoral ministry and especially with a powerful pulpit ministry.

Unique Methodology--Friday Night Public Bible Teaching

It was at Westminster Road, that Morgan got one of his important ministry insights. He began in 1895 a week night service which was focused on a series of lectures teaching the Bible chapter by chapter, and book by book (Harries 1930:52).[28] It was attended by his own Sunday School teachers and by many others from surrounding churches. This Bible School ministry within a local church became an important part of his ministry philosophy. He continued this in varied formats at every pastorate thereafter.

Albert Smith and Moody--Link To Future Public Bible Teaching

Albert Smith, a longtime friend and partner in the lay ministry days, had moved to New Jersey. In 1896 he invited Morgan to come to the states for a visit. He set up a preaching and lecturing schedule and connected Morgan to D. L. Moody and the Moody Bible Institute.[29] This three month absence would prove an important link to future ministry. It also showed the freedom which Morgan enjoyed at Westminster. Few ministers can take three months to recuperate from sickness and then three months for a trip abroad.

His ministry at Westminster was full orbed including ministry to the poor, stands on controversial issues, like the Armenian massacres of 1896 in Turkey, and a strong interest in missionary work. He began here the publishing of The Westminster Road Congregational Magazine, which took his preaching and teaching ministry beyond the immediate locale of the church. This was the forerunner of many other efforts to expand Morgan's indirect sphere of influence via materials. Morgan was able also to take this congregation out of debt. He found ways to challenge people to give.[30] Morgan was becoming a competent minister. He had a good solid approach to ministry. He had taken this church from 155 people with financial difficulties and a scattered congregation to a united church of over 430 adults with a strong ministry and reputation in the region. Morgan had expanded his sphere of influence from a small direct ministry in rural churches to a large direct influence in a region and to an indirect influence through the publishing of

---

[28]J. Morgan (1972:80) says this series of lectures became the nucleus of **The Analyzed Bible** published in 1907 and 1908.

[29]This is an example of the linking function of a *mentor sponsor*. See Stanley and Clinton (1991). This kind of apparent happenstance can significantly affect the life and ministry of the mentoree, in this case Dr. Morgan. Four years later he will be invited to become a part of Moody's on-going conference work centered in Northfield. This *chance visit* is the link to an important part of Morgan's future. J. Morgan describes in detail (1972:91-96) the meeting with Moody and its impact upon Morgan.

[30]These were in effect *ministry insights*, breakthroughs in raising money. Innovative means included giving lectures to which the public was invited. These lectures on Kingsley, Garibaldi, Savonarola and others were researched thoroughly and well attended (J. Morgan 1972:83).

Chapter 5. G. Campbell Morgan--(1863-1945)

sermons and Bible study materials for Sunday School teachers. He was ready for the next stage of ministry, an influence at national level. He received numerous calls to pastorates over the several years he was at Westminster Road but he did not accept them. It was not till after 3 and 1/2 years, a successful ministry, and a call from the new Court Congregational Church, Tollington Park, London that he felt God's challenge in it.

The decision to go was made after several months of prayer and counsel.[31] It was only finalized after a congregational meeting in which the church as a whole advised that he should.

D. New Court, Tollington Park
(1897-1901); Age=34-38

During his four years at New Court his ministry reached national prominence. He was invited to numerous pulpits and conferences including several trips during the three summers to the U.S.A. for ministry at Northfield and in numerous large cities in the states and Canada. He was established as a Bible teacher of note on these tours across the Atlantic.

Winnie Howell--Materials Production, Lifelong Helper

Morgan's first published writings began about the time of his acceptance of this suburban London pastorate in February 1897.[32] It was here at New Court that Winnie Howell joined the team. She became Morgan's administrative assistant and was responsible for the details of recording and publishing much of his material over the next almost 50 years.[33]

During these years he again did fund raising to renovate and expand facilities. He also salvaged a church, the Holloway Chapel. He also had a throat infection which required an operation and sidelined him in for about three months.[34] His ministry at New Court widened his sphere of influence and established him not only as a competent public Bible teacher and pastor but also served as a springboard to international prominence.

---

[31] J. Morgan points out again the mentor counselors Morgan confided in with regard to this important decision. They included Dr. John Henry Jowett and Mr. Frank Crossley of Manchester as well as many mature friends in the Birmingham congregation (1972:102).

[32] He is 34 when he begins to publish materials for others to use. These included in 1897 *Discipleship* and *The True Estimate of Life and How To Live It*. In 1898 there were *The Hidden Years at Nazareth, Wherein? Malachi's Message for Today, God's Method With Man*. In 1899, *Life Problems* and *The Spirit of God* appeared. Most of these were apparently either sermons, extended studies or booklets.

[33] Over the years much of his published materials was the reproduction of his oral public ministry, much like that of Watchman Nee. Miss Howell was a very important part of the recording and editing of this oral ministry and making it ready for a printed format. Such, love gifted people, as Winnie Howell make a vital difference in the overall effectiveness of a public rhetorician like Morgan. Such people who support and release the giftedness of others, especially Word gifted people, are invaluable in the Kingdom. We will see this again in the ministry of Henrietta Mears.

[34] This is another incident of *isolation processing* (Clinton 1989:274). Morgan said of it, himself, that evidently, the enforced *complete silence* for two months was to teach him to listen. Morgan commented on the importance of this isolation processing in a sermon on 2 Corinthians 1:3-7 given five years later. He saw, as Dr. Parker shared with him, of the importance of such suffering to ones spiritual authority and empathy with the congregation (J. Morgan 1972:112,113).

Chapter 5. G. Campbell Morgan--(1863-1945)   page 190

Moody Invitation--Prelude to the Future

D. L. Moody died on December 23, 1899. His son Will Moody took up his work. One of his first important decisions was to ask Campbell Morgan to come to the United States and locate in Northfield. From that base he would provide a Northfield Extension program, teaching the Bible publicly all over the United States. Morgan's explanation of his resignation from New Court shows that he had a sense of destiny, and that a search for a broader role was part of his fulfilling his destiny and allowing him to reach his maximum potential. This search for such a role would continue, after the three years in the U.S.A.

> "No other church in the world could have tempted me from a pastorate which is a peculiarly joyful one," he told his own people in explaining to them his reasons for his resignation. "This, I trust, was proved by my refusal last year to entertain the advances made to me by the Fifth Avenue Church in New York. In this Northfield invitation the case is different. I have long felt that God was preparing me for a ministry to the churches, rather than to one particular church. Now the door stands open for such work. It has not opened in my own country where I hoped and thought it would....To wait would be to choose for myself, when I wish that God would choose for me." (J. Morgan 1972:115)

His send off from England showed just how nationally prominent and popular he was. In addition to his own churches going away party there was a general farewell in London. Dr. F. B. Meyer, a warm friend of Campbell Morgan, organized the send off. Many prominent well known English pastors spoke at this farewell. It was clear that they recognized just what a loss to England was this decision to minister in the United States. When Morgan left he stated that his ministry in the U.S.A. was open ended. It was not clear to him how long he would be. He may be there a short time. He may never come back. He simply was following God's will and would continue to do so.

III. The Effective Bible Years--Wide Public Exposition
(1901-1919); Age=37-56

A. Northfield Conference Extension--1st Major Itinerant Ministry
(1901-1904); Age=37-40

Campbell Morgan and family moved to the United States and home based in Northfield and Baltimore. During these three years Morgan participated in each of the three major summer conferences: The Students' Conference (about seven hundred men in attendance); The Young Women's Conference, and the General Conference of Christian Workers (Harries 1930:74). Each of these were well attended. They were Bible conferences. People came prepared to study the English Bible and to apply it to everyday life. In addition, he taught in Bible Conferences all around the country. He also made a yearly trip for ministry to England just after the summer conferences at Northfield. He preached and taught before capacity crowds where ever he went. Packed out crowds of 6000 or 2000 or 1000 were not unusual. His most important contribution during this time of ministry was the challenging of many to study and teach the Bible. He showed them how to study it for themselves. In addition to his scheduled extension work for Northfield, he also had many pulpit appearances in important churches around the country.

He suggested small groups as a means of following up his Bible conferences. Many such groups were started. During all this itinerant ministry Morgan maintained time

Chapter 5. G. Campbell Morgan--(1863-1945)

for Bible study and thorough preparation. He continued to prepare materials for others to use including Sunday School lessons, sermons, Bible studies and even books.[35]

Revell Contact--Significant for Future Publishing

The highlights of his development during this period of time include:

1. Continued personal growth through disciplined study and preparation for his ministry.
2. His public ministry. He was without peer in the public presentation of Bible teaching. This period of time with its thousands of presentations established Morgan as the foremost Bible teacher in the world.[36]
3. Morgan made contacts everywhere he went.[37] This manifestation of networking power will prove invaluable in the future.
4. He linked many top British leaders into Northfield and other important ministry in the United States.
5. Morgan connects with Fleming H. Revell who becomes a mentor sponsor and for more than half a century published his materials--sermons, papers, booklets, and books so that Morgan's indirect sphere of influence became international and left behind an ultimate contribution.[38]

Westminister Decision--Free To Choose, God Will Bless

During the winter of 1903-4 Morgan received a number of communications from Westminster Chapel in London asking to become their minister. In fact, during his time with the Moody organization he had three calls to pulpits in the United States (J. Morgan 1972:132). Morgan declined them all including Westminster. But Westminster persisted. Murray describes the final intervention of God to clearly direct Morgan back to England and Westminster Chapel.[39] There was tremendous pressure both in the United States and in England for Morgan to minister.[40]

---

[35]During this period of time the following are listed (Turnbull, editor 1972) as being published: 1901, *God's Perfect Will, All Things New: A message to New Converts, The Ten Commandments*; 1903, *The Letters of Our Lord: A First Century Message to Twentieth Century Christians, Evangelism*, and his first major book--**The Crises of the Christ**.

[36]One indication of that recognition was the awarding of the honorary degree of Doctor of Divinity to Campbell Morgan by the Chicago Theological Seminary.

[37]The process item, a special shaping activity, described in this development is called *networking power* (Clinton 1989:240). Networking power is the unusual use by God of mentors, divine contacts, or other related leaders so as to open doors or link to resources or opportunities. The vast networks of leaders who were established in these three years will prove invaluable when Morgan comes back for his ten years of independent ministry from 1919-1929. At that time he will not be sponsored by the Moody Organization. God is sovereignly preparing for that most powerful focused time of ministry to come.

[38]Revell was a *divine contact*, one sent from God to link Morgan to resources--in this case, his own publishing firm. This example with Revell not only illustrates a mentor sponsor and a mentor divine contact but also the process of *networking power*. Fleming H. Revell was the brother of Mrs. D. L. Moody who first invited Morgan to speak at Northfield. From these early days the contact was made which was profitable for Revell's company, for Dr. Morgan, and for the Christian public (J. Morgan 1972:362).

[39]It is interesting how at critical junctures God gives such clear direction to Morgan. Again as with other important decisions Morgan consulted the advice of a number of lateral mentors, in this case: Gregory Mantle, Samuel Chadwick, Frank Fifoot and Albert Swift (J. Morgan 1972:133).

[40]J. Morgan (1972:141) records that after it was known in America that he had an invitation to Westminster Chapel he was inundated with letters. Six prominent churches offered a call. Three theological colleges offered him positions on their faculties. One wealthy American offered to back him in a Bible institute ministry. The Moody organization offered to tailor make his role to allow him ministry

I came home," he said, for a visit. I preached at Westminster. I was asked to accept the pastorate. I was committed to America for Conferences that would last at least a year. The little band of men who had held the fort at Westminster against a great deal of misunderstanding asked me to reconsider the matter in a year. I said I would, if they promised in the meantime if anyone else appeared, they would not hesitate to call him.

In that year someone else did appear, Dr. Smith, of St. Paul and Minneapolis, and they invited him. He, however, did not see his way to accept, and I came back in 1904 to look over the ground and consider the opportunity which Westminster offered. I felt at once the building was a great preaching auditorium than which none is more acoustically perfect.

I preached through the month of June, having promised to give answer to the invitation on the third Sunday. On the morning of that day I was staying in Dulwich with Albert Swift.

My father was there. When I came down to breakfast early, he said, 'What are you going to do?"

I replied, I don't know.

After a hasty breakfast, I went up to my room and got down on my knees alone, and said, Master, what shall I do?

I heard no voice replying, but I had an answer as clearly and distinctly and directly as any man ever had a word from God, and this was the answer.

Make your own choice. I am with you, whether in the States or in London. [Boldfaced emphasis mine]

It was a new experience in my spiritual life to feel I was flung back upon my own choosing, and I said to myself, How shall I choose? There came to me at once the familiar but great statement, "The just shall live by faith."

At once I felt the matter was settled.

In a certain sense, faith was not necessary if I went back to America. For instance, John Wannamaker had told me if I would stay he was prepared to put up a Bible School and Institute of which I should have charge, with an assured salary. Moreover, my arrangements with the Northfield Conferences was a settled one, as to finance. On this side nothing was arranged. The Church had no endowments. Here was the place where the activity of faith would be necessary.[41]

I chose on that principle. (Murray 1938:38-40)

This was a faith challenge. Morgan, true to his previous track records of renewing helpless churches accepts the challenge.

Albert Smith--His Positive Response Confirms Decision

Part of his reason for acceptance was the agreement of Albert Swift to come and work with him as an associate handling administration. For years, Morgan had inwardly entertained the hope of someday working closely with Albert Swift.[42] Morgan was a man

---

almost of his choice and without financial care. Individual church leaders in England as well as the Congregational leadership also put pressure on Morgan. He was desperately needed in England, they said.

[41] At that point, Westminster Chapel, with its glorious history was at its lowest ebb ever. Harries describes it vividly. "The fortunes of Westminster Chapel had now reached their lowest ebb. A few faithful souls kept the doors open, and Sunday services were conducted in one corner of the great auditorium. ...the last of this fund was expended early in the year 1902. A number of the leading preachers in the Congregational ministry had been pressed to undertake the pastorate, but one and all refused to shoulder such an onerous burden and face such a desperate situation....The place was derelict, bankrupt--the despair of London Congregationalists (Harries 1930:78,79)."

[42] Morgan makes that point clear. "The vast opportunities on the other side of the Atlantic [the tremendous offers in the U.S.A.] appealed to me with almost irresistible force, but the conviction that here was a strategic point in danger of slipping out of the hands of the church was too strong, and I came to be convinced that I, with the help of one other man, could hold it. The question was, Would he come? And

Chapter 5. G. Campbell Morgan--(1863-1945)

who recruited to his weaknesses. He always had around him a team of supportive people who could get the job done and free him to do the things he could do best.

B. Major Pastorate--1st Westminster Stint
(1904-1917); Age=40-54; A Pastoral Base + Itinerant Ministry

The new era, one in which the value of a long tenure in one place will be realized, began officially on the last Sunday of October, 1904. The ministry at Westminster can be broken down into three significant time periods. These are as follows:

1. **Organizing a Flagship Ministry**[43]--(1904-1907)
   This was a time of ministry in which Campbell Morgan and Albert Swift worked together. Morgan the dominant up front leader and Swift the organizer who freed up Morgan for his Public Bible Ministry. This period of time was concluded when Albert Swift left to accept a senior pastor role in a sister church in the London region.

2. **The Glory Years--Convergence, Pastor Based Role** (1907-1914)
   These were the years of outstanding public ministry by Campbell Morgan. This period was terminated by his famous 10th year Anniversary sermon, September 27, 1914 from Psalm 119:96. His bout with typhoid followed immediately. Morgan was not in good health the whole fall preceding this controversial sermon.[44]

3. **The Transition Years**--(1915-1917)
   Morgan goes through an isolation time including typhoid fever. After this he continues to minister but has lost his powerful drive to build at Westminster. He knows that God is moving him on to something else. He will transition into a time of convergent ministry from a parachurch role.

One could spend a whole book on the Westminster years and Morgan's accomplishments there. Rather than give details I will simply summarize what I think were achievements and developments in Morgan's life during this period of time. I realize in doing this that I will most likely overlook a number of important ventures.

1. Flagship Church
He and Albert Swift created a church model which utilized a full time multi-staff and release of numerous sodality type ministries by lay people. There was a sisterhood-- women ordained and released for numerous ministries including various social ministries in

---

when Albert Swift, my life-long friend, said he was willing to stand with me, the matter was settled. So I came (J. Morgan 1972:142).

[43] By a flagship ministry is meant a full orbed church ministry model which is having regional and national impact and becomes a pattern or ideal for other aspiring leaders to aim at. We have seen this earlier in A. J. Gordon's work in the Boston area. Westminster Chapel had social ministries, evangelism outreach, a book room and library, leadership training, and a Bible Institute ministry with extensions in 5 or 6 centers. It was involved in Bible Training associations and Missions Associations. It had a summer conference ministry. It had a Word Ministry from its pulpit which drew thousands each Sunday. Its Friday night Bible School averaged 1400. Its Senior Pastor had ministries outside the church which highlighted his Public Rhetorician contribution. His ministries outside the church included times in several countries. Today he would have been a prominent TV personality with an outside organization grossing millions as some of these do today.

[44] J. Morgan (1972:208-212) carries almost in total a letter reviewing this sermon by Reverend Samuel Chadwick which gives a balanced viewpoint on this critical turning point in Morgan's life.

the surrounding neighborhoods and even the wider region of London. There was a Bible centered Sunday School program. There was a youth institute meeting the needs of teenagers in the London area. There was an evangelistic outreach program involving training and ministry led by an evangelistically gifted Pastor, Hewitt. Morgan developed into a senior pastor who could work with, develop, and release staff. He could motivate toward vision. He had a way of seeing what something could be, not what it was.

2. Unifying Ecumenical Influence--Indirect Influence Via Associations/ Outside Ministries

Morgan was an important member of a number of number of associations which were trans-denominational including: Vice President of the World Evangelical Alliance, President of the Sunday School Union, strong supporter of the British and Foreign Bible Society, the prime instigator and promoter of the Bible Teachers Association, a staunch supporter of the Evangelical Union of South America (mission society for focusing on South America). In addition, he ran the Mundesley Summer Conference Ministry (invited so many various Christian leaders and conducted Bible School Extensions in numerous churches of differing denominations). His attendees at conferences and Bible School extensions were from all kinds of ecclesiastical backgrounds. Morgan was always one who promoted unity across church and organizational lines. Murray sums it accurately, "This man's whole life, however, has been a sermon on true unity and brotherhood." (Murray 1938:40). Morgan developed networks across denominations and partisan interests. He demonstrated in his own attitude and ministry involvements the unity of the Spirit.

3. Summer Conference Ministry

Morgan had vision for and pioneered the Summer Conference Ministry at Mundesley. He financed it and recruited the people to build it into a first class retreat center. This retreat area promoted Bible teaching and missionary work in an environment conducive to rest and renewal. Prominent Christian leaders from the U.S.A. and England influenced many at these summer conferences. Morgan models vision casting. He is able to promote a work, see it come into being and make it an effective tool to realize one of his focal values--teaching the Bible so it can impact on lives.

4. Friday night Bible School and Extensions

This activity averaged 1400. At times it was higher with as many as 2000 coming. This ministry highlighted his focal value: the Bible properly taught will change lives. Extensions[45] of this were also held in as many as six different centers in the greater London metropolitan area and even further. This was the supreme manifestation of Morgan's giftedness. He was never better as a public rhetorician than in his Friday night Bible school. This ministry had impact around the world.

5. President of Cheshunt College

This was a non-conformist theological training institute located in Cambridge. Morgan stepped in during the years from 1911 to 1914. This was in addition to his ministry at Westminster. He and his family moved to Cambridge. He commuted to Westminster for his public ministry there. He was instrumental in helping Cheshunt College recover from financial and organizational problems. He was able to take it through a building program which provided an excellent plant for the years to come.[46] Morgan, in

---

[45]The Friday night Bible school was a weekly event. The extensions were every two weeks or 1 a month for several of them.

[46]This is one of several instances in which Morgan tried to involve himself in theological institutions. None worked. His classes (practical ministry classes like homiletics were impactful) were praised but not to the extent of his public Bible teaching ministry. He attempted to reproduce his Friday night Bible class

Chapter 5. G. Campbell Morgan--(1863-1945)

my opinion, was out of his element here. His strengths were not in organizational oversight or administration. But his pattern of helping out an institution in trouble kept him from saying no to this opportunity. However, he did cut his losses. He got out while he was still ahead.

6. Missionary Giving And Interest

J. Morgan devotes a lengthy chapter to report on Morgan's missionary interest and activity. Early in his ministry at Westminster, when funds were tight, he convinced the deacons and the church of the importance of being a missions minded church. The church agreed to give 1/10 of its budget to missions.

7. Series of Sermons

During August just prior to the outbreak of World War I and just after it, Morgan gave a series of sermons which were timely and stabilizing. Two different independent sources echoed this evaluation. I include them both.

> A reviewer of the Westminster years deems that one of Dr. Morgan's greatest achievements was the series of sermons he preached in Westminster Chapel, in August, 1914. "In those days of bewilderment and alarm," he said, "when it seemed that the very foundations of our national life were shaking, Dr. Morgan's sermons with their note of confident assurance that God reigned, and that wrong would be worsted, allayed the anxieties of thousands of trembling hearts. I can recall no intervention by any preacher in a time of crisis which produced so powerful an effect. Dr. Morgan served the whole nation in that grim hour."

> Miss Jane Stoddart, Assistant Editor of *The British Weekly* ...said, "Dr. Campbell Morgan rose to his greatest heights as a preacher on the five August Sundays of 1914, before and after the declaration of war with Germany. Incomparable service was rendered by him at that time to the people of London, to the nation and to the Allied cause." (J. Morgan 1972:206)

It should be noted that many prominent politicians, public official and leaders attended Westminster Chapel.

8. Writings

In addition to his sermons and some Bible teachings which were distributed to several thousand on a regular basis through the Westminster Bible Record, a monthly publication, this was a productive time of publishing for Morgan. A number of books and other materials were published[47] including **The Analyzed Bible, Living Messages of the Books of the Bible, The Gospel According to John,** and **The Gospel of Matthew** which are generally still available today. Chadwick in his letter of

---

on campus but it didn't fly. I think all of his Bible College attempts were not as successful as his public ministry primarily due to influence-mix. Morgan was best with large groups. Seminary classes were always small.

[47] A full list, compiled from J. Morgan, Murray, Harries and Turnbull includes: 1905--*The Christ of Today, What, Whence, Whither*; 1906--*The Bible and The Child; The Practice of Prayer*; 1907--*The Simple Things of the Christian Life; The Parables of the Kingdom-Expositions of Matthew XIII*; 1908--*Christian Principles; Mountains and Valleys In the Life of Jesus*; **The Analyzed Bible Volumes I, II, III. Genesis-Esther, Job-Malachi; Matthew-Revelation** (Vols I, II in 1907--complete set in 1908); **The Gospel According to John;** 1909--**The Book of Job; The Book of Romans;** *The Missionary Manifesto;* 1910--**Isaiah Volumes I, II; The Teaching of the Lesson. A Pocket Commentary on the International Lessons for 1910; The Study and Teaching of the English Bible.** 1911--**The Book of Genesis; The Gospel of Matthew;** 1912--*Sunrise! Behold He Cometh;* 1913--**The Teaching of Christ--A Companion Volume to the Crises;** 1914--**Intercession;** *God, Humanity, and War;* 1915--**Living Messages of the Books of the Bible.**

explanation of Morgan's *10th Anniversary Sermon* mentions the importance of this aspect of achievement by Morgan at Westminster Chapel.

> There is another ministry of the ten years, that is a monument of industry and wisdom. I refer to the ministry of the pen. I wonder if Dr. Morgan has any idea of the number of studies in which there stands a long row of his works on the Bible. He is teaching teachers by the thousand every week. He has published books at the rate of three a year, besides all the public work of preaching, teaching, and lecturing. He says he feels as if he had grown twenty years older in the ten years; and no wonder, seeing he has lived at least thirty (J. Morgan 1972:211,212).

Briefly, then, these are some of the major achievements Morgan left behind at Westminster. It was a time of tremendous outpouring of energy. Morgan took a dying church and made it into an on-going vibrant ministry which would continue long into the future. In fact, he would come back to it in his afterglow years for a final contribution to it in the troubled years before World War II and during those six years of warfare.

10th Year Anniversary Sermon--Isolation Processing (Set Aside)

Chadwick refers in the previous quote to a sermon Morgan gave on his ten year anniversary. That sermon indicated probably a near state of what we would call today burnout. Physical illness and overwork led to a somewhat negative and discouraging evaluation of his ministry. This mental state and physical state led to an internal crisis and eventually resignation from Westminster.

C. Recovery From Internal Crisis
(1917-1919); Age=54-56

Essentially this is part of a boundary time in which Morgan is searching for the next major leading of God in his life. Guidance came through blocked doors. He had an call from the Collins Street Congregational Church in Melbourne, Australia, to fill its pulpit for a year, with freedom to do outside public Bible ministry (J. Morgan 1972:221). But the door was shut. He could not get permission for his family to travel with him--due to wartime restrictions. The same travel restrictions applied to ministry in the U.S.A. For two years Morgan was forced to remain in his London location. He did pulpit supply ministry[48] and some training ministry for the Y.M.C.A in Mildmay Park in North London, and a combination of pulpit supply and pastoral work in Highbury Quadrant in North London. In the summer of 1919 he was able to make arrangements to go to America.

IV. Convergence Ministry--Wide Impact
1919-1933; Age=56-69

A. Focused Role: Bible lecturer in U.S.A., Canada, England
(1919-1929); Age=56-66

Morgan's decision to go to America had been based on an offer to become part of the faculty of The Bible Teachers' Training School (became The Biblical Seminary). But

---

[48] He preached more than forty times in Westminster while they were searching for their new pastor. This was not what he wanted to do. He had hoped to separate himself from the church altogether. he also preached in the pulpit of Highbury Quadrant which had been without a pastor for 14 months (J. Morgan 1972:224,225).

Chapter 5. G. Campbell Morgan--(1863-1945)

upon arrival in New York he found the conditions of that position too restricting.[49] The networking of his previous time in America was now to come into play.

Morgan and family lived in Winona Lake, Indiana for 2 years operating out of the conference center there. They then moved to Athens, Georgia which became home base until 1926. His ministries while in these two locations were basically that of a Bible lecturer at Bible Conferences and an itinerant ministry of teaching Bible in various churches and centers throughout the U.S.A. and Canada with summer excursions to England. Everywhere he went he taught to large audiences and was well received. This was a time of his most powerful public Bible teaching ministry.

In 1926 he moved to Cincinnati in order, hopefully, to combine a pastoral ministry with a church based Bible Study Center. This did not work out.[50] He continued an independent itinerant ministry.

Morgan then received an invitation to become part of BIOLA's faculty. He was part of this institution for nearly two years. A conflict associated with the Dean, his friend, caused Morgan to resign his position in sympathetic support.

Following this short tenure (1928-29) on a Bible College faculty, Morgan again became a Bible lecturer at large. Toward the end of 1929, at age 66, he accepted a call to the Tabernacle Presbyterian Church in Philadelphia.

This period of time from 1919 to 1929 was again a time of convergent ministry for Morgan. His independent ministry was essentially a parachurch ministry. He did not formally structure an organization as most do today but essentially he operated out of his own informal organization. He was free to pursue public Bible teaching all over the U.S.A. and Canada. These were busy years. They were years of searching for some permanent base which would enhance his public Bible teaching role. They were years of great power in ministry.[51] His achievements were several among which stand out include the following.

1. World Class Bible Teacher--Role Model
Morgan modeled a Bible teaching role all over American and Canada, a role which honored the Scriptures and inspired many to study and teach it. This ministry highlighted his focal value: The Bible is the authoritative Word of God. When taught with power it will change lives.

2. Faith Challenge--Model
Morgan modeled what it means to trust God to lead and supply. During this period of time Morgan had no guaranteed source of financial means such as an organization or

---

[49]In all three of his involvements (Cheshunt College, The Biblical Seminary, and BIOLA) with training institutes it seems that he was providentially blocked from long term ministries with them. In retrospect, it seems clear now that the ideal role for him was not out of a Bible College or seminary base.
[50]This is one of those few times that Morgan did not feel receptivity for his plans and dreams and so aborted the scheme which had led him to Cincinnati.
[51]I have deliberately cut short the reporting of this stage due to my page limitations of the biographical narrative. I do not feel I have adequately treated this important convergent time in Morgan's life. I highly recommend the reading of Chapter VII in J. Morgan's biography which covers the time from page 55 to 69 years. The chapter was done with his son, the Reverend Kingsley J. Morgan and is entitled, *The Itinerant Ministry in the United States*. It covers this time period in 23 pages. An additional chapter expands on the time from 1926-1932.

church backing him. He simply trusted God to supply for him ministry opportunities and finances. He never lacked for either.

3. Taught Bible Content and Bible Study Philosophy

His ministry honored the Bible. People came to see the Bible as the authoritative Word of God. They were inspired to study this Word of God and to teach it to others. The experience of the two disciples on the road to Emmaus (Luke 24:31) became the experience of many who heard him. In short, he passed on content, information from the Bible, with gifted power so as to change many, many lives.

4. Bible Materials Left Behind

Morgan published materials which would make a long lasting contribution to the importance of Bible study and Bible teaching.[52]

B. Transition to Active Afterglow, Tabernacle Presbyterian Church (1929-1933); Age=66-70

For three years, from 1929-1932, he worked in the pastorate at Tabernacle Presbyterian Church in Philadelphia and taught as an adjunct faculty member at Gordon College in Boston (until 1931). His public ministry continued to be powerful. His classroom work stimulating. His achievements in this ministry include at least the following:

1. Bringing **renewal** to this church through a Bible centered ministry; Morgan attracted crowds who came to hear the Word taught. There was an excitement and freshness that brought new life as people from all over came to hear a master teach the Word.
2. Providing **Financial Stability**--as was his case where ever he went Morgan found ways to raise finances. He liquidated the debt of this church (relatively small loan) and raised money to renovate its main sanctuary. This in itself was a renewal effort which brought promise of better things to come.
3. Providing leadership which gave **vision** to this church on what it could be and accomplish. His years of experience concerning what a church should be and do and activities and structures which work were brought to bear in this situation.
4. Maintaining an itinerant **conference and speaking ministry**, though on a more reduced scale than in the past. Morgan still continued to speak around the country and even in England.
5. Broadening their outlook on ministry by **linking them to outside speakers** and other resources. His own sons now in full time ministry were linked to this church. After he moved on, this church called his younger son to be its pastor.
6. Providing **modeling** for a number of students at Gordon. Young students preparing for ministry need to see a godly older leader who is finishing well. Not only was his teaching important to them, but his modeling of his life, a life that had achieved much and had been lived well for Christ, was important.

---

[52]His publishing included: 1919-The Ministry of the Word; 1922--The Bible in Five Years-- A Comprehensive Outline of the Entire Bible; 1924--The Acts of the Apostles; 1926--A Series of Sermons; Searchlights from the Word--1188 Sermon Suggestions; 1927--The Gospel According To Mark; 1929--Christ and the Bible; The Gospel According to Matthew.

Chapter 5. G. Campbell Morgan--(1863-1945)

7. Continuing to **publish materials** that would live after him and be useful for pastors and Bible students.[53]

V. Active Afterglow At Westminster
(1933-1945); Age=70-81

In this section I will very briefly outline the major activities of the separate smaller time periods and then conclude with achievements summarizing the entire **Afterglow Period**.

Afterglow is a special time in leaders' lives in which there is a residual effect of their lives which rubs off on others. Leaders who have been effective and finish well usually culminate their life of activity in a form of semi-retirement. This may involve some ministry like occasional preaching, teaching, informal consultation and/or reflection and writing. It usually means no structured formal role involving strenuous responsibility.

The fruit of a lifetime of ministry and growth culminate in an era of recognition and indirect influence at broad levels. Leaders in afterglow have built up a lifetime of contacts and continue to exert influence in these relationships. Others will seek them out because of their consistent track record in following God. Their storehouse of wisdom gathered over a lifetime of leadership will continue to bless and benefit God's people.

But Morgan's **Afterglow Period** was an **Active Afterglow**. He in fact had a role which emphasized public ministry and allowed him to give the fruit of a lifetime of walking with Christ to a people who were to go through the most strenuous and challenging history of any corporate peoples--the British during the time leading up to and including World War II. Though his body was weakened, his mind was sharp and clear and full of a lifetime of wisdom. His afterglow ministry involved providing stability, courage and hope in the darkest times of the British empire.

A. 2nd Stint at Westminster; Co-minister with Simpson
(1933-1935); Age=70-72

Can an old preacher go back to a congregation he once pastored? Most would say it isn't wise. But Morgan did and providentially was there to help carry it through its most trying years since its renewal in 1904ff.

In between the time that Morgan had left Westminster a number of able pastors had filled its pulpit including J. Henry Jowett and Hubert Simpson. Simpson was the senior pastor when Morgan returned. He was elderly and not in good health. It was he who had personally invited Morgan to come back. His idea was that they would alternate pulpit time giving each a less strenuous schedule. But during this time Simpson became increasingly unable to do his part and Morgan took over more of the public ministry. His preaching was with clarity and power and again attracted. He revived the Friday night Bible School and its attendance was again around 1800.

---

[53]His publishing ministry during these years included the following works: 1930--*Categorical Imperatives of the Christian Faith*; 1931--**The Gospel According to Luke** [one of my personal favorites].

Chapter 5. G. Campbell Morgan--(1863-1945)

B. Senior Pastor at Westminster
(1935-1938); Age=72-75

When Simpson became unable to carry on the church called Morgan to be its senior pastor. His duties were limited largely to pulpit ministry. These were the years of increasing strain as it was becoming clearer that war was on the horizon.

C. Co-Pastor With Lloyd-Jones at Westminster
(1938-1943); Age=75-80

As Morgan became increasingly frail he saw that it was necessary to bring in someone younger and more able than he. Martin Lloyd-Jones was that man. He was a great leader. His association with Morgan in these final years was amiable and profitable for both. Lloyd-Jones went on to become one of the great preachers of our time. Morgan's view of a sovereign God brought tremendous encouragement during these blackest days of World War II, when it was unclear that the British empire would survive.

D. Passive Co-Ministry with Lloyd-Jones at Westminster
(1943-1945); Age=80-81

These were years of occasional input, timely messages of encouragement during the final years of the war.

Achievements during the Afterglow years include:

1. Imparting Confidence about a Sovereign God to a people undergoing tragic suffering.
2. Modeling what it means to finish well.
3. Writing--During these years he continued to write. Some of his best received works, which are still available and used today include **The Gospel According to John,** one of my favorites and one which has helped me know and understand who Christ is in a deeper sense. Other excellent devotional commentaries from this period of time include **Studies In the Prophecy of Jeremiah, Hosea: The Heart and Holiness of God,** and **The Answers of Jesus to Job.**[54]

---

[54]A full listing of his published work for the Active Afterglow period and after (some things were published after his death) include: 1933--**The Gospel According to John;** 1934--**Studies in the Prophecy of Jeremiah, Hosea: The Heart and Holiness of God;** 1935--**The Answers of Jesus to Job, Great Chapters of the Bible;** 1937--**Preaching, The Great Physician;** 1938--*The Bible--400 Years After 1538, Voice of 1200 Hebrew Prophets, Peter and the Church, God's Last Word to Man;* 1940--**The Parables and Metaphors of Our Lord;** 1944--*The Triumphs of Faith, The Music of Life;* 1946--**The Corinthian Letters of Paul: An Exposition of I-II Corinthians,** 1947--**Notes on the Psalms, The Parables of the Father's Heart;** Unsure dates: *The Bible and the Child, The Bible and the Cross, Alpha and Omega, An Exposition of the Whole Bible;* 1968--*The Birth of the Church;* Several dates: **The Westminster Pulpit**--11 volumes of Sermons preached at Westminster Chapel, London, various editions and revisions have been published--the latest being by Baker Book House. Turnbull also lists a number of items undated which are either pamphlets, sermons, booklets, or lecture series. These include: *Divine Guidance and Human Advice; The Romance of the Bible; Paul--What Shall I Do, Lord?--One Thing I do; The Purposes of the Incarnation; H.M. The King, 1910-1935; Harmony of the Testaments; Sin, Righteousness, and Judgment; The Desire of All Nations; All Things New; But One Thing; To Die is Gain; Enoch; The Fulfillment of Life; Foundations.*

Chapter 5. G. Campbell Morgan--(1863-1945)

4. Intangibles--who can say what are the after effects of a godly life in its twilight years as wisdom is imparted, courage instilled, and hope revived. I include this category because I know there are many things achieved in this period of time that I could not begin to identify nor could the biographers capture them.

I close his **Active Afterglow** years with Murray's quote of an onlooker's view of Morgan in this period of time. It is for me a capstone to a leader who finished well.

> When I have seen and heard Dr. Morgan in recent days, I could not help thinking how well he has learned to grow old gracefully, He seemed to have mellowed, to have become more tender in his tones, more generous in his outlook--not less sure but more so, yet, I daresay, more gentle in his assurance (Murray 1938:70,71).

Gentle Assurance. Almost contradictory words that challenge us.

Critical Incidents Identified, and/or Explained

Critical incidents are shaping activities which can affect values relating to all three types of formations--spiritual (leadership character), ministerial (leadership skills) and strategic (total direction in life and ministry). There is a sense in which many, many incidents in a leader's life affect values. But from that large identifiable number a few should be highlighted and recognized as very significant. Here is a list of these that I have so identified from the materials that were available to me.[55] Table 5-1 indicates these. I number them for convenience of referencing later when I comment on them.

Table 5-1 Listing Of Some Critical Incidents In Morgan's Life

Incident(s) Name	Age	Formational Type Dealing With Basic Value/Thrust
1. Early Destiny Items (see pages 178,179)	7-8	Strategic--Parents pre-birth committal, early exposure to numerous good preachers, incident of preaching to Lizzie and dolls
2. Giftedness and Pride (see pages 175,176)	15	Spiritual--Self-assessment, ego check, and recognition of source of giftedness
3. An Authoritative Word (see pages 176, 177)	19-21	Ministerial, Strategic--established the Bible as the authoritative Word of God to which Morgan could give himself for a lifetime of effort of study and teaching.
4. Forced Out (see pages 182, 183)	22-23	Strategic--He receives certainty guidance into full time Christian ministry from his teaching position in the Jewish prep school
5. Gipsy Smith (see pages 183)	22-23	Strategic--prophetic word toward role allowing individuality, initiative, and more independence--something Morgan would strive for throughout his whole ministry.

---

[55] One must always remember that data is limited. If more were available or even more viewpoints on that which is available, then more critical incidents probably could be chosen.

Chapter 5. G. Campbell Morgan--(1863-1945)

Table 5-1 Listing Of Some Critical Incidents In Morgan's Life

Incident(s) Name	Age	Formational Type Dealing With Basic Value/Thrust
6. Methodist Rejection (see pages 183,184)	25	Strategic--He is directed to a more independent ministry which will force him to study Bible for himself and develop his approach to Scriptures Spiritual--a check on his pride and accomplishments (like Joshua's Ai).
7. Conflict--Stone Pastorate (see pages 185)	25, 26	Strategic--Morgan first recognizes his call to a broader role than just a local pastorate; his outside ministries will be problematic in almost every pastorate he goes to (possibly Rugely excepted).
8. Crake Mentoring (see page 185)	25-28	Spiritual--submission to wise counsel from a mentor in the midst of his first conflict may have saved him for the ministry; Morgan learned about authority and submission to it.
9. Rugeley Pastorate; Bible Study Method Discovered (see page 186)	28-30	Spiritual, Ministerial, Strategic--Here in the midst of a warm caring atmosphere which was totally supportive, Morgan was not only free to, but almost forced to, do much study. Out of this time came habits of study and the seedbed of his original approach to the study and teaching of Scripture.
10. Ego Check--Sermons to Ashes. (see pages 186,187)	28-30	Spiritual--His surrender to serve God and not honor himself opened him to the expansion and next ministry appointment at Birmingham.
11. Friday Night Bible School (see page 188)	32-34	Ministerial--Morgan's ministry insight discovery of a means of public Bible teaching from within a church context was a breakthrough enhancing his use of giftedness and further defining his public rhetorician role. It reached its height in Westminster and in an adapted form in his itinerant ministry in the U.S.A.
12. Moody Connection (see pages 188,189)	33	Strategic, Ministerial--Albert Smith connects Morgan to Moody and the conference ministry at Northfield. This was confirmation of his broader ministry and paved the wave for both itinerant ministries in the U.S.A. (1901-1904, 1919-1929).
13. Howell Recruitment (see pages 189)	34	Strategic--Morgan is essentially a public rhetorician; speaking is his dominant form of expression. Much of what he did had permanent value. Howell was a key to expanding his oral ministry into the print medium and greatly expanding his sphere of influence and ultimate achievements.

Chapter 5. G. Campbell Morgan--(1863-1945)

Table 5-1 Listing Of Some Critical Incidents In Morgan's Life

Incident(s) Name	Age	Formational Type Dealing With Basic Value/Thrust
14. Revell Divine Contact-- Serves as Mentor Sponsor (see page 191)	38	Ministerial, Strategic--Morgan meets Fleming H. Revell, a brother of Mrs. D. L. Moody, at the Northfield Conference. Revell sponsors for 50 years the publication of Morgan's works. Dr. Morgan's books were, almost without exception, sermons and lectures reported first, then edited (mainly by Howell) for publication. This was a major factor in Morgan reaching maximum potential in terms of sphere of influence.
15. Westminster Decision (see pages 191,192)	41	Strategic--Morgan's sensitivity to God for direction reaches a new level--He can freely choose his direction and moves in light of the faith challenge and his natural predilection for restoring needy works.
16. Albert Smith Partnership (see page 192)	41	Ministerial--Smith provides the necessary organizing energy behind the foundational Westminster years and releases Morgan to pursue his beyond-the-church broader role that featured his public rhetorician role. Smith was fundamental in providing a church based convergent role for Morgan.
17. The 10th Anniversary Sermon (see pages 196)	51	Strategic, Spiritual, Ministerial--Morgan has essentially operated out of a doing base. His ministry is driven by an overactive desire to do and accomplish. God has set him aside a number of times into isolation to move him to a being base. But Morgan has not changed essentially. This critical time of processing set him aside for several years. This incident was pivotal eventually in taking Morgan to the U.S.A. for his second convergence experience in a parachurch role.
18. Repeated Blocks to Seminary or Bible College Role (see pages 196, 198, 199)	48, 56 63, 65	Strategic--Morgan's sphere of influence potential needed a public ministry with a larger influence-mix than he could get in a Seminary or Bible College context. God, I believe, providentially blocked permanent appointments in a variety of ways.

Critical incident 3, An Authoritative Word, was the major focal incident of Morgan's life. It is not always true that you can isolate just one single incident as being the focal incident. But this is the case with this incident. Out of it came a willful decision to serve God, to devote himself to the study and teaching of the Bible, and to demonstrate the divine authority and relevancy of the Bible through his ministry. The major value realized in this process can be loosely stated as the following.

Chapter 5. G. Campbell Morgan--(1863-1945)

> The Bible is the authoritative Word of God. It doesn't have
> to be defended. It can convince people if it is clearly taught in
> terms of its intent--on the whole and book by book. People
> have a sense of need to which truth in the Bible speaks.

Several sub-values flowing from this incident were added as experience with teaching the Bible grew.[56] These included at least the following:

1. Whenever the Bible is approached with a relatively unprejudiced mind, for or against, it will convincingly persuade the person of its truth, of its own accord.
2. Every person desiring to study the Bible must study it persistently and continuously, patiently expecting answers over a long haul.
3. A person studying the Bible ought to do so with a system which moves from general to particular, from extensive to intensive.
4. A student who learns from the Bible must willingly decide for and obey its moral claims or lose sensitivity to its further teachings.
5. A Bible student should begin the study of the Bible by first concentrating on gaining an accurate knowledge of each of the books making up the Bible.
6. A Christian leader should test any systematic theology by the Bible rather than vice versa.
7. Each book in the Bible to be studied should first be read repeatedly without the reference to divisions of chapters and verses but with attention to flow of story until there is a conscious impression of its content and general flow of movement.[57]
8. The Bible student should then identify the major structure of the book by condensing its flow into several major parts each with a suggestive label. This process can be repeated down to the smallest structural unit, the paragraph.
9. The Bible as a whole must be taught clearly in light of its God intended purposes.
10. Each Bible book, as a whole, should be taught clearly in light of its God intended purposes in the Bible as a whole.
11. A Christian teacher should seek to be as clear as the Bible is clear, nothing less, nothing more, nothing else.
12. A Christian leader, in public ministry, should build on what is certain so as to increase the faith of followers. Don't take your doubts into the pulpit.
13. A Christian leader must be prepared to spend much time and to work at the study and teaching of the English Bible.[58]
14. Spiritual authority and power in teaching flow from a life which has used the truth it has studied and taught.

Item 2, giftedness and pride, and item 10, Ego-Check--Sermons to Ashes, deal with an inner character issue of pride. Morgan's sensitivity to God in this and his response

---

[56] Most of these sub-values are my summarized wording that come from statements given directly by Morgan in his booklet, *The Study and Teaching of the English Bible*, 4 lectures given at the Friday night Bible School. He was answering the question posed to him so many times throughout his ministry, How should I study the Bible?

[57] Morgan said that he read books on the average 40-50 times before arriving at this impression of content and flow of movement. Most of these readings were at one sitting.

[58] When asked privately what the key to his success Morgan would answer, work, hard work and more hard work. He studied and thoroughly prepared all his life.

Chapter 5. G. Campbell Morgan--(1863-1945)   page 205

are Pauline-like.[59] God continually dealt with Morgan over his life time with regards to this issue. Morgan was not derailed by pride as some potentially great leaders are. He successfully eluded the pride barrier which keeps some leaders from finishing well.

Incidents 4 (Forced Out), 5 (Gipsy Smith), 6 (Methodist Rejection), 8 (Crake Mentoring), 12 (Moody Connection), 15 (Westminster Decision), 16 (Albert Smith Partnership), 17 (The 10th Anniversary Sermon), and 18 (Repeated blocks to Seminary or Bible College Roles) were all guidance incidents in which God's focusing activity can be traced at important junctures in Morgan's life. There were a number of divine contacts in the focusing efforts of God. There were also a number of certainty guidance episodes-- those which provide divine assurance from more than one source. It is these that become anchors as one perseveres on through the ups and downs of ministry. After the fact, perhaps not while we are in the confusing decision times, it can be seen that God's guidance is clear guidance. Such a fact can be counted on even in the confusing times. In some of these focal guidance issues Morgan had choices. In others, God blocked doors and opened them. In at least three, God forced the issue. Morgan's Biblical life motto, given him by his father at age 13 when he baptized Morgan, proved to hold true over his lifetime: Proverbs 3:6, In all thy ways acknowledge Him and He shall direct thy paths.

Incidents 1 (Early Destiny Items), 7 (Conflict--Stone Pastorate), 9 (Rugeley Pastorate), 11 (Friday Night Bible School), 13 (Howell Recruitment), and 14 (Revell Divine Contact--Serves as Mentor Sponsor) were activities that shaped Morgan toward his ultimate contribution. They led toward identification of role, ministry insights, and means for reaching maximum potential and its appropriate influence-mix.

Values And Critical Values

Below I have identified what I think are important values[60] in Morgan's life. Some seem to be crucial and appear throughout all his ministry. He seems to be more vocal about them when talking to others about the nature of ministry and his own views on it. These I call critical values. I mark them with an asterisk (*). I have grouped these values in terms of spiritual formation, ministerial formation, and strategic formation. There are some which overlap several categories--these I list last. I have identified what I think is the focal value, the dominant critical value with a double asterisk (**) and its strategic application.

Spiritual Values:

* 1. A Christian leader must maintain a personal vibrant relationship with God to enjoy real spiritual power.
* 2. A Christian leader must consciously trust God to reveal truth when studying, meditating upon, or reading the Bible.

---

[59] Paul in 2 Corinthians 12 shows God's dealing with him on this potential problem. Paul had unusual privileges and experiences with God which could easily have led him to boast and become prideful. God used the so-called *thorn in the flesh* to continually remind Paul of his need of dependence upon God.
[60] I realize that I am being highly interpretive. Values have been identified from all three biographies and from Morgan's Sermons and books which were lectures to theological students in preparation for ministry. Whenever you can get Morgan's own words you are on firmer ground. In any case I have taken what were personal value statements for Morgan, himself, and broadened them to more general statements which may have application in other leaders' lives. Just because Morgan held a value is not reason enough for someone else to hold that value. These values flow out of his personal experience and giftedness. However, some are commonly rooted in ministry and may have wide application. Certainly all are worthy of consideration for what they teach us about life and ministry.

Chapter 5. G. Campbell Morgan--(1863-1945)

- *3. A Christian leader must see the Bible as the primary book to be studied and all other books to be interpreted from its perspectives.
- 4. Christian leaders should have an element of faith in their decision making.
- *5. A gifted Christian leader must be sensitive to God's dealing with the nuances of pride that can place self and its satisfaction above the ministry of God. That is, a Christian leader should teach to exalt God and His truth so that people respond to the truth and not the speaker of it.

Ministerial Values--Personal, About the Bible, Communication, Organizational

- *1. A Christian leader must have disciplines of study and work which are prioritized to the first hand study of the Bible and its communication to others.
- 2. A Christian leader must be competent in the study of words in the original--Hebrew and Greek.
- 3. A Christian leader must have good tools for study of the Bible.
- **4. The Bible is the Word of God. It doesn't have to be defended. It can convince people if it is clearly taught in terms of its intent--on the whole and book by book. People have a sense of need to which truth in the Bible speaks.
- *5. A Christian teacher should seek to be as clear as the Bible is clear, nothing less, nothing more, nothing else.
- *6. The Bible as a whole must be taught clearly in light of its God intended purposes.
- *7. Each Bible book, as a whole, should be taught clearly in light of its God intended purposes in the Bible as a whole.
- *8. A Christian leader, in public ministry, should build on what is certain so as to increase the faith of followers.
- 9. A Christian leader should be well acquainted with literature which is faith building and helpful in understanding and using the Bible.
- 10. In public meetings, nothing should take away from the presentation of the Bible teaching or message.
- *11. One must work deliberately on the communication of truth, not just the acquisition of it. I speak freely from a brief most carefully prepared.
- 12. The knowledge of one's subject is limited by the ability to impart it.
- 13. A teacher should always seek to give the bigger perspective first, extensively, before moving to smaller portions, intensively. All should be constantly related to the whole of which it is a part.
- *14. A teacher should always move the will so that the learner responds to the truth being taught so as to bring the lives of those taught into right relationship with eternal truth (though the avenue to do so might be via emotions or intellect).
- 15. A church's organization should follow the basic principle of a minimum of organization for a maximum of work.
- 16. The organizational structure of the church should flow from the ministry of the church as needed for that ministry.
- *17. A pastor should set high expectations so that his/her people should be challenged to study the Bible and consider it a high priority in their lives.
- *18. Each Church should be a Bible School. The Bible must be taught.

Strategic Values

- **1. Value 4 under Ministerial Values was the focal value which led Morgan to an Ultimate Purpose: Morgan sought to lead people into the truth of the Bible, to have them see its nature and relevance to life, and to have them desire to understand it and use it for their lives.
- 2. The atoning work of Christ is the basis for anyone's salvation; there will be those saved in the Church through apprehension of and faith in this work; there will be

some saved by living up to the light they have though they have no light of this work.
3. The Church must declare truth to the society of which it is a part concerning matters of moral and ethical living. It should stir that society to recognize and use truth to correct its practices.
4. The Church must publish the Gospel to those needing it and nurture by teaching the Word of God those who respond to that Gospel.
5. Constructively teach the word of God in its beauty and it will draw people and unify them around the evangelical faith. As opposed to polemic ministry.
6. The unity of Christians in regards to controversy over core issues is best brought about by positively teaching the truth of the Word and not engaging in controversy over differences.
7. A Christian leader should respect differing opinions on non-core items (person and work of Christ--core).
8. A Christian leader can have fellowship with those of differing opinions if core items are observed.
9. It is the work of Christ through which people will come to God whether if they live up to the light they have or accept Him personally as their savior.
10. Leaders are responsible for giftedness and opportunities for service entrusted to them.
11. A Christian leader should prioritize ministry opportunities and choose based on experience, giftedness, and destiny.

Overlapping Values
1. Leaders and followers must have an experiential grasp of knowledge of the Bible to realize a strong faith and life in Christ.
2. Any gifted person regardless of sex, ethnicity, or social status should be permitted to exercise that giftedness in local churches.
3. A Christian leader ought to trust God's guidance in life and recognize that it will surely come to those prepared to follow it: via the Word of God, and/or an inner light, and/or circumstances sovereignly controlled.
4. Christian leaders need mentors to whom they can go for wisdom from God in times of need.

Ministry Insights, Lessons, and General Values

In my opinion, the single most important ministry insight proved to be the Friday Night Bible School discovered at Westminster Road Pastorate in Birmingham. This insight involved means, methodology, and role identification. Morgan was gifted as a public rhetorician to teach before large crowds. This weekday ministry built on several of his values. People who came to it had to be committed. His approach to study and teaching of the Bible, extensive first and then intensive, could be realized before an receptive large audience--not just exclusively to his church members. His destiny of speaking before large groups and influencing them toward his focal Bible values were realized in a role of public Bible teacher. All of Morgan's pastorates from then on would utilize some adapted form of the Friday Night Bible School. Even his itinerant ministry in the U.S.A. and Canada would apply varied forms of this Friday Night Bible School.

Christian leaders need a range of mentors throughout their entire ministry. Morgan had numerous occasional mentors to whom he would go for guidance in problem times or major decision times.[61] According to J. Morgan this was his pattern throughout his

---

[61] One wonders if Morgan during the tiring months leading up to the 10th Anniversary Sermon was getting any upward mentoring counseling. It sounds as if this were not the case. Samuel Chadwick's letter seems

ministry. He does not demonstrate the full range of the Constellation model ideally. His only upward mentoring was occasional for counsel. His downward mentoring was usually restricted to contemporary model and teacher. His correspondence was a distance form of mentoring--usually teaching or counseling. The lack of deliberate downward mentoring, however, fits the profile of a public rhetorician whose influence is dominantly a large direct face-to-face type sphere of influence.

Mentor sponsors are crucial for a leader to reach maximum potential. Several stand out in Morgan's development toward maximum potential. Gregory Mantle linked Morgan into the Westminster Road Congregational Church, a move from small rural area of influence into a large city influence. Albert Smith linked Morgan to Moody in the U.S.A. Moody introduced and backed Morgan before his first American audiences at Northfield. Later out of this conference ministry would come the link to Fleming Revell--the means for a broadening indirect sphere of influence through publishing. It is frequently difficult for an author to break in to the publishing field. Moody's son connected Moody into audiences all over America via the Northfield Extension ministry. Mentor sponsors are necessary for leaders to develop. Though potential leaders are born, effective leaders are made as a result of 1) opportunity, 2) training and 3) experience. These three components do not automatically guarantee that one will rise to become a great leader. But without them it is not likely that one will realize maximum potential. Mentor sponsors often are the doors or links to opportunity--for ministry and/or for resources. While one can not guarantee the emergence of mentor sponsors one can know their importance, the role of networking power, and be sensitive to connecting to those God brings across one's paths in the normal course of serving and ministering. One can know that vital links for the future may be made in the present.

Morgan had an amazing breadth in terms of his ecclesiology. He constantly associated with all those who believed in the person and work of Christ, no matter what denominational label they bore. His approach to unifying around the positive aspects of the Bible rather than the polemic attacks on others was both refreshing, evangelical and challenging.[62] He modeled respect and tolerance for differing opinions while still holding to his own strong convictions about the person and work of Christ and the nature of the Bible. His views on gifted people, including women, using their gifts in the church was way ahead of his time.[63] He was able to release gifted people in ministry.

---

to indicate this and gives balanced perspective after the fact. Perhaps a good upward mentor at this time might have helped Morgan avoid the painful isolation and troublesome exit from Westminster. The sermon was so uncharacteristic of Morgan. It brought his negative doubts and feelings into the pulpit--something he did not usually do.

[62] Excerpts from J. Morgan (1952) illustrate this refreshing, positive evangelical perspective. In 1905-- ...the only way to contend for the faith is to preach it in all its positive beauty (1952:241). In 1908-- Those of us who believe in the foundation truths should best occupy ourselves by preaching them and applying them (1952:241). In 1923--...I have constant sorrow in my heart over the bitter theological controversies which characterize the hour; and the saddest thing is the spirit of them...However, I never feel that I am called upon to enter into these controversies. My work is wholly constructive, and I believe that that is the only kind that is really of value (1952:244). In 1924--I am resolutely going on with positive teaching and refusing to be involved in the fight. It is not easy, and I am not sure that the hour will not come when an open cleavage, cutting across all denominations, will compel everyone to move distinctly to the right or to the left. I abhor the unethical attitude of many Modernists who remain in evangelical churches and preach rationalistic philosophy; and I hate the bitter, vitriolic spirit of many Fundamentalists. However, wherever I go I find a great multitude of souls, hungry for the Word of God (1952:244,245).

[63] He has several rather extended pieces of correspondence concerning women and ministry in which he deals with 1 Corinthians and 1 Timothy on passages concerning women and ministry. His basic value states that any gifted person regardless of sex, ethnicity, or social status should be permitted to exercise that giftedness in local churches. Like A. J. Gordon he was well ahead of his times on this viewpoint. See J. Morgan,

Chapter 5. G. Campbell Morgan--(1863-1945)

Contributions

This chapter contributes to the general field of leadership development in the following ways:

1. It portrays a very gifted leader who had focused ministry from two distinctly different ministry bases--a church base and a parachurch base.
2. It portrays a gifted leader who had an active **Afterglow Period**.
3. It affirms in classical fashion many of the leadership emergence shaping processes and patterns. It attempts to identify ensuing values flowing from these processes.
4. It highlights the importance of mentor sponsors.
5. It shows that one can have a focused ministry without long tenure in a geographic locale. Morgan's focus was around a role, which role he maintained in various geographic locations. The tenure was vested in the role and not a position or organization or geographic locale.
6. It shows that a leader can be trained in various ways. Formal training is not absolutely essential to successful ministry.
7. It demonstrates the focusing activity of God in guidance via divine contacts, sponsors, open and shut doors, certainty guidance, and providential intervention.
8. It highlights the importance of public Bible teaching to large audiences.
9. It identifies and defines a Flagship Model for a strong church ministry.[64]

What were Morgan's contributions? We are interested in both specific/ unique contributions and his ultimate contributions. His ultimate contribution set is given in diagram form below.[65] I follow that then by giving some of his specific contributions to the cause of Christ and the on-going of the Christian movement.

1952, **This Was His Faith** (excerpts from Morgan's correspondence). See 1913 excerpt on pages 118, 119; 1918 excerpt on pages 119,120; 1927 excerpt on pages 115-117; and 1941 excerpt on page 201ff.
[64] One thing that is missing from the Flagship Model is the important structural insight of decentralized small groups related to and sponsored by the church. This important insight will be seen later but was foreign to Morgan and his times.
[65] The diagram which describes his ultimate contributions in pictorial form is called a Venn Diagram. See Appendix F for an explanation of how to read Venn diagrams.

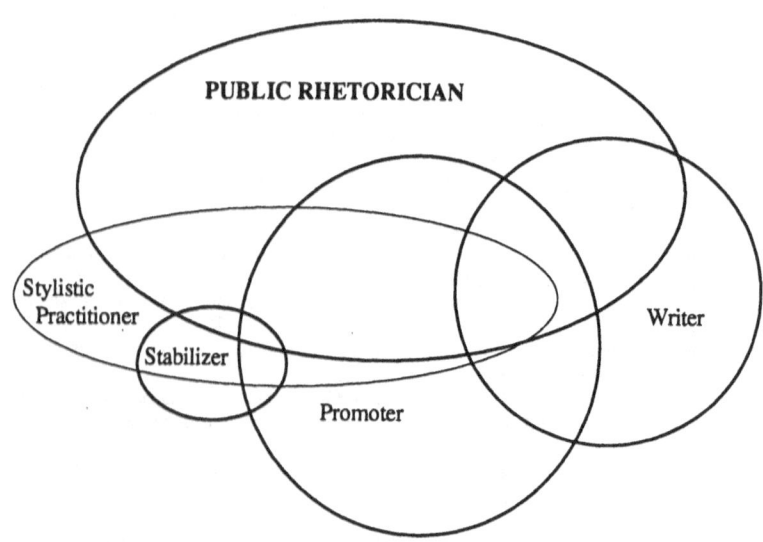

In terms of the prime types of ultimate contributions, Morgan illustrates well the above five types of ultimate contribution.

He was a **public rhetorician**. This was his dominant ultimate contribution role. He taught the Bible to large audiences.[66] He modeled gifted power as a teacher. He gave Bible insights. He inspired people to study and teach the Bible. He preached on crucial issues at critical junctures--particularly during World War I and II. Infrequently his ministry was prophetical. Always it carried a teaching focus. Early on it had an evangelistic bent. But it was the teaching of the Bible first from a macro-viewpoint and then portion by portion tracing the contextual flow and message of the book which was the highlight of his public ministry. The Bible was central to all his public ministry. His basic drive was to expose the Bible in all its beauty so that it could impact lives.

He was a **promoter**. In conjunction with his public rhetorician role he promoted various causes. The first, of course, was the place of the Bible in the life of the individual, Church, and nation. This was primary. Where ever he went people came away with a changed attitude toward the Bible. His focal values learned in critical incident 3, An Authoritative Word, dominated his promotional efforts. He was one who was able to sell his ideas about the Bible to a large public. Secondly, he was able to promote various financial causes in numerous of his ministry assignments.[67] He was able to visualize what

---

[66]His diary shows he spoke 23,400 times over his lifetime. He practically could not say no to public ministry opportunities unless he was physically incapacitated.

[67]In his leadership transition period, 1883-1888, he raised money for evangelistic efforts through public lectures. Again at the Westminster Road Pastorate he took the congregation out of debt via various methods one of which involved again, public lectures. At the New Court Pastorate he again raised funds to renovate and expand facilities. Westminster Chapel, the Mundesley Summer Conference site, and Tabernacle Presbyterian Church in Philadelphia are other examples of his ability to raise finances.

Chapter 5. G. Campbell Morgan--(1863-1945)

could be and sell that vision to backers. Third, he promoted numerous lost causes--churches and/or inner-city works that were faltering and may be lost to Christendom. He was able to restore many and to give added life to them.[68]

He was a **stabilizer**. In every pastorate he went to he brought about stability in organization usually through his relationship to church leadership. His basic notions of minimum organization arising out of need and release of people in ministry to carry out burdens they felt stood him well in every church pastorate. His ability to work with a large multi-staff during the height of the Westminster Chapel ministry illustrates this ultimate contribution role.

He was a **writer**.[69] He left behind a mass of writings, most of which are classical in nature.[70] His Bible expositions are outstanding examples of his extensive and intensive approach to the Scriptures.

He was a **stylistic practitioner**. He was not content to be just a pastor in one location for a long period of time. His lifetime of ministry was a search for an ideal role which matched his large sphere of influence as a public rhetorician and his ecumenical bias toward Christians of all kinds of denominational labels. He modeled a co-ministerial role, as a Pastor/ Public Bible teacher, which was far beyond the standard pastoral role. And yet his pastoral emphasis and local church involvement made him distinctly different from a parachurch worker such as Moody.

His contributions to the cause of Christ and the on-going of the Christian movement include at least the following:

1. He pioneered the teaching of the Bible from a macro-viewpoint. That is, he taught the Bible in terms of understanding its overall unity--how books contributed to the development of the Bible as a whole and God's work over the ages. He taught the importance of the message of each book in the Bible--how the message develops in the book and its implications for today.

2. He provided strategic follow-up to the evangelistic efforts of Moody and others. He was a man prepared for the times and contributed to them. After revival efforts there is a need to ground believers in the Word if they are to mature. Morgan stepped into that vacuum and provided Bible teaching that enabled growth.

---

[68]In New Court he salvaged the Holloway Chapel, a nearby church ready to close down. The supreme example of this was Westminster Chapel in 1904. But there were others even during his Westminster Chapel days.
[69]Though his writings were largely an overflow from his public rhetorician ministry due to the complementary support he received from Howell and others and the mentor sponsoring of Revell who would allow his oral ministry to be published.
[70]Ultimate contribution writing can be of two kinds. They can be classical or contemporary. If classical, they deal with fundamental issues which allow them to be useful even long after the author is dead. If contemporary, they deal with important issues that are important for the time in which issued but may not have later relevance. Morgan's writings were dominantly classic. Many are still in print. Even the ones out of print are useful for today because of their classical nature.

3. He modeled the validity of the in-service training track into ministry.[71] His training was largely informal and on-the-job. He was a self-starter in ministry and in his training processes.

4. He restored a number of Christian works including Westminster Chapel so that they had a continuing impact for Christ for years.

5. His ministry at Westminster Chapel during his first stint provided a Flagship Model.

6. He influenced thousands toward study of, use of and teaching of the Bible.

7. He modeled a ministry which attempted to demonstrate Christian unity not via organizational structure but via fellowship, networks including associations, and agreement on common truths of the Scriptures.

8. He left behind materials, Sermons, Lectures, Booklets, and Books which are classic in nature and have impact even today. Particularly his Bible expositions are still very effective today.

9. He helped bolster the courage of a nation under fire--both in World War I and II. His public ministry affirming the sovereignty of God was deeply inspirational to a country in desperate need.

10. He modeled a focused life and a good finish. His example may yet inspire many toward a focused life and a good finish.

Overall Lessons from the Life

Effective leaders maintain a learning posture all their lives. Morgan was primarily self-taught majoring on the study of the Bible. But he was well read. This is seen in his writings, especially in his formal lectures to Seminaries and Bible Colleges. He is an example of one whose training was on-going because of his continued study of the Word, reading, and learning from life's experiences.

We need to heed the major warnings seen in his numerous isolation processing experiences, mostly from physical breakdowns. Christian leaders need to deliberately break from the strain of ministry on a repeated basis. This involves recreational outlets, spiritual retreats, and the practice of a sabbath discipline on a weekly basis and even on a longer basis involving extracted time away from ministry for growth and renewal. Morgan tended to overwork himself until his health would break down. This happened a number of times. In each of them he was set aside. God was trying to slow him down. The most significant was the time just prior to his 10th anniversary sermon.

---

[71] In leadership emergence theory we have identified three major training patterns of leaders. The *pre-service pattern* involves formal training, that is, education for ministry, usually in a Bible College or Seminary before going full time into ministry. The *in-service pattern* involves on-the-job, informal training in which proficiency for ministry is learned as one does ministry--that is, education in ministry. Apprenticeships and other informal mentoring techniques, contemporary models, teachers and coaches as well as self-initiated learning dominate this training. The third pattern involves usually a *modified in-service pattern* of training followed by a-periodic forays into non-formal and formal training for extended periods of time. Such forays for training continue throughout life (Clinton 1989:354-358).

Chapter 5. G. Campbell Morgan--(1863-1945)

> The tempo of life which Campbell Morgan had set for himself during the Westminster years began, in 1914, to take its toll of his health. Only the careful habits of diet, and the vigilance of Mrs. Morgan, who did all in her power to make the wheels of domestic affairs run smoothly, had enabled him to continue the pace thus far. The determination not to lower his standards of preaching and teaching, or to overlook any duties of administration at Westminster or Cambridge; the oversight of the B.T.A. and the E.U.S.A., and the endeavour to accept as many outside invitations as possible, together with certain emotional strain, combined to tell upon the natural resilience of a physique which had never been robust. (J. Morgan 1972:203)

Morgan operated primarily out of a doing base--though of course his relationship to Christ was always alive and sweet. A major lesson from these repeated isolation processes is simply, SLOW DOWN or you will be put aside.

One of the more important lessons from Morgan's life concerns role adaptation. He forces us to think about roles and effectiveness. Gifted leaders will rarely find a role that enhances who they are. They will have to adapt the roles that are and make the best of them. Rarely will they even be able to adapt to an ideal role which will promote their ultimate contribution set. In adapting a role, the Christian leader must be prepared for opposition. Ideal roles or even quasi-ideal roles will usually not be traditional and there will be opposition. Frequently the hunt for an ideal role means the necessity of raising the finances to underwrite it. An ideal role for would contain a number of factors which Morgan actually saw happen. An ideal role for Morgan would include:

1. Senior Pastor of a large influential church which allowed a large public ministry. Morgan needed an anchor to hold on to and come back to in the midst of his varied external public ministry.
2. The freedom to have an influential public ministry outside the church across denominational lines. His large home base church would see this as part of their ministry to the church at large.
3. Freedom from administrative responsibility in the church.
4. Freedom to travel 4-6 months a year for itinerant ministry.
5. A church based Bible Institute in which he would have a prominent influence in terms of hermeneutical input to the students. The finances for this institute would be borne by the church. Numerous students from around the world would move into the area to receive an internship training which was largely focused on the study, teaching, and preaching of the Bible.
6. A parachurch publishing venture, either owned or controlled, so that he could publish what he wanted when he wanted to.
7. A large base of funds that could be used to help restore Christian works.

Implications for a Focused Life

What have we learned from this life that helps us understand a focused life? That is the question I attempt to answer in this section. When we study a focused life we are in fact looking for a number of issues.[72] Below I comment on a number of factors that can affect focus in a life. I weigh them relatively speaking in terms of their effect of Morgan's focused life.

---

[72] I mentioned earlier in two footnotes in the preface, 5 and 11, that I was looking for factors that make up the focal variable of a ministry philosophy. The focal variable describes those factors which help the leader prioritize life's activities around focal issues (major role, life purpose, unique methodology, and/or ultimate contribution). These given here are an initial list of such factors.

Chapter 5. G. Campbell Morgan--(1863-1945)

1. <u>Giftedness Development</u>[73]

Morgan's giftedness set is given below in diagram form.[74]

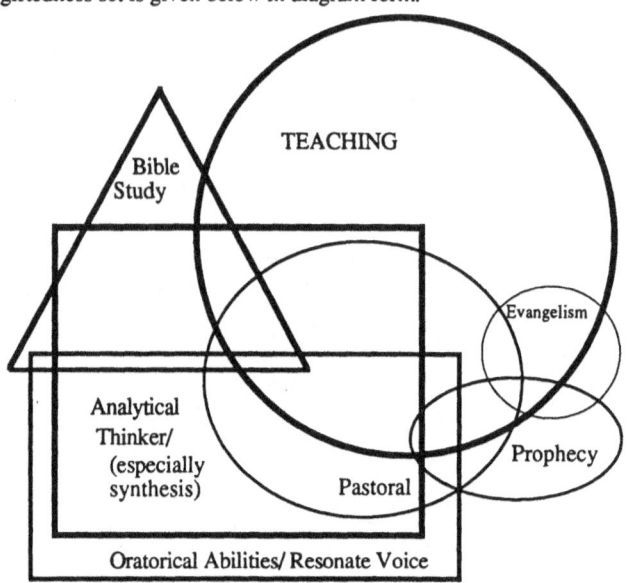

Spiritual gifts are the focal element. His gift-mix includes teaching, pastoral, prophecy and evangelism. Within spiritual gifts his teaching gift is the dominant gift of the gift-mix. Evangelism was more dominant early in his leadership transition period. It gradually paled before his teaching ministry though he never lost his desire to see people related to God through Christ. Even his strong Bible teaching gift was used occasionally to see people come to Christ. Prophecy was occasionally used, usually from the pulpit in crisis times.

Two natural abilities are worth commenting on. He has a strong analytical natural ability which flows into his Bible study skills that he was able to acquire over his lifetime. This ability fit hand in glove with his Bible study skills which he acquired and his teaching gift. His analytical ability, sharpened by his basic training increased all throughout his life. He had an oratorical bent even as a little child. He was probably strongly conditioned in this from his early visits to hear preachers. He eventually had a resonant voice which strongly enhanced his public ministry. His natural ability at speaking, especially his resonate voice, formed part of the motivational drive for a public ministry role.

---

[73]See Clinton and Clinton (1994) for descriptive definitions of the giftedness set and the skills for constructing a Venn diagram such as that given here for Morgan. That manual helps one also visualize a role that fits the giftedness diagram.

[74]The diagram which describes his giftedness set (natural abilities, acquired skills and spiritual gifts) in pictorial form is called a Venn Diagram. See Appendix F for an explanation of how to read Venn diagrams.

Chapter 5. G. Campbell Morgan--(1863-1945)

These Bible study skills included synthesis and analysis of large units: Bible as a whole, sections of Bible, individual Bible books, various contextual size units in books. He acquired word study skills both in Hebrew and Greek. His Bible study skills developed fundamentally in his first four pastorates (Stone, Rugely, Westminster Road, and New Court). He perfected these, particularly applying synthesis abilities to his Bible study skills, in his first Northfield ministry and his Westminster Chapel days. His early ministry assignments in the rural pastorates were conducive to development of Bible study skills. Starting with the Westminster Road Pastorate his Bible teaching gift began to dominate and continued to do so increasingly in the years to come.

Morgan's giftedness was a dominant factor in movement toward a focused life.

2. Destiny Processing

Destiny processing did not form a conscious factor in his focused life. Destiny processing is there, particularly the destiny preparation toward full time ministry and preaching. But it is the destiny revelation combined with guidance that leads to his focused ministry. Morgan was not so much aware of a sense of destiny as he was led into it. This would be a relatively minor factor affecting his focused life.[75]

3. Identification of Key Ministry Insights

I have already commented on the importance of the Friday Night Bible study in its affect on role and its providing a platform for his giftedness and destiny to be expressed. This single ministry insight was a most important factor in realizing of a focused life.

4. Identification Of Major Values That Uniquely Fit One's Ministry

I have pointed out the single most important value discovered in Incident 3, An Authoritative Word and the accompanying ultimate purpose that flowed from it.

> Value: The Bible is the Word of God. It doesn't have to be defended. It can convince people if it is clearly taught in terms of its intent--on the whole and book by book. People have a sense of need to which truth in the Bible speaks.

> Ultimate Purpose: Morgan sought to lead people into the truth of the Bible, to have them see its nature and relevance to life, and to have them desire to understand it and use it for their lives.

These dominant values were significant in shaping Morgan toward his focused ministry. The other ministerial statements I listed concerning Biblical values (see page 205 sub-values 1-9) also strongly focused activity corresponding to giftedness and role. This factor, values, was dominant in moving Morgan toward a focused life.

---

[75]Particularly is this so when compared with charismatic or Pentecostal leaders who usually have a strong supernatural calling related to some sort of prophecy.

Chapter 5. G. Campbell Morgan--(1863-1945)

5. Integration Of Personality Factors So As To Identify A Focused Or Ideal Role That Moves Toward Convergence

While this is not highlighted in Morgan's case it was a factor. My assessment of his Myers-Briggs fixes him as basically an ISTJ.[76] His role as senior pastor allowed for a certain aloofness which fit his personality profile. His Bible study habits, long hours in isolation, with disciplined study fit this profile. In his earlier rural pastorates he had extended times of pastoral visiting in homes. This seemed to have dropped off in the later ministries with the increase of public visibility and popularity. This was not a strong factor in focusing Morgan but could have been if his role did not fit this profile.

6. Social Base Processing

This was not a significant factor. His wife, Nancy, operated in the release pattern, that is provided the home base support which freed Morgan to pursue ministry hard.[77]

7. Ultimate Contribution Set

These elements relate strongly to Morgan's focused life though it is not clear if Morgan had explicit knowledge of them. I have already discussed these elements. See page 211, 212 for discussion.

8. Ministry Philosophy Concepts

By the time Morgan had finished his Westminster Road pastorate he had a well defined implicit ministry philosophy and a number of explicitly identified values. This local church focus was strengthened by the partnership ministry at Westminster Chapel with Albert Smith partnership. Out of those years came the broad based Flag Ship model I have previously identified. Because Morgan gave formal lecture series at Bible Colleges and seminaries we have explicit explanation of much of his ministerial values. Ministry philosophy concepts played a strong part in focusing Morgan's ministry.

9. Future Perfect Time Paradigm

Morgan usually did not have a strong vision as he went into a pastoral situation. He was open ended. Therefore he did not get vision and do vision casting. He basically did not operate from a future perfect time paradigm. Apart from basic values and his weeknight Bible School structure he operated with a strong faith that God would honor his Bible teaching and bring into being what He wanted. His ministry philosophy included the concept of allowing organizational structure to grow out of ministry needs. He did,

---

[76]For those not familiar with the Myers-Briggs profile an ISTJ is one who primarily draws his strength from being alone, who has strong observational abilities that enhance his learning, that has strong ideation tendencies, and is ordered and has well laid out plans and procedures. Whenever Morgan was on the road he preferred to stay alone in hotels rather than take the hospitality offered by host families. Murray (1938:65,66) quotes Morgan. "I don't think my friends would describe me as unsociable, but I cannot bear near me anybody who creates in me a feeling of restraint. I am slow to make friends, or to talk to strangers. What would suit me would be a house buried in the woods, a quick transit to a crowded church... and back to the woods." Murray after observing his study and his disciplined habits says, " cannot imagine him doing anything in a slovenly, slipshod way." (1938:83).

[77]See Appendix D which explains Social Base Processing in detail. Nancy Morgan was an excellent support for Morgan in hundreds of ways which released him to concentrate on his ministry. See also the Clinton position paper (1993), *Social Base Processing--The Home Base Environment out of Which a Leader Works*.

Chapter 5. G. Campbell Morgan--(1863-1945)

however, have one symptom of future perfect thinking which often permeated an optimism for what could be. He often saw what could be in a situation rather than what was. For example, when visiting Westminster Chapel in 1903, most would have seen a rundown building, dirty and in need of repair with little hope of ever filling its auditorium. But Morgan went to the pulpit, spoke, and assessed the acoustics of the place and immediately his eyes shone with the possibilities of a powerful public ministry in that place. But on the whole the future perfect paradigm was not an important factor in Morgan's focus.

10. **Boundary Processing Which Helped Focus**

Apart from guidance and reflective thinking in isolation times boundaries were not significant in determining focus in Morgan's life. The transition period out of Westminster Chapel to the U.S.A. was the only boundary in which Morgan struggled to find his next ministry assignment from God. This factor was not a significant determinant in Morgan's focus.

11. **Paradigm Shifts Which Helped Focus**

Apart from the paradigm shift represented by critical incident 3, An Authoritative Word, no paradigm shifts appear in the biographical presentations which seemingly affected Morgan's focus. Critical incident 3 and its effects were focal in shaping Morgan's ministry.

12. **Windows of Opportunity**

No windows of opportunity, except to minister stability in times of war, were noted.

SUMMARY ON FOCUSED LIFE INSIGHTS FROM MORGAN'S LIFE

Let me summarize what we have learned about a focused life from G. Campbell Morgan.

A *focused life* is
- a life dedicated to exclusively carrying out God's unique purposes through it,[78]
- by identifying the focal issues, that is, the **major role, life purpose, unique methodology,** or **ultimate contribution**,[79] which allows
- an **increasing prioritization** of life's activities around the focal issues, and
- results in a satisfying life of being and doing.

Three focal issues played an important part in G. Campbell Morgan's life. The **major role**, a public Bible teacher, dominated his focused life. But that role was used to carry out a **life purpose**, the exposing of the Bible so as to highlight its divine authority,

---

[78] I am thinking primarily of full time Christian workers who have made a second commitment beyond their salvation experience dedicating their lives to accomplish God-directed purposes through them. I am not saying that non full time Christian workers can't have focused lives. I am sure they can. It is simply that this research deals with full time workers and is primarily for them. This definition may or may not hold for non full time Christian workers. I have not yet studied them in depth.

[79] These four--*major role, life purpose, unique methodology,* or *ultimate contribution*--are called the *focal issues*. Usually one or more of them dominates a focused life. A number of other factors (like giftedness, ministry insights, sense of destiny) contribute to the divine guidance which helps these leaders to prioritize life's activities around the focal issues. Both the identification of focal issues and the processes that prioritized them are given in the studies of the eight chosen for this book.

relevant truth for today, and the necessity of its study for growth as a Christian. There were numerous **ultimate contributions** but they were secondary and flowed from these first two issues.

We have learned from Morgan's life about the importance of adapting a role to fit giftedness and destiny. There is a risk involved in role adaptation. We have seen that movement to such a role will usually involve conflict and misunderstanding from those who know only a traditional role.

We have seen that a life does not necessarily need tenure in one location or position in order to be focused. Though, tenure for a long time in a geographic location may help bring focus as is the case in 6 of the 8 we study in this book, focus can be gained by a long time of operation in a role which is carried out in different localities.

We have seen how some values force movement toward a focused life. Morgan's values were important and forced movement toward roles compatible with and enhancing use of those values.

We have observed the various focal factors and pointed out those which were more important to Morgan's focused life. Giftedness, early destiny processing, ministry insights, ministry philosophy, ultimate contribution, and the important paradigm shift with regard to the Word of God, all were significant in shaping Morgan's ministry and bringing focus.

We have identified the critical incidents and pointed out that incidents 4, 5, 6, 8, 12, 15, 16, 17 and 18 were extremely important in moving toward priorities emphasizing the focal issues of major role and life purpose. See again page 31.

We have suggested an ideal role for Morgan--many of the descriptions of the ideal role he realized in some fashion--though not all at once.

We began with the imperative, **Lets remember G. Campbell Morgan, a world class public Bible teacher.**

We have done that. We have thought back on how he lived and ministered. It remains now for us only to,

> Imitate those **excellent qualities** we have seen in his life. For Jesus Christ is the same today, as He was in the past and as He will be in the future. What He did for G. Campbell Morgan He will do for you to inspire and enable your leadership.

Where To Go and What To Do For Further Study

The following are important works about Morgan or by Morgan. Glance through my comments about them then read my suggestions for follow-up. These books about Morgan are sometimes available in used book stores. But most likely you will have to check them out from a Bible College or Seminary library. Most such libraries will have several of the following.

Harries, John
    1930   **G. Campbell Morgan--The man and His Ministry.** New York: Fleming H. Revell Company.

Chapter 5. G. Campbell Morgan--(1863-1945)

Comments: This is a biography which is complete as far as it went. It was written to commemorate 40 years of ordained ministry by G. Campbell Morgan. It is a Chronological/ Interpretive genre type. Though out of print, it can be found in Bible College and Seminary libraries.

Morgan, G. Campbell
1910   **The Study and Teaching of the English Bible.** New York: Fleming H. Revell Company.

Comments: Four lectures given at the Friday Night Bible School at the Westminster Chapel. These lay out the major values of Morgan regarding Bible study and Bible teaching.

1919   **The Ministry of the Word--The James Sprunt Lectures delivered at Union Theological Seminary in Virginia.** New York: Fleming H. Revell Co.

Comments: This was a series of lectures given to seminary students preparing for the ministry. This is an excellent series on what the pastoral ministry is all about. Morgan in this series defines spiritual gifts associated with Apostle, Prophet, Evangelist, and Pastor/ Teacher. This is a helpful treatment.

1937   **Preaching.** London: Marshall, Morgan and Scott, Ltd.

Comments: Morgan discussed preaching and sermons. He sees preaching as giving an authoritative public word that is Biblically founded and explaining and applying truth from the Scriptures. He identifies three basic characteristics of authoritative preaching: truth, clarity, passion.

Morgan, Jill
1951(1972)   **A Man of the Word--Life of G. Campbell Morgan.** Reprint in 1972 by Baker. Grand Rapids: Baker Book House.

Comments: This is the most complete biography available. It is a Chronological/ Interpretive genre type. Though out of print, it can be found in Bible College and Seminary libraries.

1952   **This Was His Faith--The Expository Letters of G. Campbell Morgan.** Westwood, N.J.: Fleming H. Revell.

Comments: Morgan, unlike many pastors or Christian workers today. maintained a thorough orderliness about his correspondence. He usually promptly answered letters by the next return mail. He noted his letters in his diary. Each of his letters were copied and filed. Once a year he would go through this file and throw away all but a few which had good excerpts on his views, Bible interpretations, etc. His correspondence numbered many thousands of letters during his lifetime. This was a form of distance mentoring which encouraged many. Of the many thousand that he wrote he saved 2000. In each of these letters was a sentence or paragraph of general interest or information to any reader, particularly to a student of the Bible or a seeker for help from the Word of God in a time of anxiety, or doubt, or need for enlightenment. These were carefully catalogued and grouped under subjects. They form the data base for this book. I used it to search for values that Morgan held--whether in the area of spiritual formation

Chapter 5. G. Campbell Morgan--(1863-1945)

(leadership character), ministerial formation (leadership skills), or strategic formation (leadership directive values).

Murray, Harold
1938   **Campbell Morgan, Bible Teacher--A Sketch of the great Expositor and Evangelist.** London: Marshall, Morgan and Scott, Ltd.

Comments: This is not a complete biography but simply observations, a few vignettes and one admiring journalist's interpretive insights into G. Campbell Morgan. It was done in 1938. Murray did quite a bit of personal interviews. He does have some vignettes not included in either Harries or J. Morgan.

Wagner, Don M.
1957   **The Expository Method of G. Campbell Morgan.** Westwood, N.J.: Fleming H. Revell Co.

Comments: This book analyzes Morgan's method of study and analysis of the Scriptures.

I suggest three approaches to get started if you are interested in having Morgan as a historical mentor. The first two involve being ministered to by Morgan in terms of his Public rhetorician role. The third involves studying his life.

One, buy one of his Gospel expositions. All are in print. Each morning go through a context that Morgan will discuss. First, read carefully the given context in your Bible noting important observations and words for study. Then read Morgan's explanation. You will be listening to a World Class Bible Teacher. You will see how he identifies the flow of thought, how he identifies the important words, and how he relates the teaching to the historical setting. You will get insight after insight even in familiar passages.

Two, buy the Westminster Pulpit, 10 volumes of some of his best sermons while at Westminster Chapel. Read a sermon each morning. Read it as if Morgan were speaking personally and privately to you. At the end of the sermon, imagine that you could ask Morgan to apply this sermon to your life. Jot down what he might say as a result of the truth he has just given you in the sermon. After a couple of months of this, reread what you have journalled at one sitting.

Three, get a copy of J. Morgan's biography. Read again my own biographical narrative to refresh yourself with the overall perspective on Morgan. Keep the time-line before you at all times as you read. Read the biography in your devotional time--a small section at a time. Jot down observations. Remember the Hebrews 13:8 mandate. For additional help in reading biographies see Appendix E, Biographical Genre and the Historical Mentor.

Chapter 5. G. Campbell Morgan--(1863-1945)   page 221

ONE BOOK	FOUNDATIONAL BIBLE YEARS-- FOCUSED INTAKE	BIBLE YEARS-- WIDE PUBLIC EXPOSITION	MINISTRY-- WIDE IMPACT	AFTERGLOW
1863	1888	1901	1919	1933 1945
Age	25	37	56	69 81
A. Family Influences (1863-1873)	A. Stone Pastorate (1889-1891)	A. Northfield Bible Conference Extension--1st Major Itinerant Ministry (1901-1904)	A. Focused Role: Bible Lecturer U.S.A., Canada, England (1919-1929)	2nd Stint Westminster: A. Co-minister with Simpson (1933-1935)
B. Basic Analytical Skills (1873-1883)	B. Rugeley Pastorate (1891-1893)	B. 1st Westminster Stint--Pastoral Base + Itinerant (1904-1917)	B. Transition to Active Afterglow, Tabernacle Presbyterian Church (1929-1933)	B. Senior Pastor (1935-1938)
C. Leadership Transition (1883-1888)	C. Westminster Road Pastorate, Birmingham, (1893-1897)	C. Recovery/ Transition to Convergence Role (1917-1919)		C. Co-Pastor with Lloyd-Jones (1938-1943)
	D. New Court, Tollington Park (1897-1901)			D. Passive Co-Ministry with Lloyd-Jones (1943-1945)

<---Strong Focused Ministry--><---Strong Focused Ministry-->
        Church Based   Quasi-Parachurch Based

Critical Incidents:

C1 Early Destiny Items
C2 Giftedness And Pride
C3 An Authoritative Word
C4 Forced Out
C5 Gipsy Smith
C6 Methodist Rejection
C7 Conflict--Stone Pastorate
C8 Crake Mentoring
C9 Rugeley Pastorate
C10 Ego Check--Sermons To Ashes
C11 Friday Night Bible School
C12 Moody Connection
C13 Howell Recruitment
C14 Revell Divine Contact
C15 Westminster Decision
C16 Albert Smith Partnership
C17 10th Anniversary Sermon
C18 Blocked Formal Training   C18   C18   C18

Chapter 5. G. Campbell Morgan--(1863-1945)   page 222

I. BORN TO ONE BOOK	II. THE FOUNDATIONAL BIBLE YEARS-- FOCUSED INTAKE	III. THE EFFECTIVE BIBLE YEARS-- WIDE PUBLIC EXPOSITION	IV. CONVERGENCE MINISTRY-- WIDE IMPACT	V. ACTIVE AFTERGLOW
1863 1888	1901	1919	1933	1945
Age 25	37	56	69	81
A. Family Influences (1863-1873)	A. Stone Pastorate (1889-1891)	A. Northfield Bible Conference Extension--1st Major Itinerant Ministry (1901-1904)	A. Focused Role: Bible Lecturer U.S.A., Canada, England (1919-1929)	2nd Stint Westminster: A. Co-minister with Simpson (1933-1935)
B. Basic Analytical Skills (1873-1883)	B. Rugeley Pastorate (1891-1893)			B. Senior Pastor (1935-1938)
C. Leadership Transition (1883-1888)	C. Westminster Road Pastorate, Birmingham (1893-1897)	B. 1st Westminster Stint--Pastoral Base + Itinerant (1904-1917)	B. Transition to Active Afterglow, Tabernacle Presbyterian Church (1929-1933)	C. Co-Pastor with Lloyd-Jones (1938-1943)
	D. New Court, Tollington Park (1897-1901)	C. Recovery/ Transition to Convergence Role (1917-1919)		D. Passive Co-Ministry with Lloyd-Jones (1943-1945)

Phase III. THE EFFECTIVE BIBLE YEARS--WIDE PUBLIC EXPOSITION

1901	1904	1917	1919
A. (1901-1904) Northfield Bible Conference Extension--1st Major Itinerant Ministry	B. (1904-1917) 1st Westminster Stint --Pastoral Base + Itinerant	C. (1917-1919) Recovery/ Transition To Convergence Role	

Chapter 5. G. Campbell Morgan--(1863-1945)

FOUNDATIONAL BIBLE YEARS--FOCUSED INTAKE	BIBLE YEARS--WIDE PUBLIC EXPOSITION	MINISTRY--WIDE IMPACT	AFTERGLOW
1863 — 1888 (Age 25)	1888 — 1901 (37)	1901 — 1919 (56)	1919 — 1933 (69) — 1945 (81)
A. Family Influences (1863-1873)	A. Stone Pastorate (1889-1891)	A. Northfield Bible Conference Extension--1st Major Itinerant Ministry (1901-1904)	A. Focused Role: Bible Lecturer U.S.A., Canada, England (1919-1929)	2nd Stint Westminster: A. Co-minister with Simpson (1933-1935)
B. Basic Analytical Skills (1873-1883)	B. Rugeley Pastorate (1891-1893)	B. 1st Westminster Stint--Pastoral Base + Itinerant (1904-1917)	B. Transition to Active Afterglow, Tabernacle Presbyterian Church (1929-1933)	B. Senior Pastor (1935-1938)
C. Leadership Transition (1883-1888)	C. Westminster Road Pastorate, Birmingham (1893-1897)	C. Recovery/ Transition to Convergence Role (1917-1919)		C. Co-Pastor with Lloyd-Jones (1938-1943)
	D. New Court, Tollington Park (1897-1901)			D. Passive Co-Ministry with Lloyd-Jones (1943-1945)

Phase IV. CONVERGENCE MINISTRY--WIDE IMPACT

1919	1929	1932

A. (1919-1929) Adapting a Convergent Role
  (1) Aborted Seminary Professor, The Biblical Seminary, N.Y., Bible Lecturer
  (2) Winona Lake (1919-1921) Bible Lecturer at Bible Conference and Itinerant Ministry
  (3) Athens (1921-1926) Bible Lecturer Throughout U.S.A. and Candada with Summer Excursions to England
  (4) Cincinatti (1926 but aborted) Church Based With Bible Study Center and Itinerant Ministry First Presbyterian Church/
  (5) Itinerant Ministry (1927, 1928)
  (6) Los Angeles (1928-1929) B.I.O.L.A. Professor and Itinerant Ministry via Extension Department (again aborted)
  (7) Bible Lecturer at Large Itinerant Ministry (1929)

B. (1929-1932) Church Based Philadelphia -- Tabernacle Presbyterian Church

Robert Jaffray
(1873-1945)

"... to preach the Gospel, not where Christ was named, lest I build upon another's foundation."

Chapter 6. Robert Jaffray (1873-1945) Missionary Pioneer Who Exemplifies Major Life Achievement After Age 55

> Remember your former leaders. Think back on how they lived and ministered. Imitate those **excellent qualities** you see in their lives. For Jesus Christ is the same today, as He was in the past and as He will be in the future. What He did for them He will do for you to inspire and enable your leadership.
> Hebrews 13:7,8 (Personal Interpretive Paraphrase)

Let's remember Robert Jaffray, a missionary pioneer who was not afraid to take up a faith challenge at age 55. He forever changed the lives of 1000s in Indonesia because of his pioneer faith. At a time when most are thinking of retirement, taking it easy, and letting the younger folks do the work, he stepped out again in faith with everlasting results. He illustrates this hopeful notion for older leaders, "**My most lasting achievement may happen in the next few years of my life.**"

Opening Illustration 1.
Can God Supply?
Will Jaffray Stick by His Leadership Committal Decision?
Age 20 (Exodus 3:7,10; 5:1))

At age sixteen Robert Jaffray was converted to Christ through the ministry of his Sunday School teacher, Miss Annie Gowan (Tomatala 1990:64) who had been trained at The New York Missionary Training Institute. He grew slowly over the next years until age 20. Then he attended a meeting in which A.B. Simpson spoke. Simpson, headquartered in New York at the training institute he had founded was touring some cities in Canada. Miss Annie Gowan had trained with him.

Simpson--The Divine Contact,[1] A Life Changing Decision

Simpson threw out the challenge. In the light of the many who knew not Christ how could a young person not be willing to give his/her life to further Christ's missionary effort in the world? Jaffray accepted the challenge. But he reasoned something like this. "I am willing but in light of my health situation I will most likely not go.[2] I can help out in other ways. But he continued to feel convicted that he should actually go." But this was not the end of it. He continued to sense those words God had used with Moses. It was as if God was saying the same thing to him through them. "I have surely seen the affliction of my people and I am come down to deliver them. Come. I will send you...and you shall say, 'Let my people go.' " (Tozer 1947:18) Finally after a period of time and inner grappling with the issue, Jaffray decided that he would go.

---

[1] Simpson was a *divine contact* for Jaffray. *Divine Contacts* (Clinton 1989:260) are special kinds of mentors. They intervene in the life of a mentoree at a timely moment to provide linkage to resources or affirm some plan of action or reinforce some touch on the life by God. The timeliness of the intervention, as well as the actual function done, validates the person as divinely sent, that is, a divine contact or means of contact with God's divine intention. Simpson will challenge Jaffray for missions, recruit Jaffray for training and eventually sponsor him to the mission field in Asia under the new movement emerging, the Christian and Missionary Alliance.

[2] Ellenberger (1985:4) points out that even as a young lad, Jaffray suffered from heart problems and diabetes. These would chronically affect him throughout his entire missionary career.

Chapter 6. Robert Jaffray (1873-1945)

Conflict and a Decision

It was not an easy decision. Jaffray had a bright future with a good job. He would have to give that up if he were to follow through on his decision to serve Christ as a missionary. But more challenging was the pressure of his father. His father had long had plans for Jaffray--plans that involved his taking over the successful business and making a career in it. Tozer describes the situation.

> Robert Jaffray, Sr. was no longer a young man. He had come up the hard way, had tasted power and had become accustomed to command. And he had his own plans for the sons. Will, the elder, he had slated to succeed him as editor and publisher of the powerful Toronto Globe, and Rob would continue in the highly lucrative insurance business. He had but to close his eyes to see Rob as Canada's richest man, and Will and his Globe as a mighty moulding force in the political future of the country (1947:20).

Jaffray certainly did not look forward to facing his father and shattering his dreams. Tomatala gives a feel for the emotions involved.

> Even though young Jaffray's decision would destroy his father's dream, he must be told. The announcement to his father was like a sudden thunderstorm in the middle of a summer day. There was an incredible contest of opposing ideals. From one perspective, it was an unequal battle with the advantage on the side of the older man. He had power and money while his son "had only his vision, his crusader's zeal and his dogged determination to obey God rather than man." (Tomatala 1990:67)

The Integrity Check--Can God Supply?

But Jaffray continued with his desire to serve Christ as a missionary. Where to train? The logical place would be the New York Missionary Training Institute.[3] Annie Gowan had trained there. A. B. Simpson, whom God had used to move Jaffray, headed it up. Jaffray knew he should be a missionary. He knew that he should be trained by those who were interested in missions. However, his father not only opposed the choice of vocation but the choice of training location as well. Note the powerful pressure he puts on Jaffray. Remember that Jaffray has always had the financial backing of his father. His needs have always been more than amply provided for.

> In view of his father's strong opposition to the initial decision to become a missionary, it is not surprising that the elder Jaffray opposed his plans to attend the Missionary Institute as well. A still greater challenge was posed by the fact that his father denied him financial support. He did, however, offer a compromise. If the younger Jaffray would but quit the Missionary Institute and enter the regular Presbyterian Seminary in the Dominion, his father promised to finance his way (Tomatala 1992:68).

In leadership emergence theory this shaping activity illustrates one of the classic types of an integrity check.[4] Jaffray had inner convictions, about serving the Lord as a

---

[3] This institute was founded by Simpson around October of 1883. It is one of the older of the Bible Institutes. Moody Bible Institute, Practical Bible Training School, and Gordon's Missionary Training Institute are all part of the Bible Institute movement which so spurred on missions and church planting. Simpson's institute was designed to equip missionaries, evangelists, teachers and pastors with practical knowledge and skill as well as an awareness of the liberal arts. It primary aim was to equip for ministry, not give theoretical theological knowledge. The Institute had a strong emphasis on world evangelization. This ambiance strengthened Jaffray's desire to go to the mission field.

[4] An *integrity check* (Clinton 1989:125) refers to the special kind of process test which God uses to evaluate heart-intent, consistency between inner convictions and outward actions, and which God uses as a foundation from which to expand the leader's capacity to influence. Integrity checks usually occur early in a

Chapter 6. Robert Jaffray (1873-1945)

missionary and about going to the New York Missionary Training Institute. Can he follow through on these convictions in light of his father's refusal to finance him? Will he accept the compromise and go to the Presbyterian Seminary? He desired to honor his father. But he knew that here he must obey God as the higher priority. So he went. And God honored him. God did meet his needs. The three years with Simpson were life changing and prepared him for the missionary future which was his destiny.[5] On such a simple decision, holding one's integrity, hinges such great future accomplishments for God. Jaffray would be a leader of character--one whom God could use greatly. That character formation can be fundamentally traced back to this important decision.

Opening Illustration 2.
Faith Challenge at Age 55, A Second Career
Will You Pioneer a New Mission Field?
Age 55 (Joshua 14:10-12)

Jaffray was sensing that maybe God was directing to open a new field. But he was old. He had served 31 years in Indo-China. Shouldn't someone else, perhaps younger, take the challenge? God directed differently at this pivotal point in Jaffray's life. Over a period of time He, in a step-by-step fashion, led Jaffray to a growing conviction about this faith challenge at such a late stage in his life. The culminating incident, deeply mystical and personal, brought the final conviction. But the process leading up to it was sustained over an extended period of time. Let me describe it.

A number of factors combined to deepen Jaffray's desires to open this new field for the Alliance. One, was Simpson's 1887 challenge to reach the islands, given so many years before. This challenge was renewed at the Christian and Missionary Alliance Annual Conference in 1926. Jaffray was part of that conference. He began to promote the idea in his itinerant speaking. He knew he would have to gain support, both prayer and financial, from the Christian and Missionary Alliance as a whole to break into a new field. A second factor was his growing desire to actually see the prospective fields. He was beginning to sense that it was God's timing to go.

> For some years I have felt a burning desire to visit the islands of the South Seas, to reconnoitre, as it were, for Him. I felt convinced that there was a great need, especially in the interior of these islands, where no Gospel witness has yet been given. The pressure of circumstances in the work in South China seemed to hold me, but at last the time seemed ripe for me to go (Jaffray 1928:2).

---

leader's development. Character is crucial and must be formed early. Followers must be able to trust leaders. Integrity is fundamental to that trust. Several kinds of integrity checks include: temptation (conviction test), restitution (honesty testing), value check (ultimate value clarification), loyalty (allegiance testing), guidance (alternative testing--better offer after Holy Spirit led commitment to some course of action), leadership backlash (follow through) and persecution (a steadfastness check). This shaping activity was the guidance test. Could Jaffray maintain consistency with his original decision? The financial offer from his father involved compromise. This shaping activity was also a *faith check* (Clinton 1989:143) for if Jaffray refuses his father he has no source of income. Can God supply?

[5]This period of about 4 years contains an excellent illustration of a major early pattern in the lives of emerging leaders. The pattern, the *positive testing pattern* (Clinton 1989:352), is threefold. God tests. The leader responds positively. God expands. The expansion is seen here not only in the financial support God provided but also in the tremendous training Jaffray got. I'll discuss this further when I describe the mentoring of Simpson in Jaffray's life. The alternative pattern, the negative testing pattern (Clinton 1989:352) is also three fold. God tests. The leaders does not discern or refuses to respond positively. God gives remedial training and retests, sometimes in varied forms.

Chapter 6. Robert Jaffray (1873-1945)

In 1928, Jaffray first made this missionary journey to survey possible work in the Dutch East Indies.[6] Three factors probably explain why he was convinced that the time was ripe. These combined to impel Jaffray in this direction. First, one of his former students, Tsang To Hang, challenged him to see Indonesia as a place to open work. Second, worsening conditions in South China, the war and strong anti-Christian biases, also led Jaffray to recognize the shortness of time left for missionary effort there. Third, the churches in South China were mature enough to stand on their own, as proved by their stands in the face of persecution from the early Communist movement in South China. Consequently, Jaffray felt released from his leadership burden for the region (Tomatala 1990:114).

You can sense the extent of his travels. On the first journey he spent almost two months. But he did not stay in any one place for more than three days. He was moving from island to island and place to place getting a feel for the various peoples and the extent of the work.[7] The burden grew as he saw the needs.

God convinced him of the need to open the work. A number of unusual encounters bristled with God's sovereign intervention. God provided seemingly impossible transportation needs at various times. One example follows.

> No regular steamers ran between the port of Sandakan and that part of Borneo where he wanted to go. At first he toyed with the idea of hiring a Chinese junk for the trip, but he soon gave it up as he said, "The journey might take two days or two weeks according to the will of the winds." So he haunted the docks on the lookout for something more substantial that might be going his way. We can believe that he did some praying. "After three days," he tells us later, "when the Lord would have me leave Sandakan, he had a steamer all ready." A Dutch oil-tanker had steamed into port and stopped over on its way to Balik-papan. It was no luxury liner, but it would float, and it was going south. So he applied for passage. His request was flatly denied by the agent. The tanker did not carry passengers. Jaffray went on board and hunted up the Captain. Him he found to be a good-natured Dutchman who spoke English, but he merely confirmed the agent's word. The tanker not only did not carry passengers but was expressly forbidden by law to do so. And besides there was no cabin anyway. This latter fact did not bother Jaffray. He wouldn't need a cabin, he explained, but he did need to get to Balik-papan. He would stand up during the trip. Would they grant him at least a standing room? The Captain's resistance went down before the courage of the missionary. "We'll do better than that," he laughed, "we'll give you a canvas cot on deck, and to avoid the technicalities of the law we'll make your Fourth Officer of the ship." Jaffray was eager but cautious. "And what are the duties of the Fourth Officer?" he inquired uneasily. "Oh" replied the Captain, "if the other three officers die, you just take over." Jaffray signed for the Fourth Officer of the S. S. Sanbodga. He paid the Captain his passage to Balik-papan and the Captain paid him his wages as one of the ship's officers (Tozer 1947:84-85).

There was a tremendous mystical prayer encounter with God in which Jaffray felt God's burden for the lost peoples of Borneo, especially the Dyaks (Tomatala 1990:122).

---

[6]This venture, a missionary survey trip, has often proved to be one of God's means of inculcating a *faith challenge* (Clinton 1989:222). It is a modern day equivalent of the Joshua words, "every place that your foot shall tread, that will I give you." I have seen this idea of a missionary survey trip used repeatedly this way. There is something about being there, seeing the needs of the people, of feeling God's burden for them that brings about a response to the faith challenge. So it was with Jaffray. For another striking example, see J.O. Fraser's trek into Lisu country in **Mountain Rain**.

[7]Tomatala (1992:118,119) mentions some of the more well known places visited by Jaffray: Balik-papan, Samarinda, Donggala, Pare-pare, Makassar, Singaraja, Surabaya, Bandung, Batavia.

Chapter 6. Robert Jaffray (1873-1945)

> On this trip away to the interior of Borneo the Lord spoke to my soul, and laid a great, heavy burden on my heart. I finally cried out with tears,--"Lord Jesus, the chiefest petition of all my prayers, I will now make second to this, Save this long forgotten Dyaks in the vast interior of Borneo." Oh, Borneo! Borneo! When will Christ be brought to your sons and daughters in the interior? When will Christ be born in the heart of Borneo, in the heart of the Dyak? Not until some one is willing at the foot of the Cross of Calvary to lay down all, and count not even his own life dear unto himself. Not until someone leaves the comfortable home and is willing to penetrate into the jungles of Borneo, to climb the mountain steep, and find the Dyak and tell him the Way of Life. Not until someone travails in earnest prayer. God is working today for Borneo and God is calling His people to evangelize the Dyaks. Will you help? How much? (Jaffray 1928:5)

One especially moving encounter enlightened him to the tremendous spiritual warfare that he must face to reach this place.

> While in Balik-papan, deep depression of spirit and a feeling of discouragement, doubt and fear, seemed to settle upon my soul. It came upon me like a dark, thick cloud of gloom, and I could not shake it off. Only His light and joy finally dispelled the darkness. It did not last long, but long enough to make me realize that I surely was on the enemy's territory. Yes, here is a place where the supreme rule of Satan has never been disputed. The Prince of Darkness has never been challenged here. No messenger of Christ has ever lifted up his voice to preach the Gospel in this place. It is a place where Christ has not been named. What utter darkness (Jaffray 1928:7).

Knowing *what* God wants and *when* God wants to do it are two very different things. Leaders frequently think they know the *Will of God*. By this they usually mean *what* God wants. But two other things are vital--*when* God wants to do it and *how* God wants to do it. Jaffray felt he knew that God wanted to lead the Christian and Missionary Alliance into this new field. He made his proposal to them. And then he waited. While the Board accepted his plan with affirmation they dragged their feet on *when* to do it.

Jaffray at first abided by their lingering decision making. While the board was apparently willing, they did not see where the finances would come from. They advised waiting. He reacted at first impassively. After all he was older. He was tired. He had done his part. Why fight it? But it was God's timing. In the midst of this time of dried up funds, He intervened and provided impetus to Jaffray to respond to the faith challenge. He would convince Jaffray with an unusual *once in a lifetime kind of experience*. It came, like Gordon's transforming experience, in the form of a dream.

> One night as he lay asleep a dream came to him, a dream so vivid and so terrible that he could never doubt its meaning. In telling about it afterwards he half apologizes. He wants us to know that he has never had many dreams to which he attached special significance. He is not a visionary, nor is he much given to the strange or wonderful, but this is different. He is sure it is from God. "It was a horrible dream," he tells us. "I thought I was at home. I thought I was a fugitive fleeing from justice, with stains of human blood on my hands. I thought the Lord Jesus was pursuing me. I was full of fear and running for my life. The pure white snow was on the ground. I stopped and tried to wash the blood stains from my hands in the snow. I looked around and ran again. I awoke, and my first words were, 'Oh, Lord Jesus, what does this mean? I am not running away from Thee. I have no blood stains on my hands. I am washed clean in Thy precious blood. Oh, teach me what this means.' At once this Scripture came unto my mind, 'Son of man, I have made thee a watchman unto the house of Israel; therefore hear the word at my mouth and give them warning from me. When I say unto the wicked, Thou shalt surely die; and thou givest him not warning, nor speakest to warn the wicked of his wicked way, to save his life: the wicked man shall die in his iniquity: but his blood will require at thine hand.' " (Tozer 1947:90 quoting from Jaffray's writings).

The *what* and *when* of God's will were now clear. Jaffray made a firm decision to enter this new field. He took the vision as a command to go forward. The decision, made by faith, brought immediate results. Two Chinese pastors responded to needs he had seen in Makassar and Surabaya. They volunteered to go. This response also brought the *how*. Jaffray had been struggling with how to open the work. Tomatala describes the insightful breakthrough.[8]

> The answer came with the positive response of S. W. Chue and T.H. Loh to go. The primary task in the East Indies is to preach the Gospel, and the first to be reached are the Chinese. Moreover, who would be better suited to the task than the Chinese themselves. Jaffray decided to establish an indigenous mission society composed of Chinese Christians. Thus, in November 1928, together with L. T. Chao and Leland Wang, Jaffray founded The Chinese Foreign Missionary Union (C.F.M.U.) (Tomatala 1992:130,131).[9]

God immediately confirmed this. The Christian and Missionary Alliance Board, just after this faith decision was made, informed him that new missionaries of the Christian and Missionary Alliance were now available.

This critical incident is amazing. Most full time Christian workers with 31 years of good experience under their belts and at age 55 are ready to move to a less vigorous role. But Jaffray responded to this faith challenge. Like Caleb he conquered his mountain. The most powerful time of his entire missionary career is just about to begin.

The Time-Line

See the time-line at the end of this chapter for a one page overview of Jaffray's life with critical incidents and other important summary information. I include location of home base since this is usually important to missionary types. Note there are three major time periods lasting 24, 34, and 13 years.

Jaffray's life is fairly straightforward. He was moving toward a business career with expectation of taking over his father's insurance business when he was waylaid by God, via A. B. Simpson. He committed himself to missions. He studied with A. B. Simpson and then departed for East Asia where he ministered with good effect until 1931. Accepting a late-in-life challenge, he opened a new field in Indonesia and ministered there

---

[8] What Jaffray saw was that there were *straits Chinese* everywhere in the islands. This vigorous group of enterprising Chinese has migrated from South China to all over the islands. In a flash, he saw that they already had been reaching Chinese in South China. Send in Chinese to reach these merchants and influential Chinese. Then from the converts that would come, they could branch out to reach the hundreds of ethnic groups in the chain of islands making up the Dutch East Indies. They would be his bridge just like the God-fearers were Paul's bridge in the New Testament. He also saw he could form an indigenous organization to send Chinese, whether or not the home office would send missionaries. This is a beautiful example of a *ministry insights* process item. A *ministry insight* (Clinton 1989:198) is a conceptual breakthrough on how to do ministry. It may be a new communication method, a new way of structuring an organization, a delivery system for evangelism or a means of motivations, etc. But these breakthroughs are often paradigm shifts. Once seen they can be used with great effectiveness. For example, Dawson Trotman's one-on-one discipleship technique was such a breakthrough concept in making disciples.

[9] Leland Wang was elected as the first president. This is an indigenous missionary agency. Jaffray was generally well ahead of missionary strategy. This shaping activity leading to how to do the ministry is called a *ministry insight* (Clinton 1989:198). It is a type of paradigm shift, new breakthrough insight, for accomplishing the ministry.

Chapter 6. Robert Jaffray (1873-1945)   page 231

from 1931 until imprisoned by the Japanese in 1942. He died in prison camp at age 71, almost 72.

Highly Condensed Biographical Narrative

The following running capsule, organized around the three major time increments of Jaffray's life indicates the important activities, people, and events that shaped Jaffray's life. Critical incidents for the life are given on page 246 and are usually indicated in the running capsule by an indented underlined title.

I. FOUNDATIONAL MISSIONARY ATTITUDE INGRAINED
(1873-1897); Age= Birth-24

A. Family/ Pioneer Spirit
(1873-1889); Age=Birth-16

Four important influences characterize the first 16 years of Robert A. Jaffray's life.

1. The genesis of his **pioneer spirit** emerged both from within, a family trait, as well as from without, catalyzed by the Canadian national scene.
2. He learned about **depth of character**, a never-give-up spirit, as he watched his father go through two major crises involving loss of business and holdings.
3. His mom modeled **character traits**--a spirituality that was captivating.
4. He faces **two debilitating illnesses** early on. After effects of these will linger all his life.

All of these helped mold Robert Jaffray at his roots.

Pioneer Spirit and Depth of Character

Robert Alexander Jaffray, Jr. was born on December 16, 1873 in Toronto to Robert Alexander Jaffray, Sr. and Sarah Bugg Jaffray. He was the second of five children. There was his older brother William and sisters Margaret, Annie, and Elizabeth. Jaffray's family was Christian, of Scottish Presbyterian tradition (Tomatala 1992:26,27). Canada's frontier was being expanded. Its cities were developing. It was a time of pioneering.

From his father he learned resilience--a major pioneer trait. At age 20 his father showed pioneer courage. He migrated from Scotland to Toronto. He possessed a strong drive to succeed. He started a business from scratch, a grocery business. The business was going well. Then disaster hit. The store burned to the ground. Along with the ashes, Robert, Sr. was left with a pile of debts. He bounced back. In a few years he paid off the debts. Real estate provided the means to get out of debt and to succeed again. In mid-life, after accumulating a lot of money, the senior Jaffray bought the *Toronto Globe*, one of the great daily newspapers of Canada. He was on his way to power. Disaster struck again. World economic depression crippled his efforts and nearly took the *Globe* to bankruptcy. He bounced back again and took the Globe to greater heights. Eventually he became involved in political activity. He amassed a large fortune which he passed on to his children. From his father, Robert, Jr. imbibed a success-oriented mentality and an entrepreneurial spirit.

Chapter 6. Robert Jaffray (1873-1945)

Spirituality of Mother

His mother took the spiritual lead in the family. She modeled a sweet Christian spirit. She saw to it that the children went to Sunday School and church. She laid the foundations so that eventually, each of her children came to the Lord.

Two Medical Problems

Two health problems plagued Rob Jaffray. Ellenberger describes.

> The life of young Rob Jaffray, as he was called, was dominated by the dual affliction of heart trouble and diabetes, which kept him from all active sports and left him a stout and pensive lad. This double millstone was to go through life with him, though he lost his heaviness and turned into a very dapper looking young man (Ellenberger 1985:4).

These two maladies taught him about suffering.

Both parents wanted their children to be respectable members of society. They got the very best education. After school, Robert joined his father at the Canadian Life Insurance Company. He started at the bottom and was well on his way toward the top. He learned about business. He learned about approaching people and selling them on life insurance. He also saw the importance of the print media and its power to influence. All of these basic insights would later be used on the mission field.

But a life changing event, coupled by a second challenge, would take hold of his plans for the future.

B. Conversion Lifelong Attitude Assumed
(1889-1893); Age=16-21

Conversion--Fruit of A Faithful Sunday School Teacher, Annie Gowan

At Sunday School, Annie Gowan influenced Jaffray to personally accept Christ at age 16. Her own life had been deeply affected by the preaching and teaching of A. B. Simpson.[10] Miss Gowan went to the Missionary Training Institute in Nyack, New York and studied under Simpson. Her walk with Christ exemplified the very best of Simpson's teaching. Her testimony and her sacrificial service as a teacher of young people broke through to Robert Jaffray. This critical incident brought about a fundamental value in Jaffray's life. His life was not his own.

He grew after his conversion. He took part in some Christian activities. But he was interested in business things as well. However, when he was about 20, he was invited to meet and hear A. B. Simpson in person. He had already heard of Simpson through Miss Gowan. This dynamic preacher was involved in a series of meetings in Canada. Revival was in the air. Simpson's fourfold gospel with its emphasis on

---

[10] He was a Presbyterian clergyman who had gone through a deeper life experience and left the Presbyterian ranks to form his own church. He needed the liberty to press the claims of Christ, the deeper life, and the place of healing in a local church ministry. He was also strongly motivated toward missions, something difficult to promote among the Presbyterian upper level leadership. He founded two enterprises--a Bible Institute, The New York Missionary Institute, which trained missionaries and the Christian and Missionary Alliance, an organization for promoting world missions and sending of missionaries.

Chapter 6. Robert Jaffray (1873-1945)

sanctification and the deeper life broke like a cool fresh wind on the Canadians. His challenge to missions affected young Jaffray.

Simpson and Decision To Go for Training at Nyack

Opening Illustration 1, contains focal incidents 2 and 3, which introduced the chapter occurred here. Jaffray responded to the character testing. He went to Nyack, N.Y. and for three years studied with Simpson.[11]

C. Early Ministry Values Imbibed
(1893-1896); Age=22-25

Simpson--Imposing Mentor

Remember, Jaffray has gone against his dad's first choice. This means he will get no financial help. Did God meet this response of faith? Yes! God provided for Jaffray in various ways, one of which was to give him a student pastorate, the Kenwood Alliance Church (Tozer 1947:24). This provision not only helped finance his schooling but also helped complement it. Here he was practicing what he was learning.[12] In addition, to this financial provision, community of support, and a place to learn ministry by doing, Jaffray also was blessed by a mentor who took a personal interest in him.

A. B. Simpson shared, taught and modeled. For three years Jaffray sat under this godly man. He interacted with him. And he learned from him more than information. Ellenberger emphasizes how Simpson's mentorship influenced Jaffray's early ministry values.[13]

---

[11]We have identified three major training patterns through which most leaders emerge. Four of the eight, Gordon, Maxwell, Jaffray, and Simeon (somewhat) fit the *pre-service pattern* (Clinton 1989:354), that is, they receive formal training prior to ministry. Three fit the *in-service pattern* (Clinton 1989:356), that is, they learn on-the-job and finally after proving their abilities take on full time responsibilities. The third is a *modified in-service pattern* (Clinton 1989:357) in which the leader gets ministry experience, then interrupts it for formal training, and then resumes it. Usually this pattern will include further interruptions for training down road. Brengle fits this pattern somewhat. There are advantages and disadvantaged to all of these patterns. In teaching these patterns we point out the advantages and disadvantages of each pattern. But we seek to move people toward the third pattern. Jaffray will do this in a quasi-form because he will begin several Bible schools in Indo-China and Indonesia. These kept him studying in an on-going fashion.
[12]From training model theory we identify four elements that need to be balanced for training to be most effective. They are input (cognitive focus), experience (using the input in life), dynamic reflection (an evaluation process which tests ideas of input with use in life and which generates new ideas from experience) and formation (that is the deliberate focus on building of leadership character, skills, and strategic thinking). Seminaries mainly focus on the cognitive. But Bible institutes, such as Simpson's do not. They focus on personally studying and using the Bible and ministering to others. Jaffray supplies the experience via this part-time pastorate. This gave some experience which helped him dynamically reflect. Because the school was so small there was lots of personal attention--meaning that Spiritual Formation was focused on strongly. See Clinton (1984) **Leadership Training Models** for Holland's Two Track Analogy which gives this balanced model for training.
[13]*Mentoring* is a relational experience in which one person called the *mentor*, empowers another person, called the *mentoree* via a transfer of resources. Nine types of mentor functions have been identified. One of these is the modeling function of a contemporary Christian leader respected by the mentoree. The *contemporary model* serves as a sort of Christian hero/heroine who inspires the young leader. The mentoree tends to emulate and imbibe values from the *contemporary model* and tends to live up to the genuine expectations that person sets out. (See Clinton and Clinton, 1991, **The Mentor Handbook**). Simpson not only served the mentoring function of a *contemporary model* but he served other mentor roles as well: *spiritual guide*, *coach*, *teacher*, and *sponsor*. Mentoring is an important shaping process that God uses in

Chapter 6. Robert Jaffray (1873-1945)

> Jaffray's three-year period of mentoring by Albert Simpson would indelibly mark his inner life and his ministry. Simpson modeled union life before him--what he called "the sanctified life." He drank deeply at the well-spring of zeal for missions which Simpson believed was not an end in itself but sprang from this sanctified life. He learned his special eschatology (that world evangelization can "hasten his coming" and "bring back the King") and his way of exegeting Scripture. He apprenticed himself in Simpson's evangelism program, observed his publications, leadership training and mission magazine ministries. Jaffray got more than a Bible education: he got a pattern of ministry (1985:19)!

Tomatala comments further on the results of this personal, in-depth mentoring.

> Thus Jaffray learned from Simpson a biblical, theological and philosophical framework, a theoretical as well as a practical approach. His Christ-centered theology, love for souls and yearning to reach the unreached millions in places where Christ had not been named, his missionary approach and methods, his emphasis on leadership training and literature work, his prayer life and many other characteristics derived from Simpson's mentorship...In short, Simpson became the primary contributor to his early ministry values, values which would later appear throughout his ministry in various mission fields (Tomatala 1990:69,70).

Jaffray's prolonged interactions with Simpson were an important, extended critical incident which shaped numerous foundational values that will serve Jaffray well all his missionary career.

Apostolic Yearning

Sometime during this three years God met Jaffray with a special call. We do not have the exact details of it. But all through the expansions in his ministry--his heartbeat was for those yet unreached. This heartbeat was repeated throughout his missionary activity. Where did it come from? When did he get it? In about 1889 he was converted. In 1893 he made a decision to be a missionary. In 1896 he went to east Asia. In 1898 he and Glover penetrated a new province--Kwang-si. In 1910 he expanded Alliance work into Indo-China. In 1928 he began the process that expanded Alliance work into Indonesia. Always his heartbeat was like that of Paul given in Romans 15:20, "I eagerly strive to preach the Gospel of Christ where Christ is not named; to break new ground." Sometime during the three years studying with Simpson, Jaffray moved from a general mission call to an Apostolic calling pulsating with a desire to reach the unreached. Tomatala (1990:70) assigns this Apostolic call to this three year period of Bible School training in Nyack. He
cites Smalley, affirming this heartbeat.

> Thus Jaffray learned from Simpson...yearning to reach the unreached millions in places where Christ had not been name...We can observe Simpson's mark... when Jaffray expressed this deep concern and yearning for missions [and here he quotes Jaffray] "In my

---

the life of a developing leader. It is interesting that both Jaffray and Maxwell were deeply impressed by mentors in a Bible School context. They learned not only values for life from the small intimate class settings and the on-campus residential intimacy but they learned a methodology to use. It was modeled for them--the Bible Institute. They saw its power in shaping lives and sending people out. It changed their own lives. Both Maxwell and Jaffray go on, not only to permeate values learned from their mentors, but to also perpetuate their methodology, that is, start Bible institutes. Maxwell founded Prairie Bible and Jaffray started at least four institutes. More on his institutes later.

Chapter 6. Robert Jaffray (1873-1945)

soul I heard his voice saying 'Other sheep I have, ... them also must I bring.' And again, 'Whom shall I send, and who will go for us?" 'Here am I send me.' (Tomatala 1990:70)

Tomatala gives two quotes from Jaffray which describe the impartation of this Apostolic Yearning in Jaffray's life. The first shows the deep respect each of his students had for him. The second, contains the kernel of the Apostolic yearning.

> As a young man having been thrilled over and over again by Dr. Simpson's missionary messages, we rather looked upon him with awe, and considered personal contact with him almost beyond our expectation (Jaffray 1935c:2).

Tomatala goes on to say before the second quote, "If asked about the most remarkable thing he remembered about Simpson relating to mission, Jaffray would say, I remember:

> ...don't think that when you reach the mission field you have accomplished it all....it is only the beginning of great things for you, if you persist in pressing on....don't settle down in a little corner by yourselves, but keep your eyes lifted up, and see the fields far distant. You can dry up even after you have reached the mission field, and wither away into comparative nothingness. Keep the vision of the uttermost parts of the earth, ...(1935c:3).

In 1887 Simpson published his vision to reach out to the unreached in one of his editorials in **The Word, The Work and the World**, his mission magazine. It was this burning missionary message that Simpson repeated throughout Jaffray's training years, 1893-1896. And evidently Jaffray was moved by it.[14]

> Jaffray's vision to enter the East Indies had its roots in Simpson's vision, when in 1887, he wrote about the islands in his mission magazine, **The Word, The Work and the World**. It took some forty years before the vision was consummated. (Tomatala 1990:115).

When mentioning the 1926 Annual Conference, at which the matter of expansion into the Dutch East Indies (Indonesia), Tomatala refers back to this publication and this vision. So, sometime during this early training, Jaffray responds to God's call on his life for a special type of Apostolic work--breaking new ground for Christ.

1898--Summary of Focal Issues and Shaping Toward Them

At this point five critical incidents have helped shape crucial values and move Jaffray toward focus. His conversion (focal incident 1) as influenced by his mother and Annie Gowan and his leadership committal (focal incident 2)--willingness to serve as a missionary, as influenced by A. B. Simpson--have given him some life changing fundamental values and a goal to move toward. His stand on integrity and his acceptance of the faith challenge (focal incident 3),when he went to Simpson's missionary training institute, was blessed of God. Finally, his training and mentoring by Simpson for three years (focal incident 4) imbedded values, a missionary vision, and gave him his unique methodology, the Bible institute, that he will use both in South China, Indo-China, and Indonesia. He has responded to God's Apostolic call (focal incident 5) on his life.

---

[14]Again while we don't have the actual incident, which I will continue to research, we do know that there was a change. And references during his times of mission expansion always seem to point back to vision gained at this time. This quote on continuing to look for the unreached certainly describes Jaffray's mindset. Simpson must have deeply influenced Jaffray with this value at this time.

Chapter 6. Robert Jaffray (1873-1945)   page 236

In terms of focal issues, at this point, he is moving from a **general missionary role**, that of missionary to that of Apostolic missionary--one who will start new works, expand into unreached territories and to unreached peoples. But it remains to be uniquely defined **what kind** of missionary role that will be. It will be connected to the Bible Institute as a methodology. He has been impressed with the power of a Bible institute as a training methodology. He will later use this **unique methodology** both for training and as a basic jumping off place for evangelization. Life purposes are still general--evangelize the world. Ultimate contribution thinking is way off in the future. But he has made some fundamental decisions. His life will be a life serving Christ and not amassing money and power in the business world in Canada. And he will pioneer new works for Christ.

II. MISSIONARY DEVELOPMENT--EAST ASIA
(1896-1931); Age=23-58

Assignment Asia/ Simpson Sponsors. Why To South China?

We have no details of this incident but we do know that Jaffray committed himself to the Christian and Missionary Alliance as a mission movement. He wanted to be under Simpson's authority and mission vision.[15]

Jaffray was posted to South China. The choice of this field for Jaffray is not clear to me. Further research may yet disclose this. But at this point I do not know the details. This is an important focal factor. That he went to South China and not somewhere else is very significant. So I will list this as a critical incident and hopefully will get details as I continue to study Jaffray.[16]

A. South China-- Early Missionary Lessons
(1896-1911); Age=23-39

Jaffray's Ai--Initial Difficulty in Cross Cultural Evangelistic Ministry

Jaffray went to China in 1896. The Alliance, as a mission, had been in China for less than ten years when Jaffray arrived. They were in about ten locations when Jaffray arrived.[17] He was given a task--move to Tung-un, do language and culture learning, do

---

[15]Tozer in describing the clash of wills between Father, Robert Jaffray Sr., and young Jaffray seems to indicate that Jaffray had already been persuaded in his heart for China--even before he went to Nyack. "By the time September rolled around things had quieted down somewhat. Rob would go to New York and work his way through school. His father was somewhat reconciled but certainly not convinced. You couldn't do anything with Rob in his present state of mind. That was evident. But things might change. He would wait and see. 'If the Alliance sends you to China,' he told his son, 'they'll pay every penny of the expense. Not a dime will you get from me.' " (Tozer 1947:21,22). Tomatala (1992:77), quoting Reynolds, points out that Simpson and seven other ministers were the leaders who commissioned Jaffray and George G. Shields on January 20, 1896 at the Bethany Chapel in Toronto, Canada. They were ordained for missionary service.

[16]Such an crucial choice is usually accompanied by a *sense of destiny* (Clinton 1989:349) experience. That is, God meets the individual in some unusual way to clearly and sovereignly direct the leader and give an awareness of His presence and choice of a leading toward an ultimate purpose. Probably Jaffray talks about this in retrospect in some of his editorials. I will continue looking.

[17]Tomatala cites Latourette (1929:399 et al). He points out that the first appointee to China, Dr. William Casidy sailed for China in 1888. He contracted smallpox in route and died. He was buried in Japan. His wife and two other women missionaries (Tomatala leaves them unnamed) followed sometime later and were the first Alliance missionaries to enter China. Less than ten years later the C.M.A. were in Kansu, Shansi, Mongolia, Kwang-si, Peking, Shanghai, and Tientsin. The Alliance was the first Protestant body to establish a permanent station in Kwang-si. Robert Glover and Robert Jaffray opened that work.

Chapter 6. Robert Jaffray (1873-1945)

evangelistic work, and establish a mission station. He was able to do the first of these--language and culture learning. But he was not able to pull off any appreciable success in evangelism nor was he able to establish a station.[18]

That he got a good start in the language can be seen by his later proficiency. Tomatala quotes Reynolds, who reports on John Salmon's trip and preaching in 1910.

> On the Lord's day I preached morning and evening through Mr. Jaffray interpreting. I learned from a missionary from another body that Brother Jaffray is the best interpreter in South China (Reynolds 1981:563).

The initial difficulty in evangelizing and establishing could be attributed to several things:

1. The initial difficulty of language and culture. One could hardly expect effective ministry in such a short time.
2. Jaffray recognizes that he does not have primary evangelistic gifts. His assignment didn't fit his giftedness.
3. Jaffray needs a ministry insight, a breakthrough, on how best to get evangelism accomplished.

Whatever the case, he learns of the difficulty of missionary work,[19] as most missionaries do in their first term. This initial set back drove him to evaluation. But like his father, he was persistent and continued steadfastly to go on in his missionary calling. He is transferred to Wuchow after about a year in Tung-un.

In the next ten years, operating from Wuchow as his base, Jaffray will establish himself not only as a solid missionary, but as a leader.

A number of important items highlight the experience he gained in these years as he moved toward leadership (Tomatala 1990:71-82). He and Robert Glover are credited with opening the Kwang-si province (1898). He meets and marries Minnie Doner (1900).[20] She was an American missionary who had come to the field two years earlier than Jaffray. She had been instrumental in establishing the church in Wuchow. He faces the strain of the effects of the Boxer Rebellion (1900). With Glover he started the Chien Tao (Wuchow) Bible School in 1900, the first CMA Bible School ever founded in a foreign field (1900). Glover was the principal. Jaffray was on faculty. In 1907 his daughter Margaret was born. I have only skimmed some of the highlights. But it was these kinds of things that pointed to or supported Jaffray's inborn leadership ability.[21]

---

[18]It was unrealistic to think he could. Today most new missionaries tackling a new language, especially a difficult one, are dedicated to that task alone. Asian languages, especially tonal ones are difficult to learn. Many western missionaries never learn them well.

[19]Missionaries go through what anthropologists call culture shock as they attempt to learn language and culture and to minister cross-culturally. Getting the language and the culture and an appreciation for it are foundational for future ministry. Jaffray did these fundamental things.

[20]At first Robert and Minnie Jaffray operated as the co-ministry social base pattern. She was an excellent missionary. She also ran a hospitality home for missionaries and visitors. When Margaret was born she basically moved to the release pattern, social base profile, though she was very active in missionary work outside the home as well. See Appendix D, Social Base Processing.

[21]In this brief paragraph I have skimmed over some very important shaping activities. The Boxer Rebellion in 1900 was a major crises. Glover and Jaffray faced death in Wuchow. They stayed until they have helped all the interior missionaries to evacuate. Then they escaped by river boat (Tomatala 1990:90). In 1911 Jaffray was captured by bandits. Again he escaped with his life (Tomatala 1990:91).

Jaffray Emerges As Field Leader

His stability, his godly life, his response to crises, his excellent social base and his apostolic nature[22] all help demonstrate his leadership qualities. The field elects him as field leader in 1910.

B. Indo-China--Expansion Lessons
(1910-1928); Age=38-55

When he was made field chairman, Jaffray was 38. He was a mature missionary. He had 14 years of missionary experience. He had helped open a new field. He had helped found a Bible School. He was well respected. He manifested the life of Christ within. Tozer describes this step forward in Jaffray's leadership development.

> Robert Jaffray continued to labor in South China, and with fuller maturity and wider experience came into greater and greater prominence. The hidden strength of the man and the smoldering zeal within him brought him naturally to the front. Over the years his influence increased and the confidence of his fellow missionaries in his inborn leadership, till, when the time came for the chairman, Rev. Isaac Hess, to retire, he was elected to the chairmanship of the South China field. This marks his real coming of age, and it was from there out that his notable work was accomplished (1947:27).

Note the words *smoldering zeal* and *coming of age* and *notable work*.. These signal passion for leadership, effectiveness, and vision.

He has now been focused in terms of role. He is an Apostolic missionary, a trainer, and now field leader, a strategic decision making position. Apostolic vision (that smoldering zeal) has a platform for demonstration. This combination Apostolic decision maker with a training focus will be the major role through which he will focus more sharply on his life purpose--reaching the unreached. Expansion always characterizes Jaffray's work. Especially is that seen from the time of his installation as field chairman.

Two means proved foundational to Jaffray's efforts at expansion. One, capitalized on previous experience from long ago. He had seen the power of the printed media, with his father's controlling of the Globe. He had seen Simpson's development of training materials, the magazine, and books to undergird the missionary movement. Jaffray started the Alliance Press in Wuchow in 1911. The second means emerged from his mentoring experiences at Simpson's Bible School. He saw the Bible School as a means for fostering a movement. Both of these means aided Jaffray's expansion efforts during these focused years as field leader.

---

[22]Tomatala consistently points out that Robert Jaffray was continually looking to the yet unevangelized. He also consistently founded new works of all kind, printing presses/ publishing ministry, Bible Schools, new missions, opens new fields, etc. His passion behind these efforts was to reach others--the Apostolic heartbeat.

Chapter 6. Robert Jaffray (1873-1945)

Ministry Insight--Expansion Efforts Via Publishing, Alliance Press

The means of expansion via the publishing effort began in 1911 when Jaffray founded the Alliance Press in Wuchow. It is easy to trace the background which helped lead to this particular focus. Tozer comments on early influences from which Jaffray imbibed values relating media and powerful influence.

> Robert Jaffray believed in the power of the printed page, and for the most of his life kept his presses rolling, turning out tons of Christian literature for distribution throughout the Orient. His publishing work was carried on with a zeal amounting to a crusader's passion.
> ...
> He had been reared in an atmosphere never free of the smell of printer's ink. The talk around the table had been of newspapers, the power of printed ideas, the influence of the press for good and for evil, and he had not forgotten anything (Tozer 1947:28,29).

Tomatala cites Niklaus (et al) as directly tying the printing means back to Jaffray's father. He also uses this citing to identify the expansion of influence for Jaffray.[23]

> Jaffray himself was "born well" into a home of affluence and culture. His father owned and published the **Toronto Globe**, one of Canada's most influential newspapers. This background perhaps influenced him to establish the South China Press and publish **The Bible Magazine**. The Chinese monthly gained wide circulation and won him international recognition throughout the Far East (1986:109).

The Bible Magazine gave him a forum to expose his long term mission strategizing and to display his values and ministry philosophy. Over the years this became one of his ultimate contributions--a reservoir of mission strategy ideas.[24]

Later after the work expands into Indo-China he will repeat this procedure (1913). And again after to moving to Makassar in Indonesia he starts still another publishing ministry (1931).

Ekvall gives high praise to this aspect of Jaffray's influence.

---

[23]It seems clear to me that the establishment of the printing ministry was two things. It was a *ministry insight* (Clinton 1989:198), a breakthrough concept for effectively increasing one's ministry. It was also an *influence-mix* (Clinton 1989:280-284) challenge in Jaffray's life. *Sphere of influence* refers to the totality of people being influenced by a leader. A closely related term is *Influence-mix* (Clinton 1989:378). This involves a profile describing how and who leaders influence. All leaders influence followers. They can influence *directly*, that is, face-to-face ministry, *indirectly*, via shaping of key individuals or via materials used by others or *organizationally* via executive leadership or committees or the like. Each leader has a profile corresponding to which of these dominates or how they relate. *Power-mix* (Clinton 1989: 378) has to do with the major means a leader uses to influence followers. Jaffray will have great indirect influence, through many key individuals in his Bible School ministry. There, he used positional power as well as personal authority, competent authority, and spiritual authority. When he became field leader he began to exert positional power at a higher level. His decisions will be a means of indirect influence on many missionaries. His publishing ministry gave great indirect influence and will lay the groundwork for his being known in places he has not yet ministered. This breakthrough concept of publishing materials and distributing them is often desperately needed by local churches. Pastors can enhance greatly the influence of a local church by creating an organization on the side for publishing and distributing materials for use in the local church. Usually it is best done apart from official control of the church leaders.

[24]Tomatala had access to nearly every issue of **The Bible Magazine** and pored over them in his study of Jaffray. They provided insight after insight in ministry philosophy values of Jaffray.

Morrison in giving the Bible to China, did the work of scores of missionaries for decades. The Alliance Press by publishing tracts, books and the Bible Magazine edited by Mr. Jaffray, greatly facilitates the spread of Bible truth and scriptural teaching on all phases of fundamental Christian belief as well as giving the distinctive aspects of the Alliance message (1939:178).

Jaffray's leadership influence certainly was enhanced by this ministry structure.[25]

Unique Methodology--Expansion Via The Bible School--1913ff[26]

In 1900, Jaffray and Glover had founded the Chein Tao Bible School. From an initial enrollment of four it continued to grow. It was the first Christian and Missionary Alliance Bible School on the mission field. The school had as its general purpose, "to produce men more thoroughly trained in head and heart." (Tomatala 1990:84) Jaffray had been involved in the school from its inception. But in 1913 when Glover was elected to the position of Foreign Secretary of the C.M.A., Jaffray succeeded him as the principal of Chien Tao Bible School (Tomatala 1990:84).

This school provided a strategic center for expanding the work in South China. Under Jaffray's leadership, the school produced hundreds of Christian leaders who later assumed leadership responsibility in the churches of South China. Three quotations show the importance of this unique methodology and its potential for strategic influence.

Tozer points out the repeated emphasis by Jaffray.

For Jaffray believed with unquenchable faith in the importance of the Bible School in the total scheme of Christian missions. Wherever he went from those first days on, as soon as a few converts had been formed into a church the next thing to receive his attention was the founding of a Bible School (1947:28).

Peter Anggu points out an underlying motive of Jaffray's drive for establishing Bible Schools. It shows his awareness of indigenous workers and their ultimate responsibility.

Jaffray's vision for a Bible school was to train the native Christians to take the Gospel to their own people and to prepare leaders for the future of the church. He fully recognized that foreign missionaries are limited in many ways, and the time would come when the national leaders would have to take over the responsibility (1986:64).

---

[25]Jaffray was multi-talented and had a large capacity for work as well as an understanding wife. He is running a Bible School. That is tremendous pressure. From 1971-1974 I was principal of the Jamaica Bible College. I can attest to the many pressures involved: recruiting both students and teachers, overseeing schedules, teaching, preaching in chapels, overseeing discipline, raising funds for housing and food needs, etc. In addition to this, he is responsible for mission administration which includes personality conflicts between missionaries, assignments of missionaries, orientation for them as they come on the field, visits to the various fields and stations, strategizing with missionaries, encouraging them, etc. And on top of these two major jobs, he was overseeing the publication of a monthly magazine with its deadlines, writing, editing, soliciting of articles from missionaries, handling the funding, making sure copy gets to press, etc. But he was ably gifted for such a stretching and effective tri-role.

[26]Remember the focused life hinges around discovery of: 1. a **major role**, uniquely tailored to the leader so as to buttress destiny, giftedness, life purposes; 2. and/or **life purposes** which clarify and move from general to more specific over time; 3. and/or a **unique methodology** used in the major role for effectively accomplishing life purposes or ultimate contributions; 4. and/or an increasingly clear picture of the end results, **ultimate contributions**, that will be left behind as a legacy of life achievements. Critical incidents pave the way by instilling key values to undergird and giving strategic guidance that narrows the leader toward these focal issues. The **unique methodology** is under focus here. It is being honed for strategic evangelization purposes.

Chapter 6. Robert Jaffray (1873-1945)

Jaffray recognized the need for both missionaries and national workers. They must work hand-in-hand to expand a work in a country.

> He knew that foreign missionaries would never be the last word in evangelization of any country. To Jaffray, the best and swiftest work would always be done by Christian nationals, and therefore, the training of national workers is very important. This truth was proven in his ministry in China, Indo-China and Indonesia (Anggu 1986:63).

Simpson's mentoring influence, particularly the modeling of a Bible institute for training, paid high dividends.

Expansion Efforts--Apostolic Opening of French Indo-China, 1911ff

There had been earlier aborted attempts to enter French Indo-China by the C.M.A. previous to the successful efforts in 1911.[27] In 1911 Jaffray sent in Paul M. Hosler and G. Lloyd Hughes. They purchased property in Danang and established the first Protestant mission in the area (Tomatala 1990:98). The securing of property proved to be the key to entry. By 1913 Jaffray had established the Alliance Printing Press in Hanoi. In 1916 he was elected superintendent for the area.

An important expansion step was the establishment of Touranne as a strategic center for missionary work. A number of important steps followed. There was the opening of the Touranne Bible School in 1918. There was the initial penetration into Cochin China in the southern part of Indo-China and Cambodia. This proved to be a stepping stone into Cambodia itself in 1922. He was instrumental in establishing the Cambodian Bible School in Battambang. He also strategically pinpointed a number of important cities for penetration and establishment of work: Hanoi, Saigon, Touranne. While Jaffray never moved his personal residence and directly instigated these advances, he did in his role as superintendent plan, sponsor, and oversee these important advances (Tomatala 1990:100).

Herendeen properly credits Jaffray's leadership in these efforts to establish the Evangelical Church of Vietnam (ECVN).

> The opening of the work in Viet Nam can be traced all the way to the vision of the founder of the CMA, A.B. Simpson, and to one of the Alliance's great missionary statesmen, R.A. Jaffray of South China. Simpson gave Jaffray the go-ahead at the turn of the century to see what could be done among that vast, yet unreached people of Indo-China. Indeed the vision included all of what today is North and South Vietnam, Laos, and Cambodia (1975:58).

Herendeen further notes the progress of the work, during the time of Jaffray's overall leadership.

> Membership growth for the ECVN rose from 183 in 1921 to 4,326 in 1927. There was an increase of over 1,000 baptized members per year between 1924 and 1927. But statistics can be dull, however important for church growth analysis. In fact, during these years, rapid membership growth frightened one pastor in the My Tho church in the delta, somewhat like some critics of church growth in our day. It seems that in 1925 the My Tho church grew from 27 members to 1017 in one year! Such growth reasoned the leadership, had to consist of rice Christians only. So they changed pastors. The roll was

---

[27]Tomatala (1990:97) mentions David LeLacheur's missionary survey trip in 1892 and a later trip by Reeves. Jaffray himself had attempted to go in following Reeves path. He also attempted to send in a French-Canadian couple in 1902. All of these efforts were aborted and had no long term effect.

purged of those who were judged to have improper motives. But surprisingly enough, 565 adults survived the purge and were baptized (1975:59-60).

In 1927 the National Church was founded in Indo-China, ECVN, Evangelical Church of Viet Nam.

One of the major lessons Jaffray learned through his leadership experience in Indo-China was the importance of the timing of God.[28] He had first tried to enter 13 years earlier. In God's timing the work broke open. This important lesson will be followed in the entrance into the Dutch East Indies.

1925--A Challenging Year to Jaffray's Leadership

Two things should be mentioned about Jaffray's leadership in 1925. One, he exerted leadership influence beyond his own normal sphere of influence. He met a crisis situation in the Philippines. Two, there was the evacuation of missionaries to Hong Kong because of the threat of war in South China.

Upon hearing that missionaries in the Philippines had become discouraged and were contemplating closing the mission work, Jaffray traveled there. He encouraged the missionaries. He transferred in some of his ablest missionaries. The work eventually turned around and today still continues. Jaffray's feeling about the Philippines express his Apostolic nature.

> The Philippine Islands should not be a small field of the Alliance, but one of the largest. The large and unoccupied areas of the islands and the many untouched islands farther south constitute one of the largest and most difficult fields of the world (Hunter 1964:170-171).

Three major leadership functions describe all leadership activity: task oriented leadership, relationship oriented leadership and inspirational leadership. Jaffray never maintained task or relational responsibility for the work in the Philippines. But his momentary inspirational leadership in 1925 may well have saved the field.

In 1925 China was in a state of near revolution. At that time, Jaffray and his missionaries were forced to evacuate to Hong Kong. Jaffray exerted leadership at this critical time. It was just such an action that forced him to think ahead to the time missionaries might not be allowed in South China. Such thinking helped spur his interest in the Dutch East Indies--the next major work he will open.

---

[28] In my study of leadership across the six major leadership eras in the Bible I have begun to identify major leadership lessons called macro-lessons. A macro-lesson is a high level generalization of a leadership observation (suggestion, guideline, requirement, value), stated as a lesson, which repeatedly occurs throughout different leadership eras, and thus has potential as a leadership absolute. One of the more important macro lessons occurring in every leadership era fits what Jaffray has learned. GOD'S TIMING IS CRUCIAL TO THE ACCOMPLISHMENT OF GOD'S PURPOSES. Jaffray is becoming sensitive to this. His prolonged boundary entering into the Dutch East Indies highlights this important macro-lesson. See HANDBOOK I. Leaders, Leadership and The Bible: Overview which is available through Barnabas Publishers. This Handbook deals with the approach to study of the Scripture from leadership perspectives.

Chapter 6. Robert Jaffray (1873-1945)

C. Boundary To Major Achievement--Dutch East Indies
(1928-1931); Age=55-58

The time when a leader moves from one major time period to another is called a boundary. Boundaries have been studied extensively.[29] Every leader goes through critical times of transition in his or her ministry. Comparative studies of such boundaries have identified three stages: 1. the entry stage, 2. the evaluation stage, and 3. the expansion stage. Boundaries can last as short as 2 or 3 months or as long as several years. The boundary time for Jaffray, in which he shifts from South China as his home base and focus of ministry, to Indonesia, and its all absorbing challenge, lasted for about six years. But there were harbingers of it even earlier than the six years. This important boundary will catapult Jaffray into the most important, most fruitful, and most satisfying time of his entire ministry. And it comes at a late stage in life; this intervention by God so encourages many of us to anticipate this same kind of intervention ahead in our lives.

A Second Career, Opens Brand New Field At Age 55

Time-wise, Focal Incident 11, Faith Challenge at age 55, which was given in the Opening Illustration 2, occurs here and is the focus of the boundary processing.

Harbingers of The Boundary

As early as 1920, Jaffray felt the stirrings of a call to the South Sea Islands (the Netherlands East Indies, or today Indonesia). There were *push factors* and *pull factors*. In both Jaffray sensed the sovereignty of God.

Push Factors

Revolution was in the air in China. Political unrest signaled a major boundary as Chinese dynasties shifted.[30] Jaffray had been aware of the political tensions the entire time he had been in China. He had gone through the Boxer Rebellion. He had been captured by bandits (minor warlords in a district). He had evacuated missionaries out of the region at the request of the embassies. But from 1920 on, he saw the political situation deteriorating more. There was strong anti-foreign sentiment and even open threats. Tozer comments.

---

[29]Richard W. Clinton (1993) did his doctoral dissertation in this area of study. See also Dr. J. Robert Clinton's position paper (1992) on this subject, *Boundary Processing--Looking At Critical Transition Times in Leader's Lives*.

[30]Tomatala (1990:105) summarizes. "The early twentieth century political situation in China was marked by uncertainty. First there was the Boxer War in 1900, then the Revolution in 1911. In the early years of Revolution, the central government was very weak. Many battles occurred in Kwang-si in the South. Three main reasons contributed to the situation. First, China had been dominated and divided among the foreigners for years. Second, there were many warlords mostly in the Northern China with private armies assisted by the foreigners. Third, China was a vast country, and it was difficult for the new government to control the whole region in the beginning stage. The only way to strengthen the new government and establish its power over China was to defeat the powerful warlords in the north. The Russians were willing to help. In 1924, they established a military academy outside Canton under the leadership of General Chang Kai Sek. In 1926, Chang started his campaign to the north. He asked the Nationalists for unity, but the unity was only a temporary concession. After succeeding in the Northern Campaign, the Nationalists moved to Shanghai. Faced by a small Communist force, they killed many of them. From that time on open contention erupted and spread rapidly. Led by Mao, the Communists proposed rural national development. The proposal won the favor of the people. He also received support from the poor peasants of the South. In 1930 the Communists took over the government in Kwang-si. This enabled the Communists to rule and unite China (KCET 1989).

Chapter 6. Robert Jaffray (1873-1945)

> Soon the whole China, but specially the coast cities, was all aflame with strong, rapidly-spreading anti-foreign feeling. As the agitation increased it was concentrated against the British more than any other foreign powers, and later took on an anti-Christian attitude (Tozer 1947:78).

This same political situation was forcing the migration of many Chinese into surrounding countries and the South Sea islands. Was not the hand of God in this? These migrating Chinese would be unsettled.[31]

Previous to 1920 Jaffray had a burden for leadership training and helping the South China church mature. That burden begins to release as he sees the leadership maturing and the church making courageous stands against the persecution it faces.

The evacuation of missionaries to Hong Kong in 1925 further impressed Jaffray with the limited time missionaries had in South China.

The Pull Factor

Jaffray's Apostolic nature constantly made him restless to take the Gospel to those who had never heard. Simpson's passion to take the Gospel to those who have not heard became a value for Jaffray which implicitly drove him on to look further afield. Typical of that passion is this Jaffray concern, quoted by Smalley.

> I have a deep burden for China's four hundred million souls. ...But the question that burns in my heart is, What about those in whose language there is as yet no Bible, no gospel text, not one messenger to tell them the Way of Life? And again he added, I am thinking of those parts of the world where no gospel light whatever has penetrated the awful darkness; places where Satan still holds absolute sway; places where no representative of the Lord Jesus has dared to go with the saving message of the Cross (Smalley 1976:21).

So then, there was **The Pull,** the inner conviction from God in general to reach out to these needy people in the South Sea Islands. And there was **The Push,** the outward circumstances.

The Entry Stage of the Boundary[32]

Somewhere around 1925 Jaffray began to more earnestly consider the Dutch East Indies. One prompt was a plea/challenge from one of his former students, Tsang To Hang, describing the situation in the East Indies.

> The Gospel was preached in this country three hundred years ago. But, the advance was very small; it was a pity. Among thousands of islands in Indonesia, the only places where the Gospel advanced were Ambon, Menado, Tapanuli and a few more areas. Still,

---

[31] Church growth experts have recognized that migratory people are unusually receptive to the Gospel just after being unsettled and attempting to get established in a new region. There is a window of opportunity which will close as they begin to succeed in the new region.

[32] Four different kinds of boundaries, under which most can be categorized, are popularly described by the titles of Surprise, The Creeping Vine, The New Glasses, The Growth Challenge. This is a Creeping Vine type. A number of issues over a period of time accumulate until there is recognition of the boundary and subsequent action taken. In the entry stage, the Creeping Vine Boundary will be signaled by negative preparation like the Push Factors already described. Frequently, there will be sovereign factors that prepare the heart for something coming.

Chapter 6. Robert Jaffray (1873-1945) page 245

the largest sections are waiting for the Gospel to shine among them. They are badly in need of salvation (1979:25).

An Apostolic type, like Jaffray, would read this with different eyes than a historian. He would see, immediately, the challenge from God to go and impact them. He would repeat over and over, "the largest sections are waiting for the Gospel to shine among them. They are badly in need of salvation."

Jaffray began to get the notion on the agenda. He spoke to fellow missionaries. He spoke to the annual conference. Though he himself was increasingly feeling the burden he needed a special touch from God and a personal appraisal if he was to convince others of this important need. So he planned a missionary survey trip. On this trip he moved, in terms of boundary stages, from the entry stage to the evaluation stage.

The Evaluation Stage of the Boundary

I have previously discussed the highlights of this first missionary journey in Opening Illustration 2. That two month trip brought both the touch from God (see the sovereign interventions, the prayer burden, the spiritual warfare, and the dream). From those he made the major decision. We must go in.[33] Immediately the ministry insight broke open; the Chinese Indigenous Mission was formed and the bridging strategy to reach the Chinese first and use this as a base to reach other Indonesians crystallized.[34]

During this trip, Jaffray displayed the wisdom he had learned in operating many years in Asia. His basic procedure included (Tomatala 1990:119,120):

1. Wherever he went he started by contacting the Dutch Officials, making sure he was on good legal ground,
2. He contacted any Christian ministers if there were any to secure support and diminish any feelings of threat and competition,
3. Being fluent in Chinese, and acculturated to Chinese ways, he sought to build contacts with diaspora Chinese for the purposes of evangelism,
4. He assessed the presence of and effectiveness of any evangelical witness,
5. He established temporary bases where there was any response to evangelism.

A typical response to item 2 above, not only did not signal any red flags, but actually gave the green light, is shown in Jaffray's report from Batavia.[35]

---

[33]Sometimes a boundary is likened to a long tunnel. As we enter it most of the light is coming from behind us, the past, as we move along there is less and less light from behind us. Sometimes there is a portion of the tunnel in which we are getting no light from behind us, the past, and as yet no light from in front of us, toward futuristic thinking. But then we begin to see the light ahead which becomes clearer as we move toward it. That signals the turning point. The turning point in a boundary is the pivotal point of the evaluation stage. From then on, we begin to move in terms of the light that is ahead of us. Jaffray's decision to go in--followed immediately by God's affirmation in the form of the two Chinese pastors who volunteered to go was just such a turning point.

[34]Frequently, a paradigm shift, such as this ministry insight, will either spur the turning point or will accompany it as a solution to move forward.

[35]You have to be a missionary who has traveled to many different mission fields to really appreciate how positive this is. Frequently, there is competition between mission agencies. Established missionaries are often threatened by the possibility of new works coming in. This is certainly heart warming to me, a former missionary, who would wish for this sort of cooperative effort as we move rapidly to the former Russian Republics and the Eastern Block and will soon go into Japan and China the same way when the big breakthrough comes. For Jaffray this was one of several very important confirmations about going in. This is a powerful instance of *ministry affirmation* (Clinton 1989:267). In *ministry affirmation* God gives

Chapter 6. Robert Jaffray (1873-1945)

> A little later on my trip, on reaching Batavia, I had the privilege of interviewing leaders of the Dutch Missions, the Methodist Episcopal Mission, and particularly Dr. Slotemaker de Bruine, the Missionary Consul. The latter was very courteous and helpful, and heartily approved of our opening work among the Chinese, and encouraged us also to occupy some of the unoccupied areas of the Dutch East Indies. He recommended the following fields, where no work has been done:--
> 1. The entire east coast of Borneo, with Samarinda and other places as centers.
> 2. The west coast of Borneo, with Pontianak and other places as centers. The object would be to reach "the wild man of Borneo," the Dyak of the interior.
> 3. The Boeginese on the coast of the Celebes, and the wild races of the interior of the Celebes, with Makassar as center.
> 4. The whole south-western coast of Sumatra.
> 5. A large number of smaller islands in the East Indies where no Gospel witness has yet been given. (Jaffray 1928:8).

Two items, which I have not previously mentioned, further conditioned Jaffray's resolve. Dr. Swemer's survey of the Malay Archipelago helped buttress his own thinking.

> Dr. Swemer, in his survey of Malay Archipelago, calls attention to whole islands and parts of islands which are without any missionary work, and includes Bangka, Madura, the Flores, Bali...; Lombok, the great island of New Guinea, and others. He estimates the unevangelized population of these islands at between six and seven million (Jaffray 1928:8).

Another striking and more alarming factor was Jaffray's almost prophet-like warning.

> If the Gospel of Christ does not soon enter these fields, the influence of Mohammedanism, which is spreading rapidly, will soon be such as to form a most effective barrier to its progress. Mohammedanism is rapidly displacing paganism. this fact surely makes the evangelization of these fields all the more urgent (Jaffray 1928:8).

His first trip eventually resulted in the decision to go in.

His decision to go in necessitated other trips to assess locations, help transition missionaries in, and expanding of further knowledge needed for strategic and tactical decisions. All in all, five missionary journeys were made from 1929 to 1931. But these more properly belong to the termination stage of the boundary.

The Termination/ Expansion Stage of the Boundary[36]

Once the decision was made to go in there were many more almost innumerable little follow-up decisions that were required. Other missionary journeys were made. Table 6-1 Summarizes these journeys.

---

clear approval of a given ministry being done or being contemplated so as to inspire and encourage the leader to continue. Sometimes this will come in a time of discouragement or criticism from others. In this case, it comes to give outward confirmation of a growing inner conviction.

[36] Once the evaluation stage is past and a major new direction set there is the follow-up activity of the termination stage. There will be many decisions that need to be made in order to follow through and move into a stable new major time period of development. Numerous decisions were made in this time. Finally, Jaffray, himself, will move into Makassar in 1931. With that move the new development phase was fully entered into.

Chapter 6. Robert Jaffray (1873-1945)   page 247

Table 6-1 Summary of Missionary Journeys Transitioning to Indonesia

Journey	When	Major Results
1.	1928 January/ February/ March	Surveys fields. Makes contacts with government and Gospel workers. Evangelizes. Sets up some temporary bases. Identifies key cities. Sees needs of Dyaks and others. Receives confirmation from God to go in. Senses timing is right. Makes proposal for C.M.A. to go in.
2.	1929 January/ February	Established first two Chinese workers--one in Samarinda (C. Y. Lam) and one in Balik-papan (K. L. Lin). Met Leland Wang in Balik-papan; he was concluding evangelistic tour. Strategized together about new efforts of new indigenous Chinese Mission. Officially named Superintendent of this new field.
3.	1929 May-August	Stations first C.M.A. missionaries. Expands mission effort beyond the "Chinese." Experiences prayer challenge[37] and conducts first baptisms.
4.	1930 January	Visits Tsang To Hang in Makassar. Two main purposes: 1. Conduct first missionary conference of C.M.A. and C.F.M.U. (the indigenous Chinese Mission). 2. Finalize plans to enter Bali. Tsang was blessed and sent into Bali to begin language learning there and established contact with a colporteur representing the British and Foreign Bible Society.
5.	1930 October, November, December	Set plans in motion to establish publishing ministry. He does this on faith as the home board was dragging its feet with regards to financing this. Gets official approval from Dutch East Indies government to enter Bali . Now moves Tsang's family into Bali.
6.	1931	Moves permanent mission headquarters from the Wuchow, South China location to Makassar.

With his 6th missionary trip, he said goodbye to Wuchow and South China, his home base for his entire missionary career.

---

[37] This special touch from God renewed his burden to continue reaching these island groups. Tomatala quotes Jaffray, himself. "On my way back to the boat that morning, I passed an old lady on the road. Her face was wrinkled with age, 'Too late to reach her with the Gospel Message, I fear,' was my thought as we passed her. 'We have come too late to reach her, even if we come at once. She will drop into a Christless, hopeless grave. God help us to do our part, to hesitate not, to delay not, to do our part to send the Gospel Light to these, who 'sit in darkness and in the shadow of death.' Reader, pray please for Bali, for Lombok, for Sumbawa" (1929a:11)

Chapter 6. Robert Jaffray (1873-1945) page 248

1931--Summary of Focal Issues and Shaping Toward Them

By 1931 Jaffray's **major role** was well defined: He was an Apostolic Missionary Field Leader with a four fold thrust: 1. Bible School work producing national workers for advancing the work; 2. Missionary Administrator--Superintendent ; 3. Publishing Ministry--both for evangelization and growth of the Church; 4. Missionary Statesman.[38] He used the **specialized methodologies**, the Bible School and the Publishing Ministry, as his main thrusts. He has completed a major life purpose--the planting and development of the Christian and Missionary Alliance Churches in South China and Indo-China under capable leadership. His **life purpose** has narrowed to the planting of the Church of Christ in the Dutch East Indies among as many unreached peoples as possible and laying the foundations for on-going growth after his ministry. His ultimate contributions already accomplished have been in the areas of PIONEER, FOUNDER, STABILIZER, RESEARCHER, WRITER and PROMOTER.[39]

With focal issues clarified and in place he is ready for a most productive finish. He will expand his Mission administrator function to co-ordinate three mission efforts: the Christian and Missionary Alliance, the Chinese Foreign Missionary Union, and the World Wide Christian Courier (a sister mission organization under Paul Rader). He will see the work expand. He will face many complex problems and much opposition. But he will do so with the wisdom of a mature leader who can trust God in the midst of tough times. He will model an inspirational leadership that is always expanding to reach more of the unreached.

III. MISSIONARY CONVERGENCE--EXPANSION IN MATURE YEARS (1931-1945); Age=58-71

A. Moving--Expanding To Indonesia and Beyond--Singapore and Malaysia (1931-1941); Age=58-68

In 1931 after 34 years, at age 58, Jaffray moved from Wuchow, South China to Makassar, Indonesia. His attention was now given fully to the ministry in Indonesia. The next several years were to be years of advance.

YEARS OF ADVANCE--1931-1941

Prior to Jaffray's move the work had begun. On a number of his missionary trips he had initiated work in several places and placed missionaries in strategic locations. In

---

[38] His publishing ministry, his growing recognition in the States among mission conscience people, his numerous trips to various strategic locations, his intervention in the Philippines, his co-founding of an indigenous Chinese mission, his relationships with the Dutch government officials as well as the Dutch Reformed Missions all made him a Missionary Statesman of growing importance. Wheaton College honored him with a Doctorate of Divinity in 1938 (they had been trying for several years to catch him in the States). This was just one token of his growing reputation as a missionary statesman.

[39] Remember that these ultimate contribution types are briefly described in Chapter 1, pages 22,23. *Ultimate contribution* refers to categories of major life achievements. Comparative study of lives has resulted in 12 prime types (some of which focus on *being* and some on *doing*). Effective focused leaders usually have several of these prime types in their make-up. We call this the ultimate contribution set. Jaffray's ultimate contribution set includes: **Pioneer** (founds apostolic type works), **Founder** (starts new organizations), **Stabilizer** (solidifies organizations), **Researcher** (develops new ideation), **Writer** (captures new ideation for use of others), and **Promoter** (distributes effectively new ideation). Knowing your ultimate contribution set early can make the difference in a proactive or reactive stance toward future development. See Clinton (1989) paper, *The Ultimate Contribution--A Life that Counts*, available through Barnabas Publishers.

Chapter 6. Robert Jaffray (1873-1945)

1931 his family moved to Indonesia. Others from Wuchow moved. New recruits also joined those on the field. The ranks grew from 9 to 14. In addition, Jaffray has relationships with the Chinese Foreign Missionary Union (the indigenous effort headed up by Leland Wang) which had about 4 units on the field.[40]

Jaffray had learned in his years in South China of the importance of the publishing ministry and the Bible School to expanding the work He began to develop both of these. Jaffray, in 1931, first expanded the publishing ministry. Gospel tracts, Bible translations, commentaries, books, and Bible magazines began to come off the press. Over the years these continued and even increased. All of these Christian materials were foundational to growth and spread of the church which was to come.

In 1932 the Makassar Bible School was opened. David Clench was installed as its first director (Tomatala 1990:146). With the Bible school Jaffray was able to train national leaders for ministry. Shortly he was involving them in the advancing work.

Pioneers often have trouble convincing superiors of their vision. Boards often are cautious. Tomatala describes such a situation.

> During the years 1928-1932, Jaffray's first concern had been to station all of his missionaries from the C.F.M.U. and the C.M.A. in strategic places. The year 1930, in particular, marked a **new advance in his bold effort to double the number of missionaries.** [boldfaced emphasis mine] The response of the Board of Managers to Jaffray's proposal showed caution.
> While we desire to press forward in intensive pioneer ministry in every field where God so leads, and we are glad for the zeal that calls for eleven new missionaries this year, and fifty in five years, yet we believe the work of the Dutch East Indies should be more fully established before deciding upon such large reinforcements, and we hope that the Chinese and the native Christians in the islands will have such a large share in the evangelizing of the islands as to make such large missionary force unnecessary (Tomatala 1990:147,148, quoting Smalley 1976:69).

Advance Into Bali In 1931

One of the most significant advances in 1931 was the entrance of Bali. This field was fraught with difficulties. Getting in with government approval was difficult. There was opposition to the work there. Eventually the field will be closed to the C.M.A. but they will be able to put in their Balinese Bible School graduates. Then there will be restrictions on Balinese students going for training. Through all of these difficulties Jaffray exerted forceful leadership.

When Jaffray changed his request before the government he was granted permission to enter. His first request had asked permission to evangelize in Bali. His changed request was to evangelize the Chinese in Bali. This was granted in early January 1931. Tsang moved his family to Bali. Jaffray persevered against the odds. Tomatala quotes Brill on this impossible task.

> It was thought impossible by the Dutch Missionary Consulate to obtain Government permission to work in Lombok, but thank God it was granted. It was also thought impossible to secure permission for a Chinese missionary to preach to the Chinese in Bali, but this also has been granted (1931:18-19).

---

[40] In mission circles today a *unit* means either a single worker on the field or a married couple on the field.

Tsang and family went into Bali with the restriction that they only work with Chinese. In February he had founded the Hok Im Tong Christian Church, the only Christian church that had ever been founded in Bali (Tomatala 1990:150, quoting Tsan 1979:34). The work progressed. Jaffray went in at the end of the year and conducted baptismal services. By the end of 1934 there were 436 Balinese Christians (Smalley 1976:214). These Christians were under growing persecution. There was such a stir and a growing antagonism that the government gave Jaffray an order to close the work. Jaffray tried appeals to higher authority. He published editorials such as "The Battle for Bali." He recruited prayer backing around the world. Eventually the C.M.A. was forced to leave Bali. After independence they returned. Most of the Christians had stood firm (Tomatala 1990:152, 153).

1933ff--Most Striking Successes--Advances in East and West Borneo

Jaffray had initially placed missionaries in East Borneo in 1929. In 1933 Jaffray placed a missionary couple, the Mouws, in Sintang in the Kapuas River region of West Borneo (Tomatala 1990:154). Then it happened--a people movement.[41] Large numbers of Dyaks (remember Jaffray's earlier prayer challenge for them?) turned to Christ. This amazing success seemed too much for people on the home front to accept. Jaffray explains.

> During the past six years of missionary work in the Netherlands East Indies among the various tribes of Dyaks in Borneo, we have been as it were, almost swamped with success. Some have considered it what is generally know as a "mass movement." Others have though that the large number of converts reported is due to the fact that some missionaries are prone to baptize people more easily and more hurriedly than others, and that the work therefore is to be considered more or less superficial. Neither of these criticisms is just or correct. It is a genuine work of the Holy Spirit in many individual hearts. Hearing the word of the gospel, conviction of sin, a decision to accept Christ, simple childlike faith in Him, the great Forgiver of sin, and resultant peace and joy of heart--these are the features that mark this work of grace in Borneo (Smalley 1976:374).

Jaffray does acknowledge the problem, however.

> It is one thing to rejoice in the birth of so many, who have believed on the Lord Jesus Christ, but it is another thing to feed with the sincere milk of the Word these "babes in Christ." (Jaffray 1936a:23)

Tomatala (1990:156) attributes the successful breakthrough on two factors: 1. the involvement of Bible School Students in evangelism. 2. The evangelism spread along kinship lines, the web of networks described by McGavran (1955).

In three short years of Jaffray's presence on the field the work had grown from 14 missionaries present in 1931 to 18 in 1933 and 14 national workers. The work among Dyaks continued to grow right up to World War II. After the war it was found that the Dyak Christians had maintained their testimony.

---

[41]McGavran, the great Church Growth Apostle, as early as 1955 had coined this phrase to describe multi-individual conversions among a group of people who decide to move toward Christ. McGavran was an expert in people movements and an avid researcher of just such great turnings to Christ. See his **Bridges of God**. People are often suspicious of these kinds of ingatherings. But careful follow-up and discipling of these groups turning to Christ will conserve them for Christianity. And their conversions can be seen as real.

Chapter 6. Robert Jaffray (1873-1945)

1937 Major Advance beyond the Borders of the East Indies

In 1937 Jaffray began to look beyond the Dutch East Indies. He sent exploratory works into the Malayan Peninsula. These efforts were eventually cut off due to World War II. But an effort which did eventually succeed was the entrance into Dutch New Guinea (Irian Jaya). The interior was discovered to be inhabited by a Dutch Oil Company explorer, F. J. Wissel. He discovered a large lake in the interior, which was named after him. In 1938 Jaffray, having heard of the find, made a pioneering survey trip to the island. The interior trip proved to rugged for the 65 year old man. But he gathered enough information to petition the Dutch Administrator and the home Board for the C.M.A. to go in.

In November 1938, during the annual missions conference, Walter M. Post and C. Russell Deibler was specially consecrated and set apart for this work. Their attempts to settle in were interrupted several times by World War II events. The missionaries were evacuated to Australia in 1943. But eventually they returned and continued their work with great breakthroughs.

Summary of Efforts--Why Was There Advance?

The C.M.A., under Jaffray's leadership continued to advance in a number of the islands belonging to Indonesia including: Borneo, Bali, Sumatra, Celebes, Lombok, Sumbawa, Dutch New Guinea. They were excluded from Java by a comity agreement.[42] Makassar was the home base for the missionary expansion in Indonesia.

Tomatala (1990:163,164) summarizes five factors that under girded the advances:

1. Jaffray primarily targeted hidden peoples.
2. A flagship, Mother church, was developed in Makassar.
3. The Bible Magazine, Kalam Hidoep, and other publishing materials were significant.
4. The Makassar Bible School was powerfully used. Students were required to have one year of field training. Evangelistic training was coordinated with evangelistic meetings held in the Mother Church in Makassar.
5. Jaffray organized a second indigenous mission society among Indonesians. This mission operated a short time but was later closed down because the Dutch government thought it subversive. But it pioneered a concept.

It is important to note that these advances took place in a period of world history in which there was a world economic depression. Support for Bible school, scholarship money for students, and support for national evangelists and full time workers all challenged Jaffray's faith. Then too the government imposed heavy taxes on missionaries working in the country. In a time when many churches and mission organizations were cutting back, Jaffray moved forward. God honored his faith.

Jaffray's initial efforts began in 1928. By 1933 when he moved to Indonesia there were 2,007 church members. By 1934 this increased to 6,857. In 1935 it was 8,340. The 1939 report showed 89 Centers of Operation, 38 C.M.A. missionaries, 141 national workers, 20 Chinese missionaries, 184 Students in Makassar Bible School, 1408 Baptisms, and 10,329 church members.

---

[42]Comity is a term referring to agreements which divide certain geographical areas among specific groups. If a group is assigned an area they can get in with government approval. Otherwise, they can not.

Chapter 6. Robert Jaffray (1873-1945)

There were hard times too. The Malayan Penisulan work did not succeed. Bali was closed down. Dutch New Guinea was evacuated though eventually returned to with great success. There was a strong challenge to Jaffray's leadership in the latter 30s.[43] Jaffray responded positively. He countered charges not by attacking but by giving the positive accomplishments involved. He also resigned his leadership post. But the Board and the majority of missionaries asked him to withdraw his resignation. They wanted his leadership.

The year, 1938, was a special year--a victorious year. Jaffray was able to get through one of his innovations, the purchase of an amphibious sea plane for use in transporting missionaries and supplies among the various locations spread out in the islands.[44] He was physically sick but saw a miraculous healing by the Lord. Dutch New Guinea was entered and Jaffray was awarded an honorary doctorate, D.D., by Wheaton College.

The future looked dark. Jaffray knew his own time was limited. He knew that the work would prosper eventually but that persecution and problems would try it as gold. Smalley's quote of Jaffray in the year 1940 catches the Apostolic spirit which looks forward yet recognizes the difficulties.

> "We must expect temporary reverses as well as continual triumph and ultimate victory." Jaffray also challenged the Christians to be involved in supporting the work. To them, he wrote, "You can help by your prayers if you really take the matter to heart." Again he said, "You can help by sacrificial giving in your missionary offerings for this all-important pioneer enterprise." (Smalley 1976:569,571)

The April 1941 Report was the last complete report given by Jaffray. It is a fitting summary to his years of advance in Indonesia. In 1939 there were 139 Centers of Operation, 29 C.M.A. missionaries (WWCC missionaries now excluded), 141 national workers, 20 Chinese missionaries, 209 Students in Makassar Bible School, 2049 Baptisms, and church membership of 13,093.

B. Last Years, World War II Intervenes--Suffering Victoriously (1941-1945); Age=68-71

Jaffray is sixty-eight, almost sixty-nine. He has lived a good life. His service to Christ spans four decades. It has been pioneer effort. His heart has been always to reach out to the unreached--to expand frontiers. He has had two major ministry periods crowned with results, 30+ years in South China and Indo-China, and now a final burst of pioneer effort--the establishment of a solid work in Indonesia--more than 13 years effort. Now

---

[43] Some C.M.A. missionaries were not happy with Jaffray's committal to administrating the other mission works (the Chinese Foreign Missionary Union and World Wide Christian Courier). They also had some other grievances. Tomatala (1990:180) lists 8 items: 1. They wanted governance by the Chairman and not a Field Superintendent, 2. They felt Jaffray's time was taken up with the Chinese work, 3. They thought Jaffray's methodologies from South China were outdated, 4. They felt that Jaffray sided with the C.F.M.U. in disputes, 5. They pointed out that Jaffray did not know the Malay language, 6. They did not feel that Jaffray was involved in direct evangelism and pastoral work--only a pioneer, 7. They did not want the Dyaks extracted for training in Makassar, 8. They did not want the World Wide Christian Courier missionaries to be accepted as associate missionaries of the C.M.A.

[44] Boards do not always agree with innovations. They had been getting along without airplanes before, why get one now. Eventually the board reluctantly agreed though their financial involvement was minor. Jaffray produced the larger part of the needed funds from his own pocket. Needless to say the airplane greatly improved the communication and transporting of goods and missionaries between stations (Tomatala 1990:171,172).

Chapter 6. Robert Jaffray (1873-1945)

what? What has God planned for this faithful servant? What will climax such a life? God planned a **victorious finish** for this old, worn-out, pioneer! The darkest days that the Christian and Missionary Alliance Mission work in Southeast Asia has ever known lie just ahead. What is needed is an encourager? One who knows God in the midst of trials? One who can see through and beyond the darkness to the hand of God in it and the victory beyond it. Jaffray will be that person!!!

God's ways, his shaping processes, often are not what we would expect. Jaffray has labored long. He has sacrificed much. He has seen much victory--much expansion of the cause of Christ in Southeast Asia. We would expect Jaffray to be put out to green pastures. He should enjoy a time of peace and reflection on God's work through him. He should spend time with his family, tell his story, recount God's victories; perhaps he will challenge new, fresh, younger ones to the mission field. But God has something else for him. It unfolds piece by piece. Three Acts describe the final play. All contribute to the theme of inspirational leadership.

First, Jaffray sensing the depth of struggle, suffering, and darkness to come will encourage his fellow workers. One of Jaffray's great Biblical exhortations comes at this time. It was written as a combination editorial/open letter to be distributed to all the field workers. Tomatala describes the gist of it.

> In 1941 the sounds of war increased as the Japanese conquered the neighboring countries to the north and continued their relentless march toward the south. Faced with the upcoming war, Jaffray determined to encourage his coworkers. To their present sufferings in the ministry would be added the sufferings of war. Jaffray, however, was determined to face the fact squarely. Using Isaiah 52:7 and Romans 10:15, regarding the beautiful feet of the evangelist, Jaffray sought to encourage his fellow laborers.
> "The reference to the feet on the mountains may well be interpreted as setting forth the necessary suffering involved in missionary work...Many a missionary has come at nightfall at the end of his day's tramp with sore, bleeding feet, but in His sight such feet are beautiful; beautiful because they bear the marks of suffering in carrying the Glad Tidings of great joy to sin-sick, weary souls." (1941:13)

Tomatala goes on to comment further.

> Although great suffering would eventually arrive, Jaffray took courage and wanted his missionaries to find the same courage to stand firm when suffering came. He believed that everything would come to an end in the glorious reign of Jesus Christ, which he saw as imminent. regarding this, he wrote the refrain:
> "One day it will all be finished and the weary feet, all scarred, bleeding, and sore will cross the last mountain, and tread the last trail, reach the last tribe, and win the last soul and then He himself will exclaim: "Well done, good and faithful servant! How beautiful the feet of him that hath brought Good Tidings and proclaimed salvation to perishing souls!" Then indeed it will be true that our Christ reigns, reigns over all the world, over every nation. Every knee shall bow and every tongue confess Him." (1941:13-14).

In leadership theory, three highly generic functions categorize all leadership efforts.[45] Jaffray was a strong task oriented leader. His Apostolic drive moved him in that direction. But he was also an inspirational leader. That particularly stands out in these closing years.

---

[45]See Clinton (1986) **A Short History of Leadership Theory**. This study surveys the five major leadership eras from 1841 to the present. In era three factor analysis studies identified the first two major leadership functions, which are independent of each other. *Task oriented leadership* (technical name called initiation of structure) provides the vision which moves forward, structures effort toward accomplishment, the carrying out of the raison d'être of the organization. *Relationship leadership* (technical name called

Chapter 6. Robert Jaffray (1873-1945) page 254

Final Choice--Decision To Stay

Second, he encouraged not only by words but by his modeling. He was due for a furlough. And, really, he was due for retirement to some less strenuous post. He was ill. Tomatala describes the inner struggle.

> Faced with personal needs and the advance of war, Jaffray struggled to discern God's will as to whether he should stay on the field or return home. No one would have blamed him if he returned home. Instead, he chose to remain in the East Indies. He explained the reason for his decision.
> "Mrs. Jaffray, my daughter Margaret, and myself all need a time of rest and change. I do not want to take regular furlough in the U.S.A. or Canada, if it can be avoided. It may be that a few months in Manila will suffice. I greatly dislike leaving the work at this critical juncture, in the midst of political unrest. You may hear from me soon from Manila, and ere long we may be back again in Makassar, refreshed and strengthened (Smalley 1976:644).

After staying in Baguio City for a few months, his health recovered. And he began to sense God's will.

> On reaching Manila the Lord's guidance seemed to be quite clear that we should stay in the Far East. The war news was even then rather serious. We did not fear any mishap on the way home, but I feared lest, during the time of our stay at home, war might break out and the Pacific would be closed and our return to the mission field be hindered, at least temporarily (Smalley 1976:684).

It becomes still clearer. While in Manila he continued to study the war situation. He kept waiting for God's timing.

> I had consciousness that when the time came to return to Makassar, the Lord would indicate clearly. The hour came, and He spoke clearly in my heart that the time had come to return to our home and work in Makassar, Netherlands East Indies (Smalley 1976:685).

So Jaffray chose to stay. The Jaffrays arrived safely in Makassar on December 6, 1941, one day before the attack on Pearl Harbor.[46]

---

consideration) provides the knitting together of people and tasks and provides the ambiance, the relational (emotional) support, people need to move toward accomplish. In the fourth and fifth leadership eras it became clear that a third function is foundational, which can co-exist with either of the two--that of *inspirational leadership*. Such a leadership function provides the values for why the organization exists and why it moves toward task. It motivates. The fourth leadership era, while validating the independence of the first two variables, showed that in fact most leaders are dominantly either a task leader or a relationship leader and not usually both. But either a task leader or a relationship leader can perform the inspirational functions. All three are needed for completion and satisfaction of leadership and followership. Jaffray was all his life primarily a task leader. He was not as relationally sensitive. This is one reason for some of his clashes with other missionaries. But he also was a strong inspirational leader. And it is with a strong focus on inspirational leadership that he closes on a triumphant note. Inspirational finishes in the midst of difficulty challenge all of us. He finished well. Task or Relational leaders vary greatly in leadership styles. See Clinton (1986) **Coming To Conclusions on Leadership Styles.**

[46]I am reminded of Watchman Nee, who also deliberately chose to stay just after World War II. He also was imprisoned. He died in prison after 20 years. While there are those who can choose to get out there are many who have no choice. The over 13,000 Christians that have come into existence in Indonesia could not. Jaffray chooses to stay with them. He will go through what they will go through. And he will model an inspirational leadership that will not be forgotten in the years to come. His story will be retold. Tomatala's dissertation and teaching at the Jaffray Seminary will keep this story alive.

Chapter 6. Robert Jaffray (1873-1945)

Third, he finished well in the midst of the most trying circumstances. The Japanese continued to advance on all fronts in the Far East. Hong Kong fell. Manila and the Philippines were taken. Singapore fell. Soon they invaded the Dutch East Indies. East Borneo fell on January 12, 1942. Tozer captured Jaffray's spirit at that time.

> The missionaries were caught in the middle of all this. With a heart for safety of his workers Jaffray immediately issued blanket permission for all who so desired to leave their post and proceed to the United States. A few fled the islands. Most of them stayed. Jaffray himself stayed with his workers. "I Cannot leave," he said, "while one missionary remains on the field." (1947:121)

Jaffray changed his seat of operation from Makassar to the mission rest house in Benteng Tinggi, Malino, some sixty miles away up toward the mountains.

The Japanese invaded Makassar on February 9, 1942. The got to Benteng Tinggi on March 13th (Tomatala 1990:188,189). They separated the men and women missionaries. The women were interned in Benteng Tinggi. The men were taken back to Makassar. For some reason (perhaps age?), Jaffray was permitted to stay with his family for almost a year. Finally he was separated from them and put into a different camp in Malino and finally to a camp in Pare-pare. As the pressure from the Allies mounted toward the end of the war, he was transferred to several other camps each more remote that the other. The rations were severely limited. He was an old man. He could not last long. The last person to have the privilege of seeing and talking to Jaffray at the end was F.R. Whetzel of the Batjan Immanuel Mission. About Jaffray he wrote.

> "One of the great blessing of my life was the privilege I had of being interned with Dr. Jaffray on the island of Celebes. I learned to love him as a great man of vision and faith." (Tozer 1947:126)

On July 29, 1945 just shortly before the war ended Jaffray heard his "Well done." He finished well.[47] His was a focused life that should inspire many Apostolic types.

Critical Incidents Identified, and/or Explained

Critical incidents are shaping activities which can affect values relating to all three types of formations--spiritual (leadership character), ministerial (leadership skills) and strategic (total direction in life and ministry). There is a sense in which many, many incidents in a leader's life affect values. But from that large identifiable number a few should be highlighted and recognized as very significant. Critical Incident 3, Can God Supply? Early Character Formation, and Critical Incident 11, A Second Career, **were the prime focal incidents** in Jaffray's life. Focal Incidents 1 (Conversion), 3 (Can God Supply?), 4 (Simpson--Mentor), 7 (Ai--Initial Difficulties), and 12 (Final Choice) were basically incidents imparting crucial focal values.

Critical incidents also frequently provide pivotal points for choices of roles, kind of ministry and locale. These focal factors provide strategic guidance. Focal Incidents 2 (Simpson Divine Contact), 5 (Apostolic Yearning), 6 (Assignment Asia), 8 (Field Leader),

---

[47] I had the privilege of hearing Rose Deibler's testimony about these prison years. She was the wife of C. Russell Deibler. Deibler was a friend and colleague of Jaffray who died in the prison camp just before Jaffray. Her testimony concerning Jaffray's testimony (for almost a year in the same camp) sparkles with godliness. His faith, his character, his response to the trying situation with the Japanese guards, all resonate with the fruit of the Spirit. We have used six characteristics to help assess a good finish. He receives high marks on all of them--10+ on Christ-likeness in character.

Chapter 6. Robert Jaffray (1873-1945)

9 (Ministry Insight--Alliance Press), 10 (Bible School Methodology), and 11 (New Field Opened, 2nd Career) all were important focal factors--shaping the strategic guidance.

Here is a list of critical incidents, some giving focal values and some providing strategic guidance, that I have so identified from the materials that were available to me. Table 6-2 indicates these. I number them for convenience of referencing.

Table 6-2 Listing Of Some Critical Incidents In Jaffray's Life

Incident(s) Name	Age	Formational Type Dealing With Basic Value/Thrust
1. Conversion (See page 232)	16	Spiritual--This incident, a focal value, brought Jaffray into a personal relationship with God. He will increasingly want to please God with his life.
2. Simpson--Divine Contact--Life Changing Decision (See page 225)	20	Spiritual/ Strategic--This focal factor also imbedded a value. Jaffray is challenged to serve as a missionary. That Christ should come first became a prime value. That he was to become a missionary would follow and was a major guidance factor.
3. Can God Supply? Early Character Formation (See page 225)	20-21	Spiritual/ Strategic. This incident provides both focal values and is a focal factor moving toward strategic guidance. Young Jaffray strengthens his integrity and learns to trust God.
4 Simpson--Imposing Mentor--Values Imparted (See page 233)	20-23	Spiritual/ Ministerial/ Strategic. This incident, a prolonged series of shaping activities, provided focal values and also imparted a methodology that Jaffray would use in his two major missionary efforts--the training of leaders via Bible institutes.
5. Apostolic Yearning (See page 234)	20-23	Strategic. This focal factor points Jaffray to pioneer breakthrough work. He will be involved in always expanding the work into new fields. Romans 15:20 becomes his heartbeat.
6. Assignment Asia Simpson sponsors. (See page 236)	23	Strategic. Jaffray had committed himself to the Christian and Missionary Alliance, especially A. B. Simpson's values and vision for world evangelism. He was assigned to Asia. His ordination on January 20, 1896 at Bethany Chapel was the formal sendoff. Simpson officiated. This is a focal factor. A missionary destiny hinges on this assignment.

Chapter 6. Robert Jaffray (1873-1945)   page 257

Table 6-2 Listing Of Some Critical Incidents In Jaffray's Life continued

Incident(s) Name	Age	Formational Type Dealing With Basic Value/Thrust
7. Ai--Initial Difficulties (See page 236,237)	24	Spiritual/ Ministerial/ Strategic. This focal incident brought values, and indirectly, long term guidance. Difficulty is often needed to take away self-confidence and to bring a deeper trust to God. So it happens with Jaffray. But he also learns that his methodology for evangelism will not be alone. He needs a breakthrough insight for opening a new region. He along with Robert Glover will next found a Bible College which takes initial labors of others and builds an evangelistic training center to send out indigenous peoples to reach their own.
8. Jaffray Emerges As Field Leader (See page 238)	38	Strategic--This focal factor moves Jaffray into a responsible decision making position. From here his influence will expand. He will be able to implement his Apostolic calling.
9. Ministry Insight-- Alliance Press (See page 239)	39	Ministerial, Strategic--This focal factor provides clarification of Jaffray's role, expands his influence, and provides a means of getting training materials for use in the Bible Schools. It also gives a platform for dissemination of ideas via **The Bible Magazine**.
10. Unique Methodology Honed--The Bible School comes of Age (See page 240)	40-45	Ministerial/ Strategic: This focal factor sharpens the focal issue, unique methodology which provides the evangelistic base and springboard for Apostolic expansion.
11. A Second Career/ Faith Challenge at Age 55, A Second Career Will You Pioneer a New Mission Field? (See page 243)	55	Strategic. Jaffray is strategically guided by this series of events in a focal factor which led him to the place and time of his most significant life contribution. This faith challenge was accepted by an older man, a tired man, against circumstances which did not encourage faith. But thank God, Jaffray responded and several hundred thousand in Indonesia today also say thank you.
12. Final Choice/ Decision To Stay/ WWII Breaks Out (See page 254)	68	Spiritual. This choice based on an important value leads Jaffray to internment in a Japanese Prison of War Camp. He will die in this camp. But he will model godliness. He finishes well.

Critical incident 3, Can God Supply? and Incident 11, A Second Career--Faith Challenge at Age 55, were the **prime focal incidents**. In the first, Jaffray passed an integrity check with flying colors. He had made a commitment to missions. He stood by it. God honored it. Fundamentally, he was sound in integrity. God had a leader with

Chapter 6. Robert Jaffray (1873-1945)

integrity.[48] In Incident 11, Jaffray accepts God's faith challenge to open a new field--something a young man with energy should do. But he more than makes up for energy in his spiritual maturity. The one big challenge to go in, leads to hundreds of little challenges along the way and finally the culminating challenge of his life--the testimony in the Japanese Concentration Camp.

Mission Values--Theological and Practical

Usually this section of material identifies the shaping of a leader in terms of spiritual formation (leadership character), ministerial formation (leadership skills) and strategic formation (the integration of values and direction in life toward achievement of God's life purposes). It identifies and labels values dealing with these three formational aspects. But since Jaffray is the only person of the eight chosen for this book who was a missionary I think it would be worthwhile to look at important values that under girded his theology of mission[49] and his philosophy of mission.[50] In addition, I want to expose his views of leadership, including leadership selection and training.[51]

Jaffray's Theological Basis for Mission[52]

Tomatala discusses 9 major ideas in analyzing Jaffray's theology of mission.

---

[48] Early on in the Scriptures, God tests a leader, King Saul, twice for integrity. Both times he fails. This is a Biblical model and warning to leaders. God can not use a leader, or will limit His use, of a leader who lacks integrity--that is, can not hold true to inner convictions. Early on God will shape leaders in terms of inner life and character. The basic tests are the *integrity check* (inner consistency), *word check* (ability to discern God speaking), *obedience check* (willingness to do what God wants), *faith check* (willingness to trust God for something), and *ministry task* (willingness to faithfully carry out an assignment). Two testing patterns can be observed with these tests. The *positive testing pattern*: God tests, the leader responds positively, God expands the leader in terms of potential, position, influence or the like. The *negative testing pattern*: God tests, the leader either can not discern or chooses not to respond positively to the test, God brings on remedial testing. When a leader has integrity, he can be trusted. Followers need this in leaders. Jaffray had it. See Clinton chapter 4, Transitional Processing (1989:123ff).

[49] I use the term theology of mission to refer specifically to Jaffray's understanding of the Bible regarding mission. I am looking at his views regarding God's whole program toward humankind. McGavran (the father of the church growth movement) defines mission as "God's program for man. Since God, as revealed in the Bible, has assigned the highest priority to bringing men into living relationship to Jesus Christ, we may define mission narrowly as an enterprise devoted to proclaiming the Good News of Jesus Christ, and to persuading men to become His disciples and dependable members of His Church." (McGavran 1987:23,26)

[50] *Ministry philosophy* refers to ideas, values, and principles whether implicit or explicit which a leader uses as guidelines for decision making, for exercising influence, and for evaluating his/her ministry (Clinton 1989:57). *Strategic formation* is the development and integration of that philosophy over a lifetime. Such an integration allows an articulation of that ministry philosophy to others.

[51] Of the eight leaders analyzed in this book, three (Simeon, Gordon, and Morgan) were senior pastors of large churches. But they directly led only a small number of people (church staffs and others voluntarily working for church). One, Brengle dominantly had a public ministry. In his convergent ministry he had essentially only one assistant under him. Mears was on staff and had a few staff reporting to her. Maxwell and McQuilkin had larger numbers of people for whom they were directly responsible to lead. Mears had a small number for whom she was directly responsible to lead. But Jaffray had large numbers of people whom he was directly responsible to lead. He had large resources for which he was responsible. He more than any other leader in this book must be studied for leadership influence of an organization. Though McQuilkin and Maxwell will also contribute to this understanding.

[52] These components of a theology of mission are adapted and abridged from Tomatala (1990:239ff). See Chapter VI. Theology of Mission.

Chapter 6. Robert Jaffray (1873-1945)

1. **Christ Centered Theology**
   Jaffray believed that missionary work was a continuation of the book of Acts, that is, the on-going work of the risen glorified Christ through the Spirit. The reign of Christ is the end result of mission. People are freed from bondage when Christ is Lord of their lives. Christ is the center of the Christian life. It is his redeeming work that saves. His resurrection provides the basis for victory in life. He intercedes for mission. He is the source of victory for doing missionary work. Christ's life, death, and resurrection provide the message that will deliver.

2. **Great Commission Mission**
   Jaffray saw mission rooted in both Old (e.g. Psalm 2:7) and New Testaments (Acts 1:8). He saw in the great commission first a promise. The Father has promised to give the Son the uttermost part of the earth. The Son asked based on the promise. The Father will answer. This means that unbelievers in the uttermost part of the earth, may potentially be reached for Christ based on this promise. In other words, the Great Commission is simply claiming Christ's inheritance in the far-flung reaches of the world. He saw secondly, a command. The Great Commission is a command to go to the uttermost parts-- the focus is the uttermost part.

3. **Two Analogies of Mission**
   Jaffray frequently talked of mission in terms of two analogies: deliverance, God's battle. He used the Exodus story as his analogy for deliverance. God sent Moses to demand of Pharaoh, "Let my people go." Israel was in bondage to Pharaoh. God empowered Moses to proclaim and deliver Israel to freedom to serve God. The process was inexorable though faced by obstacles. God's mission will ultimately prevail. As to battle, missionaries enter into battle. Their strength lies in the fact that the Lord is fighting on their behalf. The result, moreover, is already determined. We are on the winning side, because the Lord has won the battle for us. We need only to wait for His appointed time, and when it comes, we should act.

4. **World Evangelization**
   Jaffray viewed the whole Bible as the foundation for world evangelization. Evangelization involves going and residing among a people, preaching Christ to them, and establishing a church. The going is to the uttermost parts of the earth. Evangelism involves visiting the nations and taking out a people for His name.

5. **The Holy Spirit in Mission**
   The Holy Spirit is a living Spirit who empowers mission. He illuminates the heart of the Biblically illiterate so they can understand the Word of God. This same Spirit lives in the hearts of the believers through the living Word.

6. **Church Growth Multi-Individual Conversion**
   Jaffray believe that church growth is primarily the work of God. As the Word of God increases the church grows. When Christians are empowered by the living Word of God, they will multiply the Word and the church will grow.

7. Multi-Individual Conversion[53]
Peoples in tribal societies come to Christ as groups. There is a group decision to convert. Within a cohesive group all members may make the same decision. But it is the Holy Spirit working in individual hearts through the preaching of the Gospel that leads to the separate persons ratifying individually the group decision.

8. The Kingdom as a Mission Motive
Jaffray, along with Simpson, saw the proclamation of the Gospel of the Kingdom as hastening the coming of the Lord. The ultimate aim of mission is to have some from all nations, tribes, peoples singing the Redemption Song, the Song of the Lamb. To achieve this, the Gospel of the Kingdom must be preached to the ends of the earth. This will have the result of bringing about the Second Coming of the Lord Jesus. All missionary enterprise, therefore, should be done with this motive in mind--to bring back the King.

9. Power Encounter[54] and Healing Ministry
God's power must be demonstrated to make breakthroughs in peoples dominated by Satan's power. Jaffray believed in the intervention of God in healing supernaturally as well as other demonstrations of power. "We have come to feel strongly that we need such *signs and wonders* in the Name of the Lord Jesus to attest the Message of the Gospel." (Jaffray 1934b:7)

Jaffray's Philosophical Basis for Mission[55]

1. Lengthen and Strengthen (Isaiah 54:2-4)
God's people must be involved in two interlocking aspects of mission. They must be going to the ends of the earth to proclaim Jesus Christ the Savior. They must be nurturing and building up those who come to know Him in order that they too must be going and nurturing. Lengthening refers to the going. Strengthening refers to the nurturing. Jaffray sought to prepare leaders to assume responsibility for nurture and to ensure the continuity of God's mission which has been entrusted to the church. Jaffray believed that lengthening must be coupled with strengthening and vice versa if the church is to stand on its own and continue involvement in Christ's mission.

2. God's Direction and Blessing
The essential ingredient of leadership must be the powerful presence of God in the life and ministry of a missionary. Therefore, the crucial question is, "Is God in this?" The relationship of a discerning leader to God and God's will is crucial.

3. Personal Devotion
A leader must maintain a healthy devotional life, time spent with God. Time spent with God makes one more sensitive to God and to seeing his direction

---

[53] See McGavran (1987:340) for a technical and detailed discussion of *people movements* (multi-individual conversions).

[54] A *power encounter* is a technical term used in church growth theory. It refers to a special situation in which God intervenes in a supernatural manner to demonstrate more power than the forces of evil. The breakthrough even though happening in a human arena is clearly seen to be of God. People involved in such a demonstration then can choose to follow this God. Elijah on Mount Carmel against the prophets of Baal is the classic case of a Biblical power encounter.

[55] These principles have been condensed and adapted from Tomatala's (1990) Chapter 7.

Chapter 6. Robert Jaffray (1873-1945)

and blessing. Tomatala, quoting Smalley, describes his personal devotional life.

> He gave three hours to the Word and prayer daily, starting about 4:30 or 5:00 in the morning. Jaffray says "...after three hours in the word of God and waiting on Him before breakfast, I am ready for 101 duties of the day." (Smalley 1976:87).[56]

Tomatala goes on to say that Jaffray's devotional life also had a strong influence on national and missionaries who worked with him. Such modeling impacts lives.

4. **Harvest Theology**
   A missionary must sow to reap and to gather. Where the harvest is overwhelming God will provide the workers in answer to prayer.

5. **Evangelistic Priority**
   The evangelistic mandate must have priority over the social mandate. Social concern is a by-product of evangelistic results.

6. **Means And The Gospel**
   Innovations in missions which flow from modern science (inventions, breakthroughs in medicine, etc.) should be used to further effective communication of the Gospel.

7. **Mission Strategy**
   A missionary leader should have a basic strategy in approaching a given work in an area. Jaffray's included: 1. Evangelistic witnessing through preaching and other methodologies is prior. 2. Mobilize[57] all Christians to this evangelistic task. 3. Select strategic locations and place key missionaries there. 4. Concentrate workers where receptivity is greatest. 5. Establish indigenous churches as quickly as possible. 6. Train national workers and release them into ministry. 7. Publish materials widely for evangelization and training.

8. **Research and Mission**
   Strategies must be based on good information. Jaffray used survey trips to gather first hand materials.[58] These involved travel to potential key cities,

---

[56] I do not want to lay a legalistic guilt trip on leaders about studying the Bible. But I want to point out here how important the study of and use of the Bible was to Jaffray. Note the central role the Bible played in his life. Each of the leaders of this book studied the Bible regularly and deliberately all their lives. If this quote is true of Jaffray then Jaffray spent more than 5 years of Bible study over his lifetime in his devotions alone. This is in addition to special study for teaching and preaching. The Bible was important to him as it was to all these leaders selected. They studied it devotionally for their own lives. They studied it to exhort others. They studied it to know of God and His purposes and to teach them to others. This will not be true for all focused leaders. But all of the eight leaders chosen in this book were *word gifted* leaders. See Clinton and Clinton (1994) **Developing Leadership Giftedness**, where we develop the concept of word gifted, power gifted, and love gifted clusters of spiritual gifts. All eight leaders in this book had spiritual gifts as the *focal element* of their giftedness set and word gifts as the dominant spiritual gifts.
[57] Jaffray believed in holding conventions to lead Christians into the deeper Christian life and into the baptism of the Holy Spirit. He believed in leading them to seek for revival. He believed in informing them about missions. He believed in involving them in support of missions financially. He believed in challenging many to go. All of this was part of his mobilization (Tomatala 1990:281).
[58] Jaffray (1934:23) described it this way. "First, a lesson in geography, a study of the map, and the knowledge of the need. From this is begotten by the inward working of the Holy Spirit, an intense desire that new races should hear the Glad Tidings. Then comes prayer growing more and more intense, for nothing can be accomplished except through the mighty inward working of prayer, begotten by the Spirit of

Chapter 6. Robert Jaffray (1873-1945)

contacts made with many people, and initial attempts to pre-evangelize (he called these pioneer surveys-- "to spy out" the unreached lands). He utilized information from other's research.

9. **4 Step Total Evangelistic Method**
A missionary must be clear on an approach to evangelizing. Jaffray had a 4 step approach: 1. Establish contact. Find a bridge to open communication with the target audience. 2. Use proclamation evangelism as the prior methodology-- though presence evangelism may help the bridging process. Use any and/or all kinds of methodology for proclamation. Find what works. 3. Gather people responding into small groups and organize local congregations. 4. Nurture these local congregations and mobilize them for evangelistic outreach--including organizing mission structures.

Jaffray's Approach to Leadership Issues[59]

I will treat leadership selection and development, basic organizational ideas, and view of and use of authority. Jaffray had rather strong opinions and consistent practice in all these areas.

Leadership Selection And Training

Leadership selection involves the major leadership responsibility that leaders have for early recognition and facilitation of emerging leaders in their transition into leadership-- especially their early training. One of the seven major leadership lessons we have observed includes:

EFFECTIVE LEADERS VIEW LEADERSHIP SELECTION AND DEVELOPMENT AS A PRIORITY FUNCTION.

Jaffray, more so, than any other leader in this book highlights this lesson.[60]

Jaffray undertook the responsibility of recognizing and encouraging emerging leaders in every locale and people group he was involved with. Partially he was driven by his Apostolic gifting and convictions that mission was probably carried out best by indigenous peoples. Selection and training was a means to an end for him--the accomplishment of mission in the uttermost parts of the earth. In simple terms Jaffray saw the leadership selection and training process under three headings: call to leadership, leadership response, and leadership recruitment.

Jaffray believed that God **calls** leaders into ministry. Five major ideas undergirded this conviction.

1. God calls leaders. They will have convictions from Him that they are to be involved in ministry as leaders.

God. This followed by a trip of investigation, spying out the land as it were. And then, a report to praying friends, which increases the volume of prayer for these unreached islands."
[59] I am here condensing and adapting Tomatala's (1990:295ff) Chapter VIII, Leadership in Mission.
[60] Simeon manifests its heartbeat with his tremendous mentoring ministry but his actual training was minimal and not very sophisticated. His mentoring highlighted sponsoring more than training. McQuilkin and Maxwell were also involved in the training aspect but less so in selection. Mears was tremendously involved in selection but less so in training. Morgan was involved in training from a public ministry standpoint. Jaffray was involved in the whole process: selection, training, placement, on-going help.

Chapter 6. Robert Jaffray (1873-1945)

2. God sends those leaders He calls for training in ministry.
3. God sends leaders in answer to the prayer for harvest leaders.[61]
4. God wants leaders involved in the missionary task.
5. Training should thus be oriented toward the mission task.

Leaders who **respond** to God's call should have certain values. They must be concerned about the lost. They want to see them saved from an eternity without Christ. They must be especially concerned about the "other sheep," those yet unreached peoples. Finally, they must be motivated by the compassion that Christ demonstrated when he saw the masses.

While Jaffray held strongly to the fact that it is God who calls he saw that human instrumentality was involved in the process. Everywhere, in accordance with his mission as battle analogy, he recruited soldiers for the battle.[62]

Jaffray believed deeply in the power of the Bible School as a training methodology. He had been changed by that method. He established four different Bible Schools in four different areas of ministry for which he was responsible. He established them as soon as there was even a few to train. He trained both men and women for ministry. The thrust of training was nurture and mission. The training program always centered around preparation for mission. He used a formal classroom situation in combination with practical ministry experience. He also used non-formal methodologies in conjunction with Public Evangelistic Campaigns and mission conferences. He recognized the strengths and weaknesses of extraction methodology.[63] He knew that residential training was one of the fastest ways of bringing about fundamental change in a life. He knew that exposing these students to cross-cultural perspectives (many ethnic groups were represented at these Bible Schools) was in itself a preparation for mission. He sought to minimize the damage of extraction by using homogenous small groups on campus to reinforce their own cultural identities. In addition to the residential Bible Schools there were elementary Bible Schools being taught out of local churches. These were dominantly for edification of local Christians. But they sometimes functioned as part of the selection process. Most promising students could go on to residential Bible Schools.

Since Jaffray strongly viewed the end result of Bible School training as mission he mixed theoretical with practical.[64]

---

[61] Jaffray considered the Matthew 9:36-38 prayer mandate for leaders as essential to the process. "We ask God to supply the harvest/shepherd leaders needed for the great work before us."
[62] Jaffray (1936c:11) like to emphasize King Saul's recruiting view. "We too like King Saul are recruiting for the Army of the Lord. 'And when Saul saw any strong man, or any valiant man, he took him unto him." Jaffray was always on the look out for promising leaders. And he taught his leaders to be on the lookout also for emerging leaders. He was definitely involved in challenging potential emerging leaders.
[63] Jaffray used centralized residential training. That meant that students were *extracted* from their normal cultural setting and brought to this *artificial environment*. One of the complaints against his leadership in the 30s was about this point. Some missionaries believed that training should take place in the cultural location. Their experience was that leaders trained by extraction often did not want to go back. This is a valid objection.
[64] All four of Holland's components of balanced learning were part of Jaffray's schools. Spiritual formation was deliberate. Input was centered in the Bible and/or practical ministry. Input was directly related to ministry. Ministry taught basic lessons that became part of input. See Clinton (1984) **Leadership Training Models**, for Holland's two-track analogy for balanced training involving four components: input, formation, dynamic reflection, ministry experience.

Organization

For Jaffray organization was always a means to mission. Organization existed in order to accomplish this goal. But it was always subordinated to mission and could be altered in order to better accomplish mission. He was not overly concerned with sophisticated organizational structure. Like Morgan he believed that the structure should fit the task and grow out of it. The simpler it was the better it was. Jaffray believed in an indigenous church. He believed every church had the right to indigeneity from the beginning. He attempted to structure the organization of the church along the lines of the cultural patterns of organization. He felt that a Western style of organization and church constitution would not foster an indigenous ideal.[65]

Leadership Functions, Authority, and Its Use

Leadership theory has isolated three high level generic functions which are independent of each other. Leaders must **function to structure** their leadership to accomplish **task**. Leaders must create a **relational ambiance** so that followers can be supported emotional, relationally, and affirmatively in their tasks. That is, there must be created a **community** of relationships from which to carry on the task. And finally, leaders must **inspire**. They must bring hope. They must bring a sense of God's involvement. They must create a motivation toward vision. While these major concepts are independent of one another, that is, a given leader may operate in one, two, or three of them, it is usually the case that a leader is either dominantly a task oriented (structuring for task) leader, or a relationship oriented (creating the relational community working ambiance) leader. Either type can be inspirational. But usually task oriented leaders are more inspirational.

Jaffray was dominantly a task oriented leader. The mission was primary. People were secondary to this all important absorbing task. He was highly inspirational. He motivated people to the unfinished task of mission. Frequently, task oriented leaders are strongly authoritarian in their leadership style. This was the case with Jaffray. Today, such leaders are called strong leaders.[66] His power base came from several power resources including: legitimate (positional--field leader); personal (strong personality); competence (he was highly effective in accomplishing mission, methodology, etc.); persuasion (strong motivator) and spiritual authority (especially in the final ten years of his ministry (1931-1941).[67] Some of his clashes with strong leaders under him came because of his strong bias toward use of methods he had used in China without much give and take toward the opinions of upcoming leaders.

---

[65]We know his ideal views on indigeneity. However, we do not have clear examples of what the governmental structure of the national churches he established actually looked like.

[66]Apostolic types tend to be strong willed leaders. That is one of the reasons they get things done. But often it is at the expense of people. Apostolic leaders tend to use people rather than develop them. Or development is only in order to use them. Jaffray had this tendency. Fortunately most of his followers (leaders in their own right) agreed with him and saw his way as best.

[67]Three categories are used to describe leadership: influence, authority, power. I am using Dennis Wrong's (1980) power typology which sees influence as the highest generic level. Under influence comes power forms, under power forms comes various kinds of authority. Here the two higher level power forms are persuasion and authority. Under authority Jaffray uses legitimate (positional), personal (charismatic) and competent. Spiritual authority is a hybrid containing persuasion, personal, and competence. Technically, spiritual authority is the right to influence conferred upon a leader by followers because of their perceived spirituality in the leader (attributed because of a godly life, knowledge of and experience with God, and gifted power).

Chapter 6. Robert Jaffray (1873-1945)   page 265

Ministry Insights, Lessons, and General Values

Two ministry insights, both large in scope, dominated Jaffray's ministry.[68] In terms of the four focal issues, these insights became for him **unique methodologies** for accomplishing life purposes. The Bible School and the Alliance Press were integral to Jaffray's ministry.

The first of these ministry insights was the discovery of the Bible School methodology for training leaders and mobilizing them for mission. Many times Bible Schools become *ends* in themselves. Jaffray's apostolic bent kept the Bible School as a *means* for accomplishing mission. Jaffray had experienced first hand the effects of Bible School training under Simpson. He knew that rapid change can be brought about in young people in a short time with the proper mission oriented ambiance. The development of the national church in S. China and Indo-China and Indonesia were all products of a Bible School which was integrated with local churches and focusing on mission.[69]

The second of the ministry insights which dominated was the Alliance Press, Jaffray's publishing efforts. Training and evangelism needs materials. Jaffray took this challenge head on. His presses produced what was necessary to edify churches and to provide helps for evangelism. His Bible Magazines inspired, taught, and provided strategic perspective which focused on mission.

Simeon and Jaffray more than any of the other leaders in this book provide examples of the importance of **unique methodologies** as part of the focusing process. Simeon's unique methodology was the mentoring process. Jaffray's was the use of centralized Bible Schools and use of the print media.

Contributions

This chapter contributes to the general field of leadership development in the following ways:

1. It portrays an Apostolic gifted leader. His study and use of the Bible validates the perspective of different word gifted leaders relating differently to the study of the Bible. His convictions underlying his theology of mission and his philosophy of mission illustrate the notion of the Apostleship gift being a superstructural word gift.[70]

---

[68]Usually we think of a ministry insight in terms of a smaller item of some kind which helps us more effectively deliver our giftedness effectively. A Bible School is a huge conglomerate of many many smaller ministry insights. What was so powerful about Jaffray's connection with the Bible School was his use of it as a means solely focused on fostering mission. That was the ministry insight. Plenty of people have started Bible Schools. But few have used them to carry out such a powerful Apostolic ministry.
[69]As Bible Schools grow they become less effective in terms of prime ministry efforts like church planting, evangelism, and cross-cultural mission. When small, all four of Holland's components for balanced learning happen. As they grow the emphasis moves toward only the input (cognition). Ministry experience, dynamic reflection, and formation lose efficacy. Bible Schools are best when kept small and with a practical bent. Jaffray somehow always stayed within the bounds of Bible School activity. He kept them small enough that balanced learning took place. He always related them to the bigger picture of establishing churches in cultural contexts.
[70]See Clinton and Clinton (1994) **Developing Leadership Giftedness** for a detailed explanation of this notion. Briefly spiritual gifts in a can be categorized by major functions accomplished as a corporate body in terms of love gifts, power gifts, and word gifts. All eight of the leaders studied in this book were

Chapter 6. Robert Jaffray (1873-1945)

2. It presents a leader who accepted a challenge late in life and accomplished in that stage the crowing achievement of an already full life.[71]
3. It shows that a leader can have a very focused life without long tenure in a geographic locale. Jaffray actually ministered on locale in Indonesia 10 or 11 years. That is because his focus was in terms of a role which he continued and unique methodologies which he perfected to a single-minded life purpose--reaching the unreached. However, his long tenure in South China certainly conditioned him, cross-culturally for his time in Indonesia, even though it was relatively short.
4. It shows the importance of values, especially convictions, for narrowly focusing a life. Jaffray's Theology of Mission, his Philosophy of Mission, and his leadership selection and development values gave strong conviction to his undertaking mission effort.
5. It depicts a leader whose major ultimate contributions are dominantly apostolic in nature.
6. It shows the importance of a power position for bringing about change.[72]

What were Jaffray's contributions. We are interested in both specific/unique contributions and his ultimate contribution.

His ultimate contribution set, like his giftedness set, is dominated by his apostolic bent. His ultimate contribution set is one of the more tightly focused sets of all eight leaders in this book.

He was a **pioneer**. With Robert Glover he opened the Kwang-si province. He opened the whole Indo-China field. He established the work in Indonesian. He went into Dutch New Guinea. He oversaw the opening of Bali.

He was a **promoter**. He influenced a whole denomination toward missions. His influence along with Glover's did as much as anyone since Simpson for the cause of missions among the Alliance. He also moved entire fields toward mission.

He was a **founder**. At least 4 Bible Schools were started by Jaffray. He co-founded one mission organization. He initiated a number of Alliance Press Publishing Ministries.

---

word gifted leaders. That is, their spiritual gift-mixes were dominated by word gifts. All people dominated by word gifts will be much more deeply involved in the study of and use of the Scriptures than will be power gifted and love gifted people. But the extent and intensity to which the study of the Bible is a part of a word gifted person differs. Foundationally Word Gifted people (teaching, exhortation, prophecy--and combinations of these) will be involved deeply in the study of the Bible. Their main ministry is the explanation of the Bible. Superstructurally Word Gifted people (apostleship, evangelism, ruling, and pastoring) are less involved. Their ministry involves major thrusts other than the explanation of Biblical truth. But they must use the Bible as a basis for their ministry, being judged by it and motivated by it. Jaffray certainly illustrates this. Remote Word Gifted People (word of knowledge, word of wisdom, word of knowledge, faith, discernings of spirits) are even less involved with the study of the Bible. All must know the Scriptures of course. But they will interact with them with differing intensity and disciplines.

[71]Our western culture in general does not appreciate the contributions that older mature experienced people can give. The emphasis is on retiring early. Jaffray illustrates how important it is to be available to God for those final years of usefulness. Like Morgan his ministry was an Active Afterglow--really a continuation of convergent ministry.

[72]Simeon brought about change with a non-power role. His mentoring sponsorship skirted the power structure and implanted his change at the grass roots. He demonstrates that change can happen via change agents not in the top decision making positions. Jaffray, on the other hand, shows that power positions can also be greatly used to bring about change. His leadership took off after he was made field leader.

Chapter 6. Robert Jaffray (1873-1945)

He was a **stabilizer**. At a crucial moment he stepped into the Philippine's work and gave inspirational leadership to keep it going. But every work he was involved in grew. He recruited to his efforts. He brought in key people. He trained and released leaders. Works were always more productive and more stable after his presence. His stabilizing efforts did not include creating organizationally sophisticated structures. His stabilizing efforts primarily centered on focusing whole groups toward mission. During his crowning achievement in Indonesia he was coordinating three mission groups. He was Field Superintendent for the Christian and Missionary Alliance. He coordinated the Chinese Foreign Missionary Union and the World Wide Christian Courier. He stabilized all three of these groups around mission--reaching the unreached in the East Indies.

He was a **writer**. He produced a stream of training materials and evangelistic materials. He edited Bible Magazines in every field which he oversaw. He continually promoted mission in his writings including Apostolic vision for the unreached.

He was a **researcher**. His research primarily focused on the unreached. His survey trips and his studies of available information were for the purposes of getting a solid base upon which to strategize for mission.

The pictorial display of his ultimate contribution set is as follows.[73]

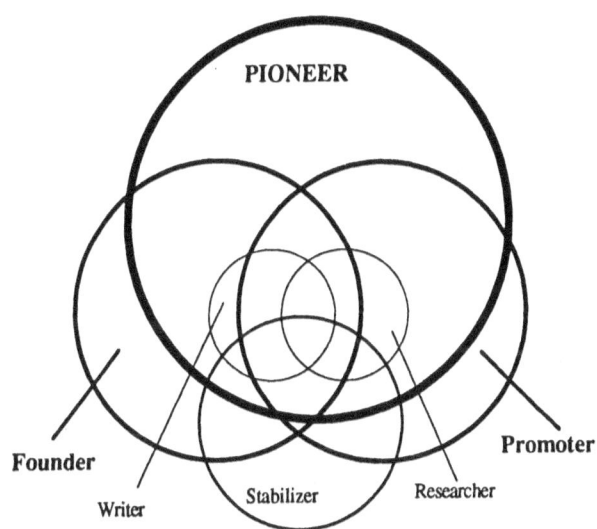

Jaffray's Specific Contributions

His contributions to the cause of Christ and the on-going of the Christian movement include at least the following:

---

[73]See Appendix F for an explanation of how to read a Venn Diagram.

Chapter 6. Robert Jaffray (1873-1945)

1. The establishment of three major fields of the Christian and Missionary Alliance: South China, Indo-China, and Indonesia. This means missionaries in there, people won to Christ, churches organized, leaders raised up, and these resulting churches mobilized for further mission.
2. The establishment of four Bible Schools for training and mobilizing indigenous workers into mission: South China (with Glover), Indo-China, Cambodia, Indonesia.
3. The establishment of three Printing ministries: South China, Indo-China, and Indonesia.
4. The modeling of an Apostolic ministry based on convictions. We are what we think. Jaffray saw among unreached persons those belonging to Christ. He wanted to reach them and set them free. And this he did.
5. The salvation of many. He was indirectly responsible for many 1000s not only coming to Christ but being responsible members of Churches who took the Great Commission seriously.
6. The modeling of a focused life with life purpose dominating, a major role with a fourfold thrust clearly identified and productive, two very effective unique methodologies--the Bible School and Printing Ministry, and solid ultimate contributions centered in his Apostolic gifting.
7. The steady output of ideation over 30+ years, some in books but the majority in his articles and editorials in the Bible Magazines he edited. He left behind written materials, generally of a contemporary nature, that focused on Apostolic ministry in East Asia. However, many of his editorials also pulsate with classic ideas underlying mission.
8. The modeling of achievement in old age. He responded to a faith challenge at 55 years of age and God blessed his mature years with great achievement.
9. The model of a life that finished well. Particularly does he exhibit the manifestation of a Christ-like life but also a life that proved his convictions.

Certainly, Jaffray is among those Cloud of Witnesses who are waving us on in the race.

Overall Lessons from the Life

In addition to the many lessons already given, I want to concentrate on five as I finalize the importance of Jaffray's ministry to us.

1. Holy Spirit Blessed Research

Jaffray used research as a stimulus for expanding. His apostolic drive kept him looking for unreached people. He studied maps. He obtained information from others. He made personal treks into locales of unreached people. He tried probing expeditions. He derived a basic methodology for entering an unreached people--including the spiritual dimension of it as well as the practical steps. His lesson to us stated **negatively**: IF WE DO NOT KNOW ANYTHING ABOUT PEOPLE WITHOUT CHRIST, WE ARE NOT LIKELY TO DO ANYTHING ABOUT THEM. **Positively**, IF WE KNOW ABOUT PEOPLE WITHOUT CHRIST AND WE ARE ENGAGED IN A CONSTANT EFFORT TO LEARN MORE ABOUT THEM, THE HOLY SPIRIT WILL EMPOWER IN CONVICTION, GUIDANCE, AND PROVISION TO REACH THEM.

Chapter 6. Robert Jaffray (1873-1945)

2. Means[74]

While Jaffray believed ultimately that God was in the work and doing the work, he never-the-less took advantage of every means, humanly speaking to carry out mission. He pragmatically identified successful evangelization methodologies--discarding those that didn't work and applying those that did ruthlessly. He used Printing Ministries and Bible School Ministries--honing them toward his purpose of Apostolic mission. He saw scientific advances as potential aids for his causes. In Moses' language, he answered the question, "What is that in your hand? Take it and use it." Jaffray did.

3. Dual Prime Focal Incidents

His two prime focal incidents almost demand attention.

The first solidified **character**. His integrity check, involving trusting God and denying compromise with his father's financial backing, set the tone for this man's life. He was a person who could live by convictions. No stronger leader in this regard is studied in this book. Character is primary. For we minister out of who we are and character is a major component of who we are.

The second affirms the notion of **always expecting God to accomplish better things for us and through us as we continue to grow in Christ**. We do not need to slacken off as we age. Perhaps we will slacken off physically as our energy diminishes. But we with Caleb and Jaffray can ask God for more mountains. The wisdom, experience, and giftedness of a lifetime can culminate in perhaps our richest experience and achievement for God. Jaffray accepted an overwhelming challenge at age 55 when circumstances, age, and physical condition would say, "Take it easy." Instead he persevered. A church was born among several unreached people groups. The path of the righteous is as a dawning light that grows brighter and brighter until noonday brightness. Jaffray shows that noonday brightness is much later in life than we think.

4. Attitude Is Everything

Tozer once intimated that the most important thing about a person is what he/she thinks about God. Jaffray was clear on what he thought about God and His purposes. His theology of mission was a prime motivating force. His philosophical bases for mission was formative and foundational and almost deterministic to how he operated. He knew what he believed. He acted upon it. It brought tremendous results. One element of a focused life is a life purpose that clarifies and becomes more specific as we grow in Christ and mature in ministry. A powerful motivating factor for life purpose is what we believe about God concerning it. Jaffray was clear. One does not have to agree with his convictions to admire and see that they brought results in his life.

5. Power Position for Bringing Change

Two leaders of the eight studied, Simeon and Jaffray were very successful change agents. Simeon brought change from a non-power position. Jaffray brought change from a power position. If gifted for it, positional authority can be a powerful means for bringing change. Too many leaders in positional power roles are not change agents. Many preserve the status quo. Jaffray demonstrates that a power position can be used to bring about very effective change.

---

[74] William Carey's great treatise was on this very thing, the use of means to promote and further missions.

Chapter 6. Robert Jaffray (1873-1945)

Implications for a Focused Life

What have we learned from this life that helps us understand a focused life? That is the question I attempt to answer in this section. When we study a focused life we are in fact looking for how God clarifies values and how God helps the leader identify a specific role, a life purpose, a unique methodology, and ultimate contributions. Below I comment on a number of focal screens (that is, potential indicators of a focused life) that can affect focus in a life. I weigh them relatively speaking in terms of their effect on Jaffray's life and ministry.

1. Giftedness Development

Without a doubt this is the most significant push toward Jaffray's focused life. We minister out of what we are. Along with character, giftedness strongly defines who we are. For Jaffray this was central. His giftedness set dominated his ministry. Without question, spiritual gifts are the focal element of the giftedness set. Apostleship dominates the gift-mix of spiritual gifts. Jaffray's apostleship gift dominated his life. His natural abilities (attitudes) synergistically fit this dominant gift. He used two acquired skills--use of materials and the Bible School to further contribute to his overall giftedness set. This is one of the tighter giftedness diagrams. This is a very focused life in terms of giftedness.[75]

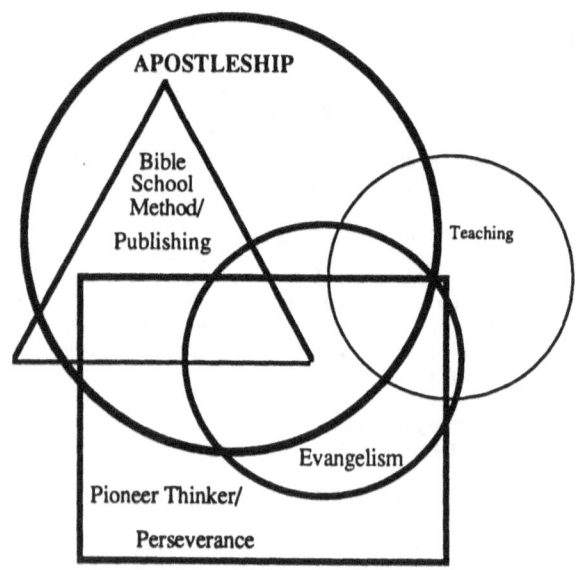

2. Destiny Processing

A number of destiny experiences, personal mystical experiences were crucial toward moving Jaffray into Indonesia (prayer burden, spiritual warfare, blood dream, and prayer challenge via the Old Woman). From the beginning he was also captured by God's

---

[75]See Appendix F for an explanation of how to read a giftedness Venn Diagram.

Chapter 6. Robert Jaffray (1873-1945) page 271

application of the Word to Moses, "Let My People Go." He did see himself as a person of destiny who would set many free. This focal screen, destiny processing, was important in Jaffray's life. All three stages of the destiny pattern, preparation, revelation, and fulfillment can be seen with concrete illustrations of each.

3. Identification of Key Ministry Insights

I have already mentioned the two most important ministry insights: the Bible School method for training and releasing indigenous leaders into mission; the use of the Printing Ministry. Both of these became for Jaffray unique methodologies. They were important to carry out his life purpose.

4. Identification Of Major Values That Uniquely Fit One's Ministry

The values flowing from his theology of mission were primary to his ministry. He based convictions and drew principles for use in ministry out of these values.

5. Integration Of Personality Factors So As To Identify A Focused Or Ideal Role That Moves Toward Convergence

Because of Jaffray's strong personality he needed a high power position from which he could make major decisions. If he had been a subordinate he would constantly have been frustrated and hampered in his drive for apostolic expansion. In the promotional blurb on the dust cover of the republished biography, **Let My People Go!** the Christian Publication's editor captures Jaffray so that we can sense the importance of his personality and the importance of a power position.

> Jaffray was a **missionary general** [emphasis mine]. His keen administrating, voluminous writing and incessant strategizing made him a natural leader.

6. Social Base Processing

Minnie Jaffray totally supported Jaffray in his multi-faceted job description. The release pattern (with some outside ministry, especially as Margaret got older) was ideally suited for Jaffray's heavy emphasis on ministry.

7. Ultimate Contribution Set

I have already commented on his ultimate contribution set. It should be restated here that his ultimate contribution set was very tight[76] and flowed from his apostolic gifting.

8. Ministry Philosophy Concepts

Jaffray had a relatively explicit ministry philosophy which he articulated in his Bible Magazines. This ministry philosophy had core values which were dominantly tied to his apostolic gifting. His ministry philosophy was the most clearly developed and articulated of the eight leaders studied.

---

[76]*Tight* means that the Venn diagram is compacted very closely with much overlap between items. That is, Jaffray's life time achievements were highly focused. All he was and did related to what he was to accomplish. His diagram is the most focused with Gordon and Mears a close second.

Chapter 6. Robert Jaffray (1873-1945) page 272

9. Future Perfect Time Paradigm

Jaffray's open letter to the missionaries just as the Japanese were advancing indicates his future perfect thinking. His teaching flowing out of "how beautiful are the feet on the mountains of them that publish good news," reveals a future perfect thinking though embryonic.

10. Boundary Processing Which Helped Focus

Jaffray's boundary lasting about six years and leading him from South China to Indonesia was a formative factor in the final focus of God's strategic guidance for him. I have previously analyzed this boundary in some detail in the running capsule, the biographical narrative.

11. Paradigm Shifts Which Helped Focus

Other than his conversion experience, no paradigm shifts seem to have played a significant part in focusing Jaffray.

SUMMARY ON FOCUSED LIFE INSIGHTS FROM JAFFRAY'S LIFE

Let me summarize what we have learned about a focused life from Jaffray.

A focused life is
- a life dedicated to exclusively carrying out God's unique purposes through it,
- by identifying the focal issues, that is, the **major role, life purpose, unique methodology,** or **ultimate contribution**,[77] which allows
- an **increasing prioritization** of life's activities around the focal issues, and
- results in a satisfying life of being and doing.

All four of the focal issues played an important part in Jaffray's life. The **major role**, had four thrusts: 1. Field Leader--a positional power role; 2. Publisher of Materials for training and evangelism and for stimulating vision; 3. Head of Bible School, a trainer; 4. Missionary Statesman--coordinated mission activities of several mission organizations and promoted the cause of missions all over East Asian and with impact on the whole Christian and Missionary Alliance. These roles were used to carry out a major **life purpose**, freeing many unreached people groups of South East Asia from the dominion of Satan and into the Kingdom of God under Christ's Lordship. His use of Bible Schools and the Printing Ministry were twin pronged powerful unique **methodologies**. Six of the **ultimate contribution** set fit him: Pioneer (dominant), Promoter, Founder, Stabilizer, Writer, and Researcher. All were related to the life purpose and supported it.

There was no natural order, that is, one focal issue developing first. Seeds of all of the focal issues were there early and developed along side of each other. But it was his appointment as field leader[78] that gelled the focal issues.

---

[77]These four--*major role, life purpose, unique methodology,* or *ultimate contribution*--are called the *focal issues*. Usually one or more of them dominates a focused life. A number of other factors (like giftedness, ministry insights, sense of destiny) contribute to the divine guidance which helps these leaders to prioritize life's activities around the focal issues. Both the identification of focal issues and the processes that prioritized them are given in the studies of the eight chosen for this book.

[78]Jaffray is an apt illustration that leaders are both born and made. Leaders are born means that leaders have inherent talent to lead. Jaffray both in natural abilities and especially giftedness had what it takes to lead.

Chapter 6. Robert Jaffray (1873-1945)   page 273

Closure--Lets Really Remember Robert Jaffray

Well, I have attempted to apply the Hebrews 13:7,8 leadership mandate.

> Remember your former leaders. Think back on how they lived and ministered. Imitate those **excellent qualities** you see in their lives. For Jesus Christ is the same today, as He was in the past and as He will be in the future. What He did for them He will do for you to inspire and enable your leadership.
> **Hebrews 13:7,8** (Personal Interpretive Paraphrase)

We have remembered Jaffray! But what challenges from his life do we take away for our own? Let me suggest two! First, notice his heartbeat in these two quotes.

> I have a deep burden for China's four hundred million souls. ...But the question that burns in my heart is, What about those in whose language there is as yet no Bible, no gospel text, not one messenger to tell them the Way f Life? And again he added, I am thinking of those parts of the world where no gospel light whatever has penetrated the awful darkness; places where Satan still holds absolute sway; places where no representative of the Lord Jesus has dared to go with the saving message of the Cross (Smalley 1976:21).

> I have tried to study the map of the World and learn where these unreached people are. I have to get in touch with the great students of World Missions, and learn from them. I have longed that an adequate "survey" of the world might be made to show us what still remains to be done ere He should say "It is enough" and come back to earth again (Jaffray 1990:163).

Jaffray had a heart to take the Gospel to all people groups of the world. He knew there would be some there that belong to Christ and would be delivered. He believed that if we learned about them and prayed about them, the Holy Spirit would burden and empower us to reach them. So challenge number 1. Would you be willing to ask God to give you a heart for mission, for seeing the Gospel go forth to the unreached peoples? If so, how would that kind of burden outwork itself in your personal situation? How could it affect your own church? your own denomination? Could I suggest the place to start, after such a surrender of heart, is with Patrick Johnstone's tremendous motivating book for mission, **Operation World--The Day-by-Day Guide To Praying For the World**. You'll want to get the latest edition. But at the time of the writing of this book, the fifth edition is out. This is 662 pages of motivational information. If Jaffray only had this! What would he do? Read this book! Use it as a prayer guide! Get groups together to pray using it! This is an excellent starting place.[79]

But he is also an apt illustration that leaders are made. That is, opportunities where leadership can excel must be a part of the context for a leader to make his mark. Jaffray existed in a time and place where there were tremendous opportunities that could make or break a leader. It seems clear that though potential leaders are born (there is inherent leadership talent there), effective leaders are made as a result of, 1) opportunity, 2) training and 3) experience. These three components do not automatically guarantee that one will rise to become a great leader. But without them it is not likely that one will realize maximum potential.

[79] If you are interested in going further I suggest you contact Caleb Project, a missionary organization that exists just to help mobilize people into mission, especially to reach unreached people groups. Just write Caleb Project, 10 West Dry Creek Circle, Littleton, Colorado 80120. Today we stand at a time in history when there are windows of opportunity open that have never before been there. And more to come!

Chapter 6. Robert Jaffray (1873-1945)

The second challenge is for older leaders. At age 55 Jaffray accepted a faith challenge. He went into a new field, opened a new work, and saw more of his life purpose realized in 13 years than in the previous 31 years (though he had seen good results). When he died in 1945 there were about 13,000 Christians in Indonesia among a number of different people groups associated with Christian and Missionary Alliance Churches. In 1990 at the time of Tomatala's dissertation, the long term results of Jaffray's work includes 496,935 members of Churches related to the Christian and Missionary Alliance. There are 1,604 organized churches. And there are 2,212 national ministers. What if he hadn't gone in? What if he had considered himself too old? But he did not. He went in. He commanded, "Let My People Go!" And today 1000s are thankful. As an older leader what are you looking forward to. Could I suggest that it might be or ought to be, "**My most lasting achievement may happen in the next few years of my life.**" That would certainly be a challenge Jaffray would want to leave with us.

Where To Go and What To Do For Further Study

Fortunately, Christian Publications (the Christian and Missionary Alliance Publishing Arm in Camp Hill, Pennsylvania) has just republished Tozer's 1947 work on Jaffray's life. It is available in bookstores or can be ordered directly from them. Buy one. Then here is what I suggest you do.

1. Read carefully again my chapter on Jaffray to refresh these ideas I have been discussing.
2. Note carefully the diagrams giving Jaffray's giftedness set (page 260) and his ultimate contribution set (page 257).
3. Read through the section on his Theology of Mission, Ministry Philosophy, and Leadership.
4. With these ideas before you read Tozer's biography and note carefully indications of giftedness, ultimate contribution, and values from his theology of mission, ministry philosophy, and leadership. Mark down in the margins notes indicating these items. You will find that if you read with a purpose, that is, to identify these items, your reading will be much more productive.
5. Ask God to impress upon your heart the challenges He has for you in Jaffray's life.

I have listed below the dissertation of my good friend Yopi Tomatala. I realize that it is only available to those in seminary libraries with inter library loan. But I felt I had to list it, even thought it is so inaccessible, because it has been such a help to me.

Tomatala, Yakob Yonas
    1990   **The Dynamic Missionary Leadership of Robert Alexander Jaffray.** Doctoral dissertation. Pasadena: School of World Mission, Fuller Theological Seminary.

Tozer, A. W.
    1947   **Let My People Go: The Life of Robert A. Jaffray.** Harrisburg: Christian Publications.

Chapter 6. Robert Jaffray (1873-1945)

ATTITUDE INGRAINED	EAST ASIA	CONVERGENCE--EXPANSION IN MATURE YEARS
1873 — 1889 — 1893 — 1896	1896 — 1911 — 1928 — 1931	1931 — 1941 — 1945
December 16, 1873		July 29, 1945
Age: 24		58 / 71

ATTITUDE INGRAINED (1873-1896)
- A. Family/Pioneer Spirit (1873-1889)
- B. Conversion Lifelong Attitude Assumed (1889-1893)
- C. Early Ministry Values Imbibed (1893-1896)

EAST ASIA (1896-1931)
- A. South China Early Missionary Lessons (1896-1911)
- B. Indo China Expansion Lessons (1911-1928)
- C. Boundary To Major Achievement Dutch East Indies (1928-1931)

CONVERGENCE--EXPANSION IN MATURE YEARS (1931-1945)
- A. Moving--Expanding To Indonesia and Beyond (1931-1942)
- B. Last Years--Suffering Victoriously (1942-1945)

Toronto, Canada → Nyack, New York → Tung-Un, S. China / Wuchow, S. China → Makassar, Indonesia / Philippines

General Role
  Role Clarifies
    Life Purpose generalized   Becomes Specific to an area
      Unique Methodology Observed
        Unique Methodology begun
          Unique Methodology Matures
            Writing Ultimate Contribution Begun

C1 Conversion--Miss Annie Gowans
C2 Simpson--Divine Encounter--Total Surrender
C3 Can God Supply?
C4 Simpson Mentors
C5 Apostolic Yearning
C6 Assignment Asia
C7 Jaffray's Ai
C8 Jaffray Emerges As Field Leader
C9 Alliance Press
C10 Unique Methodology Honed
C11 Second Career
C12 Final Choice

page 275

Robert C. McQuilkin
(1886-1952)

"Young people, believe that there is Victory in Christ! It is real! It can be life changing forever! Accept his provision and be free from your past to walk moment-by-moment with this Victorious Savior."

Chapter 7. Robert C. McQuilkin (1886-1952) A Life Dominated By A Two-Fold Life Purpose

Remember your former leaders. Think back on how they lived and ministered. Imitate those **excellent qualities** you see in their lives. For Jesus Christ is the same today, as He was in the past and as He will be in the future. What He did for them He will do for you to inspire and enable your leadership.
Hebrews 13:7,8 (Personal Interpretive Paraphrase)

Let's remember Robert C. McQuilkin who was instrumental in founding a Bible College. That school has sent 1000s on the mission field and even more into a future, whether full-time Christian ministry or other vocation, knowing the Victorious Life founded in Christ. McQuilkin modeled a victorious life.[1] He desired to know Christ and make Him known throughout the world. He wanted a center of influence for this great *Victorious Life Message*. Columbia Bible College, now Columbia International University, continues this two fold thrust, taking the *Victorious Life Message* to the whole world.

Opening Illustration 1.[2]
August 15, 1911
Charles Trumbull, Divine Contact,[3] **Life Giving Message**

Age 25 (Romans 6:6,11; 8:2)

The following is the prime *Critical Incident* in Robert C. McQuilkin's life. It represents a paradigm shift[4] of McQuilkin's view of the Christian life. It forever altered

---

[1] The title of his biography taken from the American Standard Version of 2 Corinthians 2:14 captures Robert C. McQuilkin's heartbeat, to be led **Always in Triumph**. The victorious life is known by several names among which are the *deeper life* (Keswick term), the *exchanged life* (Hudson Taylor), the *normal Christian life* (Watchman Nee) and *Union Life* (the present day movement centered in the Wheaton area and headed by Bill Volkman, P.O. Box 2877, Glen Ellyn, IL 60138). It is not a life free from sin, that is, a perfect life, but a life free to walk above the controlling authority of sin; a life demonstrating that sin does not have to dominate a life. It is a life progressively demonstrating the fruit of the Spirit as God shapes it toward the image of Christ. But at any given moment in the process, though not a perfect life, it is an abundant life vibrant with the person of Christ uniquely manifested in union with the person. See reprint of Robert C. McQuilkin's **Joy and Victory** and **Victory in Christ** for McQuilkin's ideas.
[2] This introduces critical incident 6, the prime incident of McQuilkin's life. Remember, a *critical incident* is a time of shaping by God which either instills a major value in a life or gives strategic guidance to that life toward the focal issues. See page 319 for the whole list of critical incidents.
[3] Charles Trumbull was a *divine contact* for McQuilkin. *Divine Contacts* (Clinton 1989:260) are special kinds of mentors. They intervene in the life of a mentoree at a timely moment to provide linkage to resources or affirm some plan of action or reinforce some touch on the life by God. The timeliness of the intervention, as well as the actual function done, validates the person as divinely sent, that is, a divine contact or means of contact with God's divine intention. Trumbull challenges McQuilkin with the message of the Victorious Life. It is timely. It is given in a way that the rational and logical McQuilkin will grasp and use. Divine Contacts often intertwine in lives. Trumbull will re-enter McQuilkin's life shortly and provide the base of training he will need to go deeper in the Victorious Message and to organize a ministry to reproduce it in the lives of others.
[4] This kind of experience is typical of a number of like *paradigm shifts* (See Clinton position paper, 1993, *The Paradigm Shift--God's Means of Opening New Vistas for Leaders*). This experience is a power gate which functions to open the participant to a new level of awareness of God's power in the life. Two kinds of *power gates* are typically described: *life power* and *gifted power*. This is a *life power* type. The participant wants power from God to live a righteous life. The Keswick *power gate* which is a surrender/

Chapter 7. Robert C. McQuilkin (1886-1952)

who he was, what he taught, and his life purpose. This incident primarily deals with a focal value. But a grasp of this focal value will eventually give McQuilkin's strategic direction for life as well. I am going quote at length from his testimony and his biographer since this is such a crucial incident in McQuilkin's life. I also suspect some of my readers may need this very paradigm shift for their own lives.

> Bob McQuilkin came enthusiastically down the aisle that August morning for the Institute period at New Wilmington Missionary Conference. Finding a seat near the front, he took out his little black notebook. Charles Trumbull, the honored editor of *The Sunday School Times*, was to be the speaker and he would get some good suggestions for his own Sunday school teaching, as Mr. Trumbull spoke on methods in Sunday school work.
>
> But Bob's little black notebook was soon put away for Charles Trumbull had departed from his assigned topic. And the words that were spoken that morning were written instead on his heart. Bob listened with the intensity of interest which was characteristic of him--body forward, face lifted.
>
> The testimony of defeat in his own life with which Mr. Trumbull began was what attracted the young conference delegate's attention. Why, the testimony could have been his own! He, too, had been a Christian for many years. He, too, had been active in the Lord's work. He, too, had longed after something which he did not have in his Christian life.
>
> After a brief explanation as to why he felt led to give this message, Mr. Trumbull began: "I think I am correct when I say that I have known more than most men know about failure, about betrayals, and dishonorings of Christ, about disobedience to heavenly visions, about conscious falling short of that which I saw other men attaining, and which I knew Christ was expecting of me. Not a great while ago I should have had to stop just there, and only say I hoped that some day I would be led out of all that into something better. If you had asked me how, I would have had to say I did not know. But, thanks be to His longsuffering patience and infinite love and mercy, I do not have to stop there, but I can go on to speak of something more than a miserable story of personal failure and disappointment.
>
> Mr. Trumbull in his clear logical way went on to describe the three conscious needs he had: "There were great fluctuations in my spiritual life, in my conscious closeness of fellowship with God. Sometimes I would be on the heights spiritually; sometimes I would be in the depths. A strong, arousing convention, a stirring, searching address from some consecrated, victorious Christian leader of men; a searching Spirit-filled book, or the obligation to do a difficult piece of Christian service myself, with the preparation in prayer that it involved, would lift me up; and I would stay up--for a while--and God would seem very close and my spiritual life deep. But it wouldn't last. Sometimes by some single failure before temptation, sometimes by a gradual downhill process, my best experiences would be lost, and I would find myself back on the lower levels...."
>
> "Another conscious lack of my life was in the matter of failure before besetting sins. I was not fighting a winning fight in some lines. Yet if Christ was not equal to a winning fight, what were my Christian beliefs and professions good for? I did not look for perfection. But I did believe that I could be enabled to win in a certain directions habitually, yes, always, instead of uncertainly and interruptedly, the victories interspersed

---

faith appropriation one, is one of several power gates including the entire sanctification paradigm and later the Pentecostal Experience, the Baptism of the Holy Ghost. All essentially do the same function--open the way to new experience with God. None guarantee an on-going successful ministry. They are simply gates that open the way for a new relationship with God. Here with McQuilkin we will see the Keswick type power gate. So it is also with Maxwell and somewhat with Gordon. Brengle's *power gate* experience is an entire sanctification paradigm. Jaffray, somewhat like Brengle manifests a modified form of the entire sanctification paradigm. The *gifted power gate* experience is similar except that its participant is seeking for power in ministry. Finney's, Moody's and Torrey's experiences are of this type.

Chapter 7. Robert C. McQuilkin (1886-1952)

with crushing and humiliating defeats. Yet I had prayed, oh, so earnestly, for deliverance; and the habitual deliverance had not come."

"A third conscious lack was in the matter of dynamic, convincing, spiritual power that would work miracle changes in other men's lives. I was doing a lot of Christian work--had been at it ever since I was a boy of fifteen. I was going through the motions--oh, yes. So can anybody. I was even doing personal work--the hardest kind of all; talking with people, one by one about giving themselves to my Saviour! But I wasn't seeing results."

Mr. Trumbull went on to say that as he read and heard various messages he came to believe that there was a different kind of Christian life than the one which he had been leading. He continued.

"Some months later I was in Edinburgh, attending the World Missionary Conference, and I saw that one whose writings had helped me greatly was to speak to men Sunday afternoon on 'The Resources of the Christian Life.' I went eagerly to hear him. I expected him to give us a series of definite things that we could do to strengthen our Christian life; and I knew I needed them. But his opening words showed me my mistake, while they made my heart leap with a new joy. What he said was something like this: *'The resources of the Christian life, my friends, are just--Jesus Christ.'* That was all. But that was enough. I hadn't grasped it yet, but it was what all these men had been trying to tell me....' "

But he did grasp it--less than two months later while attending the New Wilmington Missionary Conference.[5] Alone in his room after hearing a missionary bishop from India speak on the Water of Life, he had it out with God and rose from his knees with a "new Christ."

After presenting the teaching of the New Testament on union with Christ and explaining how the three needs of his life had been met, Mr. Trumbull concluded by giving two simple conditions for such an experience.

"Surrender absolutely and unconditionally to Christ as Master of all that we are and all that we have, telling God that we are now ready to have His whole will done in our entire life, no matter what the cost."

"Believe that God has set us wholly free from the law of sin (Romans 8:2) not *will* do this, but *has* done it. Upon this second step, the quiet act of faith, all now depends." (M. McQuilkin 1956:54-57)

The timing is perfect. McQuilkin is ready for this message. He identifies completely with Trumbull's words. Notice his reaction.

> As I listened to this testimony, something happened. My own problem was not solved. I did not see the full significance of all that the speaker had said about surrender and faith. But one thing I did see which was an entirely new thing for me. The thought came, 'God is no respecter of persons! What He has done for that man, He desires to do for me!' There sprang up a hope, and more than a hope--a definite expectation, that the desire of my heart would be satisfied in an utterly new experience of Christ.
>
> As quickly as possible I sought out Mr. Trumbull and had an interview with him. It was a blessing to hear him talk over the problems very quietly and pray in definite requests. But I did not enter into any new experience. Two or three days passed, and one evening I met Mr. Trumbull in the hall. He asked me if I was satisfied, and I told him, no. He suggested that we go into the prayer-room and pray together. As we walked through the hallway, there came to me this distinct impression--perhaps it was a prayer: "I am going into that room, and I do not want to come out before this matter is

---

[5]This is a relatively new experience for Charles Trumbull. The Edinburgh Conference was in 1910. It was the summer conference of that year that he entered into this experience. So he has operated in this paradigm for about a year when he gives this talk that McQuilkin hears. But there is a difference. Trumbull is an older much more experienced Christian worker. McQuilkin is a relatively young inexperienced Christian worker--in the early stages of his leadership transition. In the flush of something new, often there is great power in one's testimony. So it was in this case with Trumbull.

Chapter 7.   Robert C. McQuilkin (1886-1952)

settled, and I have take Christ as my Victory for daily living as well as my Saviour." [6]
As I went into that prayer-room there were three definite facts in my mind. First, there was the great need in my life. I was a defeated Christian. I had need for this life of constant fellowship, of supernatural victory over sin, of definite fruit-bearing and answered prayer. The second fact was that since I had taken Christ as my Saviour, the Lord was living in my heart to meet all these needs. The third fact was that on my part I was to surrender completely to him, and to trust him to supply every need.

We went into the room and kneeled down. My new friend prayed. I then prayed. But it was a different prayer from any I recall praying before. It was to be an expression of a definite transaction that would make things completely different in my life. I began definitely to do the two things I was supposed to do. First, I was to surrender, then to believe. (R. C. McQuilkin n.d.:12-15)

Now notice how methodically and logically McQuilkin proceeds to do these two things.

"From one standpoint, I would have been counted a surrendered Christian. I had offered my life to go as a missionary. Had anyone asked whether I wanted the whole will of God in my life, I should without hesitation have answered, yes, but on that day it was on my heart to make the matter a definite thing. In my prayer I expressed my surrender in a logical way. First, I told the Lord I surrendered all my sins. Second, I told the Lord I wanted to surrender the doubtful things in my life. There were some things that I did not call sins. If I called them sins, they must be given up. Now I wanted to give God the benefit of the doubt, and yielded these things to Him...."

"After surrendering the doubtful things, I surrendered the things that I counted good things, along with my life plans. I was looking forward to going to the mission field, and I yielded this to the Lord in case it should be His will for me to remain at home. I yielded to the Lord my doubts concerning this and that part of the Old Testament. I recognized what a flimsy basis such doubts had as over against the overwhelming testimony to the Bible as the Word of God."

"Then I told the Lord I surrendered my loved ones to Him. His most precious gift to me at that time was the love of a young woman to whom I was engaged. It was a real transaction when I faced the question and I told the Lord I would bow to His will in case He should want her love taken out of my life..." (M. McQuilkin 1956:57-58)

Now comes a mystical interaction.[7]

"When I had reached this point in my prayer, a question came into my mind that seemed almost like an audible voice: 'Now wait a moment. Do you think that with all those past failures in your life, with all the neglected opportunities, you can in just a moment enter into this joy and peace and victory that you have seen in other lives?' Another voice seemed to say, 'You are making a surrender. Had you not better surrender the past to the Lord?' "

"There was no emotion about this prayer, as I recall it. It all seemed like a definite business transaction. But there was a quiet sense of reality in the definite surrender of the past that I made to the Lord. I realized anew that because Christ had died and put away my sins, I could turn all the past sins and failures over to Him. I realized that He could restore the years that the locust had eaten."

"Almost immediately there came another question, as though from an outside person: 'Now do not get excited. You are here in this missionary conference. Everyone is interested in spiritual things. It is one thing to make a surrender like this now. But

---

[6] Sensitive charismatics today would recognize this as a revelatory word from God. In my terminology it is the Divine Initiative in prayer. It is the affirmation behind 1 John 5:14,15. He can pray with assurance because he is being led into prayer by the Holy Spirit.

[7] Modern charismatics would have no problem in seeing what was happening. There is revelatory information, according to their view, that is involved in this vignette. There is also interplay with the tempter or a minion. In their view, this is a supernatural experience.

Chapter 7. Robert C. McQuilkin (1886-1952)

> wait until you get back to your home. (We had tremendous problems in our home.) Wait until you get back to that church. Wait until you get back to that business office. You better wait and see how this works out before making any definite decisions to thank Christ for victory before you have tried it out to see whether the thing will work.' "
>
> "There came the answer; 'You are making a surrender. Had you not better surrender the future to the Lord?' "
>
> "It took but a few moments to pray this prayer of surrender. When I finished that part of the prayer, I had no special emotion, and I saw no vision. But it did seem to me, for the first time consciously in my life, there were just two persons in the universe-- my Lord and I, and nothing else mattered except the will of that other Person....For the firs time it seemed that there was nothing between my Lord and me." (M. McQuilkin 1956:58-59)

McQuilkin has completed the first part of the two step procedure. He has prepared himself before God. Now comes the more difficult part, accepting His provision and really believing it. "The just shall live by *faith,*" has always been true but never more true than when appropriating the provision of Union Life. McQuilkin describes it beautifully with his boat illustration. That is, a picture flashed in his mind--a living analogy, in charismatic terms a word picture. For him it was a word from the Lord, a faith challenge.

> However, I had in mind that this was just the first part of what I was to do. Since I was yielded to Christ, and He had accepted me, my part now was to thank Him that He was living in my heart, and that He was now meeting all my need. Not, He would meet every need, but He *was* meeting every need. Again, I saw no vision, and I had no special emotion. But it seemed to me that I was standing on the shore looking out on a measureless ocean that represented the boundless grace of God. There was a boat. I had one foot in the boat. The question was, would I put both feet into the boat? That is, would I thank God apart from all feelings, and upon the basis of His Word, that His grace is sufficient, that Christ is actually living in my heart, and that He is meeting all these needs? I took God at His Word and thanked Him. I put both feet into the boat. When we rose, I went out from that room with no special emotion,[8] but with a clear conviction that there was a new attitude in my life. Something had happened. I had made a decision. (R.C. McQuilkin n.d.:19)

Marguerite McQuilkin, his biographer, alluding to John 7:37-39, goes on to say, "Bob had sunk a well of his own. And for more than forty years the life-giving Spirit whom he had found flowed through him in rivers of refreshing water to those around him." (M. McQuilkin 1956:61) This paradigm shift is typical of one kind of power gate that leaders need to enter to have a ministry which essentially flows out of being. McQuilkin enters this power gate. He emerges on the other side with a new source of power for the Christian, *just Jesus Christ.*[9]

---

[8] Several times in the illustration, McQuilkin, in telling the story in retrospect, has been very careful to show that it was not an emotional experience. Several things are involved here. McQuilkin is careful to avoid taint of any kind of Pentecostal or charismatic emotional experience. He is also stressing the notion of faith in an objective Word of God--a deeper life approach to the power gate. Another thing that the illustration brings out is how God meets a person where they are. McQuilkin is logical, rational, and non-emotional. God meets him in the way that will appeal to him and draw him on into the experience. My own union life experience at a Columbia Bible College retreat on the Toccoa Falls College campus was very similar to McQuilkin's experience.

[9] Perhaps a summary is important at this point. *Power gates* are experiences with God which open a leader up to a new level of relationship with God and thus to available power for life or ministry. They do not guarantee anything for the long run. But they are a new beginning point which forms an anchor as the leader goes on to experience new power. There are two power gates, generally. The first, *life power,* is a paradigm shift with regard to power to live a holy life, a life demonstrating more fully the fruit of the Spirit. There is a pattern: Need + Surrender + Appropriation by Faith +or- a validating experience. Both the entire sanctification experience and the Keswick experience follow this pattern though the entire

Chapter 7. Robert C. McQuilkin (1886-1952)

Opening Illustration 2.
Clear Guidance--The Ship Sinks
Age 31, 32 (Psalm 27:11)

Mr. Sells, one of my Bible teachers during my first year at Columbia Bible College graduate school used to say with emphasis, "Students, God's guidance is clear guidance!"[10] And so it was with Bob and Margeurite McQuilkin who had committed themselves to the mission field. They had joined African Inland Mission. Mrs. McQuilkin was to arrive in New York city the next day. Mr. McQuilkin was already there when it happened. Lets pick up M. McQuilkin's story. The year is 1917.

It was a full year after they had been accepted by the mission that their sailing date was set. Passage was booked on the *City of Lahore*, sailing Saturday, November 30, from New York. On November 11, the glad news of the Armistice was announced, which seemed an added seal to their plans. The Princeton Conference had given its generous missionary offering to help send them forth, and so definite were their plans that the published account of the Princeton Conference spoke of the Robert McQuilkins "now serving in East Africa."

Equipment was bought and packed and shipped to New York and Mr. McQuilkin went up on November 26 to complete passport and customs arrangements. Back in Philadelphia at the second United Presbyterian Church on Race Street he gave a testimony. One who was there that night, the Reverend W. K. Rouse, recalled the incident: "A slender young man sat under the balcony in the extreme southwest corner of the church. Testimonies were being given and he arose and...after praising the Lord for what He had done for him, spoke of how the Lord had restored his wife's health and how she had been passed by the doctor and given permission to go to Africa. He had just returned from New York City and had been on board the boat, the *City of Lahore*, on which they were to sail for Africa. He told with beaming face of how he had been in the state room they were to occupy and was rejoicing in what God had done for them."

The next morning as he crossed the city on a streetcar Mr. McQuilkin glanced casually at the newspaper of a seatmate. Suddenly the headlines came alive: "*City of Lahore* sinks in Harbor!" It could not be true, but there it was. The boat had caught fire and in an effort to keep the fire from spreading to the pier and other vessels, it had been sunk.

As far as they knew their earthly possession were gone, along with their carefully laid plans. But Mrs. McQuilkin said that when her husband called her with the news, there came to her a sense of sudden joy as she realized the utter worthlessness of things. Things did not matter when they had the same faithful unchanging Lord. As it turned out, their things were not lost but were still on the dock, but they learned of this later.

---

sanctification will be filled with emotional validation while the Keswick is non-emotional with a focus of faith not feelings. The other general category of *power gate* is the *gifted power gate*. It is a seeking for power in ministry. Public rhetoricians, for example, usually need this. The pattern for this is: Need +or- Surrender+ Unusual Validating Experience + appropriating faith. The symbol +or- means it may or may not be there. McQuilkin's experience was essentially a *life power* experience which ramified to *gifted power*. Brengle's was the same--though he saw the experience in retrospect as a *gifted power* experience as well and taught it that way. See Edman, **They Found The Secret**, for illustrations of both.

[10]However, Mr. Sells would explain further. When you are in the midst of it, it may not look so clear. But in looking back in retrospect, you can see it was clear guidance. This is a frustrating bit of perspective. But it does **bring assurance**. Often he would close by praying from Psalm 27:11, Teach us thy way O Lord, *and lead us in a plain path*. (Meaning go before us and prepare the way). This assurance is manifested beautifully in McQuilkin's life with this incident and the two years of frustration as they wait to go.

Chapter 7. Robert C. McQuilkin (1886-1952)

> Thanksgiving Day that year was one of unusual significance. To them it was a day to give thanks to the Lord who orders both steps and stops and although they did not know it, the sinking of the ship was to be a turning point in their lives. (M. McQuilkin 1956:89,90).

God is looking for a willing heart that He can strategically guide. He found two in the McQuilkins.

The Time-Line

See the time-line at the end of this chapter for a one page overview of McQuilkin's life with critical incidents and other focal issue information. Notice that there are three time periods lasting 25 years, 10 years and 31 years. Dr. McQuilkin died at age 66, otherwise there would have been most certainly a long Active Afterglow period.[11]

McQuilkin was brought into the church at the age of 9 and made a leadership committal when he joined the church at 12. He was active in young people's ministries. He was further stimulated to grow at summer conferences. Because of needs in the family he forewent matriculation at the University of Pennsylvania (on a scholarship) and instead worked for Steele and Sons, a building construction company. At age 25 at a summer conference his life was transformed by the *Victorious Life Message*. He then went into full time ministry working for *The Sunday School Times* for a period of about 5 years. From there he started toward the mission field but was providentially blocked. The door was opened for him to become the head of a new Bible school in Columbia S.C. He ministered there for 31 years until his death. He left behind a legacy, now Columbia International University, still carrying out his two life purposes.

Highly Condensed Biographical Narrative

The following running capsule, organized around the three major time increments of McQuilkin's life indicates the important activities, people and events that shaped McQuilkin's life. Critical incidents are interwoven into the narrative explanation. A complete summary of the critical incidents are given in Table 7-3 on page 319.

I. Victory Commitment/
(1886-1911); Age=Birth-25)

A. Shaky Family Foundations
(1886-1895); Age=Birth to 9

Robert Crawford McQuilkin was born on the 16th of February, 1886, the second child and only boy among six sisters to Irish immigrants Robert McQuilkin and Lucy Kirkpatrick McQuilkin. There was a fairly strong religious heritage in both families in Ireland. Robert's father, at age 20, migrated to the United States from Ireland. He courted and married Lucy Kirkpatrick in 1883. We hear very little of Robert McQuilkin, the father in the biography.[12] Lucy McQuilkin seems to be a truly saintly woman who selfishly gave

---

[11]Two of the leaders studied in this book died relatively young. Dr. A. J. Gordon died at age 1959 from a lung related infection. Dr. McQuilkin died at age 64 from heart problems. All the rest were in their 70s or 80s. For McQuilkin this means a relatively short focused ministry time as his role was not finalized until the early 30s. Up until that time he was wearing the multiple hats necessary for a growing Bible College.
[12]There is one statement that indicates that the father had problems with alcohol. He also had several failures in business. And comments, later in the book, about Robert C. McQuilkin's home life not being

Chapter 7. Robert C. McQuilkin (1886-1952)

to her children and always made the best of her life. All we know of the family life is that Robert's mom and sisters were a sharing family. They were regular church goers after moving to Pastor Anderson's church. At least one of Robert's sisters went into full time Christian work later in life. We can imply that the family was living on the edge of poverty, that the father did not have a spiritual influence, and that the important godly character traits that Rob gained from the family came from his mom.

B. Church Training
(1895-1898); Age=9-12

Pastor Anderson--An Important Model for Young McQuilkin

At age 9 a very important person collared Robert and invited him to church. The Reverend William M. Anderson was the new pastor of the North United Presbyterian Church. He visited people all in the neighborhood and invited them to church. Pastor Anderson promised that there would be an excellent class for young Robert. Mrs. McQuilkin and her children began attending that church. It became their church home. Pastor Anderson modeled a genuine Christian life. He pastored in that church from 1895 to 1948.[13] He was personally appreciative of Rob and encouraged him along the way. A couple of incidents, even at an early age, show Pastor Anderson's care and give promise of the thoughtful mind that Robert McQuilkin was to bring to the study of the Bible.

> As he neared Opal Street, he saw a little lad, school books under his arm, dart into a corner grocery. Anderson followed.
> What happened to that lad who just came in here?" asked the pastor of the man behind the counter.
> "That's my son," was the short reply.
> A pale-faced boy of about nine years reappeared at once from the back of the store and the father added, "Robert, come and recite *Horatius at the Bridge* for this gentleman." ...
> Anderson smiled and put his question, "Where do you go to Sabbath school?"
> Robert replied that since they had just recently moved, he had not found a church as yet. Then followed Anderson's invitation.
> "And I can promise you a wonderful teacher too" he added, "Mr. William Parker. He has a fine class of boys."
> ...
> Sometimes after Rob joined the Bible class his teacher resigned. The pastor was astonished. What catastrophe could have happened that would make Mr. Parker willing to give up his beloved boys. When he inquired, the conscientious little man replied that he could not answer the questions the boys were asking. What kind of questions? Oh, about the authenticity of the Scriptures. And who particularly was asking such questions? Why, that little Rob McQuilkin. But the pastor could not let Parker go. This should be a challenge to him to develop the lad who showed such a deep interest in the truth of the Word of God. (M. McQuilkin 1956:21,22,23).

Pastor Anderson and Mr. Parker provided for young McQuilkin contemporary models of the Christian life. Early on, a potential leader needs to see Christianity lived out

---

good and his mother living a hard life seem to indicate that this was the case. Robert loved his mother dearly and helped out with finances in the home, for nine years, while working for Steele and Sons.
[13]Pastor Anderson and Robert McQuilkin were friends over the many years. Near the close of his life Dr. McQuilkin wrote a letter of appreciation to Dr. Anderson in which he said among many other things, "I think you know that I will never cease to be grateful for all the blessing that you have brought to my life. The training in the North Church Sunday school and church and your personal friendship was the foundation for my Christian life." (M. McQuilkin 1956:23) This strong influence of Pastor Anderson has much to do with Focal Incidents 1 and 2.

Chapter 7. Robert C. McQuilkin (1886-1952)

in a meaningful and sincere way. Both of these men befriended Robert at a needy time in his life when solid male role models are so important.

In this church, Robert had ample opportunity to demonstrate leadership. He discusses some of his early on-the-job training.

> In our small church there was one young people's society, which belonged to the Christian Endeavor movement and also to a city union of the various churches of the same denomination. When I united with the church, I was asked to join this society and did so with the desire to throw myself into the work. I recall vividly the first meeting. I had signed a pledge to take some part in every meeting aside from singing. I memorized a verse and stood up to give it, steadying myself by holding the chair in front of me with two hands. The next week, I read a 'clipping,' this time holding on with one hand. The third week I wrote out something and memorized it. I am very grateful for the training in that young people's society. All members were put on one of the committees. There was the lookout committee, the membership committee, the prayer-meeting committee, the missionary committee, and others. The active members became officers. First, you may be elected vice president, if there is a good president. Then if you are a real worker you become secretary. After you have established confidence in your carefulness and integrity, they made you treasurer. And finally, if there is not an abundance of good material, you are elected president. I went through all of the committees and offices. After some years, the city-wide union became active, and I went through the committees in the union, and through the various offices. This was at the period when the mission study movement started. We threw ourselves into this new activity, and I began to teach mission study classes as an important part of my Christian activity. (R.C. McQuilkin n.d.:2,3).[14]

Early Leadership Committal, Was It Real?

It seems clear that Pastor Anderson had made a deep impression on young Robert. After attending three years at North United Presbyterian Church, and going through catechism class, Robert united with the church.[15] This was a serious time for young Robert.

> When I was twelve years old, I united with the church. The pastor asked certain questions about Christ and His salvation and I accepted all that the Bible said about it. I felt that I was not taking Christ as my Saviour for the first time, but was confessing Him openly. I did not recall any time when I did not believe in Christ as my Saviour. I remember attending evangelistic meetings when the evangelist would ask the Christian to stand. Sometimes I would stand. At other times I would not stand. It depended on what the evangelist said it meant to be a Christian, or rather what I understood him to say. I did not go up in any of these meetings to accept Christ, as I considered it might seem a repudiation of what I felt was a true faith in Christ. At least, that was how I reasoned. My uniting with the church was a real crisis in my life, and I felt that now I must seek to do everything possible to serve the Lord and be a faithful church member. (M. McQuilkin 1956:24,25).

Further insight, especially showing the leadership committal comes from His special cousin, Bess. She recalls some of his special thoughts and words at this time.

---

[14] In retrospect, one can see already a hint of *destiny preparation* (Clinton 1989:103). God is preparing McQuilkin for an interdenominational work. Already McQuilkin is broader than just his Presbyterian denomination. We will see this again in the Erdman incident in the YMCA. This vignette also contains indications of leadership transition and most likely *ministry tasks* (Clinton 1989:142).

[15] We do not have an actual record of the catechism class. But that was standard procedure in this church. And we know Robert was a serious student from the Parker Sunday School Class incident.

Chapter 7. Robert C. McQuilkin (1886-1952)

They give indication of God's working in the heart to lead this young lad into Christian work.[16]

> Bob had a double first cousin, Bess, whom he affectionately called his twin cousin, because she was born the same day and year as he. She writes: "I remember the summer Rob and I were twelve. He was visiting us and he and I were talking quite seriously for twelve-year-olds." He said, "When I grow up I am going to be a minister; the Lord wants me." A sister also remembers this as his mother's great ambition for him.[17] (M. McQuilkin 1956:24).

God is going to honor this desire, though it will be long in coming, almost 13 years.

C. Work, Informal Training
Leadership Transition
(1898-1911)

From 1898 until 1902 Bob McQuilkin attended Central High School of Philadelphia. Here he received a sound classical education.[18] Bob graduated in the top ten of his class on June 26, 1902. He was awarded a scholarship to the University of Pennsylvania. That fall he was sick with typhoid fever. In addition, the financial needs of the family were such that Bob had to decline the scholarship and go to work to help out.

Bob McQuilkin went to work for William Steele and Sons, Co., a building construction company in June just after graduation, 1902. He was to work for this company for 8 years full-time and then almost two more part-time. This was a positive experience for both Bob and the company.[19]

The years with Steele and Company were important years for young McQuilkin. He entered as a young lad of 16, with zeal and potential. He left as man of 25, with integrity, trustworthiness, confidence, and business skills. He could be trusted with decisions that would involve hundreds of thousands of dollars. Four things stand out from this period of time.

1. **A Contemporary Model, A Mentor**
   Joe Steele, who was his boss, was a good secular business model and also a Christian. McQuilkin learned much from him. He taught McQuilkin the basic skills needed in the building construction business. He taught skills, then gave responsibilities to use them, and released Bob to do them on his own.

---

[16] We can not ignore a simple statement like this. In light of Pastor Anderson's modeling, Rob's need of a male Christian model, and his interest in the things of the church, we can see that God plants a seed which He will later water and finally bring to fruition.

[17] Knowing his mother's upright life, we suspect that she dedicated him to the Lord and prayed that he would be used in Christian work. We have no evidence of this, but I suspect it to be true.

[18] McQuilkin had to take an entrance exam to get in this school. According to M. McQuilkin (1956:26,27), the classical course involved a full range of language work including Latin, Greek, English and Either French or German. In addition, there was Mathematics, Astronomy, Physics, Chemistry, History, Drawing, Biology, Logic and Ethics. Apparently with optional courses and advanced work a student could even graduate with a Bachelor of Arts. The solid English background would serve McQuilkin well as he developed his contextual approach to hermeneutics.

[19] Nearly 50 years later Joe Steele (M. McQuilkin 1956:24), at 87 years of age and still going to the office, remembered Bob. And what he remembered was character traits. "The thing that impressed me about Bob was his earnestness and sincerity."

2. **Character Lessons**
   During this time, McQuilkin was faced with temptations in business practices which were less than honest. Once when faced with a gift (read gift with implicit attached strings--a bribe) he would not give in.[20] He continued to increase in job skills, commensurate responsibility and increased salary over the years.
3. **Continuing Education**
   The company paid him to take classes at Drexel Institute of Technology to gain perspectives and skills needed in the building construction business.
4. **On-The-Job Training--Christian Things**
   Bob was very active in lay ministry. He was an avid Bible student. He had administrative responsibilities as well as taught a large women's Bible class on Sunday afternoon (M. McQuilkin 1956:34). He was involved in activities associated with the YMCA (then a strong Christian organization). His ministry activity and participation was wider than just his Presbyterian Church. He was becoming known to persons involved in youth ministries and activities in the Philadelphia area.

Like-Attracts-Like, Dr. Erdman Demonstrates Good Teaching

M. McQuilkin, almost passing over the vignette, describes on about two-thirds of a page a critical incident that shaped Robert both ministerially and perhaps strategically. This incident demonstrates several important leadership emergence principles. It lays seeds that will bear fruit in McQuilkin's life. It will help him shape a role. It will lay foundational principles for public Bible teaching. It is a *chance* encounter, as seemingly are many interventions by divine contacts. But in retrospect, God is seen to be sovereignly controlling.

> One night as Bob waited at the YMCA for some of the fellows with whom he regularly played handball, glancing through an open door he noticed a class in session. Having a little time to spare he slipped in and took a back seat. He goes on with the story: "A venerable looking old gentleman was reading and teaching the Bible. I had come in expecting to stay five or ten minutes. I remained a regular member of the class for three years--as long as the class continued. When I came out of that first evening, at the close of the class, I said to myself; 'There is a man who really believes the Bible is the actual Word of God. And I believe he is right.' The thrill of hearing God speak was consciously mine for the first time."
> The teacher of the class was Dr. W. J. Erdman, a former pastor of D. L. Moody. Moody said o him that he knew the Bible better than any other man in America. Erdman's influence in McQuilkin's own teaching of the Word was very profound, both in eschatology and in Erdman's specialty, "The Forms of the Revelation of Redemption in the Old Testament." It may have been in connection with this class that McQuilkin told one of his friends that he had given up reading Shakespeare because he discovered how little he knew of the English Bible. (M. McQuilkin 1956:36).

At least six important items frequently seen in the development of a leader are couched in these two small paragraphs. They include:

---

[20]This is a typical *integrity check* (Clinton 1989:125). The entire *positive testing pattern* (Clinton 1989:154) can be seen here. McQuilkin is tested, responds positively with integrity, and God expands.

Chapter 7. Robert C. McQuilkin (1886-1952)   page 288

1. **Entry Context**[21]
   The Philadelphia region provides a confluence of Christian influences. There are numerous influential Christian leaders located in this region. McQuilkin is in the right place to break into a network that will expose him to numerous leaders both in the United States and Britain. Dr. Erdman is just such a man. An influential Bible teacher, noted author, and evangelical Christian--he is on the scene in his Afterglow years to provide the model that a growing lay Bible teacher needs. McQuilkin, like other potential Bible teachers, needs to see someone who is competent in the Scriptures. This will challenge McQuilkin to study the Scriptures. He will begin a more serious approach to Bible study and will acquire life long disciplines with the intent to master the Scriptures.

2. **Alive To The Word**
   At this point McQuilkin has been a committed sincere Christian for about eight years. He has had a positive church experience and a challenging Christian experience. But notice those words, "The thrill of hearing God speak was consciously mine for the first time." For the first time, McQuilkin has a Samuel-like experience in which he consciously sees God's power in the Scriptures.[22] There are many sincere Christians who have never heard God speak in the Word. Erdmans are needed all over.

3. **Mentor Coach/ Teacher**
   As a young leader is transitioning into leadership a mentor coach or mentor teacher is invaluable.[23] Erdman is in his prime. McQuilkin, an ever intent and

---

[21]*Entry contextual processes* (Clinton 1989:108) refer to the situation or time in history into which a leader is born and which will offer constraints and expansive opportunities for the exercise of leadership. There are items related to the setting, both culturally and historically, of the local, regional, national, and international situation into which a leader is born and will minister in and which will be used by God to process a leader in terms of strategic guidance, long term convergence, and sense of destiny. Philadelphia, at this point in the history of Christianity in the United States is one of the leading centers. We shall discuss more of this when we speak of *The Sunday School Times*. There were a number of important and influential Christian leaders in this locale. W. J. Erdman was one of them. He was an outstanding Bible teacher. That in his Afterglow years he should minister to an adult Bible class in a YMCA speaks reams about his love for Bible teaching. He has macro perspective, like Campbell Morgan. He can see the importance of context in the larger flow of the book's message as well as a book's message in the larger flow of the Bible. This latter especially appealed to McQuilkin, who will later develop a course on the Progress of Redemption in the Scriptures for which he will be known.

[22]In leadership emergence theory, this is significant. *Word processing*, that is, the ability to hear and perceive God speaking is one of the top symptoms of an emerging leader. A Christian leader is a person with God-given capacity, and God-given responsibility who is influencing a specific group of God's people toward God's purposes. The critical concept of leadership is influencing toward God's purposes. That means, a leader must be able to hear from God. *Word processing* then is crucial to a developing leader. McQuilkin will have the joy of imparting this same sort of *Luke 24:32 thrill* to almost countless numbers of Bible students. He experienced it first here in a simple Bible class in the YMCA. Dr. Erdman was God's instrument. It is significant that it was in a public ministry setting. McQuilkin will reproduce this same sort of public ministry.

[23]*Mentoring* is a relational experience in which one person called the *mentor*, empowers another person, called the *mentoree* via a transfer of resources. Nine types of mentor functions have been identified: mentor discipler, mentor spiritual guide, mentor coach, mentor counselor, mentor teacher, mentor sponsor, contemporary model, historical model and divine contact. Our studies have shown that ideal development requires different of these functions at different times of leadership emergence. One of these is the modeling function of a contemporary Christian leader respected by the mentoree. This needs to happen as the Christian leader is growing in ministry (and hence facing problems). The *contemporary model* serves as a sort of Christian hero/heroine who inspires the young leader. The mentoree tends to emulate and imbibe values from the *contemporary model* and tends to live up to the genuine expectations that person sets out.

serious learner, observes from this passive mentor[24] and imbibes values. This first teaching/learning experience is formative. How to read the Scriptures publicly with emphasis will be observed. How much to read will be observed (contextual units).[25] How to get the hearer's attention, how to illustrate, and how to bring closure all will be carefully noted. McQuilkin will learn as much or more about the process of public Bible teaching as he will the actual content.

4. **Like-Attracts-Like Spiritual Gifts Pattern**
Leadership giftedness research has identified six patterns helpful in assessing a leader's development.[26] One of the more important of these is the like-attracts-like giftedness pattern. Leaders, with embryonic spiritual gifts, are attracted to mature Christian leaders who demonstrate these gifts with effectiveness. Leaders with an evangelistic spiritual gift will be drawn to those exercising evangelism as a gift--even if the young leader isn't aware of the gift. So it is with teachers and prophets and apostolic types. This observed fact, not an absolute, is very helpful to leaders who are aware of it and want to offer deliberate mentoring. They recognize that many that are drawn to their ministry will have one or more spiritual gifts that they have. They can do *top down recruiting*. In this case, McQuilkin is learning from a passive mentoring situation from a public Bible teacher. But the relationship could have been personal had either or both recognized mentoring concepts and how they are established.[27]

5. **Content**
The phrase, "forms of the Revelation of Redemption in the Old Testament" give us a hint of the content of the Bible study. At least some of the Bible study was macro in scope, that is, viewing portions of the Bible in light of the Bible as a whole. Knowing one of the major courses that McQuilkin develops after 1921 in Columbia, The Progress of Redemption in the Scriptures, helps us see the importance of this content that Erdman taught. It gave McQuilkin perspective that he would use greatly in his classes at Columbia Bible College in his convergent ministry.

Erdman does this for McQuilkin. At this early stage of leadership emergence it is important to be coached and taught in terms of ministry skills needed by the developing leader. Erdman (mature teaching gift) served (passively) as a mentor coach and teacher for McQuilkin (embryonic teaching gift) (See Clinton and Clinton, 1991, **The Mentor Handbook**).

[24]Active mentoring means a deliberate relationship between mentor and mentoree. Passive mentoring means that the mentoree learns from the mentor by actively learning from the modeling going on even though the mentor may not even be aware of it. There are five mentoring dynamics that enhance a mentoring process (attraction, relationship, responsiveness, accountability, empowerment). In active mentoring they are a joint responsibility of mentors and mentorees. In passive mentoring the mentoree must supply these. (See Clinton and Clinton, 1991, **The Mentor Handbook**).

[25]Erdman was a master at identifying contextual units.

[26]These include: 1. The like-attracts-like, 2. Giftedness Drift, 3. Role-Gift enablement, 4. Complementary Giftedness-Need, 5. Giftedness Development and 6. Gift Cluster Ripening. See Clinton and Clinton (1994) **Developing Leadership Giftedness--What Leaders Need to Know About Spiritual Gifts to Develop Themselves and Their People**.

[27]How do mentors get connected up with mentorees? Three basic means include: 1. TOP DOWN RECRUITING (Mentors recruiting mentorees), 2. BOTTOM-UP RECRUITING (Mentorees recruiting mentors), 3. LINKERS (Someone with mentor eyes recognizes potential mentorees and mentors and links them in a sponsoring fashion). We do not see this happening here. The mentoring stays passive. Active mentoring at this point could have significantly speeded McQuilkin's development. We will see top down recruiting later when Kyle tutors McQuilkin in theological subjects in preparation for the mission field.

6. Ministry Insight[28]
McQuilkin sees in this simple ministry format an approach to using his teaching gift with power. The public Bible study, open to any who are interested, provides a forum for edification, for imparting perspective, for modeling, and for recruiting people and resources. McQuilkin will use this greatly in the early days of Columbia Bible School.

Pivotal Points: New Wilmington Committal and May 1909, Decision Time

These two critical incidents are part of a pattern with McQuilkin. He progressively over a period of time becomes more intensely involved in missions. Several anchors publicly attach him to deeper involvement. His progressive call includes inner times that only God knows, disclosures to intimate friends, and public times which are major stepping stones. It is the public times that serve as anchors. The May 1909 commitment was the first public commitment toward missions. I designate it as critical incident 4. However, this public stand is only part of an increasing movement toward full time ministry with a missions focus.

In 1908, the closing service of the New Wilmington Summer Conference for young people included a traditional testimony time. Bob McQuilkin gave his testimony. Essentially it was that he was willing to go. However, he felt the Lord would have him stay in the business world and help finance others (M. McQuilkin 1956:41). This was a public committal of a growing interest in missions. As early as 1903 he was concerned with missions. He had taught on it. In 1908 he makes a public committal to back missions with his business talents. Later he will consecrate himself to full time ministry, presumably as a pastor. Then he will go into full time work in a parachurch organization, *The Sunday School Times*. Finally, in a challenging time by S. D. Gordon he makes an inner committal to missions in Africa. He will join the African Inland Mission, raise his support and then be providentially blocked from going. Figure 7-1 lays this progressive calling on a time-line. The letter C on the chart indicates a step of leadership committal.

This is an important concept to recognize. For with many emerging leaders there is no *once-for-all* leadership committal. There is a growing number of steps involved in the leadership committal. Submission to each opens the door for the others.

Two things should be noted. One, there are repeated leadership committals. Two, with each call there is a progressively deeper and more specific call. Leaders who are concerned with leadership selection and development must be aware of both the repeated nature of calls and the progressively deeper committal involved. Recognition of these elements can vitally affect design of ministry application times. Leaders interested in the leadership selection will in fact design ministry times with these two notions in mind. From this case study we see that leadership committal is as much a process as it is an event.

---

[28]This is a simple example of a *ministry insights* process item. A *ministry insight* (Clinton 1989:198) is a conceptual breakthrough on how to do ministry. It may be a new communication method, a new way of structuring an organization, a delivery system for evangelism or a means of motivations, etc. McQuilkin will try a conference ministry approach for a while but will eventually settle down to a public Bible teaching approach (both in classroom and in his Friday night studies in the Sun Parlor Room at Hotel Colonia). He learned the value of that kind of ministry here under Erdman. In effect, this is an early *destiny revelation* process item (Clinton 1989:220) in seed form. It will later be clarified further.

Chapter 7. Robert C. McQuilkin (1886-1952)   page 291

```
C1       C2       C3  C4    C5    C6       C7              C8             C9
|--------|--------|---|-----|-----|--------|---------------|--------------|
1898     1903     1908 1909 1910  1911     1915            1916           1921
Age 12   17       22   23   24    25       31              32             35
```

At least nine **commitments** (C1 through C9) can be identified over these 23 years:

C1= initial destiny revelation about full time Christian work at age 12. This was seen in his statement to his cousin Bess, "When I grow up I going to be a minister; the Lord wants me." This is essentially private except his disclosure to Bess.

C2= his initial interest in missions at age 17--He taught on missions. There he worded his conviction that missions was one of the most important Christian enterprises. He taught on this publicly but his initial insights were privately recorded in a diary.

C3= his testimony at the closing service of 1908 New Wilmington Conference. Here he was publicly committing himself to the cause of missions but via financial support, prayer support and other means than directly going. This was public.

C4= in May 1909 Bob and Marge discussed going into full time ministry. The decision was made though a year would go by before Bob went for schooling. This was a private decision that both Bob and Marge made together. It was a significant step since it meant that Bob must resign from Steele and Sons Co. I designate this as critical incident 5.

C5= correspondence between Bob and Marge involved discussion that ministry might mean missions (this was over a period of longer than a year)

C6= in the fall of 1911 Bob was invited to join *The Sunday School Times* by Charles Trumbull. This was about 2 or 3 months or so after the Union Life critical incident. This is his actual movement into full time ministry. It is with a parachurch ministry and it involves mostly administrative detail, though there is some study, analysis, and some ministry via correspondence. But this role while good for training and putting Bob in a position to build up networks with Christian leaders does not enhance his main Bible teaching gift and his public rhetorician role in promoting the Victorious Life. Still it is a major step forward. This is critical incident 7.

C7= at the Princeton Conference Bob responds to an S. D. Gordon message. This is critical incident 9 and leads Bob to resign from *The Sunday School Times*. God is moving toward a role which will embrace McQuilkin's teaching gifts, his distinctive *Victorious Life Message* and his interest in promoting missions. This was a private inner response to God alone. Later he will share its implications at the office.

C8= the McQuilkins are committed to Africa. God closes the door, not to their missions involvement but to their going.

C9= the McQuilkins receive the call to a role that will allow gifting, message and mission interest to merge. They will form a Bible School which has a *Victorious Life Message* and a missions thrust.

Figure 7-1. Progressive Calling of McQuilkin

In 1910 McQuilkin entered the University full time. His background allowed him to enter as a sophomore. His fiancée, Marge, also was a sophomore at this time in Pennsylvania College for women. Bob was able to complete a little more than a year before the prime critical incident, Union Life, occurred. Eventually Bob will finish a Bachelor of Arts degree (in 1917), doing it part time while working at *The Sunday School Times*. One of the most important lessons that McQuilkin learns at the University of Pennsylvania will serve him good stead in his own teaching career. M. McQuilkin captures it.

> "I find continually that perhaps the most important influence of college is the men who are teaching. Their personality and their opinions, their view of life, constantly impress me as more valuable than the specific information they dispense. Here are eight or nine men, each in a class by himself each with a different experience in life, most of them have thought amply about life and its problems, and can't help revealing himself. Our philosophy teacher reveals himself least; I have discovered none of his philosophy of life as yet." (M. McQuilkin 1956:36)

McQuilkin feels first hand the impact of modeling. He will use this himself in his classes at Columbia Bible College.[29]

August 15, 1911, The Pivotal Point

It is at this point that McQuilkin has his life changing experience with the *Victorious Life Message* presented by Charles Trumbull which was given as Opening Illustration 1. This incident gave him an important spiritual value--the importance of appropriating Christ's life as the source of victory in the life. This message is so dominant that he will be led to structure a ministry to pass it on to others. He draws from this a life purpose--to help Christians enter in to Union Life and have a Victorious Life Testimony. At this point he has a life purpose. No major role has emerged. No methodology has yet emerged though the seeds are there--the Conference. His personal time with Charles Trumbull will provide a future invitation to full time ministry with *The Sunday School Times*.[30]

M. McQuilkin (1947:105) seems to indicate that it was at the August 15, 1911 critical incident that Bob McQuilkin received the seeds three means toward carrying out his life purposes. He longed to see connected with presenting the *Victorious Life Message*:

---

[29] Paul deliberately uses modeling as a means of influence. See Philippians 4:9 and others. Mentoring is a relational empowerment that dominantly uses modeling as part of its power base for influence. McQuilkin will model a victorious life, a teaching role, response to crises, and especially faith. His modeling will deeply impact almost every student who takes his courses. This is in essence an important *ministry insight* (Clinton 1989:198). McQuilkin never voices this as a ministry insight explicitly. But it is clear he was aware of it. His students certainly gave testimony to its impact in their lives.

[30] McQuilkin essentially operated from the same guidance principle as Gordon--*Be obedient in the things at hand. If I follow the light I have, the next will come when I need it.* And it did. The quaint King James Version of Genesis 24:27 captures the idea. Abraham's servant who has been led to find a wife for Isaac says, "**I, being in the way, the Lord led me.**" Other translations say led straight. The basic idea is we follow the Lord in terms of what we know and we trust Him to show us as we go. He will direct us to our destination. In McQuilkin's case his acceptance of the Victorious Life paradigm and his personal involvement with Charles Trumbull leads to a job offer with Trumbull. While working for Trumbull he organizes a conference ministry, called the Victorious Life Testimony, on the side to promote this wonderful ministry. At one of the conferences he receives a call to Africa. When that is blocked he ministers in conferences. In one of them in South Carolina he impresses a prayer band who are looking for a man to head up a Bible School McQuilkin's guidance opens up step-by-step as he obediently follows and ministers in what is before him.

Chapter 7. Robert C. McQuilkin (1886-1952)   page 293

1. a publication, 2. a conference, 3. a school. However, the idea of the school seems latent in 1911. None of his ministry connected with *The Sunday School Times* or outside seems to be related to this vision. It isn't until the door is blocked to Africa and the door apparently opens to Southern Bible Institute that the third element seems to emerge.

1911--Summary of Focal Issues and Shaping Toward Them

At this point, McQuilkin at age 25, has identified one life purpose and a potential unique methodology, the Conference Ministry. He knows that he will have at least a Public Rhetorician's role.[31] His 3 years with Erdman has drawn him toward it. He has a growing missions interest. He has an interest in teaching the Bible. Much needs to be cleared up for him concerning the focal issues. But he has a good start. The next step thrusts him into full time ministry--a necessary preliminary to identifying his unique role.

II. ORGANIZATIONAL APPRENTICESHIP/ MISSIONARY CALLING
(1911-1921); Age=25-35

A. Organizational Apprenticeship/With *The Sunday School Times* And Charles Trumbull
(1911-1916); Age=25-30

Trumbull--Invitation To Work At Sunday School Times

McQuilkin was studying at the University of Pennsylvania. He was still working part time at Steele's building construction company. In the late fall of 1911 Trumbull invited Bob McQuilkin to join *The Sunday School Times*, critical incident 7.[32] His role was multi-purposed. He would write, administrate, and help Trumbull in various supportive ways. He would also study, analyze, answer correspondence[33] and in general learn the skills involved in publishing a weekly.[34] Shortly after his accepting the position he and Marge were married.[35] During the next five years they will together face three critical incidents which will clarify more of the focal issues of his life. In addition, McQuilkin will grow in status, network with important Christian leaders, and become a proficient public rhetorician--particularly with respect to the *Victorious Life Message*.

---

[31]*Public rhetorician* is a type of role which represents public teaching or preaching which has effective impact on people and for which the person is remembered. McQuilkin's Friday night Bible study in the Sun Parlor of the Colonia Hotel, his conference ministry, and even his class room activity will flow from this God-directed role.

[32]There was a special mentoring relationship between McQuilkin and Trumbull. It was much like Jonathan and Saul--a lateral mentoring relationship of deep friendship and respect for each other.

[33]He frequently answered correspondence about Bible questions. Over the five years he increased his Bible knowledge, in addition to other regular disciplines, simply because he had to handle much of this correspondence. Also, as part of his regular work he read widely and wrote book reviews for publication. He constantly was maintaining a learning posture. Even if he didn't want too, the job required it.

[34]*The Sunday School Times* published a weekly Christian newspaper. It was very influential all across American. The details involved with writing, editing, and distributing this weekly newspaper were immense. During the time McQuilkin was with the weekly it grew to a peak circulation of 109,000 (M. McQuilkin 1956:81). You can imagine the many skills that McQuilkin picked up during his five years working side-by-side with Trumbull.

[35]Little is said about the social base pattern. It is assumed that the release pattern was the basic pattern. Certainly Mrs. McQuilkin was a party to all of the decision making that has led to the important choice of ministry at *The Sunday School Times*. But M. McQuilkin says very little about her mom's ministry status. See Appendix D. Social Base Processing.

Chapter 7. Robert C. McQuilkin (1886-1952)

During his time with *The Sunday School Times*, McQuilkin was influential in the paper's stand on three important issues: 1. the doctrine of the personal return of Christ, 2. exposing modernism, and 3. promotion of victorious life teaching. McQuilkin had numerous writings published on all three of these topics (M. McQuilkin 1956:81).

One other important feature should be noted. McQuilkin was one of the promoters of the organizational prayer meeting. When McQuilkin came the staff met once a week for prayer. This had a good response. In 1914 this was changed to a daily noon period. This rich time would later have its counterpart at Columbia Bible College. He will meet with his board on a weekly basis in Columbia. The roots of discovering God's will in prayer were begun here.

The Oxford Challenge, Organizing the First Conference

After Bob McQuilkin got his feet on the ground at *The Sunday School Times*, he began thinking about promoting the *Victorious Life Message*. In the fall of 1912 he and his wife began an informal prayer meeting in their home. They were asking for guidance. They knew that the life giving message had deeply impacted their own lives. They wanted to introduce others to this wonderful living Savior.[36]

An answer to their prayer came when the Presbyterian Committee for young People's work, Wendell Cleland, Jr. was asked to appoint a committee to plan for a Conference. The prayer partners were appointed as the committee. McQuilkin was the Conference Secretary. They planned for a July 19-27, 1913 date. The location for the first conference was Oxford, Pennsylvania. J. Alvin Orr, a minister of a United Presbyterian Church extended the invitation to host the conference. The Oxford Conference was the first of a number of faith challenges that the McQuilkins would face over their lifetime.[37] It set the tone. Some said that the conference should be canceled when less than twenty-five had been signed up with less than two weeks to go (including the six committee members). But the Oxford Challenge proved to be a important foundational time. Seventy-five people came. Two very distinguished Conference Speakers were on hand, Henry W. Frost, the home director of the China Inland Mission and W.H. Griffith-Thomas the noted Bible teacher from England. The conference had a strong mission interest. Several responded to go to the mission field as a result of this conference.

But more important, the committee recognized the importance of a Conference for advancing the *Victorious Life Message* and for impacting the cause of missions. God had put his affirmation on this ministry. They formed a parachurch organization for the purpose of scheduling missions and Victorious Life testimony conferences.[38] It later was named the Victorious Life Testimony. This was a key point in focusing activity for McQuilkin. He was chosen to be the corresponding secretary. J. Alvin Orr, the host pastor for the first conference, accepted the position of Conference Chairman.

---

[36] M. McQuilkin (1956:67,68) lists Bob Regester, Russell Galt, Betty Smith, Laura Forsythe, and Bob and Marge McQuilkin as the prayer partners. All had attended the conference at New Wilmington.

[37] A *faith challenge* (Clinton 1989:222) refers to those times when God's shapes a leader by challenging that leader to take steps of faith in regards to ministry. The leader who responds in faith will see God meet those steps of faith with divine affirmation and ministry achievement in such a way as to increase the leader's capacity to trust God in future ministry.

[38] M. McQuilkin (1956:69,70) points out that, from the start, they wanted an organizational broader than just the Presbyterian denomination. Freedom was needed. The Victorious Life Testimony needed to be like *The Sunday School Times* and the China Inland Mission. This meant, like those organizations, they would have to trust God to provide finances.

Chapter 7. Robert C. McQuilkin (1886-1952)

This conference ministry was carried alongside of McQuilkin's normal work with *The Sunday School Times*. Scheduling was usually during summer vacation times. This ministry had Trumbull's blessing. McQuilkin gained in proficiency at design of conferences, administrating them, and at ministering effectively at them. Table 7-1 lists the Conferences and sites.

Table 7-1. Victorious Life Testimony Conferences

Year	1913	1914-1918 (yearly)	1919-1922 (yearly)	1923 onward
Location	Oxford	Princeton[39]	Stoneybrook, Long Island	Keswick Grove, New Jersey

Networking Base

Before moving on to the important boundary processing which led to the focal issue of major role we must not leave *The Sunday School Times* ministry period without discussing the importance of networking.[40] Philadelphia was a hub of Christianity in the United States at the turn of the century. M. McQuilkin describes this.

> If Philadelphia was a kind of Christian world capital in those days, *The Sunday School Times* was its capital hill. Outstanding men from all over the world met and conferred in the *Times* offices. It was a rare privilege for a young man in his late twenties to be able to talk with such men of God. Often it fell in his pleasant line of duty to take them to lunch. It was here than he became acquainted with Dr. Melvin Grove Kyle, who later became his tutor in seminary work. He met Charles Hurlburt the director of the African Inland Mission, with whom he was to become intimately associated. The *Times* sponsored the work of the Ralph Nortons, who were founders and directors of the Belgian Gospel Mission. He met other Christian leaders as he covered the Billy Sunday campaigns in Pittsburgh, Philadelphia, New York, and elsewhere for his paper.
> It was a broader base for Christian fellowship than he would have found had he limited himself to the denomination in which he grew up. Though he was criticized by some for not giving himself wholly to the work of his own church, the Lord was grooming His servant to be a blessing to many denominations and many missions and many lands (M. McQuilkin 1956:79,80).

This time at *The Sunday School Times* was invaluable in terms of establishing a resource of contacts that will be useful in the future.

---

[39] After the 1916 conference, the book, **Victorious Life Studies**, was produced. It was an edited version of the messages of the 1916 Princeton Conference plus some articles. This was McQuilkin's first book (M. McQuilkin 1956:71). Perhaps this was first called **Victory in Christ** as indicated by Miss Laura LeFevre (M. McQuilkin 1956:71), who helped produce it. The Columbia International University Library card catalogue calls it **Victorious Life Studies** and shows 1918 as one of the publication dates.

[40] *Networking power* (Clinton 1989:240) refers to the unusual use by God of mentors, divine contacts, or other related leaders, to channel power in order to open doors or accomplish influence goals for a leader. The leader in the process will sense the importance of relationships with other leaders and will see in the future God touch through these networks of people. God is beforehand building networks that McQuilkin will be able to utilize as he founds a Bible College which will train leaders for ministries around the world. This placing of McQuilkin in Philadelphia with *The Sunday School Times* at this important juncture, when viewed in retrospect, standouts with God's sovereign working.

Chapter 7.   Robert C. McQuilkin (1886-1952)   page 296

S. D. Gordon Gives Mission Challenge; "The Joints of the Will"

Robert McQuilkin had a growing sense of the importance of missions. He had made several progressively more important decisions about missions. Each of the summer conferences from 1911 onward always had a strong missions emphasis. In 1915 McQuilkin made an important commitment. This critical incident provided a focal value and a step of strategic guidance.

> At the Princeton conference in the summer of 1915 a message had just been given by Dr. S. D. Gordon on the necessity of bending the joints of the will as well as the joints of the knees when seeking guidance. A member of the staff at *The Sunday School Times* writes of this: "After this meeting instead of attending the scheduled session, I felt compelled to go to the Prayer Room to be alone, and went to the farthest corner, seeking God's will concerning China...After some time I was conscious that someone else had entered the room also with a terrific burden which was being poured out before the Lord. When assured that God had met me with His best, I arose. As I passed this gentleman on my way out of the room, he raised his head--it was Bob McQuilkin. 'Oh, is that you, Miss Kuehn?' he asked. I answered, 'Yes,' and walked out. That was Bob McQuilkin's call for Africa and mine for China." (M. McQuilkin 1956:84,85)

McQuilkin quickly told his boss, Charles Trumbull and obtained his favor.

Mentor Teacher, Dr. Kyle--Intensive Personal Theological Training

Dr. Melville Grove Kyles was the archeological editor (part time) at *The Sunday School Times* as well as being a Professor of Theology at Xenia Seminary. He felt that McQuilkin had great gifts for the work at *The Sunday School Times*. But upon sensing that McQuilkin's leading was to the mission field he offered to give him private instruction on seminary subjects to prepare him for ministry. For a number of months McQuilkin went to Dr. Kyle's home two or three times a week.

B. Boundary[41] Processing--
(1916-1921); Age=30-32

1. Entry Stage--Mission Call/ The Ship Sinks
(1916-1918) Age=30-32

As McQuilkin was finishing five years with *The Sunday School Times*, he applied to the Africa Inland Mission. He had met Charles Hurlburt in connection with the times. The needs of East Africa were presented convincingly. In preparation for going to the

---

[41] The time when a leader moves from one major period of his/her life to the next is called a boundary. Boundaries have been studied extensively. See Clinton (1992) *Boundary Processing--Looking At Critical Transition Times in Leader's Lives*. Comparative studies of such boundaries have identified three stages: 1. the entry stage; 2. the evaluation stage, and 3. the expansion stage. Four different kinds of boundaries, under which most can be categorized, are popularly described by the titles of Surprise, The Creeping Vine, The New Glasses, The Growth Challenge. This is a combination of Growth Challenge and Creeping Vine type. McQuilkin has gifts that are not being used by *The Sunday School Times*. He is needing to move on. The missionary challenge and acceptance starts him on the way. The heart problem alerts them possibly to a change of plans. But it is the City of Lahore sinking that makes them sit up and take notice. It is one of two major turning points of the boundary. But it will take some other convincing factors before the decision leading to the next phase is made. The turning point in a boundary is the pivotal point of the evaluation stage. In this case there are two--this one, and the Conflict/ Resignation from VLT. I will use the three stages of the boundary to describe the narrative.

Chapter 7. Robert C. McQuilkin (1886-1952)   page 297

field, he resigned his position as associate editor and worked to complete his degree at the University of Pennsylvania. Eventually this was done in 1917.

The Doors Shut

They were accepted by the Africa Inland Mission and moved in the fall of 1917 to the African Inland Mission home in Hatboro, Pennsylvania (M. McQuilkin 1956:88). During this time McQuilkin was raising support. Then obstacle number 1 to getting to Kenya occurred. The mission doctor found that Mrs. McQuilkin had a heart problem that would be aggravated at the high altitude in Kenya where they had been appointed. M. McQuilkin tells how this obstacle was removed.

> A godly old blacksmith, whose shop stood just beside the train shed, where they frequently waited for transportation, heard of this, and along with others urged them to pray for God's miraculous healing. He came to their home for prayer. Several months later the doctor examined her heart again and in amazement pronounced it quite normal (M. McQuilkin 1956:89).

So they continued on.

Obstacle 2, their support was raised. In fact, one of the summer conferences helped defray their outgoing expenses. It was a full year after their acceptance that their sailing date was set. Obstacle 3, the boat sinks was the big surprise and in retrospect one of two turning points in the boundary.

2. Evaluation Stage: Waiting--Conference Ministry/ Victorious Life Affirmation
(1918-1921); Age=32-35

The Ship Sinks And Other Shut Doors

It was at this point that Opening Illustration 2, *City of Lahore*, was given.

Now notice the way God clearly directs. He has broken them loose from *The Sunday School Times*. He has tested their hearts concerning missions. They have held nothing back. They are God's. They will follow Him.

The next scheduled sailing was in January but its accommodations were smaller. Only eight of the party of twelve could go. Obstacle 4 happens. The McQuilkins were left behind. It was a time of living out of suitcases.

Obstacle 5 was a series of delays which strung out for an extended period of time. For nearly two years from 1917 to 1919 they were prepared to go. But one or another reason kept them from going. Shipping was scarce. A letter written in July of 1919 explained their assurance that God was still leading. Every delay had a purpose. In the meantime, as they waited calls came in from around the country for conferences. The Victorious Life Testimony Board of Managers wanted to extend their conference ministry to these locations. They invited McQuilkin to help them while they were waiting to go to Africa. The Africa Inland Mission Council approved of this, especially as there was no certainty of any shipping in the next several months.

Chapter 7. Robert C. McQuilkin (1886-1952) page 298

God clearly gives affirmation of the conference ministry and certainty guidance via double confirmation.[42]

> "Thus began the extension work of the Victorious Life Conference and the response was so overwhelming, the results so remarkable, and the need for the messages so crying, that I began to believe my friends, who insisted that the Lord had given me a special call for this message and this conference work that I should not leave, were right. I told the Lord that if this were the case, the decision not to go to Africa for permanent work must come from the Mission and not from myself." (M. McQuilkin 1956:89).

As he reached this conclusion the double confirmation came.

> ...a letter came from the director of the Mission advising that Mrs. McQuilkin and the children should not attempt to come as they could not stand the conditions on the field, and that the greatest contribution Mr. McQuilkin could make would be to spend a year in Africa getting acquainted with the field and return to America for deputation and conference work." (M. McQuilkin 1956:92)

M. McQuilkin evaluates the guidance and its results at this point in the McQuilkin's pilgrimage.

> It was assuring to them to trust that every prayer that had gone up toward getting them to Africa, every gift that had been given with sacrifice and love, every carefully laid plan and preparation, and every moment of time, even the waiting, were turned by the wonderful alchemy of God to the progress of the Gospel in Africa. If a ship had to be sunk in the process of brining this about, that just intimated the value God sets upon earthly things. The end of all the praying and purpose to go was that the Gospel might get out to every tribe and kindred. They had prayed, "Lord send us to Africa," and the Lord would reply, "I will send you to Africa and to China and to India and to Europe and to South American besides." (M. McQuilkin 1956:92).

And so the focal issues become clearer. Missions is an important part of their lives. But they will not go. In fact, they will send, that is, encourage, train, and stimulate many to go. M. McQuilkin (1956:92) goes on to point out than in the next twenty-five years more than 300 students would go forth to various parts of the world--even one to the exact assignment that had been the McQuilkins. But what next?

3. Termination/Expansion Stage: Mission to Central America/ CBS (1921-1922); Age=35,36

Negative Preparation/ Conflict/ Free To Go Anywhere

Should they continue the Victorious Life Conference ministry? It was the step-by-step leading they had received. They had been affirmed in it! There were opportunities all over the United States. This is an important time for McQuilkin. He is not yet at the final locale where God will use him. He has not yet identified the long term role. God has at this point affirmed two life purposes: 1. to see many Christians enter into the Victorious Life; 2. to be involved in God's great missions program. God will lead to the next step of

---

[42]*Double Confirmation* Clinton (1989:262) is a sovereign guidance shaping experience in which God clearly guides a leader to some major decision. The process is usually that the leader will get inner conviction about something. Then God will bring in an outside source independently of the leader to confirm that conviction. McQuilkin is recognizing that God has something else for him. But he has followed clearly God's leading to this point therefore he does not want to move unless he is sure it is God.

Chapter 7. Robert C. McQuilkin (1886-1952)

McQuilkin's strategic guidance. And He will use a common means to do so--negative preparation.[43] This provides the second major turning point of the boundary.

M. McQuilkin describes the sovereign guidance pressures generally.

> Into the life of every man of conviction, sooner or later, there must come conflict, whether it be in his own soul, in some personal relationship, in the policy or practices of an organization, or in doctrinal issues, it comes. Conflict does not always purify a man. It may harden or embitter or crush him--depending on what his substance is. But when the North wind blows upon the garden, and faith and hope and love are there, these spices are bound to flow out in refreshing and blessing to a parched land (M. McQuilkin 1956:93)

The time was the two years following his resignation from the mission. McQuilkin was involved in the conference ministry.

Over the years, McQuilkin had grappled with the conceptual framework which explained his August 15, 1911 Victorious Life experience.[44] His views and his teaching, in my opinion matured over the years. But he was a zealous and sincere person and taught strongly and openly what he believed at any given moment in his life. Some of his earlier views were misunderstood or mis-represented by others. Some were later modified slightly by him. Sometimes it takes time for criticism of past efforts to catch up with where a leader is in the present. In any case, the conflict that ensued was used to free up McQuilkin for that future major role that was to be his.

> The Lord had marvelously used the Testimony; the whole Christian public was being awakened to the fact that there was a Christian life immeasurably above the ordinary level at which most Christians lived. Scores and hundreds of lives were being changed at these conferences which were now being held by several teams all year round, throughout the nation and abroad. But as the months passed, it became evident that the Lord would use the doctrinal difficulties to stir up His young servant to step out again into new work, and

---

[43]*Negative preparation* (Clinton 1989:255,256) describes a guidance shaping activity of God usually in a number of incidents over a period of time. These incidents have negative connotations and are used to prepare a leader, by freeing them up from a situation in order to enter a new phase of development. Because of the negative issues, the leader will look at the new phase of development with a new abandonment and revitalized interest. He/she will be ready to embrace it and accept it. Whereas, without the negative circumstances, the leader may be content to remain in the situation and miss the expansion of potential offered by the next phase. Here, the unusual thing, is that McQuilkin recognizes the guidance and resigns from the Victorious Life Conference, before the next opportunity comes. So, he is certainly open to whatever opportunity comes.

[44]For an understanding of the experiential issues that brought McQuilkin face-to-face with the conceptual framework that underlies his experience--see M. McQuilkin's chapter 12. Conflict. This traces some of his inner life experiences with consistency in victorious living. This chapter describes the conflict, basically over the understanding of the *Victorious Life Message*, with people involved with the Victorious Life Conference. There were later conflicts with external people not involved with the movement. But this chapter deals with those who were partners in ministry. For McQuilkin's own explanation of his understanding of the *Victorious Life Message* see **Victory in Christ** which gives his personal testimony of the experience and his explanation of it. This booklet appears to be written in the late 20s or early 30s and gives a mature understanding of the doctrine. See also **Joy and Victory** which gives further explanation. Later I will comment on his description of the *Victorious Life* when I review values and contributions. But for now suffice it to say that M. McQuilkin in two chapter 12 footnotes (1956:252) points out the minor changes that came. Footnote 1: "If Mr. McQuilkin changed his doctrine at any point subsequent to this time, it was in the matter of defining the sin from which Christ could keep us as *conscious* sin. This proved a stumbling block to him and to others, and he later used the term *known* sin." Footnote 2: "He later used the expression *fill me* as more accurately describing the experience."

Chapter 7. Robert C. McQuilkin (1886-1952)

in June of 1921, he resigned from the council. This was a decision full of heartache and suffering for him, but as only the mission field could have taken him from his beloved *Sunday School Times*, only a complete break could have taken him away from the Victorious Life Testimony which was his very life. He was not the kind to drift away. His loyalties were intense. And neither *The Sunday School Times* nor the Victorious Life Testimony were to be his life's work. He was thirty-five years old when this took place, and God's time for his life's ministry was approaching (M. McQuilkin 1956:101).

The last two years had been years of living by faith.[45] They had seen God stretch them to the breaking point and then supply. These foundational lessons would be the springboard for yet greater faith lessons to come.

Call To Columbia--The One of His Choice

God has been working in Columbia, S.C. A prayer band,[46] motivated by Miss Emily Dick had been praying about two things: 1. a Bible Conference; 2. a Bible School.

In 1920 the group was praying about a Bible Conference in Columbia, S.C. They asked God to send them Mr. Charles Trumbull. They knew of his ministry at *The Sunday School Times*. One of the group added that if Mr. Trumbull could not come that the Lord would send *the one of His choice to them*. Shortly afterwards they received a letter from Trumbull who declined to come but recommended that he would send Robert C. McQuilkin in his place (M. McQuilkin 1956:102). After their first feelings of disappointment they were reminded of their prayer--*The one of His choice to them*. And so Mr. McQuilkin came for the first time. He co-ministered with Dr. Ramsey. Their ministry exceeded the expectations of the little prayer group.

Meanwhile, Miss Emily Dick had begun to minister in textile communities. Her several months at Moody Bible institute in 1917 had given her help and inspiration in her growing ministry. As her ministry prospered she wished that the young folks who were getting saved could get training at Moody Bible Institute. One night as she was praying the thought came to her. She probably couldn't get her young people to go to Chicago and study there. But they might study at a Bible institute nearby. What was needed was a Bible school in Columbia (M. McQuilkin 1956:103,104).[47] The next morning at breakfast she asked her sister, "What do you suppose the Lord wants us to have in Columbia?" To her amazement her sister told of a vivid dream she had had a few days before about a Bible school (M. McQuilkin 1956:104). This double confirmation encouraged the small prayer band to pray with conviction and to take first steps.

Two first steps included praying for a leader for the Bible School and starting some classes. There prayer became focused on a leader after Dr. James M. Gray, President of the Moody Bible Institute, visited Columbia and advised that they needed a leader to head

---

[45](M. McQuilkin 1956:100) describes a beautiful vignette in which the McQuilkin's borrowed $450 on their life insurance to reduce indebtedness of the Victorious Life Testimony. God met this step of faith 12 days later with a marvelous provision.

[46]M. McQuilkin lists Mrs. T. H. Dick, Miss Emily Dick, Miss Margaret Childs, Miss Pamela, Mrs. I. T. Stone and Mrs. Guy Tarrant as important member of this little group. Matthews (1973:7,8)) also describes this little group and its importance in the founding of the Bible College.

[47]This is another illustration of *divine initiative praying*. The "thought came to her, as from the Lord: A Bible school should be started in Columbia!" (M. McQuilkin 1956:104) It was from the Lord! It is also the front end of a *double confirmation* guidance experience (Clinton 1989:262). This is certainty guidance. They will pray with firm convictions (1 John 5:14,15) because of this certainty guidance--that is, guidance given in more than one way.

Chapter 7. Robert C. McQuilkin (1886-1952)

up the work. Ask God for one! They also rented a room in the fall of 1921 and started some classes in child study, personal Evangelism, and book studies.

By this time a committee had formed of which Mr. H. T. Patterson was the chairman. In November of 1921, Mr. McQuilkin and Dr. Ramsey were completing a tour of eight conferences on a Southern tour, in Columbia. The timing is right. Both Mr. McQuilkin and the prayer group have come to a common point in time. The group has been led to take first steps in starting a Bible School. They have been led to pray for a leader. Mr. McQuilkin has been negatively prepared to leave the Victorious Conference Testimony. He is finishing out tours that were scheduled. At this point in time there was an important informal gathering in the Dick home. M. McQuilkin records the intersection of these two needs.

> Near the close of the week the conference speakers were in the Dick home with several members of the prayer group. In the course of the conversation Dr. Ramsey was asked half-jokingly if he would consider coming to head up the proposed Bible School. He mentioned very seriously several reasons why this would not be possible. Then they turned to Mr. McQuilkin and asked, "Why don't you come and head up this work?" With his famous smile Mr. McQuilkin replied: "Because I haven't been asked." Everyone laughed, but after the guests had gone, one of the group said, "You know I believe that if we asked Mr. McQuilkin, he would consider it." Everyone was pleased with the thought, and Mr. McQuilkin was approached the very next day (M. McQuilkin 1956:105).[48]

Mr. McQuilkin was free. He was open. One last touch by God will bring about the final decision.

Reflection Time in Central America--Feeling The Mission Passion

Mr. McQuilkin promised the group he would consider their offer seriously. He told them he would give them an answer after he returned from a trip to Central America. He will see on this trip first hand the needs that missionaries have. He will return from this trip fired up by missions and inspired to train many for such a call. After two months on the field and having done much ministering and reflecting, McQuilkin came to the conclusion that God would have him respond positively to the Call in Columbia. It remained for his wife to confirm these feelings. This she did. Mr. McQuilkin returned. Together they decided that God was calling to Columbia. Mr. McQuilkin finished out his scheduled conferences on the West Coast with Dr. Ramsey. He lays out before H. T. Patterson some of his own understanding of the ground rules for his acceptance of the Call.[49]

> Dear Brother Patterson:
> The way seems clear for me to accept the gracious invitation of your Board to join you in the work of the Bible School in Columbia. I shall mention here briefly my understanding of the present plan for the school and its development, and my own relationship to it, and then you can write me your confirmation, or the action of the Board in the matter.
> We have sold our house in Glenside and expect to start for California April 6 or 7, remaining there most of the summer....We can plan to settle in Columbia in

---

[48] Again this illustrates the next step guidance pattern of both Gordon and McQuilkin. "I, being in the way, the Lord led me." It is as McQuilkin is ministering obediently in what he knows to do, that God very carefully arranges the next step for him.

[49] This wise leadership principle of getting the issues clarified and openly agreed to (in modern days, in writing) is first seen in Jephthah's acceptance of a military deliverer role for the Israelites. He will be the military leader and later political leader after delivering from the Ammonites. See Judges 11:10,11.

Chapter 7.   Robert C. McQuilkin   (1886-1952)   page 302

> September and take up the Bible School work as a permanent work for development. For some time to come it would seem best to give much of my time to conferences which would fit in admirably with the Bible School work. But the adjustment of time and such details may be left for the future as the Lord may lead, if we are clear on the main point, that I should undertake this as my life responsibility and make this the center of my work. (M. McQuilkin 1956:109,110).

He continues the letter with an unusual request. It reveals his growing faith gifting--something he shall become known for. This modeling of faith in a living God will be passed on to countless students.

> "For several years Mrs. McQuilkin and I have looked to the Lord for our support, in the sense that we have had no salary nor guaranteed allowance of any kind; there are special circumstances that make this the best plan for some of the Lord's servants, though that does not mean that it is the plan for all, nor a better plan than to have a regular income. I feel very clear, however, that for the present we should continue to look to the Lord in this way, and no appropriation should be made from Bible School funds either for the moving or for a home in Columbia. Apart from other considerations, the school is a venture of faith which in its beginning must be supported largely by the sacrifice of those who have the vision and who are giving their time and strength without any remuneration and I shall certainly want to have the privilege of joining those who are doing this and not be an expense to the work in this early stage. You may be assured that I shall feel the same responsibility for this work as though all our support were coming from it." (M. McQuilkin 1956:110).[50]

1921/22--Summary of Focal Issues and Shaping Toward Them

In terms of focal issues, much has been clarified.

Two **life purposes** have become increasingly clear: 1. to see many Christians enter into the Victorious Life; 2. to be involved in God's great missions program--recruiting, training, and stimulating people to go.

He has clarified part of a **unique methodology** for promulgating the *Victorious Life Message*--the Conference. Now he must merge that unique methodology with a Bible School base and he must adapt his conference delivery to a fixed location and on-going ministry.

He now has a central base, in his own words--"take up the Bible School work as a permanent work for development" and "that I should undertake this as my life responsibility and make this the center of my work." The **major role** will develop. It will have four major thrusts: 1. **Administration/Leadership**--including developing the Bible School facilities and recruiting quality teachers and under administrators, 2. **Teaching**--He will teach, both on campus and off, with gifted power in the area of

---

[50] As I write this chapter I have just returned from a homecoming at Columbia International University, the present outgrowth of McQuilkin's work. There were students who graduated in the 30s and 40s who had studied with Dr. Robert C. McQuilkin. One common theme that was repeated in their testimonies was that of learning to live by faith. They all attested that Dr. McQuilkin had imparted this important value to them in their time at Columbia Bible College. I spent some time in the library and studied all the catalogues from 1925 to 1952, the period of time in which Dr. McQuilkin was first Dean of the School and then the President as the school grew. One amazing fact is that during this time the School did not charge tuition of students. Students paid for room and board, for books, and some small registration fees to cover medical exams and some student records. The funds for the general budget of the school came from without from those interested in "sacrificing for the ministry."

Chapter 7. Robert C. McQuilkin (1886-1952)

Victorious living, hermeneutics, and Biblical studies--he will exhort in his preaching the importance of missions; he will be the main draw for students coming in--they will come to study with him; and 3. **Modeling**, he will live the Victorious Life and demonstrate apostolic-like exploits of faith, something many of the students will later themselves need and demonstrate in their own ministries. 4. **Mentoring**--he will link people to mission resources; he will sponsor mission groups; he will sponsor many individuals as they move into missions; he will carry on a powerful distance mentoring empowerment through his correspondence.

Ultimate contributions are yet in the future but it is already clear that **Saint, Founder, Stabilizer**, and **Promoter** will increasingly become prominent. In moving to the Bible college he has probably opted to prioritize a **Mentor** role as over against a **Public Rhetorician** role. Up to this point the public rhetorician role has dominated.

III. Life Work--Two Fold Thrust
Columbia Bible College/
Missions and Victorious Life
Ben Lippen/
(1921-1952); Age 35-66

McQuilkin spent 31 years at Columbia Bible College.[51] His development of his major role and its four major thrusts can be traced through three major time periods:

1. (1921-1928) The Formative Time--Foundations For Missions and Victorious Life Thrusts
2. (1929-1938) The Years of Steady Growth--Faith Challenges
3. (1939-1948) Mature Years of Productivity
4. (1948-1952) Final Years

A. Foundations For Missions and Victorious Life Thrusts
(1921-1928) Age; 35-42

Notice how the very first catalogue captures the life purposes of McQuilkin. The threefold purposes of the Bible college are interwoven with his specific life purposes.

1. To train for Christian Service at home and on the foreign mission field young men and women who are not able to take the more extended Seminary Courses.
2. To help any Christians who wish to study the Bible systematically, and be prepared for more effective Christian living and serving.
3. To win souls, to build up Christians in the Christ-controlled life, and to cooperate through prayer and in other ways in the work of the foreign mission fields.
(Columbia Bible School Catalogue:1925/26)

During the formative period the student body grew from 8 in 1923 to 47 in 1928. The final form of the School motto was established in 1927, To Know Him and To Make Him Known. The Colonia Hotel became its home. Gradually a faculty was recruited.

---

[51]The name was first Southern Bible Institute--when he came. It shortly became Columbia Bible School. When it leaped forward, the first Bible School to offer a degree, it became Columbia Bible College. Later during his tenure it added a graduate school. The name was later changed to show this after McQuilkin's death to Columbia Bible College and Graduate School. When it opened up a masters of divinity program it became Columbia Bible College and Seminary. Presently (1994), in order to focus on its worldwide ministry, it has become Columbia International University--a name broad enough to encompass its present ministries and other outgrowth of ministry in the future.

Chapter 7. Robert C. McQuilkin (1886-1952)

McQuilkin accomplished the following during this period of time:
1. He established a reputation as an outstanding Bible teacher.
2. He stabilized the Bible School by establishing the faith methodology as a viable means for funding, by recruiting a stable faculty, and by continuing to increase the facilities as needed by trusting in God's provision. He built up a constituency for prayer support and financial support.
3. He networked conservative missionaries, mission leaders, and other Christian institutional leaders to the Bible School.
4. He took a major step forward, both practical and far seeing, when he moved the school toward a degree program.[52]

Right from the beginning, Mr. McQuilkin's Bible teaching ministry was powerful. He had three outlets for his Bible teaching ministry: the Bible classes in the regular seminary program, the Friday night Bible class open to the public, and an itinerant off campus speaking ministry around the state and the country. This itinerant ministry (off campus and around the country) included Bible conferences, mission conferences, and speaking in churches. Part of his recruitment of both students and faculty, stabilizing of constituency, and publicizing the work of the Bible college was done via his ever busy off campus schedule.

When the school was small, at the beginning, Mr. McQuilkin at one time or another taught all the courses that were offered except music. He was an outstanding teacher. He saw his material as vitally related to life and communicated that to his students. In the early days the classes were small. There was the personal almost informal feeling. As the years went on and the school grew, Mr. McQuilkin focused on Bible book studies (frequently taught at night, hence open to townspeople who wanted to attend), hermeneutics, and a progress of doctrine course.[53]

Our Lord's Parables, first published in 1929, typifies his careful two-fold approach to hermeneutics. His intent was to teach students **how to study the parables for themselves** with a view toward **discovering truth and using it.** He carefully constructed questions which were under girded by the basic hermeneutical principles applying to the study of parables. Students received content but much more; they learned how to get that content itself. And they learned the most enduring lesson. It is truth applied that is truly learned.

Typical of his Victorious Life teaching during this period of time is his famous study on the 23rd Psalm--*The Lord is My Shepherd, The Psalm of Victorious Life.* McQuilkin's teaching on this Psalm is still available today. It is contained in the limited reprint of **Joy and Victory**.[54] He interweaves the message of victory as he exposes the beautiful figurative language of this most familiar psalm. Note his major breakdowns:

1. The Lord Is My Shepherd
2. What The Shepherd Does

---

[52]One of his early recruits to the faculty, Mr. J. A. Morris Kimber, who served as registrar, was the prime facilitator for this great step. This was the first Bible College to offer a recognized degree in Bible (Matthews 1973:23).

[53]Which was most likely the forerunner of that most popular course taught down through the ages, Progress of Redemption by Buck Hatch. The early modeling of Dr. Erdman is seen in this and the Popular Friday night Bible class in the Colonia Parlor.

[54]From time-to-time Columbia Bible College reprints this booklet (now out of print by Moody Press) in limited quantities for use of students. It is available in the Columbia Bible College bookstore.

Chapter 7. Robert C. McQuilkin (1886-1952)

    3. How The Shepherd Does It
    4. How We Enter In
    5. How We Continue

In his teaching on the 23rd Psalm and his personal testimony **Victory In Christ**, McQuilkin stresses that which is common to all Christians seeking after a transformed life which appropriates Christ's provision for Christian living. Essentially, according to McQuilkin's exposition on *What Scripture Teaches on Victory*, in **Victory In Christ** (R. C. McQuilkin n.d.:37) four steps can be identified: 1. **Need**--there is a hunger and thirst after righteousness. As this need builds there will be a moment of crisis that will lead to a paradigm shift--a change in attitude about the Christian life and how it can be lived. 2. **Awareness**--there is a paradigm shift, a breakthrough in understanding God's provision in Christ for living the Christian life. 3. **Surrender/ Removal of Barriers**--There is the removal of any barriers which would prevent acceptance of this provision. This is a step of renewal of relationship with God in which God is given absolute first place in the life. It is characterized by surrender to God for all that He has purposed for the life. It is a yielding of the life completely to Christ. 4. **Appropriation**--there is an acceptance by faith of the provision and a resulting paradigm shift in which the believer's attitude changes to believe that God is providing moment-by-moment victory in the Christian life. The strength of Mr. McQuilkin's teaching on the Victorious Life was his ability to motivate listeners to want this kind of life, to see the provision, and to move through the paradigm shift to experience it for themselves.[55]

Mr. McQuilkin, very early on, offered a Friday night Bible class, much like Morgan's, to which townspeople were welcome as well as the regular Bible College students. Joy Ridderhof, one of the members of the very first class, describes this part of Mr. McQuilkin's Bible teaching ministry.[56]

> "I remember the first Friday night class. I had gone far from my home that I loved and not without opposition and some persecution. I expected to receive a great deal at Columbia. It seemed to me on that opening night that I was in heaven. Oh, all that I hoped for or dreamed of had come to me and more, much more...I was bubbling with pure joy. It wasn't a passing sensation either; from one day to the next was to live in eager anticipation for the riches that were ours in the coming classes...I was indeed fortunate to be able to stay in the home in those days. At every meal I used to ask him questions about the Word and he would pour out his wonderful answers. I felt that he led us to think in terms of spiritual principles involved in all that we studied to such an extent that we could never forget." (M. McQuilkin 1956:116)

It is as Bible teacher and role model for the Victorious Life that most of the early students of Columbia Bible School remember Mr. McQuilkin.

---

[55]Like Brengle, McQuilkin was able to use this paradigm of the Victorious Life very effectively to see hundreds, maybe even thousands, actually enter into life power. Both Brengle and McQuilkin emphasized an *experiential* paradigm shift. All the learning taxonomies were used. For McQuilkin *cognition*, though important, was secondary. The provision step dealt with the cognitive. The *affect* was stressed in the need and surrender steps. The *volitional* was stressed in the appropriation of victory. It is the affect and volition that are key to the experiential paradigm shift leading to the victorious life as advocated by McQuilkin. See Clinton position paper, 1993, *The Paradigm Shift--God's Means of opening New Vistas for Leaders*.
[56]Joy Ridderhof founded Gospel Recordings an innovative parachurch ministry which put the basic Gospel message in many languages. A major building on the present campus is named after Joy Ridderhof. She came to the Bible College as a result of one of the California Victorious Life Conferences held by Mr. McQuilkin in California just before he came to Columbia.

Chapter 7. Robert C. McQuilkin (1886-1952)

From 1923 until 1927 the school rented space from the Colonia Hotel, an institution downtown in Columbia. As more students came to the school more of the Colonia's one hundred rooms were rented. A whole floor was used as a dorm. The year 1927 was an important time in the stabilization process during these formative years. The board and school under Mr. McQuilkin's leadership took its first major faith venture. They made a decision to purchase the entire Colonia Hotel. The asking price was $90,000. The plan was to raise $35,000 to complete the purchase and then to take a mortgage for the remaining $55,000. A prayer letter was sent out--not soliciting directly for funds but informing those who would be interested in praying for the project. There was an excellent response to the project. Many got behind it.[57]

In addition to facilities, Mr. McQuilkin's stabilizing role included the attraction of supportive people--both faculty and staff. Those who were attracted to Columbia Bible School and contributed to the development of the institution in this formative stage include: J. A. Morris Kimber, John Hehl, Betty Cridland, and Charlotte Cary (toward the end of the period). Part time teachers included Mrs. T. H. Dick, music, Miss Margaret Childs, Personal work and English, Miss Emily Dick, Practical work and Mrs. Maude Sanford, child study. Others on a less repetitive basis helped out from time-to-time.

The financial policy was indeed remarkable and radically different from most post high school training institutions. I have already mentioned how Mr. McQuilkin's basic plan was to live by faith. The first printed catalogue, 1925,26 catches how this operation by faith affected the Bible college.

> There are no fees for entrance or for tuition. The running expenses of the School being met on the plan of voluntary offerings from those interested in the work. Board and Room is provided at seven dollars a week, not including laundry, for those students living... in the Colonia.

Money was prayed in. As gifts came, frequently in the nick of time, students, staff, and faculty celebrated the goodness and faithfulness of God. They learned that God could be trusted to supply needs. After several years of this methodology, its viability was established.

McQuilkin was a master at promoting missions. Because of his wide conference ministry and his time at *The Sunday School Times* he had a wide network of contacts with mission boards and influential leaders and pastors. One of the most powerful means of promoting missions was to bring these leaders on campus. Chapel services often were graced with the presence of these kinds of leaders. They were always welcome on campus. They were hosted. Students were encouraged to meet them. The catalogues of each of the years from the mid-twenties on lists every one of the visitors who came to campus to promote missions or other ministries. Reading back on these lists is thrilling.

---

[57]Early on, Miss Emily Dick, a board member, and part of the prayer group behind the school made a simple statement of faith, "We are going to own this place some day." To the eye of faith this is possible even from the tiny non-descript beginning. The final step was by faith. But it was not presumption. This was a carefully considered plan. M. McQuilkin explains (1956:120). "Because the school would not to grow into the full use of the building for a number or years to come, it meant that a certain amount of income would be counted on through continuing to operate as a Christian hotel. The rent the Board had been paying each month was more than double the amount of interest they would pay on the mortgage. It might be added that Mr. McQuilkin did not hold the view that the total amount of money must be in hand before a building was built or a property purchased. He felt that if the Lord had given clear indication of His will that a certain property be obtained, and had given a seal by a certain sum of money, it was right to go ahead." Actually only $25,000 had come in by the purchase date. The building was bought. The mortgage was paid off early.

Chapter 7. Robert C. McQuilkin (1886-1952)

Many of the mission greats are listed. On the average between 75 and 100 of these prominent leaders came on campus each year.[58] Their challenges to students, their modeling, and their interaction with them created an ambiance for ministry that fulfilled part of Mr. McQuilkin's life purpose--the promotion of missions.

The 1929 catalogue contained a special announcement. For in 1929 the school was recognized by the State of South Carolina as a degree granting institution. The school inaugurated a four year program. The name was changed from Columbia Bible School to Columbia Bible College.

Chart 7-1 shows the expansion of the student body during this formative period.

Chart 7-1 Enrollment Figures, 1923-1928

Year	Number of Students
1923,24	8
1924,25	15
1925,26	15
1926,27	27
1927,28	42
1928,29	47

B. Years of Steady Growth--Early Faith Challenge
(1929-1938)

The first Published Catalogue, 1925,26 listed three kinds of students, the Bible School was serving. These reflected strongly Mr. McQuilkin's two life purposes connected to the *Victorious Life Message* and missions. The school has grown now. The faculty is enlarged. There is a degree program. The 1929/30 catalogue carries an expanded list of categories, 10 of them, describing the students being served. This is indicative of

---

[58]This has continued down through the years and is one of the strengths of the missions emphasis at Columbia International University. For years, the list of Visiting Missionaries and Speakers was published as part of the school's catalogue. Here is a typical list, shorter than most, which gives the range of kinds of people and places all over the world from which they came: Dr. William Ward Ayer, Calvary Baptist Church, New York City; Rev. Clifford Bammesberger, Ridgeland, S.C.; Rev. Gordon C. Beacham, Nigeria, Africa, Sudan Interior Mission; Mrs. Ruth Bicker, Peru; Carlton Booth, Providence Bible Institute, Providence, R. I.; Mrs. Louis Bowers, Liberia, United Lutheran Mission; Miss Margaret Childs, Washington, D.C.; Dr. Harry Clark, University of South Carolina, Columbia, S. C.; Dr. R. A. Forrest, Toccoa Falls Institute, Toccoa, Ga.; Miss Martha Franks, China, Southern Baptist Mission; Dr. and Mrs. Robert H. Glover, China Inland Mission; Miss Sophie Graham, China; Mr. Charles Gremmels, New York City; Dr. and Mrs. Edward N. Harris, Nigeria, Sudan Interior Mission; Rev. Jesse Hendley, Atlanta, Ga.; Miss Betty Hu, Bethel Mission, China; Rev. Maurice Jacques, Providence, R. I.; Rev. A. B. Kennedy, Columbia, S.C.; Miss Alice Lan, Bethel Mission, China; Colonel James L. McBride, Fort Bragg, N.C.; Rev. Thomas McMahan, Greenville, S.C.; Carter Morgan, Westminster, S.C.; Bernard Morris, Passaic, New Jersey; Miss Lucy Peet, Columbia, S.C.; Arnold V. Pent, York Beach, Maine; Robert Prescott; Chaplain Eugene W. Pilgrim, Fort Jackson, S. C.; Rev. Stephen Sloop, Brazil; Rev. J. Raymond Stauffacher, Africa Inland Mission; Dr. Francis Stifler, American Bible Society; Mrs. Guy Tarrant, Columbia, S.C.; William Taylor, Costa Rica; Rev. John White, Charleston, S.C.; Miss Marian Wilcox, China; Rev. J. Elwin Wright, Boston, Mass.; Jack Wyrtzen, Word of Life Hour, New York City; Mrs. Helen Duff Baugh, Christian Business and Professional Women of America, Portland, Oregon; Rev. Walter K. Beaty, Columbia, S.C.; Howard W. Ferrin, President, Providence Bible Institute.

Chapter 7. Robert C. McQuilkin (1886-1952)   page 308

the steady growth that will come. Students will come from varied backgrounds and for varied purposes.[59]

For Whom Intended

The purpose of the school as set forth in this announcement will indicate that any Christian of any age or training may profit by the study, even if a regular course is not taken. The following may be noted among the groups whom the school is seeking to serve. All of these classes have been represented in the school in the few years of its life:

1. *High school graduates, young men and women, who desire to train for Christian service and who do not plan to take the more extended college and seminary courses.* Very various are the forms of Christian service open to graduates according to the individual gifts and calling; among them may be mentioned: Foreign Missionary service, Christian Community Work in mill villages, Christian education, Sunday School work, etc. Home Missionary work, Assistant pastors, or pastors, Teachers of Bible in connection with public schools, Assistants to pastors, church visitors, etc. City mission and evangelistic work.

2. *High school graduates, training for Christian service, who plan to take further college or seminary work.* The four-year course leading to a degree may be supplemented by college courses in science and mathematics, and thus cover complete B.A. work as well as the B.A. in Biblical Education. ...

3. *High school graduates, of nineteen years or over, who enter for the two-year course,* to train for service, or as preliminary to further study in college or seminary...

4. *Men and women of any age who are not high school graduates* who desire to train for Christian service, or to secure a better knowledge of the Bible.

5. *High school graduates who are not necessarily planning to go into Christian service,* who wish to take this Bible college course as their college training, perhaps supplementing it later with further college work.

6. *College or university graduates who wish to get the work in English Bible and related subjects,* as their training for service or for Christian living.

7. *Seminary graduates and ministers* who to take more extended work than the seminary offers in English Bible and related subjects.

8. *Missionaries on furlough* who desire to continue their study of the Bible or to increase their educational equipment.

9. *Bible school graduates* who desire to take more extended work either in the Bible or related subjects.

10. *Laymen and women at work in Sunday School and church, especially in Columbia,* should take advantage of the classes to increase their knowledge of the Bible and Christian service. (1929,30 Catalogue)

This expanded list is symbolic of the coming era--one of steady growth. During this period of time, from the end of 1928 till the fifteenth anniversary year, 1938:

1. the student body will expand from 74 in 1929,30 to 198 at the beginning of the school year in 1938,39,
2. graduate classes begin,
3. the Ben Lippen conference property will be bought,
4. the Seminary will make its first purchase of property on the old Columbia Seminary property,
5. the faculty will be expanded,
6. the faith ventures will be introduced, the Thanksgiving goals.

---

[59]Note the *Victorious Life* emphasis, seemingly, is missing altogether. Mr. McQuilkin's other life purposes is there but not as strong. This does not mean they were not a part of the school's emphasis but they were not an important part of the publicity for recruiting. Note the strong Bible teaching emphasis. McQuilkin has come into his own as a recognized and powerful Bible teacher--part of his **major** role.

Chapter 7. Robert C. McQuilkin (1886-1952)

The school is no longer a one man show. Mr. McQuilkin has drawn around him an able group of staff and faculty personnel. His major life role is clarifying in all four of its aspects. The **administrator/Bible College leader** aspect of his role has clarified. He has matured in it. He is at peak form as a **teacher**. This will continue right on through his entire ministry. He is **modeling** the Victorious Life. His is a life of faith and obedience. His **mentoring**, especially the linking of people with mission resources and his personal impact on student's lives, is fruitful. His life purpose concerning the promulgation of the *Victorious Life Message* is being solidly implanted in lives. He has moved from a Conference only **methodology** as a delivery system to an on-going modeling and presentation of truth in a repetitive class room situation. His **missions life purpose** will gain momentum during the coming period of time. The first graduate to go as a missionary was in 1928. By the end of this period there will be nearly 100 missionaries out from the school. It is clear now that his legacy will be related to the Bible College. He has founded it. During this period it will be further stabilized.

The Post Office And the 1931 Bank Crash

This period of time begins and ends with faith ventures. The Ben Lippen[60] faith venture, especially 1931, showed that God could be trusted to supply needs even in the bleakest of financial times. The purchase of the Columbia Seminary property, 1938, the greatest challenge, up to this time, closes this steady growth era. There will be other faith goals in the 40s but the Ben Lippen post office experience paved the way. The Columbia Seminary property was icing on the cake.

One thing that all early graduates of the school talk about is the life of faith that Mr. McQuilkin demonstrated. Typical of this is the Ben Lippen, faith challenge of 1931. The Colonia Hotel purchase in 1927 had set the tone for faith ventures. But it is the 1931 Ben Lippen Faith Venture which highlights the focus of Mr. McQuilkin's trust in God.[61] Early on Mr. McQuilkin had looked for a site for a summer conference highlighting the Victorious Life. Ties were made to a camp site in Asheville, N.C. For seven years, the temporary arrangement--rent free use of the rustic facilities, for the conference was adequate. The property had been located. The asking price was $9000. The Bible College took up the option. But it is not the purchase of the property but the Post Office incident which challenged faith. M. McQuilkin emphatically tells the story of this faith venture. It is the story of the inn which highlights McQuilkin's faith in God.

> About the time that the plans for an inn or hotel for the new conference grounds were being made, a new post office building had just been completed for the city of Asheville. The old post office which stood at the intersections of College and Heyward streets was to be razed. A friend, interested in seeing the conference obtain this for building material, gave $1,000 to be used on condition that they get it. It would cost $3,000 to move the post office, but from it they would get an estimated $10,000 worth of material. As the Bible College had only $570 in the building fund plus this $1,000 given conditionally, the leaders were praying for some sign from the Lord as to whether they should take the option on moving the building. Before they were fully satisfied as to what the Lord's will might be, He gave a strange sign (M. McQuilkin 1956:134,135).

---

[60]Ben Lippen is the Scottish name for mountain of trust which was the name given to the mountain-like property that was to house the conference ministry proclaiming the Victorious Life.
[61]The story is told in detail in Chapter 5 Ben Lippen--Mountain of Trust, of Matthews' 50 year history of Columbia Bible College, **Towers Pointing Upward**. See also Chapter 16 The Land of the Sky in M. McQuilkin's 1956 biography. Of all the leaders treated in this book two stand out as exemplifying trust in the unseen God for financial provision. Both McQuilkin and Robert Jaffray were men of faith who in the world economic depression years of the 30s trusted God to expand their ministries.

Chapter 7. Robert C. McQuilkin (1886-1952)   page 310

The stage is now set for the faith challenge.[62] M. McQuilkin describes the disaster.

> On December 31, 1931, forty-four banks in South Carolina closed their doors! All of the Bible College funds, which amounted to about $6,000, including the money for the post office, were deposited in one of these banks. None of their bills had been paid; the allowances for half of November and all of December had not been paid, and the $1,000, given conditionally, was to be returned if the post office was not obtained. (M. McQuilkin 1956:135)

How would Mr. McQuilkin and the board respond?

> The Bible College Board had to notify the city of Asheville by January 7 if they were going to take the building. When they met on January 5, to seek the Lord's mind, someone began her prayer, "Lord, we thank thee for this bank failure!" And though they teased her about it later, this prayer brought them to face the truth that they could only cast themselves upon the Lord for His mercy. They took the verse: "O our God...we have no might ... neither know we what to do: but our eyes are upon thee" (2 Chronicles 20:12). How foolish it seemed to pray for guidance about going ahead with a new project when money for current needs was gone. But with weakness and fear they decided if the Lord should send $1500 designated for the new conference grounds by noon Thursday, they would take the old post office building. (M. McQuilkin 1956:135,136)

How will God answer this request of faith and ensure future trust in Himself? Let's get two vantage points on this time of victory.

> In the meantime the one who had given the original amount for the post office was visiting in Florida while his prayer letter telling of the great loss in Columbia lay in his post office box in new York. As prayer went up at Columbia Bible College for guidance, the Lord led this friend to a home where a copy of the prayer letter had just come. When the news was called to his attentions, the Lord reminded him of a bond which had just matured. Immediately he wired to Mr. McQuilkin something like this: "Am anxious for you to get the post office. $1500 is in the mail today!" (M. McQuilkin 1956:136)

I have stated how Mr. McQuilkin was such a staunch model of a leader who trusts God. Hear how his modeling affected one student who observed Mr. McQuilkin in this situation.

> I wondered whether Dr. McQuilkin would be quite so happy if he had all of my problems. I soon found out. One day forty-four banks in South Carolina closed their doors. The faculty had not yet received their allowances and all the school money was in the bank. Dr. McQuilkin rang the bell in the middle of the afternoon. We thought there might be a fire. He was smiling and told us to assemble in the Sun Parlor. As if nothing had happened he mentioned the fact of the banks closing and then assured us that the Lord would take care of everything and not to worry. A check came in to the Bible College within a few days that covered all the immediate bills that had to be paid (Matthews 1973:30).

---

[62] *A faith challenge* (Clinton 1989:222) is the shaping activity of God in which He expands a leader. It is an instance in ministry where a leader is challenged to take steps of faith in regards to ministry and sees God meet those steps of faith with divine affirmation and ministry achievement in such a way as to increase the leader's capacity to trust God in future ministry. This is the prime focal incident for testing McQuilkin's faith in God to provide finances--the years of campus expansion, that is, the Thanksgiving Victories and the building projects on the downtown campus in the 40s, all hinge on this testing time. It is one thing to trust when you can see God's people with plenty of resources to help out. It is another when economic conditions are tough for everyone, God's people, and many have lost all of their financial resources. But McQuilkin was not focused on people providing but on the living God providing.

Chapter 7. Robert C. McQuilkin (1886-1952)

McQuilkin's own faith was strengthened. Students saw him face the same kind of problems they did. And they saw him respond by trusting God and continuing in the life of victory.

In 1933 Mr. McQuilkin received from Wheaton College the honorary degree of Doctor of Divinity. He was a worthy honoree.

The year 1938 represented the 15th anniversary year of the Bible College. It is fitting to close this section with the faith venture which catapulted the school into the war years. Matthews describes the problem.

> Ten years carried the enrollment at CBC over the one hundred mark. By 1936 the student body was straining to the limits the facilities of the old Colonia Hotel, and dormitory space for men students had to be rented outside--first, in the Chicora College grounds, and then the Columbia Seminary campus. As the fifteenth anniversary approached, it was decided to commemorate the anniversary by purchasing the seminary campus. This was a tremendous forward step. The president called this "the greatest step forward in the development of the work since its foundation in 1923. Continuing his comments he said, "This may seem the worst time from the standpoint of human resources, to make such a venture. But since it is a venture of faith and in the will of God, it is the very best time, for it is God's time. (Matthews 1973:31)

What was involved in this faith challenge?

> The Columbia Seminary campus had four buildings with 75 rooms on a beautiful city block just a block away from the Bible College.[63] The agreement was drawn up for payments to cover a five-year period. Faith was confronted with mountain-sized financial impossibilities to be moved before the property could belong to the school (Matthews 1973:31)

Table 7-2 tells the faith story ((Matthews 1973:32).

Table 7-2 God's Faithfulness for the Columbia Seminary Campus

Date	Required	Received
6/1/38	$ 1,000.00	1,000.00
9/1/38	4,000.00	4,003.10
6/1/39	5,000.00	5,000.00
9/1/39	20,000.00	20,197.09
10/1/40	10,000.00	10,000.01
10/1/41	10,000.00	13,000.00
10/1/42	10,000.00	10,013.00
10/1/43	15,000.000	15,074.00
	$75,000.00	

> Each deadline called for an exercise of prayer and faith on the part of the board, faculty, staff, students and interested friends. The deadlines always leaped forward to meet the board with their unbending demands while the funds either dawdled by the wayside or stopped altogether (Matthews 1973:32).

---

[63] The Columbia Seminary had vacated this campus in 1926 and moved to Decatur, Georgia nearby Atlanta.

Chapter 7. Robert C. McQuilkin (1886-1952)

A typical example will show how God's people had to learn to trust and wait and believe right to the last instance. Dr. McQuilkin always modeled these qualities.

> ...the September 1, 1938, deadline...A payment of $4,000.00 was due and by August 29,1938, only $3,356.00 had been received. That meant that $644.00 had to be available for the payment in just two days. With time not pressing, it is easy to believe that the money will all be in. But with only two days to go and over $600.00 to come in--in fact, when the situation has become impossible, when faith alone is left of all our resources--then, lo! the money comes. And then too, it is only the last five minutes that counts in lessons of patience. So both faith and patience were getting a workout over the $644.00. Yes, the money came: $78.00 on August 30, $126.00 on August 31, and $443.10 early enough on September 1 to complete the payment. This particular payment was important because it was the crisis point in the transaction. It had been decided that if all the money came in, the Bible College would take this as God's signal to move forward, and would then secure the option trusting Him to bring in the total. The climax of rejoicing on the 20th anniversary, 1943, when the last payment was made, gave God all the glory... (Matthews 1973:32,33).

The two faith ventures, the Ben Lippen Post Office in 1931 and the Columbia Seminary property in 1938, were anchors of faith. They would serve as signposts of God's faithfulness in the years to come.

C. Mature Years of Productivity
(1939-1946); Age=52-60

This period of about seven years represents the mature years. They take us to the great expansion challenge. The Bible College has a solid faculty. They have a good campus. There will be need to build. But these are the years in which Dr. McQuilkin begins to see his life purposes filled with increasing effectiveness. His role, all four aspects of it are in focus. His life purposes are being fulfilled. His unique methodology using the classroom and Bible college as a means to exploit his powerful teaching/exhortation combination allows him to challenge many to the Victorious Life and missions. The victories of faith continue throughout this period. In fact, they happen with such a regularity that a lesson of correction about presumption and going ahead of the Lord has to be taught. A catalogue captures the highlights of this period.

Time	Special Highlight
1939	Enrollment goes beyond 200.
1940	Ben Lippen School inaugurated.
	Completion of Conference Inn.
1941	Number of graduates reaches 310.
1942	Alumni going to mission field reaches 100.
1943	Twentieth anniversary.
	Completion of payment for men's dormitory.
	Graduates, 405.
	Foreign missionaries, 119.
1944	Enrollment reaches 236.

Chapter 7. Robert C. McQuilkin (1886-1952)

1945   Purchase of Ben Lippen Camp.
          Enrollment reaches 258.
          Foreign missionaries, 145.
          Program of Directed Teaching Inaugurated.
1946   New dormitory and classroom building started.
          Completion of dining room extension.
          Enrollment reaches 316.
          Foreign Missionaries, 170.
1947   Completion of new dormitory and classroom building.
          Recreation ground purchased.
          Erection of Huston Hall Book Store at Ben Lippen.
          Enrollment reaches 396.
          Foreign missionaries, 190.
          Graduate School of Missions inaugurated.
1948   Foreign missionaries, 210.
          Enrollment reaches 399.
          Ben Lippen School gymnasium erected.

I could describe many of these events. Each has its story. But I want to summarize four important aspects of Dr. McQuilkin life and ministry which reached a peak during these years--his **teaching role** (including his writing ministry which permanently reproduced his teaching), the **motivating force behind his missions** thrust, his **mentoring through correspondence**, and his **character**--the manifestation of the fruit of the Spirit in his life.

His Teaching/ Exhortation Gift[64]

Dr. McQuilkin was an accomplished teacher. Included in his gift-mix was the gift of exhortation. Some teachers like Morgan have dominantly the teaching gift but not the exhortative gift. For them the thrust of the teaching is on clarifying the truth. For a teacher with exhortive gift the emphasis is not only on seeing the truth but using it. There is a drive to see truth applied in the life. Such teachers motivate students to see truth and to realize it in their lives. McQuilkin's teaching methodology involved discussion, question and answer (provided materials which stimulated this), and later in life more and more lecture format. He put his teaching in a broader perspective always carefully reviewing content in terms of the larger picture. His teaching over a period of time in a course was integrated. Years later students could remember the entire framework of a whole course. He always attempted to move the affect. M. McQuilkin (1956:201) quotes one of his famous repeated statements which reflects his intense desire to touch the affective domain of learning (the feelings). "Young people, get the thrill of this; it's real!" He helped students see the relevancy of truth, how it fits in life today.

What were his special courses? Over the years he taught a number of Bible book studies. In the early days these were often night classes which allowed non-residential students from Columbia to attend also. But if you ask a number of those who studied with him over the years they will mention: Daniel and Revelation, John and Romans, Acts and Hebrews as especially important Bible courses. They will mention hermeneutics, the course which teaches how to interpret the Bible. And then they will pinpoint several courses which apply hermeneutics to the Bible such as Parables or Christ in the Old

---

[64]M. McQuilkin devotes one entire chapter, Chapter 24 Dr. McQ, to the explanation of Dr. McQuilkin's teaching ministry. It is clear in the description and illustrations that his *gift-mix* includes *exhortation* as well as *teaching* (see Clinton and Clinton 1994 **Developing Leadership Giftedness**). His teaching/ exhortation combination impacted lives. He was effective.

Chapter 7. Robert C. McQuilkin (1886-1952)

Testament or Progress of Doctrine in the New Testament (using Bernard's **Progress of Doctrine**, the Bampton Lectures as a text).

Have I overstated his teaching/ exhortation gifting?[65] M. McQuilkin gives feedback from three students. Their viewpoint on his impactful teaching is probably typical of many students less able to articulate it. These were taken from personal letters of students to Dr. McQuilkin giving appreciation for his ministry in their lives.

> The Bible College taught me to think for myself, study for myself, and go straight to the Bible itself to learn its meaning instead of depending on commentaries or helps. There was also the balancing emphasis on staying close to the great stream of evangelical truth which the church has always held to, and the emphasis on getting added help from every possible source after I have sought the meaning first hand. (M. McQuilkin 1956:200)

> The thing which impresses me most about Columbia, I think, is that everything is given such a practical treatment. It is never learning for the sake of learning, but learning to "Know Him." Scholarship is good, but I am glad that it is not placed above spirituality. (M. McQuilkin 1956:201)

> Before I graduate I want to tell you a little of what you have meant to me as a spiritual father in the Lord.
> I don't know what all of your aims were, but there are certain trusts that stand out in my mind and I am gradually making them my own as the Holy Spirit deals with me. These are some of them:
> 1. Study the Bible first and know what it says above all else that men have written.
> 2. Get thrilled with the truth you are studying.
> 3. The personal joy of knowing that Jesus is coming is more important than the problems connected with His coming.
> 4. Israel is God's channel to pour out His blessing to all the world.
> 5. The conflict between God and Satan is real, yet is headed to victory for Jesus.
> 6. Victorious living is to be a working thing at the time of greatest darkness and not when trials are over. Rejoice!
> 7. An intellectual knowledge is worth zero to God if not controlled and centered in the Lord Jesus.
>
> I'm sure that there are many more that I could list and probably you'll wonder why I didn't think of some of the truths you've given day in and day out but these are what I think of now....The thing that has touched me most has not been just hearing the things you teach, but knowing that these are living real experiences with you...(M. McQuilkin 1956:203).

In addition to direct teaching, Dr. McQuilkin also reduced his teaching to various types of written materials including articles, book reviews, pamphlets, booklets, and books. Most of these are now out of print although some like **Joy and Victory** and **Victory in Christ** are from time-to-time reprinted for classroom use and are available in the Columbia Bible College Bookstore. For a list of his writings see the bibliography in the section, **For Further Study**.

---

[65] I probably have understated it. At the 1994 homecoming there were a large number of older alumni who had studied with Dr. McQuilkin in the 30s and 40s. I heard two things over and over--his teaching impact and his modeling a life of victory and faith--as I chatted with these old timers who had based a lifetime on the foundational values gained from Dr. McQuilkin's ministry.

Chapter 7. Robert C. McQuilkin (1886-1952)

Motivation For Mission

    Dr. McQuilkin had two life purposes which focused his life and ministry--promulgating the *Victorious Life Message* and mobilizing people into missions. His own call to the mission field and its providential blocking supply us with part of what motivated him for missions. But the major reason was a Biblical one.

    M. McQuilkin suggests that Dr. McQuilkin used to read the following passage inserting the bold faced phrase and saying it with emphasis. Then he would finish with an emphatic phrase. I have enlarged and boldfaced it so you want miss it. Read the passage as if your were in Dr. McQuilkin's class and imagine his emphasis. He would read rapidly from verses 3 to 13 with emphasis on the bold faced. Then he would read verse 14 triumphantly with slow emphasis on the final bold face.[66]

    Jesus has just predicted the fall of Jerusalem and the destruction of the temple. As soon as he was alone the disciples posed the question in verse three. Catch Dr. McQuilkin's emphasis.

> 3 And as he sat on the mount of Olives, the disciples came unto him privately, saying, Tell us **when shall these things be?**...
> 4 And Jesus answered and said unto them, Take heed that no man lead you astray. 5 For many shall come in my name, saying, I am the Christ; and shall lead many astray. **BUT THE END IS NOT YET.** 6 And ye shall hear of wars and rumors of wars; **BUT THE END IS NOT YET.** See that ye be not troubled: for these things must needs come to pass; **BUT THE END IS NOT YET.** 7 for nation shall rise against nation, and kingdom against kingdom; **BUT THE END IS NOT YET.** And there shall be famines and earthquakes in divers places. **BUT THE END IS NOT YET.** 8 But all these things are the beginning of travail. 9 Then shall they deliver you up unto tribulation, and shall kill you: and ye shall be hated of all the nations for my name's sake. **BUT THE END IS NOT YET.** 10 And then shall many stumble, and shall deliver up one another and shall hate one another. **BUT THE END IS NOT YET.** 11 And many false prophets shall arise, and shall lead many astray **BUT THE END IS NOT YET.** 12 And because iniquity shall be multiplied, the love of the many shall wax cold. **BUT THE END IS NOT YET.** 13 But he that endureth to the end, the same shall be saved. 14 And this gospel of the kingdom shall be preached in the whole world for a testimony unto all the nations; **AND THEN SHALL THE END COME.** (Matthew 24:3-14 adapted from the American Standard Version)

This Biblical truth then was one of the primary motivating factors behind Dr. McQuilkin's strong emphasis on missions.[67] By the end of 1951 there were about 737 graduates.[68] Of

---

[66] This emphasizes a value also seen in two of the major public rhetoricians in this book. Both Brengle and Morgan stressed the importance of emphatic public reading of the Scriptures. **THE BIBLE OUGHT TO BE READ PUBLICLY WITH CLARITY, PROPER ENUNCIATION, EMPHASIS AND ATTENTION GETTING POWER.** McQuilkin and Brengle were adept at adding emphatic illustration or phrases which would call attention graphically to the importance of the passage.

[67] We have seen this same emphasis as a driving force in Robert Jaffray's ministry. A.B. Simpson strongly impacted Jaffray with this Biblical value and probably Dr. McQuilkin as well. M. McQuilkin (1956:204,205) relates one of Dr. McQuilkin's favorite stories. "In the early days of the Christian and Missionary Alliance a newspaper reporter from the *New York Journal* called on Dr. A. B. Simpson, founder of that movement, with the idea of getting a story. In a very few years hundreds of missionaries had been sent out under their auspices. And although their group were folk of average income, hundreds of thousands of dollars were being given. But the special news that drew the reporter was that Dr. Simpson claimed to know when Christ was coming. The reporter asked: 'Do you know when the Lord is coming?' 'Yes,' replied Dr. Simpson, 'And I will tell you if you will promise to print just what I say, references and all.' The reporter's notebook was out in a moment. 'Then put this down: And this gospel of the kingdom shall

these, 315, or about 41% went on the mission field--an unusually high per cent. This says something of McQuilkin's effectiveness in accomplishing one of his life purposes.[69]

Mentoring Via Correspondence/ Personal Aspect of Ministry

One feature repeated in the lives of Simeon, Brengle, Morgan and Robert C. McQuilkin was the powerful personal ministry carried on with numerous people via correspondence.[70] McQuilkin used correspondence to,

1. build relationships,
2. affirm,
3. encourage,
4. impart knowledge,
5. carry on theological discussion,
6. give advice,
7. link people with people and other resources.

The extent of his correspondence is captured in a few quotes.

> A chapter devoted to his intimate friends would be long indeed, while one reproducing his vital correspondence would be book length. The hundreds of letters which poured in after his death give a little picture of the variety and reality of these friendships. They came from men of wealth, and from those who had been his servants, from doctors of philosophy and from those who could hardly spell; they came written in Spanish from friends he had met on the mission field and from Negro friends of the city and state. They came from mansion and from prison and from all between.
> These letters may be explained in art by the monumental volume and variety of correspondence which Dr. McQuilkin carried on over the years. He wrote letters of congratulations when receiving graduation, wedding, or birth announcements. A warm, chatty letter might even go in response to a brief message on a Christmas card. He wrote *bon voyage* letters sending missionaries off to the field and then again he would write welcoming them home. He answered mimeographed or form letters from individuals or organizations if the news contained unusual burdens or joys. Thank-you notes were written promptly for the smallest service, and letters of sympathy to the bereaved were tender and sincere.
> The theological discussions he carried on by mail with various men often ran for pages. On one occasion a friend replied to such an epistle: "On the number of pages, you win the argument eleven to six!"
> Frequently such allusions as this would appear in his correspondence. "I have dictated eight cylinders tonight " (approximately five letters to a cylinder). "The conference closed last Sunday and we are having a vacation with one hundred and fifty

---

be preached in all the world for a witness unto all nations; and then shall the end come' (Matthew 24:14). 'Have you written down the reference?' 'Yes, what more?' 'Nothing more.' The reporter laid down his pencil and said, 'Do you mean to say that you believe that when the gospel has been preached to all nations Jesus will return?' 'Just that,' said Dr. Simpson. 'Then,' replied the reporter, 'I think I begin to see daylight' 'What do you think you see?' 'Why I see the motive and the motive-power in this movement.' 'Then,' said Dr. Simpson, 'you see more than some of the doctors of divinity!'

[68] McQuilkin's interest in networking via individual missionaries, mission leaders, and mission organizations was a powerful means of motivating people toward mission involvement. M. McQuilkin devotes one entire chapter, Chapter 26 Affiliations, to the various mission organizations that McQuilkin was involved with. He made occasional trips to nearby Mexico or Central America where he ministered first hand.

[69] At the 1994 homecoming it was mentioned that now, over 3000 alumni had served on the mission field. There are more than 11,000 alumni and they serve in 80+ countries around the world.

[70] This is a form of *distance mentoring*, relational empowerment on an occasional basis at a distance.

Chapter 7. Robert C. McQuilkin (1886-1952)

> letters to dictate. "I want to celebrate my birthday by actually catching up on all my mail, wouldn't that be wonderful?" This week I am in Buffalo holding a Bible conference. I brought some odds and ends of letters to answer with a personal note. When I counted them I found that there were about seventy letters, so I decided to borrow a dictaphone and dictate some answers." (M. McQuilkin 1956:170-171)

One of his friends captured the sense of personal relationship McQuilkin engendered with people.

> At the memorial service held at Ben Lippen conference center two weeks after Dr. McQuilkin's death, one of those called upon to give a word of tribute made this statement: "I was speaking with a man this morning who said, 'I knew him intimately; that's why I'm here.' " Then he went on to say, "I think that there were thousands of people who knew him intimately. His ministry was very personal...he had a personal interest in what seemed to be almost everybody." (M. McQuilkin 1956:169)

Whereas, many founders and stabilizers of organizations, may see correspondence as a necessary evil of the position, or a hindrance to their real ministry, McQuilkin saw it as a means of personal ministry. Many were empowered via his distance mentoring.

Fruit of the Spirit, Importance of Character

Frequently, when one meets some Christian leader that has been admired afar off via writings or other public ministry, there is often a disappointment. Up close they don't seem to display the fruit of the Spirit that you would hope for from someone who apparently ministers in power. One would hope that a proponent of the *Victorious Life Message* would indeed not disappoint in this respect. Dr. McQuilkin did not. He was consistent through and through. Robertson McQuilkin, the son of Dr. McQuilkin gave, in my mind, the finest tribute to his father when he highlighted Dr. McQuilkin's consistency.[71] At the memorial service for his father he paid this ultimate testimony.

> The message that the Lord has laid on my heart concerns the greatest characteristic of my father's life. When people would tell me that my father was a great missionary statesman, I would swell with pride, perhaps rightfully and say, "That's my father." I believe that he deserved recognition n that field, but I'm sure that this was not his great characteristic.
> And then, when I would think of how the Lord had used him to establish a unique and mighty work for Him, my heart would fill with pride again and I would think, "That's my father." But I'm sure that these works were not the greatest characteristic of his life.
> Nor even his message of the Victorious Christian Life, although God used him in a marvelous way to bring that, could be counted his greatest characteristic.
> But I feel that the greatest characteristic of his life was this, that he lived the message that he preached. And when I have heard people say it and thought of this myself, I have not been filled with pride at all...I can only praise God that in His great mercy and love and power, ... And when this has come to me I have though, "That is my Heavenly Father." (M. McQuilkin 1956:226,227)

This consistency was modeled throughout these important years of productivity.

---

[71]During my last two years in graduate school at Columbia Bible College (1968-1970) I had the privilege of serving as the teaching assistant to this godly man. I respect his opinions. Dr. Robertson McQuilkin had every right to be proud of his father. And he has carried on in that same tradition of consistency and a godly walk that he saw in his own home.

Chapter 7. Robert C. McQuilkin (1886-1952)

D. Final Years
(1946-1952); Age=60-66

M. McQuilkin (1956:218) describes the next several years as the "time of greatest tests of faith, the greatest victories and, for Dr. McQuilkin, the greatest physical weakness." The GIs were returning home. Facilities were stretched to the maximum. The enrollment went over 300 in 1946 and neared 400 in 1947. One of the great victories of this period concerned the thanksgiving goal for the new women's dorm.

> As the leaders prayed about meeting the cost for this building they decided to ask the Lord for the first $100,000 by Thanksgiving Day, when the building was to be dedicated. One hundred thousand in a few months? Impossible! But they prayed. On October 22, $66,750 was on hand toward this, but one week before the date set the amount was still 28,000 short. The day before nearly $23,000 was still needed. Had they been presumptuous?
> On Thanksgiving morning at the worship service there was a tenseness as Dr. McQuilkin arose to make the announcement about the status of the dormitory fund. Very deliberately he reviewed the circumstances of the Lord's leading in the matter of building the dormitory; he spoke of the earnest seeking of the Lord's mind, of the tokens given, of the prayer, and of the hopes and fear. the group waited expectantly. Then as he reached the point and announced that an annuity of $50,000 had been given that morning, there was a thrill of felt joy over the great congregation! It took but a slight motion from the leader to bring the group to their feet to sing with great exultation, "Praise God from whom all blessing flow." (M. McQuilkin 1956:221)

Several other goals, like this, were established and met during this last period of ministry. Students continued to see the life of faith and victory modeled.

Dr. McQuilkin was active during these last several years of his life, including a heavy speaking ministry outside the Bible college.[72] There were, however, increasing physical symptoms that were troubling. Due to high blood pressure he was put on a strict diet in the summer of 1951 and thereafter. During the summer of 1952 while at Ben Lippen Conference in Asheville he was feeling heart pains. He was under the constant watchfulness of doctors. But on Tuesday, July 15, just after answering a phone call from his daughter, he gave the phone to Mrs. McQuilkin, laid down to rest and suffered a heart attack which quietly took him in to the presence of the Lord.

I have already mentioned the Christlikeness of character that was demonstrated over these last years. All of the six characteristics of a leader finishing well were dominant in his life and ministry at the end and throughout these last years. He maintained a personal vibrant relationship with God right up to the end. He maintained a learning posture. He evidenced Christ likeness in character as evidenced by the fruit of the Spirit. He lived out his life so that convictions and promises of God were seen to be real. He left behind several ultimate contributions. And his destiny, to be a leader greatly used of God to promote victorious living and mobilization for missions, was increasingly fulfilled. McQuilkin finished well. His was a life dominated by two life purposes. It was a focused life and a satisfying life.

Critical Incidents Identified, and/or Explained

Critical incidents are shaping activities which can affect **values** relating to all three types of formations--spiritual (leadership character), ministerial (leadership skills) and

---

[72] I'll say more about this when I talk about his ultimate contribution as a *public rhetorician* and a missionary statesperson.

Chapter 7. Robert C. McQuilkin (1886-1952)

strategic (total direction in life and ministry). There is a sense in which many, many incidents in a leader's life affect values. But from that large identifiable number a few should be highlighted and recognized as very significant. Critical incidents also frequently provide **pivotal points for choices** of roles, kind of ministry and locale. These focal factors provide strategic guidance.

Here is a list of critical incidents, some giving focal values and some providing strategic guidance. Table 7-3 indicates these. I number them for convenience of referencing later when I comment on them.

Table 7-3 Listing Of Some Critical Incidents In McQuilkin's Life

Incident(s) Name	Age	Formational Type Dealing With Basic Value/Thrust
1. Pastor Anderson/ Contemporary Model/ Divine Contact (See page 284)	9	Spiritual--Pastor Anderson's personal concern for neighborhood children leads young Bob to church and eventually to salvation as well as early ministry outlets. His early life was one given over to Christ.
2. Leadership Committal/ Joins Church/ I am going To Be A Minister (See page 285)	12	Spiritual/ Strategic: McQuilkin made a child-like committal for ministry when he joined the church. God will come back and hold him to this after a time of vocational experience in the building industry.
3. Like-Attracts- Like: W.J. Erdman Contemporary Model/ (See page 287)	20-23	Ministerial: Erdman becomes a model for McQuilkin in how to publicly teach the Bible. Erdman is a macro-contextual/ contextual Bible Teacher. His knowledge of the whole Bible gives McQuilkin the seeds of his Progress of Redemption course and his model for Friday Night Bible time.
4. New Wilmington/ Missions 1st Surrender (See page 290)	22	Strategic: This is the seed of his Mission Call. Progressive election is in view. McQuilkin puts missions first; via prayer/ giving. Later this will become a committal to go.
5. May 1909, Progressive Call; Love and Ministry (See page 290)	23	Strategic: This is part of progressive call. Now to ministry full time, later to missions.
6. August 15, 1911/ Union Life Experience; Trumbull, Divine Contact (See page 277)	25	Spiritual, Strategic: McQuilkin goes through a paradigm shift which alters forever his life and life goals. He will now always have the victorious life message as part of his thrust in ministry. This connection with Trumbull will lead to the next step in strategic guidance. McQuilkin gets seeds of life purposes and vision to carry it out: publish *Victorious Life Message*; Conference Center for Promotion of *Victorious Life Message*; Bible School for propagating *Victorious Life Message*.

Chapter 7. Robert C. McQuilkin (1886-1952)   page 320

Table 7-3 Listing Of Some Critical Incidents In McQuilkin's Life continued

Incident(s) Name	Age	Formational Type Dealing With Basic Value/Thrust
7. Trumbull--Invitation To Join *The Sunday School Times* (See page 293)	25	Strategic: McQuilkin will apprentice to a contemporary model who will teach many ministry skills (publishing related) as well as network into leading evangelicals in U.S. and Britain.
8. Oxford Challenge/ Victorious Life Testimony Founded (See page 294)	26	Ministerial/ Strategic: McQuilkin and like-minded friends found sodality, Victorious Life Testimony to promote *Victorious Life Message* in eastern Pennsylvania. This will continue as a secondary ministry while he is at *The Sunday School Times* and will become primary while waiting for mission field after influence-mix challenge.
9. S. D. Gordon/ Divine Contact / "The Joints of the Will" (See page 295)	29	Spiritual/ Strategic: McQuilkin responds to an S. D. Gordon challenge for mission field. Available to go. McQuilkin will in the future challenge many to go on the field. He needs to have made this surrender himself in order to challenge others.
10. Dr. Melvin Kyle, God's Provision for Training, Mentor Teacher (See page 296)	29	Ministerial: When McQuilkin committed to the mission field, Dr. Kyle, a Professor of Theology at Xenia Seminary offered to tutor McQuilkin in theology. For several months while waiting to go overseas, McQuilkin met two or three nights per week in Dr. Kyle's home.
11. The *City of Lahore*, Ship Sinks/ And Other Shut Doors (See page 282)	31	Spiritual/ Strategic: A series of blocked doors gives strategic guidance. An influence-mix challenge is part of the back swing from the attention getting slamming of the door, the ship sinks. Double confirmation is necessary. The mission has the final decision. They release McQuilkin for conference ministry.
12. Negative Preparation/ Conflict/ Where To Now (See page 298)	33	Spiritual/ Strategic; McQuilkin takes up the conference ministry full-time with Victorious Life Testimony, the parachurch group he had helped found. His ministry is very successful. Then comes conflict--differences over interpretation of the *Victorious Life Message*. McQuilkin grows through the struggles over these issues. And strategically he is guided to the next ministry, his career role.
13. The One of His Choice/ Dr. Ramsey--Divine Contact/ Prayer Band/ Open Doors/ The Call (See page 300)	34	Strategic: McQuilkin, the answer to prayer, goes to hold a Victorious Life/ Bible Conference teamed with Dr. R. J. Ramsey. This will eventually lead to the Call to come as Dean of Southern Bible Institute soon to become Columbia Bible School.

Chapter 7. Robert C. McQuilkin (1886-1952) page 321

Table 7-3 Listing Of Some Critical Incidents In McQuilkin's Life continued

Incident(s) Name	Age	Formational Type Dealing With Basic Value/Thrust
14. Reflection Time/ "How Beautiful Are The Feet"/ Central America (See page 301)	36	Strategic/ Ministerial: McQuilkin gets first hand taste of Mission field and its needs. He needs this in order to lay foundations at Columbia Bible School of mission and Victorious Life thrusts. This time also settles for him his decision to go to Columbia-- though the final decision will not be made till after he talks with wife in Pennsylvania after return.
15. Ben Lippen, the Post Office and the 1931 Bank Crash (See page 309)	45	Strategic: McQuilkin models true faith in God to supply in circumstances which do not support such a faith. This faith challenge accepted and passed paves the way for many similar victories in the future when the campus will be expanded.

Critical incident 6 was one of three primary focal incidents. It shaped a value, "Christians can enter in and have a victorious life in Christ." This value will permeate all of Dr. McQuilkin's future ministry. It will develop into a life purpose which will focus his life activities. It was an experiential paradigm shift. Later he would work out over the years the cognitive explanation of it. The other two primary focal incidents gave strategic direction. Critical incident 11, The Ship Sinks and critical incident 13, The Call, gave him his mission emphasis and the location and incipient major role which later became full blown and entailed 4 thrusts: **academic administrator/ leader; teacher; model--** Victorious Life, faith; **mentoring**--personal ministry.

Several things should be noted about these critical incidents. One, there were a number of contemporary models or divine contacts who deeply influenced McQuilkin including: Pastor Anderson (critical incident 1), Dr. W. J. Erdman (critical incident 3), Charles Trumbull (critical incident 6), S. D. Gordon (critical incident 9), Melvin Kyle (critical incident 10), and R. J. Ramsey (critical incident 13). Two, a number of them were incidents which impressed focal values upon McQuilkin: Incidents 2, 4, 5, 6, 9, 14, and 15. Three, there were a large number of strategic direction incidents: Incidents 3, 7, 8, 11, 12, 13, 14. Incident 15 was fundamental in affirming in McQuilkin the walk of faith which was demonstrated increasingly over the next 20 years.

Three Dominant Critical Values

This section is usually devoted to a listing of values under three categories: spiritual (character forming), ministerial (skills), and strategic (life long direction). I then identify some of the more critical of these values. With McQuilkin I want to list three important focal values. These values were interwoven into the fabric of his life and ministry. They emerge in numerous ways.

McQuilkin lived a life which was focused around two life purposes--Victorious Living and missions. A dominant value can be drawn from each of these life purposes. A third dominant value arose in the context of working out one aspect of his major role, academic administrator/ leader. As he established the campus facility, recruitment of faculty, and the financing of the work he demonstrated a trustworthy God. He lived a life of faith. He was a model that many would follow in their own life work.

Chapter 7. Robert C. McQuilkin (1886-1952)

1. **Victorious Living**
   A Christian should have a relationship with the living Christ so as to walk above the controlling authority of sin in a life. Provision is available. A surrendered Christian who is willing to appropriate that provision by faith can have this kind of satisfying life--not a perfect life, but a life pleasing to God and demonstrating the power of Christ in a life.

2. **Missions**
   Every Christian should be looking forward toward Christ's return and thus must be deeply committed in doing his/her part in carrying out the Great Commission. The mobilization of people toward this goal is deeply satisfying.

3. **Faith**
   A Christian leader must be willing to trust God for provision for needs in his/her ministry and thus demonstrate the presence and power of God in his/her ministry in a way to inspire faith in the living God. The essential ingredient of leadership is the presence and power of God in the life and ministry of a leader. Exhibiting faith in God for provision is one way to demonstrate this.

Contributions

This chapter contributes to the general field of leadership development in the following ways:

1. It portrays a leader whose life was dominated by two life purposes which he merged.
2. It shows the importance of long tenure in one locale. His 31 years thawed, broke through, and developed the concept of an interdenominational Bible centered institution in an otherwise denominational locale.
3. It shows the importance of life purposes for focusing a life. The motto of Columbia Bible College interrelates the two important life purposes--To Know Him (Victorious Living) and To Make Him Known (missions). Major role, uniquely methodology, and ultimate achievement flowed from these life purposes.
4. It highlights the drift pattern toward an ultimate contribution set.
5. It shows how God honors heart intent and yet providentially blocks as well as opens doors to lead to the major role.
6. It depicts a leader for whom three focal values dominated his life.
7. It shows the importance of a parachurch ministry linking closely to the church and demonstrates that each helps complement the other.

Dr. McQuilkin's contributions to the cause of Christ and the on-going of the Christian movement include at least the following:

1. He led many Christians into a Victorious Life experience.
2. He mobilized a number of Christians directly into missions and/or the support of missions.
3. He models the in-service track of preparation for ministry.
4. He founded or helped found and/or stabilized four organizations: Victorious Life Conference; Columbia Bible College, Mexican Indian Mission, Ben Lippen High School.
5. He modeled an impactful teaching ministry--grounding many students in the study and importance of the Word of God.

Chapter 7. Robert C. McQuilkin (1886-1952)

6. He provided materials in the area of crisis experiences, hermeneutics, and some important theological topics.
7. He finished well and left a model for others to follow.

Overall Lessons from the Life

There are many important lessons of life that could be identified in Dr. McQuilkin's life. From those I want to list and emphasize seven.

1. **Character is Critical.**
   Early on McQuilkin faced an integrity check in the business world. His response showed him to be a person of integrity. Leaders must have this. He exemplified the importance of integrity all his life. He consistently lived by his conviction.

2. **Victorious Living Testimony**
   Consistency is a must for advocates of victorious living. When a person claims to have an experience with Christ which radically transforms a life, that person will be scrutinized by others. Consistency is crucial. In my opinion, mature Christians don't expect perfection from leaders who are under the public eye. But they do expect consistency. McQuilkin was consistent.

3. **Response To Crises**
   McQuilkin demonstrated in numerous crises (ship sinking--major change in life direction, conflict in understanding of *Victorious Life Message*, loss of two children, the Bank Crash, the Thanksgiving goals, etc.) that responses to crises in life are as just as important as the solutions to them. The modeling of response, that of trusting God for His best in these situations, probably had as much impact as the actual decisions finally made with respect to them. Leader's lives are always on display.

4. **Commitment Insights**
   A leadership commitment can be progressive over a lifetime. McQuilkin was progressively led into a deepening leadership commitment. As we as leaders select emerging leaders we must recognize that our touch in their lives may be simply to move them along to the next level of commitment in a lifetime of God's dealings with them. While we may want them to go the entire distance in one fell swoop, we may in fact be the instrument to take them only to the next level. If we run ahead of God in this we may in effect thwart His on-going activity and put it back a step or two.

5. **Faith Situations**
   Probability should not affect faith. A person demonstrating a full blown spiritual gift of faith can trust God in unfavorable circumstances as well as favorable circumstances. The probability that such and such a thing can happen will not add to or deter a person exhibiting the gift of faith. Dr. McQuilkin's ringing the bell in the 1931 bank crash and joyfully trusting God highlights this beautiful truth.

6. **Power of Group Prayer**
   McQuilkin practiced prayer as an important part of his leadership influence. He was an active participant in the noon hour prayer band of *The Sunday School Times*. He was formative in the small group of individuals who had experienced the life transforming paradigm shift in Victorious Living in the

1911 summer conference. They formed a prayer band which prayed into existence the Victorious Life Testimony--a parachurch group to promote Victorious Living. He saw the power of a small band of prayer warriors when he received the Call to Columbia. He prayed weekly with the board of the Bible College which emerged out of that earlier prayer band. He instituted monthly days of prayer at the Bible College in order to instill that basic habit in the lives of students. He was part of the faculty and staff intensive praying that was part of the faith goals that were set to expand the campus facilities. Now while this emphasis differs from leader to leader and may be tied somewhat to gifting, never-the-less, McQuilkin consistently saw intercessory prayer answered throughout his life time.

7. **Expect Criticism**
One lesson learned from a simple reading of Nehemiah is, **Expect Criticism in your leadership.** When you are leading a work that spans across parachurch organizations and denominations there will be conflict. M. McQuilkin captures just the tip of the iceberg when she shows the difficulty of pleasing across a continuum of opinions.

Perhaps it was in the questions of church policy and doctrine that his bitterest conflicts came. If it had not been so sad, it might have been ludicrous when, for instance, one group accused him of being an extreme dispensationalist, while another blamed him because he was not. One group accused him of being anti-denominational and another blamed him because he was not, and so on. Perhaps the criticism along some lines would not have been so great had he settled in a different part of the country. The South knew little of interdenominational work and looked at such with suspicion. He felt that a denominational loyalty that came first was dishonoring to Christ. He often said, "When I met Christ, I lost every speck of denominational pride that I ever had!" These were hard words for some groups (M. McQuilkin 1956:216).[73]

These lessons demand reflective thought by leaders--especially those less tied to giftedness. Lessons 1, 3, 4, 6, and 7 may well apply across the board, regardless of giftedness and life purposes.

Implications for a Focused Life

What have we learned from this life that helps us understand a focused life? That is the question I attempt to answer in this section. When we study a focused life we are in fact looking for a number of issues. I use the following screens to help me perceive aspects of the focused life. Only a few of these factors were dominant in McQuilkin's life.

---

[73]This ecumenical viewpoint, founded on core convictions, was also a trademark of Simeon (who fellowshipped with evangelicals whether or not they were Anglicans), A. J. Gordon (his conference ministry was beyond Baptist circles), Samuel Brengle (who was much broader than just the Salvation Army), and G. Campbell Morgan (constantly ministering beyond his church setting to others).

Chapter 7. Robert C. McQuilkin (1886-1952)

1. <u>Giftedness Development</u>[74]

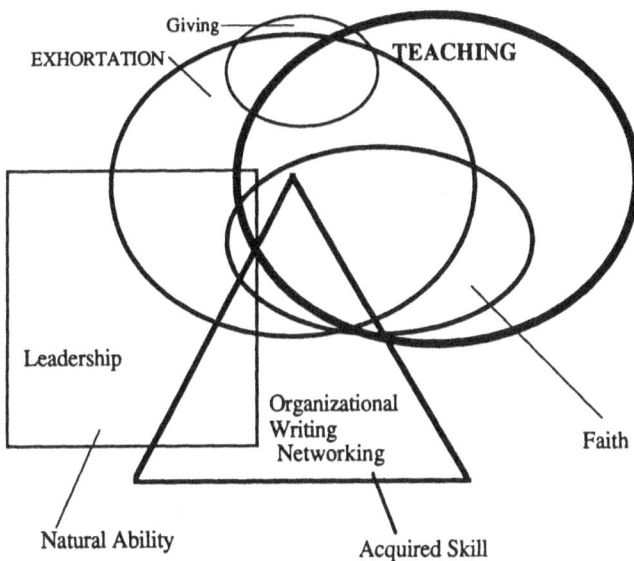

Giftedness development was a very important factor in bringing focus. God led to the major role which would enhance all of the elements of the giftedness set. Note that spiritual gifts are clearly the focal element of the giftedness set. The four fold thrust of the major role allowed freedom for all parts of the giftedness set to be used with power. The faith and giving gifts were crucial to his stabilizing ultimate contribution.

2. <u>Destiny Processing</u>

This factor did not play an explicit part in focusing Dr. McQuilkin. The destiny pattern can be demonstrated but it was not dominant.

3. <u>Identification of Key Ministry Insights</u>

Key ministry insights do not seem to play any role in focusing Dr. McQuilkin with the possible exception of a public Bible teaching ministry modeled by Dr. Erdman.

4. <u>Identification Of Major Values That Uniquely Fit One's Ministry</u>

This was a very important factor in bringing focus. See under critical values where I identify three that shaped the focus of McQuilkin's life: Victorious Life, Missions, Faith.

5. <u>Integration Of Personality Factors So As To Identify A Focused Or Ideal Role That Moves Toward Convergence</u>

This factor apparently does not affect the focus.

---

[74]The following is a pictorial diagram of the giftedness set. See Appendix F for explanation.

Chapter 7. Robert C. McQuilkin (1886-1952)

6. Social Base Processing

Mrs. McQuilkin was very supportive of Dr. McQuilkin's ministry. The release pattern, which was dominant throughout Christian circles in this period of time was followed. The testimony of Robertson McQuilkin, the commitment of children to the mission field, and the testimony of those who knew the family indicate a solid social base situation.[75]

7. Ultimate Contribution Set[76]

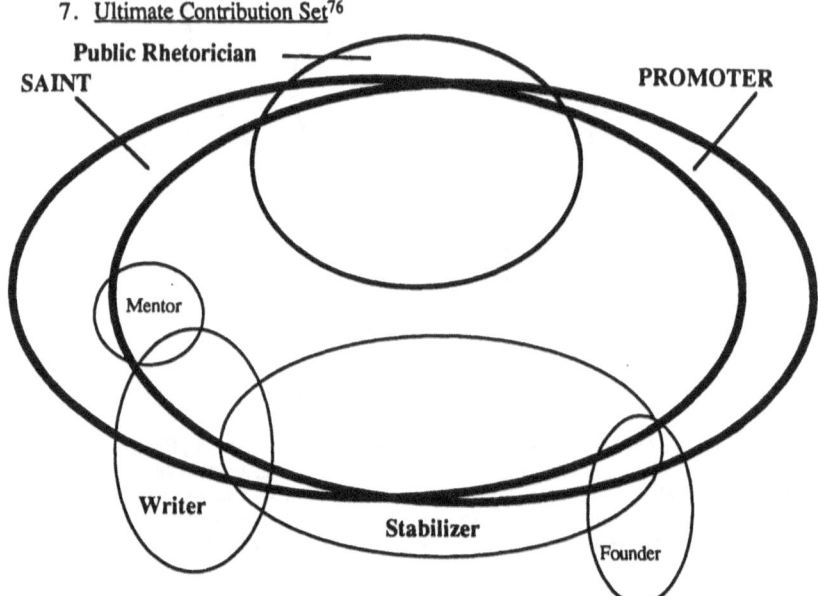

In addition to the specific contributions I have already given, I have identified six ultimate contributions that form his ultimate contribution set. Four were more dominant: **Promoter** and **Saint** were most dominant. **Public Rhetorician** and **Stabilizer** were next most important. **Writer** and **Founder** were also a part of the set. However, Dr. McQuilkin followed the drift pattern in all of these ultimate contributions. These happened as a result of other things and were not the dominant target of his activities as in the deliberate pattern. I have included a **Mentor** category.

1. Promoter

McQuilkin was a strong advocate of missions and the *Victorious Life Message*. This contribution was brought out in the biographical section.

---

[75] M. McQuilkin devotes a whole chapter to insights on the family, Chapter 19 1015 Gregg, which affirms this solid social base.

[76] The following pictorial diagram of the ultimate contribution set is called a Venn Diagram. See Appendix F for help in interpreting.

Chapter 7. Robert C. McQuilkin (1886-1952)

2. Saint

He lived a life which modeled what he believed about the Victorious Life. This contribution was also discussed previously. See items on modeling, mentoring, consistency, fruit of the spirit, and Victorious Living Testimony which touch on this contribution.

3. Public Rhetorician

In addition to public ministry at chapels and other occasions within the school, Dr. McQuilkin had at one time or another extensive ministry outside the Columbia Bible College setting. M. McQuilkin (1956:145ff) describes these. Some of his outside ministry included:

1. a weekly ministry in Columbia--Business Men's Bible Class--also broadcast on the radio,
2. a Bible Class on Friday nights in the Sun Parlor of the Colonia Hotel,
3. an evangelistic booth at the South Carolina State Fair,
4. many conferences. He averaged 8 or 10 Conferences a year over his 40 years of ministry, at times like from 1932-1942, he averaged 12-14.

His conference ministry including evangelistic services, deeper life meetings, and Bible exposition. For five successive years during the 30s he was the speaker at the winter evangelistic services held at Wheaton College. He spoke at Dr. Walter L. Wilson's Kansas City Bible Conference. On these kinds of ministry excursions he was kept busy speaking to numerous groups in addition to the plenary speaking at the conference. He had a strenuous summer ministry at his own Ben Lippen site every year. M. McQuilkin (1956:148) mentions that he appeared on most of the large conference platforms of the nation as well as many of the smaller ones. He was described as having a clear and penetrating voice. He was an energetic speaker who used body language for emphasis. His public reading of the Bible constantly was used to gain attention. One example about his reading of Scripture, Matthew 24, the 2nd Coming, was previously given.

His public ministry in addition to its direct results, whether evangelism or edification, always performed secondary functions. He built a good public image of the ministry of Columbia Bible College. He also forwarded his two life purposes. Like Brengle and Morgan, Dr. McQuilkin could have ministered full time as a public rhetorician. But in God's providential guidance, this ministry was to complement his life ministry at Columbia Bible College.

4. Stabilizer

He left behind two solid organizations which have continued and grown: Columbia Bible College and Ben Lippen High School. He was an administrator/ leader. He skillfully built both of these organizations to the point where they had God-given vision, property, and people--the essentials to continue.

5. Founder

McQuilkin was part of the instigation of several organizations. Though his founding work was usually in concert with others. His need to found organizations was not a primary drive for him. But in the normal course of his ministry certain organizational entities were needed. He helped facilitate those. The Ben Lippen school was a case in point.

Chapter 7. Robert C. McQuilkin (1886-1952)   page 328

6. Writer

I have mentioned that he wrote pamphlets, booklets, book reviews, and books. In addition, for a number of years he wrote the Sunday School lessons for *The Sunday School Times*. I list his books and other works in the bibliography at the end of this chapter. Most are now out of print though two **Joy and Victory** and **Victory in Christ** are reprinted from time-to-time.

7. Mentor

McQuilkin had personal relationships with so many. During the formative stages of the school while it was still small, McQuilkin had powerful relational ministry with students as contemporary model, teacher, and counselor. His correspondence ministry over the years frequently demonstrated mentor sponsoring and mentor counseling.

8. Ministry Philosophy Concepts

Other than the major values I have previously listed I have not been able to integrate a ministry philosophy though I intuitively feel this was important to Dr. McQuilkin's focus.

9. Future Perfect Time Paradigm

This concept apparently does not play a role in focus for Dr. McQuilkin.

10. Boundary Processing Which Helped Focus

I discussed in detail the boundary which led away from *The Sunday School Times* toward the mission field but ended up in Columbia. This was a very significant shaping force in his focus.

11. Paradigm Shifts Which Helped Focus

The Victorious Life paradigm shift which was entitled August 15, 1911 was probably the most important force to focus Dr. McQuilkin's life and ministry. I have discussed this in much detail throughout the biographical narrative.

12. Window of Opportunity

Following World War II there was an opportunity for training veterans. However, while there was some expansion, Columbia Bible College was not as vigorous in taking advantage of this opportunity as compared to Prairie Bible Institute.

SUMMARY ON FOCUSED LIFE INSIGHTS FROM McQUILKIN'S LIFE

Let me summarize focused life concepts from McQuilkin. A focused life is a life dedicated to exclusively carrying out God's unique purposes through it, by identifying the focal issues, that is, the **major role, life purpose, unique methodology,** or **ultimate contribution,**[77] which allows an **increasing prioritization** of life's activities around the focal issues, and results in a satisfying life of being and doing.

---

[77]These four--*major role, life purpose, unique methodology,* or *ultimate contribution*--are called the *focal issues.* Usually one or more of them dominates a focused life. The identification of focal issues and the processes that prioritized them are given in the studies of the eight chosen for this book.

Chapter 7. Robert C. McQuilkin (1886-1952)

Life purpose dominated the focusing activity of God in McQuilkin's life. The promulgation of the *Victorious Life Message* was the first life purpose that McQuilkin gave himself too. A second life purpose that of mobilizing for missions became intertwined with the first. It was people who knew Christ in Victory who could take that message to others--the missions thrust. These two ideas captivated McQuilkin's attention. Following several means to do them led eventually to Columbia and the Bible College which he developed. His **major role** grew out of who he was and included at least four major thrusts: **administrative/ leadership** of the Bible College--all aspects but dominantly its academic excellence and its financial base; **teaching**--hundreds of lives were moved toward his life purposes; **modeling**--this was an indirect role but one that powerfully affected all those with whom he came in contact--this was the basis for his **Saint** ultimate contribution, legacy; **mentoring**--like Brengle his ministry was effective both in public and because of his personal interest in people. Of secondary importance in his focus were **unique methodology** and ultimate contributions, though his **ultimate contributions** are a living legacy--visit Ben Lippen and Columbia International University today and you will see vividly that legacy.

Closure--Lets Really Remember Robert C. McQuilkin

Well, I have attempted to apply the Hebrews 13:7,8 leadership mandate.

Remember your former leaders. Think back on how they lived and ministered. Imitate those **excellent qualities** you see in their lives. For Jesus Christ is the same today, as He was in the past and as He will be in the future. What He did for them He will do for you to inspire and enable your leadership.
Hebrews 13:7,8 (Personal Interpretive Paraphrase)

We have remembered Robert Crawford McQuilkin! But what challenges from his life do we take away for our own? Let me suggest two I believe he might make to us today.

1. **Victory**
   Today, with our modern emphasis on dysfunctionality, 1000s are bound by a past which will not allow them to live freely. Without wanting to negate the complexities of these foundational shaping events and people in our pasts I do want to say that there is provision for Victory in Christ. Healing does not always have to be a prolonged and painful dredging of the past. I can almost hear Dr. McQuilkin saying, "Young people, believe that there is Victory in Christ! It is real. It can be life changing forever! Accept His provision and be free from your past to walk moment-by-moment with this living Victorious Savior." His own past was not conducive to a Victorious Life. But God gave it to him. And he modeled it for us. I believe he would want that emphasis to be resurfaced.

2. **Missions**
   Missions is much more complex today than at any point in history. But we have greater windows of opportunity than ever in the history of the Church. And Asia promises to open as never before to the up coming generation. I believe Dr. McQuilkin would challenge us to be a part of this great expansion of the Gospel to every nation. **AND THEN THE END WILL COME.**

Chapter 7.   Robert C. McQuilkin (1886-1952)   page 330

Where To Go and What To Do For Further Study

The following are important works about Dr. McQuilkin or by Dr. McQuilkin. For the most part you will have to go to a Bible College or Seminary setting to get at them. Three of these, marked with an asterisk, are reprinted from time-to-time. Buy these from the Columbia Bible College Bookstore when available. I am hoping they will do more of these reprintings. I am encouraging the leaders there to do so.

Let me give two suggestions for follow-up: 1. Get a copy of **Victory In Christ** and read it.[78] Ask God to challenge your heart about your walk with Christ. 2. Visit the Columbia International University campus, chat with students, talk to faculty, attend some of the chapel services and catch the ambiance of an institution committed **To Know Him and Make Him Known.**

Bibliography

Matthews, Arthur
    1956   **Towers Pointing Upward.** Columbia, S.C.: Columbia Bible College.

McQuilkin, Marguerite
    *1956   **Always In Triumph.** Westwood, N.J.: Fleming H. Revell Company.

McQuilkin, Robert C.
    *n.d.   **Victory in Christ.** Columbia, S.C.: Columbia Bible College.

    1918   **Victorious Life Studies.** Philadelphia: Christian Life Literature Fund.

    1929   **Our Lord's Parables.** 1980 edition--Grand Rapids: Zondervan.

    1931   *What is Pentecost's Message Today.* Columbia, S.C.: Columbia Bible College.

    1932   *Can We Trust the Old Testament.* Columbia, S.C.: Columbia Bible College.

    1938   *The Lord is My Shepherd.* Columbia, S.C.: Columbia Bible College.

    1941   *Let Not Your Heart Be Troubled.* Columbia, S.C.: Columbia Bible College.

    1943   *Lord, Teach Us To Pray.* Columbia, S.C.: Columbia Bible College.

    1943   *Why Is It Right For a Christian To Fight.* Columbia, S.C.: Columbia Bible College.

    1947   **The Message of Romans.** Columbia, S.C.: Columbia Bible College.

    1950   *Be of Good Cheer--Christ's Five Victory Commands.* Columbia, S.C.: Columbia Bible College.

    *1953   **Joy and Victory.** Chicago: Moody Press.

    1958   **God's Law and God's Grace.** Grand Rapids: Zondervan.

---

[78]Write to the Columbia Bible College Bookstore, P.O. Box 3122, Columbia, South Carolina, 29230-3122. Reprints are available from time-to-time.

Chapter 7. Robert C. McQuilkin (1886-1952) — page 3

Timeline

1886	1895 1898	1911 1912	1918 1916<--B1--->	1921	1928	1938	1946 1952
Age 9	12	25	32	35			66

Summary of Focal Issues:

A. Shaky Family Foundations (1886-1895)
B. Church Training (1895-1898)
C. School, Work, Leadership Transition (1898-1911)
  Work--9 years at Steele Builders 1902-1911
  1910 to U. of Penn. (part time for Steele) Age=24

A. Organizational Apprenticeship--The Sunday School Times (1911-1916)
B. Boundary Processing (1916-1921)
  1. Entry Stage: Mission Call/ The Ship Sinks (1915-1918)
  2. Evaluation Stage: Waiting--Conference Ministry/ Victorious Life Affirmation (1916-1921)
  3. Termination/ Expansion Stage: Conflict/ Mission To Central America/ SBI (CBS) (1921/22)

Two Life Purposes Unfold Emerges: 1. Reproduce Victorious Life in people; 2. Publish this Message; How? Train People in Bible School with this Message.

LP1= Publish Message *Sunday School* Times
LP1=Victorious Life--Unique Methodology =Victorious Life Testimony/ Conference Develops
LP2= Missions Interest Develops

A. Foundations For Missions and Victorious Life Thrusts (1921-1928)
B. Years of Steady Growth--Early Faith Challenge/ Great Faith Victory (1929-1938)
C. Mature Years of Productivity (1939-1946)
D. Final Years/ Greatest Tests of Faith, Greatest Victories, Greatest Physical Weaknesses (1946-1952)

Major Role Develops: Bible Leader/ Teacher/ Mentor/ Model

LP1 =Ben Lippen Conference Asheville
Bible School As Unique Methodology for LP2 Bible College as Sending Base, also becomes Ultimate Contribution

Critical Incidents

C1 Pastor Anderson/ Age 9 — Contemporary Model
C2 Leadership Committal/ Age 12 — Joins Church a
C3 W. J. Erdman/ Age 20-23 — Contemporary Model/
C4 New Wilmington Challenge/ Age 22
C5 May 1909, Age 23
C6 August 15, 1911/ Age 25
C7 Trumbull Invitation/ Age 25 S.S. Times
C8 Oxford Challenge Age 27 Victorious Life Testimony Formed
C9 S. D. Gordon/ Divine Contact Age 29 "The Joints of the Will"
C10 Dr. Melvin Kyle--Mentor Age 29
C11 City of *Lahore* Sinks/ Age 31 And Other Shut Doors
C12 Conflict/ Negative Preparation Age 33
C13 The One of His Choice/ The Call Age 34
C14 Reflection time Age 36
C15 The Post Office/ Age 45 Ben Lippen Victory

Henrietta Mears
(1890-1963)

"If you place people in an atmosphere where they feel close to God and then challenge them with His Word, they will make decisions."

Chapter 8. Henrietta Mears (1890-1963), Teacher
A Destiny for Challenging Emerging Leaders

Remember your former leaders. Think back on how they lived and ministered. Imitate those **excellent qualities** you see in their lives. For Jesus Christ is the same today, as He was in the past and as He will be in the future. What He did for them He will do for you to inspire and enable your leadership.
            Hebrews 13:7,8 (Personal Interpretive Paraphrase)

Let's remember Henrietta Mears whose vibrant life and influence inspired many potential leaders to leadership committals which have forever changed the face of Christianity in the United States and beyond. We still feel the results of her influence today through many of the leaders she challenged and the organizations they initiated.

Henrietta Mears was an unusually strong woman leader who wielded great power and influence in her ministry. The following two opening illustrations give insight into the source of this power--two power gate experiences[1] in her progressive call and a special sensitivity and awareness to her sense of destiny derived both from her heritage and her own experiences with God.[2]

Opening Illustration 1.
Progressive Leadership Committal[3]

Ages 17, 20, 26, 38 (Matthew 4:19, 2 Timothy 2:2)

Henrietta Mears received a series of progressive calls over a period of 21 years. They eventually led to the role and life purpose which dominated her ministry efforts. Each call was responded to with a committal which opened the way for the realization of the next. Two were directly related to power in her life and ministry. The third dealt with a clarification of her life purpose. The fourth concerned the place and major role through which her leadership would be exercised with a long tenure and great effectiveness. I tie these together and offer them as an introduction to one whose entry into full-time ministry although delayed was exceedingly productive.

While still a senior in high school, Henrietta attended a series of meetings led by Dr. Riley, the senior pastor of the Baptist church she attended. He culminated the series with a challenge to all who would respond to serve as full-time Christian workers. The thrust was a surrender to go where ever and to do what ever the Lord wanted. Henrietta

---

[1] *Power gate* experiences are unusual times when a leader seeks from God power for life or ministry. I'll describe these more fully after giving Mears' illustrations.
[2] A *sense of destiny* (Clinton 1989:349) is an awareness of God's hand on the life for special accomplishments. I give more on this later when I talk about the importance of her heritage in shaping her life.
[3] We have already seen the notion of a progressive leadership call in the case of Robert C. McQuilkin. However, he went into full time ministry early on in the series of progressive calls which led toward the mission field and finally to his life work. Mears' call into full time ministry was the fourth in a series of committals over 21 years. Mears entered full time Christian ministry at age 38, after 15 years as a high school educator. This is quite late compared to all studied in this manual: Simeon (23); Gordon (27); Brengle (23); Morgan (23); Jaffray (23); McQuilkin (25); Maxwell (27). Yet she accomplished a great deal for she entered into full time service as a competent worker. The rest who entered early on developed proficiency after a number of years in full time ministry. She was proficient and productive immediately.

Chapter 8. Henrietta Mears (1890-1963)

and her friend Evelyn Camp both responded with a public committal (Roe 1990:69). Roe captures the willingness but lack of decisive call for Henrietta Mears.

Initial Call--Wait

> In time, Evelyn developed a deep concern for Japan, feeling the Lord would have her serve Him there. But, try as she would, Henrietta felt no such urge to go and work with the Japanese people. She saw the need in Japan and felt a deep concern for that country and its people, yet she did not feel led to serve there.
> Henrietta prayed, lest something was wrong in her life, keeping her from wanting to go to Japan, too. "Is something wrong with me?" she asked herself again and again. Yet not one to jump into action without divine direction, she waited and prayed, abiding the Lord's time.
> Her only solution, she felt, was to search out for herself how she could appropriate God's power and find His direction for her life. For weeks, she scoured the Bible for references to Christ's presence, particularly for those concerning the ministry of the Holy Spirit. She closeted herself with God.
> Then a divinely revealed truth began to take shape in her mind, as the object of her search gained focus in her thoughts: It was God Himself she was seeking. In Him lay her call. But how to acquire the full measure of His presence, His will, His power? What needed to be done? What discipline to take up? What efforts of mind and will to reach for?
> Then suddenly, a cascading flood of light rushed into her soul, illuminating darkened corners, transforming her questions into understanding and confidence, as the controlling insight of her life dawned upon her: She could do nothing more to obtain God's presence and power than to receive the fullness of His Holy Spirit as a gift. By faith then, she reached out and took what God had for her--Himself (Roe 1990:69-70).[4]

Her call to full-time ministry was tied up with her friend Evelyn's call. She will again comparatively come to grips with her call when Evelyn Camp returns from Japan on furlough. In the meantime, God challenged again, this time, toward a power gate experience. Henrietta Mears was overwhelmed and knew she could not accept that challenge without God's power.

Riley's Mantle Challenge--Need

Three years later, in her sophomore year at college, her mom died. At her mom's funeral, after a tremendous eulogy for her mother which reviewed her life and ministry, Pastor Riley challenged Henrietta Mears to take up the mantle of her mother.

> In Henrietta's second year of college, when she was 20 years of age, her mother fell critically ill. Henrietta remained out of class to care for her, but on December 29, 1910, just a few days after Christmas, Mother Mears died. Following her mother's death, Henrietta went through a period of loneliness and great grief....
> Henrietta at this time wrestled with more than just grief. She thought often of Dr. Riley's words on the occasion of her mother's death when he said "Henrietta, I am praying that your mother's mantle will fall upon you." How, she wondered, could she possibly measure up to such high expectation (Roe 1990:73,74).

---

[4]Henrietta Mears had made an early public decision for Christ as her savior as a young girl at about age 7 (Roe 1990:61). As is typical in churches where children receive Christ at an early age, there is usually a second committal in the teen years in which God meets the youngster in terms of Lordship. This is true here of Henrietta Mears. She is open to what ever God wants. He meets her with a revelation of Himself as her source of power. His presence is enough. It is all she needs. He will clarify later.

Chapter 8. Henrietta Mears (1890-1963)   page 335

There was a prolonged build-up of this overwhelming challenge until the need became great enough to press Henrietta Mears toward God for a solution. God responded with a mystical experience which encouraged and inspired confidence as well as empowered with the Holy Spirit.

> Then one winter night, alone in her room, as she knelt in prayer, she felt she "saw the Lord." In a total surrender of herself and of everything she held dear, she finally experienced closure in the matter of her mother's death and entered into a life of total dependency upon the Lord. That matter was now settled for all time and would never trouble Henrietta again.
> The room was still and her heart was quiet before the Lord as she then asked God for spiritual power that she be fully used of Him in the might of the Holy Spirit. (Roe 1990:74)

Powers (1957:114) records that at this point a verse was impressed upon her heart, "How much more shall your heavenly Father give the Holy Spirit to them that ask him." She sensed God speaking to her. She asked and received by faith the fullness of the Holy Spirit and had confidence that it was so.

> Assured in her spirit that her request had been honored, she expressed her gratitude for His goodness to her. "Thank you, Lord, I accept by faith the filling and the power of the Holy Spirit, just as I accepted Christ as my Savior." (Roe 1990:74)

From that moment on she began to experience that power in her life.[5]

> She would later describe this encounter with the Lord in this way:
> I [had] felt absolutely powerless from the thought that I could possibly live up to what my mother had been and had done, and I prayed that if God had anything for me to do that He would supply the power. I read my Bible for every reference to the Holy Spirit and His power. The greatest realization came to me when I saw that there was nothing I had to do to receive His power but to submit to Christ, to allow Him to control me.
> I had been trying to do everything myself; now I let Christ take me completely. I said to Christ that if He wanted anything from me that He would have to do it Himself. My life was changed from that moment on. (Roe 1990:74)[6]

The third part of the progressive leadership challenge occurs upon Evelyn Camp's return from the mission field.

---

[5]These two experiences, critical incident 4 and 6, illustrate power gates. Power gates function to open the participant to a new level of awareness of God's power in the life. Two kinds of *power gates* are typically described: *life power* and *gifted power*. Critical Incident 4 is a *life power* type. Mears wants to sense God in her life. This experience is similar to a Keswick *power gate* which is a surrender/ faith appropriation experience. It is one of several power gates including the entire sanctification paradigm and later the Pentecostal Experience, the Baptism of the Holy Ghost. All essentially do the same function--open the way to new experience with God. None guarantee an on-going successful ministry. They are simply gates that open the way for a new relationship with God. Incident 6 represents a *gifted power gate* experience which is similar except that its participant is seeking for power in ministry. Mears was overwhelmed by her mother's life and ministry. She knew she could not accomplish what her mother did without God's special enabling power in the life.

[6]This is a typical example of the positive testing pattern. The three fold pattern of challenge, positive response, and expansion are clearly seen. Here Henrietta is challenged by God to appropriate the Holy Spirit in her life for power in ministry. She responds appropriately by asking for the Holy Spirit and believing by faith that God has given. Her ministry begins to see power in it. She started a Bible class on campus for women. From a few at the beginning the class quickly expanded to 60 or more (Roe 1990:74,75). Her following ministry in the rural towns of Beardsley and North Branch also manifest power in her evangelistic and Bible teaching ministries.

Life Purpose Clarified

Henrietta had surrendered her life for full-time service. It was not yet clear where or how. The question of power had been settled. God now clarifies for her a life purpose which focuses her life.

About this time[7] Evelyn Camp, returned home on her first furlough from Japan. She shared her ministry experiences with Henrietta's Fidelis Class.[8] Later, when Evelyn returned to Japan, the president of the class went with her. And other class members also went into missionary service.

As Henrietta observed one after another of her Bible students answering the call into Christian service, she realized God was speaking to her. He was clarifying her own calling in the Christian field by confirming what she was already doing for him:

She had been called to train leaders and to nurture the spiritual growth in thousands who could go in her place to penetrate the world with the Gospel of Christ. Only one Henrietta could have gone to Japan--or to anywhere else (Roe 1990:90,91).

Final Clarification of Call

The fourfold critical incidents leading to her call culminated in a major decision time in 1928. Pastor Steward P. MacLennan who had previously met Henrietta Mears on a trip to Minneapolis in 1925 offered Miss Mears the post of Christian Education Director in the First Presbyterian Church of Hollywood, an exciting and growing church. After a sabbatical time from teaching including a European tour and two visits to First Presbyterian Church of Hollywood, Henrietta Mears accepted *this clear God-given call* to full-time ministry. There was certainty guidance from God which clinched the decision.[9]

Henrietta's pilgrimage to full-time ministry was a long one. But she was always involved in productive ministry where ever she was. She knew God's power in ministry. She knew the major focus of her ministry--challenging emerging leadership into ministry. And finally it became clear, in God's timing, of the place and role to which she was to accomplish her life work.

---

[7]About 1916 or 1917. Henrietta Mears is 26 or 27. This is some 8 or 9 years after her initial surrender with Evelyn Camp for full time ministry. Evelyn has gone on to be a missionary. Henrietta has not. Surely this was a time of evaluation.

[8]This Fidelis class also illustrates Miss Mears moving in power following her filling of the Spirit experience about 5 years previously. Baldwin and Benson (1966:46) points out that after first returning to Minneapolis Henrietta was asked by her sister to take over a small class which had been a frustrating experience for her. Within five years this class swelled to over 500. New facilities had to be built at the church just to house this one class.

[9]Certainty guidance means special confirmation by God. Sometimes this is a double confirmation, that is an inner conviction by the leader, followed by an external confirmation by someone else who has no knowledge of the original conviction. In this case, it was a special type of fleece. Henrietta asked that her house (Margaret's too) be sold for $2000 more than the asking price and in a time when things were not moving very well. God met this request almost instantly (Roe 1990:94). She also had to be released from her teaching contract--which she was.

Chapter 8. Henrietta Mears (1890-1963)   page 337

Opening Illustration 2.
Destiny Trip, The Expendables

Age 56,57 (Esther 4:13-16)

Henrietta Mears' whole life was a life of destiny.[10] It is clear when her life is analyzed in retrospect. But the fruitfulness arising out of this destiny experience, critical incident 19, is the peak productivity of her destiny fulfillment.

The year was 1946. Henrietta needed a break from ministry. During the war years there had been a heavy load, especially due to the absence of so many males off doing battle. She and her sister, Margaret, decided on a sabbatical tour[11] to Brazil. Henrietta, frequently used just such sabbatical tours for inspiration, rest, renewal, and new vision. So it was off to Brazil they went. Note the anticipatory build-up as this tour unfolds.

> On the calm beaches of Brazil, she sought to recoup her energies. As her strength returned and Americans began receiving visas for Europe--closed to tourists until late 1946--Teacher began to think about visiting the fields of war where hundreds of her college boys had served. As always, thought led to action, and she applied for the necessary visas.
> "Impossible!" responded the American ambassador in Rio de Janeiro. "Only official persons are receiving visas to Europe."
> "But I am official," Henrietta remonstrated. "Over 700 young men from our church fought in Europe, and I want to see for myself what conditions prevail there, so I can better counsel them as they return home." (Roe 1990:274, 275)

The American ambassador after almost superhuman effort did in fact get the necessary visas. Now, Roe foreshadows the significance of this critical tour.

> They were fatigued from all their last-minute preparations but satisfied that they were on their way to Europe at last. Margaret lay in bed with a severe cold. Henrietta spent most of the days on the ship resting, reading her Bible and praying, *not realizing*

---

[10] Over a lifetime God increasingly shapes a *sense of destiny* in effective leaders. A *sense of destiny* is a growing awareness that God's hand is upon a leader in a special way to accomplish His purposes through that leader. Usually there is a three fold pattern as a sense of destiny progresses. First, there are indications of *destiny preparation*. Then there is a clarification of the destiny, called *destiny revelation*. Finally, the pattern culminates in *destiny fulfillment*. At this point in Mears' life she has already been fulfilling her destiny of challenging emerging leaders into ministry. But this experience, critical incident 19, is the peak experience of her life in which her life purpose of fulfilling leadership selection takes on a heightened dimension due to the window of opportunity available. More is accomplished in the next few years of her life than all of the previous time--though that time has been very fruitful. The dam bursts here and her influence multiplies due to the revival-like breakthrough.

[11] There is something very instructive here. Powers (1957) in chapter 3 lists some 11 of these sabbatical tours (1927, 1931, 1935, 1938, 1940, 1942, 1946, 1949, 1952, 1954, 1956). Later I will give a table describing them and the results of them. Powers (1957:34) indicates that these sabbatical travel tours accomplished three purposes in Mears' life: 1. they were times of relaxation and refreshment, that is, a change of pace from her intense ministry; 2. they were also times of discovery of new insights or renewal or new vision for ministry--these were an on-going continuing educational experience taken in lieu of formal study; 3. they were an opportunity to visit and minister to her many students and missionaries around the world. Miss Mears was a high energy person who accomplished much in a three fold demanding role. But she also almost periodically took lengthy sabbaticals from this demanding ministry. She did not burn out. She accomplished much. Usually leaders today do not have planned sabbaticals. These are necessary for continued accomplishment. Mears serves as an excellent example that these are not only possible but very profitable.

Chapter 8. Henrietta Mears (1890-1963)

> *that God was preparing her for the most significant work of her life* (emphasis mine). (Roe 1990:274, 275)

Devastation and tragic conditions awaited Margaret and Henrietta as they traveled across war torn Europe. Henrietta reflected on what had happened from the standpoint of a sovereign God. She surmised that when nations repudiate God that moral judgment will fall. When character fails, nations fall. The world was on a downhill slide. She sensed that unless there was a renewed vision of an omnipotent God and a turning from the ruins to Him there was no hope for the world. She began to sense a growing awareness that God was about to do something about these conditions of despair.

> Henrietta Mears saw a renewed vision of the omnipotent God ascending from the ruins that lay about her, rising like the fabled phoenix bird from its own ashes to live again. As she and Margaret boarded the boat on their return to America, Henrietta felt a growing awareness of God's leading. She spent the days on the high seas in quiet meditation.
> As she read the story of Queen Esther she was impressed with the seemingly hopelessness of the situation when the decree went out for the Jews to be annihilated (Roe 1990:278).

It became clear to her that Esther's hopeless situation and her own in seeking to help Europe were similar. Esther 4:13-16 seemed to come alive to her. She was beginning to sense that she, like Esther, faced a window of opportunity for God to work. But it was not yet clear what or how. There is a growing awareness of an urgency, a moment of destiny.

> Although once again involved with her many tasks in Hollywood, Henrietta felt she was being moved forward by an unseen hand. She had known power in her life before, but this was something beyond any previous experience. Here messages were filled with urgency. She spoke of what she had witnessed in Europe and what she thought was God's solution to the chaos. Those about her saw a vitality and commitment in her that they had not known before. She was living on the tiptoe of expectancy, but what she was expecting was not yet clear (Roe 1990:278,279).

During the spring of 1947 there was an increased commitment to prayer for God to reveal what must be done. Roe describes the first power breakthrough.

> On Thursday night, June 24, 1947, during the Gospel Light Teacher's Training Conference at Forest Home, God broke through and His power was released. Henrietta ascended the platform with a controlling sense of God's presence. As the hundreds of Sunday School workers, pastors and young seminarians listened, she spelled out all that she had seen abroad.
> The seeds of destruction had been long in bringing forth their fruit. Atheism and moral expedience had been at work for centuries before Hitler's rise to power. There is no mystery as to what has happened to Germany. It can all be traced out step-by-step.
> And the same is taking place in America today. There must be a Christian answer to the growing menace of communism. Leaders are predicting that within another generation or sooner we will have entered World War III, which could bring an end to civilization.
> God has an answer. Jesus said that we must make disciples of all men. We are to take His gospel to the ends of the earth. We must become evangelists, even through evangelism is not recognized in our day as a valid program. And we must present the full doctrine of Christian truth.
> God is looking for men and women of total commitment. During the war, men of special courage were called upon for difficult assignments, often these volunteers did not return. The were called "expendables." We must be expendables for Christ (Roe 1990:279,280).

Chapter 8. Henrietta Mears (1890-1963)

The challenge continued. And there was a response. Many were moved to consider themselves as expendables. Four rising young leaders responded wholeheartedly to this challenge. They decided to do something about it. They requested prayer time with Miss Mears in her cabin. Richard C. Halverson, Louis H. Evans, Jr., Jack Franck, and Bill Bright prayed deep into the night (Roe 1990:280,281). After much confession, asking God for guidance and recognition of inadequacy, the insight from God came. The college campuses contained the key to world leadership. Such young leaders full of energy could be used of God to bring revival. The four young leaders envisioned a week long conference for collegiates from all over America. Such a meeting would provide the backdrop for God's challenge. Roe describes the almost impossible situation.

> The sheer audacity of what they contemplated--a national collegiate conference with only two months to prepare--was breathtaking. Still, the immensity of the challenge swept over them and gripped them. What a great undertaking for God this would be!
>
> As they began anticipating the many logistics involved in pulling together a conference of this magnitude in such a short time, their thoughts--whipped by winds of inspiration--rushed together like waves and then crested on rocks of yet unanswered questions. yet the vision had come; God had spoken clearly, and they had heard. Teacher and the four young men went out into the early light of morning, transformed, commissioned, expendable. Theirs was a world to conquer for Christ and the time for conquest was now! (Roe 1990:281,282)

Further prayer and planning resulted in the design of a covenant, which could be signed by those who would respond to be expendables for God. Those signing the covenant and committing themselves to its statements would be part of *The Fellowship of the Burning Heart* (Roe 1990:282). All four leaders, Halverson, Evans, Franck, and Bright signed it immediately. Their enthusiasm for the commitment and their surrender to God were evident.

The bottom line was that they pulled off the conference and God greatly challenged young emerging leaders from campuses all over America.[12] Numerous Godly leaders came and spoke. The 1947 College Briefing Conference, as it was known, became the seedbed for revival and an on-going movement to reach campuses for Christ. This conference became the forerunner of many other such conferences over the years. Hundreds of young people committed themselves to the covenant. Organizations were begun. Great was the fall out from this Spirit-led conference. Henrietta Mears was the leader. Her inspirational messages, her networking with Christian speakers, and her status and prestige made this conference possible. And it was the trip, the growing awareness of a moment of destiny and her willingness to take a risk with these young leaders that God blessed. Truly it was for such a moment as this that Henrietta was in place and ready for God's blessing.[13]

---

[12] Bill Bright went on to found Campus Crusade for Christ. Certainly this period of time was a time of destiny preparation and revelation for him.
[13] I have talked first hand a number of times with Bob Munger, one who was part of this conference and its aftermath. This was a tremendous time of empowerment. Munger recalls with an almost awe-like memory these times. He speaks so highly of Miss Mears leadership in this movement. Bob Munger has served as Pastor to the faculty of Fuller Theological Seminary in his afterglow years. He, himself, like Henrietta Mears became a facilitator of leaders--encouraging many to go on the mission field and into pastorates. Mears was an encouraging model for Munger. He was also a leader in this conference.

Chapter 8. Henrietta Mears (1890-1963)   page 340

The Time-Line

See the time-line at the end of this chapter for a one page overview of Mears' life with critical incidents and sabbatical tours listed. Notice that there are three periods lasting 23 years, 15 years, and 35 years. There is no recognized afterglow period as Miss Mears was relatively active throughout the 35 years as a full-time Christian worker.

The unusual thing about this time-line is the very late entry into full time Christian ministry. During the last three years of her college time Henrietta Mears was actively engaged in ministry as a Bible teacher on campus and Superintendent of a Sunday School department. Her next 15 years were essentially bi-vocational. Though she was an educator in a high school, the central meaning of her life was derived from her ministry. So that when she entered into full-time ministry, she was already an accomplished Sunday School worker, administrator, a Bible teacher of note, and a personal worker in terms of evangelism. She was a competent leader before she entered her full-time ministry at First Presbyterian church of Hollywood. Upon entering, her ministry accelerated greatly.

Highly Condensed Biographical Narrative

The following running capsule, organized around the three major time increments of Mears' life indicates the important activities, people and events that shaped Mears' life. Critical incidents are interwoven into the narrative explanation. A complete summary of the critical incidents are given in Table 8-3 on page 370.

I. A LINEAGE OF FAITH
(1890-1913); Age= Birth-23

A. Character Foundations
(1890-1896); Age= Birth to 6

Henrietta Cornelia arrived on October 23, 1890, the seventh and last child born to Ashley and Margaret Mears. The family was located in Fargo, North Dakota. Henrietta's dad owned a chain of 20 banks across the Dakotas. In 1893, a depression hit in which numerous businesses went under. Many banks across the country closed including a number owned by Ashely Mears (Roe 1990:58).

Henrietta's mom was 42 years old when she was born. She and her husband Ashley had known sorrow. Their first child, a son, had died unexpectedly at age 20. Their second child, a son, at age fourteen was stricken with spinal meningitis and suffered the after effects of deafness for life. A son was next, their third child. Their fourth was a girl. This first daughter died at seven of typhoid. The fifth child was a boy. The sixth was Margaret who was to partner with Henrietta in ministry. She was eleven years old when Henrietta was born (Roe 1990:58). Henrietta's mom was certainly experienced as a mother by the time this baby daughter arrived. She was also at the peak of her spiritual experience, a significant factor in Henrietta's development.

Rich Heritage, Parental Modeling

Roe, quoting Henrietta Mears, first, and then Powers second, capture one of the two most important shaping factors in Henrietta Mears' life.

> I'm amazed to see how many of my own policies and beliefs trace back to my grandmother. The same thinking, the same ideas and approach. She taught them to my mother, and I was almost unconsciously reared upon these same precepts (Roe 1990:55)

Chapter 8. Henrietta Mears (1890-1963)

"Thou shall keep therefore his statutes, and his commandments, which I command thee this day, that it may go well with thee, and with thy children after thee..." Deut. 4:40.

A short time ago, when Henrietta Mears was on a speaking engagement in Texas, she stopped by the Baptist bookstore in Dallas and asked the clerk, "I was wondering if you have the **Pastor's Handbook**, written by Dr. W. W. Everts? It was written well over a hundred years ago and I realize that it is very old."

"Why," said the clerk, "that's like stopping at a super market and asking if they have salt and pepper! It may have been written over a hundred years ago, but it's still selling."

"How amazing," said Miss Mears, smiling happily as she looked at the copy. "My grandfather wrote it. Grandfather Everts. He was pastor of the First Baptist Church of Chicago." (Powers 1957:82)

Powers goes on to point out the important implication of this simple incident and the awareness of grandmother's influence.

One thrilling thing to me about the life of Henrietta Mears is the great spiritual heritage she has received. The scope of her life has been tremendous; even more tremendous is the spiritual influence of her forebears, which can be traced back through at least five generations, and the spiritual "mantle" has been handed down on the maternal side from one generation to the next. Truly, this is a witness to the Scriptural promise "that it may go well with thee, and with they children after thee.

The biographies of Henrietta Mears' grandfather and grandmother have both been published and have made available many details of her spiritual inheritance. Deuteronomy 5:29 says, "O that there were such an heart in them, that they would fear me, and keep all my commandments always, that it might be well with them, and with their children for ever!" Without a doubt there was just such a heart in Miss Mears' ancestors. We can definitely trace and delineate this great spiritual heart in Henrietta's mother, her mother's mother, her maternal grandfather, his mother, and his mother's mother, Henrietta's great-grandmother, of whom it has been written, "She walked with the Lord and her voice was lifted continually to give praise to God." This great spiritual inheritance was received by each succeeding generation. (Powers 1957:82,83).

The first important shaping factor on Henrietta's life was the destiny on her life from this spiritual heritage. Her very heritage foreshadowed a sense of destiny for her. She came from a long line of Christians who were known for their strong testimonies for Christ.[14]

The second most important shaping factor in Henrietta Mears' life was the modeling of her parents, particularly her mom. Roe points out how ready Henrietta's mom was for this influence.

---

[14] One major lesson we have identified with effective leaders states: EFFECTIVE LEADERS HAVE A GROWING AWARENESS OF THEIR SENSE OF DESTINY. A *sense of destiny* is an awareness that God's Hand is on the life for special purposes and will lead to and enable those purposes. We have identified a three fold pattern: destiny preparation (Clinton 1989:104,104), destiny revelation (Clinton 1989:220), and destiny fulfillment (Clinton 1989:350). Destiny preparation involves incidents that foreshadow and point to a destiny. Destiny revelation clarifies the path, the things to be accomplished, the methodology, etc. Destiny fulfillment sees them come to pass. A long line of staunch Christians, especially praying ones, often pray for the future generations and influence their life choices God ward. In this Godly heritage of Henrietta's there were certainly those who prayed for the future generations. This heritage was definitely destiny preparation. The hand of God was on Henrietta's life. Pastor Riley's challenge of the mantle was with spiritual discernment and in line with the heritage. Proverbs 20:7 was true for Henrietta. This is one of the most significant shaping factors in her life.

Mrs. Mears' influence on Henrietta reflected the practical wisdom she had gained in the rearing of her other six children. Coupling this knowledge with her own rich heritage, she was able to share with her daughter all the treasures of a deeply spiritual and experienced mother. And with the sensitivity of the very young, her own innate curiosity and keen interest in everything, Henrietta soon sensed that her mother's life was different from any other around her. At first, she wondered why. (Roe 1990:59)

Then she found out. Point one given below was one of the discoveries about her mother which she knew made her mother different. I include all of the shaping influences of her mother here in this time period although they do occur throughout the first two time periods right on up to age 18. The following are ten of the most important ways that Henrietta's mom shaped her life:

1. **She modeled an effective prayer life.**

   Noticing her mother going regularly to her room every morning, Henrietta toddled after her one day to see what her mother did in there. In the room, she found her mother on her knees, her hands folded and her lips moving. Imitating her mother's actions, Henrietta knelt beside her, folding her chubby hands and made her lips move too. Putting her arm around her daughter, Mrs. Mears explained that she was talking to God, that God loved Henrietta and would also hear her when she talked to Him.

   The mother then prayed that the Lord would make Henrietta a good girl that day and always be with her. Satisfied, Henrietta jumped up and was quickly off about the many things that filled her busy childhood days. but she never forgot her mother on her knees talking to God, and her great ambition was to spend an hour in prayer, just as her mother did each day (Roe 1990:59,60).

2. **Early on she modeled the centrality of the Bible to a life. She introduced Henrietta to the Bible and the importance of reading the Bible.**

   Before she could read words for herself, Henrietta loved to listen to her mother read the Bible aloud. Sometimes her mother would attempt to simplify the words-- endeavoring to clarify the meaning for the little tyke beside her--but Henrietta would stop her and ask her not to change them, assuring her that she understood them as they were. Surprisingly for one so young, Henrietta's favorite portion of Scripture even then was Paul's mighty classic, Romans, the book she most frequently taught in later years. (Roe 1990:62).

3. **She modeled the importance of using the Bible by making practical applications of Bible truths in everyday life. She also modeled teaching the Bible with power in her well attended Sunday School class.**

   Forgiveness and retribution, for example, were carefully defined. Whenever a child did wrong and duly expressed his sorrow, he was forgiven. But he also had to learn that repentance was not enough' someone had to pay for the wrongdoing.

   To pay the penalty for one of her children's offenses, Mrs. Mears would deny herself butter for a stipulated number of meals. At the dinner table, whenever the children noticed their mother was not taking butter-which she greatly liked--a pall of silence and guilt fell on them all, causing the culprit to cringe in shame. When sufficient time had elapsed for her fulfilling a particular child's punishment, Mother Mears would ask the erring child to pass her some butter. Invariably, the child would scramble to get the butter to her as quickly as possible. Young and impressionable, Henrietta never forgot these incidents nor the lessons learned for them. (Roe 1990:62,63).

Chapter 8. Henrietta Mears (1890-1963)   page 343

4. **She modeled control of the tongue.**[15]

Both parents were outstanding in discipline concerning the tongue. Their words were carefully calculated to edify and not hurt. At her mom's funeral, Henrietta's dad commented to Henrietta that in his whole married life he had not once heard her mother ever use words in a derogatory, disparaging, or discouraging fashion with or about people. She always focused on the positive, the best that could be said about or to people.[16] She was always consistent with the children. When she said something she always meant it. Miss Mears was later to remark that the secret in discipline for children was to be consistent. Children should know that parents mean what they say.

5. **She modeled concern for social outcasts, the poor, and those who had suffered tragedies in life.**

Always socially concerned Mother Mears frequently visited, among other places, the Florence Crittenden Home [a home for unwed mothers]. When she felt Henrietta was old enough to understand that tragedies were part of life, she took her daughter with her to the home where they give little gifts to the young residents. The experience of coming into contact with these hapless women made its mark on Henrietta's 10-year old mind. Not long afterwards, she and her cousin Margaret formed "The Willing Workers," their private social service organization "to do good for unfortunates." (Roe 1990:64).

Powers (1957:98) remarks that there was always one or more small boxes on the kitchen shelf in which money was saved for various people in need. Traditionally the family would invite a poor family to a major holiday meal like Christmas as well as make up food baskets to hand out. Henrietta carried on this tradition (Powers 1957:111,112).

6. **She was deeply concerned for the lost and modeled the gift of evangelism in natural ways during the normal course of life.**

Henrietta's later effectiveness as a personal worker was a quality first nurtured in her by her mother. In the Mears' home, a stack of New Testaments--each with salvation verses clearly marked--were placed near the front door. Salesmen and other visitors to the home were each given one with a gracious word of encouragement to study it.

Mother Mears would often make some such comment as this to a young man who came to the door to sell something: "I am always so interested in young men. I have four sons of my own, and I am concerned not only with their preparation for this life but for the one to come. I was wondering if you have ever accepted Christ as your personal Savior." From her mother's example, Henrietta learned a kind and sympathetic approach in inspiring people to seek God (Roe 1990:64).[17]

---

[15]Both her father and mother were disciplined in this sometimes lax area of life. Mrs. Mears said of her husband (Roe 1990:64), "If the Bible says that every man who bridleth his tongue is a perfect man, then your father is a perfect man. I have never heard him say an unkind word. The Lord knew I needed someone to see the silver lining in every cloud, for I am more serious. He always sees the funny side of every situation." Henrietta drew from her father a sense of humor and the ability to see the positive things in situations.

[16]The discipline of the use of the tongue is one that mentors should early on instill in mentorees. Two of the six barriers which prevent leaders from finishing well are related to discipline of the tongue (pride, abuse of power). See especially the discipline of Secrecy in **The Mentor Handbook--Detailed Guidelines and Helps for Christian Mentors and Mentorees** (1991). Apparently Henrietta Mears imbibed this important value from her mom and dad and reflected it all her life.

[17]Powers (1957:105,106) tells of a particularly moving illustration of Mother Mears' concern for people knowing God. "Norman Mears (her son) and his cousin, Charles Buckbee, were co-founders of the Buckbee-Mears engraving firm in St. Paul. One day his mother asked him, "Norman, are the men in your employ Christians?" To which Norman replied, "Mother, I really don't know." "I'm going to write each

7. **She taught Henrietta to read to learn.**
Roe (1990:66) illustrates this. "Mrs. Mears, when seeing her daughter engaged in a book, would come up to her without warning, close the book and ask the girl to tell her what she had been reading. Henrietta might remonstrate, 'But Mother, I've only been reading for 10 minutes.' 'My dear,' Mrs. Mears would reply, 'if you have been reading that long, you certainly should have learned something. Now tell me what you have read.' This ability to focus and gain something from reading was to be honed to a very fine skill in her college years due to her physical problems with eyesight.

8. **She instilled a sense of urgency about life, particularly in redeeming the time.**[18]
This was particularly applied to procrastination concerning difficult or distasteful jobs. For example, homework must be done as early as possible on Friday so as not to interfere with enjoyment of the weekend. Laziness was not tolerated. Sleeping in was discouraged. Verses from Proverbs on the sluggard were often quoted (like 6:9 How long will you lie there, you sluggard? When will you get up from your sleep?). Even on vacation the children had tasks to do which centered on more than just pleasure.

9. **She taught responsibility for making things better.**
It is an easy thing to complain when events and things are not going well. It is another thing to take the initiative to make them better. Those who criticize should be willing to also suggest alternatives. This valuable lesson was learned repeatedly and early by Henrietta.

> Whenever Henrietta came home from a party or a meeting at church, her mother would ask her how it had gone. If Henrietta ever complained that it hadn't been very good, her mother immediately asked, "What did you do to make it better?" "But Mother," Henrietta would complain, "it wasn't *my* party (or it wasn't *my* meeting). I wasn't in charge. I had nothing whatever to do with it!" Bit if it was a social party that had failed, the mother reminded Henrietta that she could have suggested a game to play, or played the piano for them, or looked around to find some opportunity to make the occasion more fun for the others. If it was a meeting at church, the mother reminded her that she could have offered a testimony or a prayer, or shared a Bible verse or looked for a place to use her initiative to make it a more effective meeting. So Henrietta early learned a social obligation to every group in which she participated, a sense of obligation that has never left her. No matter in what circumstance or situation she finds herself, she feels a social responsibility to join in and contribute in any way she can to make it more effective and enjoyable for others (Powers 1957:103).

10. **She believed in a mighty God who could intervene supernaturally in life.**
At least three times during her lifetime Henrietta experienced the healing touch of God on her life. The first was when she was 12.

---

one of them a letter then," she said. After her death, Margaret saw a letter on the desk of one of the artists in her mother's handwriting. The artist, said, "Margaret, would you like this letter? It is the most wonderful letter I have every received in all my life." Then he showed it to her. This letter exudes kindness yet concern for the spiritual welfare of the man. It is a beautiful illustration of the Gospel presented in an attractive way.

[18]Powers (1957:105) mentions that her mother saw time like a great river passing by as one observes it. As the water passes it is gone forever. So too with time. The immediate moment of time must be used or it is passes by and is gone forever. Fragments of time were used to memorize poetry or Bible verses or to practice a few minutes on a musical instrument.

Chapter 8. Henrietta Mears (1890-1963)

When Henrietta was only 12 years old, she contacted a painful, crippling case of muscular rheumatism. Many other cases were also reported in their region that year her friends, who contracted the disease at the same time, died from it. In constant pain, young Henrietta was almost completely immobile, having to be carried about from place to place.

Her family feared for her life, for during this siege, she began to suffer repeated nosebleeds. Claiming Philippians 4:19, "But my God shall supply all your need according to his riches in glory by Christ Jesus," Mother Mears took God at His word. She asked Henrietta if she would like Mr. Ingersoll, a family friend and member of a Presbyterian church, to come and pray for her nosebleeds. Henrietta agreed.

When Mr. Ingersoll arrived, he said, "Henrietta, do you believe the Lord can heal you?" Henrietta looked up at him and said, in her direct way, "He created us. I see no reason why He cannot heal us."

Mr. Ingersoll prayed for the bleeding to stop completely. God heard and answered, for the bleeding stopped and never occurred again in her lifetime.

The rheumatism, however, not only continued but became more painful with time. One afternoon, Henrietta, now 14 called her mother to her bedside and asked "Do you think Mr. Ingersoll would come back and pray for my rheumatism?"

Within a few hours, Mr. Ingersoll was again in Henrietta's room, asking once more for God's intervention. As he prayed, Henrietta was suddenly filled with confidence that she was completely healed. All the pain was gone. Tears of relief flowed down her cheeks as she raised her voice in prayers of thanksgiving.

Her road to full recovery was swift and sure. She regained her strength rapidly and, to build up her muscles, Henrietta energetically took up horseback riding and swimming. Within three months, her body was free of any trace of the illness. And throughout her life, she never had a recurrence of rheumatism (Roe 1990:67,68).

Summary of Modeling Intent

Mom Mears had a clear cut philosophy on rearing her children to know and serve God.

Her mother said that the childhood years were the years when the children's lives were like plastic clay and the mother's fingers were molding the shape, determining whether the life would be a shallow dish or a deep bowl capable of holding great blessings to overflow to others. Right after breakfast the family had family prayer, Bible reading, and hymn singing. As the years brought changes in schedule for the various members of the family, the mother was there, ready for each child as he went off at a different hour. She would rise early to pray with one, then the other, as they left for the day (Powers 1957:95).

Mrs. Mears was God's most significant influence in the shaping of Henrietta. Pastor Riley commenting on the example of her life, at her funeral brings out what an important model this preacher's kid was.[19]

Margaret Burtis Mears, daughter of Dr. W. W. Everts, pastor of the First Baptist Church in Chicago, passed away last week. In intellect she had few equals, keen, inquiring, aggressive, confident. She literally reveled in the Word of God and came as nearly walking according to its sacred precepts as is possible in the sinful flesh. As a Bible teacher she had few equals in the city of Minneapolis and in the practice of the presence of God she had no superior. Like Martin Luther of old, one and two hours a day she spent upon her knees. When she appeared before a great class of young women on Sunday they gave audience to one they knew had been in the presence of God, believing that her

---

[19] I have been personally touched by this woman, Henrietta's mom. In my comparative searching of the three biographers for her modeling impact how I wished there was a biography on her life. We need to hear of case studies of lay leaders (especially women) who have impacted for God. She is certainly one worthy of being remembered in a biography.

message was direct from the Spirit. When she visited the homes of the poor or talked with the convicted sinner, they alike understood that a messenger from the Holy One was at work for Him. ... The Thursday night prayer meeting following was a Memorial Service. The chapel was filled, and every person present seemed to be a mourner but scores bore testimony to her beneficent influence. ... The church is poorer for her going but rich in her ministry and in the influence certain to abide forever (Powers 1957:106,107).

Because Henrietta was a tag-along, a late joyful surprise--like Joseph and Benjamin, a child of relatively old age--her mother had more time to spend individually and personally with her. And she did this. She spent much time with her. At the time of Henrietta's birth her mother was also a very competent spiritual leader with much influence and a well defined ministry philosophy including her views on child rearing. Without doubt it can be said that she poured the very best of her own life's experience into Henrietta's life. An absorbent sponge was filled. A piece of clay was molded. A vessel for God's use was shaped. A mom mentored a daughter.[20]

B. Early Modeling Leading To Leadership Committal
(1896-1908); Age= 6-18

Contemporary Pastoral Modeling--Pastor Riley

By the time she was 6 years old, the Mears family had relocated to Minneapolis. Here was where Henrietta received her basic education, all the way through high school.

But fundamentally more important here is where she received her basic education in ecclesiology--what the church is.[21] Her family united with the First Baptist Church of Minneapolis. They were very active members. This church was pastored by Dr. W. B. Riley, "a man of stature and great influence, a thoroughly evangelical scholar." (Roe 1990: 60) During her years from 6-18, Pastor D. B. Riley modeled an effective pastoral ministry with an evangelistic emphasis. His ministry included challenging young people into leadership--a value which would later become a dominant life purpose for Miss Mears. Emerging Christian leaders need to early on see someone whom they respect as a Christian leader. This on-going series of incidents lays an incipient value concerning challenging

---

[20]*Mentoring* is a relational experience in which one person called the mentor, empowers another person, called the mentoree via a transfer of resources. Nine types of mentor functions have been identified. One of these is the modeling function of a contemporary Christian leader respected by the mentoree. The *contemporary model* serves as a sort of Christian hero/heroine who inspires the young leader. The mentoree tends to emulate and imbibe values from the *contemporary model* and tends to live up to the genuine expectations that person sets out. (See Clinton and Clinton, 1991, **The Mentor Handbook**). Henrietta's mom not only served the mentoring function of a *contemporary model* but she served other mentor roles as well: *discipler, spiritual guide, coach,* and *teacher*, Mentoring is an important shaping process that God uses in the life of a developing leader. While some of these functions were non-deliberate much was deliberate. The close personal relationship between the two enabled great empowerment even from the contemporary modeling which is usually a very passive form of mentoring.

[21]It is especially significant that all of Mears' experiences with church life were positive ones. Her growing up years were connected with First Baptist of Minneapolis. Her two years in rural high schools were experiences with two rural Methodist works. She brought life and renewal to both situations. Then upon her return to accept a position at Central High of Minneapolis she again affiliated with First Baptist and had an increasingly powerful ministry as a Sunday School teacher and enthusiastic Sunday School leader. When she was called into full time ministry it was to Hollywood Presbyterian church, a very successful and lively church setting. She was broader than a single denomination. She expected great things to happen. That had been her experience. Positive experiences with church situations lays a base for faith expectancy in other situations.

Chapter 8. Henrietta Mears (1890-1963)

leadership. Pastor Riley, was not only an excellent contemporary model but also came into play as a divine contact[22] at three critically important junctures in Henrietta's life. Because of his modeling he had the respect of Henrietta. She would respond positively to his later challenge into full-time Christian ministry, his mantle challenge, and his suggestion for a sabbatical time of reflection.[23]

A Healing Touch--Nosebleed and Muscular Rheumatism

I have described this incident previously when I covered Mom Mears modeling influence concerning a God who intervenes. At age 12 Miss Mears learned that the unseen God can intervene in the seen world. Her two experiences in a two year period, in which God stopped her nosebleeds and then finally completely healed her muscular rheumatism strengthened her faith in an invisible God. In later life she will receive God's healing touch concerning deterioration of eyesight. Here she is opened to the supernatural work of God. This is a focal incident resulting in an important value about God. God can intervene in the lives of His needy children. But she also learned that healing is not automatic. Sometimes God has other purposes which supersede healing. Her poor eyesight which was to plague her throughout life was a case in point. Miss Mears had a balanced view of healing. God can heal. But He does not always heal.

Leadership Committal--Gave Life to Full Time Work at 17

In opening illustration 1, I mentioned this critical incident as the first of four leadership committal type happenings which shaped Miss Mears. Around age 17 or 18 Miss Mears was in her senior year of high school. She was challenged by Dr. Riley, a timely divine contact, to full-time Christian service along with her friend Evelyn Camp. On the surface it was a commitment to go where ever God wanted. But deeper, it was a commitment to be what God wanted. This anchor becomes part of an on-going challenge by God which eventually leads to full-time service in First Presbyterian Church in Hollywood, California. This is a strategic incident.[24]

---

[22]A *divine contact* (Clinton 1991:11-7) is a special kind of occasional mentor whose intervening presence is perceived as timely and from God.
[23]While many *divine contacts* usually only show up once in a life it is equally true that a given person might be interwoven into a life and serve the *divine contact* function several times over a lifetime as God brings them back into the life at critical junctures. Pastor Riley intervenes significantly as a *divine contact* in critical incident 4, *leadership committal* (Clinton 1989:146). This is a response to serve God in where ever, when ever, and how ever He wants, will be basic to a life of accomplishment by Henrietta Mears. God will build upon this as He later directs.
[24]Sometimes we may tend to think these teen-age decisions are light things and that everyone has them. But these experiences like A. J. Gordon's at sixteen, Robert C. McQuilkin's at 12, and Henrietta Mears at 18 validate early calls. Rather than pooh-pooh these we should be seeking to identify, reinforce, and celebrate them as significant as anchor experiences to build upon. Like A. J. Gordon's family we should put all our family force behind helping the youngster build toward a future with God.

Eyesight Crisis--Senior Year in Highschool[25]

Miss Mears even as a young child suffered poor eyesight. She was very near sighted. But during her senior year in high school her eyes began to deteriorate appreciably. She faced a crisis. Her doctors recommended that she forego any future studies. Otherwise they felt she would be blind by age 30 (Roe 1990:72). Henrietta Mears displayed a courageous learning posture which reckoned with the possibility of blindness.

> Deeply concerned, her mother asked Henrietta what she was going to do. Would she accept their advice...? Her unhesitating reply was typical: "If I am going to be blind by 30, then blind I shall be! But I want something in my head to think about. I'm going to study as hard as I can as long as I can." (Roe 1990:72)

She decided to go on to the University of Minnesota. She learned many ways to compensate for her eye condition including increased powers of concentration, studying in daylight only, reviewing a classroom lecture immediately after class, focused listening skills, reading comprehension skills for digesting a book at one reading, etc. (Roe 1990:72). She honed her listening skills so that upon an immediate review she could repeat almost verbatim what have been given in a lecture.

God does not always heal. Miss Mears responded well to this crisis with a very positive view of God's sovereignty in her life. An important value, *God is sovereignly controlling our lives*, is settled here. This crisis became an on-going process. That Miss Mears responded well is captured in this important quote repeated by all her biographers.

> When asked about her lifelong struggle with extreme myopia, general eye weakness, irritation and other vision problems, Henrietta would remark, "I believe my greatest spiritual asset throughout my entire life has been my failing sight, for it has kept me absolutely dependent upon God." (Roe 1990:72).

In the very latter stages of life she will face her most serious crisis concerning her eyesight. God will meet her with healing which enables her to finish out her ministry.

C. Power gate/ Teaching in University
(1908-1913); Age=18-23

Henrietta Mears was a good student at the University of Minnesota. At this point in her life none of the focal issues have been settled. She has made a commitment to full-time ministry but has not received any further guidance as to what that will entail. In the meantime she has gone on to prepare herself to teach.

At this point in ministry development, she has gained experience as a Sunday School teacher and Sunday School administrator. At 12 she taught her first Sunday School class in a mission Sunday School (Baldwin and Benson 1966:44). As a freshman in college, she gained experience as superintendent of a junior department. Both of these are harbingers of what is to come. She will influence Sunday Schools all over the world.

She had recognized a teaching gift by this time as well as a leadership gift. But it would take another crisis experience to launch her into a power gate experience which would be the anchor point for unusual power in her ministry.

---

[25]*Crisis* processing (Clinton 1989:210) refer to those special intense situations of pressure in human situations which are used by God to test and teach dependence. Dependence is certainly seen here.

Chapter 8. Henrietta Mears (1890-1963)　　　　　　　　　page 349

2 Incidents: Power For Ministry and Accept the Challenge

I have previously described in detail in the opening illustration 1 this critical incident. Again for the second time Pastor Riley serves as a divine contact. His simple almost private challenge, "Henrietta, I am praying that your mother's mantle will fall upon you," stirred up an inner response of inadequacy in Henrietta. She responded by going deeper with God. It was a twofold response. She received spiritual comfort and brought closure to her mom's death and she asked for and received an inner filling of the Holy Spirit which enabled her to take up her mother's mantle.

Evidence of this fullness of the Spirit for ministry can be traced in ensuing ministry. In the following year, as a junior, she had an exciting Bible class on campus which grew to 60. Her ministry following graduation in two rural situations were both powerful. She motivated youth, led many to Christ, and challenged many into ministry. Her Bible teaching ministry again was powerful. After these first two years in ministry she returned to Minneapolis. Her small class which she took over from her sister quickly jumped to over a hundred in the first year and on to 600 in the next five years. Truly this infilling by the Holy Spirit for power in ministry was realized. She indeed took up the mantle of her mother. Like Elisha of old she parted the waters.

Divine Contact, Need for Grace--Paul Rader's Teaching

Simultaneous with incidents 6 and 8 which were on-going and spaced over a year's time there was a hunger for God awakened in Henrietta.[26] God sent along a divine contact, Paul Rader. Henrietta was ready to experientially hear and learn of God's grace. Power's describes this critical learning time and suggests it later fruitfulness in Henrietta's life.

> Sometimes it takes a time of death, which is an experience rather than a fixed date, to give the impetus for great spiritual comprehension. The Bible says, "When King Uzziah died, I saw the Lord." When her mother died, Henrietta, in her loneliness and grief, turned to the great spiritual truths with new comprehension and "saw the Lord." For it was at this time that Paul Rader, minister at the Moody Church in Chicago, came to hold meetings in Minneapolis, and it was a significant spiritual milestone for her. She would come over from classes at the university and slip into the meetings. He was a strong, forceful speaker, suing such marvelous illustrations that afterwards she could recall the entire sermons almost word for word.
> She was greatly impressed with Paul Rader's concept of the grace of God, the love of God, and of spiritual freedom from the law provided by what Christ had done in freeing us from obligation; and she was thrilled with the potential of living the life under grace. From understanding gained now, she later developed her strong lesson from the sixth chapter of Romans: know, reckon, yield, gain the knowledge, and act upon the knowledge, let go and let God (Powers 1957:113).

The year and a half following her mother's death was filled with three intense shaping activities. Henrietta received power for ministry, accepted the challenge of taking up her mother's mantle, and was grounded in the basic victory truths of Romans 6 which she will use all her life. She is now ready to embark on a secular teaching career--essentially as a bi-vocational worker--which will center around her ministry of reaching young people for Christ and motivating them into ministry. The focal issues are not yet clear but the servant is certainly being prepared to minister competently when the door finally opens wide.

---

[26]This was undoubtedly part of the grieving process at the loss of her mom who had been so close and was such an important person in her life.

II. INFORMAL PREPARATION
(1913-1928); Age= 23-38

A. Rural Schools/Powerful Witness
(1913-1915); Age= 23-25

Her first two appointments as a teacher involved both administration and teaching in high schools in rural work. She enthusiastically gave herself to both high school work and ministry. This bi-vocational commitment would continue for 15 years.

Early on she displayed an inclination for motivational ministry insights.[27] Typical of her genius for such breakthroughs is her effort to motivate her young people in the church to give to missions. She had already won the hearts of these young people by her earnest endeavors to organize a high school football team and by her Bible teaching ministry. They respected her. In the midst of war years when the economy was tight and money was scarce she motivated her gang to give. I give these two vignettes of her early experience which is symbolic of hundreds more throughout her career.

> Her methods were original, and her enthusiasm infectious. One Sunday night, when she could not get any of her youngsters to stand and give a testimony, she asked the entire group to rise and sing a hymn. They stood. After the hymn, she announced that any who testified could sit down. The humor of what she had done broke the ice for all, and one by one the members of the group began expressing themselves and sharing their faith with one another.
>
> These were depression years, and money was scarce, making it hard to raise even the smallest amount of money. Few members of that Beardsley church had much to give that year when the annual campaign for missions was announced. But Henrietta was undaunted.
>
> She challenged her young people with a plan that inspired and excited them. "I want you to work and earn as much money as you are able," she said. "Do everything you can to bring in money for our missionaries. And I will match you dollar for dollar."
>
> Eager to outdo the other groups and one another, the young people charged out on their assignment. Townspeople marveled at the sudden interest of their youth in running errands, doing chores, tackling odd jobs and every other task they could find that generated a little income. And they all saved their earnings.
>
> When missionary Sunday arrived, the youth class could barely sit still in the pews as the other classes reported their collections: $1.27, $3.00, $15.50. Then the minister called out, "Miss Mears' Young People's Class."
>
> Charlie--one of the harder working members of the class--leaped to his feet and shouted, "$120!" Such an amount for missions was unheard of in those times, and the young people were jubilant in the triumph of their near-miracle (Roe 1990:76,77)

This early use of a matching fund creatively motivated young people to accomplish an almost impossible feat. This kind of activity was demonstrated repeatedly hundreds of times throughout Miss Mears lifetime. Later in Table 8-2, I will include a number of ministry insights used to motivate or accomplish her ministry.

---

[27]*Ministry insights* (Clinton 1989:198) refer to breakthroughs in delivering one's ministry effectively. Mears, time after time, throughout her lifetime came up with structures, events, creative happenings, or ways of doing things which motivated and challenged young people to join in and give their all to something. Often these breakthroughs involved identifying with the young people in things they were interested in. Frequently, as in this case, she displayed an experiential grasp of the social dynamic sometimes called Goodwin's Expectation principle. *Emerging leaders tend to live up to the genuine expectations of leaders they respect.* Miss Mears did believe in her young people. Her challenges were right on target. They motivated because they were reachable yet sometimes seemed beyond reach.

Chapter 8. Henrietta Mears (1890-1963)   page 351

In addition to gaining valuable ministry experience, probably the most significant things that happened to Henrietta Mears in these two years of transition to adulthood on her own were two obedience checks which established her integrity and the fact that God was absolutely first in her life.

Two Singles Tests

In Beardsley, a young man, a handsome Harvard graduate was attracted to Henrietta and vice versa. They began seeing each other regularly. They went out for long drives. They dined together. They talked a lot. Henrietta shared how important God was to her life and how serving Him gave meaning to what she did. He listened and responded by promising to attend church with her. Something like what happened could only take place in a small town, a community in which everyone knew each other and all that was going on. But it does shows God providential care.

>Then one day the president of the school board called on her. Henrietta could tell from the gravity of his manner that he had come on a matter of some seriousness. Coming directly to the point, he questioned her about the man she had been dating.
>"What kind of a young man is he, Miss Mears?"
>"Why, just wonderful," she answered. "He is very intelligent, gracious, polite-- very charming in every way."
>"Well, I always knew that someone, some day would find a good side to him," he agreed. "The trouble is that he has such a bad reputation that if you continue going with him the town simply will not believe that you are reforming him, but instead--! You see, he has the worst reputation in town. I always felt he had possibilities, but it seemed there was never anyone to challenge him. But you will ruin your reputation instead of improving his."
>Henrietta was stunned, dismayed and almost disbelieving what she had just heard. Yet, unable to doubt the principal's counsel, she knew she would have to act on what he had told her. That night, when her Harvard man called her, she told him he could not come to see her again. Not easily put off, he told Henrietta that whether she consented or not, he was coming over because he had to talk with her at least once more. He came to the house, and Henrietta agreed to only a brief conversation with him.
>"I know what you've heard," he said miserably, "and the trouble is, it's true. I know it would be too much to try to live down, so I'm going to leave town. I didn't care until I met you. Now I'm sorry."
>"It's too bad that you didn't have enough courage to be true to yourself," she said gently.
>"I know. I want to make a fresh start. At least I want to thank you for making me want to start over again somewhere else."
>And then he was gone, leaving town abruptly. Some days after he left, his mother visited Henrietta and thanked her for giving her son reason to change and for inspiring him to become something better. Henrietta was grateful to God that He had used her to make a difference in a genuinely promising life (Roe 1990:77-79).

God checked her intent and her loyalty to Him with an obedience check via a counselor mentor. She obeyed, recognizing that a union with this man would take her away from God. An important value was implanted. God must be first in the life.

A second like experience occurred the next year. She had finished her one year contract in Beardsley and moved on to another one year contract in North Branch, another rural town. Again her ministry and school teaching were very effective. The test came again, this time with a Dartmouth graduate.

>Her vivacious personality, keen sense of purpose, spontaneous humor and immense capacity for appreciation attracted many a rugged and ambitious fellow. However, there

Chapter 8. Henrietta Mears (1890-1963)

was only one young man whom she ever loved and considered for marriage. He was tall, handsome, black-haired, intellectually challenging and a delight socially, a graduate of Dartmouth, and now a young banker, but he was of a different faith. As the friendship developed and love grew, a fear struck her hear, and she knew she would have to terminate this relationship. He tried to make her see that he admired her religious convictions; he tried to persuade her that they could establish their home, and she could go on and believe and o just as she wanted, and she wouldn't have to change in any way. A home had always been very important to Henrietta. She loved children and companionship, she loved entertaining and the social life, and she loved the young man who was doing the persuading (Baldwin and Benson 1966:42).

The issue is set before her. She clearly saw it for what it was.

> Yet wouldn't she be compromising her faith, her beliefs, to share her life with someone who had a different faith from hers? As the months slipped by, Henrietta could not get away from the thought: It would be like establishing a home and deciding that the husband would eat each night in the dining room, and she would eat in another room. They would both have an excellent meal, but they would have no fellowship together. If in the matter of their faith they could not sit together at the same table and have fellowship, their relationship would be impossible. The conflict was great (Baldwin and Benson 1966:42).

Her surrender in this matter to the Holy Spirit prompted conviction was deep.

> There was only one place she could turn. In the solitude of her own room, she prayed, "Lord, you have made me the way I am. I love a home, I love security, I love children, and I love him. Yet I feel that marriage under these conditions would draw me away from you. I surrender even this, Lord, and leave it in your hands. Lead me, Lord, and strengthen me. You have promised to fulfill all my needs. I trust in you alone." The friendship was terminated (Baldwin and Benson 1966:42,43).

Later I will come back to these two incidents and comment on the character issues involved and these two processes as important leadership tests. But first I want to relate Miss Mears' testimony later in life concerning reflection back on this last incident and the ensuing single life she led. The testimony is worth relating in its entirety since it can be so encouraging to those who will remain single and minister freely before the Lord.[28]

> The marvelous thing has been, that the Lord has always given me a beautiful home; he has given me thousands of children; he has supplied every need in my life, and I've never felt lonely. Since I am a very gregarious person, I though I would have a feeling I didn't belong. But I've never had it, never! I've never missed companionship. Through one experience after another the Lord has shown me that he had something special for me to do. After I went through that final door, where it was just the Lord and I, into wide open

---

[28]Two of the characters in this book remained single for life. Both used their singleness and the freedom it gave to focus intensively on ministry. Both accomplished great things for the Lord. Both looked back on their lives at the end and had no regrets about their choice but were satisfied with their lives. Charles Simeon and Henrietta Mears both illustrate that God's choices are best and that singles can be satisfied with God's choices. Simeon's motivations for remaining single came out of his own family experiences growing up and his observations on families in his early ministry. There are negative connotations involved in these motivating factors. For him it was not necessarily a sacrifice. But Henrietta's choice had no such negative connotations. Hers was a sacrifice, yet a sacrifice of joy. For God gave her a full life. Indeed she enjoyed the many social activities involved in marriage and the security of a loving home. She did miss having children of her own but God gave her many spiritual children. In my years of teaching at Fuller I have seen numerous single women grapple with this problem of singleness. Some have opted for marriage. Some have not. I have observed that there can be many social base situations worse than being single. Henrietta Mears, in this Dartmouth thing, chose the better option in my opinion.

Chapter 8. Henrietta Mears (1890-1963) page 353

spaces of people and things and excitement, life has been one great adventure. It has been a tremendous thing to see how the Lord has filled my life so abundantly with lovely things, and I want to tell everyone that wherever the Lord puts you--even alone on an island--he absolutely satisfies you. So often young people will say to me, "Oh, Miss Mears, I want to be just like you! You are so happy! I, too, never want to get married." And I say to them, "Nonsense! The Lord intends for you to marry; that is the way he has made us. It just so happens that in my case that wasn't his will." But it has pleased me to know that young people have been able to see my happiness and my complete satisfaction in the life that God has given me (Baldwin and Benson 1966:43).

Early on, as a leader begins to emerge in leadership God usually works on character issues. Both of these incidents, 9 and 10, illustrate this.[29] The positive testing pattern, which solidifies character, involves three stages: the test, recognition of and positive response to the test, and expansion. The contrasting negative testing pattern, which reveals character flaws and weaknesses, involves three stages also: the test, either lack of recognition of the test or deliberate willful failure to respond as God wants, and remedial treatment (or eventually God's discipline including even perhaps ultimately removal). In Mears' case both tests involved the positive testing pattern. Manifestations of the expansion is seen almost immediately when she moves back to Minneapolis. Critical incident 11 is a partial answer and the powerful ministry success that ensued is also a partial indication of God's acceptance and expansion of her leadership capabilities.

B. Central High School, Minneapolis, SS Work, Competent Bible Teacher (1915-1927); Age= 25-38

Social Base; Margaret's Decision--Enablement for Ministry

When Henrietta had completed her initial teaching experiences she moved back to Minneapolis and applied to teach at Central High. After first being denied, she was finally accepted as a chemistry teacher and served with distinction for more than ten years.

Upon arriving back in Minneapolis, her sister Margaret, senior by 11 years, offered to partner with her. Sensing that God's hand was on Henrietta's life and that God was going to use her in a mighty ministry, Margaret offered to devote the rest of her life to her sister's care--especially taking care of the household, hospitality, and details of living. This would free up Henrietta to give herself to ministry without the details of providing for social base needs.[30] This is the first of a team of workers who were attracted to Henrietta Mears and would enable her to reach maximum potential in her ministry. Margaret had been working in the family business for years and continued to do so while maintaining the social base in Minneapolis. Later when Henrietta moved to California, Margaret left this job and moved to California to manage household affairs as a full-time job. This partnership was to last for 35 years. Eventually this will become an ideal social base from

---

[29] Two fundamental shaping processes are involved, the *integrity check* (Clinton 1989:125) and the *obedience check* (Clinton 1989:125). If God is going to use a leader, that leader must be able to take stands on principles and convictions and not waver when they are tried. The *integrity check* enables God to confirm and solidify these convictions and the ability to take stands on them. Frequently, the issue comes down to knowing what is right and obeying what God wants, *the obedience check*, in the issue. Mears demonstrates in these two fundamental issues that she can obey God. Leaders need this. For they will be influencing followers who must trust them. Character is essential to that trust. God works on this early in leader's lives. Careful reflection on many of the numerous leaders who have fallen in recent years usually involves tracing back from the fall to fundamental integrity checks and obedience checks that were failed.

[30] See Appendix D for explanation of Social Base Needs. All leaders must operate out of some home base environment and must have basic needs met: Emotional Support, Economic Support, Strategic Support, and Social Support--Physical Needs.

Chapter 8. Henrietta Mears (1890-1963)

which to minister as others are recruited to Miss Mears team. Roe describes this pivotal point.

> Margaret was always a wonderful contrast to Henrietta. She was a very successful businesswoman in her brother's firm and in other establishments for over 20 years. Her keen practical approach to everything kept all projects on a solid foundation. She had a sharp, dry wit, and a stimulating humor that kept everyone intrigued...She could meet anyone in any stratum of society. She was interested in everyone, had no inhibitions, and immediately established a rapport with the person with whom she talked. Her sly sarcasm in good-natured fun kept everything on an even keel.
>
> A delightful hostess and a superb cook, Margaret took complete charge of their home, providing the necessary physical setting for her sister's spiritual concerns and needs.
>
> Margaret took every physical responsibility from Henrietta: she paid the bills, did the shopping, ran the household, bought all of Henrietta's clothes, hats and accessories, shoes, gloves and purses. Henrietta never had to give a thought as long as Margaret was alive for what she "should eat, or drink, or wherewithal she would be clothed." Margaret would never marry, for she felt that her responsibility was to Henrietta, to help her devote full time to her unique Christian ministry (Roe 1990:84,85 using some quotes from Powers).

I believe that Margaret's decision was part of the expansion of the testing process back at North Branch. God was showing Henrietta that He would meet her needs just as she had been led to expect in her surrender to God's will about the banker.

A second expansion and a manifestation of Holy Spirit power, accepted by faith in critical incidents 6 and 8, occurred with the 18 year old girls class that she inherited from Margaret. This was a problematic class for Margaret. Henrietta saw all of the original members of the class, relatively small, eventually go into lay leadership in the church. In addition, the class grew quickly to over a 100 in the first year. Henrietta and Margaret did neighborhood visitation and personal work with these girls. Eventually over a five year period this class grew to be over 500 (Baldwin and Benson 1966:46). As Margaret surmised, God's hand was indeed on Henrietta's life.

Life Purpose Clarified; Evelyn Camp's Furlough

During these years Henrietta grew in several areas of her potential as seen by powerful demonstrations of the spiritual gifts of teaching, evangelism, and leadership. Her missions interest was keen. Over and over again she was able to challenge and see people in her ministry go into Christian service some as lay leaders and some as full-time.

This continual pattern became clear to her as she reflected back on her life and compared it to Evelyn Camp's life. Both Evelyn and Henrietta had made decisions as 17 year olds to go into full-time Christian service. Evelyn had received a call to Japan and had gone. Henrietta had struggled for a while to discern what her full-time ministry should be. But instead of giving her a clear ministry locale or function for full-time work, God had met her with life-giving power in a Holy Spirit power gate experience (critical incident 4). All she needed was God's presence and on-going guidance, not an identification of role or geographical call. Still when Evelyn came home on furlough and visited her ministry, Henrietta was forced to evaluate. Powers and Roe validate this as an important clarification for Henrietta Mears. I go further and call it a pivotal critical incident--for her **life purpose** was clarified. From now on she deliberately and proactively pursues this. It becomes a priority with her.

Chapter 8. Henrietta Mears (1890-1963) page 355

About this time Henrietta's old friend, Evelyn Camp, returned home on her first furlough from Japan. She shared her ministry experiences with Henrietta's Fidelis class. Later when Evelyn returned to Japan, the president of the class [Ann Kludt], went with her. And other class members also went into missionary service.

As Henrietta observed one after another of her Bible students answering the call into Christian service, she realized God was speaking to her. He was clarifying her own calling in the Christian field by confirming what she was already doing for Him:

She had been called to train leaders and to nurture the spiritual growth in thousands who could go in her place to penetrate the world with the Gospel of Christ. Only one Henrietta could have gone to Japan--or to anywhere else.

Instead of sending her, God was asking her to multiply herself in the lives of the many others whom He would then send out in her place (Roe 1990:90,91).[31]

This was a very important part of God's strategic guidance for Henrietta Mears. Her **life purpose** was the first of the focal issues to fall into place. Henrietta clarified her life purpose. She sensed correctly that God would use her to channel others into Christian service. She would motivate, recruit, and release into leadership many. She herself will not go but will stimulate others to go. She will deliberately and proactively focus on recruiting and challenging young male leadership into Christian ministry. Her influence will be felt around the world and in many Christian organizations.

MacLennan--An Able Recruiter, Divine Contact, and Link to Future

Miss Mears had an increasingly productive ministry for a number of years. In the course of this time she and Margaret hosted many visiting missionaries and speakers who came to First Baptist Church. She grew in competency in all three of her major areas of giftedness: evangelism, teaching, leadership. God was about ready to move her on to her life work. How to link her to what is to come? Two divine contacts provide the way. The first was Pastor MacLennan from the First Presbyterian Church of Hollywood, California.

Pastor MacLennan was a visiting speaker in 1925 on one of Pastor Riley's absences. His sermon on "The Love of God" deeply impressed Margaret and Henrietta (Roe 1990:91). They hosted him for a noon meal and spent the afternoon talking about ministry and particularly about Bible teaching topics, including an upcoming series on the person of Christ. Both the Mears sisters and Pastor MacLennan were mutually impressed with each other's devotion to and service for Christ. Pastor MacLennan invited the two of them to come to California and see the work God was doing at First Presbyterian of Hollywood. Already he had his eye on recruiting these two. He sees in Henrietta Mears leadership that has great potential, only needing the right opportunity to unleash it. This contact will be renewed almost three years later with the challenge that will clear up the second of the focal issues--a role for carrying out her life work, one that will maximize her fulfillment of her life purpose.

Pastor Riley, Divine Contact, Wise Advice; Decision Time

The time was 1927; Baldwin and Benson (1966:48) points out that Dr. Riley was aware that Henrietta was going through a restless period and was seeking to determine if

---

[31] Essentially this is the same kind of thing that happened to McQuilkin, when the ship sank. Instead of going he was to train many others to go in his place. Both Mears and McQuilkin will be involved in training and releasing leaders. McQuilkin will do it from a formal training situation; Mears from an informal. A major difference was that Mears not only trained but she recruited heavily. The flagship church, informal environment, was conducive to that.

Chapter 8. Henrietta Mears (1890-1963)

she should remain in high school educational work or go full-time into Christian ministry.[32] He suggested for her what was to become a ministry insight[33] for her.

> Some time later, Dr. Riley, knowing that Henrietta was seeking to know whether the Lord wanted her to remain in public school teaching or if he had full-time Christian work for her to do, suggested that during her sabbatical year she and Margaret travel. "It may give you a vision of this world that will determine the direction of your life." And so she and Margaret left for Europe (Baldwin and Benson 1966:48).

Over the years she will make some eleven such sabbatical tours, many of which will be significant to her ministry. Later I will come back to comment on this ministry insight.

> With some of their sabbatical still before them, they returned to the United States and ventured to California to spend the winter there. Of course they looked up Dr. MacLennan and attended his church. They were delighted with all they saw. Dr. MacLennan had taken a little country church near Hollywood and Vine and had built it up to one of the most influential of Presbyterian pulpits. Wednesday evening prayer meetings saw hundreds in attendance. From five hundred to a thousand men met in a special Bible class called "Macsmen." The emphasis of the church was on the young, and there were some four hundred or more in the church school. The Mears sisters tingled with excitement as they beheld this work being carried on in a city bursting with the strength and bluster of its youth. Dr. "Mac" had Henrietta speak on several occasions, and the response to her messages was immediate (Baldwin and Benson 1966:48).

Dr. MacLennan had confirmed what he has thought almost three years previously. Henrietta Mears was a powerful leader. She simply needed a platform from which to greatly influence. He quickly invited her to come and minister. Notice how he pursues her. He believed in her. He let her know she was important. He let her know she had an important role to play. He wanted her for the ministry she could contribute to the church. This was no half hearted attempt to determine the will of God. It was settled as far as he was concerned. Later results validated his perspective.

> He finally offered her the position of Director of Christian Education. But it was out of the question. All of their ties were in Minneapolis, and whatever successes she might have had were there. Besides, Margaret was involved in business. They owned their own home. And Henrietta was scheduled to return to her teaching post. In a few weeks the two sisters were back in Minneapolis. But Miss Mears' thoughts gave her no peace, and neither did Dr. MacLennan. He wrote--he telegraphed--he telephoned! (Baldwin and Benson 1966:48,49).

Henrietta was challenged, interested, and yet undecided. This is a pivotal decision that will take her away from all that she has been familiar with. She is feeling what many she will

---

[32]It is clear in retrospect that she was in the front end of a boundary time and was being prepared by God for release into full time ministry. The time when a leader moves from one major period of his/her life to the next is called a boundary. Boundaries have been studied extensively. See Clinton (1992) *Boundary Processing--Looking At Critical Transition Times in Leader's Lives*. Comparative studies of such boundaries have identified three stages: 1. the entry stage; 2. the evaluation stage, and 3. the expansion stage. Four different kinds of boundaries, under which most can be categorized, are popularly described by the titles of Surprise, The Creeping Vine, The New Glasses, The Growth Challenge. This is a combination of Growth Challenge and Creeping Vine type. McQuilkin has gifts that are not being used by *The Sunday School Times*. He is needing to move on. This is an example of a combination of two types, Growth Challenge and Creeping Vine type. To develop to maximum potential Mears needs the right role and geographical locale for influence. First Presbyterian Church of Hollywood provided these.

[33]A *ministry insight* (Clinton 1989:198) is a breakthrough that facilitates one's ministry. The concept of a sabbatical for renewal, new insights, reflection, and rest will be greatly used by Miss Mears. She never burns out in ministry because she regularly took sabbatical tours.

Chapter 8. Henrietta Mears (1890-1963)	page 357

later challenges into ministry must have felt. So she made one more trip. It was on this trip that it was clear to her that God had already decided. It took an unusual incident to open her eyes.

> One noon, she and dr. MacLennan went to the Pig 'n Whistle restaurant on Hollywood Boulevard for lunch. As they approached the door, it silently opened before her. She had never seen a door controlled by an "electric eye." She was greatly amazed and impressed. As they ate their lunch and talked about the possibilities of the work that could be done in Hollywood, Miss Mears, without realizing it, found herself saying, "If I were going to do such-and-such, I'd..." She finally saw that her own door had opened as silently and effortlessly as the electric-eye door had opened when she had entered the restaurant (Baldwin and Benson 1966:49).

Immediately upon returning home she asked God to validate what she was feeling and had in essence already decided. God sold her home almost immediately and for $2000 more than they were asking--something Henrietta had asked God to do to validate His leading. She was also released from her teaching contract. This clear and sovereign pivotal point in her life led to the first of her major roles.

III. LIFE WORK--ONE AIM, PRODUCING LEADERS
THREE FOLD MAJOR ROLE--CHURCH LEADER/ TEACHER; PUBLISHER OF S.S. MATERIALS; FACILITATOR OF RETREAT CENTER MINISTRY
(1928-1963); Age 38-73

With a move from Minneapolis to California in 1928 and a major change from a bi-vocational ministry to a full-time Christian ministry, the second of the focal issues begins to fall in place. Henrietta had already visualized a **life purpose**--challenging young people into leadership. Now was to come the development of her **major role**. As to focal issues, it was **life purpose** which dominated, but **major role** was a close second and certainly supplied the means for achieving her life purpose.

Now Miss Mears was to develop her **major role**--having a three pronged thrust which was to influence hundreds of thousands of people. Her position as Christian Education Director for a successful church provided the status and the platform for developing this three fold thrust.

First she became a leader in the Sunday School movement. Her leadership broadened outward from her own church. This involved teaching a very successful college age class,[34] directing a whole Sunday School program, and eventually inspiring thousands of Sunday School programs in the U.S.A. and abroad through her conference speaking and Sunday School Associations' work.

Second, she published Sunday School materials and books for Sunday School teachers. Eventually this led to the founding of Gospel Press, a successful publishing venture. She was the executive director of this ministry.

---

[34]She taught this class with power for almost the entire 35 years of her ministry at First Presbyterian Church. It was one of her most important means for challenging and releasing leaders. It was as a result of this ministry that she received the honorific sobriquet, Teacher. She was a superb teacher both by training, experience and spiritual gifting. It was the dominant gift of her gift-mix.

Chapter 8. Henrietta Mears (1890-1963)

Third, she founded Forest Home, a retreat center in the California mountains. She directed the philosophical thrust of its programs. It was at this center that a major campus movement challenged and launched many young leaders into ministry.

Through this complex major role, with a three pronged thrust, she was able to see her major **life purpose** realized--to challenge, motivate, train, and free up numerous young people into ministry. The use of the retreat center to see many lives committed to Christ and His service was as close to a **unique methodology** as she had, apart from her forceful teaching ministry and motivational ministry insights.

A. Initial Success--Sunday School Ministry (450+ to 6000+) (1928-1933); Age= 38-43

God's hand was on her life. This was seen in the next five years in two major ways. One, He brought to her side a team of co-workers who were to devote their abilities to enabling Miss Mears to achieve her God-given potential. Two, He blessed her work greatly and gave her favor and influence with many others involved in Sunday School ministry.

The Team Forms--Ethel May Baldwin and Esther Ellinghusen

Within a space of just a few years two critical players on Henrietta Mears team came along side to take responsible supportive roles that would complement and/or supplement Miss Mears and help her to work not only effectively but efficiently.

Ethel May Baldwin had met Henrietta Mears on one of her former visits to the church and immediately felt drawn to minister with her in the area of Christian education. She responded to Henrietta's cry for administrative help. As her talent was recognized she moved from secretary to executive assistant to co-laborer handling almost all of Miss Mears administrative needs and program details. She was to be an almost indispensable person on the team that was to free up Miss Mears to focus on her giftedness without distractions.

A second important person on the team, Esther A. Ellinghusen joined efforts with Miss Mears after about two years of ministry. A growing Sunday School, and it was growing, needed leaders trained and materials they could use. Esther was a talented educational expert with a flair for designing and writing materials. After Gospel Light Press was formed, still down road a few years, Esther was along with Miss Mears the major producers of materials.

In just under three years the Sunday School grew from around 450 to over 4200. By 1933, just five years later it went over 6000, one of the most successful in the world. Eventually it topped out at 6500 (Roe 1990:142). Why? Let me suggest nine important reasons for this tremendous rapid success. There are probably more. I almost hesitate to give these since I am sure to miss some important ones. However, even this small list can be instructive and challenging. These standout to me even upon first glance at this period of her life.

1. **Henrietta Mears was gifted for her Sunday School leadership role.** Experience had honed her giftedness. Spiritual gifts were the focal element of her giftedness set. Evangelism, teaching, and leadership flourished. Her expanding adapted role enhanced this gift-mix, one of the symptoms of

Chapter 8. Henrietta Mears (1890-1963) page 359

convergence.[35] Her team of workers around her enabled her to adapt her role to fit more closely her giftedness.[36]

2. **She was a value based leader.** She had learned some important spiritual values, leadership values, and strategic values which she put to use. I will seek to identify some of the values in a later section of this chapter.

3. **She modeled all that she espoused to others.** This was true in the smallest details of her teaching and personal relationships with others as well as with Sunday School programs as a whole. She had experienced what she recommended to others. It carried weight--spiritual authority, because God's hand of blessing was seen it. She was a powerful mentor, howbeit if only mainly non-deliberate in the passive role of a contemporary model.[37]

4. **She developed and released leaders.** She basically recruited from within, set up strict acceptability for training, organized the training and carried it out. As capable people developed they picked up the training.

5. **She developed training materials and solid Bible based content that emerging leaders and Sunday School teachers could use.** At first her materials were mimeographed. Word of mouth advertising began the initial distribution. Her educational background, both training and experience, made her a capable designer of materials to fit groups of people.

6. **She used creative ministry insights to give breakthroughs in her own personal ministry.** I mentioned one incident in her earlier ministry in the rural setting (motivational matching fund). There were hundreds like that, except expanded to meet the target groups she ministered to. I will later pinpoint some of these when I summarize her leadership.

7. **She operated out of a future perfect paradigm.**[38] She was goal oriented. She saw what she wanted out there in front of her in the future and then capably motivated and inspired others to help her reach those goals.

---

[35]*Convergence* (Clinton 1989:378) is a time of very effective ministry as several factors come together. Here, in Miss Mears' case, role and gift-mix, ministry philosophy, and potential for influence-mix are in place. She is also in a geographical location where effective ministry can happen. Her two power gate experiences have an important effect on her personal bearing and conduct of ministry. All of these factors increasingly come together to make for a very effective time of ministry for her.

[36]In the *giftedness set* composed of natural abilities, acquired skills and spiritual gifts, one usually dominates. That one is called the *focal element*. In this case it was spiritual gifts (evangelism, teaching, leadership). Further, the gift-mix is mature, that is what a *gift-cluster* is, working together. See Clinton and Clinton 1994, **Developing Leadership Giftedness**. For Mears, teaching is the dominant gift of the gift-mix with evangelism and leadership close seconds. Her leadership gift is probably the prime motivational force and shows up both in evangelism and teaching (probably even stronger than would an exhortation gift). Her evangelism gift was dominantly personal rather than public. Note that her team around her allowed her to focus on using her gift-mix. She was even freed from the details usually accompanying use of a leadership gift. She could freely work on the motivational aspect of it--for which she was especially gifted.

[37]*Mentoring* is a relational experience in which one person called the *mentor*, empowers another person, called the *mentoree* via a transfer of resources. Nine types of mentor functions have been identified. One of these is the modeling function of a contemporary Christian leader respected by the mentoree. The *contemporary model* serves as a sort of Christian hero/heroine who inspires the young leader. The mentoree tends to emulate and imbibe values from the *contemporary model* and tends to live up to the genuine expectations that person sets out. (See Clinton and Clinton, 1991, **The Mentor Handbook**). Henrietta was such a person to many. In addition she also served in a mentor coach, teacher, and sponsor. Her heavy individual and relational ministry made this mentoring effective even though all the mentoring dynamics were not necessarily in place.

[38]The *future perfect paradigm* refers to a way of viewing something in the future as if it were already in place. Such a visualization by faith sees the reality in place and works from that picture by attacking the *beforemath* issues that flow back into the present from such a reality realized. You can catch this kind of

Chapter 8. Henrietta Mears (1890-1963)   page 360

8. **She was a good change agent.** She knew how to get ownership[39] with the change participants. Her opening session with her Sunday School workers demonstrated that she knew how to get ownership.[40]
9. **She was never daunted by restrictions but worked around them.** For 22 years she never had the educational plant or facilities she really needed but she made do with what she had. Eventually she would see numerous educational buildings constructed to house the mammoth Sunday School program.

Even early own these leadership characteristics made themselves known. And as she continued to grow they became even more effective.

B. Wider Ministry--Gospel Light and Sunday School Associations (1933-1938); Age= 43-48

A Ministry Challenge--Gospel Light is Born

As her Sunday School materials began to get wide distribution and as her team of Ethel May and Esther began to take hold the need for a publishing venture became evident.

---

thinking as you listen to Henrietta Mears first thoughts as she came to First Presbyterian of Hollywood. "The first thing I did in Hollywood," she said, "was to write out what I wanted for my Sunday School. I set down my objectives for the first five years. They included improvements in organization, teaching staff, curriculums and spirit. I wanted a closely graded program, a teaching material that would present Christ and His claims in every lesson, a trained teaching staff, a new education building, choirs, clubs, a camp program, a missionary vision, youth trained for the hour." Over and over she repeated that she was not out to build a bigger Sunday School but a better one. She believed that a quality Sunday School program that had the person and work of Christ central would be a growing program. Hers was, in all three areas of church growth: quantitative, qualitative, and organic.

[39]Because she was so goal oriented, a future perfect thinker, she was implicitly conscious of the notion of a *bridging strategy*. Her motivational strengths in her leadership gifting and her people skills allowed her to work with people in getting them to have *ownership* (that is, personally commit themselves to the changes and actually participate in bringing them about as if they were their own ideas). See Clinton (1992) **Bridging Strategies--Leadership Perspectives for Introducing Change.** Mears operated implicitly as a natural change agent and manifested many of the dynamics and principles covered in this change dynamics manual.

[40]Her opening session shows her natural ability with change agent skills. She had received a word from God, which strengthened her just prior to this session. This is also typical of her ministry. ...Henrietta Mears walked into the first teachers' and officers' meeting...They came eagerly, for word had already gotten around about the new director. Some had heard her teach on her earlier visits and were anticipating great things for the Sunday School. Others were doubtlessly skeptical, thinking, "No one could be as good as they are making her out to be!" Speaking in soft, friendly tones, her eyes dancing with enthusiasm and goodwill, she said, "I believe I know just what you are thinking. I think I might feel the same way if I were in your place: 'Another director of the Sunday School--new plans, new ideas, her way of doing things! Now everything is going to be changed again!' 'If I have to reorganize my class once more or try out some fancy new theory, I'll just die!' 'What does she know about Hollywood anyway?' Her audience broke up in laughter, probably more at themselves than at their new leader, for she had caught them off guard. "You don't like changes and neither do I," she continued. "You've been getting along without me up to now, and it would certainly be a great burden for me to have the responsibility of rushing in here to try and reorganize everything overnight. So here is what I thought we might do: We'll relax for six months and use the time for observation, and then we'll sit down and evaluate the situation and decide together what we need to do. You undoubtedly will have some ideas, and I might just possibility have a suggestion or two myself." Those present could hardly wait for her to close the meeting before they rushed to the platform. "Oh, Miss Mears, we can't wait six months! Our department just has to have something done about the teachers. We are having a terrible time. No one wants to teach three-year-olds." And on and on. She had won the first round. For now they had invited her into their departments themselves (Roe 1990:100,101).

Chapter 8. Henrietta Mears (1890-1963)

At first it was a three woman show. But eventually able volunteers with different kinds of expertise were added to the team. Roe entitles one chapter of his book about Henrietta, "Thank Mr. Falconer." Henrietta credits him with providing the spark to go into the publishing business. He was one of those Sunday School superintendents from another Presbyterian church (in Anaheim) who almost forcefully and repeatedly finally extracted promises from Miss Mears for Sunday School materials.

The publishing venture grew rapidly because there was such a great need for good materials. The wider aspect of her major role--Sunday School movement leader--began to take off with this distribution of materials. From a small garage based work the ministry grew until by 1937 over a quarter of a million books had been sold. Harry Rimmer (a self-publisher) and Cary Griffin (a printer) gave helpful advice which got the small venture off on a good foot.

By 1938, the publishing venture was more than a useful expedient. It had become a business. Full time executive and administrative help was added as the Gospel Light Press was formally recognized as a major business. Henrietta would little-by-little have less direct oversight as the years went by but she still maintained an influence in its philosophical underpinnings.

As her reputation as a competent Sunday School worker spread, Henrietta began to take part in Sunday School workshops, rallies, and even large national conferences. She became one of the prime movers in bringing renewed interest to the Sunday School ministry in churches. She helped found the National Sunday School Association. She took part in the leadership of other related Sunday School organizations as well.

C. Forest Home/ Revival Fires/ Seeds of Widespread Influence (1938-1951); Age= 48-61

Henrietta Mears' sphere of influence continued to expand. Her **major role** became clearer: 1. she was a leader in the Sunday School renewal movement. She taught in Sunday School and organized curriculum. 2. She began a publishing venture which greatly aided her Sunday School leadership. From the very first, Henrietta Mears saw the vital importance of taking young people out of their normal environment and placing them in a nature setting. In such a setting they could reflect on their lives and life purposes. It is this need, a location to do this, that brings into focus a third thrust of her **major role**. It also overlaps with one of her **unique methodologies** for motivating leaders toward Christian service.

A Faith Challenge--Forest Home is Born

In Chapter 12, Give Me This Mountain, Roe describes the faith challenge[41] which eventually became Forest Home. This became a sacred, holy place, where many decisions to follow and serve Christ and to accept greater challenges were made by *cream of the crop* leaders.[42] Many of these have significantly affected the generations of Christians who lived from the 50s through the 80s. The value underlying the need for this place is

---

[41] A *faith challenge* (Clinton 1989:222) is the processing God does to expand a leader to trust the unseen God for greater things than ever before. Such a challenge, positively responded to, will usually accompany an expansion in ministry and sphere of influence. This challenge to purchase the Forest Home property in economically lean times was such a shaping activity by God. Mears responded positively. God greatly blessed.
[42] Billy Graham, Bill Bright, and Bob Munger are just a few which are typical of many who were deeply influenced by Henrietta Mears at Forest Home.

Chapter 8. Henrietta Mears (1890-1963)

captured in the Mears quote, "If you place people in an atmosphere where they feel close to God and then challenge them with His Word, they will make decisions."

Henrietta experimented with a variety of camps over several years including Switzer's camp in the San Bernardino mountains, Mount Hermon near San Jose, and Camp Bethel near San Dimas. But it was in the summer of 1937 that she was led to consider a piece of property in the San Bernardino Mountains called Forest Home.[43] Here is some of the inner play she voiced to Bill Irwin the contact that knew about the property. This is what led up to the acceptance of the faith challenge. Note the timing! God is in this.

> Oh, Bill, that is the most elegant place I ever saw, but I just knew we couldn't afford it, so we didn't even get out of the car. We just drove up past all those stone buildings and turned back on the highway at the round house. What could we ever do to run such a big place, even if we could afford to buy it--and we can't afford it!
>
> *A reasonable offer.* But Bill Irwin had some interesting facts to reveal. The owner was very sick and quite old, and he was facing major surgery. It was not all certain he could survive the operation. His son did not want to chance the possibility of having to meet the inheritance tax on a place valued by the bank at $350,000. The tax could wipe him out completely.
>
> Bill thought that a reasonable offer would be considered. The "reasonable offer" was $50,000, so an option on the property was taken (Roe 1990:244).

Henrietta accepted the challenge and began to motivate others toward it. But in her heart she knew that it probably couldn't be done--there simply was not evidence of enough money to do all that needed to be done to the property. They could possibly buy the property but not develop it. It would be more expedient to keep on renting. So the option was dropped. But God is not through yet. He is going to use this place for His glory and to inspire great Christian leaders who will for 40 years dominate the American Christian scene. Roe catches the sovereign working.

> And on the mountain top, God said, "I want this place for My glory to dwell in." So He reached out to the sky and called around Him the thunderclouds. All day and into the night they gathered, billowing like the smoke from an immense furnace. A moment of hushed suspense fell over the earth as nature waited for the command.
>
> Then the God of glory thundered, His voice shaking giant boulders from their beds and causing towering pines to bend to the ground in worship. Bolts of lightning crashed like heavenly spears from cloud to cloud, unlocking the suspended floods that now swept earthward like steeds racing to war. Down the torrents fell, forming into a gigantic wall of water.
>
> The welling tide, bolstered by enormous rocks hurling along in its waters, uprooted trees, crashed against buildings and cut into mountainsides. from wall-to-wall of the valley, the roaring current leaped onward, its unbridled fury leaving disaster in its wake. On the Forest Home Resort property, three cabins down by the stream were washed away and a fourth was left hanging over the bank. Yet, though the surrounding countryside lay in the ruins, the rest of the campsite remained relatively unharmed.
>
> In the silence after the storm, the shrill tones of the telephone bell could be heard. Bill Irwin was calling and asking to speak to Henrietta Mears. The son of the owner of the resort grounds had phoned and offered to sell Forest Home for $30,000 (Roe 1990:245,246).

---

[43]Bill Irwin was the contact who recommended the property and encouraged her to go for it, especially after she had first looked at it and thought it beyond her dreams.

Chapter 8. Henrietta Mears (1890-1963)

With the encouragement of a number of young seminarians[44] and a convincing word from God to Henrietta (Joshua 1:3) the project was launched.

The ministry associated with Forest Home was to become the third and a most powerful thrust of Miss Mears' **major role**. This place became a place of destiny for her in which her life purpose to challenge and free up leaders to serve God was fulfilled in a remarkable way.

Through the years Miss Mears had numerous retreats and conferences at Forest Home. Hers was a powerful ministry there. It was a public ministry of teaching followed by challenge to committal. It was a personal ministry of individual counseling. It was a ministry of prayer for God's will in the lives of numerous potential leaders. It was a ministry which stimulated young people to believe that they could make a difference in the world. It was an effective ministry.

One unique methodology that brought closure and an on-going anchor was her technique, *the book of remembrance*. Roe describes this.

> After making a public of Christ in Victory Circle, each young person moved to a small table nearby where Teacher [the honorific name for Miss Mears] presided over a *Book of Remembrance*. Believing that writing one's name down after making a public decision helped to crystallize it in the mind, Henrietta Mears would hand the individual a pen with an invitation to sign the book, quietly encouraging him or her with a gentle, "God bless you.," This scene was repeated many, many times in Teacher's lifetime (Roe 1990:251).

This Forest Home ministry was intriguing. Miss Mears was able to run it, participate in many of the events there and still coordinate it with her on-going ministry out of First Presbyterian Church. I am tempted to tell many of the stories of her ministry here but I will pass on--after all this is an interpretive presentation. I can not present the details as I wish I could. Instead I am going to jump a number of years to the culminating significant critical incident.

The Europe Destiny Trip; The Expendables

In connection with Forest Home occurs one of the most momentous ministry times of Miss Mears entire life. I have already given the story of this critical incident in opening illustration 2. The important thing to see is its timing. Henrietta Mears is 57 years old. She is at the very peak of her ministry. All three of her thrusts of her major role are in place. Her life purpose is clear. She has seen great things happen already in many individuals lives at Mount Forest. Things are ripe for two kinds of vignettes. One, she can plateau and gradually taper off in her ministry. For after all, she has almost 20 years of fruitful full-time ministry on top of 15 years of good lay leadership. Two, she can be energized by God for a final push which will culminate her life work with a powerful finish. It is vignette 2 which occurs.

One reason for it was Henrietta Mears sensitivity to God in terms of a sense of destiny. The Sabbatical trip, number 7, which keyed this sense of destiny. There is a

---

[44]Dave Cowie and Bob Munger are cited especially as recommending this and offering their help. Both were to have a vital part in the powerful ministry which was culminated by the revival outpouring around 1947 (Roe 1990:246).

mystical sense[45] of destiny attached to her trip to Europe. Step-by-step leading as this destiny unfolds eventually releases great numbers into ministry and changes the face of Christianity both in the U.S. and around the world. This Esther-like opportunity, accepted, was probably the great destiny fulfillment of her life.

D. The Castle--Final Years
(1951-1963); Age= 61-73

It was during the fifties that the major educational plants were planned and completed. Several major building projects were carried out. These were really necessary to house the more than 6000 Sunday School members.

Her sister Margaret died in 1951 ending a long fruitful partnership. Miss Mears shortly thereafter moved into a home, the Castle, near the UCLA campus with Bill and Vonette Bright who were in the opening stages of the development of Campus Crusade. For these last years she maintained a fruitful personal ministry in many lives and continued her college class and various small group training with emerging leaders.

She finished well. Especially notable was her word centered faith and her fulfilled sense of destiny--two of the six characteristics of finishing well.[46]

Summary of Leadership

Now I would like to summarize some aspects of her leadership which cross over the time periods and so were not handled in any one part of the narrative.

<u>Sabbatical Tours--Breaks From Intensive Ministry Are Necessary</u>

In 1927 Dr. Riley suggested that a tour to Europe might be a special time for Henrietta Mears. That was a prophetic insight full of wisdom. For throughout her lifetime sabbatical tours played an important role in her life. In my opinion, one of the reasons she never plateaued, as is the usual case with competent leaders who stay in one place a long time, was these sabbatical tours. These times:

1. provided a needed change of pace from heavy intensive ministry, and thus resulted in a refreshed attitude upon return,
2. sometimes brought renewal,[47]

---

[45] Wiersbe (1993:227) points out four characteristics of an evangelical mystic. The evangelical Christian mystic has 1. a consciousness of the spiritual world beyond the physical, 2. a success standard which focuses on pleasing God rather than those in the world, 3. a bent toward developing an intimate relationship with God and its concomitant an unusual sense of His presence everywhere; and 4. a mindset toward constantly relating this unusual experience with God to the practical things of life. Normally because of her outgoing personality one would not think of Mears as a mystic. But she had a real consciousness of God in things. She sensed Him speaking often in her Bible reading and study and in timely events.

[46] *Finished Well* can mean different things to different people. Six characteristics of finishing well are given in Appendix C. Of these six Mears scores high marks on all six: personal vibrant relationship with God, learning posture, Christ likeness in character, Word centered faith, ultimate contributions, fulfilled sense of destiny. She is one of five including, Simeon, Brengle, Morgan, and Maxwell who died in peaceful circumstance and were able to look back in old age with satisfaction on a purposeful focused life well lived.

[47] *Renewal* is a specially meaningful encounter with God in which He communicates with *freshness* various kinds of things needed by a leader such as: 1. insights about Himself, 2. affirmation--both personal

Chapter 8. Henrietta Mears (1890-1963)

3. frequently brought new insights about ministry,
4. was used by God to give her cultural sensitivity,
5. kept her missionary vision alive,
6. allowed for ministry among missionaries and former leaders she had influenced to go into ministry,
7. served as a major means of continued education for her.[48]

Table 8-1 Contains a list of these sabbatical tours. They certainly dispel the notion that a leader is indispensable and can't be missed from ministry. In fact, they reinforce the notion that leaders should absent themselves from their ministries from time-to-time to test the stability of their work as well as for personal benefit.

TABLE 8-1 LIST OF SABBATICAL TOURS

When	Where	Who With	Duration	Results
1. 1927	Europe	Margaret	1 year	Major decision to go into full-time ministry in California.
2. 1931	Panama	Ethel May	several mos.	Renewed interest in missionary enterprise
3. 1935	Around the World	Ethel May	several mos.	Educational/ Cross-cultural/ awareness
4. 1938	Caribbean	Ethel May	few mos.	Refreshment/ Ministry/ cross-cultural education in near cultures

---

and ministry, 3. inspiration to continue, 4. breakthrough concepts which inspire one to try them in ministry, 5. a sense of His personal presence and/or power, 6. an unusual sense of intimacy--can be tied to some symbolic thing (like a place, physical object, etc), 7. perspective on time, now and/or the future so that ones faith is increased to see God in what is happening and will happen, so as to give the leader another anchor upon which to build a sense of a new start, a beginning again, and a desire to rededicate and continue on in following God. I have already mentioned two major renewal experiences that Henrietta Mears had in her two power gate experiences. The sabbatical trip of 1946,47 was also a major renewal experience. But a number of these tours brought about minor renewal experiences in Mears' life. Effective leaders will need several repeated renewal experiences over their lifetimes in order to continue and finish well. The classic cases of renewal leadership in the Old Testament are Abraham and Daniel, from which the renewal definition was derived.

[48] We have identified three major training patterns through which most leaders emerge. Four of the eight, Gordon, Maxwell, Jaffray and Simeon (somewhat) fit the *pre-service pattern* (Clinton 1989:354), that is, they received formal training prior to ministry. Three fit the second pattern, the *in-service pattern* (Clinton 1989:356), that is, they learned on-the-job and finally after proving their abilities took on full time responsibilities. Morgan and McQuilkin fit here. Mears started here. The third pattern is a *modified in-service pattern* (Clinton 1989:357) in which the leader gets ministry experience, then interrupts it for formal training, and then resumes it. Mears transitioned to a quasi-form of this pattern by use of the sabbatical tours. Usually this pattern will include further interruptions for training down road. Brengle fits this pattern somewhat. In these complicated times and complex ministry settings in which things learned often are outdated quickly, it is clear that the third pattern the *interrupted in-service* is necessary for survival and effectiveness. We highly recommend planned and continued learning throughout life and ministry. Henrietta Mears, like so many things she did, operated this way naturally.

Chapter 8. Henrietta Mears (1890-1963)   page 366

TABLE 8-1 LIST OF SABBATICAL TOURS continued

5. 1940	South	Ethel May	several mos.	Refreshment/ cross-cultural education
6. 1942	Mexico Cuba	Margaret	several mos.	Renewal/ Refreshment/ cross-cultural education/ viewed first hand, Bible Translation work
7. 1946	South America, War Torn Europe	Margaret	several mos.	Major Renewal/ sense of destiny experience/ Mission thrust/ leadership challenge/ window of opportunity seen
8. 1949	Around the World	Louise James	several mos.	Refreshment/ cross-cultural education/ ministry to missionaries/ renewal of interest in missions
9. 1952	Around the World	Esther Ellinghusen	several mos.	Grieving Process after Margaret had died. Renewal.
10. 1954	Europe London	unclear who	few months	Visit Billy Graham campaign; contacts for ministry in Forest Home, refreshment
11. 1956	Africa Europe	Ethel May	several mos.	Renew missionary vision/ cross-cultural education/ minister to missionaries/ enjoy fruit of previous labors

With world travel so accessible today, world conferences and other non-formal training workshops, seminars, and conferences so available, can you imagine what Miss Mears travel sabbaticals would look like if she were living and ministering in our day?

<u>Identification of Some Ministry Insights--Her Creative Leadership</u>

Table 8-2 lists some of the ministry insights[49] I have identified in Miss Mears ministry. If I could have seen her first hand I am sure I would have identified many more for I feel she had an unusual God-given creative ability to come up with these insights, at least at tactical level, with on-the-spot spontaneity.

---

[49]Remember that *ministry insights* (Clinton 1989:198) are break through concepts which allow penetrating effectiveness in ministry. Mears' leadership gift included a creative/enthusiastic aspect which allowed her to visualize ways and means to penetrate a situation.

Chapter 8. Henrietta Mears (1890-1963)

TABLE 8-2 SOME MINISTRY INSIGHTS

Location/ Group	When	What/ Results
1. Beardsville youth ministry	1913	Matching Fund/ Challenge to Earn to give to missions/ highest giving to missions of any group
2. North Branch teaching	1914	Use of Goodwin's Expectation Principle with Everett, the class problem person/ changed Everett
3. Women's Class--18 year olds, Minneapolis	1915	Restructuring to meet class; personal visitation/ use of greeter for recruiting/almost entire first class into lay ministry/ second class grew to be over 500/ offshoot class, Dorcas, focused on mission support
4. Sunday School, First Presbyterian, Hollywood	1930s	Introduced graded classes and curriculum/ Eventually classes for all ages and materials that fit them
5. Sunday School, First Presbyterian, Hollywood	1930s	Introduced concept of Worship Services into Sunday School work/ children learned importance of worship at early age
6. Sunday School, First Presbyterian, Hollywood	1930s	Rabbit Hutches; portable, movable class rooms/ solved temporarily need for educational plant
7. Sunday School, First Presbyterian, Hollywood	1930s	Supplemented Sunday School Classes with clubs, interest groups, socials, camps, choirs and activities that met the needs of the various young people
8. Sunday School, First Presbyterian, Hollywood	1930s	Introduced selectivity requirements for Hollywood Sunday School teachers/ better teachers[50]/ better quality teachers
9. College Age Class, First Presbyterian, Hollywood	1930s	Decentralized Authority Structure; students expected to take up responsibility for functions/ every student accounted for somewhere and emerging leadership develops/ every student contacted on some regular basis

---

[50] Her selection screens (Roe 1990:122-129) included particularly these three: 1. an evident and productive relationship with Christ; 2. a willingness to spend time in lesson preparation and in training classes; 3. a desire to model Christian living as well as to teach God's Word.

Chapter 8. Henrietta Mears (1890-1963)　　　　　　　　page 368

TABLE 8-2　SOME MINISTRY INSIGHTS continued

10. College Age Class, First Presbyterian, Hollywood	1930-1960	Variety of Meetings with different functions-- **Sunday morning**: teaching of word; **Wednesday**: Evangelism, prayer, testimonies, discussion groups for Bible study; **Sunday evening College Hour**: forums, panels, musicals, testimonials, interaction, productive creativity; **Monthly youth night**: program put on for whole church by youth.
11. Intercessory Backer, Mother Atwater	1930-1960	Early on she saw the necessity of Wagner's intercessors for leaders; she personally developed a relationship with a prayer warrior who not only prayed for the class but did visitation evangelism with Henrietta Mears on a regular once per week basis/ many young people personally led to the Lord over the years/ breakthroughs in ministry due to answered prayer
12. Hands-On-Training in Evangelism	1940s?	She taught evangelism with practical hands-on-exercises in which what was learned was used. People won were funneled into the class immediately and hence were reproducing right away/ many personal evangelist raised up and trained
13. Creative Club in Home	1930s	Gathering of aspiring musicians, writers, artists, poets; stimulate and encourage their creativity/ many into specialty ministries using creative talents
14. Timothean Club	1950s?	Monthly Gathering of potential full-time ministers; question/answer forum with visiting ministers/ ministerial formation of emerging pastoral leaders
15. Summer Seminarians	?	Summer internships for five or six seminarians during their summer days; practical ministry experience with feedback/ seminarians trained for ministry

Chapter 8. Henrietta Mears (1890-1963)

TABLE 8-2 SOME MINISTRY INSIGHTS continued

16. Meals with Visiting Spiritual leaders in her home/ invited young leaders	?	Miss Mears frequently invited important leaders who were in town or speaking at First Presbyterian Church to have a meal in her home; she invited select emerging leaders from her collegians and seminarians to come to and interact/ modeling, stimulating of emerging leaders.[51]
17. Saturday Morning Prayer time in her home	?	Directors in college class participated; the elite informal atmosphere in the home was motivating to many of these emerging leaders/ prayer modeled, openness modeled
18. Structured/ informal counseling	?	Always available after prayer time to meet with individual students for personal needs/ powerful mentor counselor influence
19. Closure Technique/ Book Remembrance	1930-1960	At camps people making decisions signed their names in a Book of Remembrance to bring a sense of finality to their decision/ many went on from this place with their decision as an anchor point for the future

<u>Observations on Her Motivational Means</u>

Miss Mears was a powerful motivator. Partly I think this was due to her leadership gifting. Partly it was due to her conviction about her life purpose. But there were other factors involved in her powerful motivational effect on emerging leaders. I list a few of my observation with a disclaimer, that this is scratching the surface at best. Still it may prove helpful. Some observations about her motivating include:

1. She had an attractive winsome personality that saw the best in people.

2. She modeled what she expected of others.

3. She selected the right people to motivate. She had an uncanny ability, a God-given discernment for spotting potential leaders early on.

4. She used Goodwin's Expectation Principle effectively. Emerging leaders tend to live up to the genuine expectations of older leaders they admire or respect.

5. She taught with expectation. Her God-given power in teaching was used to bring impact in the life. She always moved for decisions of the affect and the will and she expected to see these as a result of her teaching.

6. She used creative means to gain attention and activities that would attract and create an ambiance for God to work.

---

[51] Roe (1990:214,215) mentions such names as Dr. Harry Rimmer, Dr. J. Edwin Orr, Dr. Wilbur Smith, Dr. William Evans. There were many others of like stature. The impact of these kind of leaders on emerging leaders is tremendous, particularly in their leadership transition period.

7. She realized that certain structures were more conducive to powerful motivation than others.

8. She was not afraid to take a risk with emerging leaders. This in itself was a huge factor why leaders were challenged by her to try things.

Mears' leadership is filled with motivational insights. In a day when inspirational leadership is so desperately needed she is especially worth remembering.

Critical Incidents Identified, and/or Explained

Critical incidents are shaping activities which can affect values relating to all three types of formations--spiritual (leadership character), ministerial (leadership skills) and strategic (leadership vision, that is, total direction in life and ministry). There is a sense in which many, many incidents in a leader's life **affect values**. But from that large identifiable number a few should be highlighted and recognized as very significant. Critical incidents also frequently provide **pivotal points for choices** of roles, kind of ministry and locale. These pivotal incidents provide strategic guidance.

Here is a list of critical incidents, some giving focal values and some providing strategic guidance. Table 8-3 indicates these. I number them for convenience of referencing later when I comment on them.

Table 8-3 Listing Of Some Critical Incidents In Mears' Life

Incident(s) Name	Age	Formational Type Dealing With Basic Value/Thrust
1. Rich Heritage (see page 340)	1-6	Spiritual--Mears sees in her father one who uses words only to build up; She sees in her mother a model of Christian reality (powerful values) and of a Bible Teacher/ Evangelist/ personal worker. This early shaping deeply impacted her life and ministry. Numerous values are imparted including the practice and power of prayer and the naturalness of witnessing evangelistically to people. Christianity affects how we think, live, and relate to others.
2. Contemporary Model Pastor Riley (see page 346)	6-18	Ministerial--Pastor D. B. Riley modeled an effective pastoral ministry with an evangelistic emphasis. His ministry included challenging young people into leadership--a value which would later become a dominant life purpose for Miss Mears. Emerging Christian leaders need to early on see someone whom they respect as a Christian leader. This on-going series of incidents lays an incipient value concerning challenging leadership.
3. A Healing Touch (see page 347)	12	Strategic--At age 12 Miss Mears learns that the unseen God can intervene in the seen world. An early healing of muscular rheumatism. In later life she will receive God's healing touch concerning deterioration of eyesight. Here she is opened to the supernatural work of God. This is a focal incident resulting in an important value about God.

Chapter 8. Henrietta Mears (1890-1963)

Table 8-3 Listing Of Some Critical Incidents In Mears' Life continued

Incident(s) Name	Age	Formational Type Dealing With Basic Value/Thrust
4. Leadership Committal (see page 347)	17	Strategic--Around age 17 or 18 Miss Mears is challenged by Dr. Riley to full-time Christian service along with her friend Evelyn Camp. On the surface it was a commitment to go where ever God wanted. But deeper, it was a commitment to be what God wanted. This anchor becomes part of an on-going challenge by God which eventually leads to full-time service in First Presbyterian Church in Hollywood, California. This is a strategic incident.
5. Eyesight Crisis (see page 348)	18	Spiritual--Henrietta Mears displays a courageous learning posture which reckons with the possibility of blindness. God does not always heal. She responds with a very positive view of God's sovereignty in her life. Important value on God's sovereignty settled here.
6. Crisis: Mom's Death; Prophetic Mantle Challenge; Grieving by going deep Spiritually (see page 334)	20	Spiritual/ Strategic--Pastor Riley challenges Henrietta at the funeral to take up her Mom's mantle. She responds by going deeper with God; seeking spiritual comfort. Important value, that of recognizing God's call to a deeper spiritual life is seen here.
7. Divine Contact Paul Rader (see page 349)	20	Spiritual/ Under Paul Rader's timely preaching, Miss Mears receives spiritual consolation and deeper understanding of the grace of God.
8. Mantle Accepted; Power gate experience; Gifted Power; (see page 334)	21	Spiritual/ Strategic--Henrietta accepts by faith Holy Spirit power to minister as her mother did. She has mystical experience with the unusual sensed presence of Christ and resultant infilling of Holy Spirit.
9. First Singles Test, Beardsley; Divine Contact, President of school board (see page 351)	24	Spiritual--A young man, one not walking with the Lord is attracted to Henrietta and vice versa. God gives obedience check via a counselor mentor, a divine contact. She obeys, recognizing that a union with this man will take her away from God. An important value is implanted. God must be first in the life.

Chapter 8. Henrietta Mears (1890-1963)

Table 8-3 Listing Of Some Critical Incidents In Mears' Life continued

Incident(s) Name	Age	Formational Type Dealing With Basic Value/Thrust
10. Second Singles Test, North Branch (see page 351)	25	Spiritual--Another young man, one of a different religious view courts Henrietta. Again she is led by God to recognize an unsuitable match in terms of a life long pursuit of God. Here a compromise of values is the issue.
11. Social Base; Margaret Opts to minister with Miss Mears (see page 353)	25	Strategic--Miss Mears older sister opts to partner with Henrietta and maintain the social base support that will free up Henrietta to focus on a Word ministry. This partnership will last 35 years. Eventually this will become an ideal social base from which to minister as others are recruited to Miss Mears team.
12. Life Purpose Clarified; Evelyn Camp's return stimulates reflection (see page 354)	27	Strategic--Henrietta clarifies her life purpose. She will be a channel to motivate, recruit, and release into leadership many who will go. She herself will not go but will be the stimulus for many going. She will deliberately and proactively focus on recruiting and challenging young male leadership into Christian ministry. Her influence will be felt around the world and in many Christian organizations.
13. Divine Contact; Stewart P. MacLennan (see page 355)	35	Strategic--Pastor MacLennan provides the opportunity to link to a broader ministry. He sees in Henrietta Mears leadership that has great potential only needing the right opportunity to unleash it. This contact will be renewed almost three years later with the challenge.
14. Divine Contact; Pastor Riley (see page 355, 356)	37	Ministerial/ Strategic: Pastor Riley at a timely moment suggests that a sabbatical tour may be a reflection time in which God will give insights. This was true and led eventually to a full-time position at First Presbyterian Church in Hollywood. But it also gave Miss Mears an insight to use in ministry which would keep her renewed throughout her ministry years.
15. Decision Time; Sabbatical Travel Abroad; Opportunity of a lifetime. (see page 356)	38	Strategic--Miss Mears chooses between further education and a career in public education and Christian Ministry. The sabbatical tour plus visit to Hollywood, First Presbyterian Church, provided stimulus for reflection and a major decision. Certainty guidance clarifies God's intent in it.

Chapter 8.   Henrietta Mears (1890-1963)

Table 8-3 Listing Of Some Critical Incidents In Mears' Life continued

Incident(s) Name	Age	Formational Type Dealing With Basic Value/Thrust
16. Ethel May Baldwin Recruited (see page 358)	38	Ministerial/ Strategic--Miss Baldwin is recruited to Henrietta's team. She will supply executive administrative backup which will greatly increase Miss Mears ministry. The sphere of influence that Henrietta Mears will wield necessitates a team of people who can handle details and free her up for her motivational Word ministry.
17. Esther A. Ellinghusen Recruited; Opens Way for Gospel Light Press to Develop (see page 358)	40	Ministerial/ Strategic--A vast explosion in the Sunday School ministry necessitates training and Sunday School materials. Henrietta Mears will do this along with other ministry. But what is needed is someone to focus on just that. Esther Ellinghusen is just that person. The team is almost complete. Great potential will be released because of this complementary group of leaders.
18. Ministry Challenge Mr. Falconer; Harry Rimmer Cary Griffin (see page 360)	43	Ministerial/ Strategic--Gospel Light Press is developed in order to meet increased demands for S.S. materials. Volunteer labor from knowledgeable support people helps broaden the team. This ministry will have tremendous impact on Sunday Schools all over the world and will eventually publish all kinds of Christian literature.
19. Faith Challenge; Forest Home; Book of Remembrance (see page 361)	48	Ministerial/ Strategic--Miss Mears has long used retreat settings to motivate young people to accept Christ and to give their lives for ministry. She now has the base for tremendous ministry over the years, particularly the setting for the 1947,48 revival and challenge of young leaders into the window of opportunity after World War II.
20. Europe Destiny Trip; The Expendables; Peak Motivational Ministry realizing life purpose. (see page 337)	57	Ministry/ Strategic--There is a mystical sense of destiny attached to her trip to Europe. Step-by-step leading as this destiny unfolds eventually releases great numbers into ministry and changes the face of Christianity both in the U.S. and around the world. This Esther-like opportunity, accepted, was probably the great destiny fulfillment of her life.

This array of critical incidents is filled with potential lessons and various confirmations of concepts seen elsewhere in leadership emergence theory. Let me detail a few:

1. **IMPORTANCE OF MODELS EARLY ON IN A LIFE**
    Comparative study of lives reveals that for every leader at least 10-15 people are identified as playing very significant mentoring functions over their lifetimes. Early on, when the discipleship habits are being formed and when there are first steps in ministry, contemporary models are very necessary. For Miss Mears

critical incidents 1 and 2 affirm this important observation. Her mother was the single most important factor in determining Henrietta's leadership.[52] She saw that a lay person, even a female, could have a powerful ministry over a life time. It was not only possible. It was admirable. Her pastor modeled what a full-time minister ought to be and do. His wisdom, godly life, and evangelistic emphasis all impacted Henrietta. From these two she learned much about leadership. She was not afraid to challenge lay people to lead. She was not afraid to challenge lay people to go into full-time Christian work. She was not afraid to lead people to Christ.

2. **IMPORTANCE OF DIVINE CONTACTS IN A LIFE**
Another type of mentor, a very passive one[53] is the divine contact. Such a person intervenes in the life of a mentoree at a propitious moment so as to give what is perceived as God-given advice. Critical incidents 6, 7, 9, 13, 14, 18 and 19 illustrate this. Pastor Riley (6) challenged Henrietta to carry on a God-given heritage. This challenge overwhelms her and drives her to seek God in a new way. She experiences a life power paradigm shift which will flow throughout all her ministry to come. Paul Rader (7) met her with God's message of grace in a moment of grief. His victory message became her own. The school board chairman in Beardsley (9) courageously confronted Henrietta concerning a serious but unworthy suitor. Her decision to obey God's voice in this set the tone for living a life pleasing to God and trusting Him to meet her social needs. Stewart MacLennan (13) provides the link to the setting in which her major role will develop. He was a recruiter. He saw in her potential that could be developed and used greatly for the kingdom. He sponsors Henrietta into the full-time ministry that will allow her to fulfill her destiny. Pastor Riley (14) makes a key suggestion at an important and critical juncture. His advice on self-isolation and reflection not only led to the decision to go full-time into ministry but provided a ministry insight, the concept of the Sabbatical tour, which was to play such a renewing effect in Henrietta's life. Falconer, Rimmer, and Griffin (18) are illustrative of how God brings the right people along to help Henrietta make decisions when expansion of ministry is in order. She takes the plunge to publish. God brings along the right people at the right time to meet needs. This same sort of example is seen in the major faith challenge (19) when Bill Irwin was the link to timely knowledge that allowed the transaction to be pulled off which provided a retreat center that later would be part of Henrietta's fulfillment of destiny. Just simply reviewing the place of divine contacts in her life can alert us and make us more sensitive to God's

---

[52]There was also a very important personality mix seen in Henrietta due to both parents' influence, either genetically or from early imitation modeling. Her mother was highly disciplined, very structured, very serious and wholly concerned with counting for God. She was effective in spiritual matters. But her life is almost too legalistic. But her father had a powerful sense of humor and was able to enjoy spontaneity in life. Henrietta was a good balanced mix. She was effective and goal oriented and focused on spiritual matters (her mom's influence). But she was creative, spontaneous, fun-loving and had a winsome personality (all seen in her dad) so as to mix business and pleasure in a most effective way to motivate people.

[53]See **The Mentor Handbook** where nine types of mentor functions are outlined. Three (discipler, spirituality mentor, coach) are active mentoring relationships. For active mentoring, all the dynamics of mentoring are operating at least at some level (attraction, relationship, responsiveness, accountability, empowerment). Three (counselor, teacher, sponsor) are occasional. Some of the dynamics are in place. Three (contemporary models, historical models, and divine contacts) are passive. The dynamics are not there unless supplied by the mentoree. Henrietta's divine contacts with the exception of Pastor Riley who intervened several times specifically at critical junctures are very passive and occurred only at a God-given moment to influence Henrietta toward some important strategic decision.

working in our own lives through divine contacts. It can encourage us to believe that God will meet us in our timely need with His answers through His messengers. It also leads us to see, in a strategic sense, the wider interdependence of the body of Christ.

3. DOUBLE POWER GATE EXPERIENCES

Miss Mears emphasizes both the importance of power in a life to live a victorious Christian life and power in a life to operate with gifted anointed power. Critical incidents 6 and 8 illustrate this. Usually a leader will experience one or the other of these power gate experiences. Miss Mears knew both. The first one (6) is of special interest. Miss Mears was seeking a specific answer to the **what** of ministry. She had surrendered to full-time ministry. But what. God showed her that the what of ministry was not the vital need. It was a special relationship with Himself. It was being not **doing** that was in focus. This early lesson will begin to imbed an important ministry value: Ministry essentially flows out of being not doing. Doing is not the goal but the by-product of the goal of being. But most important, her experiences validate the crises needs for power that leaders will face in their lives and ministry. All leaders will need power for life and ministry. Sooner or later their need will drive them to appropriate it from God.

4. FREED TO MINISTER

Critical incidents 11, 16, and 17 show how a loving God not only meets needs but goes beyond those needs (Ephesians 3:20, exceedingly abundantly above what we ask or think). In response to two tests, critical incidents 9 and 10, God fully meets Henrietta's social needs by providing a loving home environment (11) watched over and run by Margaret, a beautiful complement to Henrietta. She is **freed up** to operate in her giftedness without a worry as to the majority of her social needs. But God answers beyond just the social needs. This same **freeing up** is seen in incidents 16 (Ethel May) and 17 (Esther) where God brings along people who take responsibility for carrying out details so that Henrietta again can focus on her primary giftedness. This same principle, God bringing alongside others to free her up, is seen throughout her ministry of teaching, publishing and operating a retreat center. God also gave her the freedom to release ministry to those He raised up.

5. MINISTRY CHALLENGES FLOW OUT OF MINISTRY NEEDS

Among the many smaller challenges that Henrietta faced there were two great ones--the publishing venture (18) and the Forest Home purchase (19). Two principles, seen in leadership emergence theory are confirmed here. One, great ministry challenges flow out of great ministry needs. Problems can be opportunities if they drive us to God for solutions. As leaders we merely have to look around us and see the major problems as potential for opportunities for God to act. We must then be sensitive to perceive what God is saying in them. We wait while He confirms, possibly through divine contacts. Then we act. Two, great ministry challenges involve in a special way the timing of God. This is seen in critical incidents 18 and 19 and in a more spectacular way in the Europe trip/ window of opportunity (20). When God's timing has come, a leader must courageously and with power proclaim it, expecting God to move. Like Robert Jaffray (age 58), Henrietta Mears was challenged at age 57 to expect God to move to meet the leadership needs facing a world bankrupt after World War II. Late in life, almost 20 years in to her full-time ministry, she was challenged to expect the greatest fulfillment of her ministry. And God greatly blessed her obedient faith expectancy.

Chapter 8. Henrietta Mears (1890-1963)

Two of the incidents stand out as pivotal. Incident 12 in which her life purpose was clarified--she was to recruit, motivate, equip, and release leaders into ministry--settled for her the dominant focal issue of her life. She lived with that purpose dominating her decisions and ministry. The second pivotal incident was the Social Base one (11) in which Margaret committed to partner with Henrietta. She saw on Henrietta's life the blessing of God and wanted to free her up to accomplish all that the blessing entailed. Henrietta Mears had the best social base situation of all the leaders studied in this book. God more than made up to her all that she forewent in opting to remain single. He satisfied her inner needs. He provided functional substitutes for family and heritage. He blessed her greatly. She was a female Daniel whom God greatly blessed as a single.

Along with Samuel Brengle and Robert Jaffray she best illustrates not only the destiny pattern but destiny fulfilled (20). Along with Simeon she changed the course of Christian history because she fulfilled her life purpose of supplying quality leaders to the cause of Christianity.

Finally, the incidents taken as a whole remind us of God's strategic timing in our lives. Henrietta Mears did not go into full-time ministry until age 38. All during the time preceding this momentous decision she was obediently ministering very successfully as a lay leader. When the timing was right, God led her into a full-time ministry that blossomed much more rapidly than one could ever expect or hope for. As leaders our focus should be on relating to and obeying God not seeking convergence. Convergence and fulfillment of our destiny is a by-product of the major goal--seeking and knowing God. Henrietta Mears exemplifies this.

Values And Critical Values--Quotes from Mears

I usually reserve this section for a listing of values categorized in three areas: spiritual (leadership character), ministerial (leadership skills), and strategic (leadership vision, that is, life long leadership direction). Mears was unusual in that she motivated so many young people into leadership ministries along the lines of her life purpose of raising up leaders. Much of her value system is captured in quotes sprinkled throughout her teaching and writing. Rather than explicitly identifying values I want to simply quote Miss Mears and leave you, the reader, to draw out the values contained implicitly in the quotes. These quotes have challenged many. Here are a number of quotable quotes which contain powerful leadership values imbedded in them. Can you spot the values?[54] I will group related quotes--dealing with like values.

Quotes Relating to Future Perfect Thinking

Goals are never met by happenstance (Roe 1990:202).

You must decide what you want to build and then proceed with the plans (Roe 1990:20).

Only that which is directed toward definite goals, which in turn are founded on sound educational philosophy, can be ultimately meaningful. The principles must always precede the activities (Roe 1990:99,100).

---

[54]In addition to these quotes which can be copied out put up on a bulletin board or on a desk as a reminder, I am going to give Henrietta Mears 10 commandments for a teacher. I will include this as a closing challenge from her life just prior to her time-line. I will also give her personal points for personal workers. These two appendix like features highlight her two of her major gifts: teaching, evangelism.

Chapter 8. Henrietta Mears (1890-1963)   page 377

There is no magic in small plans. When I consider my ministry, I think of the world. Anything less than that would not be worthy of Christ nor of His will for my life (Roe 1990:17).

Enthusiasm starts a hard job. Determination works at it. Only love continues until it is finished (Roe 1990:18).

Quotes Relating to Leadership Selection

God has a job for every Christian, and no one else can fulfill it (Roe 1990:191).

This is our supreme task as Christian educators; to gear youth into Christian service-- regardless of what the specific occupation may be--and to encourage the utmost skill in the fulfillment of this service (Roe 1990:195).

Our duty is to understand youth, but more, to help them understand themselves that they may release their varied abilities in the service of Christ and his Kingdom. We must help them to discover a life work, not work for life (Baldwin and Benson 1966:141).

What is the goal of our Sunday School? ... Our job is to train men and women, boys and girls, to serve the Master (Roe 1990:191).

What you are is God's gift to you. What you can become is your gift to Him (Roe 1990:20).

Quotes Relating to Ambiance and Motivation

God must have time to talk to people (Roe 1990:254).

If you place people in an atmosphere where they feel close to God and then challenge them with his Word, they will make decisions (Roe 1990:227,252,253).

As I travel around the world, I meet scores of people who say to me, 'I love that old pile of bricks on the corner of Gower and Carlos: It was there I met my Savior, my friends and my wife, and there I found my life's calling.' I have tried to create in our college department an atmosphere that God could use to draw young people unto Himself and to train them for His service (Roe 1990:151).

Quotes Relating to Teaching Ministry

I have discovered that if the Bible is taught the way it should be that it will be like a powerful magnet drawing youth unto the Lord Jesus Christ (Roe 1990:126).

Every child is born with a great capacity for knowledge. We cannot make capacity, but we can cultivate that which is God-given (Roe 1990:17).

You teach a little by what you say. You teach most by what you are (Roe 1990:18).

Quotes Related to Evangelistic Ministry

Personal work is one person finding another person and bringing him to the personal Saviour (Baldwin and Benson 196:103).

Chapter 8. Henrietta Mears (1890-1963)

Kindness has converted more sinners than zeal, eloquence or learning (Roe 1990:18).

Quotes Relating to Purposeful Closure in Ministry

Will is the whole man active. I cannot give up my will; I must exercise it. I must will to obey. When God gives a command or a vision of truth, it is never a question of what He will do, but what we will do. To be successful in God's work is to fall in line with His will and to do it His way. All that is pleasing to Him is a success (Roe 1990:71)

The greatest of a man's power is the measure of his surrender. It is not a question of who you are or of what you are, but whether God controls you (Roe 1990:19).

Miscellaneous Quotes Dealing With Various Values

I know not the way He leads me, but well do I know my Guide (Roe 1990:18).

An efficient leader may, through his knowledge of his job and the magnetism of his personality, greatly increase the efficiency of others (Roe 1990:19).

God does not always choose great people to accomplish what He wishes, but He chooses a person who is wholly yielded to Him (Roe 1990:43).

If you would be pure, saturate yourself with the Word of God (Roe 1990:227).

The Christian life is not merely the remembrance of a historical Christ in the past, but it is fellowship with a living Christ--with us now (Roe 1990:19).

Nothing will satisfy one made in the image of God except God Himself (Roe 1990:19).

Remember that leadership values are statements of ought or must or should. You will find it a profitable exercise if you seek to reduce these quotes to a value statement which begins like this,

A leader should...
or
A leader ought to...
or
A leader must ...
or
It is necessary that ...

Mears was a powerful motivational leader. Her quotes moved people. That is because they were so value laden. There were always identifiable principles underlying what she did.

Contributions

This chapter contributes to the general field of leadership development in the following ways:

1. It portrays a very gifted leader who had about 15 years of lay leadership before becoming a full-time Christian worker.
2. This leader had a single dominant life purpose involved with leadership selection and development. This chapter therefore shows the importance of a life purpose for focusing a life.

Chapter 8. Henrietta Mears (1890-1963) page 379

3. It depicts a leader who had very positive experiences in local church setting.
4. It depicts a leader whose motivational abilities highlighted her inspirational leadership function.
5. It depicts a leader whose ministry was powerful because it was value based.
6. It shows the importance of releasing leaders into ministry.
7. It portrays a leader with an almost tri-focal spiritual gift-mix: teaching, evangelism, leadership and shows how the leadership gift so aptly complemented both the evangelism and teaching gifts.
8. It shows how a natural change agent can bring about change through a powerful motivational ministry.
9. It shows the importance of creative ministry insights to bring life to ministry.
10. It introduces another methodology for maintaining an on-going learning posture and thus fulfilling the interrupted in-service training pattern.

Her contributions to the cause of Christ and the on-going of the Christian movement include at least the following:

1. She personally led many persons to the Lord and motivated many to do the same.
2. She stimulated Sunday School ministry in the United States and around the world bringing renewal to a waning movement.
3. She developed materials for Sunday School teachers to use and to increase their effectiveness.
4. She also published Biblical materials that greatly impacted teachers.[55]
5. She showed the importance of ministry setting to motivate people. Her Forest Home ministry facilitated 1000s of decisions either for Christ or for Christian service.

Overall Lessons from the Life

Three lessons from Henrietta Mears' life and ministry should be emphasized. More than any of the others of the leaders studied in this book she operated a value based ministry, continued to develop ministry insights throughout her life, and showed the importance of future perfect thinking as part of her motivational power.

Henrietta Mears was trained as a secular teacher. She knew the importance of curriculum. She knew the importance of designing training. She knew the importance of learning taxonomies. She stressed the volitional and affective taxonomies as a means to challenging leaders. Her cognitive input was always strong but sublimated to the movement of the affect and will. She also stressed the experiential taxonomy. Her modeling and on-the-job training approach instilled the importance of integrating affect, volition, and cognitive inputs in the life. Her ministry was filled underlying values some gained in her educational training and much gained in her lay leadership ministry prior to her work at First Presbyterian of Hollywood.

Early in her ministry Henrietta Mears demonstrated an almost unique ability to come up with creative ministry insights which motivated people and penetrated deeply. As the years went by and as the age differential became greater between herself and the collegiates

---

[55]None of her biographers listed any bibliography of her materials. However, I have in my own library one book, **What The Bible Is All About** first published in 1953 (at age 63) by Regal which has over 1,250,000 copies in print. That alone is very significant. I suspect there were other titles that also had impact.

Chapter 8. Henrietta Mears (1890-1963)

to whom she ministered so powerfully she recognized she would need special grace to continue to challenge these young people.

> When the Lord made it clear to Teacher that she was to remain at her post year after year--for over 30 years, she used to say,
> "Lord, as long as you see fit to keep me in that college department, you must make me attractive to those young people, and you must give me the message for this day and age that you want them to have (Roe 1990:330).

I have previously listed a number of ministry insights (see Table 8-2) that arose in her ministry. I am sure that I have only tapped the surface. This ever dependent attitude was one of the secrets to on-going challenging ministry insights both means and material to use.

I have listed five quotes which symbolize her goal oriented thinking. Henrietta dreamed big.[56] The unique thing, however, was her ability to carry it out. She built a Sunday School to over 6000+ which over the years carried the main continuity of values of First Presbyterian Church of Hollywood as three Senior Pastors ministered. She empowered Sunday School teachers all around the world. This empowerment flowed from a dream to have materials available to them to make them effective teachers. She saw numerous leaders released into ministry. It was the fulfillment of a dream. No other leader in this book used future perfect thinking so powerfully.

Implications for a Focused Life

What have we learned from this life that helps us understand a focused life? That is the question I attempt to answer in this section. When we study a focused life we are in fact looking for a number of issues. Below I comment on a number of factors that can affect focus in a life. I weigh them relatively speaking in terms of their effect on Mears' focused life.

---

[56]In fact, **Dream Big** is the title of Roe's biography. Several chapters highlight this future perfect thinking, that is, visualizing something in the future as a reality, and then working to see it happen. Chapter 6 Making Dreams Happen, Chapter 11 Leading Men To Leadership, Chapter 12 Give Me This Mountain, as well as Chapter 14 The Expendables all capture this future perfect bent of Henrietta Mears.

Chapter 8. Henrietta Mears (1890-1963)

1. <u>Giftedness Development</u>[57]

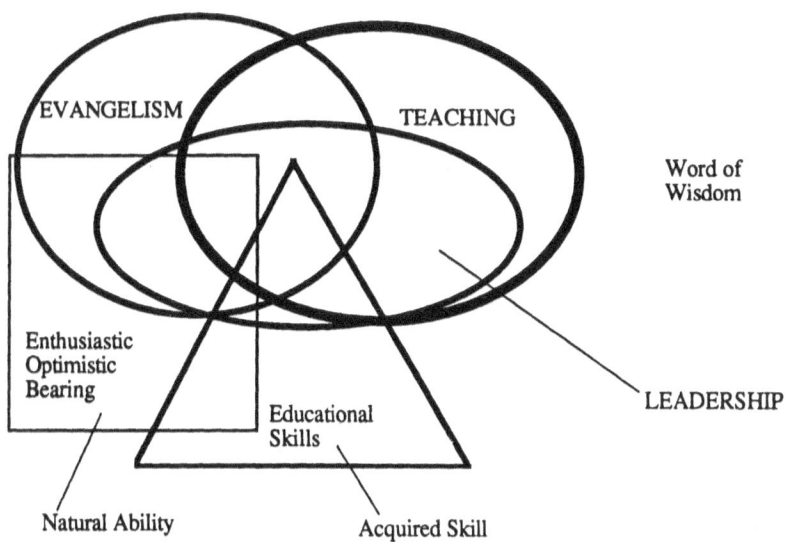

This gift-mix is unusual for two reasons. One, it is somewhat rare for a teacher to be so evangelistically gifted. Teachers dominantly edify and usually do not see many come to Christ personally. Evangelists usually see people come to Christ but can't do much to edify them. Henrietta Mears did both and did it powerfully. Two, she had a strong spiritual gift of leadership which shows up in her motivational ministry. Both in teaching and evangelism she was a powerful motivator. This is a very tight diagram and symbolizes a very synergistic gift-cluster. Such a profile will have a highly focused life--if there is a role which enhances it. And there was for Miss Mears.

2. <u>Destiny Processing</u>

Critical incident 20, points to a powerful destiny moment and led to the destiny fulfillment which so satisfied her life purpose.

3. <u>Identification of Key Ministry Insights</u>

Table 8-2 lists some 19 ministry insights. The creation of these to meet tactical situations was a regular part of her focused ministry.

4. <u>Identification Of Major Values That Uniquely Fit One's Ministry</u>

In the major lessons from her life I have indicated that Henrietta Mears was highly value driven in her ministry, in fact, more than any other leader in this book. Her values gained over the years helped structure the focus of her ministry.

---

[57]The following is a pictorial diagram, called a Venn Diagram, of Miss Mears' giftedness set. See Appendix F for an explanation of how to interpret it.

Chapter 8. Henrietta Mears (1890-1963)

5. Integration Of Personality Factors So As To Identify A Focused Or Ideal Role That Moves Toward Convergence

Personality played an important part in Miss Mears accomplishment. Her positive, buoyant, enthusiastic, winsome personality was one of the keys to her motivational ministry and hence her inspirational leadership.

6. Social Base Processing

Critical incidents 9, 10, and 11 deal directly with social base processing. Miss Mears is one of two leaders in the book who operated out of a singles pattern. Her social base was the ideal of all the leaders seen in this book.[58]

7. Ultimate Contribution Set[59]

Her major contributions like Gospel Light and Forest Home simply grew by necessity in order to meet her expanded ministry needs.

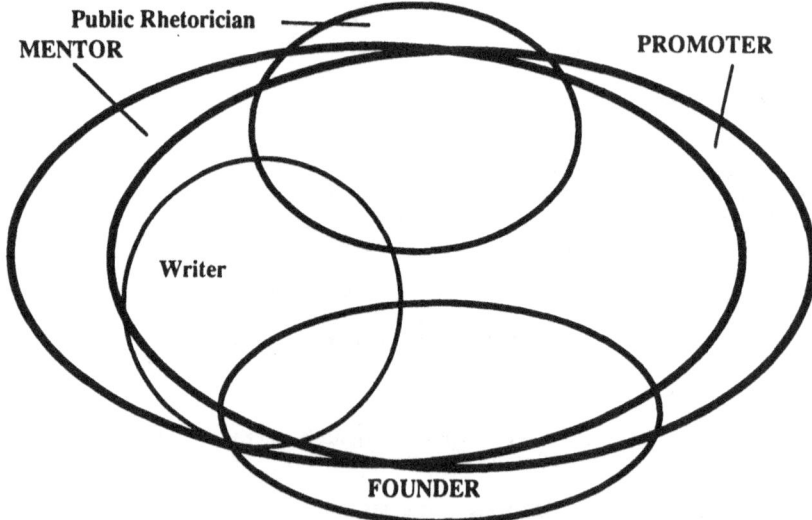

The **Mentor** and **Promoter** ultimate contributes dominate what she left behind. Her ministry was very personal. She recruited, trained and released so many leaders. She promoted (remember her motivational bent) Sunday Schools, Bible Teaching, and leadership. She **Founded** a powerful Christian Education Department, a publishing company, and a retreat ministry. She **Wrote** Sunday School materials, teacher training materials, and Bible materials. Her speaking ministry, including an on-going Bible

---

[58] See Appendix D for an explanation of social base issues. God uniquely and most wonderfully met Miss Mears in terms of her social needs. Her social base actually enhanced and brought more focus to her ministry.

[59] The following is a pictorial diagram, called a Venn Diagram, of her Ultimate Contribution set. See Appendix F for an explanation of how to interpret.

Chapter 8. Henrietta Mears (1890-1963)   page 383

teaching ministry to collegiates and conference ministries, as well as her speaking around the world on her trips was significant. She was an outstanding **Public Rhetorician**, but it didn't dominate her ministry.

8. Ministry Philosophy Concepts

In addition to being a strong value based leader, Mears has done the best job of articulating her ministry philosophy, particularly in terms of her Christian Education thrust. I include two samples of articulation at the end of this chapter.

9. Future Perfect Time Paradigm

In the overall lessons from her life I commented on this item. Mears is the strongest leader in this book using future perfect thinking.

10. Boundary Processing Which Helped Focus

The boundary processing connected with critical incident 15 was significant in focusing Miss Mears. It was the boundary that took her out of her secular educational career track and put her into full-time ministry.

11. Paradigm Shifts Which Helped Focus

Essentially this category was not strong in determining her focus. Her two power gate experiences were important but not so much from new insights as appropriating what already was known.

12. Windows of Opportunity

The time period following critical incident 20 was an unprecedented window of opportunity which Henrietta walked right through. Only Robert Jaffray and L. E. Maxwell of the leaders studied in this book saw similar windows of opportunity. This window of opportunity for Henrietta Mears brought her into the fulfillment of her sense of destiny.

SUMMARY ON FOCUSED LIFE INSIGHTS FROM MEARS' LIFE

Let me summarize what we have learned about a focused life from Mears.

A *focused life* is
- a life dedicated to exclusively carrying out God's unique purposes through it,
- by identifying the focal issues, that is, the **major role, life purpose, unique methodology**, or **ultimate contribution**,[60] which allows
- an **increasing prioritization** of life's activities around the focal issues, and
- results in a satisfying life of being and doing.

---

[60]These four--*major role, life purpose, unique methodology,* or *ultimate contribution*--are called the *focal issues.* Usually one or more of them dominates a focused life. A number of other factors (like giftedness, ministry insights, sense of destiny called focal screens) contribute to the divine guidance which helps these leaders to prioritize life's activities around the focal issues. Both the identification of focal issues and the processes that prioritized them are given in the studies of the eight chosen for this book. As the book has developed the 12 screens have been categorized into four major pointers. I present this in the final chapter.

Chapter 8. Henrietta Mears (1890-1963)

Three of the focal issues played an important part in Mears' life. **Life purpose**, the stimulation of and release of many quality Christian young people into leadership dominated her life. As to **life purpose**, how did she do?

> Ever mindful that God had called her to train leaders, Henrietta continually sought out leaders among her young people and trained them, all her energies, ambitions and abilities dedicated to helping each one achieve his maximum development. Her God-given ability to spot leadership potential in an individual seemed almost instinctual at the time.
> ....Leadership was her theme and she voiced it at conferences, meetings, Bible classes and in a thousand conversations. (Roe 1990:197)

In the course of her career in Hollywood, over 400 collegians heard God's call and turned their energies to pulpits in America or to missionary stations scattered around the world (Roe 1990:199).[61] Note her impact, via her retreat center ministry. This anecdotal evidence of her fulfillment of life purpose could be multiplied hundreds of times.

> One of the prominent Baptist ministers in southern California said one year, "I have 22 of my young people studying in Baptist schools for the ministry. They all made their decisions at Forest Home. (Roe 1990:257)

Dr. Harold John Ockenga, the first president of Fuller Theological Seminary of Pasadena, California pays tribute to her fulfillment of her life purpose.

> What a work you have done! There is no young people's or Sunday School work in the nation equal to yours. When I think of the tens of thousands of people who have studied the Bible under your leadership, of the thousands of young people who have faced the claims of Christ and made a commitment to Him, of the hundreds of young people into Christian service, I cannot but stand back in amazement (Roe 1990:199).

Her major role as a Christian educator in a powerful mega-church enhanced her life purpose. Her founding of a retreat center ministry also powerfully brought focus to realization of this life purpose. Five of the **ultimate contribution** set fit her: Promoter, Mentor, Founder, Writer, and Public Rhetorician. All were related to the life purpose and supported it.

There was a natural order of development. The **life purpose** came first. **Major role** came second and enhanced the life purpose--particularly when the role was adapted to include a publishing ministry and a retreat center ministry. **Ultimate contributions** were by-products of the other two focal issues.

---

[61]In the early 1950s Henrietta was musing about the organizations that had been influenced by her. She began to make a list of organizations who had leaders that she had impacted. The list quickly grew to over 50. Her team, amazed at the list suggested they have an open house and invite these organizations and leaders in for a time of celebration. So there was a gathering of leaders from Christian organizations who had been influenced by Henrietta Mears. Hundreds came. In 1962 just a year before her death there was a special gathering of leaders at Forest Home. Over 40,000 delegates from 40 different denominations and hundreds of churches and groups came (Roe 1990:336). This too was symbolic of the overflow of her ministry. "People must be called by God," she said, and she prayed the Lord of the harvest to send forth His laborers." (Roe 1990:336) This gathering was partially an answer to her prayers and efforts at raising up leaders.

Chapter 8. Henrietta Mears (1890-1963)	page 385

Closure--Let's Really Remember Henrietta Mears

Well, I have attempted to apply the Hebrews 13:7,8 leadership mandate.

> Remember your former leaders. Think back on how they lived and ministered. Imitate those **excellent qualities** you see in their lives. For Jesus Christ is the same today, as He was in the past and as He will be in the future. What He did for them He will do for you to inspire and enable your leadership.
> **Hebrews 13:7,8** (Personal Interpretive Paraphrase)

We have remembered Mears! But what challenges from her life do we take away for our own? Let me suggest two!

Her life challenges us to:

1. Teach with **power and for results** that are life changing. She focused on the will and the affect. She was interested in hooking people in to serving the Lord no matter what vocation they chose. Because she was purposeful and expectant she saw results.

Her collegiate class was probably the most outstanding illustration of the above challenge. She was respectfully called **Teacher**, a fitting sobriquet!

2. Use our ministries to **select** and **develop** emerging leaders.

From time-to-time I have mentioned seven major leadership lessons. The following is one of those seven:

EFFECTIVE LEADERS VIEW LEADERSHIP SELECTION AND DEVELOPMENT AS A PRIORITY FUNCTION IN THEIR MINISTRY.

While almost all leaders in this book somewhat touched on this in their lives there are five other leaders beside Henrietta Mears who were at least partially involved in this major leadership lesson in their lives: Charles Simeon, A. J. Gordon, Robert Jaffray, R. C. McQuilkin, and L.E. Maxwell. All but Jaffray were dominantly involved in the development of leaders and not so much in the selection process. Jaffray was involved, as an apostolic leader, in both the selection and development of leaders. But it is Henrietta Mears who is head and shoulders above all the rest in **selecting** and developing leaders. She released significant quality leaders into the life stream of American Christianity. Only Simeon comes close in terms of releasing leaders.

She was the best of the eight studied in this book. And I think she would want to leave us with this challenge.

THE ON-GOING VITALITY OF CHRISTIANITY IS DEPENDENT ON CONSTANT FRESH LEADERSHIP EMERGING.

WHAT ARE YOU DOING TO STIMULATE THIS?

Chapter 8. Henrietta Mears (1890-1963)

Where To Go and What To Do For Further Study

There are three good biographies on Henrietta Mears. I have profited greatly from all three of them and quote from all three.[62] I list them below. Two of them are out of print. But the third by Roe is available. Her book on the Bible is sometimes available in used book stores. I obtained my copy that way. I am sure those of you with a teaching gift will want to get it.

I would suggest that for further study you first read the two attached ministry philosophy descriptions--one on teaching and one on evangelism. Then I would suggest you get Roe's biography. You may want to browse my chapter again then read Roe. Use the following suggestions as you read.

Read it to identify:

1. Values,
2. Ministry Insights,
3. Motivational ideas,
4. for inspiration, she was an inspirational leader.

Bibliography

Baldwin, Ethel May and David V. Benson
    1966   **Henrietta Mears--and how she did it!** Glendale: Regal.

Mears, Henrietta
    1953   **What The Bible is All About.** Ventura, Ca.: Regal Books.

Powers, Barbara Hudson
    1957   **The Henrietta Mears Story.** Westwood, N.J.: Fleming H. Revell Company.

Roe, Earl O., Editor
    1990   **Dream Big, The Henrietta Mears Story.** Ventura, Ca: Regal Books.

---

[62]Sometimes quotes appear in more than one book though I acknowledge only one. The latter biographies quote from earlier ones sometimes without actually marking the quote as such. Only because I read the earlier works last did I note this. I simply note the one in which I first saw the quote.

Chapter 8. Henrietta Mears (1890-1963)

Articulation of Personal Ministry Philosophy--Sunday School Teaching[63]

When I was just a girl in college, the Lord entrusted me with a large Sunday School class. Many times I faced what I ought to do as a teacher to please the Lord, but somehow I just did not carry it out. One night I awoke from a restless sleep and determined never to fail the Lord again.

So I got up and wrote down what I still call "My Own 10 Commandments." I decided to say what I *would* do, not just what I ought to do. There have been times, when it was agony to carry these out, but by God's grace they have been the pattern for my teaching. God has honored it.

1. *I will win the personal allegiance of every student in my Sunday School class to the Lord and Master* by talking, writing, and prayer. I will expect a decision on the part of each one, and I will make sure that that decision is based on facts. No boy or girl will I ever give up on as unreachable.

2. *I will not think my work over when my pupil has made his decision for Christ.* I will help him to realize how necessary daily Bible reading and prayer are. I will also put helpful books in is hands and will encourage him to unite with God's people. I will show him the importance of church work. In all this, I will stay close until he is established, remaining at all times accessible to him.

3. *I will see that he finds a definite place in some specified task.* I will not rest until every student is an out-and-out aggressive Christian, for God has a place for each one to serve.

4. *I will bring Christianity out of the unreal into everyday life.* I will show my students the practical things they should be doing as Christians. The ministrations that the world needs so much today--meat for the hungry, drink for the thirsty--are judgment-day tests of genuine Christianity (Matthew 25).

5. *I will seek to help each one discover the will of God, because the Master can use every talent.* I will try to see in them what God sees. Michelangelo saw the face of an angel in a discarded stone. Christ saw a writer in a tax gatherer, a preacher in a fisherman, a world evangelist in a murder. He takes the foolish things and the weak and despised to work His purposes.

6. *I will instill a divine discontent into the mind of everyone who can do more than he is doing,* not by telling him the pettiness of his life, but by giving him a vision of great things to be done enthusiastically, passionately.

7. *I will make it easy for anyone to come to me with the deepest experiences of his inner life,* not by urging, but by sympathy and understanding. I will never let anyone think I am disappointed in him.

8. *I will keep the cross of Christ central in the Christian life.* It is great to be out where the fight is strong, to be where the heaviest troops belong and to fight there for God and man.

9. *I will pray as I have never prayed before for wisdom and power,* believing God's promise that "if any of you lack wisdom, let him ask...and it shall be given him" (James 1:5).

10. *I will spend and be spent in this battle.* I will not seek rest and ease. I will not think that freshness of face holds beauty in comparison with the glory of heaven. I will seek fellowship with the "man of sorrows...acquainted with grief" (Isaiah 53:3), as he walks through this stricken world. I will not fail Him.

---

[63] This is copied from Roe's book where it is an appendix. These also occur in Baldwin and Benson's book.

Articulation of Personal Ministry Philosophy--Evangelistic Work[64]

1. *A soul winner must be a Spirit-led man or woman,* not only in the matter of soul-winning, but in all things.
2. *A soul winner is made, not born.* Anyone can do it if he is willing to make the effort.
3. *The place to start is right where you are now.* Don't think about becoming a missionary across the sea if you are not a missionary at home.
4. *Let the holy Spirit guide you to people.* Be sensitive to his leading; never rush ahead of His initiative.
5. *Realize also that he is working not only in your heart but in the person to whom He is directing you.*
6. *Whenever possible, deal with a person alone* and never interrupt when someone else is working with a person.
7. *Start where the person is*--with his interests, his knowledge.
8. *Hold him to the main point of receiving Christ as his personal Savior,* don't let the conversation wander.
9. *Allow him to talk about his problems so that he will see his need.* Don't jump in with your own ideas about what he should do. Your job is to lead him to Christ.
10. *Do not try to convince by argumentation.* He is not to accept a creed, but Christ. Just introduce him to your Friend.
11. *Tell what Christ has done for you;* no one can argue against your own experience.
12. *Don't force a person to accept the whole Bible right off.* Lead him to Christ first of all and let the Bible's truth become self-evident.
13. *As you explain salvation, allow him to read the passages of the Bible for himself.*
14. *Don't be impatient; let God work in his heart.*
16. *Let your reliance be wholly on the Spirit of God and on the Word of God,* and not on yourself.

---

[64]This is copied from Roe's book where it is an appendix. These also occur in Baldwin and Benson's book.

Chapter 8. Henrietta Mears (1890-1963)   page 389

PREPARATION

```
|----|----|----|----|----|----|----|----|----|----|----|
1890 96  1908 1913 1915  1927 1928  1933  1938          1951      1963
Age       23                  38                                   73
                         <--B1-->
```

A. Character Foundations (1890-1896)   A. Rural Schools   A. Initial Success--Sunday School Ministry
B. Early Modeling--->Leadership   (1913-1915)   (1928-1933)
   Committal (1896-1908)   B. Central High School,   B. Wider Ministry--Gospel Light and Sunday
C. Powergate/Teaching in University   Minneapolis, SS Work   School Associations
   (1908-1913)   Bible Teacher   (1933-1938)
                                               (1915-1927)   C. Forest Home/ Revival Fires
                                                                          (1938-1951)
                                                                       D. The Castle--Final Years
                                                                          (1951-1963)

Sabbatical
Trips   Europe   Panama World   Caribbean Mexico/Cuba   World
                                      (1927)   (1931) (1935)   (1938)   (1942)   (1952)
                                                                     S. America Brazil/World
                                                                     (1940)   (1946/7)

                                                                                         C19 Forest Home, Age 48,
                                                                                                              C20 Destiny Trip
                                                                                                  The Expendables, Age=57

C1 Rich Heritage, Ages 1-6
   Contemporary Models
     C2 Contemporary Model,   C9 1st Singles Test, Age =24
        Pastor D. B. Riley, Ages 6ff
          C3 A Healing Touch, Age=12   C10 2nd Singles Test, Age =25
             C4 Leadership Committal Age=17 C11 Margaret Supports, Age =25
                Powergate: personal life power   Social Base Provided
                C5 Crisis--Eye Sight, Deep   C12 Evelyn Camp/ Reflection/ Age= 26,27
                   Learning Posturem Age=18   Realization/Life Purpose
                   C6 Prophet Mantle,   C13 Divine Contact, Age = 35
                      Mom dies, Age = 20   Stewart P. MacLennan
                      C7 Divine Contact   C14 Divine Contact, Pastor Riley, Age=37
                         Paul Rader, Age 20   C15 Decision Time/ Sabbatical
                         C8 Ministry Powergate,   Travel/ Reflection/ MacLennan
                            Mantle Accepted, Age 21   Offer, Divine Approval; Age=38
                                                                     C16 Recruits Ethel May Baldwin, Age=38
                                                                         C17 Recruits Esther A. Ellinghusen, Age = 40
                                                                             C18 Ministry Challenge, Gospel Light, Age = 43

L.E. Maxwell
(1895-1984)

"The man who beats the drum does not know how far the sound goes."

Chapter 9. L. E. Maxwell (1895-1984)
The Deeper Life[1]--The Central Hub of This Focused Life

> Remember your former leaders. Think back on how they lived and ministered. Imitate those **excellent qualities** you see in their lives. For Jesus Christ is the same today, as He was in the past and as He will be in the future. What He did for them He will do for you to inspire and enable your leadership.
>
> **Hebrews 13:7,8** (Personal Interpretive Paraphrase)

Let's remember Leslie Earl Maxwell,[2] who in a most unlikely location to become a Christian center of influence on the world, the prairies of Alberta, Canada, began a Bible Institute. It became a center for rugged training and discipline for many *missionaries to be* who wanted the touch of Christ in their lives along with practical help to get the job done around the world. His biographer, Stephen Maxwell Spaulding, quotes an apt African proverb under the picture of Leslie Earl Maxwell in his dissertation. "The Man who beats the drum does not know how far the sound goes." Let's explore the sound of the drumbeat, this roar of the lion of the prairie, one who mobilized many to missions.[3]

Opening Illustration 1.
Sovereign Connection--How About Considering Daddy Steven's?

Age 24 (Proverbs 20:24)

God's sovereign work, especially timing, is often very crucial in the development of a life. L. E. Maxwell's life exemplifies this more so than any other though McQuilkin and Mears are a close second.[4]

---

[1] Maxwell, himself (and McQuilkin also), preferred not to use terminology such as this because he believed that to live a holy life was well within the reach of every Christian and should be the norm. I almost used *The Normal Christian Life*--but that is a phrase associated so closely with Watchman Nee as to distract or confuse. Whatever the case, the Cross and its Victory for the Christian (including the death there and the resurrection there) were all part of L.E. Maxwell's message, whatever you call it. His was a clarion call for Christians to live up to all that was theirs in Christ's work at the Cross.

[2] I will refer to Leslie Earl Maxwell as L.E. or Maxwell or sometimes Leslie just for variety sake.

[3] Spaulding quotes this African proverb which is taken from a letter from Joseph F. Conley, Executive Director of the Regions Beyond Missionary Union congratulating Mr. Maxwell on the 50 years celebration (1972) of Prairie Bible Institute. Stephen Maxwell Spaulding entitles his thorough leadership analysis, an unpublished dissertation, **Lion on the Prairies: An Interpretive Analysis of the Life and Leadership of Leslie Earl Maxwell**. I have relied heavily on Steve's work. Being a grandson he had access to personal papers, interviews with many who worked with Mr. Maxwell, and of course many personal conversations with relatives. He also had access to Don and Carol Richardson's accumulated data which they have been amassing in preparation for a biography on Maxwell. At this date there is no published biography on L. E. Maxwell. This is a relatively objective study which paints the picture "warts and all." It is essentially a Type 4 Chronological Interpretive Biographical presentation. It is both thoroughly scholarly yet with devotional and teaching appeal. It is skillfully done.

[4] In my study of leadership in the Bible I have identified macro-lessons, that is major lessons which seem to apply in many of the six leadership eras in the Bible. One such is the timing lesson. EFFECTIVE LEADERS ARE INCREASINGLY AWARE OF THE TIMING OF GOD'S INTERVENTIONS IN THEIR LIVES AND MINISTRY. THEY MOVE WHEN HE MOVES. THEY WAIT, THEY CONFIDENTLY EXPECT. Maxwell in reflecting back on this early pre-service training could easily see the hand of God as to timing. This Midland Bible School only lasted for a few years. "Daddy" Stevens and

Chapter 9. L. E. Maxwell (1895-1984)

At this point in his life, Maxwell was 24 years of age. He was saved out of a radical background at age 20 primarily due to the influence of Aunt Christina. He had served in the Army in World War I for the last two years of that conflict. He had grown as a Christian through those years--maintaining a witness in a difficult time. His Aunt Christina had gotten him a job in Kansas City in the banking industry. He was learning accounting. He was demonstrating responsibility. His father had passed away so he, as the oldest son, felt the need to help his mother financially. Spaulding gives us a feel for the immediate background leading up to this almost chance destiny guidance.

> Spiritual nurturing for Leslie was due in great part to the watchful concern and prayers of his ever-present aunt. She acquired new employment for him first at the Kansas City Clearing House and later at the National Fidelity Bank. These were her places of work and therefore meant greater interaction and accountability with her favorite nephew. It was at these jobs that Leslie passed early tests of his own "fidelity" and financial responsibility, writing checks of up to $1,000,000 which in those days was an enormous sum. He worked hard, earned little, and with the passing of his father after the war, sent large regular amounts of his earnings to his needy mother back in Salina.
> Leslie spent his Sunday afternoons pouring over Scripture and praying, building a deep spiritual foundation and a lasting relationship with his new-found heavenly Father.
> Two years after his conversion, he found himself in an army uniform sailing for Europe. Once again it was Aunt Christina who encouraged him to place a placard over his bed in those unfriendly barracks, for all to read: "The blood of Jesus Christ, His son, cleanseth us from all sin": (1 John 1:7). He was not yet a bold witness, but he planted his flag and drew the appropriate criticism and respect. It was what he needed at that juncture in his Christian pilgrimage (Spaulding 1991b:37,38).

He came back from the war with needs--personal and family. A last minute remark at the end of a serious conversation opens the door to the situation which will open to him his life purpose, unique methodology, and major role. Catch the sovereign hand of God in the incident that follows.

> The pastor of the Baptist church in Kansas City which L.E. was now attending recommended to the growing young Christian that he attend Bible school. He [the pastor] had gone through Moody Bible Institute, yet for Maxwell this was out of the question. His father had just died, leaving mother to cope with a large family still in Salina (Spaulding 1991b:279).

Maxwell was having some struggles in his life with sin. He wanted help. The pastor, unnamed by Spaulding, proves to be a divine contact,[5] one who linked Maxwell to the mentors who would do more to shape his life than any others. Notice the almost after thought suggestion.

Dorothy Miller were led to Iowa for a short few months--long enough to connect to Pearl Plummer. Maxwell was in a major crisis in his own life--needing victory in it. He was in Kansas City due to the influence of his Aunt. All of these things come together for a brief moment in time--just long enough to touch Maxwell's life and send him on to his destiny. This same sort of timing is especially seen also in McQuilkin's life. The need for the Bible School in Columbia *just happened* to coincide to the need in McQuilkin's life for God's means of carrying out his missionary mobilization and training ministry. Henrietta Mears is a well trained experienced Sunday School worker at age 38. The First Presbyterian Church in Hollywood was ready for her type of ministry. She was at the point of making a major career decision. Five years earlier she would not have been ready, nor would the church. Timing is critical.
[5]The concept of *Divine Contact* (See Clinton and Clinton 1991), a special kind of mentor who gives a timely intervention perceived from God, is frequently seen at crucial guidance points. This advice from the unknown pastor linked Maxwell to the mentors, Stevens and Miller, who would shape the initial understanding of the focal issues of his life.

Chapter 9. L. E. Maxwell (1895-1984)   page 393

> In response to Leslie's urgent spiritual hunger for new victory in the Christian life, this same man suddenly recalled that he was on the board of another fledgling school in the Kansas city area, which had been founded by W. C. Stevens of Nyack Bible Institute. Knowing the older man's true spirituality, he counseled the young downcast Maxwell, "Old Daddy Stevens is deep, deep in the Word; why don't you go talk to him." Little did Leslie Maxwell know the future impact of this new relationship. (Spaulding 1991b:38).

W. C. "Daddy" Stevens and his co-worker, Dorothy Ruth Miller, both ex-faculty members at Nyack, were experienced mature Christian workers who had a passion for missions and knew that Bible Schools could be used greatly to mobilize young people into missions. In the latter period of his life Daddy Stevens felt led to go to some rural areas for transient Bible School work. Dorothy Miller felt led to accompany him and help him in the latter years of his life.[6] L.E. contacted "Daddy" Stevens. He shared from the depths of his heart his problems--his up and down Christian life, his struggles with sin--so illustrated in Romans 7. He had lost 15 pounds of excess army fat in this deep struggle for inner peace against the power of sin and spiritual defeat (Spaulding 1991b:280). Spaulding captures very simply the next step of guidance but with an emphasis on its destiny import.

> When Steven's counsel from the heart of the book of Romans met Leslie's inner needs, it was the most reasonable next step to enroll in the institute. The next three years would have monumental significance for history (Spaulding 1991b:38,39).

Maxwell had been introduced to the victorious life. It was the beginning of a power gate experience which would be amplified, clarified, and take root in his life over the next three years.[7] Maxwell's young pastor friend had recommended that L.E. go to Moody. But it was out of the question due to the family situation. The personal need of Maxwell and an almost afterthought connect Maxwell to Stevens and the little known Bible School, Midland Bible Institute.

---

[6] Spaulding gives us something of the timing factor and calling of Stevens and Miller to this work. "Stevens was a unique man. Having been trained as a Bible scholar, he was familiar with the theological debates of his day. He was well versed in theological and biblical scholarship and yet had chosen pioneer-type ministries overseas and in North America. He was committed to A. B. Simpson's young Christian and Missionary Alliance movement, not 40 years old, when he established the Midland school with his sidekick, D. R. Miller. Miss Miller was also a respectable student of the Bible, having written texts in Biblical history and other Bible study material. She was a stately woman who would carry her teaching influence with L. E. much further than anyone imagined at the time." (Spaulding 1991b:280). Recently I interviewed E. V. Thompson, founder of WorldTeam (my former mission). He too attended Midland Bible Institute just after L. E. Maxwell. He, too, spoke highly of "Daddy" Stevens as a man of God who in his last years, his Afterglow period, made his life count. Though Midland Bible Institute was only in existence for a few years, out of it came E. V. Thompson and L.E. Maxwell, great men of God, one who founded a mission and a Bible School on the mission field and the other who founded a Bible School in Canada.

[7] The notion of power gates are important for Christian workers. Power gates function to open the participant to a new level of awareness of God's power in the life or ministry. Two kinds of *power gates* are typically described: *life power* and *gifted power*. This particular type, Maxwell's need, is a *life power* type. Maxwell wants to sense God's power over sinful habits which bind him. This experience is similar to a Keswick *power gate* which is a surrender/ faith appropriation experience. It is one of several power gates including the entire sanctification paradigm and later the Pentecostal Experience, the Baptism of the Holy Ghost. All essentially do the same function--open the way to new experience with God. None guarantee an on-going successful ministry. They are simply gates that open the way for a new relationship with God. It was Maxwell's DEEP NEED which prepared him to claim and appropriate the inherent power in the Cross.

Chapter 9. L. E. Maxwell (1895-1984)   page 394

Opening Illustration 2.
Mentors Stevens and Miller Impact--3 Results of their Modeling
Age 24-27 (2 Timothy 3:14)

>Rather than one short-in-time incident, this critical incident is made up of a series of influences which take place in a relatively short intensive period of time in Maxwell's life. He, in response to a deep need in his life for Victory was drawn to "Daddy" Stevens. He decided to study at his Bible School. It is in this three year time of study, in which a relatively pliant young man, caught his destiny.

>Spaulding entitles this section of the biographical narrative, *The Obscure Bible School*. This little Bible School was only in existence for a few years.[8] Yet it had profound effect. In the short space of three years, Maxwell was to be deeply impacted by "Daddy" Stevens and Dorothy Miller.[9] Why did this small school with its overworked two person faculty have such an impact? Spaulding suggests that four components, at least, partially answer this question. He labels them **mentoring, message, method,** and **mission**.

>As to **mentoring,** catch the mixture of heart and mind that comprise the balance of the two mentors--"Daddy" Stevens and Dorothy Ruth Miller.

>>First, the school was very small and would last only a couple of years after L.E. graduated. The smallness of the school mean intimate mentoring of each student by the committed faculty. "Daddy" Stevens was a Bible scholar whose training included the German theologians and other great biblical scholars. His spiritual heritage was conservative coming out of the young Christian and Missionary Alliance movement. He and Miss Dorothy Ruth Miller had spent eleven years on the faculty of Nyack Bible

---

[8]Spaulding makes a statement (1991b:39). "Midland Bible Institute graduated only one male student from Kansas City. That was L.E. Maxwell. What he experienced at Midland was to be the sum of his formal training for all of his illustrious life as an educator and mobilizer of missionaries and Christian workers." I have not been able to verify this one way or the other. I have mentioned that E. V. Thompson also studied there, the founder of the West Indies Mission (now WorldTeam). In any case, this points out that L.E. Maxwell came from a *pre-service training pattern*. He, A. J. Gordon, and Robert Jaffray are prime examples that there can be power in this pattern of training. Maxwell almost seemingly flaunts my statement of the need for balanced learning (input, experience, dynamic reflection, and formation--See Clinton 1984, **Leadership Training Models**). His training had very little of the experience or dynamic reflection components. Yet from the very start he had power in ministry--even with little experience. I think he is the exception--he was an older adult when he entered Bible School.

[9]*Mentoring* is a relational experience in which one person called the mentor, empowers another person, called the mentoree via a transfer of resources at a sensitive time so that it impacts development. Note the "sensitive" aspect of the definition. This is a very sensitive accelerated learning time for Maxwell who is entering into the Victorious Life and is attracted to these gifted Bible teachers. Nine types of mentor functions have been identified. One of these is the modeling function of a contemporary Christian leader respected by the mentoree. The *contemporary model* serves as a sort of Christian hero/heroine who inspires the young leader. The mentoree tends to emulate and imbibe values from the *contemporary model* and tends to live up to the genuine expectations that person sets out. (See Clinton and Clinton, 1991, **The Mentor Handbook**). Both Stevens and Miller were contemporary models. Both provided discipling, teaching, and counsel mentoring. The school is so small that there is much personal interaction between these two powerfully gifted people, one in the Afterglow stage of ministry and the other in the Competent stage of ministry. At the end of the three years Stevens will act as a mentor sponsor and link Maxwell into the locale of his life work. Miller will move to Prairie after the Midland Bible Institute closes and will for more than 20 years provide powerful teaching and at least a continued co-mentoring influence on L.E. Maxwell.

Chapter 9. L. E. Maxwell (1895-1984)   page 395

>Institute in New York city, A. B. Simpson's training base for Alliance missionaries. They were both able and devout leaders, strangely sent by God to the American prairies for a handful of years in the early 1920s (Spaulding 1991b:39).

Though Spaulding doesn't explicitly list two factors, that I see, he does in passing mention the important **linking function** which Stevens and Miller played, and the **timing** of their ministry in New York, Iowa, and Kansas City. Stevens and Miller were in Kansas City at just the appropriate moment for L.E. Maxwell and had previously impacted two different parties who were to play a major role in Maxwell's future.[10]

>While in New York they had made a profound impact on a couple of young people whose family had moved from Ontario to the prairie provinces in western Canada. Just before coming to Kansas City, Stevens and Miller spent a very short period of time teaching young people in Boone, Iowa, another strange and short-lived placement. It was in Boone that they influenced a young girl, Pearl Plummer, of solid Christian roots, to follow them in their founding of the bible institute in Kansas. Pearl, the quiet, mature girl from Iowa, who had in her early teens prayed that she would love no other man than the one she was to marry, and who had by the age of fifteen committed her children and grandchildren to the Lord, this girl was to meet Leslie Maxwell and be convinced that he was "that man" at the moment of first encounter (Spaulding 1991b:39,40).

These apparent coincidences pile up, giving evidence of the hand of a sovereign God who will guide His young servant to his place of anointed service.

Spaulding goes on to give the second of his reasons why this little Bible School so impacted L.E. Maxwell, the **message**.

>Stevens had a **message** for this tiny group of eager students. It had its roots in the "deeper life" passages of Pauline writings such as Romans 6 through 8 and Galatians 2:20. The principles of death to self and the exchanged life of those like Hudson Taylor and Amy Carmichael were indelibly impressed on the students' minds and motivations (Spaulding 1991b:40).

This message, later after deeper experience with it and further clarification of it, will become the root conceptual paradigm which dominates Maxwell's major writings: **Born Crucified, Crowded to Christ, Abandoned to Christ.** It was learned here, in its essence, from two who believed it and lived it. The great need in his own life for just such a life-giving paradigm was probably a major reason why this school had such a lasting impact on L. E. Maxwell.

Spaulding goes on to enumerate the third reason why this school so impacted Maxwell. It had to do with a Bible teaching **method**.

>Stevens had a **method** which he developed over the years of his teaching. The era was one of great tension between the higher learning of the modernistic seminaries of Europe and the States and the profound needs of the common people in the pews. There was an enormous lack of credible, simple, Bible believing and Bible teaching ministers who were trained from their own study of the Word of God, rather than experts in the higher critical and heavily intellectual methods of the majority of seminaries. A. B.

---

[10]Geographical locale is one of the important factors for some leaders. They must be in the right place to flourish. This is clearly seen with Simeon as well as Maxwell. Maxwell needed a conservative rural setting in which to develop from a relatively inexperienced minister to one with great power. A sophisticated setting may have caused an abbreviated entry--one of the frequent patterns of ministry drop out which occurs in the first five years. The previous connections to Canada will allow the linking.

Simpson and Dwight L. Moody represented an American answer to this vacuum via the Bible School Movement. Steven's method was the genius of a comprehensive inductive Bible study course, involving "search questions" compilation of studies from Genesis 1 to Revelation 22. Students over the course of several years were put to the task of inductively learning the "whole counsel of Scripture" by answering questions dealing directly with the Word of God, mainly referenced by the Word, as opposed to a host of outside commentary or critical aids. Maxwell picked up the method and used it as a basic educational tool (Spaulding 1991b:40, 41).

As has been noted repeatedly with all of the leaders studied[11] the original study of the Bible was crucial to their spiritual formation over a lifetime.

Stevens and his faculty had a mission as well. Rooted in the Christian and Missionary Alliance, and with an obedience-oriented approach to Scripture, he brought a continuous stream of furloughing missionaries through the school to influence students regarding the vast unfinished task of world evangelization. This was to have a permanent effect on all the students. Pearl Plummer received what she felt to be a clear call to Africa through the message of one missionary statesman.[12] Leslie, on the other hand, had a growing conviction that God might be calling him to be a true sender, a motivator and mobilizer of others into the harvest field of the world (Spaulding 1991b:39,40).

Two important things are seen here. One has to do with a theological truth. The other had to do with a motivational means.

One is the ministry philosophy value involving missions. The great commission is still in effect. All Christians are to relate to it somehow. We must go. We must tell. We must find lost people. We must disciple. We must incorporate them into groups of effective Christians who will have this same mission passion.

But the other has to do with how to impact this message on young people--and that is to bring around these young people dynamic people, apt models, who are out there doing it. Missionaries with their tales of God's working deeply impress young people and often are the major reasons for mobilization into missions. This same dynamic was seen in McQuilkin's sister school, Columbia Bible College, in Columbia, S.C. Both schools made it an important part of their informal curricula to have missionaries regularly on campus to challenge and interact with students.

---

[11] I want to point out here as I have done in the other biographical chapters, and as I will do again in the final chapter of the book, of the central role the Bible played in the eight leaders studied in this book. Each studied the Bible regularly and deliberately all their lives. They studied it devotionally for their own lives. They studied it to exhort others. They studied it to know of God and His purposes and to teach them to others. This will not be true for all focused leaders. But all of the eight leaders chosen in this book were *word gifted* leaders. See Clinton and Clinton (1994) **Developing Leadership Giftedness**, where we develop the concept of word gifted, power gifted, and love gifted clusters of spiritual gifts. All eight leaders in this book had spiritual gifts as the *focal element* of their giftedness set and word gifts as the dominant spiritual gifts. Maxwell learns here a methodology which he will use all his life to study the Scriptures and which he will pass on to countless students. The essence of the methodology, the dynamic of it, is not the search questions but that students must react to the Scriptures directly and to dynamically reflect on them for meaning themselves. It is this which gives life to the method.

[12] This presents an important issues that needs research. Whose call predominates? Spaulding does not elaborate on this possible tension. How did Maxwell and Plummer iron out these differences in call? Obviously they did since they married and went to Prairie. Differences in call such as these two also call into question the issue of how we hear and know God's will.

Chapter 9. L. E. Maxwell (1895-1984)	page 397

As To Effect on this Pliable Life

Let me summarize this intense period of time which was so critical in shaping Maxwell's personal values, ministerial values, and strategic values. In addition to Spaulding's 4 items I add three others. Let me summarize the entire 3 year period in terms of the critical issues. There was a deep **need** in Maxwell's life for the message he was to hear about victory. He was a relatively new Christian and basically untaught in the Word. But he had a desire for victory in his life. This set the stage for the critical processing. He saw two **mentors** who obviously, at least to his mind, had answers to satisfy that need. They provided not only a **message** of victory but the source of answers for victory and a host of other questions about life and ministry--the Bible. Not only did they stress the life giving importance of this authoritative Word, but they gave a simple **method** for studying it. In addition, they gave a major motivational reason for being a Christian--**mission**, the alignment with God's purposes to complete the unfinished mission task given in the great commission. And probably most significant they did two other things. They modeled a major methodology, the **Bible School**, for mobilizing young people in ministry--*put them in the environment of a Bible School with godly teachers and godly missionaries. Then teach them the Word and its importance and challenge them with the unfinished task of missions.* God will bless this methodology. And finally, they provide the link and **sponsor** Maxwell to the locale which will allow him to blossom and fulfill his destiny.

The focal issues come fast for this young developing leader.[13] In this obscure Bible School Maxwell picked up in embryonic form three of the focal issues. He gets **unique methodologies** to use--the Bible School and the inductive method of studying the Bible. He got a **life purpose**--mobilizing young people into missions, and he is introduced to his **major role**--a Bible teacher in a Bible School environment.

The Time-Line

See the time-line at the end of this chapter for a one page overview of Maxwell's life with critical incidents listed. Notice that there are four periods lasting 27 years, 22 years, 16 years and 24 years. The last period of time was an Active Afterglow period. Maxwell gradually cut back to only a teaching role which he maintained until he was physically incapacitated.

There are two unusual things about this time-line. One has to do with tenure. The other has to do with diminishing leadership influence with age.

One, like Simeon's time-line, there is the extended time in one locale. Maxwell, like Simeon, actually put down roots and never moved. At age 27 he settled down in Three Hills, Alberta, Canada. From 1922 to 1984, some 62 years, Maxwell ministered in one locale and basically in one ministry, that of leading Prairie Bible Institute. This long period of time reinforces what we have seen previously about **long tenure**--the accumulated build-up of influence which can crescendo with powerful effect, as it does in Maxwell's case. With an unusual long ministry in one place there is also usually some trouble in pinpointing the major phases but these broke fairly nicely due to the war and the window of opportunity that opened up immediately after it leading to the explosive decade.

---

[13] Remember that the focal issues refer to one or more of the following around which one prioritizes activities in order to fulfill a satisfying life: major role, life purpose, unique methodology, or ultimate contribution. These exist only in the earliest of formative ideas but they are there for Maxwell. He will unfold them quickly on the Prairies of Canada--once he commits himself to an on-going ministry there, which happens after the integrity check at the end of the first year.

Chapter 9. L. E. Maxwell (1895-1984)   page 398

Two, the title for the final phase, *Fall: Return To The Soil*, seems to capture the notion of decreasing ministry, which in fact it was.[14] God sovereignly brought about an abating leadership influence over this period of time which is potentially instructive for some strong leaders.

I follow Spaulding's time-line in its entirety, including unique labels and all.[15] His identification of phase changes is based on the natural important happenings of both Maxwell's development and the organizational development of Prairie Bible Institute.

Highly Condensed Biographical Narrative

The following running capsule, organized around the four major time increments of Maxwell's life indicates the critical incidents made up of important activities, people and events that shaped Maxwell's life. To be especially noted are the last two, incidents 19 and 20 which typify something unusual and unique. Both these incidents are typical of the latter portion of Maxwell's life. Over his entire life he had taught the Victorious Life. Usually the pattern is that important values are shaped early and tested in the middle portion of ministry for consistency. Then the latter portion of life is a display of the fruitfulness of these values. And while this is true in general for Maxwell there is an unusual amount of testing of the values in his latter life. And the testing even more firmly embedded and showed these values.

I. WINTER: BARREN ROOTS
(1895-1922); Age= Birth to 27

While there are obviously advantages when a leader is born into a heritage of leaders one can not overlook how God turns a less than ideal background into strengths for his own purposes.[16] Such is the case with the first 20 years of Maxwell's life.

A. Rugged Youth
(1895-1915); Age= Birth to 20

Leslie Earl Maxwell was born July 2, 1895 in Salina, Kansas. Neither his mother or father were strong Christians. In fact his father was rather godless. Spaulding gives us a description of the social base into which Maxwell was born.

> The Kansas prairies in the 1890's were a rather rough and tumble place to be born and raised. The family into which L. E. Maxwell was born was no exception. Rugged farm life and a godless home welcomed Leslie Earl into the world in 1895 in

---

[14]The question often comes with a strong founding leader, How do you remove such a leader when efficiency is waning? Spaulding identifies an important concept regarding this aspect of leadership transition. He calls one of the processes of this period of time that Maxwell went through, *influence reversal challenge* (Spaulding 1991b:338). More on this later when I discuss the biographical narrative of this time period. One thing that can dampen the accumulated crescendo effect of long tenure can be the negative connotations of a power struggle when rising leadership seeks to get rid of older leadership.
[15]Spaulding says this about his choice of labels on the time-line. "The four major development phases of his life seemed to parallel the seasons of the year, beginning with winter. Maxwell's 'roots' were spiritually and socially barren, much like the cold and lifeless quality of the winter season. His life flowered suddenly into the fullness of spring, on into the fruitful summer zenith and then quietly 'returning to the soil' in an autumnal recess" (Spaulding 1991b:30). I think it especially fitting since he came from a Kansas prairie and labored among Canadian farmers. They would see the parallels quickly.
[16]Jephthah is certainly a classic Old Testament case.

Chapter 9. L. E. Maxwell (1895-1984)

Salina, a nondescript dot on the map of the central American wheatlands. The Bible was never read in the home. Prayers were rarely said. L. E.'s father was a gruff, unfeeling and an unabashed sinner (Spaulding 1991b:31,32).

It gets worse.

When Leslie was a young teenager, his father decided that the family needed economic rescue, so he moved to Kansas City and took up a pool-hall business. Pool halls in those days[17] were centers of illegal gambling, drinking and other "adult" entertainments. Soon Leslie, who had been a decent student in school, was spending his days racking balls and getting a reputation for being a local shark, "playing ball, playing pool and playing the fool," as he was to describe it ever after. His schooling went downhill as did his lifestyle. "We were such a bunch of hoodlums," he would say, characterizing his behavior and the company he kept: cousins, brothers and other riff-raff (Keller 1966:26).

Yet God was not without His representatives who had not bowed the knee to Baal. In the extended family there were three who countered this godless influence.

Heritage--Two Grandfathers and Aunt Christina

Spaulding points out how in the midst of a godless situation, godly relatives can make an impact.

There were individuals in the extended Maxwell clan who were genuine Christian believers and who took notice of Leslie, the eldest of nine children in this godless home, and set their wills to pray for this lad that God might intercept him from a life of predictable wanton folly. Both of his grandfathers were men of faith who left their impression on the boy through visits with the family and through years of intercession. L. E. remembered distinctly when Grandpa Maxwell took a renewed stand for Christ at the age of sixty, proving his inner transformation by the fact that his terrific smoking habit was now conquered (Spaulding 1991b:32,33).

But the most important influence was Aunt Christina.

...the relative who would have the greatest single influence for Christ on this otherwise derelict young man was his aunt Christina. He was to discover much later that she prayed daily for his spiritual well-being for over twenty years! (Spaulding 1991b:33)

She did five major things that paved the way for his conversion:

1. She modeled an active concern for his spiritual welfare. He knew she was concerned for his spiritual life.
2. She prayed regularly for him.
3. She influenced him to leave the debilitating environment (the pool hall and home).
4. She invited him to attend the Presbyterian church she frequented.
5. She sponsored him into two excellent "entry point" jobs in the banking industry.

---

[17]You might remember one of the lead songs in the popular musical 76 Trombones in which Professor Harold Hill bemoans that there is **Trouble** in River City, trouble with a capital **T** and that rhymes with **P** which stands for **P-O-O-L**, which points out the fact that pool halls in those days were a seedbed of immorality.

Her concern was genuine and active. Obviously she sensed potential in the oldest child in this family. By taking him out of his downbeat locale and linking him into a church and job she paved the way for the conclusion of a number of destiny interventions God had led L.E. through on his way to conversion. It is this conversion that serves as the culmination of Aunt Christina's efforts and becomes the boundary that will lead to ministry training. I discuss this boundary as the introductory portion of the next period of time.

B. Accelerated Ministry Preparation (1915-1922)

Destiny Preparation--An Accumulation of Incidents

Spaulding identifies a number of incidents over several years, each of which taken separately may have carried no apparent significance. But in retrospect they had an accumulative effect. They reflect something of a persistent God who is patiently pursuing Maxwell (Thompson's "Hound of Heaven") to offer him the chance of breaking out from a hopeless life to a satisfying life. These incidents accumulate over time, adding to his sense of destiny:[18]

1. **The Dream**
   Maxwell recalls that as a young lad he had a dream in which he saw himself looking over a vast extent of land and sensing that he would be the monarch over all his eyes could survey (Spaulding 1991b:32).
2. **The *No Escape* Scriptural Phrase**
   His mother though not a confessing believer in Christ, taught Leslie a phrase from a verse of Scripture (Genesis 18:13), "Thou God see me." This verse both haunted him and inspired him through the years into his adult spiritual quest (Spaulding 1991b:32 quoting Keller).
3. **Aunt Christina's Efforts**
   I have already mentioned the five major things Aunt Christina did to help facilitate Maxwell's conversion.
4. **Two Painful Incidents**
   Between the ages of eight to ten Maxwell experienced two painful incidents, one physical and one emotional, which caused him to think of life after death and his own unpreparedness for it. He accidentally spilled an entire pot of boiling tomatoes on himself, scarring his chest for life. Shortly thereafter he caught a cold and his brother Ernest replaced him working at his father's side. Ernest was a good child and well respected for his goodness by all the family. He was fatally crushed under the wheel of a loaded wheat wagon, which normally Leslie would have driven. His father was deeply moved, the only demonstration of emotion that L.E. ever refers to. His father made a statement, "they say if they die before they know better, they go to heaven" (Keller 1966:23). By contrast, L.E. knew that he, a total opposite from Ernest, the innocent brother, was thus not fit for heaven and on his way to hell.

---

[18]These shaping activities are part of a destiny process item, called *destiny preparation* (Clinton 1989:103,104), the sense of God's involvement in directing the life. These are indications foreshadowing what is to come. Cumulative recognition of a number of these process items will build a *sense of destiny* (Clinton 1989:349), an awareness that God's hand is on the leader in a special way. That Maxwell vividly remembers these in old age indicates their importance and his awareness of God in them. The dream is especially significant. Like Joseph's dream it was not clear what it meant at the time. But later when looking back and surveying Prairie Bible Institute with it land and buildings and its stream of graduates on the mission field it will became clear.

Chapter 9. L. E. Maxwell (1895-1984) page 401

5. **Two Itinerant Methodist Preachers**
Once, Maxwell visited an evangelistic meeting in which a husband and wife team were the preachers. They were described as "hell-fire and brimstone" preachers. The woman was the more dramatic, actually portraying the condition of sinners falling into hell by falling face down on the platform of the meeting place. Maxwell was both spell-bound (entranced by such a display) and frightened to death because he was further convinced he would never make it to heaven.[19]

6. **Forty Eight Hours in Hell**
Once his father brought home a set of books, unheard of in the Maxwell home. One had a chapter in it entitled "Forty Eight Hours in Hell." Its description of a man's experience of death and a visitation in hell like Dante's **Inferno** left L.E. further convicted of the fear of hell (Spaulding 1991b:35).

These incidents did two things over the long haul. They seeded this life with the sense of God's call to salvation and they hinted of a hidden destiny with God.

At one of the evangelistic meetings as a teenager he went forward. But immediately afterward he returned to his old ways. But with his Aunt's example and encouragement he was to experience a true conversion.

A Simple Conversion--It Takes

At age 20 Maxwell was primed for his conversion experience. He was in Kansas City and under the influence of his Aunt Christina. She had arranged for his job, in fact, had actually created a job for him there. Once in Kansas City, she invited him to join her at the Lynwood Presbyterian Church which she attended. Note the sovereign touch. A mother's dying request is complied with by a pastor, probably not even a believer. But his compliance creates a tension in L.E.'s life which can only be relieved by conversion.

> The pastor, though likely not a true man of faith, at the end of each service simply made the invitation: Come to Christ and the Church. This was later found to be the fulfillment of a vow he had made to his dying mother, something which he would not likely have initiated on his own. But the words drove themselves deep into Leslie's consciousness and he returned home each week under great conviction. It was not long thereafter that he was to cross the great divide (Spaulding 1991b:277).

This time his conversion experience was not public, not a going forward in a tent meeting. It would take. Spaulding describes the simple transaction which sealed Maxwell's pilgrimage to find God.

> At the time of his humble conversion, on his knees in his apartment, Maxwell's prayer had been simply, "O God, forgive my sins." A burden rolled from him that was

---

[19]This special destiny preparation item is significant for several reasons. One, its message added to the cumulative effect of conviction that was building in Maxwell's experience. Two, it is one more of a series of times he was under conviction--God is continuing to woo him. Three, it is a woman who demonstrates powerful gifting. In fact, consider the following: his mother quotes a scriptural phrase which stays with him; his Aunt has powerful influence on his life; this Methodist woman preacher demonstrates leadership gifts; Dorothy Miller deeply influences Maxwell concerning Bible teaching and the Victorious life. No wonder that in later years he will opt for women in ministry just as A. J. Gordon does. Women played such an important part in his salvation and growth! Note also Brengle's experiences with his mom and wife to be. Mears own experience with the modeling of her mother certainly created within her an expectation that God would use her in leadership. And four, the dramatic flair for illustrating truth will become his own. He saw it modeled here by this Methodist woman preacher.

Chapter 9. L. E. Maxwell (1895-1984)

> palpable. He knew at that moment that all of his boyhood dreams would become a reality. Somehow, being right with God would bring about the fulfillment of that childhood vision of becoming a monarch over everything before his eyes (Spaulding 1991b:277).

Spaulding goes on to give some interpretive comments on this--showing this to be a continuation of the destiny preparation previously described.

> It is often at moments of heightened committal or conversion that emerging leaders are given a vision into the future which fires the imagination and is indelibly impressed on the mind as part of God's special revelation to them about their merging with the greater purposes of God in salvation history.
> L.E.'s conversion was surprisingly undramatic, given the type of life he had lived and the dramatic turns his life was yet to take. Yet God visited him in such a way as to make his salvation experience truly a point-in-time decision and a milestone. He experienced newness and a radical change, a merging of his will with God's. His view of conversion was essentially the evangelical one of emphasis on decision, repentance and a receiving of God's gift--point in time. The assurance that his boyhood dreams would come true was to carry with him throughout life and be a steady source of encouragement as the Bible school mushroomed on the prairies (Spaulding 1991b:277).

Earlier in his life, as a teenager, Maxwell had made a "decision" for Christ. It did not hold. Will this one? The answer is yes. He began to study the word. He spent his Sunday afternoons pouring over the Scriptures and praying. He began to build his personal spiritual foundation. This early foundation was tested. He went into the Army for two years, the last two years of World War I. With his Aunt's prompting he made an early stand and continued to grow all during his two years in the service.

A Baptist Preacher Connects to Stevens and Miller

Upon his return from service he began attending a Baptist Church which had an evangelical pastor. That pastor had been trained at Moody Bible Institute. It is at this point that critical incidents 4 and 5 occur, given in the Opening Illustrations 1 and 2, which lead Maxwell to "Daddy" Steven's Midland Bible Institute. The Baptist preacher proves to be the link to two excellent mentors.

After graduation from that 3 year Bible Institute, Maxwell was led to the prairies of Canada. But first there was an important incident which shaped Maxwell's character. It was a precursor to his opportunity in Canada.[20]

---

[20] It is clear to me that this brokenness experience was part of a testing pattern. Maxwell is going to lead a Bible School which will shape the character of thousands of young people. If he, himself, can not be shaped how can God use him in the lives of others. And so, a bit brash, arrogant, and self-righteous this rising leader must learn some important lessons about character and judgment. This particular episode follows the three stage *positive testing pattern*. There is the test, stage 1. After a wrong judgment and a wrong accusation Maxwell must recognize his wrong and do something about it. There is the response, stage 2. He responds properly. He is remorseful, repentant and actually broken about his wrongdoing which nearly ruined another's life. He obeys the convictions on his heart and makes a public disclosure, partially righting the wrong. He is broken by the experience. There is the expansion, stage 3. Immediately comes the request. "Daddy" Stevens recommended Maxwell. Apart from this brokenness experience I do not believe Stevens would have recommended him. Note the sovereign timing of the request--just after the positive testing pattern.

Chapter 9. L. E. Maxwell (1895-1984) page 403

Brokenness and Renewal--A Fresh Start

Spaulding describes a critical incident which in my opinion is pivotal to the furtherance of Maxwell's development as a leader. Maxwell is 27 years older. Generally he is older than the rest of the students in the school. He is a military veteran. He is an authoritarian type person. He is almost ready to graduate. What is to happen now is called by Spaulding, Maxwell's Waterloo experience. Can Maxwell display character in a situation in which he has failed. Spaulding describes.

> It was in his last few months at school, after L. E. had received a degree of respectability and leadership as a student, that he experienced his most memorable "Waterloo." Having nosed his way into another student's affairs, and feeling himself quite righteously justified in so doing, he went to the authorities of the school and passed on the "needed information" in order that discipline might be swiftly administered. It was to his utter horror to discover shortly thereafter that his sources had been wrong, that he had almost been the cause of the fellow student's unnecessary dismissal from the school and that his principal and mentor was thoroughly disgusted with his poor judgment (Spaulding 1991b:42).

Maxwell has operated almost impetuously, like Peter, and now must correct the wrongs he has brought about. Can he do it? I believe his whole leadership future hinges on this response.

> After a swift but sound correcting, Leslie was overwhelmed with conviction and stood broken and weeping before the entire student body and faculty, confessing his wrongdoing and utterly convinced that he had fully fallen from grace in all their eyes (Spaulding 1991b:42).

It his here, at this point in time, that his mentor "Daddy" Stevens models wisdom.

> "Daddy" Stevens' response was gentle and restoring. This was a never-to-be-forgotten correction and a new beginning for L.E. (Spaulding 1991b:42).

To his credit Maxwell responded well. He learned a valuable lesson. He experienced the power of forgiveness. Several times during his ministry at Prairie Bible Institute he will make statements or write things which were wrong or at least unwise. But, under conviction from God about them, he would make public confession before the faculty, staff, and students. The lesson learned early here stayed with him throughout his whole life. Wrongs must be confessed. Forgiveness must be known. God will forgive.

This incident was Maxwell's spiritual diploma. God has graduated him on to the next phase of life--the founding of a Bible Institute.

A Macedonian Call--J. Fergus Kirk Appeals For Help

The big thing has happened. Integrity of character has been tested. But two more links in the chain of destiny must be forged before Maxwell is on his way. God has shaped Maxwell for a particular place and role. But God has also been at work a thousand miles away on another front preparing the place for Maxwell.

> At about the same time, John Fergus Kirk, a young, shy farmer in Alberta,[21]
> having fully benefited from "Daddy" Stevens' correspondence course, wrote the principal

---

[21] A partnership is to form. Kirk (and other relatives) and Maxwell are to begin a partnership that will bring in to existence a training institute. Kirk was a hard working, sacrificial farmer who had dedicated his life to serving God. He lived simply and gave heavily of his earning from farming. This missions minded

Chapter 9. L. E. Maxwell (1895-1984)	page 404

about his need for a teacher to come and help with the spiritual direction of the young people in his district. This letter was the product of a conversation he had had with his sister who had also benefited greatly from Daddy Stevens' and Miss Miller's teaching while at Nyack. Stevens' response was immediate and forthright; Maxwell was the one for the task (Spaulding 1991b:42).

Spaulding (1991b:43) points out how Stevens, Miller and Kirk's sister formed a chain of providential linking that gave Maxwell guidance. I have previously commented on the timing of all these things. The sovereignty of God is seen in the timing. Spaulding goes on to comment that such sovereign guidance is frequently seen in the movement of a leader into a meaningful role.

Maxwell accepted the call. Why would he have accepted such a call? There was no security in it? It was an unpromising rural farming area on the plains of Canada. There was no established church which guaranteed him a salary as a pastor. Instead there was a need to teach the Bible and minister to young people. In the past Maxwell had said that he didn't want a prominent preaching or teaching role and that he didn't want to go to a rural area. He wanted to avoid a cold climate. And yet he goes. I think that as a result of his brokenness experience he was really willing to go anywhere that God wanted. I also feel that the rural area to which he is called was just the sort of situation which would allow this country boy to develop. A sophisticated city ministry might well have done him in. But God sovereignly took him to the locale in which he could flower. I think he was aptly prepared for what was to come. His own background growing up in the Kansas wheatfields as a farmer with rural conservative people had trained him. His education was more than adequate. His previous experiential knowledge of rural conservative people fit beautifully into the situation to which he was called. And then there is the persuasive influence of his mentor. His expectant recommendation carried strong weight.

On the other side of the fence, why would they want him? At this point, there is no indication that the inexperienced Maxwell has gifts for preaching or teaching or doing Bible School work. There is, however, the mentor's judgment. And a respected mentor sponsor can influence as "Daddy" Stevens did. However, he can only get initial acceptance. Maxwell must prove out on his own in the actual ministry setting.

Maxwell was going into a cold climate, a rural situation, and one which would demand a pioneering perseverance. But at this point he was approaching it as a one or two year commitment only. He was twenty-seven. One thing, he still needed. He needed a wife, who was godly and could help provide a Christian social base that he himself never experienced. God met that need.

Pearl Is To Be Your Wife

Frequently during these Bible School days Maxwell had prayer times with his Aunt Christina. Perhaps this wise Christian observed in the rising young leader a need. Perhaps she had been praying about it. In any case God gave a word.

> In one of the prayer times which Leslie shared with his aunt, a prophetic word came to his mind very clearly, that "Pearl is to be your wife." (Spaulding 1991b:44, quoting from Keller).

---

man will form a symbiotic partnership with Maxwell which is the rural equivalent of the Charles Simeon/ Charles Grant partnership. I will relate more details of Kirk as I speak of the Bible Institute's development.

Chapter 9. L. E. Maxwell (1895-1984)   page 405

Previously I had mentioned that God had shown Pearl that L.E. Maxwell was to be the man she could love and marry. She had not confided this to anyone but had kept it as her secret for several years. Now there came the external confirmation.[22]

But they are careful and wait to make sure God is in it. On his way to Canada, Leslie, having proposed by letter, stopped in at Boone, Iowa and paid his new fiancee a visit. They would not see each other again for three years--at their wedding. During the three years of their correspondence their feeling for each other grew and they knew indeed that God had brought them together.

II. SPRING: LIFE FROM DEATH
(1922-1944); Age= 27-49

A. Arena for Faith
(1922-1931); Age= 27-36

And so in the fall of 1922 L.E. Maxwell, having left his fiancée behind in Iowa, journeyed to the prairies to be met at the train in the small town of Three Hills by J. Fergus Kirk and others of the clan.

Who were these people with whom Maxwell would partner? Who were the Kirks who had called for help from "Daddy" Stevens? Spaulding describes the other half of the partnership to which Maxwell linked.

> God had sovereignly prepared the small community of staunch Scottish Christians in the Three Hills area for the young Bible teacher in many ways...
> These people...were of such sterling character and Christian faith, with such a Spartan life-style and generous spirits, that they created the perfect climate in this rugged territory for the man of God's appointment to come in and begin the fledgling institute. Andrew and Maria Kirk, the parents of the clan, had through tremendous adversity and hardship traversed the Canadian prairies from Ontario early in the century for the purpose of reaching out in missionary fashion to the many unbelieving peoples of the plains.
> The family had a long tradition of successful farming, and it was farming which the young son Fergus (J. Fergus Kirk), was to bring to the birth of the Bible school. He met God over the issue of his investments in the farming business and never turned back. As the one who initially called for a Bible teacher from Kansas, J.F. Kirk was the humble "president" and director of the board of Prairie Bible Institute for many years. It was his family's commitment to the evangelization of the community and of the world though humble means and simple life-styles of gospel preaching and generous giving that the stage was set for a great work of God through the Bible training school which emerged (Spaulding 1991b:45,46).

These people knew how to give.[23] It was their sacrificial living and giving which paved the way for expansion in the depression years to come.

---

[22]This is an example of certainty guidance. Frequently leaders, particularly early on in ministry, need to know beyond the shadow of a doubt that God is in something, that He in fact is orchestrating the guidance. *Double Confirmation* (Clinton 1989:262) is one kind of certainty guidance. God directs a person by any of a number of internal ways to arrive at some conviction. He then directs someone else who has no knowledge of that previous guidance to arrive at the same conclusion. He then brings the two together to give confirmation. Here, Pearl who has long been praying and preparing herself for the role of a godly wife and mother receives the word in an intuitive judgment when she first saw Maxwell. She waits. If it is truly of God He will have to convince L.E. too. God does.

[23]Spaulding (1991b:389-399) includes as Appendix I, an article by the Reverend Hector Kirk, *First Things First*, which describes some of the impressions of his mom and dad, Andrew and Maria Kirk and their lives of service and sacrificial giving. They were the fountainhead for the whole solid Kirk clan which served

Chapter 9. L. E. Maxwell (1895-1984)   page 406

> In one year alone, the senior Kirk family lived on $80 total living expenses while sending another $1000 to the foreign missionary cause (Spaulding 1991b:47).

It was to this kind of hard working, loyal, and sacrificial people that Maxwell went. Almost immediately Maxwell emerged as a gifted leader--a powerful teacher and preacher. Listen to the description.

> L.E. Maxwell emerged overnight as a gifted teacher and public speaker. In his own words, he had arrived at Three Hills and "hadn't preached a dozen sermons in my life!" From the simplest of settings, surrounded by a gang of humble farm folk and teenagers, Maxwell budded into an energetic, highly gregarious, forthright speaker, teacher, expositor and prophet. It was without question from the beginning that his earlier revulsion of public speaking was to be short-lived. It is one of the amazing things of his life that he never wearied of teaching or preaching and seemed from the start to have a special anointing of God in his speaking ministry. All of the local people were shocked at first by this Kansas boy's excited histrionics, gesticulating, jumping, acting out various illustrations from Scripture. He had no end of energy once he was before a captive audience, but it was not wasted or ostentatious activity. The students were deeply impressed and blessed by the impact and fresh truth of the message. There was spiritual authority which rang of earlier testing and provings of godly character and a deep relationship with Christ (Spaulding 1991b:52,53).

A series of three major decisions now seem to cascade one upon the other. The first opens the way very naturally for the second. The third flows from the other two. They, together, open the way for a long term ministry. Two have to do with strategic guidance. One has to do with a value which will be foundational to the institute and in line with the simple lifestyle and sacrificial giving of the Kirk clan.

Pivotal Decision--Stay and Tough It Our or Leave And Enjoy Security

Maxwell had taught for a year. The response was good. He was blossoming as a powerful word gifted leader. But so far there is no permanent organizational structure. He has been operating in a quasi-Bible Institute mode. In his own mind, he has committed himself for one or two years to this sort of ministry. At this point God challenged him with an important choice. Spaulding gives the background to this important test, which is pivotal to his destiny. On such simple choices do whole lifetimes of ministry sometimes hinge.

> No sooner had L.E. taught a motley group of teenage young people for one year in Three Hills than an offer came from nearby Edmonton for him to consider a paid pastoral position at a good sized city church with a stipend for furthering his training at the city's university. This was certainly a valid temptation for the young Maxwell. After all, his commitments to the little group in Three Hills were not well defined. He and they had considered this to be a one or two year stint with no long-term goals in place.
> L.E. candidated at the church and then went back to Three Hills to wait an answer. A great inner wrestling went on within his soul. In one moment, though, he knew that he must remain with the struggling rural school (Spaulding 1991b:47).

God with unusual sensitivity to sacrificial giving. This is a challenging article, which indeed does put *First Things First*. A reading of this article will give you the ambiance of the spirit of sacrifice that made Prairie Bible Institute possible.

Chapter 9. L. E. Maxwell (1895-1984)

In his own mind Maxwell had become convinced that God wanted him to stay and commit himself to this struggling ministry. So he committed himself to it. Notice now the special test that came.[24]

> God so timed it that no less than a day after he determined to remain at the little teaching post, a letter of acceptance came from the city church pressing him with the advantages of the lucrative and prestigious position. This timing was enough to convince L.E. that he had made the right, though difficult, choice (Spaulding 1991b:47,48).

Maxwell stood behind his decision. He was committed to develop a Bible School in partnership with the Kirks.

Planned Poverty, Hoping for Nothing

Maxwell had made a decision to stay with the Bible teaching ministry hoping to develop it into a Bible School, much like the institute he had attended under "Daddy" Stevens. He had turned down a ministry which would provide adequate financial security and even a scholarship for further education in a local university. The next step comes almost easily on the heels of this first one.

> Along similar lines, it became clear to young Maxwell that he was headed into a ministry that did not guarantee clear monetary resources. In his first summer of extension ministry out on the prairies in 1923, he was tested regarding the source of his daily income, turned down a small home missionary allowance offered by the sponsoring agency, and began to live in the shadow of the little phrase "hoping for nothing." He would hope for no salary in return for the Lord's work he was doing. This would be with him and the institute throughout his career. In his own words, "I was to commit myself to planned poverty from that day forward" (Spaulding 1991b:48).

This simple sacrificial value would also undergird the institute's policies which would develop. It would apply to the salarying of workers at the school. They would share alike in what God brought in. It would affect the debt-free policy which would condition all expansion of buildings and programs.

Within two years he was tested on this issue. He was leading a missionary conference which mainly was composed of the sacrificial farmers of the region. He knew he would have to challenge them to give beyond their means. He was also conscious that he was to make the trip to Boone, Iowa to pick up his fiancée, Pearl Plummer. These same folks would have to finance that. He was tempted to cut back on the push for missionary giving in order to make sure he would have enough money to make his own trip. But he was convicted of this selfish attitude. He confessed openly to the conference. They gave mightily. On the trip back from Iowa after the wedding God showed that He could supply.

---

[24] In leadership emergence theory this is known as an *integrity check* (Clinton 1989:125). It is a process whereby God tests heart intent to evaluate consistency between inner convictions and outward actions. This is a foundational part of character shaping. Kinds of checks include temptation (conviction test), restitution (honesty testing), value check (ultimate value clarification), loyalty (allegiance testing), guidance (alternative testing--better offer after Holy Spirit led commitment to some course of action), persecution (steadfastness check). It is used to see follow-through on a promise or vow, to insure burden for a ministry or vision, to allow confirmation of inner-character strength, to build faith, to establish inner values very important to later leadership which will follow. In this case it was a guidance type (alternative better offer after a commitment to giving up ambition and doing whatever God wanted). We have seen this previously in the life of Brengle, who was also offered a prestigious pastorate as opposed to an itinerant evangelistic ministry to which he had committed himself. The end result of this kind of test is a leader who will stick with his/her calling through thick and thin knowing it is what God wants.

Chapter 9. L. E. Maxwell (1895-1984)   page 408

> The long trip back to Canada after their wedding in Iowa was a further test in the area of finance. Visits with Leslie's relatives in Kansas and various other potentially supportive groups all the way west to Seattle--including a $3.50 "love gift" offering--all proved to be unpredictable in their giving, so that upon arrival in Three Hills, the Maxwells had $20 to their name. This was to be a lesson, with finality, of the uncertainty of human resources and the full reliability of God alone to provide for financial needs (Spaulding 1991b:48).

One final decision needed to be made. What kind of Bible School will it be? And where is the best place to locate it?

Build At Three Bumps?

It was not an easy decision to build in Three Hills.

> At the same time [as the Maxwell's experiences of living by faith] there came a crucial decision by the founders of the little school as to where they should locate permanently. A school needed buildings and a physical plant. It became apparent that against all logic, God had intended that this be a rural school. Its roots were with the Kirk clan and Three Hills seemed the best place to put down roots. "Dare we build at Three Hills...Three Bumps, Alberta... and tie ourselves down here and never be able to move out...and regret forever that we ever started to build in a town like this?" (Spaulding 1991b:48).

In addition to location, there was also the decision as to what kind of school it should be. Spaulding sheds light on the decision making processes.

> When the first few leaders of the little Bible school met to discuss the future of this enterprise, they had no idea or vision of the scope of ministry into which God was leading them. There was some debate as to the value of building any structure or school building so far out in the country, 60 miles from the nearest city. Even the name of the town, Three Hills, had a "nondescript" quality about it. The young board consisted mostly of Kirk/McElheran family members. Board chairman J. Fergus Kirk was initially outspoken against the idea of building, period. He was "too heavenly minded " to think of any permanent structure suitable to God's work on earth. When he arrived at a complete change of thinking, the board was unanimous in its support of building in the Three Hills area.
>   It was a brave step in those days of relative poverty for an unsupported group of struggling farmers to begin buildings of an "undenominational" Bible school in a sparsely populated area of western Canada.
>   Maxwell's first inclination had been to establish, if they were to be an incorporated school, a Christian and Missionary Alliance institute like Nyack in New York. This was firmly resisted by the local people who were now his trusted friends and advisors. This would be their school and would be open to as many of the various local traditions as possible.
>   Primarily this was a challenge to the faith of the founding families and their leader, now 29. Difficult, faith-stretching decisions made in the formative stage of a movement or work of God elicit powerful energy and sacrifice, much akin to the effect of Nehemiah's rallying the lethargic Jews of post-exilic Jerusalem levels of accomplishment.
>   Years later, secular and church leaders alike would hail the "miracle on the prairies" in acknowledgment of the unusual beginnings and persistence of this "school in the wilderness." An attitude was developed which could laugh at the impossible (Spaulding 1991b:294).

Maxwell during this time also went through a faith stretching experience in which he considered the Biblical warning, "not to begin to build something you can't finish."

Chapter 9. L. E. Maxwell (1895-1984)   page 409

The arena is now set. It is to be an arena of faith. A powerful and firm partnership has begun. This work which will emerge will be a work of faith. Simple Bible believing people will trust God to lead and supply for this work.

The foundations have been laid. There will be a Bible School. It will emerge because of the sacrificial faith of simple Bible believing conservative Christians. The record of the Bible School during these years is of solid continual growth. Eventually the school under Maxwell's leadership attracted full time staff and faculty. But for the early years they made do with what they had.

> The prevailing atmosphere on campus in those early days was one of serving. It was to be some time before a recognizable staff of full-time, humbly paid workers was to be part of the school infrastructure. So much of what went into the buildings, the classes, and the ministries of the school was simply an extension of the early work done by the pioneering Kirks, McElherans, Davidsons and other farmers in the community. Large donations of time, land, materials and energy were the building blocks of the entire Prairie Bible Institute project through the 1920s and 1930s (Spaulding 1991b:54).

During these years Maxwell continued to grow as a powerful Bible teacher. He also did quite a bit of public rhetorician ministry in churches and conferences all over Canada. The reputation of Prairie Bible Institute continued to grow. A publishing ministry began relatively early, this came to be known eventually as *The Prairie Overcomer* which in the 70s reached an audience of over 40,000. Maxwell of course wrote for the periodical.

One of the outstanding means of mobilizing for missions were the annual conferences. Maxwell had seen the importance of having missionaries on campus in "Daddy" Stevens ministry in Kansas City. Eventually there came to be two of these per year. Students were challenged to commit their lives to God, to enter into the Victorious Life, and to identify themselves with the great commission. Many who went on the mission field could trace their call back to one of these annual conferences. Money, was raised at these conferences for missions. Prairie Bible Institute is one of the few Christian organizations which gives money to other Christian mission organizations.[25]

B. Drawing of Boundaries
(1931-1944); Age= 36-49

Expansion In the Midst of Depression--the Faith Stretching Years

The key phrase describing this time period is, **Development in Difficult Times.** At the conclusion of this time period Maxwell and partners will have built a training institution which is ready for the *Window of Opportunity* that follows World War II with its aftermath of the explosive decade. Like Jaffray's expansion into Indonesia during the depression years, Maxwell and the board, expanded when secular businesses and most Christian churches and organizations were cutting back because of the difficult times. The arena of faith, founded in the early years from 1922-1931, was tested and found

---

[25]Kirk mentions in his article (Spaulding 1991b:389,398) which accounts for a little over 50 years of ministry that nearly 2000 graduates had gone on the mission field and that $4,500,000 had been given to interdenominational faith missions. This is certainly a shining example flowing from Grandma and Grandpa Kirk's model. Few, if any other training institutions, can match this giving to missions. No Christian organization that I have been associated with and none that I know of (except perhaps George Muller's) has such a track record. Most organizations struggle to raise finances for their on survival and not to help others. Perhaps herein is some corporate organizational lesson concerning giving and getting.

faithful. Spaulding in his section entitled, *Great Depression Years,* describes and gives a touch of reality in a simple vignette.

> It is one of the great monuments to faith coming out of that period in Prairie's history that they built a new structure every year during the Great Depression to meet the growing needs of a burgeoning institute. At a time when everyone else was yearly cutting back or hunkering down, waiting for better economic times, Prairie went through an unprecedented expansion.
> Classroom buildings, large dining room, new meeting center ("tabernacle"), and dormitories were all erected as the numbers of the graduating classes moved up past 50. Outsiders were duly impressed or dumbfounded by this kind of growth. The no-debt policy was a strength and a disciplining factor at this point. According to L.E., another reason for such unbroken growth at a time of such economic disaster was the type of lifestyle which the founders had maintained throughout the 1920's. They lived so simply that when the world around them was cutting back on all but the strict essentials, the institute people had already been living at that level and hardly felt the difference.
> But there were also great moments of launching out "into the deep" without knowing where the next provision would come from. On one occasion, the pounding of nails literally shut down until the daily mail arrived and Miss Dorothy Ruth Miller walked out to the building project and waving a $5 piece, informed the head carpenter that he could resume his work once he bought the necessary nails (Spaulding 1991b:298).

What can we learn from such a faith stretching testimony? Spaulding gives his interpretive comments on this series of expansions. They are worth our reflection.

> In cooperation with the leaders of the institute, L.E. pushed the limits of his faith in a God who was bringing ever more students to his school and who logically therefore had the divine prerogative to supply these growth needs. Too often leaders wait for predictable growth and rarely step out by faith in the confidence that God is leading them far beyond their logical calculations. On the other hand, without policies like a no-debt agreement among the leadership, Christian organizations claiming to act in faith can often so over-extend themselves as to become the laughingstock of the world. L.E.'s combination of organizational discipline and the exercise of faith kept these extremes in tension and saw divine provision and a growth of his overall influence (Spaulding 1991b:298,299).

These steps of faith over these difficult years built upon and affirmed the decisions made in the early years when the Arena of Faith was being founded.

Life Message Consolidated

I have mentioned several times in previous chapters an important enhancement to a leader finishing well.[26]

EFFECTIVE LEADERS MAINTAIN A LEARNING POSTURE THROUGHOUT THEIR LIVES.

L.E. Maxwell had learned the basics of the message of Victory at "Daddy" Stevens feet some 16 years previously. He continued to build upon what he had learned about the

---

[26]This is one of the five enhancements to finishing well (learning posture, life perspective, renewals, disciplines, mentoring--See Appendix B). It is simultaneously one of the six characteristics describing one who finishes well (learning posture, vibrant relationship with God, Christ-likeness in character, live by convictions, leave behind ultimate contributions, and fulfill a sense of destiny--see Appendix C).

Chapter 9. L. E. Maxwell (1895-1984) page 411

Christian life. His life message had matured. The Christian life was put in the perspective of the Bible as a whole. Spaulding described Maxwell's continued learning posture.

> In the winter of 1935, L.E. presented a new course into the Bible curriculum entitled "Law and Grace" which represented years of development and reflection on these themes of Scripture and their interaction. It became a tough course for the senior students, but a favorite as well. Many were coming from highly dispensational, fundamentalist or other denominational backgrounds which put the Old Testament in an inferior light, insinuating that the people of God were somehow "saved" by a keeping of the law while the New Testament fold experienced the wonders of grace.
> L.E. stood strongly opposed to the dispensational line in this matter, causing a cleavage with such groups as Dallas Seminary, Moody bible Institute and various fundamentalist denominations and publications. It meant a new liberty for students, many of whom could say that for the first time, they walked out of Law and Grace with a whole Bible (Spaulding 1991b:302).

I consider from this point onward that Maxwell operated as a fully competent teacher both in methodology and power (which he had been demonstrating from the start) with an integrative **life message**--which this course demonstrated.[27]

While probably there is much that could be discussed during this preliminary preparatory time about Maxwell's development I will focus on two incidents which were important to the long lasting impact of Prairie Bible Institute's ministry. Both were part of the preparatory foundational blocks that would allow the Bible School to be used so mightily in the explosive decade to come.

The first, a seemingly local educational problem, prompted a stand for Christian truth and resulted in the formation of a Christian High School which became a feeder for the Bible School as well as a place for less qualified students to do remedial work in preparation for entrance to the Bible School.

The second had to do with God's means of countering organizational plateauing. Major spiritual breakthroughs are a must in an on-going ministry otherwise the organization will follow the normal institutional deterioration pattern.[28]

---

[27]In terms of focal issues, life message will generally relate to the focal issue of *life purpose*. It usually consists of an integrated articulation of a cluster of values, those ministry philosophy values that dominate a life. It relates in Maxwell's case to the content of his teaching to bring people into Victory and a perspective on the Christian life. Spaulding (1991b:302,303) comments on this development of a life message. "Leaders develop a 'life message' over a lifetime. Through literary items, divine contacts with Christian leaders and thinkers and their own personal reflection, prayer and processing, they arrive at an integrated theme which is a driving force behind all that they teach. L.E., after studying the Scripture as thoroughly as anyone over the years, and having been self-taught in many of the conservative classics especially from Britain and the U.S. came to a moderately Calvinistic theology which saw the Old Testament Law as Galatians 3:24 speaks of it, the tutor which brings people to Christ. Even in the New Covenant, then, there is a role for Law, that powerful conscience-touching, searing divine standard which 'crowds us to Christ' and gives us no peace until we find rest in the person and work of Christ, the fulfillment of the Law, our Peace. The 'Law and Grace' course was a great gift to all who came under his teaching and usually a spiritual milestone for the serious student of Scripture."

[28]See Adizes' **Corporate Life Cycles** and Clinton's **Bridging Strategies** which describe organizational time paradigms. Organizations usually move through several stages toward maturation and then begin to deteriorate as institutional bureaucracy builds up. Counters to this include, from the Christian viewpoint, breakthroughs from God such as this renewal generated by Oscar Lowry's ministry.

Conflict Leads to Founding of Prairie High School

An incident which at the time had no apparent strategic implications, just simply the solving of a problem, occurred during this period of time. It demonstrates again, faith, organizational as well as personal integrity, and God's providential means of leading toward strategic achievement. It also forced the introduction of an innovation as well as taught lessons on bringing about change in society. Listen to Spaulding's description of the problem.

> Certain staff children brought home some questionable literature texts from the town school one day. After meeting with the town authorities and coming to an impasse, the institute leaders, led by L.E., decided that they needed to start a Christian high school, free from godless and otherwise useless "literature" and "science" (Spaulding 1991b:299).

This was a stand, against the current educational policy in the province.

> Once the school had been established, J.F. Kirk was summarily jailed, being the first parent to send his two sons to a non-certified school. Although he was quickly released, he had led the Maxwells and others in the community against a powerful opposition (Spaulding 1991b:299).

The local problem was solved. A Christian high school would eventually be approved. But it was more than that. There were strategic implications.

> The establishing of first a high school (later accredited with the province) and then a grade school meant a whole new parameter for the institute. Many of the incoming Bible school students were farmer's children who were ill prepared for post-secondary study. The newly formed high school filled a need, then, not only for staff and student children but also for those Bible school students who needed to complete their high school education before moving on (Spaulding 1991b:299).[29]

The 1941 Spring Conference: Oscar Lowry's Renewal Ministry

I need to reemphasize an important principle. One of the five kinds of enhancements that have been correlated to leaders who finish well includes the notion of renewals.[30] Leaders who finish well will have experienced several unusual renewal type

---

[29] At this point in his dissertation, Spaulding adds an interesting tidbit of personal information. "Because of the disciplined environment for which Prairie was no famous, other parents sent their children to the high school from as far away as the States, just to reform their 'wayward kids.' This writer's father was just such a case in point!"

[30] Remember that *renewal* is a specially meaningful encounter with God in which He communicates with *freshness* various kinds of things needed by a leader such as: 1. insights about Himself, 2. affirmation--both personal and ministry, 3. inspiration to continue, 4. breakthrough concepts which inspire one to try them in ministry, 5. a sense of His personal presence and/or power, 6. an unusual sense of intimacy--can be tied to some symbolic thing (like a place, physical object, etc.)., 7. perspective on time, now and/or the future so that one's faith is increased to see God in what is happening and will happen, so as to give the leader another anchor upon which to build a sense of a new start, a beginning again, and a desire to rededicate and continue on in following God. Effective leaders will need several repeated renewal experiences over their lifetimes in order to continue and finish well. The classic cases of renewal leadership in the Old Testament are Abraham and Daniel, from which the renewal definition was derived. Maxwell obviously was deeply moved by this unusual working of God.

Chapter 9. L. E. Maxwell (1895-1984)

experiences. I have already mentioned in Maxwell's life three such renewals:

1. First Encounter with "Daddy" Stevens, enters into Victorious life,
2. Brokenness Experience in Senior Year at Midland Bible Institute,
3. Hoping For Nothing Testing at Conference just prior to wedding.

The conferences at Prairie Bible Institute, fall and spring, along with so many visiting speakers provided plenty of fuel for renewal in the lives of faculty, staff, and students. There were many touched by God through such speakers. But one stands out. It also readied Prairie Bible Institute spiritually for the expansion that was to come.

> The well known evangelist/ revivalist, Oscar Lowry, was invited to the Prairie conference [Spring Conference 1941], now gathering thousands each spring, for a crusade. For many students, this man's unabashed prophetic use of Scripture and penetrating application to sinful lives, was a turning point, a personal contact divinely appointed for the moment. Revival took hold of many people not only at Prairie but throughout the western provinces of Canada at the time.
> This was a man who was loved by L.E. and who returned that love. His vision was large and his method was as unashamed as Maxwell's. Those were days, says one former student from that era, when "we kids got right with God." They also caught some of the evangelistic zeal and enthusiasm which this man exuded (Spaulding 1991b:303).

I want to close this section by highlighting some of L.E.'s development that I have not otherwise covered.

1. **Hearing From God--Pithy Word Summaries That Clinch Truth**
   Throughout his lifetime, God spoke to L.E. from time-to-time with "strong phrases" which summed up some experience that he was going through with God. Two such from this period of time include: 1. "Hoping for nothing" the agonizing answer to living on the ragged edge of ruin that Maxwell experienced; 2. "If you just exist to GIVE instead of to GET you will get along alright," given by "Daddy" Stevens in an address to the student body during his only visit to the school, in its early years.
2. **Literary Processing**[31]
   During this phase Maxwell learned from a number of mentors (Spaulding 1991b:304). Some of his favorite authors include: Horatius Bonar, Catherine Booth, Amy Carmichael, Samuel Chadwick, Oswald Chambers, Robert Glover, Frederick Louis Godet, Jonathan Goforth, Adoniram Judson Gordon, Ernest Gordon, David Gracey, Madame Guyon, F. J. Huegel, Jamieson/ Faussett/ Brown (commentators), J. Gregory Mantle, F.B. Meyer, G. Campbell Morgan, Handley C.G. Moule, Andrew Murray, William R. Newell, David Morrieson Panton, A.T. Pierson, Samuel Rutherford, Charles Simeon, A. B. Simpson, W.C. Stevens, Gerhard Tersteegen, William Henry Griffith Thomas, Paget Wilkes, and Sam Brengle.

---

[31]*Literary processing* (Clinton 1989:184,185) refers to the vicarious learning that comes through interacting with godly authors. God greatly uses, at least in a culture which stresses literacy as opposed to an oral culture, writings to influence the growth of leaders. Early on, Maxwell, who otherwise did no further formal training discovered the importance of informal learning through reading. He read a breadth of authors including devotional, deeper life, missionary, and some Biblical ones. Though he never got advanced degrees he continued to learn.

3. Organizational Values

The challenge to build in the midst of depression years came about in conjunction with the growth of conviction concerning certain values. Listen to Spaulding's assessment:

> Ministry expansion during this period of time can best be seen through the challenges to build. Around these challenges emerged the ministry philosophy values of: **team work**, so essential to the progress of Prairie Bible Institute given the barren prairie farmland and necessity of outside help--a teamwork which required self-sacrifice and unanimity; **prayer work**, rallying all institute members and supporters around urgent needs of the school; **faith work**, knowing that only God would keep the school from becoming the laughingstock of the community ("This man began to build, but was unable...").
>
> It was around the challenges to build that many of the institute's long-range parameters were set in those early days as well. First, the Bible School, then the Conference meeting place, then the high school, farm, grade school, printing press, radio studio, staff housing, etc. Each building project represented a growth challenge and ministry priority of the overall institutional leadership (Spaulding 1991b:305).

What were the characteristics then of this school which was now prepared for the most fruitful and explosive ministry of its existence. Spaulding (1991b:305,306) pinpoints eleven:

1. **Bible-centered Curriculum**
   They were part of the Bible School movement. The study of the English Bible was the integrating factor of all curriculum.
2. **Authority of Bible**
   The school held unquestioned authority of the Bible in all its claims.
3. **Inductive Bible Study**
   The school used a "search-question" method to force students to inductively draw out truth from the Bible.
4. **World Missions Thrust**
   The school emphasized reaching the unreached.
5. **Strong Discipline**
   The school was training disciplined soldiers for Christ. Character shaping via strong discipline was the norm.
6. **Spirit Filled Victorious Christian Life**
   There was a powerful emphasis on living the Spirit-filled Victorious Christian life. This entailed dying to self--seeing The Cross in all of life.
7. **Separation**
   The school believed in separation from the world and liberal religious traditions.
8. **Social Regulations**
   Part of the discipline involved strict social regulations for students living in the Prairie Bible Institute community.
9. **No Debt Policy**
   The school practiced a no debt policy. When God supplied, they built, otherwise, they waited for God's supply.
10. **Student Gratis Work**
    As part of their learning discipline and because it was needed to survive, students did gratis work.
11. **Hoping For Nothing**
    The faculty and staff shared what God provided for living. There were no guaranteed salaries.

These values were to carry the school into the 40s, 50s, and 60s.

Chapter 9. L. E. Maxwell (1895-1984)   page 415

As to L.E. Maxwell personally, the dominant ministry philosophy model he learned experientially during this period of time was the Servant Leadership model.[32] His partners, the Kirk clan greatly influenced him with values of Servant Leadership. Spaulding emphasizes this influence.

> These simple farm folk served the interests of the school so self-sacrificially, they literally emptied their pockets many times just to see the institute carry on successfully. Maxwell learned from them and developed a generosity of his own which was equal to theirs. He raised his family, students and staff to give "hilariously" especially to the Lord's work overseas where the laborers were always struggling with less than enough. Servanthood is also a universal biblical leadership model, one which is required of any who "would be great among you" (Spaulding 1991b:306).

The summer time is coming for Maxwell and the school. There will be much fruit. They have been prepared. They are ready.

III. SUMMER: ABUNDANT FRUIT
(1944-1960); Age= 49-65

Overview

This was an explosive time in the life of the institute and the life of Maxwell. Spaulding brilliantly and candidly summarizes this period of time. I will quote his summary of this time as a backdrop for reading an abbreviated version of the critical incidents which come during these time periods. First comes the breathtaking positive side.

> Here, without question, begins the fullest, busiest, and most explicitly fruit-bearing period of L.E. Maxwell's life.
> Within a fifteen year period, the school would emerge as a world leader in missionary training. L.E. was to publish the bulk of his books, introduce two new regular publications for the institute, take five major trips overseas, introduce ever larger crowds of people to his conferences, embark on a new series of Keswick conventions, and see his own household emptied by the post-war missionary surge (including by this time 1200 from Prairie)--all between 1945 and 1960.
> Meanwhile he would continue his full administrative responsibilities over the institute and the Bible school, carry on his heavy teaching load and continue as senior pastor of the Prairie Tabernacle congregation. He was in greater demand around the continent as a conference speaker and enjoyed the unique privilege of speaking to the very first groups of post-war students in Toronto, which became the Urbana convention of Inter-Varsity Christian Fellowship. Among the students in attendance was Jim Elliot. (Spaulding 1991b:309).

Now comes the tougher down side.

> These stellar years for the man were clouded by three kinds of testing. The first were the crises which any institution goes through in the midst of terrific growth. Both "natural" and personal tragedies were to strike L.E. at the school level. Institute buildings would die in their birth. Ambitious men would threaten his authority. But probably the more sinister dilemmas were unfolding on the home front.

---

[32] I identify 5 dominant philosophical models of leadership in the New Testament in my **Handbook I. Leaders, Leadership, and the Bible--An Overview** (1993): Steward, Servant, Harvest, Shepherd, Intercessor. Here Maxwell is grasping the essence of Servant leadership--a set of foundational values that apply to all Christian leadership.

Chapter 9. L. E. Maxwell (1895-1984)   page 416

As the latter "era" of his children were now going through their teen years, the father's neglect due to extreme busyness began to catch up with him. His son Paul became the focal point because of his overt rebellion, but the others, especially his wife Pearl, were also suffering damage which would take its toll in time.

Lastly, he was to go through two cataract operations near the end of this bright, explosive era which would begin to sound a warning that the stress and speed of the ministry might short-circuit his effectiveness or even the ministry itself.

But none of these testings should cloud the overwhelming success of those days in the perceptions and development of the many students who surged through Prairie's ranks at this time. For them, in their preparation for one of the most difficult tasks on earth, this man embodied the life they were setting out to live. The authority, pathos, spiritual depth, humor, frankness, holiness and fiery zeal of L.E. rubbed off on hundreds of the world's next generation of missionaries and church leaders (Spaulding 1991b:309).

Probably the greater leadership lessons will be learned from the three kinds of testings than the successes. I will come back to these lessons when I summarize lessons from L.E.'s life.

...There is no overt indication that he resorted to a proud, fleshly means of power or leadership once he began to reap the benefits of renown in the Evangelical world. He had a single focus which he had retained from the beginning.

Yet a cloud seems to gather over the latter end of this period of great external success and popularity which points to the final testings of his life. The cloud may be merely physical suffering, the toll on the eyes of too many years in the books, or it may relate to ministry structural or relational insights which L.E. was blind to. But that remains a mystery. It is without question that God used L.E. in these peak years in many, many people's lives, directing them either into a deeper devotion to Christ and/or launching them into the training of God's Word for usefulness in his vineyard.

L.E.'s sphere of influence grew geometrically during this time. He moved from heavily direct to greater indirect means of influence. The dominant training models which he employed were still classroom oriented with the first hints of a latter period of mentoring beginning in the late 1950's. His prophetic ministry all over the continent, while not "training" per se, was a direct, modeling influence on thousands, while just the publishing of **Born Crucified** alone had a powerful indirect influence on many thousands of others including a few key Christian leaders in the English-speaking world (Spaulding 1991b:309).

With this overview in mind I will identify and examine four critical incidents during the explosive decade and only touch lightly on the lead-in to it, the growing awareness of the *window of opportunity*.

A. Highlights Amid Losses
(1944-1950); Age= 49-55

Why did Spaulding title this lead-in time as *Highlights Amid Losses*? One important reason, which helps identify the closing of a time period, was the death of Dorothy Ruth Miller. She had co-mentored L.E. and faithfully taught in the school for more than 20 years. That was certainly a striking loss. But there were gains too. And this pattern of highs and lows, this contrastive set of opposites carry on through the entire period including the explosive decade and to a different degree in the final period of his life. Table 9-1 lists some of the Highlights and Losses derived from Spaulding's description (1991b:61-64).[33] This is certainly not an exhaustive list. More certainly could be added but it does show the contrasting processes which shaped Maxwell during these years. I

---

[33] Spaulding (1991b:62) mentions that there is some debate on some of these dates but that they are within a six month window of that indicated.

Chapter 9. L. E. Maxwell (1895-1984)   page 417

show it here for the entire period because it first began to appear in this time period but it continues onward.

Table 9-1.[34]   Highlights Amid Losses--1944 Through 1950 and Continued

Time	Item
1. 1944	Miss Miller's death by cancer.
2. 1944	Renewal of publishing ministry effort. Periodical renamed *Prairie Overcomer*; will enjoy great success in the years to come.
3. 1945	**Born Crucified** published.
4. 1946	Partially constructed C-Dorm collapses.
5. 1946	Armen Gesswein renewal ministry.
6. 1946	Plenary speaker in Toronto--forerunner of Urbana Conference.
7. 1947	Incredible publicity. McLean's magazine article, "Miracle at Three Hills" puts Prairie on map.
8. 1947	Charles E. Fuller visit.
9. 1948	Newly completed infirmary fire; total loss.
10. 1948/49	Land expansion. Acquisition of additional 240 acres. "Prairie Heights" developed.
11. 1949	Plenary speaker again in Inter-Varsity forerunner of Urbana Conference.
12. 1949	Eleanor departs. Vacuum deeply felt by Pearl.
13. 1950	Difficult termination of staff member due to sexual misconduct.
14. 1950	**Crowded To Christ** produced. Some consider his best work.
15. 1950-59	Five major overseas trips. Missionary renewal experiences.
16. 1951	Maxwell relationship with son Paul very strained.
17. 1954	Maxwell relationship with cousin stretched and broken.
18. 1956	First cataract operation.
19. 1957	Larger tabernacle constructed (seating 4300).
20. 1956/57	Faculty uprising incident.
21. 1958	Second eye surgery.
22. 1958	Boiler House Fire.
23. 1962	Pearl Collapses.
24. 1964	Low point in L.E.'s personal ministry trips (California and New York).
25. 1966	L.E.'s *Dark Night of the Soul*--near death experience.

Obviously Maxwell experienced during these years both the great affirmations from God which encouraged him to continue in his destiny and as well he was *crowded to Christ* and kept humble amidst the success.

B. The Explosive Decade
   (1950-1960); Age= 55-65

   Window of Opportunity--Faith Check

   They began returning immediately after World War II. Many who had been scattered by that great world tragedy felt the call of God and came to the Prairie campus to

---

[34] I have mentioned in Chapter 1 that all biography is somewhat biased and interpretive even if the author is against interpretive biography. The choice of what to put on a list such as this one is a case in point. I am sure that many more positive things could be added and probably many more negative. Yet I think the list does point out the concept of the *Highlights Amid Losses* pattern which shaped Prairie and its leader.

Chapter 9. L. E. Maxwell (1895-1984)   page 418

be trained and sent on their way. Spaulding describes this great testing time for Maxwell and the leaders of the institution.³⁵

> The ranks of students returning from the Second World War in 1945-46 swelled the Prairie campus to the bursting point. So many had now seen the world firsthand with its suffering, death and spiritual darkness; Bible school training for missionary work was the natural next step. The school was also sponsoring much larger evangelistic and revival crusades in its meeting places. Armin Gesswein and Charles E. Fuller were two men who came through Three Hills in the summers of 1946 and 1947 back-to-back.
>
> With this unexpected influx of students and visitors came a sudden need for larger staff, faculty and physical plant. Two large new dorms were quickly erected. An efficient infirmary was needed. And the existing Tabernacle was being steadily overcrowded.
>
> A better water supply and sewerage disposal system had to be brought in, all costing more than the institute was prepared to pay. It was a time in which L.E. and the leaders at Prairie were much in prayer and, like George Muller of Bristol, were simply trusting God for daily bread and large financial provision just to keep the institute functioning.
>
> With the "hoping for nothing" catchword of the founding days as their charter, the saw God provide even through the crises. On one occasion, in January of 1949, a check for $20,000 came to Three Hills from a virtual stranger, a Christian member of the Ottawa government who had heard of a need at the school and had promptly responded (Spaulding 1991b:311).

Spaulding goes on to give his interpretive comments on this processing by God. It is apparently clear that corporate institutions as well as individuals are shaped by God. They go through integrity checks and faith checks just as leaders do. Their response, if positive, will be blessed by God with expansion just like for individuals. Such was the case with Prairie Bible Institute.

> These checks of faith kept the atmosphere of the school lively and expectant. For L.E., answered prayer was never taken lightly. He was quick to let the entire school establishment know of God's specific provision. It seems that the building of faith is one of the integral, life-long lessons, for leaders, like all believers, must live by faith and walk by faith. It is the sign of life and growth that a leader, even late in life, is being exercised in his/her faith to greater heights of trust and accomplishment (Spaulding 1991b:312).

Philip Howard, Divine Contact, Urges Writing Challenge

In addition, to the faith challenge making up the *Window of Opportunity*, Maxwell received a special challenge to expand his own personal leadership influence. He had a tremendous direct sphere of influence through his face-to-face teaching ministry and his public rhetorician ministry in conferences and churches all over. Now God will challenge him to influence many whom he will never see, a challenge to expand his indirect sphere of influence. Note how the encouragement from a respected publisher stimulates Maxwell into a wider sphere of influence.

---

³⁵A *faith check* (Clinton 1989:143) represents a time of shaping by God in which a leader is challenged to experience more of God's enablement and to expand his/her influence or ministry or combination. God's reality and faithfulness will be tested and seen to be true and form a confidence builder for later trusting God with bigger issues. Usually the test comes in five steps: 1. a stimulus to faith; 2. recognition that having faith in God is the issue; 3. insight as to what God wants to do or can do in the situation; 4. response which believes God will intervene; 5. the results through which faith in God is vindicated. Maxwell and the board experienced these divine growing pains. They responded positively. God blessed greatly. Over the explosive decade nearly a 1000 missionaries went out from Prairie Bible Institute.

Chapter 9. L. E. Maxwell (1895-1984)

> L.E. published his first book, **Born Crucified** eventually through Moody Press...It was at the recommendation of Philip Howard, then editor of the **Sunday School Times**, that L.E. put together a series of messages and articles he had given over the years concerning the "cross in the life of the believer." This teaching, which really flowed directly from L.E.'s own life experience and crises, was an easy-to-read expanded exposition of such passages as Romans 6 through 8, Galatians 2:19-20 and many others. It was a thematic treatment of the believer's identification with Christ in the cross and the ramifications for daily sanctification (Spaulding 1991b:312).

This influence challenge to give a wider audience access to the core of his life message was responded to positively. This obedient response, I think, is one of the reasons for the expansion via the McClean article which is to come. That Maxwell responded so well to this ministry insight is seen in his renewed interest in influencing through the **Prairie Overcomer**, and the books which came from his pen in 1950, 1953, 1954, 1955, and 1958.

Miracle At Three Hills--God's Sovereign Divine Affirmation

God blessed the positive responses to the *Window of Opportunity* which further opened it up. An unexpected boost from a secular periodical, Maclean's magazine, gave widespread and positive publicity to Prairie Bible Institute. The article was complimentary and captured in a positive way the import of the discipline and strong fundamental stand of the school. This incident was God's affirmation of the Spartan styled school. Many more were influenced to come to Prairie and become part of the explosive decade.

Unexpected blessings come our way when we find ourselves responding to God's challenges. Maxwell's ministry demanded wider exposure. He wrote. In turn, God honored that response giving His own wider exposure.

Conflict--The Balancing Force

I have mentioned that throughout this period there were the blessings and there were the contrasting down sides. Several items of conflict challenged Maxwell's values and consistency. Several were challenging hidden areas of his life that needed improvement, but which he was blind to. Others challenged his strong tendency to put his views of interpretation over his relationships with others. Some challenged his leadership and the eventual need for change, for leadership transition. Maxwell apparently did not learn all the lessons from this shaping activity of God. This will become more apparent as he is further tested in the latter period of his life.

I could talk of each of these recurring conflict experiences at length but I have selected one, which was probably most critical to the on-going ministry of L.E. Maxwell. Spaulding describes it well.

> There were at least two men on the faculty during the explosive decade at Prairie who were convinced that the school should become a liberal arts Christian college offering various fields of study beyond the Bible, music and missions. After all, by this point, a number of the great State-side schools of the Bible college movement had made the transition and held their distinctly Christian dynamic.
>
> David Enarson led the way in this open pursuit of change.[36] L.E. was convinced that this was completely out of step with the distinctives which God had given

---

[36] I tend to think his ideas were probably right. The Colonial mentality, the era of pioneer missionaries being accepted in countries now opting for independence, was passing rapidly. Incoming expatriates were to be increasingly limited. Governments would soon require more sophisticated training before it would give

Chapter 9. L. E. Maxwell (1895-1984)

him and the board in the formative years. Prairie's sole purpose was to train men and women for the mission field or full time ministry. If students pursued other careers after Bible school, fine and well, but Prairie was about the Great Commission and the teaching of the whole counsel of Scripture.

There seemed also to be a pursuit of political power behind the lobbying for change. This was one of L.E.'s weak points. He considered resigning from his position in the interests of keeping the peace, or just out of insecurity in the face of such aggressive resistance to his leadership. It was J.M. Murray, his close friend and administrative colleague who confronted L.E. on this issue, not fully knowing the facts, but insisting that God had called L.E. to the school in the first place, and he needed to stand his God-appointed ground. This was the encouragement he needed. Soon thereafter, when the man threatened resignation if things didn't begin to move his direction, L.E. accepted it on the spot (Spaulding 1991b:319,320).

Spaulding seems to imply that L.E. did not learn well from conflict processing of which this is an example.[37]

L.E. went through the greatest agonizing of his years of ministry in times which involved such conflict. He hated to confront the men who were in the wrong. He never wised to offend individual staff members and was mortified if he was shown to have done so. He was so quick to confess wrongdoing. Therefore in this case he almost capitulated to pressure from such strong competing and capable leadership. This man was young, popular, a good Bible teacher. The outcome of his ouster was the appointment of the young T.S. Rendall to teach Bible 2. The man went on to establish a strong Christian liberal arts college in British Columbia. But the issue of Prairie's educational and training philosophy would return many times, and L.E.'s conservative stand would be brought into question by the entire generation of students coming to Prairie after the explosive decade (Spaulding 1991b:320).

This conflict incident along with others and various other crises will eventually result in what Spaulding identified as the reverse influence challenge, the leadership transition phenomenon in which God challenges a leader to turn loose of leadership responsibility little-by-little until leadership transition is finally smoothly accomplished.

If the second major time period was characterized by the Servant Leadership philosophy model it would be fair to say this major period was characterized by the Harvest Leadership philosophy model. It was an explosive time in terms of ups and downs.

---

visas to incoming expatriates. But his ideas were ahead of the time, at least for the power bloc controlling Prairie. And perhaps better change dynamics could have brought his ideas in, with some delay. If so, perhaps the delay in moving in that direction would not have been as long as it has been. And perhaps there are other sovereign reasons, like the shaping of his character or the need for another school in British Columbia. Or perhaps it was to allow a young leader like Ted Rendall to move forward to assume leadership which otherwise might have been blocked.

[37]*Conflict shaping processes* (Clinton 1989:276) is one of the mighty shaping forces God uses to mellow strong leaders. Two types of closure should be sought for: 1. relational, attempting to bring reconciliation and insure that forgiveness of each other and acceptance of each other does not in fact build into a root of bitterness that will be an on-going problem; 2. learning of lessons which will affect our leadership in the future. While we can not always get satisfactory closure of type 1 (two are involved; from our side we can assure that no root of bitterness is there), we can always get closure from type 2. With careful reflective thinking and probing of God's intent we can learn lessons and assimilate values that can decidedly influence positively our on-going leadership.

Chapter 9. L. E. Maxwell (1895-1984) page 421

IV. FALL: RETURN TO THE SOIL
(1960-1984); Age = 65-88

An overview of this period identifies a number of issues affecting Maxwell's leadership. I identify only one critical incident since it could have seriously affected whether he would finish well. However, there are a number of items that require at least a brief comment. Spaulding carefully touches on most of them.

> The last major phase of L.E. Maxwell's life, corresponding to our use of the seasons of the year, is entitled "Fall: a return to the soil." If this connotes a quieting, downward trend, it is intentional. Yet this is not meant to be negative. More like the actual season, L.E.'s latter years seemed to be a closer experience of the actual "dying of Christ," which he had preached up to this point from a position of relative strength. Now he was to experience with a new acuteness the crucified life of his teaching and writing, a slow burial under the weight of personal, family and institutional losses.
> L.E. was 65 in 1960, the year most men retire. He was to teach for 15 more years. Certainly the "great years" of multiple ministry and broad influence were to steadily diminish from this point onward. Causes for this are many, physical limitations leading the way. Geographical isolation of the institute would also lose its power in the school's resistance of change, allowing for hallowed traditions of a bygone "Maxwell era" to be questioned and replaced.
> But in this longest and last phase of his life, L.E. was to shine in a number of significant new ways. While the activity was greatly reduced, the learner posture was still in place, if not heightened. If Christian suffering is the doorway into deep fellowship with God, L.E. was given every opportunity to step into that way. He suffered physically, emotionally, spiritually--in ways which all his simple, Spartan, godly life had not afforded in those early golden years. Now the leader was reduced to sideliner, the proud father was brought to bereavement, the busy president was reduced to bed-ridden patient, the eloquent teacher to a sputtering, coughing old man. Success gave way at times to deep feelings of utter failure. But through it all he did not ultimately falter. And there were grand moments of reward as well. His ministry was crowned with an afterglow and widespread acclamation which few men ever enjoy. It was to be a sixty year experiment in the giving of oneself for others.
> Waning strength, organizational shifting within the institute structure, the enigma of the 60's within conservative Canadian culture, a series of deaths and crises in the family, all wore heavily upon L.E. But he came through to his own "coronation" with a quiet, strong triumph of surest victory. The servant had finished his work.
> The primary development task of this final phase for L.E. was a deep processing for the purpose of a renewed spiritual formation at the end of life. While there would be several rewarding destiny fulfillment experiences (i.e. 50 wedding anniversary) the bulk of major events would come as trials or severe testings: to mellow the saint, creating a new understanding of Christian victory, of the fellowship of the saints, of "weaker vessels" and the compassion of God (Spaulding 1991b:328, 329).

A. Internal Crises
(1960-1966); Age= 65-71

While Maxwell continued to lead and teach his focus turned more inward particularly as the crises came. During this period the most serious crisis involved his wife's collapse. Through it he learned more of compassion and a correction from an outward *ministry-only* dominance. This crisis was part of his mellowing processing.

On the positive side, during this period of time, he selected young Ted Rendall as Vice-Principal and an on-going leader.[38] Rendall was a brilliant and loyal follower who had shown Maxwell the importance of a theological education. He had had sound Biblical training in the British seminary environment. His sound scholarship and methods of Biblical study were eventually seen as not countering the inductive methodology so long an honored tradition at Prairie but in fact putting it on a more solid footing. Maxwell entered a time of informal mentoring of Rendall. They had a close relationship.

B. Mellowed Teacher
(1966-1980); Age= 71-85

Dark Night of the Soul, Will He Finish Well?

In 1966 a detached retina sent him to the hospital. His experience there included poor hospital care which nearly resulted in his death. It is in conjunction with this experience that he experienced his "dark night of the soul" (Spaulding 1991b:78). "Dark night of the soul" is an expression arising in Catholic spirituality circles. It is a term describing a deep inner processing, involving penetrating introversion and the asking of difficult spiritual questions. Questions dealing with suffering, failure or deep loss are agonizingly explored with God--though frequently there is the absence of the sense of God's presence in the reflection. Spaulding describes some of the inner turmoil.

> This was L.E.'s "dark night of the soul." He had more time than ever before in all his years at the school; time to reflect on his work, successes and failures. Failures came to the fore. He was haunted and driven down by thoughts of personal failure. When he recovered, no one would question that here was a different man. Physically slowed, he took months getting back into his rigorous exercise routine, and never regained his old self. Suddenly L.E. knew again what it was to suffer, something he had not experienced in this way for himself since childhood (Spaulding 1991b:79).

Afterwards, he was heard to comment, "From this point on, I don't want to say an unkind thing to anyone" (Spaulding 1991b:324). The entire staff and student body saw a transformation toward an internal quiet and "mellowing" toward gentleness. He came through this testing a processed man who went on to finish well.

His leadership responsibilities were cut back one-by-one till he finally was only teaching, his great love. Spaulding honors this old warrior in his final remarks on Maxwell's teaching ministry.

> Teaching was by far the most difficult role for L.E. to give up. He remarked in his last days that if he had his life to live again, he would ask for those "58 years" of teaching ministry, that he would gladly pay students to hear, "if only they would listen!" The real corpus of his writings are better seen from his classroom lecture notes than from the famous sermons or books. His teaching ranged through the entire Bible, borrowed from a host of godly evangelical scholars from Britain, Canada and the U.S. and yet gloried in the simplest stories which would encourage or further enlighten the student in the understanding and embracing of key truths.
>
> His teaching had been punctuated by profoundly heart-rending glimpses into the heart of God and the plight of man and the high truths of Scripture. There was wit, sarcasm, hilarious laughter, weeping, prayer, soul-searching, and intellectual stimulation--

---

[38] This selection, which was apparently reversed later (1968) because of board pressure for a Maxwell to continue it, will eventually be followed. The reversal was an especially trying time which led to Rendall's being set aside for a period of almost ten years. This is an important time of conflict in power structures but it essentially did not concern L.E. so much as Prairie Bible Institute. So I do not discuss it here.

Chapter 9. L. E. Maxwell (1895-1984)   page 423

all going on regularly under the rubric of teaching. He took the preparation of ministers and missionaries seriously and considered it a high honor and calling not to be squandered on boredom, sentimentality, impractical scholarship or simple communication of data.
Though at times he would holler into the far away looks of a hundred students: "ink it, don't think it!" he truly intended that each concept be thought through, prayed through and conquered, not just absorbed and spit back. For this and other reasons, it was the classroom which he gave up last--that which he had begun first in October of '22 (Spaulding 1991b:339).

C. Final Testings
(1980-1984); Age= 85-88

During these final years their was on-going testing that drove Maxwell further into the sovereignty of God. In 1980, his granddaughter Lorraine Hartt, a nursing school senior in Chicago died after a painful bout with cancer. Her personal buoyancy was a special testimony to those who saw her suffer. She was an unusual saint at age 22. While there was a tremendous sense of loss in the family, her parents Brad and Ruth deeply responded to God in this crisis as did L.E.

In 1981, J. Fergus Kirk passed away. His death was not a shock. But this lifelong partner in ministry was sorely missed. It was a reminder that things would never again be as they had once been. In that same year word came from Brazil that his eldest daughter had suffered a nervous breakdown. Sacrificial effort and a heavy workload had taken a toll.

But a most troubling crisis involved Ernest and Freeda. Ernest was his oldest son, a missionary in Africa. While on furlough in Canada, in 1982, they were killed instantly in a head-on collision on an icy road in northern Alberta, just hours from their parents' home.

All of these incidents stretched L.E. but his prayer response at the funeral is a powerful model to us all, "Lord, you don't owe us any explanations!" (Spaulding 1991b:342).

Finally, the culminating testing. L.E. was diagnosed as having Parkinson's disease in his early eighties. In these latter years it began to progress. He was isolated, again shut up to a fresh time of experiencing depression and feelings of failure. These times were never prolonged. Like Amy Carmichael, one of his favorite writers, he was to spend these last days in helpless dependence upon God. And these days put the final touches on his character.

Maxwell finished well. The New Testament philosophical model which he demonstrated in this last phase was the Shepherd Model. This is not to say that his Harvest mentality ever weakened. But he moved more toward a gentler approach toward believers in their own development while his involvement in the world mission scene waned.

Chapter 9. L. E. Maxwell (1895-1984)

Critical Incidents Identified, and/or Explained

Critical incidents are shaping activities which can affect values relating to all three types of formations--spiritual (leadership character), ministerial (leadership skills) and strategic (leadership vision, that is, total direction in life and ministry).

There is a sense in which many, many incidents in a leader's life **affect values**. But from that large identifiable number a few should be highlighted and recognized as very significant. Critical incidents also frequently provide **pivotal points for choices** of roles, kind of ministry and locale. These pivotal incidents provide strategic guidance.

Here is a list of critical incidents, some giving **focal values** and some providing **strategic guidance**. Table 9-2 indicates these. I number them for convenience of referencing later when I comment on them.

Table 9-2 Listing Of Some Critical Incidents In Maxwell's Life

Incident(s) Name	Age	Formational Type Dealing With Basic Value/Thrust
1. Heritage: Prayer/ Two Grandfathers/ Aunt Christina (see page 389)	Early	Strategic--Even though his immediate family was pagan in his extended family were his grandfathers who prayed regularly for L.E. One of his grandfathers was saved at about 60 years of age and his break with some sinful habits made an impression on Maxwell. But most important in his extended family was Aunt Christina who prayed regularly for 20 years for his salvation. Then she did her utmost to get him out of the pagan situation and in to a place where Christian influence was possible. Her impact can not be over exaggerated.
2. Destiny Preparation/ Ernest's Death/ Methodist Preachers/ Monarch Dream (see page 390)	11	Strategic--Early as a young lad before he was saved L.E. had a dream that "he would be monarch over all that he saw." This was a sense of destiny in embryonic form. In later years Maxwell recalled this dream vividly and knew it had a bearing on his Christian life. A series of events continued the destiny preparation. God continues to pursue L.E. One important one was his brother's death which helped prepare him for his own salvation. He feared an eternal punishment. Two Methodist circuit preachers capitalized on the fear motive. One of them, the woman, deeply impressed Maxwell with a lively emphatic histrionic communication--something he would later use in his own ministry. All of these little by little led him not only to conversion but to a sense of destiny.
3. Conversion (see page 391)	20	Spiritual Formation--A repeated invitation Sunday after Sunday to come to Christ finally got through to L.E. who was deeply sensing a need for solving his moral dilemmas, his need for forgiveness for his sins, and eternal life with God in heaven.

Chapter 9. L. E. Maxwell (1895-1984)   page 425

Table 9-2 Listing Of Some Critical Incidents In Maxwell's Life continued

Incident(s) Name	Age	Formational Type Dealing With Basic Value/Thrust
4. Divine Contact, Baptist Preacher Links to Daddy Stevens (see page 381)	24	Strategic/ Spiritual--Maxwell's pastor suggests Bible School and links L.E. to a new, small Bible school whose teachers "Daddy" Stevens and Dorothy Miller deeply impact Maxwell and set the direction of his life work.
5. Mentors/ Daddy Stevens/ Dorothy Miller (see page 384)	24-27	Spiritual/ Ministerial/ Strategic--Maxwell is linked to two mature Christians who have a passion for missions and for the Victorious Christian Life and who believe small Bible Schools are a major way to mobilize young people with these two major emphases. Three focal issues emerge from this short three year experience: two unique methodologies which Maxwell will use all his life (inductive Bible study--search questions; Bible School as means for training and mobilizing young leaders); his life purpose (to mobilize Victorious Christians for missions involvement); major role--he will be linked to a situation where a Bible School is needed which he will found. But he saw it here first in action--a mobilizer/ trainer from a highly controlled environmental setting.
6. Brokenness/ Restoration (see page 393)	27	Spiritual/ Strategic--An incident in which Maxwell wrongly accuses a fellow student is not founded on facts. Maxwell, who thought it was, sees that he nearly ruined the reputation of a potential leader by his careless accusation. He repents before the whole student body. This obedient response is part of the reason he will be recommended to Kirk in Canada.
7. The Call--Kirk's Plea/ Partnership (see page 393)	27	Strategic--A Godly family, the Kirks, on the prairies in Canada appeal to "Daddy Stevens" for help. He responds by recommending Maxwell who in background and temperament is just the person for the situation.
8. Prophetic Word/ Pearl Social Base Stability (see page 394)	27	Strategic--God gives double confirmation to Pearl about marriage to L.E. Maxwell when he receives a word of knowledge that she is the one. She provides the social base situation that allows Maxwell, perhaps a difficult partner, to accomplish much in ministry. She is one of the keys to his success.

Chapter 9. L. E. Maxwell (1895-1984)

Table 9-2 Listing Of Some Critical Incidents In Maxwell's Life continued

Incident(s) Name	Age	Formational Type Dealing With Basic Value/Thrust
9. Integrity Check/ Strategic Guidance (see page 396)	28	Spiritual/ Strategic--Infrequently God will often allow the testing of allegiance to His steady calling on a leader's life through an attractive alternative offer. Maxwell was offered a pastorate in Edmonton which was financially attractive and would allow for further education. But the call of God, the inner conviction prior to this offer was to stay at Three Hills and develop this pioneer Bible Institute. Maxwell could look back on this as a pivotal point.
10. Planned Poverty / Hoping For Nothing/ (see page 397)	28	Spiritual/ Strategic--A simple obedience check established a major value that was to permeate L.E.'s life and Prairie Bible Institute. In a moment of testing concerning finances, L.E. saw that he must look to God alone and not trust that which he could work out with men. Thus began a life of trusting God for finances. This entailed adopting deliberately a simple life style and avoiding debt.
11. Three Hills?/ Strategic Location/ (see page 398)	29	Strategic--In a joint decision with the conservative rural board members with whom a deep partnership was forming, Maxwell decides to locate the Bible School in Three Hills rather than moving it to a more populous urban region that has large potential resources for influence such as networking and wealth. This Spartan/ survival-like environment will prove an outstanding locale for training the pioneer missionary types who during the window of opportunity following World War II will spread all over the world and be forced to live in similar sacrificial environments. These conservative leaders also decided on an interdenominational work rather than an institute aligned with the Christian and Missionary Alliance.
12. The Faith Years/ Depression Expansion (see page 399)	35-45	Spiritual, Ministerial and Strategic Formation-- Like Jaffray, Maxwell expanded in depression years. God faithfully honored the no-debt policy.
13. Life Message Consolidation (see page 400)	40	Spiritual/ Ministerial--Maxwell's teaching on the Christian life broke forth with increased maturity in his development of the Law and Grace course which he began to teach at age 40.
14. Educational Stand/ Forms Prairie High School/ (see page 402)	42	Strategic--Maxwell's prophetic bent was highlighted in his stand backing J. F. Kirk which eventually led to the formation of Prairie High School. This institution would later be used by many to overcome educational deficiencies prior to entering the Bible School.

Chapter 9. L. E. Maxwell (1895-1984) page 427

Table 9-2 Listing Of Some Critical Incidents In Maxwell's Life continued

Incident(s) Name	Age	Formational Type Dealing With Basic Value/Thrust
15. Spring Conference '41/ Oscar Lowry (see page 402)	46	Spiritual/ Ministerial--Leaders and institutions both need a-periodic renewals in which God breaks in with an unusual intervention and challenges, reaffirms, and brings renewal which gives new life. Oscar Lowry's preaching which brought revival was just such a moment. Without it perhaps there would have been an institutional time of plateauing and/or such a time in Maxwell's life.
16. Window of Opportunity (see page 407)	50-54	Strategic--Following the tremendous tragic fall out from World War II was an unprecedented Window of Opportunity for mobilizing young people and returned veterans into missionary service. Maxwell and Prairie sensed this window and took advantage of it, responding to God's challenge. The explosive decade followed in which Prairie Bible Institute began to send missionaries around the globe.
17. Philip Howard/ Divine Contact/ Result: **Born Crucified** (see page 408)	50	Ministerial/ Strategic--Maxwell responds to an influence-mix challenge which personally expands his indirect sphere of influence and provides a spark to recruit many to Prairie to get this message first hand.
18. Miracle at Three Hills (see page 409)	52	Strategic--The publicity associated with this secular media push brought in more recruits and was part of the expansion that formed the explosive decade. This was a sovereign act of God. Maxwell could not have orchestrated it.
19. Conflict/ Introduction to Leadership Transition to Come/ (see page 409)	62	Spiritual/ Strategic-Part of the leadership transition that would be necessary for Maxwell is stimulated by this time of conflict. It is one of many similar kinds of problems which lead to the influence reversal challenge which step-by-step removes Maxwell from various leadership responsibilities.
20. Isolation/ Dark Night (see page 412)	71	Spiritual--In order to finish well Maxwell must go through some difficulty family processing and physical suffering. His concept of the Victorious Life will be tested in the latter stages of his life.

Critical incidents 5 and 6 are prime incidents--one a strategic incident and the other a focal value. On these two incidents hinge Maxwell's whole ministry at Prairie Bible Institute. Incidents 4 and 7 are secondary prime incidents--they were links in the strategic guidance. I am going to eliminate comment on critical incidents. They are fairly straightforward and I want to spend more space on the section involving lessons from his life.

Chapter 9. L. E. Maxwell (1895-1984)

Interpretive Insights--Implications for Values

Spaulding, in Part II, Analysis of Patterns and Themes, spends five chapters, the longest section of the dissertation, in analyzing the strengths and weaknesses in Maxwell's leadership. These chapters yield valuable information for leadership lessons and implications for values. Tables 9-3, 9-4, 9-5, 9-6, and 9-7 summarize the important lessons seen from these important interpretive chapters, the strength of the dissertation.

Table 9-3 Warnings and Lessons From Maxwell's Life

These lessons are written, today, with much hindsight and the value of comparative study of many, many leadership cases. Were we to live in Maxwell's time, we would probably have faced and perhaps reacted much as he did without the discovery of these important lessons, warnings, and implications for values.[39] I state the lessons and warnings from the positive standpoint.

Chapter	Title	Statement of Lessons
5	Negative Patterns	1. **OVERALL BALANCE** A leader must learn to prioritize the three major responsibilities of God, family, and ministry to fit the dynamics of the situation.[40]
5	Negative Patterns	2. **BURNOUT AVOIDANCE** A strong leader with a strong work ethic must balance overwork tendencies with isolation from ministry experiences: either vacation, planned recreation, or spiritual disciplines involving solitude and silence. To avoid this balance is to chance nervous breakdown, physical burn-out, or eventual removal from ministry.[41]
5	Negative Patterns	3. **DELEGATION** A strong leader must learn to select, train, and delegate leadership responsibilities as the ministry

---

[39] I have summarized these lessons from the major sections of the chapters. I do not know if Spaulding would concur with my interpretive statement of the lessons. His descriptions of the situations certainly allow for these interpretations, even if he, himself, might not state them this way.

[40] Some experts recommend a fixed order of God first, family second, and ministry third. Maxwell dominantly followed a pattern of God first, ministry second, and family third. Or more properly he focused on ministry and assumed his wife would focus on family. I am suggesting here that once a committal has been made which sees God first in all things then family and ministry will vie for time. Depending on a discerning of God's will in a dynamic situation a leader may put family first or ministry first depending on the needs of either--whichever are demanding. Over a period of time these will probably oscillate depending on needs. A major factor involved includes the choice of social base pattern. L.E. and Pearl Maxwell were operating in the basic release pattern which was common to those days. Typically, in those days, this meant that the male almost abdicated responsibility for the family to focus on ministry. This was usually fraught with problems for the children growing up. Such was the case with the Maxwell family according to Spaulding's analysis.

[41] Spaulding (1991b:99) identifies three major episodes of temporary setting aside from ministry due to some sort of breakdown in the first 13 years. He implies that other incidents may have happened also. Maxwell took up a strong physical regimen after one of them. His lifelong habits of vigorous exercise probably prevented further incidents. Though it appears to me that there was lacking a proper balance between overwork in ministry things and relief from ministry.

Chapter 9. L. E. Maxwell (1895-1984)   page 429

Table 9-3 Warnings and Lessons From Maxwell's Life continued

		grows rather than over engage in every activity and function of the ministry.
5.	Negative Patterns	4. **PRE-SERVICE**[42] **IMBALANCE** A leader involved in training must move with deliberateness toward a balanced model of learning.[43]
5.	Negative Patterns	5. **IMBALANCE TENDENCIES** Crusades for truth sake often go to extremes which in turn lead to over emphases which miss truth.[44]

Spaulding describes in a succinct paragraph tendencies toward imbalance in seven areas.

> L.E.'s most popular maxim was "Maxwell 1:1--The hardest thing in the world is to keep balanced." This stood him in good stead as I will point out in his greater life's work. But one man's balance is another man's excess. While Maxwell's balance derived from a stubborn insistence on inductively derived biblical values, several areas of emphasis which he stressed seem "over-balanced" from this perspective and time. I address here his avowed anti-intellectualism, his militant fundamentalism, the pedagogical training model, a theology which encouraged legalism or "misled crucifixions," a weak human Christology, a lack of strategic missiology (cultural/contextual), and a hermeneutic which was silent on many social issues. While this appears to be a formidable list of theological weaknesses, it is my conviction that they are far outweighed by his spiritual and theological strengths (Spaulding 1991b:105).

In chapter six, Spaulding exposes these imbalances--"the theological weaknesses."[45] In chapters seven, eight, and nine he offsets these negative emphases by highlighting the "spiritual and theological strengths." Rather than commentary on these imbalances in detail I will simply identify them and point out the most important lesson. I think the most important thing we can learn concerns balance. We can not afford to neglect truth simply because it is abused. Intellectualism in Maxwell's day often tended toward liberalism. But anti-intellectualism which excluded any truth discovered by intellectuals was not the

---

[42] Training can be categorized (Clinton 1984) in terms of **when** with respect to use of input. *Pre-service* refers to training which is given prior to use of input. It is training that hopefully anticipates use in the future. Such teaching often lacks dynamic reflection and experience which bring closure to learning.
[43] Maxwell was pedagogically oriented (teacher-oriented, teacher-based methodology). As the school grew in numbers the teaching became more input oriented with less chance for dynamic reflection or experience of the concepts in practice. Formation was toward inner character only and lacked ministerial formation and strategic formation. See the balanced learning model (input, formation, dynamic reflection, experience), called Holland's Two-Track analogy in Clinton (1984) **Leadership Training Models**.
[44] Maxwell lived during the time of the major battles between liberals and fundamentalists. He came down on the side of the fundamentalists. His position, while strongly advocating an authoritative Word of God often lacked a thoroughness of intellectual pursuit of truth and a tendency toward separation even from whatever good might be in other positions.
[45] Of all the biographical materials studied on the characters treated in chapters 2-9, Spaulding's analysis is the most candid in terms of the negative as well as the positive. Yet, while treating the negative, he does so with an excellent bent which seeks to learn rather than criticize. And he points out as well the strengths of the man's life as well as the weaknesses. His biographical analysis follows the more modern approach of the 80s and 90s which tends to paint the picture "warts and all." And it carries with it the accompanying credibility.

answer. Such a position led to imbalances in other areas for Maxwell. Table 9-4 lists Spaulding's identification of imbalances.

Table 9-4 Imbalance Tendencies in Maxwell's Life

Area of Imbalance	Tendency
1. Pedagogical	Tended toward imbalance often seen in centralized residential programmatic training--over stresses input from a pedagogical (teacher-only directed position). Lacks andragogical emphasis (learner directed aspect).
2. Anti-intellectualism	Avoided truth found in liberal positions. Crusaded against higher education.[46]
3. Militant Fundamentalism	Strong separatistic tendency aided a rift between conservatives and more mainline groups, many of which had significant numbers of believers.
4. Legalisms	Application of the deeper life message in a centralized residential context with dominantly pre-service students frequently led to "pharasaic legalisms on the one hand and morose introspections on the other" (Spaulding 1991b:108).
5. Christology	Fundamentalism as a whole, to counter the liberal tendency to downplay the deity of Christ, in turn tended to de-emphasize the humanity of Christ. Maxwell was no exception.
6. Non-strategic Missiology	Maxwell while stressing a strong mission emphasis, from the standpoint of call fulfilling the great commission, did not concern himself with the science of missions. Spiritual preparation for missions was the emphasis. Anthropological and cross-cultural issues as well as the complexity of the mission task were not highlighted.
7. Abuse of Gifting	Maxwell used his position of influence and prophetical voice to denounce many in the various publications which came from Prairie. His strong words often made enemies. His strong prophetical stands, however, did not address the social injustices of his times but usually focused on the fundamentalists/ liberal debate.[47]

Spaulding gives a final summary in his chapter on negative patterns which brings an ameliorating balance to this negative critique.

---

[46]In later years, T. S. Rendall helped overcome this imbalance. His intellectual honesty had the credibility of one who followed hard after God, was loyal to Maxwell, and yet profited from truth where ever it was found.

[47]Spaulding (1991b:113) comments on Maxwell's own recognition of his misuse of tongue and his lifelong approach to correction of its abuse. "Happily, his misuse of the tongue, which had become his powerful weapon for good, was something for which L.E. had no patience. He corrected himself all through life until in his old age, he was a completely mellowed man. He demonstrated a learner's posture in these weaknesses and faults and was the better for it in the end."

Chapter 9. L. E. Maxwell (1895-1984)

It is likely unfair to judge a man for theological leanings which reflect the exigencies of his time. It is also difficult to substantiate the essential wrongness of a style of leadership for which he had no other alternative exposure. For this reason it would be well to stress his own family neglect and the abuse of his power of speech as the dominant negative patterns in his life. It is worthy of note that even with his family, L.E. acted out of ignorance more than calloused neglect (Spaulding 1991b:113).[48]

In one of the stronger chapters of analysis, Spaulding describes the powerful model for good that Maxwell was. Table 9-5 captures the essence of his modeling represented by a coined epigram:

> The life of Jesus Christ was central to the life of Maxwell. As I have examined the patterns and "integrated life message" of the man, I have coined the following descriptive epigram: The CHARACTER of Christ, brought about in the life by the CROSS of Christ, for the fulfilling of the COMMISSION and COMMAND of Christ, from within the COMMUNITY of Christ. Each of these components seem to me to be integral to Maxwell's overall "life bent." (Spaulding 1991b:114)

Table 9-5 Maxwell's Modeling

Category of Modeling	Qualities Seen/ Realization
Character of Christ	Passion for Life, Obedient Servanthood, Habits of Personal Discipline, Commitment to the Word, Active Faith, Personal Holiness, Passion for People, Tenderness to the Spirit Humility, Simple Lifestyle Godly Authority
Cross of Christ	Demonstrated living reality of dying daily that the life of Jesus would be manifested (2 Corinthians 4:11)
Commission of Christ	The Great Commission was a central theme as seen in: 1. Friday night young people's missionary meetings, 2. annual pre-graduation conference, 3. curriculum of Bible school, 4. printed matter coming out of Prairie.
Community of Christ	The almost isolated centralized resident institution allowed: 1. demonstration of interdependence, 2. demonstration of teamwork, 3. demonstration of mutual support, 4. demonstration of communication, 5. Mentor-modeling with and for students.

---

[48]Spaulding (1991b:113) goes on to give an illustration of this opinion. "He was accompanying his son, Paul, on a family counseling seminar on one occasion in the latter years of his life. After Paul had completed his teaching, L.E. confided in him his own bewilderment with the question: 'Is that the way it should have happened?' Shaken by the possibility that he really had failed his family, it was evident that L.E. was not even fully aware of his wrongdoing in this area as it occurred. Nevertheless it stands as one criticism against an entire era that the fathers and ministers lacked genuine sensitivity to their wives' and children's needs for them."

Chapter 9. L. E. Maxwell (1895-1984)   page 432

Spaulding captures the essence of Maxwell's educational/ training philosophy in five components (1991b:135-150). Maxwell was a product of the Bible school movement. This forever flavored his approach to training.

> The training method or educational philosophy of L. E. Maxwell was basic. In a period in which the seminaries were failing to produce missionaries for an unprecedented world harvest, L.E. was proud to announce that Prairie Bible Institute offered the most basic, simple missionary training method possible. This he could do partly because of the context in which he found himself in Western Canada. His own background also dictated a simplicity and rather utilitarian, pedagogical, that is, teacher-focused approach to missionary training (Spaulding 1991b:135).

Table 9-6 Maxwell's Educational Philosophy--5 Components

Component	Explanation
1. Atmosphere--Spiritual Encounter	Maxwell felt that an individual was ill-equipped for any serious ministry if he/she had not met God in a deep and transforming way--beyond the experience of conversion. To him it was the experience of dying to the self life and being renewed for fruitful service in an entirely new awareness of one's identity in Christ's death, resurrection and present ascended Person. Maxwell cherished the moving of the Holy Spirit among the students and gladly canceled classes when there was the genuine appearance of revival. Sometimes class sessions became times of group prayer, intercession, confession of sin, in short--mini-revivals. Meeting with God in a life changing experience was a dominant factor in Maxwell's educational philosophy. All of curriculum and activities supported this notion and carried an ambiance of spiritual encounter (Spaulding 1991b:139,140).
2. Curriculum--Inductive Bible Study	The inductive method of the study of Scripture was the backbone of the curriculum. This was a streamlined, non-scholarly, inductive study method, which used search questions and spanned the entirety of Scripture. This method forced the student to interact directly with the Scriptures, themselves, regardless of any predisposed particular theological grid the student may have begun with (Spaulding 1991b:140).
3. Mission--the World Challenge	Prairie was an institution that mobilized for mission. Evangelistic extension ministries, mandatory weekly missionary meetings, daily missions prayer groups, annual missionary conferences (the highlight of the year), regular missions course, and visiting

Table 9-6 Maxwell's Educational Philosophy--5 Components continued

Component	Explanation
	missionaries all brought strong focus on mobilization for mission.[49] (Spaulding 1991b:141-143)
4. Soldierly Discipline	The military ethos common to the era was imposed on a Bible institute in rural Canada. It was sensible and highly productive. The soldier motif of Scripture and Spiritual Warfare were part of the ethos of the school. Living conditions were Spartan. Dress and social standards were parallel to military standards but provided structure and discipline for a more focused, undistracted time of study, worship and training. Student gratis work and required ministry assignments were further means of imposing external discipline. Imposed times for eating, sleeping, personal quiet time, study hours and worship were all part of the rigorous, military style of stripping the self of needless independence and rebellion (Spaulding 1991b:143,144).
5. Structure: Committed Community	The school evolved from a family to an institution. Hence it became a residential, extractive, full-time, rural institution basically isolated from the world. It was a non-parish, para-church with a non-denominational church for the students and staff on campus. In short, it was a sodality model of a 20th century Protestant monastery. The community was autonomous, self-supporting like the Hutterite townships in the same region. It was monastic in its self-imposed disciplines, regimentation of social life, dress standards, eating, sleeping, working, studying and worshipping times. Its overall ambiance of spiritual encounter and the engendering of inner spiritual renewal--with a goal for missionary outreach--is a close approximation to the early Celtic missionary monasteries which were the center which radiated out to reach Europe. As a training methodology, the isolated, military-style Bible school was highly effective in the war years of the mid-century. It was seen as time away, a kind of self-imposed isolation for serious study and encounters with God for the crafting of fruitful workers in the difficult fields of the world (Spaulding 1991b:145,146).

Spaulding in seeking to assess Maxwell's ministry philosophy first identified an overall umbrella statement (see boldfaced portion below) which he further explained. This

---

[49] Spaulding notes (1991b:143) that, "At the peak of Prairie's highlight years in the 1950s, the school was putting out at least five percent of the entire Protestant missionary force from North America. Though the following is more of an exception than a rule, fully eighty percent of the members of the class of 1949 [the early part of the Window of Opportunity] were in full time mission work overseas within three years of their graduation. Percentages for each year of this period are not accessible, yet it is certain that at its best, Prairie was putting out about thirty-five percent of its alumni into foreign missionary service. Another large percentage were entering pastorates all over North America."

Chapter 9. L. E. Maxwell (1895-1984)

explanation provides the foundation out of which ministry values were identified and articulated. Table 9-7 labels some of the more important ministry philosophy components.

> I now offer a summary of those elements in L.E. Maxwell's expressed thought and active ministry (those ideas, values and principles) which were evident guidelines for his decision-making processes, his exercise of influence and his own ministry evaluation.
>
> ...
>
> L.E. Maxwell's own philosophy of ministry may not have been articulated as such in one formula. It is without doubt that his was a philosophy which derived directly from his "model life" and personal life message. I have perceived his model life consisting of: **The CHARACTER of Christ, brought about in the life by the CROSS of Christ, for the fulfilling of the COMMISSION and COMMAND of Christ, from within the COMMUNITY of Christ.** Each of these components seem to me to be integral to Maxwell's overall "life bent."
>
> From this character and whole-life-style base came the teaching content and training methodology which L. E. Maxwell implemented without significant structural change for five decades.
>
> The cross of Christ was central to his life message and teaching. The cross as a focal point of the life of the believer is understood as an experience which the individual must undergo both by way of crisis and in daily living for entrance into a level of victory in the Christian life. Maxwell's rendition of this life is best expressed in his books, **Born Crucified** and **Crowded to Christ**.
>
> The character of Christ was what he ultimately desired within his own life and those of his followers, knowing that all other issues would stand or fall upon this one. The development of this character was based largely on his utter commitment to the Scriptures as normative for Christian experience.
>
> Once the believer was rooted in the Scriptures, and having experienced the work of the cross of Christ in a transformation of the will in surrender to God's will, a new communication of truth in boldness merged, rooted also in the experience of deep interaction with the Spirit of God.
>
> The cause into which all these spiritual energies were to flow was the fulfillment of the Great Commission and Command of Christ. This mandate was, like the character of Christ, rooted in a full understanding of the Scriptures and obedient application to the life (Spaulding 1991b:185,186).

This driving force in Maxwell's life expressed itself in the institutional life of Prairie.

Table 9-7 Significant Elements of Maxwell's Ministry Philosophy

Philosophical Value	Further Explanation
Scripture as normative.	The Word of God was seen as a powerful, living active Word which was the final authority in all matters of decision-making for individual and institute alike. The Bible remained central to curriculum, preaching, teaching and living at the school (Spaulding 1991b:187,188).
Faith as risk.	God can be trusted to intervene in his work. Prairie would be a place that would never survive unless "God came through." (Spaulding 1991b:188,189).
Guidance as situational.	In addition to the efficacy of the written word Maxwell believed in the dynamic presence and leading power of the

Chapter 9. L. E. Maxwell (1895-1984)

Table 9-7 Significant Elements of Maxwell's Ministry Philosophy continued

Philosophical Value	Further Explanation
	Spirit of God to speak specifically into a situation needing specific direction. God's answer was available for each situation. This contrasted to the dispensational dampening of the work of the Spirit held to in those days. L.E. had a more "charismatic" understanding and experience of guidance as directed through the immanence of the Holy Spirit in conjunction with the listening of the Bible-informed believer (Spaulding 1991b:189,190).
Character development as Primal	Maxwell stressed development of character as a primary thrust of training (Spaulding 1991b:189,190).
Leadership development as servanthood	"God's way up is down." To learn submission to the will of God, often through a crisis of wills on the human or organizational level, was a secret to effectiveness in leadership. The realization of union life (the crucified life) was a prerequisite to servant leadership (Spaulding 1991b:190, 191).
Trust God for finances	Maxwell's early experiences taught him that both personally and institutionally God could be trusted to provide finances to meet needs. He committed himself to a simple lifestyle, gave heavily to missions, and saw God provide needs (Spaulding 1991b:191).
Train primarily for missions	Maxwell was committed to training primarily for missions rather than the pastorate. Pioneer missionaries were needed who could live in poverty countries in hard conditions (Spaulding 1991b:191).
Women in ministry	Maxwell was committed to the promotion of women in ministry and defending his position from Scripture, history, and pragmatics (Spaulding 1991b:191).
Boldness in ministry	Maxwell understood the Spirit's anointing on a life that was identified with Christ and which engages the enemy in conflict. His personal life was legendary in its bold denunciation of evil and authoritative calling of individuals to complete submission. He operated in gifted power (Spaulding 1991b:194).
Balance	Maxwell would rather hold conflicting texts in tension with unresolved finality than to choose one group of texts at the expense of wresting a meaning. It was a balance which drew the respect of students from many divergent denominational backgrounds and drew the criticism of those to whom he sought to bring correction in their stilted positions (Spaulding 1991b:195,196).

Chapter 9. L. E. Maxwell (1895-1984)   page 436

Spaulding concludes his chapter on Maxwell's ministry philosophy by noting his over emphasis on spiritual formation resulting in a lack of ministerial and strategic formation including a glaring lack in emphasis on Christian leadership issues. He counter balances this by pointing out that Maxwell was responsible for the missionary training of a large and highly effective group of North American missionaries over half a century.

Contributions

This chapter contributes to the general field of leadership development in the following ways:

1. This study depicts a leader who had an integrative life message which resulted from a combination of three factors: (1) the successful internalization of God's sovereign processing toward union life in his early development; (2) the articulation of this process and entry into union or "deeper life" in a well-formulated creedo, amplified through writings, mentoring, teachings and other leadership influences; (3) the application of this articulated life orientation to his ministry situation and leadership methodology. In short, this chapter shows a highly focused leader whose life purpose was encapsulated in a life message which greatly accelerated a narrow focused life.
2. This study depicts a leader who took advantage of the Window of Opportunity just after World War II and mobilized almost a 1000 leaders into missionary effort.

In addition to the ultimate contribution set, which I will describe later, Maxwell had at least the following specific contributions to the cause of Christ and the on-going of the Christian movement:

1. He (along with J. Fergus Kirk) founded Prairie Bible Institute, which became a major center for mobilizing young people into ministry. He was its principal for 55 years.
2. He motivated many through his writings and speaking ministries, both on radio and in person, to make life changing decisions either to enter into a life of Victory or to go into ministry--many of them to the mission field.
3. He taught many students over a period of 58 years the basics of Pauline, Petrine, and Johannine literature as well a courses on evangelism, missions, homiletics, doctrine, Christian living, and ministry.
4. He was the public rhetorician for the Prairie Tabernacle for 55 years and hence modeled for students a public ministry that had impact.
5. He contributed greatly to the on-going of two major movements: Victorious Christian living via the identification/ death/ life message of Romans; missions. He traveled widely in North America and overseas as a highly respected teacher and preacher, contributing significantly to the spiritual renewal and missionary mobilization of the mid-20th century.
6. He took advantage of the window of opportunity just after World War II to challenge, recruit, train and mobilize hundreds to the mission field.
7. His evangelistic efforts and radio and writing ministries had a direct influence on the spiritual and social climate of the western Canadian provinces.

Overall Lessons from the Life

From Maxwell we learn of the importance of developing a ministry which flows with the contextual pressures and utilizes them to enhance ministry. His Bible institute was

Chapter 9. L. E. Maxwell (1895-1984)   page 437

part of a movement which sought to hold onto conservative values. Its rugged discipline fit the rural region of which it was a part as well as the soldier-like mentality of the times.

We also recognize that when a life purpose becomes clearly enunciated in a life message which encapsulates that purpose then there will be a high degree of focus in the life.

He shows the dangers of a ministry which is not balanced. He was concerned with balance in doctrine and Christian life but lacked an emphasis on balance of the three major elements of family, God, and ministry. I have suggested elsewhere that all are equally important and that situational dynamics may at a given time force prioritization of one over the other. But over time each will have dominance at one time or other. In value, if not in time, God will be prioritized over all else.

He shows the challenges to finishing well that come in mid-and late life. Usually convictions and character are formed early in life and tested as to validity and persistence in middle life. Having stood the test of time they usually blossom in the end game. Maxwell was sorely tried in the end game with deep processing. He is a leader who persisted well in latter testing.

Implications for a Focused Life

What have we learned from this life that helps us understand a focused life? That is the question I attempt to answer in this section. When we study a focused life we are in fact looking for a number of issues. Below I comment on a number of factors that can affect focus in a life. I weigh them relatively speaking in terms of their effect of Maxwell's focused life.

1. Giftedness Development[50]

Giftedness played a very important role in focusing Maxwell. His spiritual gifts developed very rapidly once he went into full time ministry. He operated in gifted power almost from the start. Spiritual gifts were the focal element of the set. And teaching was the dominant spiritual gift of the gift-mix. Note the faith gift. This was significant in the development of the institution, particularly in the depression years.

---

[50]The following is a pictorial diagram, called a Venn Diagram, of his giftedness set. See Appendix F for an explanation of how to interpret it. Like McQuilkin, his faith gift was important.

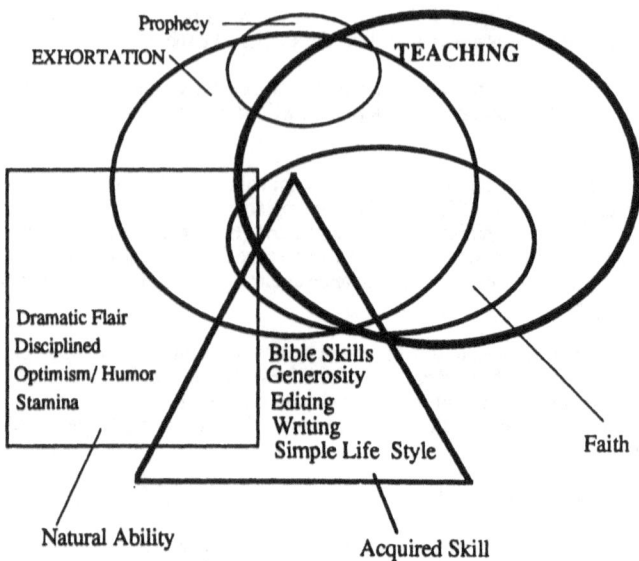

2. Destiny Processing

Though relatively unimportant in determining focus, this factor did bring strong affirmation of that focus as it developed.

3. Identification of Key Ministry Insights

Apart from the major ministry insight of a Bible institute and its power for mobilizing people into missions and the inductive Bible study method, ministry insights with paradigm breakthroughs were not so significant. The use of an annual Conference as a focal point for motivation and mobilizing for missions probably was a ministry insight for Maxwell. Conferences at Prairie down through the years were powerfully used to bring renewal as well as motivate and mobilize for missions. Many commitments were made at these annual events.

4. Identification Of Major Values That Uniquely Fit One's Ministry

The crucified life, first learned through "Daddy Stevens" and Dorothy Miller at the Midland Bible Institute became the dominant value of his ministry and the kingpin of his life message. A second value came through his observation of the Methodist woman preacher who dramatized her message so as to emphatically strike her audience. Maxwell's teaching approach allowed for use of methodology which would communicate with impact--including all kinds of acting, body language, and platform movement.

5. **Integration Of Personality Factors So As To Identify A Focused Or Ideal Role That Moves Toward Convergence**

While his personality, was probably tied to his giftedness in teaching, there were no special focusing that came because of personality.

6. **Social Base Processing**

There was a lack in the area of social base processing. Maxwell generally prioritized ministry above family, or rather relegated family matters to his wife.

7. **Ultimate Contribution Set**

In addition to the specific contributions already mentioned L.E. Maxwell's ultimate contribution set profile looks as follows.[51]

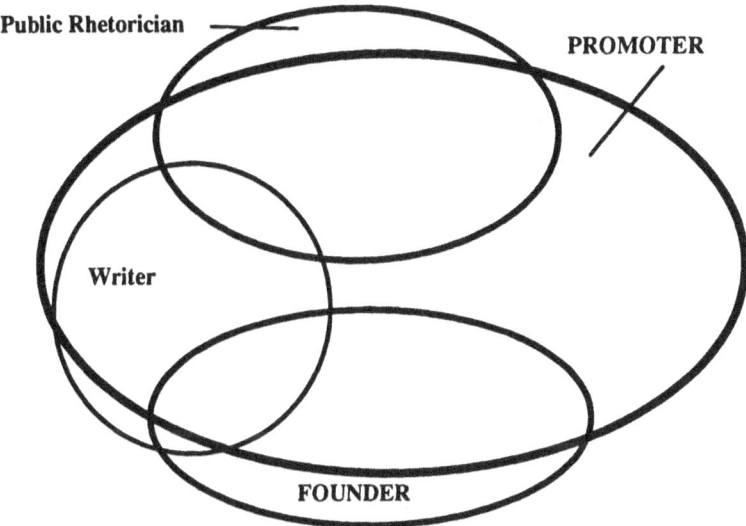

Maxwell was a powerful **promoter**. He promoted most powerfully the crucified life (union life message) and the cause of missions. One of his powerful means of promotion was via his role as a **public rhetorician**. He traveled widely in Canada, the U.S.A. and on several mission fields. His pastoral role at the tabernacle also allowed for this ultimate contribution. Many individuals made commitments and had transformed lives as a result of his public ministry. His speaking ministry was effective. As a **writer** he primarily promoted the crucified life. His major books, **Born Crucified** and **Crowded to Christ** enjoyed wide exposure and are still having impact today. And most significantly he **founded** a Bible institute which became a mobilization center for missions. Prairie Bible Institute still exists today. While making major moves toward

---

[51]This pictorial diagram, called a Venn Diagram, relates the elements in terms of importance (size) and location (central being more focused). See Appendix F for an explanation of how to interpret.

Chapter 9. L. E. Maxwell (1895-1984) page 440

relevant ministry in its present day context, it still has a number of Maxwell's core values at its heart.

8. Ministry Philosophy Concepts

I have commented in depth on some of the elements of Maxwell's ministry philosophy (see Tables 9-6 and 9-7). Ministry philosophy was very important in integrating Maxwell's life purpose and life message into an institutional setting.

9. Future Perfect Time Paradigm

This was not a significant factor in Maxwell's life in bringing focus.

10. Boundary Processing Which Helped Focus

This was not a significant factor in Maxwell's life in bringing focus.

11. Paradigm Shifts Which Helped Focus

This was not a significant factor in Maxwell's life in bringing focus.

12. Window of Opportunity

Along with Henrietta Mears, Maxwell stands out as a person who took advantage of the window of opportunity that took place just after World War II. In just over a decade the output of Prairie Bible Institute graduates who were on the mission field jumped from 300 to over 1200. The period taxed the facilities to the limits. Constant new buildings had to be erected, by faith in accordance with the debt free policy. God greatly challenged and blessed Maxwells positive response to this window of opportunity. Prairie graduates have made their mark on the course of missions around the world.

SUMMARY ON FOCUSED LIFE INSIGHTS FROM MAXWELL'S LIFE

Let me summarize what we have learned about a focused life from Maxwell.

A focused life is
- a life dedicated to exclusively carrying out God's unique purposes through it,
- by identifying the focal issues, that is, the **major role, life purpose, unique methodology,** or **ultimate contribution**,[52] which allows
- an **increasing prioritization** of life's activities around the focal issues, and
- results in a satisfying life of being and doing.

All four of the focal issues played an important part in Maxwell's life. **Life purpose**, the motivation of many to enter the crucified life and the mobilization of many onto the mission field, dominated his life.

---

[52] These four--*major role, life purpose, unique methodology,* or *ultimate contribution*--are called the *focal issues.* Usually one or more of them dominates a focused life. A number of other factors (like giftedness, ministry insights, sense of destiny, etc.), called focal screens, contribute to the divine guidance which helps these leaders to prioritize life's activities around the focal issues. Both the identification of focal issues and the processes that prioritized them are given in the studies of the eight chosen for this book. As the book has developed the 12 screens have been grouped into four major pointers. I present this in the final chapter.

Chapter 9. L. E. Maxwell (1895-1984) page 441

His **major role** which included head of the Bible institute, the dominant teacher in it, and traveling public rhetorician in behalf of victorious living and missions allowed for the fulfilling of life purpose. His Bible Institute as a mobilizing center was the unique methodology he used both for mobilizing missionaries and for challenging into the victorious life. Four of the **ultimate contribution** set fit him. They each were a significant part of his focus: Promoter, Founder, Writer, and Public Rhetorician. All were related to the life purpose and supported it.

There was a natural order of development. He first experienced the power of his **unique methodology**--the use of a Bible institute as a mobilizing force. It was during this exposure to his unique methodology that he, himself, experienced the power of the crucified life and the need to take this message to a lost world. Thus his **life purpose** was first experienced and then later clarified and articulated. **Major role** came third and enhanced the two fold life purpose--moving people into the victorious life paradigm and mobilizing them for the mission field. Finally, as his unique methodology developed into a permanent institution, Maxwell more clearly saw it as a major legacy he would leave behind--an **Ultimate contribution.**

Closure--Let's Really Remember Leslie Earl Maxwell

Well, I have attempted to apply the Hebrews 13:7,8 leadership mandate.

Remember your former leaders. Think back on how they lived and ministered. Imitate those **excellent qualities** you see in their lives. For Jesus Christ is the same today, as He was in the past and as He will be in the future. What He did for them He will do for you to inspire and enable your leadership.
Hebrews 13:7,8 (Personal Interpretive Paraphrase)

We have remembered Maxwell! But what challenges from his life do we take away for our own? Let me suggest two!

His life compels us to:

1. Explicitly challenge, with expectant power, people to enter into the Victorious life. The *crucified with Christ message* as a life process is desperately needed today as it was in Maxwell's 50 plus years of ministry.

2. Maxwell especially challenges us to recognize and use methodology which flows with the contextual forces of our times, in order to enhance our ministry.

His type of Bible Institute in a rural setting where conservative, disciplined, hard working people lived was relevant for its time, its location, and the tremendous opportunities that beckoned. What we need to do is find the ministry structures that fit our times and will allow us to take advantage of the great window of opportunity that is opening to us.

Probably the most important thing learned about the focused life from this study on Maxwell concerns life purpose. Life purpose can so be clarified as to be reduced to a **life message**. The clearer is the life message, the more intense is the focus of the life. Spaulding coined the phrase, *life message*. He also identified that life message for

Chapter 9. L. E. Maxwell (1895-1984)   page 442

Maxwell. Succinctly stated it is: **The CHARACTER of Christ, is brought about in the life by the CROSS of Christ, for the fulfilling of the COMMISSION and COMMAND of Christ, from within the COMMUNITY of Christ.**

WHAT IS YOUR LIFE MESSAGE?

Where To Go and What To Do For Further Study

The following are important works about Prairie Bible Institute, about Maxwell or by Maxwell. At this point no biography has been published. One suggestion for follow-up, perhaps a remote one, is simply, why not visit Prairie Bible Institute today and catch its changing ambiance which is yet rooted in many of Maxwell's values?

Bibliography

Callaway, Bernice
1973   **Legacy--The Moving Saga of Our Prairie Pioneers.** Canada: MacCall Clan.

Epp, Margaret
1973   **Into All the World--The missionary Of Prairie Bible Institute.** Three Hills, Alberta: Prairie Press.

Keller, Phillip W.
1966   **Expendable!** Three Hills, Alberta: Prairie Press.

Kirk, Hector A.
1966   **With God on the Prairies: The Miracle of Prairie Bible Institute.** Three Hills, Alberta: Prairie Press.

Maxwell, Leslie
1945   **Born Crucified.** Chicago: Moody Press.

1950   **Crowded to Christ.** Grand Rapids: William B. Eerdmans Publishing Company.

1955   **Abandoned To Christ.** Grand Rapids: William B. Eerdmans Publishing Company.

Schaufelberg, Jeanne
1984   *A Comparative Study of the Doctrine of the Christian Life as Set Forth By Dr. Robert C. McQuilkin and Reverend Leslie E. Maxwell.* Unpublished Master's thesis. Columbia, S.C.: Columbia Bible College.

Spaulding, Stephen Maxwell
1991a   *A Leadership Emergence Study of L.E. Maxwell.* Unpublished case study. Pasadena: School of World Mission.

1991b   **Lion On the Prairies: An Interpretive Analysis of The Life and Leadership of Leslie Earl Maxwell, 1895-1984.** Unpublished pre-doctoral dissertation. Pasadena: School of World Mission.

Chapter 9. L. E. Maxwell (1895-1984) — page 443

Timeline

ROOTS		DEATH			TO THE SOIL	
1895	1915	1922	1931	1944	1950	1960	1984
Age	20	27	36	49	55	65	88

1895–1922 (ROOTS)
- A. Rugged Youth (1895-1915)
- B. Accelerated Ministry Preparation (1915-1922)

1922–1944 (DEATH)
- A. Arena for Faith (1922-1931)
- B. Drawing of Boundaries (1931-1944)

1944–1960
- A. Highlights Amid Losses (1944-1950)
- B. The Explosive Decade (1950-1960)

1960–1984 (TO THE SOIL)
- A. Internal Crises (1960-1966)
- B. Mellowed Teacher (1966-1980)
- C. Final Testings (1980-1984)

Checkpoints

- C1 Heritage Prayer/ Two Grandfathers/ Aunt Christina
- C2 Destiny Preparation/ Ernest's death/ Methodist Preachers/Monarch Vision
- C3 Conversion Age 20
- C4 Divine Contact, Baptist Pastor, Moody Graduate links to Daddy Stevens Timing/Dad's Death Age 24
- C5 Daddy Stevens/Mentor/ Unique Methodology/ Bible School/ Inductive Study Method Unique Message/ The Normal Christian Life/ Mission Minded Life Purpose, Age 24-27
- C6 Brokenness/ Restoration Age 27
- C7 The Call--Kirk's Plea, Age 27 Partnership Kirk Family
- C8 Prophetic Word/ Pearl, Age 27
- C9 Integrity Check/ Age 28 Strategic Guidance
- C10 Planned Poverty Age 28
- C11 Three Hills? Age 29,
- C12 The Faith Years Age 35-45 Depression Expansion
- C13 Life Message Consolidation
- C14 Educational Stand Prairie H.S. Age 42
- C15 Spring Conference, 1941 Age 46 Oscar Lowery, Revival
- C16 Window of Opportunity, Age 50-54
- C17 Philip Howard, Age 50 Born Crucified
- C18 Miracle at Three Hills Age 52
- C19 Conflict Age 62
- C20 Isolation/ Dark Night Age 71

Chapter 10. Focal Findings

> Remember your former leaders. Think back on how they lived and ministered. Imitate those **excellent qualities** you see in their lives. For Jesus Christ is the same today, as He was in the past and as He will be in the future. What He did for them He will do for you to inspire and enable your leadership.
> **Hebrews 13:7,8** (Personal Interpretive Paraphrase)

We have remembered eight great leaders who led very focused lives. Without doubt they qualify as Hebrews 13:7 *faith leaders* whose excellent qualities should be emulated. We have remembered each **individually**--long chapters on each life. Now we want to remember them **comparatively**. Having seen each of these focused lives, now what observations can we make by comparing and contrasting our findings across all eight?

I will group my findings--observations, lessons, and other concepts--under four headings:

1. **Comparative Analysis,**
2. **Clarification of Focused Life Concepts,**
3. **Miscellaneous Observations,**
4. **Challenges.**

COMPARATIVE ANALYSIS

I have been looking at the concept of focus in the life. Several comparisons are worth considering, all of which touch on basic issues of the focused life. How does giftedness affect focus? What important lesson can we learn from a comparative study of ultimate contribution in these lives? Do the major lessons on effective leaders shed any light on the focused life? How did these focused leaders finish? This section gives observations on these comparisons. The comparative analysis is not for purposes of seeing who was better or worse but what can be learned from an overall perspective of these lives as seen through these various frameworks.

<u>Giftedness and Focus</u>

The chart below compares the word gifts of the eight. All eight had spiritual gifts as the focal element of the giftedness set.[1] Five checks means powerfully gifted--world class. Four checks means the dominant spiritual gift. Three means the second dominant. Two means prominent but not dominant. One check means present but less dominant.

---

[1] I want to point out here as I have done in the other biographical chapters of the central role the Bible played in the eight leaders studied in this book. Each studied the Bible regularly and deliberately all their lives. They studied it devotionally for their own lives. They studied it to exhort others. They studied it to know of God and His purposes and to teach them to others. This will not be true for all focused leaders. But all of the eight leaders chosen in this book were *word gifted* leaders. See Clinton and Clinton (1994) **Developing Leadership Giftedness**, where we develop the concept of word gifted, power gifted, and love gifted clusters of spiritual gifts. All eight leaders in this book had spiritual gifts as the *focal element* of their giftedness set and word gifts as the dominant spiritual gifts. The giftedness set is composed of three elements: natural abilities, acquired skills, and spiritual gifts. Any of the three can be the focal element, that is, the dominant force around which the life is oriented. For all eight, spiritual gifts were the focal element; and within that element the Word gifts were dominant.

Chapter 10. Focal Findings

Table 10-1 Comparison of Word Gifts of the Eight

Person	Apostleship	Prophecy	Evangelism	Pastoral	Teacher	Exhortation	Faith	Wow
Simeon			√√	√√√	√√	√√√√		
Gordon			√√√√	√√√	√√	√√√√		
Brengle			√√√√	√√		√√√		√√
Morgan	√√	√			√√	√√√√√		
Jaffray	√√√√√		√√√√		√√			
McQuilkin					√√√√ √√√			√√√
Mears[2]			√√√√√		√√√√ √√√			
Maxwell	√√				√√√√ √√√			√√√

Notice that all but one of these leaders, the exception being Brengle, had strong teaching gifts. This probably points out a sub-conscious bias on my part. I am drawn to teacher types since one of my own important gifts is teaching.[3]

In our previous research on Word gifted leaders we have categorized Word Gifts, in terms of disciplined study of the Bible as a lifetime habit. Three categories emerged: Foundational, superstructural and remote as described in Figure 10-1 below.[4] This is in recognition of differences of knowledge of the Word needed by leaders and to help prevent gift projection.[5] Remember, the word gifts have a primary function in the body of Christ

TO CLARIFY WHO GOD IS AND WHAT HE EXPECTS FROM US.

Because of the *fact that every leader we have studied so far has at least one word gift in their giftedness set,* we have looked at the word gifts and asked the question: how grounded in the Scriptures should a leader be if they operate in the word gifts? The answer

---

[2] Mears also had five checks in leadership (ruling), a quasi-word gift which I did not include on the chart for space reasons and because leadership is usually a natural ability or sub-sumed in apostleship/ prophecy/ evangelism/ pastor/ teaching as a subsidiary function of those giftings. However, it is a part of the Romans list for a local church and is mentioned in 1, 2 Timothy as a local church gift. Mears certainly manifested powerful leadership gifting--whether it be natural or subsumed under other word gifts or a local church gifting. She was powerful in getting ideas, vision, and setting goals which she then motivated people toward.

[3] This in once sense validates the like-attracts-like gift pattern. See Clinton and Clinton (1994), **Developing Leadership Giftedness**. The single exception to this gift-pattern is Brengle. I am attracted to him not so much for his giftedness as his modeling of a victorious life.

[4] The following discussion in taken intact from Clinton and Clinton (1994:190,191), **Developing Leadership Giftedness**. It is included here since these focused leaders seem to demonstrate these concepts about Word gifts so strongly.

[5] Gift projection describes the tendency of strong Word gifted leaders to expect those around them to operate in the same Word gifts as they do and to operate with the same style and same disciplines. Hence people with differing gifts feel frustrated and like 2nd class Christians. Recognition that people differ, and that there are different levels of knowledge of the Word which vary with giftedness, is a helpful concept preventing gift projection.

Chapter 10. Focal Findings

to this question has strong implications for developmental thinking. It has repercussions for discipleship. It has repercussions for how we train others. It will affect gift projection, a tendency of all strong leaders.

We believe that there are various levels of word gifts in relationship to the importance of knowing the Bible. Every leader who operates in a word gift needs to be grounded in the Bible. It is our primary source and ultimate authority of revelation about who God is and what He expects. However, in our opinion, leaders operating in certain word gifts need to be grounded more thoroughly than other leaders operating in other word gifts. We have broken the word gifts up into three levels. Figure 10-1 depicts the levels of word gifts.

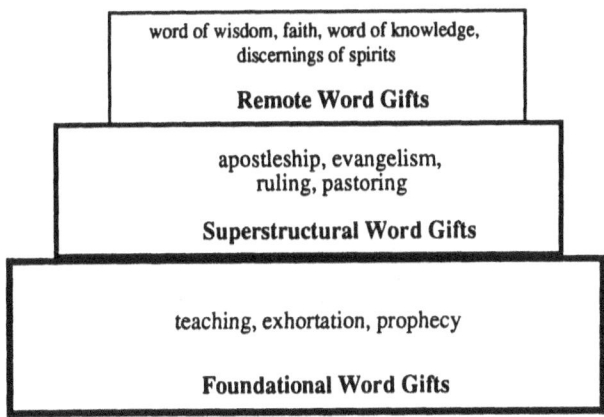

Figure 10-1 Three Levels of Word Gifts

Foundational word gifts are said to be foundational because the **major thrust of these gifts is the explanation of God and God's will.** The operation of these gifts depend very much on one's knowledge of God's revelation of Himself and His ways in the Scriptures. Leaders with foundational word gifts must continually be deepening themselves in their knowledge of God by studying and understanding the written word of God. It must be their primary source for the operation of their gifts. They must have detailed disciplines for the study of the word of God on a regular and on-going basis. Foundational gifted people have a tendency to project their detailed disciplines on others; it seems so natural to them and they have profited and grown so much by doing them. But they should recognize these projection tendencies. They should see that rather than have all the other word gifted (and even non-word gifted) people emulating their programs they should see their place in the body and provide the rest with their gains and the fruit of their labor. Simeon, Morgan, McQuilkin, Mears and Maxwell all represent leaders who dominantly operated with Foundational Word gifts. You would expect their discipline and study habits to involve strong analytical skills and most likely result in writings which expose their findings. And such was the case. Morgan was pre-eminent as a disciplined analytical student of the Bible. Gordon functioned with both a Foundational Word gift focus and a superstructural word gift focus.

Superstructural word gifts are said to be superstructural because their major function is not the clarification of God's word **but using God's word to accomplish**

Chapter 10. Focal Findings	page 448

other major tasks in the body of Christ. These leaders need to know the written word of God well enough to know that what they are building or accomplishing in ministry is firmly founded on the principles and revelation of God's word. For leaders with these gifts, **carrying out the tasks related to their gifts** is the focus rather than amassing an understanding of God's written word. These types of leaders need to rely on foundational word gifted leaders to provide correction, principles, values and guidance based on their more in-depth study of the word. Brengle and Jaffray fit here. A study of Jaffray's use of Scripture to validate his Apostolic vision is a case in point. And Brengle moved for decisions of the will and the affect in his public ministry--a ministry which used the Word of God for that purpose--rather than expounding upon and teaching or clarifying the Word. Gordon functioned with both a Foundational Word gift focus and a superstructural word gift focus. His conference ministry and writing ministry frequently was with a Foundational Word mode. His preaching ministry and pastoral role frequently operated in the Superstructural mode.

Remote word gifts are said to be remote because in the operation of these gifts the **primary dependency is on the Holy Spirit** and not an accumulated body of knowledge. This does not mean that these gifts should be inconsistent with the written word but the focus is on the immediate ministry situation. These gifts deliver a situational word from God in a specific ministry situation. Dependence on knowing the written word of God is secondary. Leaders operating with remote word gifts need to know the written word of God at a level so that the Bible operates as a tether or a yardstick for their situational words. God speaking to a situation through a leader would not contradict His written word or principles based on the written word of God. Of the eight , only Brengle operated regularly and strongly in remote Word gifts--his personal work both in evangelism and counseling toward holiness frequently utilized Word of Wisdom.

While all were strong students of the Bible, their disciplined study differed. All had a strong devotional life. Some were much more mystical in their relationship to God than others. And some studied as a discipline to learn. Others studied to use the Scriptures. On a continuum of analytical disciplined study of the whole of Scripture from strongest to less strong: Morgan, Simeon, McQuilkin, Mears, Maxwell, Gordon, Jaffray and Brengle. Devotionally rather than analytically from deepest or more mystical in relationship to less deep or mystical: Brengle, Gordon, Jaffray, McQuilkin, Mears, Maxwell, Simeon, and Morgan.[6]

Implications

1. Not all leaders need to be grounded in the word at the same level. There should be levels of depth of teaching and equipping in the word in a given situation.
2. Nor do all followers, non word gifted types, need the same level of teaching.
3. In terms of Bible study disciplines and goals, the various groupings of leaders will need different approaches and goals. Foundational will need the most exhaustive disciplines and approaches. Superstructural the next most and remote the least.
4. Almost all leaders are multi-gifted and will sometimes overlap among these three categories. The higher category should dominate their equipping philosophy.
5. All leaders are word gifted and need the equipping that can only come from the word.
6. Recognition of levels of word gifting will help ease the projection tendency of strong word gifted people.

---

[6]These are highly subjective opinions. I would not argue with any who differed. All did good analytical disciplined study. And all had strong devotional lives.

Chapter 10. Focal Findings

The question we should ask ourselves relating gifts and focus is this: If we know the giftedness set of a leader, particularly the gift-mix, can we predict an ideal role that will allow focus with it? In other word for each of the eight if given the gift-mix as shown for that specific leader, if we were to develop an ideal role to enhance it, what would it be? The role should at least enhance the most dominant gift and ideally the supportive gifts of the mix as well. While there might possibly be alternative roles other than what these leaders operated in that would bring focus with the given gift-mix, I think we would have to at least agree that the roles they were led to or developed did in fact match their giftedness. Giftedness is a significant factor in focus. This is true whether the leader knows explicitly about giftedness and hence deliberately moves toward or tailors a role or whether the leader implicitly drifts toward those matching roles. Ideally, however, awareness of giftedness should enhance a more direct career path toward a focused role.

Summary of Giftedness and Focus

Most likely there are some strong ties between giftedness and focal issues. Apostleship and evangelism correlate strongly to or inherently contain life purpose. Jaffray, Gordon, Brengle, Mears and Simeon all had at least a distinctive aspect of life purpose which flowed from their gifting--Jaffray, apostleship, and the rest evangelism. Jaffray demonstrates most vividly the correlation between gifting and life purpose. That is, life purpose will flow out of gifting. This same observation would probably hold for a person who was dominantly gifted with prophecy. None of these eight studied were strongly gifted with prophecy so I can not assert this from our study here.

Conversely, strong gifting having combinations to do with pastoral, teaching or exhortation (as the majority of the eight have) will need life purpose to focus these gifts. You could have, for example, a very strong teaching gift but without some life purpose to focus it there may be only hit-and-miss effectiveness. Rather than life purpose flowing from gifting and hence gifting determining life purpose as in apostleship, evangelism, and prophecy there is another effect. It is the other way round. Life purpose needs these gifts of teaching, exhortation, and pastoral to synergistically support it. The gift flows to the life purpose rather than from it.

Comparison of Standard Ultimate Contributions

The chart below shows in one overview the comparison of ultimate contribution sets. Remember each of these great leaders also had many unique special contributions in addition to the standard evaluation via the 12 ultimate contribution categories.[7] Three checks means outstanding legacy accomplished and/or left behind in the category. Two check means a very important legacy accomplished and/or left behind. One check means an important legacy accomplished and/or left behind.

---

[7] In order to get the types on one chart I am abbreviating the categories as follows: Ste=Saint; S. P.= stylistic practitioner; Mntor=mentor; P.R.=public rhetorician; Pionr=pioneer; Crusdr=crusader; Art.=artist; Fndr=founder; Stab.=stabilizer; Rschr=researcher; Wrtr=writer; Prom=promoter. See the Clinton paper(1989), *The Ultimate Contribution--A Life that Counts*.

Chapter 10. Focal Findings

Table 10-2 Ultimate Contribution Sets, Compared

Person	Ste.	S.P.	Mntor.	P.R.	Pionr.	Crusdr.	Art.	Fndr.	Stab.	Rschr.	Wrtr.	Prom.
Simeon			✓✓✓	✓							✓✓	
Gordon	✓✓	✓✓✓	✓	✓✓✓	✓	✓✓	✓	✓	✓✓	✓	✓	✓✓✓
Brengle	✓✓✓		✓✓	✓✓✓							✓✓	✓✓✓
Morgan		✓✓		✓✓✓				✓			✓✓✓	✓✓
Jaffray				✓✓				✓✓✓	✓✓	✓✓	✓✓	✓✓✓
McQuilkin	✓✓✓	✓	✓✓✓					✓	✓✓✓		✓✓	✓✓✓
Mears		✓✓✓	✓✓					✓✓✓			✓✓	✓✓✓
Maxwell		✓✓✓						✓✓			✓✓	✓✓✓

    The most important observation drawn from this chart is, that these great leaders had lives that really counted. They knew how to *number their days* and see *the Lord establish the work of their hands* (Psalm 90:12,17). Their lives counted. One strong motivational incentive for studying and using focused life concepts is that the more focused are our lives the more certain we are of effective leadership that will outlive us. Our legacies may not be great like these--we need not compare ourselves to them. But if we move toward focus--that is, ministering out of being--we too will have effective lives and leave behind legacies commensurate with our God-given capacities.

    A second observation recognizes that ultimate contribution is not as dominant in focusing a life as life purpose or major role or unique methodology--at least in the earlier stages. Unless an ultimate contribution happens to be part of a life purpose it is not as dominant. Ultimate contribution seems to take hold later in life, like 50s on. From that time on a leader begins to look more stringently at the finishing of life and leaving behind a life that counts. My hope is that raising awareness levels about ultimate contributions can allow for an earlier identification of them and hence a more proactive approach to them.

Summary On Ultimate Contribution and Focus

    Certain types of ultimate contribution types probably relate strongly to some focal issues.

    Saints, like Gordon, Brengle, McQuilkin and Maxwell, are concerned that their lives be what they are espousing to others. Most, because of genuine humility, would not claim a saint category for ultimate contribution. But implicitly they are concerned with demonstrating the efficacy of the message they preach. These efforts toward seeing people mobilized into victory in their lives are strongly related to **life purpose**.

    Mentors usually will correlate to some **unique methodology** for empowering people. Simeon's personal mentoring techniques utilizing levels of intimacy and capitalizing on the informal penetration theorem certainly demonstrate them. Mears' various innovative techniques and multi-faceted activities to reach, select, and develop young collegiates also demonstrates this.

Chapter 10. Focal Findings

Public rhetoricians usually require a strong **major role** in order to see their gifting flower and reach its potential. Brengle's role as *national spiritual special* carried organizational backing, giving an inherent positional authority, which he utilized along with his spiritual authority to enable a powerful public ministry. Morgan's backing by Moody along the American Conference circuit in his first tour in the U.S. first gave him a nationally recognized informal major role. He was able to parley this into a major ministry during his second tour, lasting 13+ years. Gordon's status as senior pastor of a flagship church in Boston provided the springboard for various itinerant jaunts to conferences and churches around the country. Charles Simeon's prestigious assignment to a University church gave status to his public ministry elsewhere, especially in his Cambridge lectures.

Pioneers usually are apostolic in gifting and therefore relate closely to a strong **life purpose**. Jaffray strongly illustrates this.

Crusaders will have ministries that are cause oriented--hence, will relate closely to a **life purpose** or **ultimate contribution**. Gordon's stands on various issues, freedom of speech, prohibition, and women in ministry were cause oriented and part of his life purposes which was enabled by his standing in the religious community and his status as senior pastor of a multi-ministry influential flagship church.

Founders will generally over time become concerned with **ultimate contribution** in order to conserve what they have begun. Maxwell was engrossed with this as seen in his attempt to mentor an upcoming leader to replace himself. Mears was able to transition her major external institutions, Regal Press and Forest Home, to leadership which stabilized them for on-going ministries. Jaffray founded many Bible institutes. This effort resulted in an on-going interest for selecting and developing leaders so that a major seminary still exists today in Indonesia to carry on his powerful values.

Writers, while at first simply writing to meet the need of the moment and provide materials for use in ministry, will eventually become concerned with capturing ideation for its on-going effect on the Christian world, an **ultimate contribution** focus. This may be an implicit direction or done explicitly. Morgan's work strongly illustrates this.

Promoters will most likely strongly relate to a **life purpose**. Maxwell and McQuilkin, both promoters, had strong dual life purposes related to victorious living and mobilization for missions. Simeon promoted renewal in the Anglican church as well as the cause of missions--even parachurch operations. Both were facets of his life purpose. Gordon promoted missions both within the Baptist denomination of which he was a part and on the American scene as a whole. He also pushed the doctrine of the second coming both for its renewing effect and for its implications for missions. These were tied to his broad life purposes flowing from his senior pastor role. Mears pushed for mobilizing emerging leaders into ministry a strong realization of her life purpose. Morgan strongly promoted a Bible centered ministry--an outflow from his value on the authority of the Bible, which became the bedrock of his life purpose. Jaffray, with his dominant apostolic gifting, strongly promoted the cause of missions to the unevangelized--always reaching out to those who had never heard. His life purpose, the life and breath of his ministry, was at the heart of his promoter interest.

Comparative Study--7 Major Lessons

From time-to-time I have mentioned the 7 major leadership lessons derived from many case studies. Table 10-3 lists these lessons for your immediate reference. Then Table 10-4 shows how these lessons were demonstrated. Three checks means an outstanding example of the lesson is seen in the life. Two checks means it was a prominent part of the

Chapter 10. Focal Findings

leader's life. One check means that it did occur. Not all leaders manifest all of these lessons. Usually one or two of the lessons will be a dominant force. Two more may be present and perhaps three were not observed in the life. Leaders who have more of these in the life, in general, are more effective, say, than those who comparatively have fewer or none.

Table 10-3 Seven Major Lessons of Effective Leaders

Lesson	Label	Statement
1	Perspective	Effective leaders view present ministry in terms of a life time perspective.
2	Learning Posture	Effective leaders maintain a learning posture throughout life.
3	Power Base	Effective leaders value spiritual authority as a primary power base.
4	Changing Philosophy	Effective leaders have a dynamic ministry philosophy.
5	Selection and Development	Effective leaders view leadership selection and development as a priority function in their ministry.
6	Relational Empowerment	Effective leaders see relational empowerment as both a means and a goal of ministry.
7	Sense of Destiny	Effective leaders evince a growing awareness of their sense of destiny.

Table 10-4 Comparative Analysis--8 Leaders and the Major Lessons

Leader	No. 1	No. 2	No. 3	No. 4	No. 5	No. 6	No. 7
Simeon		√√	√		√√√	√√√	
Gordon	√	√√√	√	√√	√√		√
Brengle	√√	√√√	√√√	√		√√	√√√
Morgan		√√√	√√√	√	√		
Jaffray	√	√√		√	√√√	√	√√
McQuilkin	√	√√√	√		√√	√	
Mears	√	√√		√√	√√√	√√	√
Maxwell		√√			√√√		√√

General Tendencies Between Lessons and Focal Issues

Lesson 1, on perspective, will most likely relate most closely to **ultimate contribution**. As a leader grasps his/her point in time, ministry-wise, within an entire lifetime, the result will be a more proactive stance toward ultimate contribution. Brengle, of the eight, most clearly points this out.

Lesson 2, on learning posture, will be evinced by all leaders living a focused life. In fact, it is not too much to assert that a leader must have a learning posture to move toward a focused life. The more focused the leader the more likely that a strong learning posture will be evinced. Learning posture probably relates most closely to adaptation of a

Chapter 10. Focal Findings

role toward a **major role** and recognition of **unique methodology**. All the eight leaders were strong in demonstrating this principle. All were tremendous learners. Their learning was fed back into their ministry in a formative on-going way.

Lesson 3, on power base, will relate most closely to **major role**. Most Christian leadership deals primarily with a voluntary followership. Spiritual authority is crucial to effective influence. Brengle and Morgan, with their transient public ministries, fully illustrate this principle.

Lesson 4, on a dynamic ministry philosophy,[8] relates most closely to values which dominate a ministry. These values can ensue in **life purpose** or **unique methodology**. Gordon, probably most aptly demonstrates this. His value laden and constantly expanding ministry broadened his original pastoral **life purpose** and built a flagship model, a very complex **unique methodology**.

Lesson 5, selection and development, will strongly relate to **unique methodology**. Mears standouts from the eight in illustrating this connection. Jaffray and Maxwell, with their Bible Institutes and McQuilkin with his Bible College also point this out.

Lesson 6, on relational empowerment, will also relate most closely to **unique methodology**. Simeon most strongly shows this connection.

Lesson 7, on sense of destiny, will probably have long range indications for **life purpose**, or at least will affirm it. Brengle most strongly demonstrates this connection.

General Observations on the Eight and Ultimate Contribution

Several observations should be noted.

None of the eight manifested the *perspective lesson* very well. A developmental perspective is a relatively late breaking concept. It has only been in this century that child developmental theory and adult developmental theories have developed. These secular concepts have helped Christian leaders view leadership development with a long term perspective. People of earlier times did not normally think in terms of a whole life perspective and development over the life time. In terms of Biblical characters those with a strong sense of destiny sometimes had a better grasp of a life time perspective. None of these eight leaders were strong in perspective. Brengle did Biblical studies of characters and hence had a better intuitive grasp of the concept of a lifetime of development. His early loss of wife (in his mid-50s) also sobered him to think of life and what remained ahead of him.

Sense of destiny was not a driving force, with the exception of Brengle, in these lives. None of the eight leaders studied were from charismatic or Pentecostal leanings. A leader from those persuasions has a tendency to sense God's revelatory work in his/her life more readily than do non-charismatic or non-Pentecostal leaders. Hence they tend to resonate with sense of destiny concepts rather strongly. This is not as strong among these eight. Again Brengle moves more mystically and sees this more readily. Of these eight

---

[8] By dynamic I mean one that changes. There will be a core of values and methodologies that do not change but as the leader grows in understanding of giftedness, the Bible, and faces new leadership situations ministry philosophy will expand to meet these new realities. It is dynamic in the sense that it is constantly being added to in order to meet leadership demands and personal growth. See Clinton (1992), *A Personal Ministry Philosophy--One Key To Effective Leadership*.

Brengle is the exemplar of sense of destiny. Maxwell saw fulfillment of an early boyhood dream. But awakening to a sense of destiny was more of a by-product than a driving force. As sense of destiny experiences came they basically affirmed focused direction already taken rather than determined it. But this should be a growing force to be reckoned with in terms of a focused life in our day. As you might expect, leaders of the last 25 years of the 20th century, have been much more exposed to Pentecostal and charismatic thinking--even if they are not from that persuasion. There is therefore more evidence of present contemporary leaders manifesting sense of destiny than of the eight studied here.

Note also that *learning posture* was a strong facet of each of these leader's lives. Imagine how this powerful trait would be seen in these lives if they lived today with all the learning opportunities we have. Even so they set a good example. This is probably one of the dominant forces in these lives and a behind-the-scenes stimulator of focus. People who live focused lives must have such a learning posture.

Six of the eight were strong in either *selecting or developing* emerging leaders (or both). Mears was the pre-eminent one in selection and development. She mobilized many into ministry. While stronger in selection, she was weaker in development. Her training was highly informal. Because of her strong selection emphasis she was very strong in relational empowerment. Simeon was just a step behind her in selection and development. He was more focused in his selection. And he was more systematic about development. But quantity wise, no one touches Mears. Gordon was tuned to selection and eventually began to move in systematic development--though he was cut off before maturing in this. Maxwell, McQuilkin, and Jaffray were strong in development but not as strong in selection. Morgan and Brengle, focusing on public rhetorician ministries did not have a selection focus. Though Morgan did have a strong developmental focus via his night Bible schools.

Notice that the two major public rhetoricians, Brengle and Morgan, were strong in *spiritual authority*, a necessity since they had no other power base (other than competency and charismatic personality) for influencing the transient groups they influenced. They certainly had no positional power.

Comparative Study--Finishing Well Characteristics

While I am sure there could be many various approaches to assessing a good finish, the following are based on the concept that the ideal leadership posture is one which involves **gifted power and accomplishment** as well as **mature godly character**. It is an on-going synergistic balance between being and doing. In practice you will see gifted power exercised by leaders who fall far short of character ideals. This will probably frustrate you. You will also see some who focus on character, perhaps in a move toward monastic solitude, with a corresponding lack of gifted power and achievement. The following characteristics reflect a bias toward a both/and rather than an either/or approach to being and doing. Table 10-5 lists the six characteristics. Table 10-6 lists how our eight leaders reached them. Three checks means a major strength; two means good; one means it was there.

Chapter 10. Focal Findings

Table 10-5 Six Characteristics of Finishing Well

Characteristic	Statement
1	They maintain a <u>personal vibrant relationship</u> with God right up to the end.
2	They maintain a <u>learning posture</u> and can learn from various kinds of sources--life especially.
3	They portray <u>Christ likeness in character</u> as evidenced by the fruit of the Spirit in their lives.
4	Truth is lived out in their lives so that <u>convictions</u> and promises of God are seen to be real.
5	They leave behind one or more <u>ultimate contributions</u> (saint, stylistic practitioners, mentors, public rhetoricians, pioneers, crusaders, artists, founder, stabilizers, researchers, writers, promoters).
6	They walk with a growing awareness of a sense of destiny and see some or all of it fulfilled.

Table 10-6 Eight Leaders and the Six Characteristics

Leader	No. 1	No. 2	No. 3	No. 4	No. 5	No. 6
Simeon	√√	√√	√√√	√	√√√	√
Gordon	√√	√√√	√√√	√√	√√√	√
Brengle	√√√	√√√	√√√	√√√	√√√	√√√
Morgan	√√	√√√	√√√	√√√	√√√	√√
Jaffray	√√√	√√√	√√√	√√√	√√√	√√√
McQuilkin	√√√	√√√	√√√	√√	√√√	√√√
Mears	√√√	√√√	√√√	√√√	√√√	√
Maxwell	√√	√√	√√√	√√	√√√	√√

Even a cursory glance at the chart will point out that these leaders finished very well. There was balance in their lives--beingness and doingness are reflected in their finish. In fact, they were chosen for that very reason. They faced all the complexities, conflicts, and crises of leadership that we face today. Yet they learned to trust God and walk with Him. They should encourage us that it can be done. We may not accomplish what or as much as they did, but we can finish well, living up to the potential God has given us. Be encouraged--these were people with feet of clay, in fact, they became clay pots through whom God shone (2 Corinthians 4:7). And so can you.

CLARIFICATION OF FOCUSED LIFE CONCEPTS,

Three major concepts emerged or were clarified over the long haul of the study. A fourth was introduced. The results of these concepts, as they stand at the end of the research, are given below.

Chapter 10. Focal Findings   page 456

<u>Defining The Focused Life</u>

The definition of focused life and focal issues emerged rapidly. Each of the focal issues became more definitive as the study progressed and there were more illustrations of them. In fact, the definition of a focused life grew and was modified as I went. New insights discovered in succeeding chapters was fed back into the original definition. Look again at this definition in its final form and let's trace its evolution.[9]

A <u>focused life</u> is
- a life dedicated to exclusively carrying out God's unique purposes through it,
- by identifying the focal issues, that is, the **life purpose, unique methodology, major role,** or **ultimate contribution** which allows
- an **increasing prioritization** of life's activities around the focal issues, and
- results in a satisfying life of being and doing.

I originally began with the notion of a life dedicated to exclusively carrying out God's unique purpose (an Ephesians 2:10 concept) as clarified by a **life purpose, major role** or perhaps an **end of life goal** of leaving some special legacy. Previous studies had helped me clarify some standard legacies, that is, the twelve ultimate contributions that effective leaders accomplish. As I studied each life I held the definition up. Each life helped affirm or modify or clarify or add to the original definition.

The order of the lives studied were Morgan, Brengle, Gordon, Simeon, Jaffray, McQuilkin, Mears and Maxwell. Morgan's life was dominated by life purpose and a vacillating search for a major role that would allow him to reach his very large potential. But otherwise the definition held. The ultimate contribution was less important but was there especially in terms of restoring older works to usefulness and leaving them behind. Brengle lived well into old age and saw destiny fulfilled and reviewed over his life in old age. Several of his writings explained what he saw. He was a man who could say, "You are looking at a fulfilled person. I look back over life and am satisfied with how God has led me and what I have become and done for Him. I am happy with the results of my life." From him was added the last major concept of **satisfying life of being and doing**. He also, with his use of penitent form, introduced me to the concept of a **unique methodology** as an important force for focus.

So I went back and added unique methodology as one of the four major focal issues. I then reflected back on Morgan with this new definition. I saw then that his night Bible school was a unique methodology which he used in one form or another throughout his life time. In fact, his itinerant ministry in the United States and Canada was built on content and methodology drawn from the night Bible school. The final definition of a focused life was essentially set after study of Morgan and Brengle. Each added character studied clarified each of the major concepts or affirmed them in new ways. Figure 10-2 organizes the final definition in terms of importance in focusing the life.

---

[9]I am using a grounded theory approach to research. Such an approach studies a situation and conceptualizes from what is seen. This concept is then examined comparatively in a new situation which may abrogate, modify, or clarify the definition. This comparative approach is continued until a concept saturates, that is, new situations do very little to change it or until the concept is seen not to hold up. The original definition came from earlier studies. It was tested on these eight whom I knew fit other categories of an effective life which finished well. These concepts are not nearly saturated and will be the continued object of comparative study. I expect they will be further refined. But they are a very good start.

Chapter 10. Focal Findings   page 457

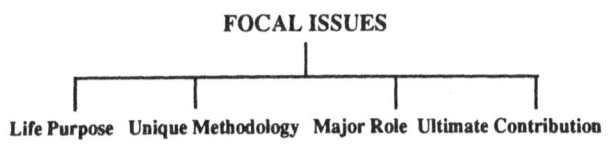

Figure 10-2 Focal Issues Ordered in Terms of Most Influential

    A focused life is usually dominated by one or more of these focal issues. The issue becomes increasingly clear over the life and dominates how the life becomes and what it accomplishes. **Life purpose** usually has most to do with setting focus. **Unique methodology**, if one or more exist, usually is second in importance. **Major role** is next in importance--though the initial role that starts focus is usually modified over a lengthy time to become a role which enhances giftedness. Finally, **ultimate contribution**, if a dominant factor at all in focus, becomes prominent in later life.

    Let me clarify where I am, at least at this point in the research, in defining or describing each of these focal issues.

    A **life purpose** is a burden-like calling to fulfill something, to see something done. It usually starts with a general burden and becomes more specific over the years. It may come very early in life in terms of some value personally experienced. How to get that value into the lives of others becomes a driving force that eventually results in a more definitive life purpose as the leader grows. Frequently leaders will have one to three dominant life purposes or some combination of one or more or at least an umbrella one which is clarified by more detailed sub-purposes.

example: My purpose is to challenge, motivate, and enable--via teaching, modeling, and available resources and materials--high level leaders to finish well.

    A **unique methodology** is some ministry insight around which the leader can pass on to others the essentials of doing something or using something. This methodology becomes a major means which moves people toward results in line with life purposes or ultimate contributions.

example: I will use personal counseling, one-on-one, with a framework derived from Larry Crabb to help people move to wholeness.

example: The basic methodology for moving people in literacy is captured in the phrase, each one teach one. This will be the major force of my efforts.

    A **major role** is the official or unofficial position, or status/ platform, or leadership functions, or job description which uniquely fits who a leader is and lets that leader effectively accomplish life purpose(s), by enhancing giftedness and by using unique methodology, in order to leave behind special contributions or ultimate contributions.

example: An itinerant public Bible teacher at national level who teaches different large groups of 1000 or more in face-to-face ministry on a repetitive basis.

    A major role will usually have to be adapted. Organizations rarely define such a role to fit a person. They hire to positions or qualification rather than hiring people and

Chapter 10. Focal Findings

defining the position in terms of the people. That is, they have a tendency to use people rather than enhance their development. The major role may be a combination of formally recognized issues and informal ones done implicitly.

An **ultimate contribution** is a legacy that a leader will leave behind after life is over. Leaders usually have several of these.

example: I intend to leave behind an organization and leadership which embraces my basic leadership values and mission and can perpetuate my major values.

example: I have outlined a series of writings, including position papers, self-study books, texts and other writings which deal with classical issues which I intend to leave behind as a legacy for those who will be teaching and helping leaders develop over their lifetimes.

Clarifying Critical Incidents

A second idea which became more firmly defined was the notion of a critical incident. Critical incidents were more carefully distinguished in terms of their function:

1. producing a dominant value or
2. pinpointing a key strategic directional factor (or occasionally, both).

From a list of critical incidents I then learned how to distinguish prime incidents, those which are supercritical to the overall focus of the life--usually prime incidents are dominated by strategic direction interventions by God, though some are dominant values which pervade.

I consistently made disclaimers that if more data were available or even varied perspectives on the data that probably more critical incidents would be identified. And yet even from the critical incidents that were identified some could be seen to be more crucial to the way the life developed. These were called prime incidents. Look again at the final definition of this concept. Then note in Figure 10-3 their major functions.

definition A <u>critical incident</u> is a special intervention (could be a series over time) in which God gives a *major value* that will flow through the life or will give *strategic direction* to narrow the leader's life work.

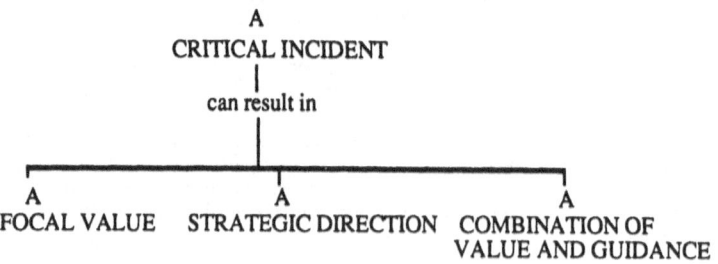

Figure 10-3 Three Basic Results of Critical Incidents

Chapter 10. Focal Findings

These major concepts are further described or defined as follows:

definition
: A *focal value* is a dominant controlling perspective (a leadership value) which interweaves itself throughout a person's ministry and usually can be traced to a critical incident.

definition
: *Strategic direction* refers to God's intervention which helps move a leader along toward the focal issues: role, life purpose, unique methodology, or ultimate contribution of the leader. That is, it is God's guidance directing toward life work.

definition
: A *leadership value* is an underlying assumption which affects how a leader behaves in or perceives leadership situations or issues.

Some examples of such values include:

Example 1   Small group structures are necessary in the church for believer's to learn about their spiritual gifts.
Example 2   Spiritual authority must dominate a leader's power bases--i.e. those means used to influence followers toward God's purposes.
Example 3   Ministry must be personal.

Values can affect all three of the kinds of God's shaping formational activity:

1. spiritual formation: leadership character,
2. ministerial formation: leadership skills, and
2. strategic formation: leadership strategic thinking.

Critical incidents will almost always yield values. In addition, they may strongly give strategic guidance.

While all critical incidents add to the focused life some of these are more crucial to the actual accomplishments of the completed life. In looking back over critical incidents those which are most crucial are identified as prime incidents.

Categorizing Screens[10]

Three, the eleven screens listed in chapter 1 for helping look at a focused life became twelve screens. Window of Opportunity emerged as an important focusing factor in three lives (Simeon--patronage opportunities; Mears--leadership needs after World War II; Maxwell, missionary mobilization after World War II). I quickly fed this information back into chapter 1 and updated all of the chapters. Further, over the course of the study I saw how these 12 individual factors could be grouped into four higher level categories. I describe that next under the concept of focusing parameters.

Let me begin by first looking at the 12 screens and grouping them into a more manageable taxonomy.

---

[10]This is an initial attempt. I am not totally satisfied with these four groups. There is overlap. Further comparative analysis will probably help definitively isolate the categories or at least further define them. But they are a start which I will use in my further grounded theory research.

Chapter 10. Focal Findings

Focusing Parameters

In chapter 1 I introduced the format for organizing the biographical chapters. In that format I introduced first gave 11 screens, that is, prompts that help us screen information for focusing ideas. Quickly I discovered another one, windows of opportunity, which was added. Then I attempted to look at each of these leader's lives asking myself how this screen was seen in the life and if the screen played a factor in focusing the life. My study of the eight characters with all of these screens has led me to simplify these categories into four broader ones which encompass all twelve of the smaller ones and attempts to delineate in terms of the 4 major focal issues. The following tree diagram, Figure 10-2, shows this reduction.

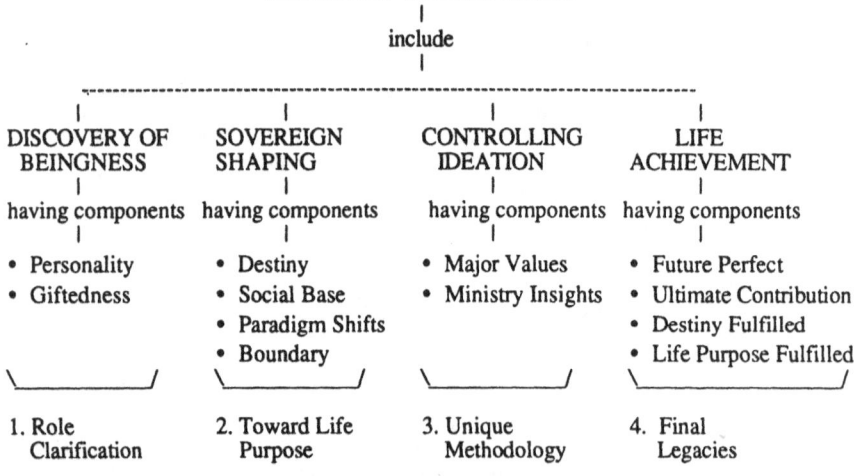

Figure 10-2 Focusing Parameters Which Group the Twelve Screens

Using these 4 categories I can now identify the prime incidents in each of the leader's life in terms of which of the four categories was the prime incident most related. Critical incidents are abbreviated by C1(V/SD), etc. Where C1 refers to the actual critical incident on the critical incident table of the leader. (V) means that the critical incident resulting in a dominant value. (SD) means that the critical incident resulted in strategic direction. (V/SD) means both a value and strategic direction were involved. A boldfaced critical incident is the pivotal prime incident. Once I relate these prime incidents to categories, I will follow by suggesting what can be seen regarding order.

Chapter 10. Focal Findings   page 461

Table 10-7 Prime Incidents in terms of Focusing Parameters

Categories

	Discovery of Beingness 1. Role Clarification	Sovereign Shaping 2. Toward Life Purpose	Controlling Ideation 3. Unique Methodology/ Viewpoint	Life Achievement 4. Final Legacies
Leaders				
Simeon	C3(SD)	C1(V)	C4(V); C12(SD)	C7(SD);
Gordon	C1(SD)	C12(V)	C6(V); C7(V)	C8(V/SD)
Brengle	C3(SD/V)	C12(SD)	C6(V)	C7(V)
Morgan	C4(SD); C6(SD)	C3(V)	C11(V)	C15(SD); C17(SD)
Jaffray		C4(SD/V)	C3(V); C10(V)	C11(SD)
McQuilkin	C7(SD) C11(SD)	C6(V)	C9(V)	C13(SD)
Mears	C13(SD)	C6(V/SD) C12(V)		C11(V/SD) C20(V/SD)
Maxwell	C7(SD)	C5(V)	C5(V)	C16(V/SD)

Life Message

At this point I have given the three concepts which were clarified in the study: definition of focused life, critical incidents, and focusing parameters. A fourth concept, that of **life message**, was introduced by Spaulding in his study of Maxwell. This important concept is integrally tied to the notion of an encapsulated life purpose. In attempting to use focused life concepts more proactively, the notion of life message will be a helpful concept. I will do further research on how to reduce to writing personal mission statements which combine findings about life purpose, unique methodology, major role, ultimate contribution and life message.

Order and Narrowing of Focus--Clarification of Focal Issues

Once the concepts were clarified or modified or added, as I have described above, further aspects or facets of them were suggested. For example, as the definitions for focal issues became clearer, I could then look for things like order. Which ones came first? Which ones came later? When in life do the focal issues began to emerge? For each of the people studied which of the focusing parameters were more prime? I next give my comparative analysis of the eight in line with these questions.

For Simeon--Tracing Prime Focusing Incidents

Simeon at age 19 was converted (C1 New Creature). This critical incident, a paradigm shift, gave him a major value concerning relationship with God. He longed to help others in the established church also experience this kind of relationship with God. He desired a position in a Cambridge church from which he could introduce this evangelical concept into the Anglican Church. At age 22 he was appointed to a key church in a critical incident which set his direction as to role (C3 Against the Odds). From this position and location he developed his role as an influential pastor in a University church and as a fellow on campus.

Chapter 10. Focal Findings   page 462

His development was speeded, if not protected altogether, with his mentoring relationship with Henry Venn (C4 Early Contemporary Mentor). Values and ministerial skills were imbibed through this relationship. This critical incident started when Simeon was 23 years old and continued till age 37.

Ten years after the mentoring had begun, at age 33, Simeon met Charles Grant and began a partnership that led him into a strong missions involvement--a second major aspect of life purpose.

Finally, at age 54, Simeon was introduced to a methodology, acquiring of patronages, which would allow him to take a deliberate proactive stance toward accomplishing one of his life purposes--renewal in the Anglican Church, which had been rooted in his own conversion. Notice that three of the incidents provided strategic direction and two gave under girding values.

In summary these prime incidents occurred at ages 19, 22, 23, 37, and 54. Focus toward **life purpose** (age 19) came first. This was followed by focus toward **role** (age 22). As he began to operate in that role he was led into a **unique methodology** (age 23-33), that of mentoring which was to help him fulfill his life purpose. He connected to Charles Grant in a partnership to promote missions, which helped him focus on a second aspect of life purpose (age 33). Much later he was led into another **unique methodology** (age 54), use of patronage which helped him not only accomplish a part of his life purpose but served as a springboard into a major **life achievement**, seeding the upcoming generation with evangelicals.

<u>For Gordon--Tracing Prime Focusing Incidents</u>

At age 16 Gordon committed himself to a **major role** (C1 Early Destiny heritage and Call). That role was a general pastorate and primarily as he understood it, the image of a rural pastor in a small church. Over the years that major role changed drastically to a full orbed senior pastor role in a flagship church with multiple staff and ministries. But the stage was set in that initial decision at age 16.

Around age 36 he experienced a mystical revelation of Christ in a dream (C6 When Christ Came to Church). This imparted a value, a controlling ideation for any **methodology**, which from then on characterized his standard of evaluation of his church ministry.

Shortly thereafter a powerful evangelistic minister with a passion for souls and an intercessory ministry for them impacted his life (C7 Uncle John Vassar--Revival Foundations). From Uncle John he learned the value of prioritizing evangelism as a primary purpose for a church. He also learned prayer skills and visitation evangelism skills, toward a **methodology**.

At age 41, he went through a paradigm shift with regard to power in ministry (C8 Revival Power--God Breaks Through in Boston--the Moody Campaign). This controlling ideation led to **life achievement** and enhanced his giftedness, part of **role** clarification.

Finally, his **life purpose** and **life achievement**, as regards missionary outreach was typified in his efforts to save the Belgian Congo mission (C12 The Belgian Congo--A Missions Passion).

In summary these prime incidents occurred at ages 16, 36, 36, 41, and 48. Focus toward **major role** (age 16) came first. This was followed by focus toward **evaluation**

Chapter 10. Focal Findings	page 463

of methodology (age 36). As he began to operate in that role he was led to prioritize evangelism and to develop **methodology** for it(age 36). He went through a power gate, a paradigm shift, which affected **role clarification, life purpose,** and **final legacies** (age 41). Finally, the mission thrust of his life purpose developed as he sensed its burden more deeply and as his influence broadened (this was there throughout his whole life--see his destiny preparation via his name, Adonirum Judson). Though a lifelong interest it really carried great power from age 48 onward.

For Brengle--Tracing Prime Focusing Incidents

All of Brengle's incidents seem linked together. Even less critical incidents perform prerequisite tasks which allowed the prime incidents to focus. However, I have narrowed critical incidents for Brengle to four, two of which gave major values which dominated. One gave strategic direction, in fact led to an ideal **major role**. One critical incident gave both strategic direction and a major value.

It was his surrender to God for ministry (C3 The Call, Harnessing Ambition, The Call), at age 22 which initiated in-depth focus in his life. This critical incident set **strategic direction.** It would be ministry and not politics that dominated his life. It also dealt with a value, the importance of having Holy ambition, and not just ambition. This value clarification was repeated in various incidents throughout his life to reinforce it and otherwise control the pride of this talented public orator.

At age 25, he experienced a paradigm shift with regard to power and holiness (C6 Personal Pentecost). His personal experiential paradigm shift imparted a deep value which dominated his **life purpose**--to have others enter into this fullness and desire for holiness.

Shortly after this, at age 25, he was challenged by God, again dealing with personal ambition and pride (C7 Attractive Offer, The Faith Challenge). His surrender, wholly to God on this issue, deeply imparted a value which dominated his inner life and his decision making toward **ministry roles**. This eventually affected **major role** and led to the Salvation Army, the group among which his life work developed.

Finally, at age 37, God providentially provided an ideal **major role** which greatly enhanced his **life purposes** (C12 National Spiritual Special) and brought about his **ultimate contributions.**

Brengle stands out as having entered into all aspects of his focus life by age 37. He therefore ministered with increasing power for almost 40 years. His entrance into a full fledged focused life was the earliest of any of the eight. His focused pattern was an accelerated pattern. And the beautiful thing is that he did not manipulate the major role which brought powerful focus. He submitted himself to God's assignments. God honored that submission. For Brengle it was **life purpose** and **unique methodology** which first brought focus. Preliminary roles led to an ideal **major role** and **ultimate contributions.**

For Morgan--Tracing Prime Focusing Incidents

At age 21, following a two year time of isolation, with God alone in His Word doing the convincing, Morgan was impacted with a major value which forever focused his life (C3 An Authoritative Word). I repeat it here because it was so revolutionizing to him.

Chapter 10. Focal Findings   page 464

> **THE BIBLE IS THE AUTHORITATIVE WORD OF GOD. IT DOESN'T HAVE TO BE DEFENDED. IT CAN CONVINCE PEOPLE IF IT IS CLEARLY TAUGHT IN TERMS OF ITS INTENT--ON THE WHOLE AND BOOK BY BOOK. PEOPLE HAVE A SENSE OF NEED TO WHICH TRUTH IN THE BIBLE SPEAKS.**

So it was a **major value** which led to an increasingly clear **life purpose**--he would teach that Word to many in all its power--which first pushed Morgan to a focused life.

At age 23, in seeking certainty guidance, God clearly led him out of secular teaching into full time ministry (C4 Forced Out). This was strategic direction toward a **major role**. This was the pivotal critical incident as far as strategic direction is concerned. He vacillated for the next 46 years as he sought to identify an ideal role. Crisis experiences with two World Wars and an ambiance which was not conducive to the adaptation of his role probably prevented him from reaching the ideal role. Never-the-less, in two differing major roles he, for different periods of time, operated with great focus.

At age 25 the door was closed to work with the Methodist (C6 Methodist Rejection) which further set strategic direction. For Morgan's potential to develop, he needed a denomination that would allow for interdenominational ministry. This block actually opened the door for Morgan to pursue a pastoral **role** in the Congregational church, which allowed him more freedom for a broader ministry.

At age 29, Morgan discovered the **unique methodology** (C11 Friday Night Bible School) which would dominate his delivery from then on. His **life purpose** now had an important delivery system through which it emerged with increasing power.

At age 41, Morgan made a decision (C15 Westminster Decision) which identified for him one of his **major roles** that allowed use of his unique methodology and fulfilled life purpose desire. That **role** was senior pastor of an old revered but dead church. He restored that church, one of his implicit life purposes, to the status of a flagship church. He operated with great focus during a period of about 13 years.

At age 51, an important boundary time led him to pursue another **major role** to fulfill his **life purpose** (C17 The 10th Anniversary Sermon). His itinerant ministry of public Bible teaching in a conference format in every major city in the U.S. and Canada allowed a powerful focused ministry that fulfilled **life purpose**. His **unique methodology** modified for a more transient ministry provided a powerful delivery system for his ministry.

In review, Morgan faced prime incidents at ages 21 (a dominant **value** leading to **life purpose**), 23 (strategic direction out of secular world into ministry--toward **role**), 25 (strategic direction via a block, toward a broad based **major role**), 29 (the dominant **delivery system** for his ministry--enhancement of giftedness) 41 (strategic direction toward first **major focused role**), and 51 (strategic direction toward second **major focused role**).

For Jaffray--Tracing Prime Focusing Incidents

At age 21 Jaffray broke strings of dependency to his father and learned to trust God by faith to supply (C3 Can God Supply?). This prime critical incident imparted a value, God can be trusted to lead and supply. This response by Jaffray and God's faithfulness

Chapter 10. Focal Findings

not only paved the way to this important value but gave strategic direction for it led to a mentoring experience and training under A. B. Simpson (C4 Simpson--Imposing Mentor--Values Imparted). This short three year period led Jaffray to **unique methodology** (the Bible School as a means of mobilizing and carrying out Apostolic ministry) and his **life purpose**--an apostolic ministry. This training paved the way for a cross-cultural ministry overseas--the very thing that allowed his apostolic gifting to flourish.

By age 40, Jaffray had honed his **unique methodology** (C10 The Bible School Comes of Age). He further enhanced his apostolic ministry via his field leadership. **Major role** for Jaffray was threefold, head of field, head of Bible institute, and head of supporting ministries such as materials publishing.

Finally, at age 55 (C11 A Second Career) in line with his **life purpose** of apostolic ministry, he started all over. He moved to a new field, Indonesia, after 31 years in south China. And there he was able to greatly use his previous experience in defining his **major role, unique methodology** to concentrate and bring cumulative results in a short time--the most important 13 years of his ministry.

For McQuilkin--Tracing Prime Focusing Incidents

McQuilkin, at age 25, experienced a life transforming event-process (C6 August 15, 1911). Out of this experience a value developed--Christ can bring victory in a life. From this flowed a **life purpose**--to mobilize people into this wonderful relationship and life. This was the pivotal critical incident of his life. From then on his life was dominated by this value.

The discovery of a **major role** from which to fulfill this life purpose took McQuilkin through a varied number of experiences, each of which were preliminary to finding his life work. Preliminary strategic direction occurred via Charles Trumbull (C7 Trumbull--Invitation To Join *The Sunday School Times*) at age 25, and via S. D. Gordon (C9 The Joints of the Will) at age 29. Both of these experiences broadened the notion of role and life **purpose**.

Strategic direction was finally offered at age 31 (C11 The *City of Lahore* sinks). This shut door forced a search for the **major role** that would pull these various experiences together. At age 34, McQuilkin found his life work (C13 The One of His Choice). His acceptance of a call to the fledgling Bible institute provided the stage for his developing a **major role** that would fulfill his **life purposes** of mobilizing Christians into victorious life and onto the mission field.

In terms of focal issues, **life purpose** (mobilizing toward the victorious life) emerged first, pieces of **major role** little by little over time began to clarify (parachurch and not church, teaching and not pastoring, strong missions interest). In the midst of clarification, a second **life purpose** (mobilizing for mission) emerged. He and his wife were not to go, but to mobilize many others to do so. The Bible College as a **unique methodology** for mobilizing occurred late in the process. And finally, the Bible College as an **ultimate contribution**, a legacy which could carry out his life purposes after his own pilgrimage was over increasingly dominated McQuilkin as he sought to recruit faculty for it and stabilize it for future ministry.

For Mears--Tracing Prime Focusing Incidents

Movement toward a focused life for Mears differs from all others studied. For she was a lay leader till relatively late in life. Everything, all shaping toward values and

Chapter 10. Focal Findings   page 466

strategic direction, was preliminary until she was age 38. At age 20, in a time of destiny clarification, she knew she would have a powerful ministry like her mother (C6 Prophetic Mantle). At age 25 her sister began a partnership which would free Mears for service (C11 Social Base; Margaret Meets the Needs). At age 27, her **life purpose** was clarified ; it was not to be a missionary life but a life of mobilizing leadership (C12 Life Purpose Clarified).

But all of these were preliminary to the pivotal incident s(C13 MacLennan, Divine Contact and C15 Decision Time) which were to take her into full time ministry at age 38. Then with a rapid accelerated momentum she sped into the focused life--developing a **major role**, increasingly fulfilling **life purpose**, and developing **ultimate contributions** which enhanced her life purpose.

Finally the icing on the cake occurred at age 57 (C20 Destiny Trip; The Expendables) in which God gave a renewed charge, a vision of destiny, which propelled her into a widespread mobilization of young collegiate leaders which seeded the evangelical movement with leaders which would minister powerfully for almost 40 years. Her **life purpose** was increasingly fulfilled in those latter years of her ministry.

<u>For Maxwell--Tracing Prime Focusing Incidents</u>

Maxwell, between the ages of 24 to 27, was led providentially to two mentors, "Daddy" Stevens and Dorothy Miller at the Midlands Bible Institute (C5 Mentors). He studied with them for three years in preparing to go into ministry. There he was not only shaped in character but was introduced in embryonic form to his **life purpose, unique methodology,** and **major role**. All of these were modeled for him. He went through an initial brokenness experience (C6 Brokenness/Restoration) which not only gave him an important value (forgiveness/ restoration) but introduced him experientially to the nature of character shaping--something he would major on later in his own Bible Institute. This brokenness experience was pivotal and a necessary prerequisite to his call which is to come.

At age 27 upon graduation Maxwell was called to the prairies of Canada in Alberta (C7 The Call). For an extended time he developed a Bible Institute, like the one he attended. This institute allowed him to develop his **major role** and carry out his **life purposes** which like McQuilkin involved mobilizing into the crucified life and into missions. This isolated Bible Institute on the prairies became a **unique methodology** for mobilizing. When the window of opportunity came after World War II, this institute was prepared for the expansion. Maxwell left it behind, a major **ultimate contribution**.

Like Jaffray, Maxwell in his pre-service training in a small personalized Bible Institute environment received all three of his major focal issues: **life purpose, major role,** and **unique methodology**. The advantage of going to a small Bible institute is that it is seen as a transferable concept. Those attending them can easily reduplicate them later in their own experiences.

Table 10-8 gives a comparative overview of the order of focal issues and age when discovered or developed. The entry designates which came first and the age at which it first became a factor in focusing the leader's life. Frequently, the age at which it first becomes a factor only initiates the item. It may take years to develop more specifically.

Chapter 10. Focal Findings   page 467

Table 10-8 Ordering of Focal Issues and Age When First Discovered

	Life Purpose	Unique Methodology	Major Role	Ultimate Contributions
Leaders				
Simeon	1 (age 19)	3 (age about 30) 4 (age 54)	2 (age 22)	5 (age 54+)
Gordon	2 (age 36) 4 (age late 30s)	3 (age 36)	1 (age 16)	5 (age 50+)
Brengle	1 (age 22) 2 (age 25)	3 (late 20s)	4 (age 37)	5 (age 50+)
Morgan	1 (age 21)	3 (age 29)	2 (age 25) 4 (age 41) 7 (age 51)	6 (age 42)
Jaffray	1 (age 22)	2 (age 24)	3 (age 38)	4 (age 40s) 5 (age 55)
McQuilkin	1 (age 25) 2 (age 29)	4 (age 40s)	3 (age 34)	5 (late 40s)
Mears	1 (age 27)	2 (age mid 30s)	3 (age 38)	4 (age late 40s)
Maxwell	1 (age 24)	2 (age 27)	3 (age early 30s)	4 (mid 60s)

From this chart it should be noted that 7 of the 8 (Gordon excepted) first happened upon **life purpose**. The earliest to discover life purpose (at least in embryonic form) was Simeon at age 19. The latest to visualize life purpose was Gordon who in his mid 30s was struck with the value that he would use to evaluate ministry and life purpose.

Gordon first discovered his **major role** at the young age of 16. At that time his understanding of it was very simple. It grew to become very sophisticated as he developed his flagship church. Life purpose came second.

After first getting life purposes, Jaffray, Mears, and Maxwell began to develop **unique methodologies** as their second focal issue. Unique methodologies are discovered throughout the life time of a leader. Many are discovered early on in the provisional and growth stages of ministry development.[11]

Simeon and Morgan moved toward **major role** as their second focal issue.

All moved toward **ultimate contribution** rather late in their ministry.

For Simeon the order of discovery of focal issues was: life purpose, major role, unique methodology, a second unique methodology, and finally ultimate contribution.

---

[11] The provisional ministry phase begins from the time a leader goes into full time ministry and lasts 4-8 years. The growth period follows and can last from 5-10 years.

Chapter 10. Focal Findings   page 468

For Gordon the order of discovery of focal issues was: major role, life purpose, unique methodology, and a second life purpose. Ultimate contributions which were many and great were by-products of an influential ministry and did not readily contribute to the focus. Perhaps if Gordon had not died early these would have come into play.

For Brengle the order of discovery of focal issues was: life purpose, a second life purpose, unique methodology, major role and finally ultimate contribution.

For Morgan the order of discovery of focal issues was: life purpose, major role, unique methodology, another different major role, and finally ultimate contribution.

For Jaffray the order of discovery of focal issues was: life purpose, unique methodology, major role, ultimate contribution and finally a second major ultimate contribution.

For McQuilkin the order of discovery of focal issues was: life purpose, a second life purpose, a major role, unique methodology, and finally ultimate contribution.

For Mears the order of discovery of focal issues was: life purpose, unique methodology, major role, and finally ultimate contribution.

For Maxwell the order of discovery of focal issues was: life purpose, unique methodology, major role, and finally ultimate contribution.

Final Summary of Focused Life Concepts and Implications

Let me first describe my summary and then state it concisely in the form of implications.

It is obligatory that to realize a focused life, a leader must have a life purpose. The more specific or detailed it is the more likely a tight focus will result. There can be no focus without a strong life purpose. But a strong life purpose needs either a unique methodology for carrying it out or a major role with facets directly related to life purpose or an ultimate contribution that dominates and relates to life purpose.

A major role is not enough. A major role without life purpose usually will result in a diffused life which may have some effective streaks diluted by many ministry red herrings. The same is true for a dominant unique methodology. A unique methodology is primarily a means to an end. Life purpose provides the end that gives ultimate meaning to the means. Ultimate contribution should inherently have life purpose under girding it.

1. Life purpose is the **dominant focal issue** and is core to any focused life. It is usually discovered relatively early in some experiential way. It is clarified cognitively, added to, and fine tuned usually over a life time moving from an umbrella-like concept to a general notion as reflected in one to three specific detailed ways. There is no focus without life purpose.

2. Life purpose and unique methodology alone can essentially produce an effective focused life.

3. Life purpose and major role alone can essentially produce an effective focused life.

Chapter 10. Focal Findings

4. Life purpose and ultimate contribution can produce an effective focused life, but the ultimate contribution will usually lead to a major role.

5. Unique methodology and major role alone, without life purpose, will usually lead to a scattered or diffused life, perhaps effective and perhaps not.

6. Ultimate contribution will increasingly play a most important function in moving leaders toward proactive decision making concerning their lives and ministries. This is so because more and more leaders are being introduced to a life long developmental perspective. With perspective, leaders begin to strategically make decisions which will move toward ultimate contribution.

MISCELLANEOUS OBSERVATIONS, Special Findings

I include here a series of miscellaneous observations which do not necessarily relate to each other.

Place of Mentors

I was impressed with just how important **mentors** were in the lives of these eight great leaders. Each of the eight leaders had ten or more mentors who strategically affected their lives. These mentors operated over a range of mentor functions including discipling, spiritual guides, coaches, counselors, teachers, sponsors and contemporary models. In addition, a number were divine contacts whose timely intervention was the difference in the focused life.

Must They Come From Heritage Backgrounds?

Focused leaders can come from Christian heritage backgrounds and from non-Christian backgrounds or mixed backgrounds. Simeon and Maxwell came from essentially non-Christian backgrounds. Jaffray was converted in his late teens. His father was not Christian. His mother was. Brengle had a godly mother but his step-father was not. His mother died early. So that his pilgrimage was not based strongly on heritage. On the other hand, Gordon, Mears and Morgan came from a strong Christian heritage.

What About Transitional Training Patterns?

Focused leaders can develop from any of the three training patterns. I have identified three major training patterns through which most leaders emerge. Four of the eight, Gordon, Maxwell, Jaffray, and Simeon (somewhat) fit the *pre-service pattern* (Clinton 1989:354), that is, they receive formal training prior to ministry.

Three fit the *in-service pattern* (Clinton 1989:356), that is, they learn on-the-job and finally after proving their abilities take on full time responsibilities. Morgan, Mears, and McQuilkin moved into ministry without a preliminary time of formal training.

The third is a *modified in-service pattern* (Clinton 1989:357) in which the leader gets ministry experience, then interrupts it for formal training, and then resumes it. Usually this pattern will include further interruptions for training down road. Brengle fit this pattern somewhat. Jaffray, though initially a pre-service pattern, moved toward pattern three, at least in a quasi-form, because he began several Bible schools in Indo-China and Indonesia. These kept him studying in an on-going fashion.

There are advantages and disadvantaged to all of these patterns. In teaching these patterns we point out the advantages and disadvantages of each pattern. But we seek to move people toward the third pattern. However, these leaders show that God can take any kind of training pattern as a background from which to develop a leader to a focused life.

Social Base Patterns[12]

Two of the leaders, Simeon and Mears, deliberately chose single life styles. This life style is most conducive to a focused ministry. As a result they had extremely focused lives which totally were immersed around their ministries.

The rest of the leaders were married. Most operated in a release pattern with the wife dominantly devoting herself to the raising of the family and the husband dominantly devoting himself to ministry. The release pattern is probably one of the most problematic for developing a focused life because of the husband's tendency to ignore family and the possibility of a family crisis which can waylay the ministry. The husbands of these studied varied in their time focus with Maxwell on the end of one scale devoting most of his time to ministry and very little to family development. At the other end of the scale Gordon spent a good deal of time with his family. The others did some of both. For example, in his itinerant ministry in the U.S.A., Morgan would spend whole blocks of time with his family in between trips. And on trips he often traveled with someone from his family.

But the observation to note is that God can develop a focused life from any social base pattern. Each pattern has its advantages supporting a focused life and some disadvantages that make a focused life more difficult.

Concept of Accumulated Influence

Two of the leaders studied, Simeon and Maxwell, had extremely long tenures in one role and one geographical locale (more than 50 years). Both were very effective leaders. A phenomena appearing in both lives was an accumulated influence which like a critical mass seemed to accelerate toward the latter part of their lives. That is, the latter years of their life saw them accelerate their influence because of the long tenure--and associated things that happen with long tenure. This same effect was seen in the life of Brengle who had a long tenure (almost 40 years) in a specific focused role though he operated in different geographical locales. He did operate in the same organization in the same role for an extended time--a long tenure of a different sort.

If these observations hold for other similar cases then there is something to be said for persevering in a ministry locale and or major role for a long time. There may be opposition or even a slow receptivity at first. But one who is in focus or moving toward it can expect in the latter part of the long tenure to have influence beyond what would normally be expected.

Leadership Transition

For a person with a long tenure there is often a difficult time involved in transitioning in a new leader to take over. Frequently, there is a power play to oust that

---

[12]See Appendix D for explanation of social base patterns. The two major patterns demonstrated in the lives studied are the extremes. You would expect the single pattern to support a focused life. And the release pattern can be problematic. All the rest of the social base patterns fit somewhere in between these two in terms of ease or difficulty toward a focused life.

Chapter 10. Focal Findings
page 471

older leader who is reluctant to lose power and influence. This often involves conflict and can actually dampen the accumulated influence effect.

There is a tendency to hold on to old values and traditions which are no longer relevant for meeting the needs of the present generation. Few leadership transitions go smoothly. Spaulding pinpointed an unusual pattern over time in which Maxwell was constantly challenged by God to give up pieces of his leadership pie. Spaulding called this phenomena, the reverse influence-mix challenge. Maxwell, little-by-little, whether he wanted to or not, was sovereignly directed to drop various leadership functions until in his very last years he was reduced to teaching only.

Most of these leaders did not have actual afterglow years.[13] They continued in ministry until they died or were incapacitated physically or imprisoned. McQuilkin and Gordon died relatively early of physical complications. Simeon, Morgan, Mears and Maxwell continued their ministry basically in their formal roles right up to physical incapacity. Jaffray was imprisoned, otherwise he too would have continued. Does that mean that people with focused lives actually plan on ministering until they drop? Can they transition out from responsibility?

Focused leaders need to be aware of leadership transition and move with God to back off and enjoy their Afterglow years.[14]

Satisfied Lives

Recently at a national conference in Colorado I heard one of the plenary speakers make a statement that thrilled me. He has ministered for more than 55 years, 43 in an outstanding leadership training seminary. He is a well known and popular leader who has walked in integrity all these years. He is finishing well. He said, toward the close of one of his plenary talks, as a means of challenging us as leaders to desire to live lives that count, "Folks, you are looking at a leader who is fulfilled. I am satisfied with how my life and ministry has turned out." Read the definition of a focused life again.

A focused life is
- a life dedicated to exclusively carrying out God's unique purposes through it,
- by identifying the focal issues, that is, the **life purpose, unique methodology, major role,** or **ultimate contribution** which allows
- an **increasing prioritization** of life's activities around the focal issues, and
- results in a satisfying life of being and doing.

Notice that last concept--*results in a satisfying life of being and doing*. How many of the focused lives studied herein actually voiced such notions? Two died unexpectedly, relatively early--Gordon and McQuilkin. So they did not have time to think back and reflect on their ministries. One, Jaffray, died in a prison of war camp after several years of suffering. Apart from this hard ending he did look back. He saw 31 years of outstanding

---

[13] Afterglow is a period of time late in life. Supposedly a leader is retired from formal positions of responsibility. But they continue to exert influence upon others due to relationships and prior ministry. Afterglow can last 10-15 years.

[14] Most of the leadership transition case studies in the Scriptures are negative. Several are positive and for that reason need to be studied carefully. The Moses to Joshua transition is a positive case study which involved 11 stages over a number of years. See Haubert and Clinton, The **Joshua Portrait** (1990). The Elijah to Elisha while being a fairly positive transition does not give much detail. In the New Testament, the Barnabas to Paul leadership transition is exemplary. See Raab and Clinton (1985), **Barnabas: Encouraging Exhorter--A Study in Mentoring.**

ministry capped off with 13 years of wonderful expansion in a new field. He without a doubt was satisfied. Simeon, Brengle, Morgan, Mears and Maxwell all died in old age. All reflected back on their ministries. All were satisfied with their lives and expressed this satisfaction in differing ways. Brengle was the clearest in revealing this. Several of his articles in this latter portion of his life treat the concept of finishing well and being satisfied with God's leading and goodness in those latter years. To look back and be satisfied, that is the goal, of a focused life.

Gentleness

I was particularly struck by the comments describing at least several of these leaders in their old age. Simeon, Brengle, Morgan, and Maxwell especially were described as having mellowed with God's processing over the years until in their old age they were described as gentle leaders (2 Timothy 2:24). I was thrilled with this. One, these were strong leaders. They were ambitious leaders with lots of talent. And yet they were gentled over the years with God's processing. Two, I see numerous strong leaders today who are not gentle. We need to see models of leaders who are effective yet gentle.

Odds and Ends

Here are some observations that may stimulate your further thinking.

Most Important Transferable Concepts

A transferable concept is an idea which can most readily be applied to other people's ministry. I have identified several of these transferable concepts and wish to list them in order to stimulate you to think along these lines. You probably will see others.

1. (A Simeon Concept)
   When bringing about change find a precedent in the system which can be used to aid you in your change.
2. (A Simeon Concept)
   Find a center of influence and commit for the long haul.
3. (A Simeon Concept)
   Deliberately find ways to transfer literary resources to those who can use them.
4. (A Simeon Concept)
   Use public lecture series to affirm the values already present in the system rather than denouncing the system.
5. (A Simeon Concept)
   Affect the grassroots over a long enough time and you will affect the whole system.
6. (A Gordon Concept)
   Take responsibility for your training. If you are attending a school which has lacks in training, then you fill in those lacks by self-initiating learning and experience that will round out your training. Don't expect the training to adequately train you. No formal model will. Hence, don't blame the training for any of your lacks after completing it. Supply what you need yourself.
7. (A Gordon Concept)
   If you want power in your ministry get some vital relevant experience with someone who expects and sees power in his/her ministry.

Chapter 10. Focal Findings   page 473

Transferable Concepts continued

8. (A Gordon Concept)
    If you want to develop a broadbased ministry, like a flagship ministry, you must develop a strong confidence in your own self-worth, so that you are not threatened by rising leaders and you can release them to minister. Many of them will bypass you as they move on to reach their potential.
9. (A Gordon Concept)
    Don't be afraid of and hence neglect a truth, like God healing people supernaturally, because of its abuse. Gordon operated a low key ministry of praying for people for healing.
10. (A Brengle Concept)
    If you don't minister for decisions, you probably won't get them. Contrary, if you expect to see people make decisions then you should develop methodology that by God's grace can be used to stimulate decisions.
11. (A Brengle Concept)
    Don't assume that public oratory comes naturally. You must work, even if you have talent, to develop an effective public ministry.
12. (A Brengie Concept)
    Transient ministries which repeat the same thing over and over tend to force a leader to plateau. You must counter this deliberately by mixing personally with the people you minister to and by deliberate disciplines to grow and develop.
13. (A Brengle Concept)
    In public ministry the most important preparation is not the message you will articulate but the preparation of your heart, that God would use you.
14. (A Brengle Concept)
    Vitalize your public reading of Scripture so as to rivet attention on it.
15. (A Morgan Concept)
    Don't defend the Word. Instead use it with expectant power. When taught as it should be it will bring results.
16. (A Morgan Concept)
    Wherever possible capture your ministry in written form that can be passed on to others long after you leave them.
17. (A Morgan Concept)
    Always find the larger perspective into which some Bible book or context fits. Teach the smaller always in light of the larger to which it is contributing.
18. (A Morgan Concept)
    Expect God to give guidance and as you mature to give you more freedom in choosing that guidance.
19. (A Morgan Concept)
    When you find a ministry structure that helps you effectively deliver your ministry, work it to death. Find ways to transfer the dynamics of it into new situations.
20. (A Jaffray Concept)
    Recognize that leaders are late bloomers. Do not be in a hurry to push your leadership on others.
21. (A Jaffray Concept)
    Facts are the fingertips of God. Do your homework, research, on anticipated new ministries. Then use your findings to motivate others.
22. (A Jaffray Concept)
    Expect opposition to advance in new areas. Be prepared to do spiritual warfare as you advance.

Chapter 10. Focal Findings

Transferable Concepts continued

23. (A Jaffray Concept)
Keep your eyes on those who have not been reached. You must be a part of the onward expansion of the Great Commission no matter what ministry you are in.
24. (A McQuilkin Concept)
Don't be satisfied with less than victory in your life.
25. (A McQuilkin Concept)
God may take you through increasing steps of commitment.
26. (A McQuilkin Concept)
Don't be discouraged if you are led into many experiences including shut doors, for all will help you in the long run. All of life is real but all of life is preparing us for all the rest of life. There will be a life work for you which integrates your experiences.
27. (A McQuilkin Concept)
The most important mobilizing method is to put students in the presence of people who are doing it and will challenge them to do so also.
28. (A McQuilkin Concept)
Faith challenges accepted and answered by God provides a powerful model to train people affectively in trusting God.
29. (A McQuilkin Concept)
Expect criticism in your leadership if you hold to an evangelical position.
30. (A Mears Concept)
If you are not certain about going into full time ministry then seek to prepare yourself spiritually and wait; God will make certain when and if and what that full time role should be.
31. (A Mears Concept)
Recruit people around you who will support you and free you to use your giftedness.
32. (A Mears Concept)
Extended times away from ministry in travel can be greatly used not only for renewal but for a continuing educational experience.
33. (A Mears Concept)
Ambiance has much to do with motivating people. If you put people in the presence of God, proper ambiance, and then challenge them with His word they will make decisions.
34. (A Mears Concept)
Little faith brings little results. If you would see big results then by faith expect big results.
35. (A Mears Concept)
Develop what ever means you must in order to provide for your ministry (Regal Press and Forest Home). But be open to the possibility of God developing that embryonic means into an ongoing institution beyond your original needs to accomplish His purposes.
36. (A Maxwell Concept)
Interact directly with the Scriptures and teach others to do so. Find a methodology that will allow potentially Word gifted people to directly study the Scriptures for themselves.
37. (A Maxwell Concept)
Opt for a simple lifestyle.

Chapter 10. Focal Findings   page 475

Transferable Concepts continued

38. (A Maxwell Concept)
    Form partnerships with lay Christians. Together you can have ownership and see God work synergistically through the combination.
39. (A Maxwell Concept)
    Take advantage of windows of opportunity. They may not come again.
40. (A Maxwell Concept)
    God can bring the publicity you may need to promote your work, especially to take advantage of windows of opportunity.

Women in Ministry

Three of the eight were far ahead of their time in their view of women in ministry. Morgan clearly stated that gifts of the Spirit were not gender oriented. That is, women could receive and exercise any of the gifts of the Spirit. He appointed women to sodality-like ministries within his flagship set-up in Westminster. He did not go so far as to talk about women in positional authority such as the pastorate. But it is clear he had a high view of women in leadership. Gordon and Maxwell were even stronger, not only believing that women could have all of the spiritual gifts, but that they also could operate positionally. Gordon and Maxwell were certainly concerned with women on the mission field. Both saw them not as a stop gap because men weren't there but as gifted by God for ministry and therefore fully capable of leadership. Gordon's strong paper on women in ministry saw them operating both abroad and home. Maxwell co-authored a book on women in ministry.

Mears while not an advocate for women in leadership (not against either) certainly demonstrated that a woman could operate powerfully in a pastoral setting with powerful gifting from God.[15]

Simeon's times did not permit or even think about women in ministry--though his functional equivalent of Wesley's lay orders did allow for them to minister in visitation and benevolence ministries.

Brengle operated with The Salvation Army--which fully endorsed women in ministry. His own wife was a full fledged minister with the Salvation Army. Several of the full Generals heading this group over the years have been women.

We do not know of Jaffray's views on this except to recognize that men and women operated in the south China field--in fact, his wife, before her marriage was part of a church planting team. McQuilkin was part of a Bible College which trained men and women, many of which went into sodality ministries.

At least three of the eight strongly encouraged women in ministry. One reason for their effectiveness in the selection and development of leaders was simply that they were willing to play with a full deck. If you limit leadership selection to males only, you are starting out with a pool of potential leaders somewhat less than 50% in most church and parachurch situations. These leaders by their willingness to recognize, select, and train women leaders as well as men had a much larger pool from which to draw leadership.

---

[15]Granted, she herself, preferred to focus on raising up men leaders since the pragmatics of the situation were that if men would lead others would follow--females--and not vice versa.

Chapter 10. Focal Findings   page 476

Most Focused To Least Focused--A Subjective Opinion

All of these leaders were focused. All were effective. All left behind powerful legacies. But can they be ranked as to who was most focused? Here is my opinion. From most focused to least focused: Jaffray, Maxwell, Mears, Simeon, Brengle, McQuilkin, Gordon, and Morgan.

Most Innovative

Mears and Simeon were most innovative in their ministries.

Largest Direct Sphere of Influence

Morgan and Brengle had the largest direct sphere of influence. Mears, Maxwell, and Gordon followed close behind.

Largest In-Direct Sphere of Influence

Simeon, Mears, and Morgan in that order had the largest indirect sphere of influence. Simeon and Mears deeply affected many individual lives with their values. These lives then indirectly influenced many others. Morgan's writings affected many.

Giving To The Kingdom

While all were relatively liberal in their giving to Kingdom work, three were outstanding. Simeon used personal funds to give to benevolence ministries. He lived relatively simply. This allowed him to use money inherited and raise money for buying patronages. These in turn provided funding for evangelical ministers in key location all over England. L.E. Maxwell probably lived at the simplest level in terms of home environment, etc. He also saw to it that his institution was involved in giving. More than $4,000,000 were given to various mission causes from Prairie Bible Institute. Jaffray, whose father was wealthy (though opposed to Jaffray's missionary call) frequently used his own funds, particularly in the depression years to expand ministry in South China. He gave heavily for mission causes. Morgan, though known for receiving high honoraria, also was very liberal in giving though this was often done individually and not known to many.

Interest in Jewish Work

Two of these leaders, Simeon and Gordon, expressed special interest in Jewish missions and helped promote parachurch organizations to reach the Jews.

Stressed the Second Coming in Their Ministry

While all stressed somewhat the second coming in their ministries in order of importance of this doctrine in their ministry philosophy and ministry I would rank these leaders as follows: Jaffray, Gordon, McQuilkin, Simeon, Brengle, Maxwell, Morgan, and Mears.

Were Mission Minded

Missions dominated a number of these leaders and was part of their life purpose. All had a vital interest in missions--the work of expanding the Gospel across cultures. I

Chapter 10. Focal Findings page 477

would rank these leaders as follows in terms of missions interest: Jaffray, Maxwell, McQuilkin, Gordon, Morgan, Simeon, Mears, and Brengle. Missions in some form or fashion was part of the life purpose of each of these leaders.

CHALLENGES

I mentioned in my preface, when I described my theme for this book that the study of these eight leaders would "reflect insightful lessons and values helpful to present day leaders." It is my belief that God can greatly use a study of leaders, like these eight who certainly qualify as *faith leaders* of Hebrews 13:7, to challenge us. It has been so with me. I hope it has been so with you. By way of modeling this I want to share five ways God has used Simeon to challenge me, to enlighten me, and to motivate me to move toward a focused life. I will do the same from Gordon's life. I could easily have done this for all eight. Then I will show you some personal follow-up projects that I have generated because of my study of these leaders. I am hoping that you too will have some follow-up projects. Finally, I simply want to reassert that these lives can help you.

How These Studies Have Helped Me Personally

During the writing of the chapters I would from time-to-time sense that some important concept or illustration had special significance for me. That is, I sensed that God wanted to teach me personally some of the lessons or to draw application from some of these ideas. So after completing all of the chapters I took time to go through each, one-by-one, asking God to point out the important applications for me in my life. I want to illustrate how these leaders have helped me. I will choose two to illustrate. But I easily could have done this for each leader. The following are the important concepts that helped shape my thinking or suggested application for my own life from Simeon and from Gordon.

From Simeon

My personal study of chapter 2 identified some 12 applicational items for my own life. Let me share how five of them affected me.

Idea 1. Continuing on With Important Ideas Even If Not Recognized By System

Charles Simeon was able to bring about change in a system that essentially was opposed to his evangelical ideas. Because he was loyal to the system and had a stable position within it, he was able to weather the opposition that lasted for a period of almost 30 years. Because he kept changing individuals and sending them in to the grass roots of the system over a long period of time, 54 years, he was able to bring about major change even though many in the system were opposed to his evangelical ideas. His position was certain; he could out wait opposition and continue to minister toward his goals.

As a result of my recognizing the two factors, loyalty to the system and stable position, which were true for me too, I was encouraged to continue working in my own system which does not understand my own approach to teaching, writing, or ministry. Rather than seeking to get approval within the system or to change the system I simply have to continue doing very well what I am doing. It will pay great dividends in the future. Previous to my own study of Simeon I was considering leaving my system and going elsewhere, where I am appreciated for my teaching and writing ministry. But one does not have to be appreciated or approved by the system. Simeon was never accepted by the system as a whole for his evangelical beliefs until he had transformed much of it at the

Chapter 10. Focal Findings   page 478

grass roots. Yet he was effective in his ministry. I too am changing lives even though the system does not know this or appreciate it.

Idea 2. Pray Regularly At Each Mentoring Time

I was encouraged by Venn's always taking time to pray with Simeon. This very event impacted Simeon. I have therefore endeavored since reading that to always have prayer with my mentorees whenever we meet. And I do a lot of mentoring. In fact, I am seeking to pray a leadership blessing into their lives.

Idea 3. Find Alternative Ways At The Edge of The System To Experiment With Change

Simeon always found alternative ways to get something done. Often, he was pushing the edge of the envelope of what was accepted in the system. It became clear to me that at the fringes of the system it is not always clear just what is acceptable. It is there that innovative ways can be introduced. It is much more difficult to introduce innovative things in the center of the system which is usually much more rigid. For me the application lies in identifying what the fringes are. Where can I attempt to do some things that would be blocked by the center of the system. Where can I introduce alternative means?

Idea 4. Get Out Written Materials into Centers of Influence for Long Range Influence

I was particularly impressed by Simeon's giving ministry. He gave to needy parishioners out of his own pocket. In fact, he systematically set aside funds for benevolence giving each year. I was particularly impressed in terms with his giving away of resources that would help individuals in ministry and centers of training. He bought 40 copies of the expensive and important study Bible (Brown's Study Bible) and sent them to 40 poor pastors. When he published his major homiletics text, **Horae Homilectae**, which certainly emphasized Biblical preaching, he made sure it got in to all the centers of influence. He donated copies to important political figures, including an autographed copy personally presented to the king. He sent copies to all of the major libraries. I was challenged by his action. I have captured much of my ideation in numerous booklets, books, handbooks, manuals, and papers. Upon reading that, I decided to:

1. identify from all my written materials those resources which contain the most classic ideas (that is, ideas that deal with fundamental dynamics and so will still have application way into the future) and select the five to eight most important ones,
2. get packets of these classic items into libraries of Bible colleges, seminaries, parachurch groups and other learning resource centers around the world,
3. raise funding to send these packets free of charge.

I want my ideas to be used. Why not select the best of them and get them out?

Idea 5. Deliberately Design and Use Equivalents of Simeon's Levels of Intimacy

I was impressed by Simeon's levels of intimacy as a selection means for penetration training. I have drawn his circles and have identified what for me would be functional equivalent activities. I intend to deliberately and systematically employ this concept to give in-depth training to past mentorees and as a selection means for processing new mentorees. I have already envisioned two special ways of his doing two of his inner most levels and have people in mind to invite to them.

Chapter 10. Focal Findings   page 479

These are five of the 12 ideas I saw in Simeon. I intend to write an article or series of articles in the future detailing all 12 of the ideas and show how Charles Simeon, My Friend and Historical mentor, influenced my life.

From Gordon

In my second run-through of Gordon I saw 16 ideas that were striking to me. Most of these had to do with values. Gordon's ministry was a value driven ministry. He was a Christian leader of breadth and balance. What were the important ideas from Gordon that struck me? Let me select five as representative.

Idea 1. Foundational Evaluation Standard

In his dream, (C6 When Christ Came To Church), at age 36, Gordon learned a most important fundamental principle. Christ was always present in his ministry. And it is his approval of what we do in ministry that is most important. Gordon was seeking to bring about change in his church situation. There were a number of things he wanted to correct. But they did not necessarily meet with the approval of some in the church. This mystical experience showed him the final standard of approval for ministry. Both the presence and the approval are critical values that must be experienced by a leader. I am no exception. I was challenged to recognize the presence of Christ in my ministry and to deliberately can consciously minister knowing that presence.

Idea 2. Support of Early Committals

At age 16, almost 17, Gordon committed himself to become a pastor. He was just a teenager. Those around him could have said, "He is just a teenager. He will forget this commitment as he grows older." But they didn't. They supported his decision. In fact, they planned for how he could follow-up. The laid out a developmental plan for getting him educated. This was in a time when few went to University. In fact, few graduated from high school. The family sacrificed to enable him to go on for further training. They backed him in prayer. They corresponded with him getting feedback on how he was doing. And he progressed and prospered and went on to become a great pastor and an influential leader. From this, I learned that early committals by teenagers should be taken seriously and supported. Whenever we see young people responding to a missionary call, or rededicating their lives to serve Christ or committing themselves somehow to Christian work we should immediately think, How can I affirm and support this initial step?

Idea 3. Rapid Early Development--Spiritual Formation in Focus

Gordon developed rapidly in his provisional leadership phase, that is, the first five years in ministry. This is a period of time in which many leaders from the pre-service training pattern drop out from ministry after experiencing the disappointments of these early years. One reason for this drop out concerns the heavy concentration on ministry activity and not spiritual formation. The young leader is learning about giftedness, about how to influence, about ministry activity and the importance of relationships to ministry. There is a tendency to lose a personal emphasis on spirituality in the hubbub of trying to make a success in ministry. In short there is an emphasis on doing rather than being. Gordon's first years are in stark contrast to this. God graciously led him (in a step-by-step way which would become a pattern with Gordon) to a pastoral situation in a sub-urban area--in fact, it was a rural-like pastorate on the edge of a metropolitan area. The situation was such that Gordon could choose to involve himself in all kinds of activity to change this situation. Or he could take time to be with God and build himself up and go slowly in activities. Gordon did three things over the next several years. He immersed himself in historical and literary mentors to develop his inner life. He immersed himself in the Scriptures concerning the provision of Christ for victory in his own life. And he became part of a lateral mentoring group of Christian workers who met on a regular basis to stimulate growth and hold each other accountable for growth and ministry. In short, he kept being as the foundation of his ministry as he developed the doing side.

All leaders, no matter where they are along their personal developmental time-lines need to be reminded of the importance of the inner life. Gordon will maintain this priority all throughout his life. I constantly meet and counsel with mid-career Christian leaders who are all along the time-line. And I find that many have lost the priority of spiritual formation in their lives. I need to be reminded of this for my own life. What does it profit a person to gain the whole world (ministerially speaking) but lose his/her own soul (spiritually speaking)? Gordon stands ever before me to challenge me concerning my spiritual formation.

Idea 4. Influence Means--Board Participation

Simeon exerted great influence on the Anglican church but not from an organizational base. He chose not to become a part of the hierarchical structure. Gordon chose another route. He did become involved in organizational leadership. He became a distinguished member of and strong participant on several important boards of organizations and movements. Simeon and Gordon were both powerful in their influence yet from different approaches. Simeon worked from below and not in the power structure. Gordon worked from above--influencing the strategic direction by being a part of its highest level of leadership. Both means are important. These contrasting means of influence should alert us to the fact that change is complex. It can come via different approaches.

Probably the most important thing about Gordon's organizational influence is that he was a real participant on the boards. His was not a token participation. He actively participated in the decision making, in the vital interests of the organization, and in sponsoring it to others.

Idea 5. Balance--Values

I was impressed again by the 10 critical values seen in Gordon's life. Particularly was I cognizant of the major areas of life and ministry that were represented in these values. Gordon's ministry was value driven. Of the eight studied, only Mears comes close to this same approach to ministry. His constant study of and use of the Scriptures as well as his learning from others and life led him to major convictions which he consistently followed in life. Gordon was balanced. He challenges me afresh to ask the question, "What underlies what I do?"

These are five of the sixteen ideas I saw in Gordon. I intend to write an article or series of articles in the future entitled, A. J. Gordon--A Value Driven Leader.

Personal Follow-Up

At the end of each biographical chapter I have suggested some follow-up ideas for you. My own follow-up projects which have resulted from these studies are three. Let me describe each of my three major follow-up projects.

1. PROJECT 1. HANDBOOK ON FOCUSED LIFE CONCEPTS

I intend too write a handbook which will be used in tandem with **Focused Lives**, to help leaders begin to identify focus in their lives. I have already done the rough draft outline which includes: Chapter 1. Getting the Data: The Time-Line (This will describe how to construct one's own unique time-line, how to identify critical incidents, and how to summarize shaping processes); Chapter 2. The Major Concepts (This will define the following major concepts and give feedback exercises to apply them to the reader's lives: Focused Life, Focal Issues, Normal Order, Life Purpose, Unique Methodology, Major Role); Chapter 3. The Focusing Parameters (This chapter will apply the fourfold parameters to help the reader personally evaluate progress in focus as suggested by the various screens); Chapter 4. Personal Focus Statement (This chapter will help the reader synthesize a personal mission statement which takes into account focusing information gained in the first three chapters); Conclusion.

2. PROJECT 2. POPULAR ARTICLES FOR EXPOSURE

I intend to do articles, at least one on each leader studied. I will write in a popular mode to demonstrate the importance of what can be learned from leaders like these

3. PROJECT 3. FURTHER VOLUMES

I intend to challenge various denominations and parachurch groups to consider volumes like this one for their historical leaders. I will help edit some of these and even contribute biographical chapters to them. I have already challenged one such parachurch group. I believe we need many examples of lives who have finished well to challenge us. I believe also that groups should celebrate their history by remembering their heroes/ heroines. In addition to these specialized groups that I will challenge I want to do various volumes which will be dedicated to: church planters, single women in ministry, lay leaders, business leaders who have been influential for God, etc.

Here, then, is some of what I expect to do because I have read this book and I want to grow. The question is, What will you do?

A Final Word

I had three purposes in mind when I wrote the book Two major ones included,

1. Purpose 1

I wanted my readers to enter into the concepts of the focused life and use them for themselves. I believe there are a lot of leaders who are frustrated because of their non-integrated scattered hit-and-miss ministries. The focused life concepts can bring great freedom to them and release them into purposeful effective ministry. They can minister out of being in the way God intended them to and for the purposes God has for them.

2. Purpose 2

I wanted my readers to recognize the importance of historical mentors. Leaders who have finished well can be a great source of encouragement to present day leaders. Historical mentors are always available.

Chapter 10. Focal Findings

3. **Purpose 3**
   The first two were major purposes. This one is a minor one, but very important to me. I want to expose readers and trainers of leaders to the interpretive genre of biography as a viable, useful approach to profit from lives. I am hoping to encourage other trainer of leaders to begin to study leader's lives from a good framework and then write up those analyses from their interpretive viewpoints. We need many more biographical treatises of leaders.

How well have I done on these purposes? Only you can answer this.

Let me finish by referring back to where I began. I mentioned in the preface that if you condensed the whole book to a thematic statement it would be:

FOCUSED LIVES, AS SEEN IN THESE EIGHT CHRISTIAN LEADERS, include some common elements such as

- long term ministries in a major role crafted to fit the leader, or an expanding, changing role in a long term geographic locale, and/or use of a unique methodology to accomplish purposes which may include,

- a lifelong involvement of serving Christ to fulfill some specific destiny purpose, and/or

- a concentration on achieving certain important goals which left behind legacies for the on-going work of Christ, and

- an importance on the Word of God for personal growth and ministry, and

- the shaping work of God to move these leaders toward their focus, all of

which reflect insightful lessons and values helpful to present day leaders.

How well have I accomplished this theme? Only you can evaluate this.

Here were two ways I suggested that your study of these lives would profit you. Read them again. How can you profit? You should profit by:

1. **Using the Leadership Mandate, Hebrews 13:7,8**
   The Hebrews 13:7,8, leadership mandate gives one answer. As you meditate on these leader's lives you will see *excellent qualities* in their leadership such as values, principles, methods, ministry insights, and perspectives which you can apply to your own life and ministry. As the mandate states, you can trust Jesus to enable you to use these in your own situation.

2. **Proactive Use of Concepts**
   Seeing the many concepts of a focused life defined, described, and illustrated in these lives will give you a working grasp of these ideas. This in turn will allow you to be more proactive in using them in your own life. That is, you can recognize symptoms of these concepts in your own life and can begin to make decisions based on this discernment which will deliberately advance you toward your focused life. You will sense God's affirmation as you deliberately take steps to focus your life around His unique purposes for you. This may mean adapting a role, clarifying a specific life purpose and using it to choose your

Chapter 10. Focal Findings

role and sift your activities, or to clarify achievements you want to accomplish and leave behind as your legacy. Again, because of familiarity you will be sensitive to God's shaping and guidance activities that help you identify and prioritize around these focal issues.

Has the book profited you in these ways? Will it continue to do so? Only you can judge.

Let me close by reminding you of two biblical truths you already know. But perhaps by juxtaposing them they will carry more weight.

We have so many heroes and heroines of the faith who have gone before us and left us their faithful testimonies. These encompass us and speak to us even now. They should impel us to cast aside the barriers that would keep us from finishing well. With renewed vigor we should set for ourselves the task of finishing well, persevering with marathon-like determination, and joining with them.
Hebrews 12:1 (Personal Interpretive Paraphrase)

Remember your former leaders. Think back on how they lived and ministered. Imitate those **excellent qualities** you see in their lives. For Jesus Christ is the same today, as He was in the past and as He will be in the future. What He did for them He will do for you to inspire and enable your leadership.
Hebrews 13:7,8 (Personal Interpretive Paraphrase)

Glossary of Important Terms

Acquired skills	part of the giftedness set; refer to those capacities, skills, talents or aptitudes which have been *learned* by a person in order to allow him/her to accomplish something.
Ai Syndrome	an experience usually early on in a new ministry challenge in which a leader fails so significantly that it is evident that the leader must not trust in self to lead. The leader is desperately thrust back upon God for leadership. Pride is usually dealt with in this shaping process.
apostleship	a spiritual gift in the word cluster; refers to a special leadership capacity to move with authority from God to create new ministry structures (churches and para-church) to meet needs and to develop and appoint leadership in these structures.
ARTICULATION VARIABLE	one of the three ministry philosophy umbrella-like concepts which describes the oral and/or written integration of ones values, principles, and the like into a ministry philosophy.
Artist	an ultimate contribution label describing a person who makes creative breakthroughs in art, literature, communication or the like and sees it enhance ministry. The creative breakthrough is the legacy left behind.
authority	according to D. Wrong one of four major power forms (force, manipulation, authority, persuasion). It has major sub-parts: coercive authority, inducive authority, legitimate authority (positional), competent authority, personal authority (charismatic). Various combinations of these make up a person's power-mix.
authority insights	a shaping activity of God dealing primarily with ministerial formation and in which a leader learns more about the positive and negative ways of influencing followers.
Balance	a technical term in giftedness theory used to describe a proper relationship between manifestations of love, word, and power clusters operating in a given context so that God's witness in that situation can be adequate.
balanced training	training which involves all four components of learning: 1. Input (dominantly cognitive--though skills are sometimes involved), 2. experience (use of input), 3. dynamic reflection (interactive thinking assessing input and experience), 4. formation (deliberate activities toward shaping of spiritual, ministerial, and strategic formations).
BLEND VARIABLE	one of the three ministry philosophy umbrella-like concepts which describes the accumulation of values for life and ministry via God's shaping processes.
bottom-up recruiting	in mentoring, a form of connecting mentor and mentoree in which a mentoree recruits a mentor.
boundary processing	the special shaping activities that occur in the critical transition time a leader goes through as he/she goes from one major development phase on his/her time-line to another. Four typical overall boundary patterns are seen enough to merit names: The Surprise, The Creeping Vine, The New Glasses, The Growth Challenge.
bridging strategy	the integrated approach to bringing change into a system which assesses the system as it is and recognizes where the system ought to be and supplies the game plan for bridging it from where it is to where it ought to be.

Glossary

catalyst	the special role of a change agent who sees the need for change in a system and stimulates change in that system via different means.
change agent	the technical name describing one who is proactively involved in bringing change into a system. Four major types are categorized: catalyst, resource linker, solution giver, and process helper. synonym: person of change.
Christian mystic	according to Wiersbe a person who has: 1. a special consciousness of the spiritual world beyond the physical, 2. a success standard which focuses on pleasing God rather than those in the world, 3. a bent toward developing an intimate relationship with God and its concomitant an unusual sense of His presence everywhere; and 4. a mindset toward constantly relating this unusual experience with God to the practical things of life.
churchman	a term in the church of England which describes someone who works within the proscribed bounds of rules, traditions, and politics of the system.
Coach	one of the nine mentoring types: an active form of mentoring in which a person helps another learn skills in Christian life or ministry and motivates that person to use them.
co-ministry social base	a married social base in which each spouse is involved full-time in the same ministry. They share the major social base responsibilities.
comity	refers to territorial agreements between mission agencies as to which areas each will minister in.
complementary giftedness-Need	one of six important giftedness patterns which describes how sometimes gifted people are drawn to others who need their gifts in order to complete their effectiveness. This happens whether or not the person being drawn even knows of the gifts they possess (which may even be in embryonic form at their stage of development).
conflict	shaping activities of God which usually have to do with others in ministry but which are directed toward the person of the leader rather than the leader's ministry.
Contemporary Model	one of the nine mentoring types: a passive form of mentoring in which a person models life and ministry values so as to impact a mentoree.
convergence	an advanced phase along the generic time-line of a leader in which the leader experiences an increased effectiveness in ministry du to the coming together of a number of factors including giftedness, role, maturity, cogent ministry philosophy, sense of destiny, ideal influence-mix, geographical locale, special opportunity.
Counselor	one of the nine mentoring types: an active form of mentoring in which a person helps another by giving timely advice.
crises	shaping activities by God which have great potential to bring about life maturing. These are times in which unusually intense situations create a sense of desperation without remedy unless God breaks in.
critical incident	a special intervention (could be a series over time) in which God gives a *major value* that will flow through the life or will give *strategic direction* to narrow the leader's life work or a combination of value and direction.
Crusader	an ultimate contribution label describing a person who seeks to right wrongs in society or the church.

Glossary

destiny fulfillment	shaping processes used by God in the latter stages of a leader's life in which the leader sees a sense of destiny coming to pass.
destiny preparation	shaping processes used by God in the earliest stages of a leader's initial awareness of a sense of destiny which hints at destiny.
destiny revelation	shaping processes used by God in which He reveals something of His purposes for a leader in such a way as to inspire that leader to go on and serve God knowing that God's hand is on his/her life.
direct influence	one of the three major ways of sphere of influence which describes direct face-to-face ministry.
discernings of spirits	a spiritual gift of the power cluster; The discernings of spirits gift refers to the ability given by God to perceive issues in terms of spiritual truth, to know the fundamental source of the issues and to give judgment concerning those issues; this includes the recognition of the spiritual forces operating in the issue.
discipler	one of the nine mentoring types: an active form of mentoring in which a person helps another learn the basic habits of Christianity so that they can continue to walk with Christ and grow.
distance mentoring	a form of mentoring in which mail, faxes or computer networks are used to connect mentors and mentorees who are separated geographically. Any of several of the mentor types can be done via distance mentoring.
Divine Contact	a special kind of mentor who appears at a timely moment and intervenes in the life of a leader to impart information, perspective, direction, resources or whatever so as to significantly affect the leader usually in a strategic sense and does so with what is perceived as God-given authority.
dominant gift	part of the gift-mix; refers to that gift in the gift-mix or gift-cluster which is more central to the person's ministry.
double confirmation	a certainly guidance shaping experience in which God assures a person via more than one channel of His intent. Usually it is an inner conviction affirmed by some outside source unaware of the previous inner guidance.
evangelism	a spiritual gift in the word cluster; The gift of evangelism in general refers to the capacity to challenge people through various communicative methods (persuasion) to receive the Gospel of salvation in Christ so as to see them respond by taking initial steps in Christian discipleship.
exhortation	a spiritual gift in the word cluster; the capacity to urge people to action in terms of applying Biblical truths, to encourage people generally with Biblical truths, or to comfort people through the application of Biblical truth to their needs.
extraction training	refers to the method of training which takes emerging leaders from their normal cultural setting and puts them into a somewhat artificial environment for their training--like a residential Bible school. Such an extraction makes it difficult for the trained person to re-enter the situation. But it enables major and rapid change among the leader being trained.
faith	a spiritual gift of the power cluster; The gift of faith refers to the unusual capacity of a person to recognize in a given situation that God intends to do something and to trust God for it until He brings it to pass.

Glossary

faith challenge	a shaping process in which God challenges a leader to trust Him in a special way in ministry. A positive response brings an expansion in ministry and builds a stronger base for trusting God in the future. Earlier shaping experiences of this nature are referred to as faith checks since they are directed toward testing and initially building faith in a life. Later experiences are called challenges since they are not so much directed toward building faith as they are in expanding ministry into some new realm.
flagship church	a church which sets an example for other churches. It has a full orbed ministry and is influencing regional and nationally.
focal element	refers to the element of a person's giftedness set that is dominant and to which the other two elements operate in a supportive way which enhances the dominant element.
focal issues	The four items which help focus a life for accomplishments of God's purposes, that is, narrow a leader toward his/her lifework: life purpose, unique methodology, major role, ultimate contribution.
focused life	a life dedicated to exclusively carrying out God's unique purposes through it, by identifying the focal issues, that is, the **life purpose, unique methodology, major role,** or **ultimate contribution** which allows an **increasing prioritization** of life's activities around the focal issues, and results in a satisfying life of being and doing.
focal screens	perspectives which help one reflect and discover the focal issues. These include such things as: personality and giftedness which help one discover beingness and hence leads to major role clarification; destiny, social base, paradigm shifts, boundary processing which represent sovereign shaping leading toward clarification of life purposes; major values and ministry insights which lead one to the controlling ideation of the life and hence perhaps discovery of unique methodology; future perfect paradigm, ultimate contribution, destiny fulfilled, life purpose fulfilled-the components leading to life achievement and final legacies.
focal value	a dominant controlling perspective (a leadership value) which interweaves itself throughout a person's ministry and usually can be traced to a critical incident.
FOCAL VARIABLE	one of the three ministry philosophy umbrella-like concepts which describes the ways that God focuses a life via values and strategic guidance.
force	according to wrong one of four major power forms (force, manipulation, authority, persuasion).
founder	an ultimate contribution label describing a person who begins organizations which are left behind as a legacy.
future perfect paradigm	an approach to viewing the future whereby a leader by faith sees how something will be in the future and makes decision based on that future reality in terms of the issues which flow back from that reality. There is a dynamic tension between what is and what is to be. The leader negotiates this tension but always affirming all that agrees with the future reality.
gift-cluster	a term describing a leader who has matured in understanding of and use of his/her gift-mix. The individual gifts of the gift-mix are seen to operate synergistically.
gift-cluster ripening	describes the last stages of the standard giftedness development pattern. This is when the gift-mix is maturing and operating synergistically.

Glossary

gift projection	the tendency of strong gifted leaders to lay expectations (even guilt trips) on followers to operate in the same gifts in which these leaders are strong.
gifts of governments	a spiritual gift of the love cluster; The gifts of governments involves a capacity to manage details of service functions so as to support and free other leaders to prioritize their efforts.
gifts of healings	a spiritual gift of the power cluster; Gifts of healings refer to the supernatural releasing of healing power for curing all types of illnesses.
gifts of helps	a spiritual gift of the love cluster; The gifts of helps refers to the capacity to unselfishly meet the needs of others through very practical means.
giftedness development	the major pattern which describes how giftedness elements are discovered over time.
giftedness drift	one of six important giftedness patterns which describes the tendency for people to drift toward ministry tasks or assignments which utilize their giftedness--even though that giftedness might not be explicitly known.
giftedness discovery process item	refers to any significant advancement along the giftedness development pattern and the event, person or reflection process that was instrumental in bringing about the discovery.
giftedness set	a set of three elements seen in a leader's life: natural abilities, acquired skills, and spiritual gifts.
giftedness time-line	a horizontal display of the discovery and acquisition of natural abilities, acquired skills, and spiritual gifts by identifying the actual date in which there was some recognition or discovery.
gift-mix	a label that refers to the set of spiritual gifts being used by a leader at any given time in his/her ministry.
giving	a spiritual gift of the love cluster; The gift of giving refers to the capacity to give liberally to meet the needs of others and yet to do so with a purity of motive which senses that the giving is a simple sharing of what God has given.
Goodwin's Expectation principle	a social dynamic which states that emerging leaders tend to live up to the genuine expectations of leaders they respect. Wise mentors use this with great power to change lives.
Harvest leader model	a philosophical model founded on the central thrust of Jesus' teaching to expand the Kingdom by winning new members into it as demonstrated in the agricultural metaphors of growth in scripture.
Historical Model	one of the nine mentoring types: a passive form of mentoring in which a biography or autobiography of a person is used to impart life and ministry values so as to impact a mentoree.
ideal role	a role which matches giftedness, personality, influence-mix, experience and fits destiny so as to enhance a person's ministry.
independent social base	a married social base in which each spouse is involved full-time in a different ministry from the other. They share the major social base responsibilities.

Glossary

indirect influence	one of the three major ways of sphere of influence which describes a leader who influences significant individuals who influence others or non-face-to-face influence like that via writings or other media.
influence-mix	the profile of direct, indirect, and organizational influence which a leader has at any given time. Includes for each category: extensiveness (numbers), intensiveness (penetration), or comprehensiveness (breadth).
influence-mix challenge	describes the shaping activity of God to expand a leader in terms of people being influenced. This could be a change of profile in terms of direct, indirect or organizational or in terms of extensiveness, intensiveness, or comprehensiveness within each kind of influence. God has created each leader with a potential influence-mix. His intent is to shape until that level is reached.
influence-mix reversal challenge	describes the shaping activity of an older leader who is challenged by God to release areas of influence to up and coming leaders. Little-by-little areas of responsibility will be removed if the leader is sensitive to God and developing leaders to take these responsibilities. Finally, the leader, in Afterglow, influences dominantly by spiritual authority and networking power rather than positional.
inner life growth	a preliminary stage in the time-line of a developing leader in which one of the symptoms of an emerging leader is seen, that of response to God in terms of character shaping, the transformation of the inner life. The next stage involves transition into leadership.
in-service pattern	a transitional training pattern in which a person basically learns ministry by on-the-job training.
Inspirational Functions	one of three leadership functions; leadership activities that leaders do to motivate people to work together and to accomplish the ends of the organization.
integrity check	an early shaping process used by God to help a leader learn to hold and live by convictions. Positive response is usually followed by deepening of character and expansion of ministry potential.
interpretation of tongues	a spiritual gift of the power cluster; The gift of interpretation of tongues refers to the ability to spontaneously respond to a giving of an authoritative message in tongues by interpreting this word and clearly communicating the message given.
intrapreneur	a leader with new and creative insights who works within a system and introduces change into the system as opposed to an entrepreneur who usually starts his/her own organization to utilize the creative instinct.
isolation	shaping experiences, eventually perceived of as from God, in which a leader is set aside from ministry in order to be deepened in relationship with God.
Joseph syndrome	a description of the frequently seen pattern, *the way up is down*, in which God's sovereign activity seems to take a leader through difficult shaping experiences in preparation for a powerfully expanded ministry.
Joshua affirmation syndrome	an experience with God, usually close after an appointment to a new ministry challenge, in which a leader is seen to be affirmed by God and to have spiritual authority. Such an experience brings the leader acceptance by followers and highly motivates the leader toward the new ministry challenge.
last straw syndrome	the recurring pattern seen when a change process has been long and hard in which after the change comes in the change agents become discouraged with further involvement in the changed system because of perceived ramifications which occur.

Glossary

leader	a person with God-given capacity, and God-given responsibility who is influencing some of God's people towards God's purposes.
leadership	a dynamic process over an extended period of time in various situations in which a leader utilizing leadership resources, and by specific leadership behaviors, influences followers, toward accomplishment of aims mutually beneficial for leaders and followers.
leadership committal	a special moment in which a leader or emerging leader responds to God's shaping processes of that moment with an all out surrender to do what God wants in leadership. This can be repeated over a lifetime as God reveals new leadership assignments.
leadership function	general activities that leaders must do and/or be responsible for in their influence responsibilities with followers. Three major functions under which all other leadership activities can be grouped include: task oriented leadership, relationship oriented leadership, inspirational leadership.
leadership value	an underlying assumption which affects how a leader behaves in or perceives leadership situations or issues.
life crises	a special case of crises shaping in which loss of life is imminent and threatened. This causes reevaluation of life purposes and the meaning of life.
life purpose	the central focal issues which describes a burden-like calling to fulfill something, to see something done.
Like-Attracts-Like gift pattern	describes an early giftedness recognition pattern frequently seen in potential leaders in which those potential leaders are intuitively attracted to leaders who have like giftedness even though the giftedness in the potential leader may be very embryonic.
Linker	a form of connecting mentor and mentoree in which a third person recognizes needs and someone who can help and instigates the connection.
literary processing	God's use of printed materials to shape a leader by vicarious learning experiences. The leader benefits from someone else's experience.
loose Venn diagram	describes a Venn diagram in which there is in general a lack of over lap between elements and items. Usually there will be some elements or items not relating to others.
love gifts	a cluster of gifts; one of the three corporate functions of gifts; these are manifestations of God's love through practical ways that can be recognized by a world around us which needs love. They demonstrate the reality of relating to this God.
macro-lesson	a high level generalization of a leadership observation (suggestion, guideline, requirement, value), stated as a lesson, which repeatedly occurs throughout different leadership eras, and thus has potential as a leadership absolute.
major role	the official or unofficial position, or status/ platform, or leadership functions, or job description which uniquely fits who a leader is and lets that leader effectively accomplish life purpose(s), by enhancing giftedness and by using unique methodology, in order to leave behind special contributions or ultimate contributions.

Glossary

page 492

manipulation	according to wrong one of four major power forms (force, manipulation, authority, persuasion).
mentor	an ultimate contribution label describing a person who has a ministry thrust which is directed toward individuals through relationship means. These people who have been relationally empowered are the legacy left behind.
mentoring	a relational process in which one person, the mentor, empowers another person, the mentoree, by a transfer of resources.
mercy	a spiritual gift of the love cluster; The gift of mercy refers to the capacity to both feel sympathy for those in need (especially the suffering) and to manifest this sympathy in some practical helpful way with a cheerful spirit so as to encourage and help those in need.
mini-convergence	a term describing some effective ministry of a leader in which several factors fit together to enhance ministry--example: role and giftedness go together.
ministerial formation	the shaping activities of God which are directed toward building leadership skills and knowledge in a person's life.
ministry affirmation	an experience perceived as from God in which the leader is affirmed by God in terms of ministry effort. It is a renewal experience in which the leader senses God's approval and hence rededicates himself/herself to serving God.
ministry assignment	describes a ministry experience usually of 1-3 years duration which is more permanent than a ministry task yet has the same basic pattern of entry, ministry, closure, and transition out of the ministry situation and through which God gives new insights to the leaders so as to expand influence capacity and responsibility toward future leadership. One can trace developmental progress across a ministry assignment by noting before and after evaluation of various measurement items.
ministry challenge	a shaping process, one of the expansion cluster, which God uses to expand a leader's ministry in terms of a wider sphere of influence and further development toward realization of potential leadership influence.
ministry insights	refers to breakthroughs in how to carry how ministry with effectiveness.
ministry conflict	shaping activities of God which utilize adverse reactions in a given ministry situation to teach a leader valuable lessons.
ministry philosophy	refers to ideas, values, and principles whether implicit or explicit which a leader uses as guidelines for decision making, for exercising influence, and for evaluating his/her ministry.
modified in-service	a transitional training pattern in which a leader is first trained via on-the-job training and then interrupts ministry some time later for a time of mid-career training. This interruption type of training may be repeated.
ministry task	an assignment from God (not always recognized as such) which primarily tests a person's faithfulness and obedience and allows use of ministry gifts in the context of a task which has closure, accountability, and evaluation. Self-initiated tasks are highly indicative of leadership.
natural abilities	part of the giftedness set; refer to those capacities, skills, talents or aptitudes which are *innate* in a person and allow him/her to accomplish things.

Glossary

negative preparation	a special shaping activity used by God which uses negative circumstances to prepare a person for a new situation. Such a person so prepared moves very freely to the next situation.
negative testing pattern	an early integrated shaping process used by God to correct a leader. God brings or uses a situation in the life of a leader (obedience check, faith check, integrity check, word check or ministry task) to challenge the leader. The pattern is threefold: the test comes, the leader responds negatively or does not discern the testing, God brings remedial shaping to repeat the test or after repeated trials severely disciplines the leader.
networking power	God's use of relationships in a leader's life so as to use these connections to further the development and ministry of a leader.
non-vested gifts	spiritual gifts that appear situationally and may not necessarily be repeated. Sometimes described as come-and-go gifts imparted by the Holy Spirit in a group situation where they are needed at the time.
obedience check	an early shaping process used by God to help a leader learn obedience. Positive response is usually followed by deepening of character and expansion of ministry potential.
organizational influence	one of the three major ways of sphere of influence which describes a leader who operates on boards, committees or other networks to control organizations.
paradigm shift	a major change of perspective which significantly affects how a leader views some aspect of life or ministry thereafter.
pastoring	a spiritual gift in the word cluster; The pastoral gift is the capacity to exercise concern and care for members of a group so as to encourage them in their growth in Christ which involves modeling maturity, protecting them from error and disseminating truth.
people movements	a church growth term which refers to multi-individual conversions when Christianity sweeps through a tightly grouped homogeneous unit of people. It almost appears like a mass movement. Decisions in such societies is usually group oriented.
Pioneer	an ultimate contribution label describing a person who begins new ministries to meet unmet needs such as Apostolic ministries to unreached peoples.
positive testing pattern	an early integrated shaping process used by God to expand a leader. God brings or uses a situation in the life of a leader (obedience check, faith check, integrity check, word check or ministry task) to challenge the leader. The pattern is threefold: the test comes, the leader responds positively, God expands the leader.
power gate	refers to an unusual experience with God in which the leader appropriates divine power for life or ministry. Such an experience is usually recognized as a special sense of destiny experience which will deeply affect the person's walk with Christ. Where the experience is primarily directed toward enablement for Christian living, it is called life power. Where the experience is primarily directed toward enablement of effective Christian ministry it is called gifted power. Leaders usually go through one or the other (sometimes both) as they move on to a focused life.
power ministry	refers to use of gifts from the power cluster in a given ministry setting so as to authenticate the reality of the power and presence of the unseen God.

Glossary

power-mix	refers to the profile, that is, the combination of power bases a leader uses to influence followers including: force, manipulation, authority (coercive, induced, legitimate, competent, charismatic), and persuasion.
power gifts	a cluster of gifts; one of the three corporate functions of gifts; a cluster of spiritual gifts that demonstrate the authenticity, credibility, power and reality of the unseen God.
pre-service pattern	a transitional training pattern in which a leader studies for ministry prior to entering it full time.
primary gifts	gifts that are vested gifts and are currently being demonstrated as a significant part of the gift-mix.
process helper	the special role of a change agent who sees the entire cycle of bringing change into a system and can coordinate the roles of various change agents and participants so as to implement a bridging strategy with the least trauma.
process item	a technical term used in leadership emergence theory which describes the shaping activity of God. This shaping activity usually involves three kinds of formation: spiritual formation (leadership character), ministerial formation (leadership skills), and strategic formation (leadership values and direction).
Promoter	an ultimate contribution label describing a person who is adept at motivating people toward a cause.
prophecy	a spiritual gift in the word cluster; A person operating with the gift of prophecy has the capacity to deliver truth (in a public way) either of a predictive nature or as a situational word from God in order to correct by exhorting, edifying or consoling believers and/or to convince non-believers of God's truth.
Public Rhetorician	an ultimate contribution label which describes a person whose public ministry effects lives. The lives so effected and the model of that public ministry are the legacies left behind.
release pattern	also called internal/ external ministry pattern. A social base pattern in which one spouse concentrates on internal ministry, mainly social base needs, while the other concentrates on external ministry.
renewal experience	a specially meaningful encounter with God in which He communicates with *freshness* various kinds of things needed by a leader such as: insights about Himself, affirmation--both personal and ministry, inspiration to continue, breakthrough concepts which inspire one to try them in ministry, a sense of His personal presence and/or power, an unusual sense of intimacy--can be tied to some symbolic thing (like a place, physical object, etc)., perspective on time, now and/or the future so that ones faith is increased to see God in what is happening and will happen, so as to challenge the leader to have a renewed desire to continue on, to start afresh, and to rededicate and continue on in following God.
Researcher	an ultimate contribution label describing a person who studies people, events, ministry and the like in order to develop ideation that can help others in ministry.
role-gift enablement	one of six giftedness discovery patterns. It describes how God sometimes puts a person in a role which needs gifts not yet known or possessed. God then enables by giving temporarily those gifts or permanently imparting those gifts or bringing the gifts into the situation to someone in the corporate group.

Glossary

ruling	a spiritual gift in the word cluster; A person operating with a ruling gift demonstrates the capacity to exercise influence over a group so as to lead it toward a goal or purpose with a particular emphasis on the capacity to make decisions and keep the group operating together.
Saint	an ultimate contribution label which describes a person whose life is a model of godliness for others to emulate.
secondary gifts	gifts that were at one time primary gifts but are no longer being demonstrated as part of the current gift-mix.
sense of destiny	a growing awareness by a leader that God's Hand is on his/her life for special purposes and will lead to and enable those purposes. This growing awareness occurs over a lifetime via a threefold pattern: destiny preparation shaping, destiny revelation shaping, and destiny fulfillment shaping.
Servant leader model	a philosophical model which is founded on the central thrust of Jesus' teaching on the major quality of great Kingdom leaders. That is, a leader uses leadership to serve followers. This is demonstrated in Jesus' own ministry.
Shepherd leader model	a philosophical model which is founded on the central thrust of Jesus' own teaching and modeling concerning the responsibilities of leadership in caring for followers as seen in the various Shepherd/ Sheep metaphors in scripture.
social base	the home environment out of which a leader operates and which meets the four basic needs: emotional, economic, strategic, physical.
sovereign guidance	the label describing those shaping activities, those divine moments of guidance when God circumstantially opens and closes doors behind the scenes.
sphere of influence	the totality of people being influenced by a leader including those directly, indirectly, or organizationally influenced.
spiritual authority	a power base a leader uses to influence followers. It is the right to lead granted by followers to a leader because of their perception of spirituality in the leader. Usually this recognition comes through acknowledgment of the leader's deep experiences with God, the leader's knowledge of God and what God wants, and via gifted power.
spiritual authority discovery	a shaping activity of God dealing primarily with ministerial formation and in which a leader learns more about the positive ways of influencing followers using spiritual authority as a power base.
spiritual formation	the shaping activities of God which are directed toward building character and spirituality in a person's life.
spiritual gift	a God-given unique capacity which is given to each believer for the purpose of releasing a Holy Spirit empowered ministry either in a situation or to be repeated again and again.
spiritual guide	one of the nine mentoring types: an active form of mentoring in which a person helps another evaluate and progress in spiritual maturity, especially with reference to centrality, interiority, Spirit sensitivity, and uniqueness.
Sponsor	one of the nine mentoring types: a passive form of mentoring in which a person helps link a person to opportunity and resources and in other ways helps promote a person to reach potential and move along career paths that otherwise may not have happened.

Glossary

Stabilizer	an ultimate contribution label describing a person who can help maintain an organization and minister so as to ensure its effective survival.
stewardship model	a philosophical model which is founded on the central thrust of several accountability passages, that is, that a leader must give account of his/her ministry to God.
Strategic direction	refers to God's intervention which helps move a leader along toward the focal issues: role, life purpose, unique methodology, or ultimate contribution of the leader. That is, it is God's guidance directing toward life work.
strategic formation	the shaping activities of God which are directed toward guiding the leader into life work and imbedding the values and ministry philosophy out of which that lifework will flow.
Stylistic Practitioner	an ultimate contribution label which describes a legacy left behind by a person who models a ministry that others can use to stimulate their own ministry efforts.
synergism	and related words (synergistic, synergistically) all refer to a process in which items work together to produce a united effort which is greater than just the sum of the individual efforts.
teaching	a spiritual gift in the word cluster; A person who has the gift of teaching is one who has the ability to instruct, explain, or expose Biblical truth in such a way as to cause believers to understand the Biblical truth.
tertiary gifts	gifts that are now non-vested gifts or come and go due to spontaneous activity of the Holy Spirit.
tight Venn Diagram	A Venn diagram in which there is much overlap of elements and items with the major part of the diagram focused about the more important elements.
tongues	a spiritual gift of the power cluster; The gift of tongues refers a spontaneous utterance of a word from God in unknown words (to the individual giving the word) to a group of people.
top down recruiting	a form of connecting mentor and mentoree in which the mentor recruits the mentoree.
transferable concepts	ideas seen in the lives of these focused leaders which may easily be applied to modern day ministries.
ultimate contribution	a legacy that a leader will leave behind after life is over. Leaders usually have several of these.
union life	a label expressing the quality life of a leader who has gone through a life power paradigm shift. It is a life in which the Spirit of Christ manifests itself in a unique expression of the leader's personality portraying godliness. It also goes by such names as The Normal Christian life, The Exchanged Life, The Deeper Life, The Crucified Life, The Victorious Life. Wesleyan expressions, though slightly different, include such labels as The Pure Heart, The Heart of Love, etc.

Glossary

unique methodology	a ministry insight for delivering one's ministry. This allows the leader to pass on to others the essentials of doing something or using something. This methodology becomes a major means which moves people toward results in line with life purposes or ultimate contributions.
Venn Diagram	A pictorial display of one's entire giftedness set or ultimate contribution set which relates importance of elements and items by size, spacing, and symbols. Larger size means more relative importance. Overlaps means things work jointly. Non-overlap means they work exclusively. In the giftedness Venn diagram rectangular is used for natural abilities. Triangles for spiritual gifts. Circles for spiritual gifts. In the ultimate contribution Venn Diagram circles or ovals are used for each of the contribution types.
vested gift	a spiritual gift belonging in a leader's gift-mix, which is repeatedly used or seen in the ministry of the leader.
word check	an early shaping process used by God to help a leader learn to hear and respond to God's revelation. Positive response is usually followed by deepening of character and expansion of ministry potential.
vested gifts	spiritual gifts that appear repeatedly in a person's ministry and can be repeated at will by the person.
word gifts	a cluster of gifts; one of the three corporate functions of gifts; they clarify the nature of this unseen God and what He expects from His followers. People using these gifts both communicate about God and for God.
word of knowledge	a spiritual gift of the power cluster; The word of knowledge gift refers to the capacity or sensitivity of a person to supernaturally perceive revealed knowledge from God which otherwise could not or would not be known and apply it to a situation.
word of wisdom	a spiritual gift of the power cluster; The word of wisdom gift refers to the capacity to know the mind of the Spirit in a given situation and to communicate clearly the situation, facts, truth or application of the facts and truth to meet the need of the situation.
workings of power	a spiritual gift of the power cluster; The workings of powers, gift of miracles, refers to the releasing of God's supernatural power so that the miraculous intervention of God is perceived and God receives recognition for the supernatural intervention.
Writer	an ultimate contribution label describing one who is able to capture ideas and publish them for others. Writers are of two kinds: those who write for the times in which they live, called contemporary, or those who write cataloguing issues which will be classic, useful long after their times.

Appendix A. 6 Barriers to Finishing Well

While the reasons why leaders get sidetracked and/or finish poorly are varied and complex, many can be traced at the root to the following 6 which can often prove fatal.

Barrier 1. FINANCES--THEIR USE AND ABUSE

Leaders, particularly those who have power positions and make important decisions concerning finances, tend to use practices which may encourage incorrect handling of finances and eventually wrong use. A character trait of greed often is rooted deep and eventually will cause impropriety with regard to finances. Numerous leaders have fallen due to some issue related to money. Frequently it includes borrowing from the till with intent to pay back. And this continues until it is beyond remedy. Integrity in finances can not be too great. Measures to insure integrity in finances must be in place in church and parachurch organizations. Responsible leaders will do this.

Biblical Examples: Gideon's golden ephod; Ananias and Sapphira.

Barrier 2. POWER--Its Abuse

Leaders who are effective in ministry must use various power bases in order to accomplish their ministry. With power so available and being used almost daily, there is a tendency to abuse it. Leaders who rise to the top in a hierarchical system tend to assume privileges with their perceived status. Frequently, these privileges include abuse of power. And they usually have no counter balancing accountability.

Biblical Example: Uzziah's usurping of priestly privilege.

I have interviewed numerous leaders at the top of hierarchical systems such as senior pastors of large Flagship types of churches or heads of parachurch organizations. Many of these types of leaders are entrepreneurial or apostolic in make-up. They do not like accountability or submission to anyone else. Some claim to have it with a board which they have discipled or hand-picked from within their own ministry. In fact such a board usually sees itself under the spiritual authority of the top leader who picked it. Such a board usually can not discipline the top leader. Many of these of course are in a deep relationship with God and hence are sensitive to His correcting voice via the Holy Spirit. But whether or not this is true, such a leader stands in a very vulnerable position which depends only on himself/herself. Let the one who stands in such a position take heed lest he/she fall.

Barrier 3. PRIDE--Which Leads To Downfall

Pride (inappropriate and self-centered) can lead to a downfall of a leader. As a leader there is a dynamic tension that must be maintained. We must have a healthy respect for our selves, and yet we must recognize that we have nothing that was not given us by God and He is the one who really enables ministry.

Biblical Example: David's numbering.

Frequently strong leaders do not even realize they are dealing with pride issues that could be harmful. They may best be detected by outsiders (external mentors) to the system in which the leader is operating.

Barrier 4. SEX--Illicit Relationships

Illicit sexual relationships have been a major downfall both in the Bible and in contemporary cultures. Joseph's classic integrity check with respect to sexual sin is the ideal model that should be in leaders minds. Often these relationships start out innocently but build till conscience and ethical issues are cast aside. It is tragic to see a whole lifetime of sacrifice and ministry go by-the-by because of indiscretion along these lines. Is it worth it? No! David's example below was a pivotal point from which his leadership never fully recovered. It was all downhill from here on.

Biblical Example: David's sin with Bathsheba

Appendix A. 6 Barriers to Finishing Well   page 500

Again what can we do by way of preventive suggestion, rather than remedial help. I suggest that we understand and insure the building of healthy social bases for each leader in our organizations.[1]

Barrier 5. FAMILY--Critical Issues

Problems between spouses or between parents and children or between siblings can destroy a leader's ministry. What is needed are Biblical values lived out with regard to husband-wife relationships, parent-children, and sibling relationships. Of growing importance is the social base profiles for singles in ministry and for married couples.

Biblical Example: Ammon and Tamar. Absalom's revenge. Eli's sons. Samuel's sons.
The suggestion under Barrier 4 applies as well here. Social base processing deals with both family--critical issues and sex--illicit relationships.

Barrier 6. PLATEAUING.

Leaders who are competent tend to plateau. Their very strength becomes a weakness. They can continue to minister at a level without there being a reality or Spirit empowered renewing effect. Most leaders will plateau several times in their life times of development. Some of the 5 things for enhancing a good finish will counteract this tendency. There again is a dynamic tension that must be maintained between leveling off for good reasons, (consolidating one's growth and/or reaching the level of potential for which God has made you) and plateauing because of sinfulness or loss of vision.

Biblical Example: David in the latter part of his reign just before Absalom's revolt.

Recognition of plateauing is a subtle thing. And even if one recognizes such a thing there is a built-in tendency because of the plateauing to feel powerless to do anything about it. Usually outside help (mentoring or other kinds--paradigm shifts, renewal experiences, or the like) is needed

Conclusion

Awareness of these barriers is a first step in avoidance of them. A study of the 5 enhancements to finishing well is also helpful since they deal with measures to overcome these very barriers.

---

[1] See *Social Base Processing--The Home Base Environment Out of Which A Leader Works* (1993) paper by Dr. J. Robert Clinton. Available from Barnabas Publishers. Some organizations have studied these concepts with their leaders and spouses and have agreed on a written covenant to which the organization pledges itself with regard to monitoring, evaluating, and helping its leaders with social base issues.

Appendix B. 5 Things To Enhance Good Finishes

Just as we can learn from those who didn't finish well we can also study those leaders who finished well and learn some things that happened to enhance their good finishes. There are items which help leaders continue well and to finish well in ministry. Five such items are repeated in a number of leader's lives who finished well. Not all five are in every life but most of them usually are.

Enhancement 1. PERSPECTIVE.

We need to have a lifetime perspective on ministry. **Effective leaders view present ministry in terms of a lifetime perspective.** This is one of 7 major leadership lessons seen in effective leader's lives.[1] We gain that perspective by studying lives of leaders as commanded in Hebrews 13:7,8. I have been doing intensive study of leader's lives over the past 13 years. Leadership emergence theory is the result of that research. Its many concepts can help us understand more fully just how God does shape a leader over a lifetime. My findings are available in two books, **The Making of A Leader,** published by NAVPRESS IN 1988 and a lengthy detailed self-study manual, **Leadership Emergence Theory,** that I privately publish for use in classes and workshops. In addition, my latest research is available in position papers published by Barnabas Publishers.

Enhancement 2. RENEWAL.

Special moments of intimacy with God, challenges from God, new vision from God and affirmation from God both for personhood and ministry will occur repeatedly to a growing leader. These destiny experiences will be needed, appreciated, and will make the difference in persevering in a ministry. All leaders should expectantly look for these repeated times of renewal. Some can be initiated by the leader (usually extended times of spiritual disciples). But some come sovereignly from God. We can seek them, of course, and be ready for them. Let me define renewal as I have observed it in effective leaders' lives.

definition Renewal is a specially meaningful encounter with God in which He communicates with *freshness* various kinds of things needed by a leader such as:

- insights about Himself,
- affirmation--both personal and ministry,
- inspiration to continue,
- breakthrough concepts which inspire one to try them in ministry,
- a sense of His personal presence and/or power,
- an unusual sense of intimacy--can be tied to some symbolic thing (like a place, physical object, etc).,
- perspective on time, now and/or the future so that ones faith is increased to see God in what is happening and will happen,

so as to challenge the leader to have a renewed desire to continue on, to start afresh, and to rededicate and continue on in following God.

---

[1] The other six include, Effective Leaders: 1. maintain a learning posture throughout life; 2. value spiritual authority as a primary power base; 3. recognize leadership selection and development as a priority function; 4. have a dynamic ministry philosophy; 5. evince a growing awareness of their sense of destiny; 6. see relational empowerment as both a means and a goal of ministry. These were also part of the selection criteria for the eight chosen in this book.

Appendix B. 5 Things To Enhance Good Finishes

Most leaders who have been effective over a lifetime have needed and welcomed renewal experiences from time to time in their lives. Some times are more crucial in terms of renewal than others. Apparently in western society the mid-thirty's and early forty's and mid-fifty's are crucial times in which renewal is frequently needed in a leader's life. Frequently during these critical periods discipline slacks, there is a tendency to plateau and rely on one's past experience and skills, and a sense of confusion concerning achievement and new direction prevail. Unusual renewal experiences with God can overcome these tendencies and redirect a leader. An openness for them, a willingness to take steps to receive them, and a knowledge of their importance for a whole life can be vital factors in heeding step two for finishing well. Sometimes these renewal experiences are divinely originated by God and we must be sensitive to his invitation. At other times we must initiate the renewal efforts.

Enhancement 3. DISCIPLINES.

Leaders need discipline of all kinds. Especially is this true of spiritual disciplines. A strong surge toward spirituality now exists in Catholic and Protestant circles. This movement combined with an increasingly felt need due to the large number of failures is propelling leaders to hunger for intimacy. The spiritual disciplines are one mediating means for getting this intimacy. Such authors as Eugene Peterson, Dallas Willard, and Richard Foster are making headway with Protestants concerning spirituality. See also my section on spiritual guides and the appendix on the disciplines in **The Mentor Handbook,** available through Barnabas Publishers. Leaders without these leadership tools are prone to failure via sin as well as plateauing.

Helpful categorizations for me which I derived from my study of Willard include the following:

1) Disciplines of abstinence such as solitude, silence, fasting, frugality, chastity, secrecy, sacrifice;
2) Disciplines of engagement such as study, worship, celebration, service, prayer, fellowship, confession, and submission;
3) Some other miscellaneous disciplines such as voluntary exile, keeping watch, Sabbath keeping, practices among the poor, journaling, and listening.

I have defined many of these disciplines and given some practical suggestions for them in my spiritual dynamics course I teach at Fuller Seminary. See Dallas Willard's **The Spirit of the Disciplines** and Richard Foster's **Celebration of Discipline.**

We need to guard our inner life with God. The spiritual disciplines have proven helpful in this regard to many earlier generations of leaders. Spiritual disciplines can be generally defined to include activities of mind and body which are purposefully undertaken in order to bring personality and total being into effective cooperation with the Spirit of God so as to reflect Kingdom life.

I concur with Paul's admonitions to discipline as a means of insuring perseverance in the ministry. When Paul was around 50 years of age he wrote to the Corinthian church what appears to be both an exhortation to the Corinthians and an explanation of a major leadership value in his own life. We need to keep in mind that he had been in ministry for about 21 years. He was still advocating strong discipline. I paraphrase it in my own words.

Appendix B. 5 Things To Enhance Good Finishes

I am serious about finishing well in my Christian ministry. I discipline myself for fear that after challenging others into the Christian life I myself might become a casualty. 1 Corinthians 9:24-27

Lack of physical discipline is often an indicator of laxity in the spiritual life as well. Toward the end of his life, Paul is probably between 65 and 70, he is still advocating discipline. This time he writes to Timothy, who is probably between 30 and 35 years old.

...Take time and trouble to keep yourself spiritually fit. Bodily fitness has a limited value, but spiritual fitness is of unlimited value for it holds promise both for the present life and for the life to come. (1 Timothy 4:7b,8 Phillips)

Leaders should from time to time assess their state of discipline. I recommend in addition to standard word disciplines involving the devotional life and study of the Bible other disciplines such as solitude, silence, fasting, frugality, chastity, secrecy. My studies of Foster and Willard have helped me identify a number of disciplines which can habitually shape character and increase the probability of a good finish.

Enhancement 4. LEARNING POSTURE.

The single most important antidote to plateauing is a well developed learning posture. Such a posture is also one of the major ways through which God gives vision. I will describe more about how to do this in the commentary which follows.

Another of the major leadership lessons is *Effective leaders maintain a learning posture all their lives.* It sounds simple enough but many leaders don't heed it. Two Biblical leaders who certainly were learners all their lives and exemplified this principle were Daniel and Paul. Note how Daniel observed this principle. In Daniel 9 when he is quite old we find that he was still studying his Bible and still learning new things from it. And he was alert to what God wanted to do through what he was learning. Consequently, Daniel was able to intercede for his people and become a recipient of one of the great messianic revelations. Paul's closing remarks to Timothy show he was still learning. "And when you come don't forget the books Timothy!" (2 Timothy 4:13).

In western culture, maintaining a learning posture usually involves reading. Countless materials are available on leadership. You should acquire skills which will allow you to read broadly and selectively the many resources that are now being published. I have learned selective reading techniques which have allowed me to learn what I need to know without reading every word of a book. This has helped me to increase the range and number of books I read. I have developed a reading continuum which identifies different techniques for approaching the reading of a book for information. The continuum moves from less intense and less in-depth reading to highly intense and in-depth reading. Methodologies along the continuum include scan, ransack, browse, pre-read, read and study levels. Each type of reading has different goals and employs different techniques for getting information leading to those goals. See my **Reading on the Run--A Continuum Approach to Reading** available through Barnabas Publisher.

A helpful accountability model I have used is the *buddy reading model.* I have a reading buddy. We covenant together to read a book, do certain exercises in conjunction with the book, and then meet to share our learning. We alternate choices of book. My buddy picks it for one month. I do so the next month. This model could be generalized to any kind of special learning activity like listening to tapes and experiential visits to ministry

Appendix B. 5 Things To Enhance Good Finishes

happenings or the like. The dynamics of the model include co-mentoring, accountability, committal to learning and some kind of learning experience. This model could be generalized to any kind of special learning activity like listening to tapes and experiential visits to ministry happenings or the like. The dynamics of the model include co-mentoring, accountability, committal to learning and some kind of learning experience.

There are many non-formal training events available such as workshops, seminars, and conferences covering a variety of learning skills. Take advantage of them. A good learning posture is insurance against plateauing and a helpful prod along the way to persevere in leadership. An inflexible spirit with regards to learning is almost a sure precursor to finishing *so so* or *poorly*.

Enhancement 5. MENTORING.

Comparative study of many leaders lives indicates the frequency with which other people were significant in challenging them into leadership and in giving timely advice and help so as to keep them there. Leaders who are effective and finish well will have from 10 to 15 significant people who came alongside at one time or another to help them. Mentoring is also a growing movement in Christian circles as well as secular.[2]

The general notion of mentoring involves a relational empowerment process in which someone who knows something (the mentor) passes on something (wisdom, advice, information, emotional support, protection, linking to resources) to someone who needs it (the mentoree, protégé) at a sensitive time so that it impacts the person's development. The basic dynamics of mentoring include attraction, relationship, response, accountability and empowerment. My observations on mentoring suggest that most likely, any leader will need a mentor at all times over a lifetime of leadership. Mentoring is available if one looks for specific functions and people who can do them (rather than an ideal mentor who can do all). God will provide a mentor in a specific area of need for you if you trust Him for one and you are willing to submit and accept responsibility.

Simply stated a final suggestion for enabling a good finish is find a mentor who will hold you accountable in your spiritual life and ministry and who can warn and advise so as to enable you to avoid pitfalls and to grow throughout your lifetime of ministry. I will deal with this more fully in my workshop times today.

Conclusion

A simple awareness of these 5 enhancements can greatly encourage a leader to move more deliberately and proactively to experience them.

---

[2] See my manual co-authored with my son, **The Mentor Handbook**, available through Barnabas Publishers and my book co-authored with Paul Stanley, **Connecting**. Both of these explain in depth the concept of mentoring and how it can be used in churches.

Appendix C. 6 Characteristics Of Those Finishing Well

For those who have finished well I have done comparative study and have identified 6 descriptors. The classical Old Testament character who exhibits all of them is Daniel. The classical New Testament Church leader who exhibits them is Paul.[1] There are gradations of finishing well. Some finish well but not quite having all six or lesser intensity on one or the other major characteristics.

While I am sure there could be many various approaches to assessing a good finish, the following are based on the concept that the ideal leadership posture is one which involves gifted power and accomplishment as well as mature godly character. It is an ongoing synergistic balance between being and doing. In practice you will see gifted power exercised by leaders who fall far short of character ideals. This will probably frustrate you. You will also see some who focus on character, perhaps in a move toward monastic solitude, with a corresponding lack of gifted power and achievement. The following characteristics reflect a bias toward a both/and rather than an either/or approach to being and doing.

Characteristic 1.

They maintain a personal vibrant relationship with God right up to the end.

Characteristic 2.

They maintain a learning posture and can learn from various kinds of sources--life especially.

Characteristic 3.

They evidence Christ likeness in character as evidenced by the fruit of the Spirit in their lives.

Characteristic 4.

Truth is lived out in their lives so that convictions and promises of God are seen to be real.

Characteristic 5.

They leave behind one or more ultimate contributions (saint, stylistic practitioners, mentors, public rhetoricians, pioneers, crusaders, artists, founder, stabilizers, researchers, writers, promoters).[2]

Characteristic 6.

They walk with a growing awareness of a sense of destiny and see some or all of it fulfilled.

---

[1] I am sure John and Peter would too. We don't have quite enough Biblical information to speak for all the characteristics though they do reflect some of them. Jesus in the pre-church era of leadership, of course, evinces the synergistic ideal between being and doing and manifests all of the characteristics.

[2] See position paper on *Ultimate Contribution* available from Barnabas Publishers for explanation of these types.

Appendix D. Social Base Processing

All leaders operate out of some home base environment. The more stable that environment is the more likely the leader is to move toward a focused ministry. A weak or ineffective social base setting can detract from a focused life. Below are given some minimum constructs about social base issues drawn from a lengthy position paper on this subject.[1]

Social Base, Social Base Processing, and Social Base Needs

DEFINITION Social base refers to the personal living environment out of which a leader operates and which provides:
- emotional support,
- economic support,
- strategic support, and
- basic physical needs.

DEFINITION Social base processing is a very general category referring to the means God uses to lead to a given social base configuration as well as His use of critical incidents with regard to social base issues and their effect upon leaders.

The simple fact is that all leaders have personal social needs that must be met. Social base processing has to do with God's shaping with regards to those needs. Here are some basic needs I have identified. Perhaps there are others.[2] Perhaps a different taxonomy could be developed. This is simply what I have seen and I have found it useful in talking to leaders about what is happening in their lives. Table 1 lists the 4 social base needs.

Table 1. 4 SOCIAL BASE NEEDS

1. **EMOTIONAL SUPPORT** (Companionship, Listener, Recreational Outlets, Empathetic Understanding, Affirmation of Personal Worth, etc.)

2. **ECONOMIC SUPPORT** (Financial Base which covers living expenses, medical, educational, basic physical needs like food, clothing, and transportation, recreational reprieves, etc.)

3. **STRATEGIC SUPPORT** (The backup for giving meaning to life; affirming that what we do is important. The sharing of ministry or career ideas, philosophy, problems, personal development--in short giving the big picture which encompasses our major choices in life.)

4. **SOCIAL SUPPORT--BASIC PHYSICAL NEEDS** (The necessities of life--how do we eat, sleep, have clean clothes, meet our physical drives. Where do we stay? Are we safe? Is it a place of retreat, refreshment, etc.?)

---

[1] See Dr. J. Robert Clinton, *Social Base Processing--The Home Base Environment Out of Which A Leader Works* (1993), available from Barnabas Publishers. This is a position paper which treats this subject in detail. Two of the barriers to finishing well relate directly to social base issues.

[2] Perhaps a psychologists or sociologist majoring in this field would have a more integrated typology. Perhaps Maslow's taxonomy could be probed in terms of this definition. Not being an expert in these fields I have simply described what I have seen. I am certainly open to more rigorous identification of such a taxonomy. My criterion is simply, "Will it help us as leaders to understand ourselves more and to become better leaders?"

Appendix D. Social Base Processing

Various leaders meet these needs in various ways. In western cultures the social base revolves around singleness and its support elements or the nuclear family, and various other family patterns that are emerging in modern society. In western missions, spouses are often very influential in the development of the partner. Many relational lessons and other important insights crucial to development of a leader come via the causal source of a spouse or other important member of the social base and relates to social base needs.

In non-western society the social base may relate very strongly to an extended family or other kinship network. Various societies meet social base needs in culturally specific ways. The four social base needs (economic, emotional, strategic, and physical) will vary in terms of importance. In one culture one may have priority. In another culture a different need may have priority.

Social Base Patterns For Singles--3 Elements

Social base patterns for singles involve various configurations over time of the three basic elements shown in Table 2.

Table 2. THREE ELEMENTS INVOLVED IN SINGLES SOCIAL BASES

1. ISOLATION

a. Solo Isolation--live alone, provide own emotional, economic, strategic, and social support needs primarily by one's self.

b. Quasi-Isolation--same as solo isolation with aperiodic retreats into some other friendly social setting.

2. PARTNERSHIPS

a. Same Sex--develop a partnership with another member of the same sex, following along the lines of patterns for married couples.

b. Opposite Sex--this can be dangerous, but partnerships along the lines of the co-ministry pattern with the exception of totally meeting the social support--basic physical needs.

3. GROUPS

a. Part of a Team--be part of a team committed to each other and to providing social base needs.

b. Part of a Family--be adopted into a family (seen in missionary situations on field)--more deliberate proactive use of forays seen in the quasi-isolation element b. above.

c. Live in Community--groups formed with singles and couples who opt to live out of the same physical set-up.

Simeon was a single who had a quasi-isolation profile though his housekeeping needs were met by maids and he had frequent social interaction due to the campus type situation and occasional hospitality with parishioners. Frequent mentoring met emotional and strategic needs.

Mears was a single who had a social base that was a combination of a partnership (her sister) and team (she had several executive type secretaries who were committed to enabling her in ministry).

Appendix D. Social Base Processing

SOCIAL BASE PROCESSING--MARRIED WORKERS

THE ELEMENTS--6 PROFILES

Table 3 lists several potential profiles focusing on how spouses arrange roles to meet the four social base needs--with a primary focus on economic and physical needs. I do not attach values to these profiles. I simply describe them. I believe all are legitimate-- that is, one is not necessarily more Biblical than the other. I do not indicate which are more prevalent today. There are real illustrations in life which I have seen of all of these though I admit that several of them are rarer. These profiles can be organized into several configurations over time to form patterns. I will attempt to describe some of these later.

Table 3. SOCIAL BASE PROFILES--6 Profiles For Marrieds

1. INTERNAL/EXTERNAL MINISTRY PROFILE (synonym: release pattern)

The basic idea:	This profile applies to a married couple with children. One spouse concentrates on external ministry (career) providing economic support; the other spouse concentrates on internal ministry to the family including a special care for the social thus *releasing the first* to freely engage in external ministry; both dabble in the other needs.
Spouse #1:	heavy engagement in external ministry, emotional support, economic support, (strategic support)
Spouse #2:	not heavy external ministry--some on the side, sees children as a focused ministry--internal ministry, emotional support, (economic support), (strategic support), social.

2. CO-MINISTRY/PARTNERSHIP PROFILE

The Basic Idea:	There are two profiles for this. One when the couple has no children and one when the couple has children. Both spouses see themselves operating in the same ministry (career) setting together. Each has a significant role in the setting.

a. No Children--each spouse has a full time external ministry focus

Spouse #1:	heavy direct ministry, share economic, provide strategic support, share social, emotional
Spouse #2:	heavy direct ministry, share economic, provide strategic support, share social, emotional

b. Children--each spouse views ministry as a partnership in external and internal ministry

Spouse #1:	part time direct ministry, share economic, provide strategic support, share social, emotional
Spouse #2:	part time direct ministry, share economic, provide strategic support, share social, emotional

3. INDEPENDENT MINISTRY PROFILE

The Basic Idea:	Both spouses give themselves to full time ministry (career) in different settings which are relatively independent of each other.
Spouse #1:	heavy direct ministry in different area from spouse's ministry, share social and economic support, (strategic)
Spouse #2:	heavy direct ministry in different area from spouse's ministry, share social and economic support, (strategic)

Table 3. SOCIAL BASE PROFILES--6 Profiles For Marrieds continued

4. ALTERNATE MINISTRY PROFILE
    The Basic Idea: The spouses alternate the release profile, internal ministry, for varying portions of time. Each releases and helps the other develop the external ministry or career for significant portions of time.

5. DELAYED MINISTRY PROFILE
    The Basic Idea: Both spouses had ministries before marriage. One spouse enters the release profile dropping ministry and concentrating on mainly providing social needs.
    Spouse #1:   heavy direct ministry, emotional, economic, (strategic)
    Spouse #2:   emotional, (economic), (strategic), provides social support until such a time as they can both enter heavy direct ministry either co-ministry or independent ministry.

6. DYSFUNCTIONAL PROFILE
    The Basic Idea: One or the other of the spouses opposes the other's role or in some significant way hinders fulfillment of potential. Can simply not provide relevant needs whether emotional, economic, strategic or social.

Most of the social base patterns for the married couples included in this book for the majority of the effective focused ministry times were profile 1. After Brengle's wife died he maintained a singles social base. His ministry was largely itinerant and though it is not absolutely clear it seems as if he operated for the most part out of his childrens' homes as his main social base, though he was on the road a good bit.

Appendix E. Biographical Genre and the Historical Model

This is information that can help you study biographical literature. It defines a historical mentor, talks about the 5 types (genre) of literature, and tells you how you can profit from a historical mentor. This material, used by permission, occurs in **The Mentor Handbook** by Drs. J. Robert and Richard W. Clinton and published by Barnabas Publishers.

HISTORICAL MODEL

introduction	Historical models provide a gold mine of virtually untapped mentoring resources.[1] Essentially historical models do what contemporary models do but they do it through the pages of a book rather than via a live demonstration. The below given examples are nine important ones from many that have mentored to me personally.
definition	The **historical model** refers to a person now dead whose life or ministry, at least in part, is written in a biographical or autobiographical form, and is used as an example to indirectly impart skills, lessons of life and ministry, and values which empower another person.
examples	Hudson Taylor, **Hudson Taylor's Spiritual Secret**. J.O. Fraser, **Mountain Rain**. Jonathan Goforth, **Goforth of China**. Jim Elliot, **Under the Shadow of the Almighty**. Amy Carmichael, **Amy Carmichael of Dohnavur**. Adoniram Judson, **To The Golden Shore**. Watchman Nee, **Against the Tide**. Samuel Logan Brengle, **Samuel Logan Brengle: Portrait of a Prophet**. Adoniram Judson Gordon, **Adoniram Judson Gordon, A Biography**.
comment	When we study lives that have counted for Christ historically we are on solid ground. For we are applying the leadership mandate of Hebrews 13:7,8 in a broad way.

---

[1] For seven years I(Bobby) have surveyed leaders in my classes concerning how many biographies they have read. I go for total read, the number that have impacted their lives and the number that have been reread. The overwhelming majority of leaders have read five or less biographies. Almost everyone has been helped in some way by at least one biography. But most have not seen it as an on-going means of development in their lives. Most have never reread a biography.

Appendix E. Biographical Genre and the Historical Model   page 512

FEEDBACK ON HISTORICAL MENTOR

1. Exercise. One way of finding biographies of interest is to scan books which survey a number of lives. Scan one of the following and list 5 biographies you would like to do follow-up work on. An interesting exercise would be to compare the people treated in these five books. Which ones occur in 2, 3, all 4?

    They Found The Secret. V. Raymond Edman
    From Jerusalem To Irian Jaya. Ruth Tucker
    Powerlines. L. Chan
    Walking With Giants. W. Wiersbe (or any of his *Giants* series)

2. What happens when a Christian leader does not take advantage of historical mentoring? Can you suggest some implications from failure to get help from historical mentors?

3. How would you evaluate your own past use of historical models? Select the category below which describes how many biographies (or autobiographies) you have read. Then check the evaluation phrases which best describe you.

    a. I have read approximately the following biographies:

    ____ 0-5   ____ 6-10   ____ 11-20   ____ 21-40   ____ 41-100   ____ 100+

    b. I would say that,

    _____ (1) biographies have had little or no impact on my own leadership development

    _____ (2) biographies have somewhat helped me

    _____ (3) biographies have been significant to my development

    _____ (4) biographies have been extremely important to my development

    c. I have reread approximately the following biographies:

    ____ 0-2   ____ 3-4   ____ 5-6   ____ 7-8   ____ 9+

Name the three most important ones.

ANSWERS------------

1. Your choice.
2. Failure to learn vicariously from the lives of others (learning in a substitutionary manner through their experiences) will leave one to learn from first hand experiences only. And there isn't enough time nor situations for you to experience all you will need to know as a Christian leader. Perspective comes when we have a broad range of leadership experience. Much of this we can get from others with out having to go through it first hand.
3. Your choice.

Appendix E. Biographical Genre and the Historical Model

5 BIOGRAPHICAL TYPES ACCORDING TO WRITING GENRE

introduction   Biography differs in quality, underlying philosophy, and presentation methodology. Some biographies are highly popular. Others are strictly academic. And many are in between. *You can learn from all kinds.* Writers differ on how they choose what to write, how much they seek to interpret, and the end results they write for. There always is the temptation to "paint the picture" better than it is or to say it another way, to leave out the down side when showing the up side of a life. Biographical values generally took a shift in the late sixties. Writers from this era and after seek to paint people "warts and all." The idea is that such a presentation carries with it much stronger credibility. And I must confess that it generally does for me. Writers use different methodology for presenting their material. I have identified several presentation formats which may help you as you choose biographies. Table 10-1 shows these basic classification of biographical types.[2]

TABLE 10-1. BIOGRAPHICAL TYPES--PRESENTATION GENRE

Type	Description
1. Vignettes	This type simply presents interesting vignettes from the life of a person. There is no discernible selection criterion, nor chronological flow or order nor interpretation.
2. Linear Vignettes	This type picks from many certain vignettes which represent in some fashion the different phases of the life. The vignettes will be ordered chronologically. Very little interpretation is given. Perhaps there will be explanation to fill in the holes between the selected vignettes.
3. Critical Vignettes	This type picks out the critical vignettes and arranges them chronologically. There will be explanation and a minimum of interpretation of the meaning and impact both of the vignette on the shaping of the person and the person as to meaning and impact of the life.

---

[2] For a technical report on biography, see Norman K. Denzin's **Interpretive Biography** in the qualitative Research Methods Series put out by Sage Publications, Newbury Park, California.

Appendix E. Biographical Genre and the Historical Model   page 514

TABLE 10-1. BIOGRAPHICAL TYPES--WRITING GENRE continued

Type	Description
4. Chronological/ Interpretive	This type seeks to first of all give a combination of interpretive/ narrative flow of the life in chronological sequence. There will be interpretation interspersed in the narrative flow. Vignettes or mini-illustrations will both be explained to show the flow and for illustration of the interpretation. Following this basic narrative flow will come major themes drawn from the life usually with major units devoted to each theme. These units are highly interpretive and are seeking to give meaning and impact to the life. Usually there will be some sort of summary section/units pointing out the ultimate contribution of the life.
5. Themes of a Life	Some biographers prefer to organize their work around the major themes of the life. Whatever is necessary (narrative, vignettes, illustrations) will be self-contained in the explanation of the theme.
comment	I personally prefer type 4 biographies. Hall's work on Brengle, one of my historical mentors, is this type.
comment	However, don't let the writer's selectivity, nor philosophy, nor interpretation nor method of presenting material rob you from the benefit of a historical model. The question you are seeking to answer, when you are looking for vicarious mentoring through models is not, *Is this absolutely true?* No writer can give you that kind of material. The question you are seeking to answer is, **If this were true, whether or not it is, what would God want to teach me through it?**

Appendix E. Biographical Genre and the Historical Model   page 515

HOW TO PROFIT FROM HISTORICAL MENTORING

introduction Biographies can not be scanned or ransacked as other information types of literature can. Biographies need to be read in their entirety. A two sweep procedure is recommended. Sweep one involves a rapid read through of the entire biography to simply get a feel for the overall. Of course you should jot down notes in the margin as you go. This read through will also help you identify the kind of biography it is, type 1-5. Sweep two involves a slower more careful reading which includes analysis, devotional, and applicational emphases. Below are given some suggestions for Sweep two reading.

I. ANALYSIS EMPHASIS

From your sweep one reading and a careful analysis of table of contents, preface, foreword, and dust cover information make a tentative identification of the biography type. This kind of analysis requires disciplined study time. Sometimes it can be done in conjunction with a devotional time as suggested in Step II. Sometimes it will require in-depth concentration and time.

IF TYPE 1

1. Study individual vignettes for processing, lessons, values. Jot notes throughout the vignette. You will have to do this without reference to an overall perspective.

2. Summarize the most important insights on 1-3 pages and fold and paper clip to the inside cover sheet where it will always be available.

IF TYPE 2 OR 3

1. Construct a time-line from table of contents or first few paragraphs of each chapter.

2. For each chapter draw the time-line in at the top of the first page up to the time of the chapter. This helps you keep the chapter in its perspective.

3. Study vignettes for processing, lessons, values. In addition, be alert to possible patterns. Repeated processing, lessons, or values usually points to a pattern.

4. Summarize the most important insights on 1-3 pages and fold and paper clip to the inside cover sheet where it will always be available.

IF TYPE 4

1. Identify the Major Sections: time-line, interpretive themes, ultimate contribution.

2. Scan the time-line chapters and construct the time-line. Pencil in the portion of the time-line at the top of each chapter which leads up to the chapter.

3. Study each phase in the time-line for processing, lessons, values.

Appendix E. Biographical Genre and the Historical Model   page 516

HOW TO READ BIOGRAPHIES continued

4. Look for patterns across the phases.

5. Read the theme sections: for each chapter identify the major philosophy of ministry value being highlighted. Notice any processing that led to it.

6. Study carefully the summary section for its identification of ultimate contribution.

<u>IF TYPE 5</u>

Repeat steps 4-6 of type 4. You will not be able to pinpoint thematic emphases in times of a time-line perspective.

II. DEVOTIONAL EMPHASIS--HISTORICAL MENTOR, JOURNAL TECHNIQUE

It is suggested that you do this part of your historical mentoring in your devotional time. Your Sweep 1 read through will have identified portions of the biography which are more appropriate for journaling

1. Keep a journal. Date your reading and identify the pages read.

2. Read small portions that make up a whole unit and meditate on them.

3. Imagine that the historical mentor is listening as you read. Have him/her answer the following question. Having seen what I have read, and knowing me as I know myself, what would you say is important for me from this section just read. What advice would you give me about what was just read? Then journal the imaginary response. Make them personal. Make them applicational. Identify needs in your own life and information, values, perspective from the reading to meet them.

4. From time-to-time review your applicational entries from the mentor and evaluate yourself on how you are doing.

III. APPLICATIONAL EMPHASIS

Remember, we are talking about a mentor situation from whom you are going to learn attitudes, skills, lessons, and values   for your own life. You alone will be responsible to see that you actually do learn.

1. Write down your applications. Indicate how you intend to use things you are finding out in your reading and analysis.

2. Find a person with whom you can share your journal entries and applications with. Do this regularly. Once a week is ideal but monthly is better than none at all.

3. If at all possible do the biographical study with a partner who is also doing the study. The both of you can then hold each other accountable for learning.

Appendix F. Venn Diagrams and How To Interpret Them

A Venn diagram is a means of combining pictorially separate elements in terms of importance and their relationship to one another.

Explaining the Giftedness Venn Diagram

Giftedness Venn diagrams use three elements to communicate information.

<u>Symbols</u>: We use three different symbols to display giftedness.

▢ natural abilities

△ acquired skills

◯ spiritual gifts

<u>Size</u>: The size of the symbols is important. Bigger size denotes more importance. Smaller size denotes lesser importance. For example:

| Leadership abilities | clear thinker | word of wisdom |

In this example, there are two natural abilities listed and one spiritual gift. The leadership abilities are being displayed as more important than the natural ability of clear thinking. The word of wisdom gift is larger than the leadership abilities and the clear thinking natural ability. It is the most important. The natural abilities next most important.

<u>Spacing</u>: Spacing is the most complex feature of a Venn diagram. When you space the symbols on the diagram you are showing the relationship between the symbols. If two elements of the giftedness set are seen as working together, they would be placed in such a way as to demonstrate the relationship. Overlap means that some of both occur simultaneously. Where there is no overlap it means that the item also occurs alone. The most important elements are the largest ones and are placed in the center of the diagram.

Appendix F. Venn Diagrams and How To Interpret Them   page 518

For example:

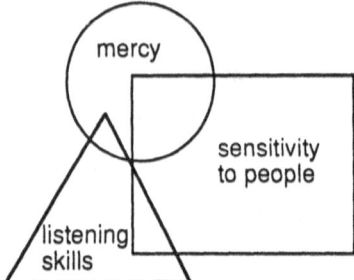

In this example, this person is demonstrating a relationship between three different elements of the giftedness set. The dominant feature is the natural ability called, sensitivity to people. It is placed in the center of the diagram and is the largest symbol. The spiritual gift of mercy enhances the operation of this natural ability in ministry situations. God takes the person's natural sensitivity and empowers this with His Holy Spirit and releases the love of God in the situation. This person has acquired some skills in the area of listening. One would summarize this diagram by saying that this person uses his/her natural ability to release a spiritual gift usually through listening to others.

Here's another example:

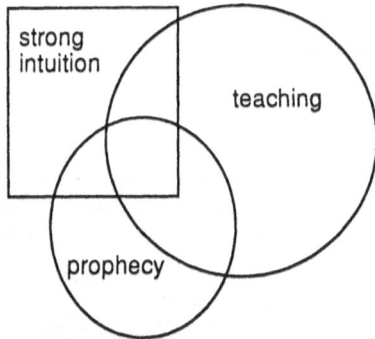

In this example the person is demonstrating that there are three elements that relate closely. The spiritual gifts work hand in hand together. There is a large amount of teaching that is not prophetical. But there is a strong overlap between teaching and prophecy meaning the teaching has strong admonition or correction and/or could be actual teaching on prophecy. The teaching gift is dominant but has a prophetic touch to it. The natural ability of intuition influences both the teaching and the prophetic gifts. But there is a large part of intuition which takes place out of the teaching and prophetic context.

Explaining the Venn Diagram--Ultimate Contribution Set

The ultimate contributions set is displayed using one basic symbol, an oval shaped symbol. Again the size is important. An element which is more important is shown by a larger size, probably heavier lines. Again the more centered an element is the more it is probably the

Appendix F. Venn Diagrams and How To Interpret Them   page 519

dominant force in the diagram. Where two ovals overlap it means that both elements occur together. Where an oval has space alone it means only that represented by the oval.

Let's use Simeon's diagram to explain.

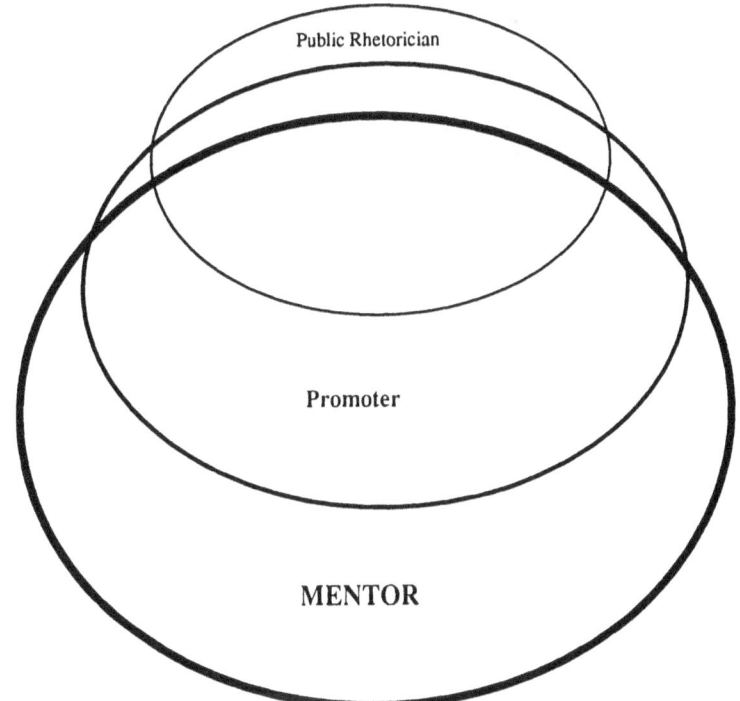

His ultimate contribution set includes four elements: mentor, promoter, and public rhetorician. Obviously the mentor contribution is the most important. This is shown by the heavy dark line, by the fact it is the largest, and by its being located in the ver central portion of the diagram. There is some mentoring which is not connected to his promotional work or his public rhetorician work. This is a farily large amount. It means he did some mentoring which was individual in nature and was not related to his pulpit ministry. Nor was this mentoring promoting missions one of the casues he espoused. There is a large overlap between mentoring, public rhetorican, and promotion. This means there was a large amount of mentoring that was promotional of the evangelical cause or of missions and which probably used public ministry to attract mentorees. There was also some promotional work which involved public ministry but was not mentor in its functioning. There was also some public ministry which was not promotional or mentoring in nature.

Remember size, thickened darkness of lines, and a central place indicates importance. Overlaps between ovals means all functions of the separate ovals are working together. Non over laps means that just the element is being emphasized.

References Cited or Mentioned and Not Listed in Chapter Bibliographies[1]

Books

        Mountain Rain. Singapore: OMF Books.

Adizes, Ichaak
        Corporate Life Cycles.

Clinton, Dr. J. Robert
- 1984   Leadership Training Models. Altadena: Barnabas Publishers.
- 1986   Coming to Conclusions on Leadership Styles. Altadena: Barnabas Publishers.
- 1986   A Short History of Leadership Theory. Altadena: Barnabas Publishers.
- 1988   The Making of a Leader. Colorado Springs: NavPress.
- 1989   Leadership Emergence Theory. Altadena: Barnabas Publishers.
- 1992   Bridging Strategies--Leadership Perspectives for Introducing Change. Altadena: Barnabas Publishers.
- 1993   Handbook I. Leaders, Leadership, and the Bible--An Overview. Altadena: Barnabas Publishers.
- 1993   Handbook III. The Big Picture: Leadership and the Bible as a Whole--Macro Studies. Altadena: Barnabas Publishers.

Clinton, Dr. J. Robert and Dr. Richard W. Clinton
- 1991   The Mentor Handbook. Altadena: Barnabas Publishers.
- 1994   Developing Leadership Giftedness. Altadena: Barnabas Publishers.

Denzin, Norman K.
- 1989   Interpretive Biography. Newbury Park: Sage Publications.

Edman,
        They Found The Secret.

Eliot, Elizabeth
        No Graven Image.

Hodgkinson, Christopher
- 1991   Ecucational Leadership--The Moral Art. Albany: State University of New York Press.

Lewis, Hunter
- 1990   A Question of Values--Six Ways We Make The Personal Choices That Shape Our Lives. San Francisco: Harper and Row

Matthews, Arthur
- 1973   Towers Pointing Upward. Columbia, S.C.: Columbia Bible College.

McGavran, Donald
- 1955   The Bridges of God.

---

[1] Materials from Barnabas Publishers, both books and papers, are available from Barnabas Publishers, 2175 N. Holliston Avenue, Altadena, CA, 91001. Write for catalogue of materials available.

References Cited/Mentioned--Not Listed in Chapter Bibliographies page 522

Mintzberg, Henry
   1983   **Power In And Around Organizations.** Englewood Cliffs, N.J.: Prentice Hall.

Raab, Laura and Dr. J. Robert Clinton
   1985   **Barnabas, Encouraging Exhorter--A Study in Mentoring.** Altadena: Barnabas Publishers.

Stanley, Paul D. and J. Robert Clinton
   1992   **Connecting--The Mentoring Relationships You Need To Succeed in Life.** Colorado Springs: NavPress.

Simon, Sidney B., Howe, Leland W., and Kirschenbaum, Howard
   1972,1978   **Values Clarification--A Handbook of Practical Strategies for Teachers and Students.** New York: A & W Publishers, Inc.

Taylor, Paul W.
   1961   **Normative Discourse.** Westport, Connecticut: Greenwood Press.

Wrong, Dennis
   1979   **Power--Its Forms, Bases, and Uses.** San Francisco, CA: Harper and Row

Papers

Clinton, Dr. J. Robert
   1981   *Structural Time--A Change Dynamics Variable.* Altadena: Barnabas Publishers.
   1989   *The Ultimate Contribution--A Life That Counts.* Altadena: Barnabas Publishers.
   1989   *Listen up Leaders!* Altadena: Barnabas Publishers.
   1992   *A personal Ministry Philosophy--One Key to Effective Leadership.* Altadena: Barnabas Publishers.
   1993   *The Paradigm Shift--God's Means of Opening Up New Vistas for Leaders.* Altadena: Barnabas Publishers.
   1993   *Social Base Processing--The Home Base Environment Out of Which A Leader Works.* Altadena: Barnabas Publishers.
   1993   *The Time-Line, What It is and How To Construct It..* Altadena: Barnabas Publishers.
   1993   *Getting Perspective, By Using Your Unique Time-Line.* Altadena: Barnabas Publishers.

About the Author

Dr. J. Robert (Bobby) Clinton and his wife Marilyn make their home in Altadena, California where they have been a part of the School of World Mission of Fuller Theological Seminary since 1981. They have four children, all of whom are walking with God. Bobby is Professor of Leadership and Marilyn is Director of Operations.

Bobby has been researching leadership emergence theory since 1981. **Focused Lives—Inspirational Life Changing lessons From Eight Effective Christian Leaders Who Finished Well** is the result of a year long sabbatical in which each of the eight were studied in-depth using leadership emergence theory concepts. Bobby's life purpose is **to challenge, motivate, and enable**—via study and development of leadership concepts both empirically and from the Scriptures, by teaching of leadership concepts, by modeling of them, by mentoring of select leaders in them, and by providing available resources and materials—**high level leaders all over the world to finish well.**

Focused Lives demonstrates that it is possible to finish well. Bobby's research and writings seek to identify what it means to finish well, to expose barriers to finishing well and to point out enhancements to finishing well. His Biblical work on leadership has also generated values, guidelines, and principles that will motivate and encourage leaders to do just that—Finish Well! Most of Bobby's leadership materials are published by **Barnabas Publishers** whose motto is *Developing Materials to Help Others Develop.*

www.ingramcontent.com/pod-product-compliance
Lightning Source LLC
Chambersburg PA
CBHW021824220426
43663CB00005B/122